THE LETTERS OF FRANK LOESSER

THE LETTERS OF
FRANK LOESSER

EDITED BY
DOMINIC BROOMFIELD-McHUGH
AND CLIFF EISEN

YALE UNIVERSITY PRESS
NEW HAVEN AND LONDON

For information about this and other Yale University Press publications, please contact:
U.S. Office: sales.press@yale.edu   yalebooks.com
Europe Office: sales@yaleup.co.uk   yalebooks.co.uk

Set in Minion Pro by IDSUK (DataConnection) Ltd
Printed and bound in the UK using 100% renewable electricity at CPI Group (UK) Ltd

Library of Congress Control Number: 2025935743
A catalogue record for this book is available from the British Library.
Authorized Representative in the EU: Easy Access System Europe, Mustamäe tee 50, 10621 Tallinn, Estonia, gpsr.requests@easproject.com

ISBN 978-0-300-25074-9

10 9 8 7 6 5 4 3 2 1

CONTENTS

ILLUSTRATIONS

Unless otherwise specified, images are courtesy of the Loesser family, with permission.

PLATES

1. Frank Loesser, 'Birthday Greetings for his Mother', c1915.
2. Souvenir programme for Frank Loesser's *Skirts: An All-American Musical Adventure in 15 Scenes*, 1944. Editors' collection.
3. Frank Loesser, George Abbott and Ray Bolger during the production of *Where's Charley?*, 1948.
4. Ray Bolger in *Where's Charley?*, 1948.
5. Vivian Blaine and Sam Levene in the original Broadway production of *Guys and Dolls*, 1950.
6. The Crapshooters in the original production of *Guys and Dolls*, 1950. Frank Loesser Enterprises, with permission.
7. Original poster for *Hans Christian Andersen*, 1952. Editors' collection.
8. Frank and Lynn Loesser, early 1950s.
9. Frank and Susan Loesser, early 1940s.
10. Advertisement for Glacierware shakers, tumblers and coolers found among Frank Loesser's papers. Frank Loesser Enterprises, with permission.

IN THE TEXT

PREFACE

Writing to Frank Loesser in December 1953, the great playwright and director Moss Hart joked: 'Well, sir, all I can say is: "Scratch a composer and you find Voltaire." I loved your letter and this may be the beginning of a whole new Holmes–Laski correspondence.' Hart's reaction to a recent communication from Loesser refers to the 1953 publication of the correspondence of Associate Justice of the Supreme Court Oliver Wendell Holmes Jr (1841–1935) and English economist and political theorist Harold J. Laski (1893–1950) that reveals not only the brilliance of two famous intellectuals but also the social and political climate in which they were writing.

Seventy years on, Hart's suggestion that Loesser's letters, at least, should one day be published has finally come true – and his astute recognition of the importance of Loesser's correspondence seems even more convincing with the passage of time. Starting with letters from his childhood and through to his final months (he died of lung cancer aged fifty-nine in 1969), this volume does not simply reveal the creative mind of the man who wrote the score to *Guys and Dolls* and standards like 'Baby, It's Cold Outside' but also his relationship with the music profession, the development of theatre and film, and the changing face of American society during his lifetime, especially during the 1950s and '60s. From his experiences of growing up in a Jewish household in New York in the 1910s to his establishment as a major songwriter and publisher in the Broadway community in the

1950s, Loesser's letters reveal him to be the product of an optimistic period in which ambition and talent could take a member of an ordinary immigrant family and turn him into an American giant.

In fact, Frank was not the only member of his birth family who rose to significant success. His half-brother Arthur was an accomplished concert pianist who not only gave public recitals but was also known as an authority on the keyboard. He published the standard text *Men, Women, and Pianos: A Social History* and served as head of the piano department at the Cleveland Institute of Music for the final part of his life. His expertise became unexpectedly useful to Frank in 1962 when he asked Arthur to advise on which brand of piano to buy for his office:

> Little did I know, when I first saw daylight, that I had been born the brother of the world's leading literate authority on pianos. But I guess there was a good reason for God's will in this matter, because here I am wanting to know something about the Yamaha piano. I feel reasonably sure that you will know more even than the Nippon Gakki Co. Ltd. of Hamamatsu, Japan on this subject. It is my experience that in 1920 you knew more than Jules Verne about rocket space craft, and more about zoology than Horowitz. Anyway, I depend on you, dear brother, to tell me what you know about this instrument (am enclosing their brochure). I need a piano for my work downtown and am being asked to consider one of this make.

The correspondence from Frank to Arthur is consistently warm and tender throughout their lives (both died in 1969). Arthur was sixteen years older, and when their father died in 1926 he regularly sent money to his stepmother and half-brother, who was still a teenager. By 1933, Frank was able to bring this support to an end:

> I have managed to gather in enough funds out of [the] song business to keep the roof on, and even <u>real</u> cream in the coffee. I never have said anything directly to you about how awfully swell I thought you have been to keep us going these years . . . but I have

been doing a lot of thinking about it. Now, the quicker I try to relieve you of the burden we must be, the better and more effectively I can say thanks.

Early letters from his father Henry to Arthur mention that Frank had an instinctive attachment to music from childhood, and songwriting allowed him to escape poverty. But one of this book's key revelations is Loesser's skill and insight as the leader of several successful businesses, starting with the establishment of his publishing company Frank Music in 1950 (he had previously created a personal publishing company, Susan Publications, in 1948, named after his eldest daughter). This was the foundation of many of his activities until the end of his life: he used it to develop and exploit new talents and also represented some more successful names who appreciated his approach. The correspondence suggests his biggest achievement in this domain was the career of Richard Adler and Jerry Ross, whom he discovered in about 1951, promoted to the producer John Murray Anderson (who put them to work on his revue *Almanac*) and mentored through their two Tony-Award-winning Broadway musicals, *The Pajama Game* (1954) and *Damn Yankees* (1955). Ross died in November 1955 at the age of twenty-nine, bringing an abrupt end to a partnership that had produced multiple song hits (including Tony Bennett's recording of 'Rags to Riches' and the showtunes 'Heart' and 'Hey There') and surely had the potential for many more. Loesser also published the standard 'Unchained Melody' by Hy Zaret and Alex North and became mentor to another major Broadway team, the more established Robert Wright and George Forrest, who wrote the hit *Kismet* (1953) during their time with Loesser.

It's unclear whether it's just a coincidence or a reflection of the importance of the relationship, but by far the most voluminous surviving correspondence is that between Loesser and another mentee, Meredith Willson. Willson and his second wife Rini socialised with Frank and *his* second wife Jo, which meant that some of their back and forth is on everyday matters such as Christmas presents, travel plans and health issues. Willson and Loesser clearly had the greatest respect and affection for one another, but on several occasions there was tension between them on business topics. Loesser was inclined to offer Willson career advice, and to be extremely honest in his comments. Sometimes, this was easily dealt with: Loesser wrote in August 1958 to apologise for a lack of enthusiasm about Willson's idea for a sequel to his 1957 hit *The Music Man*, explaining: 'It seemed to me that you were sort of bent on typing yourself . . . What I am scared about is that you may be electing for yourself too narrow a path – one seemingly designed to fit the trimmings rather than one first designed and then trimmed.'

On other occasions, there was significant mistrust. Loesser and Willson discussed forming a company in 1960, but a telegram from Loesser reveals that Willson was approaching the situation with suspicion: 'AFTER OUR CONVERSATION TODAY I LEARNED THAT THERE WAS A RELENTLESS AUDIT NOW IN PROGRESS CONCERNING YOUR ROYALTY ACCOUNTS WITH US. I SINCERELY BELIEVE THAT YOU SHOULD SATISFY YOURSELF THAT WE ARE HONEST BEFORE EVEN CONSIDERING A PUBLICATION DEAL WITH OUR COMPANY NO MATTER WHAT THE TERMS MAY BE.' At this point Loesser was irritated with Willson. He had often stepped in to carry out the older song-writer's wishes even when he did not always agree with him: in one instance, Willson would not give permission to Sammy Davis Jr, then at the height of his fame, to record 'Trouble' from *The Music Man*, and Loesser brought this subject up in the same telegram ('IT COST ME SEVERAL HOURS OF TIME AND SEVERAL LIGHT YEARS OF EMBARRASSMENT TO SPEAK IN YOUR BEHALF TO SAMMY DAVIS, JR. ABOUT OMITTING TROUBLE.'). On the other hand, Loesser sometimes went to extremes in pointing out Willson's faults, climaxing in a remarkable 58-page handwritten letter in late June 1964. Loesser explained the need to create a body of works for a writer to be perceived as 'important' and implied Willson was guilty of 'laurel resting', even providing an illustration of the laurels (he was a prolific doodler). Loesser's assessment of Willson's career is incredibly sharp, but it's a sign of their closeness that it does not seem to have damaged their relationship – indeed, Loesser went on to provide artistic comments and business advice on Willson's final musical theatre work, *1491*.

Of course, Loesser himself left an important body of diverse works, but it is striking that there is more quality than quantity in terms of his own musicals. *Guys and Dolls* (1950) and *How to Succeed in Business Without Really Trying* (1961) were enduring hits that ran for over 1,000 performances, the earlier show winning the 1951 Tony Award for Best Musical and the latter winning the 1962 Pulitzer Prize for Drama. *Where's Charley* (1948) and *The Most Happy Fella* (1956) were respectable successes that played on both sides of the Atlantic, but *Greenwillow* (1960) was a flop that caused him to comment to a fellow writer: '. . . I did such a dopey job on *Greenwillow* – letting the book sit there in rugged shreds hoping to illuminate it effectively with the ditties. I think this will result in confirming for me a principle I forgot to stick to last time. In short, it is: IT SELDOM DOES ANY GOOD TO PUT A PINK SEQUINED BALL GOWN ON A YOUNG LADY WHO HASN'T BATHED.' As for *Pleasures and Palaces* (1965), his last produced show, it closed in Detroit before even reaching New York. When his friend Cy Feuer – who had produced *Guys and Dolls* – was about to open a new musical at the same theatre in Detroit soon after, Loesser sent him a telegram: 'DON'T SKID ON MY BLOOD.'

To these four successes and two flops we can add his one-off songs and his work for Hollywood. These include 'Baby, It's Cold Outside', 'On a Slow Boat to China', 'Spring Will Be a Little Late This Year', 'What Are You Doing New Year's Eve?' and many others, as well as the scores to the ever-popular *Hans Christian Andersen* (1952) and contributions to mostly-forgotten films made by all the major studios (*Neptune's Daughter*, MGM, 1949; *Variety Girl*, Paramount, 1947; *Thank Your Lucky Stars* to music by Arthur Schwartz, Warner Bros., 1943; and *Strange Triangle*, Fox, 1946, to name only some). He was active during the Second World War in writing topical numbers, including 'Praise the Lord and Pass the Ammunition', 'Rodger Young' (the source of which he discusses in several of the letters published in this volume), and 'What Do You Do in the Infantry?'. He also wrote the words to some important songs with other composers, including two hits with Hoagy Carmichael ('Two Sleepy People' and 'Heart and Soul').

Still, it's not a huge output for a man of Loesser's limitless creativity. Anyone reading this book will immediately see why: his immersion in his businesses – including not only his publishing company but also Frank Productions (which was involved in producing *The Music Man*) and Music Theatre Inc. (which remains a global force in renting out the materials for musicals under the name Music Theatre International) – clearly took him away from writing full-time. He was absent from Broadway (in terms of new musicals) between the opening of *Guys and Dolls* in 1950 and that of *The Most Happy Fella* in 1956, with another hiatus before the opening of *Greenwillow* in 1960. (Admittedly, this gap was partly occasioned by the time spent on *Dream People*, a collaboration with writer-director Garson Kanin that was abandoned after writing the book and roughly half the score: 'I have to assume that either you have tried and failed to make some new golden geetis out of our show – or else you have abandoned interest in it in favor of the many other things you get called on to think about. Or maybe both', he wrote to Kanin in March 1959, the last mention of the project in the letters.) He was simply too busy overseeing international productions of his own and others' musicals (he had to intervene on various aspects of the London production of *The Most Happy Fella*: 'It comes to my attention (quite alarmingly) that I might not be allowed to bring a conductor to England for the run of "The Most Happy Fella"'); supporting Adler and Ross, Wright and Forrest, Willson and others in their new works; managing requests for the recording rights to his company's catalogue of songs; managing his staff; and, of course, family life required attention too, becoming more complicated after his divorce from his first wife Lynn and his marriage to Jo Sullivan, the lead of *The Most Happy Fella*. He also had health concerns to address, as he revealed in a letter to his brother in 1957:

I have had my throat cut again – NOTHING SERIOUS – just the result of neglect on my part (SMOKING + TALKING) after the last job. What I had was a recurrence of discrete (Oxford Engl. Dict. Pathol. Definition – sub-definition #c) polyps on the vocal cords.

I now have to shut up and smoke less.

Loesser's sense of humour is in evidence in nearly all the correspondence, regardless of whether it was personal or professional – indeed, he is often at his most amusing when delivering a put-down. And the art of letter writing was clearly something of which he was conscious. To fellow songwriter Irving Caesar he commented, 'I am a notoriously bad letter writer and a remarkably good songwriter. I am so busy being the latter these days that I suppose this note to you suffers as a work of art. Please forgive me.' To his musical director Herb Greene he closed one letter: 'Suffice it to say I am never content unless I am pissing in an otherwise clear puddle.' And advising writer Paddy Chayevsky on the title of his play about Stalin, *The Passion of Josef D.*, Loesser joked:

Remember that the 'passion' is that of the Lord and it is only according to – let us say Matthew – that we hear of it. I don't think it can be called Saint Matthew's passion. Please think of this and weigh it carefully before that good Catholic Walter Kerr, and that probably Catholic Bob Coleman, and that maybe once Catholic John Chapman start quarreling with the point you are trying to make.

Before you do anything please check with some real authority other than me. Being an atheist I am highly unreliable, biased, badly informed and already in hell. The hell here at the moment on the beach at Santa Monica consists of fireworks and jazz music and jazz barbecues just about evenly divided as to smoke and decibels between my left and right side neighbors. Anyway hell is getting my kids tan at about $8,000 a month. I better write something commercial.

Here and in numerous other letters, Loesser foregrounds his Jewish identity. He often signs off letters as 'Frank Loesser, President [of Frank Music]' and then adds a footnote: 'Who said a Jew couldn't be President?' In numerous letters he uses yiddish words, including 'mayven' (expert), 'nachis' (pleasurable pride), 'ferschtoonkene' (contemptible), and so on. Being culturally Jewish is something he jokes about a lot, most extremely in a letter to his staff in which he writes about the Crucifixion in relation to a terrible script they have sent him to read ('Suffer with me, you dirty fucks!'). It is also a subject of some seriousness when it comes to aspects of family life: his parents were German, and during the Second World War he and his brother took steps to bring his mother's half-brother Paul over to America. He was also an attentive uncle to his nephew Teddy Drachman, to whom Loesser regularly corresponded as the President of the (joke) Rotten Kid Klub.

Every aspect of Loesser's life is represented in these letters. Nevertheless, the availability of sources means that some topics, projects or periods are less well represented than others. There is nothing, for example, on the writing of either *Where's Charley?* or *Guys and Dolls* – although the latter is represented through some fascinating letters on the film adaptation, including tension between the two Franks (Loesser and Sinatra) and on Marlon Brando's reluctance to record an album. Much better represented are *The Most Happy Fella* (comments to the director a particular treat), *Greenwillow* (correspondence with Joy Chute, who wrote the novella on which it was based) and *How to Succeed* (tensions with the producers). But it seems to be the general pattern that he preferred to work in person with his book writers, and of course he wrote both lyrics and music to all his Broadway shows and didn't need to write letters to himself about it, so there is very little discussion of the creation of the content of his best-known work. On the other hand, there are numerous letters in which he advises other writers on how to write a Broadway musical, revealing his approach to aesthetics, structure, integration, style, characterisation and so on, and these effectively stand in for correspondence that reveals the development of his own work.

• • •

Although we conducted archival research across the USA for this project, the majority of the letters come from the office of Frank Loesser Enterprises. Unless otherwise indicated, this is the source for the documents reproduced in this book. Editorially, we have provided short commentaries to link or contextualise groups of letters and have also tried to identify the names referred to in Loesser's writings. If we have not provided a biographical note it is either because we feel the figure is too well known to need an introduction or because we could not determine their details with confidence. We made a small number of edits (indicated by [...]) to remove outdated or problematic references in the correspondence, and because so many of the letters have been transcribed from unsigned office carbon copies, we have not indicated whether each letter is signed or not. A crucial source for us was *A Most Remarkable Fella*, the biography of Loesser by his daughter Susan, who reproduced some important letters from her father to her mother Lynn. We were unable to locate the originals but have decided to include the transcriptions here in order to fill in some important gaps. We are also grateful to the International Piano Archives at the University of Maryland for providing copies of the correspondence between Arthur and Frank Loesser.

It is more than fifteen years since the last book on Loesser (Thomas L. Riis's fine study of his Broadway musicals) and more than thirty since the only biography (Susan Loesser's personal account of her father's life and work). These, plus *The Complete Lyrics of Frank Loesser*, have been invaluable reference volumes for us when creating this volume, but a new publication on his work was long overdue. Following on from books of the letters of Alan Jay Lerner (2014), Cole Porter (2019) and Oscar Hammerstein (2022), *The Letters of Frank Loesser* at last provides a window into the private and professional worlds of one of Broadway and Hollywood's most beloved songwriters.

Dominic Broomfield-McHugh and Cliff Eisen
September 2024

TIMELINE

1910	Frank Loesser born (29 June) to Henry and Julia Loesser; siblings: Arthur (1894–1969) and Grace (1907–1986)
1926	death of Henry Loesser
1931	first published song, 'In Love with a Memory of You', music by William Schuman
1936–1948	marries Lynn Garland (19 October 1936); active mainly in Hollywood for Universal Studios and Paramount Pictures, among others
1942–1945	enlists in US Army, assigned to Radio Productions Unit at Santa Ana, California (from 1943 assigned to Army Special Services Division, New York); composes patriotic songs and stage works for US troops
1948	*Where's Charley?* opens at the St James Theatre, New York (11 October)
late 1940s	founds Frank Music Corporation
1950	wins Academy Award for Best Song for 'Baby, It's Cold Outside' (*Neptune's Daughter*, MGM, 1949); *Guys and Dolls* opens at the 46th Street Theatre, New York (24 November)
1951	wins Tony Award

1952	film *Hans Christian Andersen* released (RKO Radio Pictures)
1956	*The Most Happy Fella* opens at the Imperial Theatre, New York (3 May)
1957	divorces Lynn Loesser
1959	marries Jo Sullivan
1960	*Greenwillow* opens at the Alvin Theatre, New York (8 March)
1961–1962	*How to Succeed in Business Without Really Trying* opens at the 46th Street Theater, New York (14 October); wins 1962 Pulitzer Prize
1965	*Pleasures and Palaces* closes out of town before Broadway premiere; work begins on *Señor Discretion Himself* (abandoned 1968)
1969	Frank Loesser dies (28 July)

CHAPTER ONE

Early Life to 1949
('I AM A GOOD BOY')

Frank Loesser was born on 29 June 1910 in Manhattan. His father, Henry Loesser (1858–1926), who had immigrated to the United States from Germany, was a piano teacher; his mother, Henry's second wife, Julia Ehrlich (1881–1978), was a lecturer in the arts. Henry Loesser was first married to Julia's older sister, Bertha (1869–1902); their son Arthur, Frank's half-brother, was born on 26 August 1894. Bertha died in childbirth in 1902, and in 1907 Henry married Julia. Their daughter Grace (1907–1986) was born that same year, Frank three years later.

Loesser was musically precocious. By the age of two he was a budding singer and by the age of four he could play the piano well by ear. Among surviving letters from Henry Loesser to Arthur Loesser, Frank is mentioned twice, his developing musical interests noted each time. Both letters were written when Arthur was in Berlin, launching his career as a pianist; Arthur had studied with the pianist and composer Zygmunt Stojowski (1870–1946) at the Institute of Musical Art, New York (later incorporated into the Juilliard School of Music). Aside from providing insights into the physical layout of the family home, Henry also offers advice and encouragement to Arthur. And as it happened, Loesser often followed some of his father's advice to Arthur: Loesser's musicals mix the familiar with the novel, the traditional with the new, include contrasting characters and – from a technical point of view – different tonalities, as well as entertaining

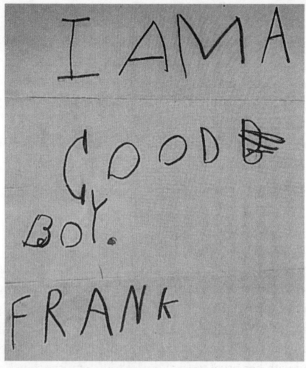

1. Undated note but, from the appearance of
the handwriting, possibly c1915.

and elevating his audiences. Both letters are written in German with
the exception of part of a postscript from his mother (starting 'Big
brother') in the first letter and a long quotation in the second letter:

3 December 1912: Henry and Julia Loesser to Arthur Loesser[1]

My dear Arthur,

We wait and wait to get further news from you. Arthur, we
received your interesting letter from Plymouth and your few lines
from Berlin.

We were very pleased with your description of your travels – the
letter made the rounds of all our acquaintances. I especially admired
your correct German style and grammar – there was not a single error

---

1 International Piano Archives, University of Maryland, Arthur Loesser Collection.

to be found. That you have come to an agreeable understanding with the aunts was very good to hear; I only hope that the aunts will not get the short end in this affair – I hope you informed yourself about what the usual conditions for room and board are elsewhere in Berlin; if you should find you are not paying enough please increase your board to what is usual.

That we are interested in absolutely everything, what you have seen, where you have been, you can imagine very well. I would only be too happy to react to it in a letter. We really miss news from you. I particularly want to know what new pieces you have added to your concert repertoire and what you are studying at the moment. Here everything is now in perfect order. The apartment has been redone and some structural changes have also been made, especially the famous folding bed has been changed into a very respectable chest of drawers which Mother is using for linen and at the same time I use it for a music cabinet. This transformation of the furniture has cost me ten dollars. Gretl[2] has a very nice bungalow bed with a new horsehair mattress and is now sleeping in her own room, which Mama has furnished with her usual taste and useability. The couch in the back parlor which needed repair is very beautiful and is now really a monument for the room and in the parlor there is a new rug which was a present from the Gallineks and the former parlor rug is now in the dining room and adds a great deal to making the room liveable. Maybe Mama will write to you details about the changes – I can't think of anything more. Uncle Spegelthal is as before a full-time boarder – he has still not found anything which would give him an income. He is after all too old and will probably have to end his days in an old people's home but it is also very difficult to get into one. My season is at present still quite good. But in my profession one should never praise the day before the evening.

The children are growing to be more delightful every day. Little Gretl is very clever, she can calculate and recite and recognize the letters of the alphabet but doesn't want to read. Frank is getting to be

---

2 Loesser's sister Grace.

more and more charming, he is very musical, especially as far as singing is concerned, but is absolutely unwilling to speak German and if he is forced to do it, he sounds as if he were the son of exotic – but not German – parents.

The musical season here is in full bloom. Godowsky had immense applause; Stojowski played in a few lesser important concerts; Mischa Elman is still a prime attraction; Sarah Bernhardt is going to appear in vaudeville, first in Chicago and later on here; Bella Alten has had her first concert here accompanied by her husband on 24 November.[3] We had to tell her about all the details of your trip and Mr. Deri and she were very pleased. They wrote down your address in Berlin and will probably write to you directly and maybe give you information about Vienna where Miss Ida Alten is living, she is a photographer. They gave me, for you, the address of Louis Sachs (address in Berlin) as well as Dr. Bogumil Zepler[4] (address in Berlin). You should visit the latter and bring greetings from Bella Alten. Mrs. Sachs was the former patroness of Bella Sachs and has a very intellectual and artistic house. Maybe you remember that she talked to us about these people. You can also visit her, or wait until Bella Alten has written to her about you. Then maybe she'll get in touch with you.

Now enough my little boy. Mother wants to write something to you too. Be cheerful and happy and kiss the aunts for me. Your Father.

P.S. You forgot to tell us what happened to the figs which friend Henschel gave you on the trip.

Dec 4th
Big brother
    My letter to you is so long it won't be ready tomorrow, but you should at least have this one. Big brother, you bad boy, confirm immediately all telegrams which you got on board the President Grant.

3 Leopold Godowsky (1870–1938), Lithuanian-American concert pianist; Mischa Elman (1891–1967), Russian-American violinist; Sarah Bernhardt (1844–1923), French actress; and Bella Alten (1877–1962), Polish operatic soprano, who in 1912 married the banker Hermann Deri (?–1941).
4 Bogumil Zepler (1858–1918), composer.

People want to know whether you got the cables or not. I don't even know from whom you got them. You have to write immediately to Mr. Kempner c/o Jennie Marl. Today I had a letter from Miss Brazier. She is surprised not to have heard anything from you. Papa is very annoyed about your negligence to Dr. Damrosch.[5] Write to him immediately. As a rule you have to confirm all letters, all presents, all cables as soon as possible. You have no idea how interested our friends are in you. They come and ask how you are and what we hear from you. Arthurchen, you have to write at least a card – you must not be ungrateful. Albert Henschel always asks about you. Aunt Tinchen, Frau Radau – they all want to know something about you. [in English:] You see, dear, this habit of scolding is innate with me, but don't mind it, only write to your loving mother.

Arthur Loesser's teacher, Zygmunt Stojowski, contributed an article, 'What Interpretation Really Is', to James Francis Cooke's *Great Pianists on Piano Playing* (Philadelphia, 1913).[6]

14 February 1914: Henry Loesser to Arthur Loesser in Berlin[7]

Dear Arthur

Enclosed is a letter of recommendation which was incorrectly addressed and came back and therefore you receive it after a delay. Yesterday I was with Stojowski. He was very pleased with my visit and to hear what I had to tell him about you. He read your last letter and he says that you are wrong if you believe that your reviews cannot be used for publicity because there is also some unfavorable comment. He says one never repeats the whole review but only the places

---

5 Walter Damrosch (1862–1950), Prussian-American conductor known in particular for his performances of Wagner.
6 Other famous pianists and composers who contributed articles to *Great Pianists on Piano Playing* include Wilhelm Backhaus, Ferruccio Busoni, Leopold Godowsky, Percy Grainger, Josef Hofmann, Josef Lhévinne, Vladimir de Pachmann, Ignaz Jan Paderewski, Sergei Rachmaninov, Emil Sauer and Xaver Scharwenka.
7 International Piano Archives, University of Maryland, Arthur Loesser Collection.

which praise you with the date and the name of the newspaper. They will be translated here and used for publicity. Further, he gave me a book for you by the title of "Great Pianists on Piano Playing" – a series of personal confessions. It also has an article by him. I am still reading it but will send it to you next week. Don't forget to thank him for it. Stojowski says he thinks he is now in your debt because he hasn't answered your very nice letter so far. His mother also sends you greetings.

We have winter for the first time since yesterday, a colossal snow-fall while the temperature previously was 4 degrees below zero. The children are very happy because of sledding. By the way, Frankie is developing more and more into a musical genius. He plays any tune he's heard on the piano and can spend an enormous amount of time at the piano, he always wants attention and an audience. Gretl remains far behind him but she spends more time with literature. She is very strong in Greek mythology and reads everything which comes under her eyes but her writing is as usual very bad.

We just got your card in which you say you're going to give another concert on March 8th. We are very pleased about it because this is after all the only way to open the eyes of the audience and to interest the reviewers. The agents will then pay attention to you and then chances for more engagements will become great for Germany as well as for other countries. Stojowksi thinks you should also go to other cities – Dresden, Leipzig, Hamburg – but this is a little more difficult because one doesn't know what the income will be from ticket sales. Stojowski feels you should not select programs that are too heterogeneous. Bloomfield-Zeisler[8] writes about it this way in the book he gave you:

[in English:] "Skill in the arrangement of an artist's program has much to do with his success; the program must contain certain works which interest concert goers, it should be neither entirely conventional, nor shouldn't [sic] contain novelties entirely, the classics should be repre-

---

8 Fannie Bloomfield Zeisler (1863–1927), Austrian-born American pianist. The reference is to an interview with her in James Francis Cooke, ed., *Great Pianists on Piano Playing* (Philadelphia, 1917).

sented because the large army of students expect to be especially bene-
fited by having these performed by a great artist. Novelties must be
placed on the program to make it attractive to the maturer habitués of
the concert room. There must be contrasts in the character and tonal
nature of the compositions played, they must be so grouped that interest
of the hearers will not only [be] sustained to the end, but will gradually
increase. It may truly be said that program making is in itself a high art. It
is difficult to give advice on this subject by any general statement.
Generalizations are often too misleading. <u>I would advise the young artist
to study carefully the programs of the most successful artists and to
attempt to discover the principle underlying their arrangement</u>. One
thing that should never be forgotten is that the object of a concert is not
merely to show off the skill of the performer, but to instruct, entertain
and elevate the audience. The bulk of the program should be composed
of standard works, but novelties of genuine worth should be given a
place on the program."

[in German:] Altogether this very successful artist gives very
important hints for the young artist for his successful development,
but you will read it yourself. Write more immediately about your
upcoming concert, what you think about staying in Berlin or Europe
more permanently. I refer you to my last letter: source and work must
be the most important agents in your life.

With a thousand greetings and kisses from your father.

Frank's early unwillingness to speak German already attests to his
sometimes intractable, stubborn and occasionally contrarian nature.
And handwritten letters or notes that he wrote to his mother during
his childhood are often sassy if nevertheless affectionate.

Undated: To Julia Loesser

Dear mother
    Please dress me and I will give you a kiss and I will go out and I will
not bother you any more and I will play and play and not cross the
street.
    Frank

Undated: To Julia Loesser

Dear mother, you said I was late. But you are very much mistaken. I was very early. Amen.
From Frank

Undated: To Julia Loesser

Dear mother,
Heartiest congratulations for your wedding anniversary. I hope you may prosper all your life. As I cannot afford a check of 100,000,000,000, I will give you a gold pianola. My pen [?] is great! Well so long.
Kisses xxxxxxxxxxxxxxxxx amen
Your Loving
Frank

March 1910s: To Julia Loesser[9]

TO Mama
FROM Frank

roses are red
violets are blue
sugar is sweet
And 32 years are you

On 2 September 1917, First Lieutenant Joseph Meyer (1894–1987) – a family friend and later a collaborator of Loesser's[10] – wrote to the seven-year-old Frank Loesser from Fort Benjamin Harrison, Indiana,

---

9 The dating of this letter is problematic. An annotation on the note, not in Loesser's hand, reads '1918 March', which cannot be correct: Julia was born in 1881 and turned 32 in 1913. At the same time, it is implausible that Loesser could have written a note like this when he was only two years old.

10 Loesser's collaborations with Meyer were the songs 'Junk Man' and 'I Wish I Were Twins' (both 1934).

with news from the camp and offering him a soldier suit, a pistol or a sabre. Loesser wrote back in December, blaming his mother for the delay.

23 December 1917: To First
Lieutenant Joseph Meyer

Dear Lt. Meyer

I wrote a letter long ago but my mother tore it up because she could not find a postage stamp. I remember that you asked me if I wanted a soldier suit. I need size 7. And you asked me too if I wanted a sword or a [sic] automatic pistol. I would rather have the pistol. I think it's very kind of you to want to send me these things. Wishing you a Merry Christmas and a Happy New Year.

   From
   Frank

Loesser spent part of the summer of 1923 at Camp Wigwam, about 15 miles west of Lewiston, Maine, on the shores of Bear Pond, in the foothills of the White Mountains. Founded in 1910 by Abraham 'Mandy' Mandelstam and Arnold 'Pop' Lehman as a summer camp for boys, Camp Wigwam was sold in 1964 to Ned and Helen Strauss, whose descendants, Bob and Jane Strauss, continue to run the camp – still as a camp for boys. The area was well known for summer musical activities: in addition to Camp Wigwam, it was the head-quarters of the Bristol School of Music and Grand Opera, and nearby Harrison, Maine,[11] was the summer home of singers Marie Sundalius (1884–1958) and Charles Harrison (1878–1965); Richard Rodgers spent part of the summer of 1916 at Camp Wigwam. Several letters by Loesser, addressed to his parents, document camp life and activities. His handwriting is not always legible.

---

11 Anon., *Harrison: Picturesque Region of Maine* (Portland, c1910).

3 July 1923: To Henry and Julia Loesser

Dear Mother and Dad.

This is the life! Every morning we get up at 6:45, endure 5 minutes of callisthenics, and then take a 30 second dip in the lake. During this time, our beds are airing and when we come back we make them and fix our tents. This takes about 15 minutes, after which we go to assembly, during which we arrange activities for the day. By the time we come back our tents have been inspected and commended.

We then go to our counsellors and are assigned duty in what ever subject we take. I ... [unreadable] ... Wigwam.

In the afternoon we play ball and take another swim, and the [sic] eat and go to bed.

Everything O.K.

5 July 1923: To Henry and Julia Loesser

[page 1 missing]

nature study I think is the best educational activity in camp. We have different Indian tribes[12] and hold contests in specimen gathering.

We also have hikes and "paper chases."

Julian Rochelle[13] is an awfully nice fellow and were [sic] still tent mates he is taking dramatics and is a fine actor. (one of the best).

Today we're having a swimming meet between Reds and Grays and also a Track meet.

Tonight will be a song contest between the two teams. Please pray for our team (Reds).

Your loving son,

Frankie

---

12 Local Indigenous groups are the Maliseet, the Micmac, the Passamaquoddy and the Penobscot, collectively known as the Wabanaki, or 'People of the Dawnland'.
13 Possibly the Julian Rochelle who in 1929 starred in a Yale University production of R. J. H. Powell's *Brief Candle* and who was a director of the Association of Junior Leagues' Little Theatre in the early 1930s.

7 July 1923: To Henry and Julia Loesser

Dear Mother & Father.

This place is the cat's! It seems that I can't stop doing something [?]. [. . .]

At 11:15 we all went in for a beautiful dip in "Bear Lake." The water was not the least bit cold. The weather is also warm and I'm writing now with only a jersey, trunks and sneakers (Uncle Dick's), which were delivered to my tent.

I have for tent mates Julian, Ralph Elias, John Dearman, all of whom are very nice fellows.

How's this for a lunch menu – Chicken soup, . . . [unreadable] . . . potatoes, beans, chicken, gravy, ice cream and cake.

I am writing now during rest period which is . . . [unreadable] . . . after lunch either [?]

When you answer this letter put on the envelope "Tent 3."

Having nothing more to say —

Blaa blaa blaa etc ......

Your affectionate son,

Frankie

P.S. Please send

envelopes

stamps

25 August 1923: To Henry and Julia Loesser

Dear Mother and Father,

I suppose you know already that I have been sick. Thats [sic] why I couldn't write sooner.

This is Red and Gray week and the whole camp is divided into Red and Gray teams. I'm on the Red team but the Grays are winning. We have baseball games and tournaments between each other. It's lots of fun.

Lots of love

Frankie

Late August 1923 (Monday): To Henry and Julia Loesser

Dear Mother + Father,

It seems that the time has flown terribly quickly. Red and Gray Week (last week of Camp) is half over. So far the Red Team (mine) is winning by about 3 points.

I'm getting awfully sunburnt now. When I come back you'll ask me [to] say "Laverne, call for the garbage please." (Is that the way to spell "Laverne"?)

Do you know that there was a song contest among the girls' camps the other day. Sister's camp won and sister almost died with joy. (They won a big cup.)

I want to say that I will be home Sat. 8.15 a.m. Grand Cent Station.

Yesterday night the whole camp had a birthday Party in Honor of Mrs. Lehman and Big Brother. Their birthdays are on the same date.

Every month had its own table[,] our table was decorated with pink and white bunting and ribbon with a card board Wedding cake in the middle.

The best decorated table won a big cake. (we didn't win.) We had ice cream, cake, soda and chicken salad.

Wednesday night will be banquet night in which will be about twice as much grub as the birthday party.

An undated letter to Loesser's mother may post-date 1923 – the handwriting appears more mature than the letters written from Camp Wigwam.

[?after 1923]: To Julia Loesser

Mother darling!

Happy landing – and try to find the gin wrappers, cigarette butts, corpses and other household effects you are wont to expect.

I have gone out into the bleak to do things with Joes. Sister will be home about 6.30 or so.

(Note soap carving by Loesser in the living room)

I will be back about 5.30 maybe. love, Frank

[in a box, lower left corner:] I have been a good boy.

Loesser attended the Townsend Harris High School for gifted children and, subsequently, the City University of New York. But he was expelled from CUNY in 1925 for failing every subject except English and gym.[14] And following the unexpected death of Henry Loesser in 1926, Frank took on a variety of jobs, mostly unsuccessfully, including as a process server, an advertisement salesman for the *New York Herald Tribune*, editor of the *New Rochelle News*, and the knit-goods editor for *Women's Wear Daily*, among others – none of which are mentioned in his earliest surviving letters to Arthur.

13 July 1926: To Arthur Loesser[15]

Dear Arthur,

Your Bolshevratic [?] version of the fire on Fort Sumter arrived yesterday morning in time for a bassoon accompaniment to the arsenal explosion at Dover, New Jersey.[16]

They are the berries, I think although sister[17] says gorgeous, papa takes one look and says Vundershoën [sic] and mamma walks over

---

14 John L. Cogdill, 'Loesser, Frank' in *American National Biography*, https://www. anb.org/display/10.1093/anb/9780198606697.001.0001/anb-9780198606697-e-18 00746?rskey=fA6XjI&result=15 (accessed 7 June 2023). According to Arthur Loesser, 'We [the family] bullied him into trying a year at the College of the City of New York, but he was a total casualty after the battle of the first semester.' Arthur Loesser, 'My Brother Frank', *Notes* 7/2 (March 1950), 219.

15 International Piano Archives, University of Maryland, Arthur Loesser Collection.

16 *New York Times*, 11 July 1926: 'LIGHTNING BOLT BLOWS UP NAVY MUNITIONS NEAR DOVER, N.J.; EXPLODING SHELLS FIRE, ARMY ARSENAL HALF A MILE AWAY, 50 MAY BE DEAD . . . Dover, N. J., Sunday, July 11, 2 A.M. – A series of terrific explosions caused by lightning striking a magazine at the United States Naval Ammunition Depot, Lake Denmark, N. J., six miles north of this town, at 8 o'clock (Daylight Saving Time) last evening, shook the country for thirty miles around, tore houses from their foundations, hurled automobiles off the highways and darkened the sky with twin barrages of burning débris and smoke.'

17 Grace Loesser.

and says splendid and something to the effect that Arthur is always so nice and everything, to which we all agree. Thanx loads "Arturchien."

Listen, I went hiking with Jud Briefer over the week end of the 4th. We went to Honesdale, Pennsylvannia [sic] and got put up in a dump farm house for the night.

Last week end we hiked again, this time to Elberon New Jersey. We did it back and forth in 6 hours.

We got high hat all of a sudden and decided <u>not</u> to see the Elmans.

We took a swim in a swell kosher dump known as "West End Casino."[18]

We may try Cleveland if I get a week off.

Anyway, I have to beat it now or get fired from my swell job. I will think of you while mopping the floor of the office.

Love and thanks

again

Frank.

3 May 1929: To Arthur Loesser[19]

Ach Bruderlein,

what with mother and sister out at a concert, no camels[20] left and a strong desire to do something mother is liable to deem useful, I take my Underwood in hand and punch away.

---

18 The no-longer-extant West End Casino in West End, New Jersey, was founded by Henry (?–1994) and Bernice Kempler (1921–2020). According to the *Jewish Daily Bulletin* for 31 May 1934: 'The sad thing about the West End Casino at West End, N.J., is that you've got to go there! I may rave for half a page and you'll not get the point, which is that this hotel is different. You've got to see the Casino itself . . . to dip in the surf or swim in either of the twin salt water pools. You've got to bask 'neath the sun on an expansive, immaculate beach or hide in the shade of a huge umbrella, exhilarated by invigorating ocean breezes. You've got to dance to the soft strains of Phil Harris' orchestra on the deck or in the ball room 'mid tropical palms and flowers. In short, you've got to go there to find out that nothing has been overlooked to assure you a pleasant vacation at this most exclusive watering place.'
19 International Piano Archives, University of Maryland, Arthur Loesser Collection.
20 That is, cigarettes.

Today I made only one mistake at the office – but corrected it myself before anyone saw it. Mr. Polk asked when you were coming to New York and I told him the middle of april. Is that right?

[asterisk in margin] Our little darling has packed his duffle and fiddle and gone to Toronto where he expects to give a concert. That saves Mamma a lot of grapefruit anyway. He is coming back soon however. These Colonials have a habit of coming back. (Colonial – meaning Native of Cologne ... which, I have discovered lately is his birthplace.)

Arthur, old klimperer,[21] for the first time in my life I have dragged me down to Sax's[22] and bought me a nifty suit WITHOUT THE FINANCIAL OR ADVISORY AID OF MAMMA ... which is quite a feat in itself.

The Goodman bros. and Lucille were here the other night and we had the first swell feed in a long time. Lucille is getting real slangy and affects sudden strong desires for Chesterfields.[23] The brothers are ultra childish Babbits[24] in modern dress and a touch of quelque fleurs. One is a wow at the piano and the other a shark at chess. The Edw. Ehrlichs[25] were at the house too. Uncle Eddie is very spry and very dumb and Minner is so coy and oh sooo very very intelligent. As the boy friend – (namely your bro.) would say – they are a peach of a pair ... where upon sister would yap, "old fruit, I think you've got your dates mixed . . . . and so on throuought [sic] the drupe family or perhaps the GOOP family

---

21 'Tinkler', as in 'tinkle the ivories'.
22 Saks Fifth Avenue.
23 Chesterfield cigarettes.
24 Slang for 'a person and especially a business or professional man who conforms unthinkingly to prevailing middle-class standards' (Merriam-Webster). The term had its origins in Sinclair Lewis's best-selling novel *Babbitt* (1922). A silent film *Babbitt* was released in 1924 (Warner Brothers) and a sound version in 1934 (First National Pictures).
25 Edward Ehrlich (1877–1964), Julia Loesser's brother, Frank Loesser's uncle. He was married to Minna Ehrlich (née Kohn, 1880–1966); they had two children, John (1907–1991) and Evelyn (1914–1996).

Amreadind [sic] a swell book by one Ethel Dell whose name is probably not familiar to you.[26] It has lots of sex in it, and Everything From Herring recipes to Voodo [sic] rituals. (the book, not the name)

Arthur, it is getting late and I have to take my bath or the bath will take me – which has no significance at all and only goes to indicate the sleepiness of my little mind.

anyway, write me a long letter soon, but dont [sic] make the mistake I have just made . . . that is to say – Use a small piece of paper and write large . . . it requires less effort – to say nothing of ink.

Old bean, I am exhausted . . .

yrs. aff.

F. L.

per. F.L.

(conf. sec.)

  * "Fireman" (Feuermann)[27]

Loesser's first copyrighted song, 'Alone in Your Class (Little Girl)' – set to music by the obscure Carl Rice (dates unknown) – was written in 1929. And between 1929 and 1931 he collaborated with his friend, the later well-known composer William Schuman (1910– 1992), on 'Doing the Dishes', 'Where the Grass Grows Green' and 'In Love with a Memory of You' (Loesser's first published lyric). In 1932, Loesser and Schuman considered writing an operetta; a copy of the typescript libretto survives among the William Schuman papers at the Library of Congress, but no music. Schuman later recalled one of the lost lyrics: 'We once started on an operetta based on the life of da Vinci and Frank had some wonderful lyrics. Then a few years ago I wrote a choral work, in which I wanted to bring in some old American tunes. I felt I ought to have a waltz, and suddenly a waltz tune I had written with Frank for the da Vinci show came to mind. The work

---

26 Ethel May Dell Savage (1881–1939, pen name Ethel M. Dell) was an English writer of more than thirty romance novels and short stories.

27 A handwritten note, possibly by Arthur Loesser, on the back of this letter reads: 'Rummaging thru a drawer I found this valuable M.S. It is undated, but from the contents it is evident that it was penned – no – typed – in 1927 [sic]. His little mind has not changed since. His letters + editorials are just like this to this day.'

was first performed by the New York Philharmonic. There they were playing the waltz – a rousing tune – and I'll tell you what the real words were: "Here comes that drunken da Vinci again, all filled with highballs, stewed to the eyeballs." [28] Schuman later said that 'Frank Loesser has written hits with Hoagy Carmichael [1899–1981], Burton Lane [1912–1997], Jule Styne [1905–1994] and other Hollywood grand dukes, but I have the distinction of having written a flop with him.'[29] Some years later, in 1948, Loesser wrote a reminiscence of Schuman:

10 April 1948: To Vincent Persichetti[30]

Dear Vincent:

What I remember about Bill Schuman as a boy hasn't much to do with his professional career. Maybe remotely it has, but I am not well enough acquainted with his doings today to see how my boyhood companion of West 107th Street turned out to be THE William Schuman, with a middle initial.

When I first met Bill we were both about eleven and he was much larger and stronger than I. He kept punching me all the time. It was only right since he was taller. That was, and I am sure still is, one of the rules, even on the enlightened West Side. So it is to Bill's credit that he let me slug him back once in a while. I think this might have been the gesture by which he conceded parity. According to the rules he didn't owe me this but he gave it. Also, he never hurt me very badly. It may have been prompted by a sense of our intellectual rapport which hadn't started to exist then but was going to someday. Our first discussion which did not involve fisticuffs or a baseball occurred two years later in the fall. He had just come back from a boys' summer camp called Cobosee and I had just come back from one called Wigwam. We were comparing summer experiences and fell to regaling each other with samples of camp song and cheer lyrics, and

---

28 Robert Kimball and Stephen Nelson, *The Complete Lyrics of Frank Loesser* (New York, 2003), 5.
29 Ibid.
30 Vincent Persichetti (1915–1987), American composer.

when I went crazy over his Cobosee favorite both of us knew that we would enjoy such things together. The words he sang, as well as I can remember were –

>Here's to our head counselor
>The bastard's name is Gordon
>He thinks he is the monkey's tits
>But he is only the Warden

There passed a stretch of many years during which we lost track of each other. We met again when we were about eighteen through a mutual friend named Frances Prince to whom, as you know, he is now married. Having been hustled off all through my youth to hear recitals by various musical wunderkinder, my pictures of a boy musician was a sort of composite of Shura Cherkosky (spelling?), Yehudi Menuhin and both Ricci brothers.[31] Bill was a short-haired personality slightly on the Rogers-Peet[32] side. Ideal margin clerk material except that he laughed too much and too loud. (This was 1928).

I can't recall the exact circumstances, but one day in the Franconia Hotel Apartment on West 72nd Street where he lived with his family, he went to the piano and started to play a piece. It was obvious from the very first bar that this boy would have to become a composer or at least a conductor, as his piano playing was an abomination. What interested me greatly was the finger technique. He caressed the keys with his finger tips the ways fiddlers do on a bare string – hoping vainly against hope that he too could produce a pleasing vibrato in this fashion. I asked about this and he said he had studied the violin and that this technique, however fruitless, was a result of habit. Whereupon he produced a violin and played for me. Once again it was painfully clear that Bill Schuman had better not become an instru-

---

31 The Russian-American pianist Shura Cherkassky (1909–1995) gave his first private performance at the age of thirteen, in March 1923; violinist Yehudi Menuhin (1916–1999) first appeared in public at the age of five, in November 1921; violinist Ruggiero Ricci (1918–2012) first performed in public at the age of ten, in 1928. Ricci's brother, George (1923–2010) was a cellist; the date of his first public performance is unknown. 32 Rogers Peet was a men's clothing store founded in 1874. It is referenced in 'Marry the Man Today' from *Guys and Dolls*: 'Slowly introduce him to the better things / Respectable, conservative, and clean / Readers Digest / Guy Lombardo / Rogers Peet'.

mentalist. But Schuman, too, was well aware of his lack of prowess as a playing musician. The tremolo business with the fingers was not merely hangover violin technique. What Schuman was doing in his mind was orchestrating. He was hearing sounds that weren't there physically. I should have known then and during the year that followed that he'd never be happy as Tin Pan Alley songwriter. I should have known that he would always have the little finger wiggling vainly on the keys in a desperate wish to hear music that couldn't possibly be produced through such a medium. Schuman <u>did</u> know although he never spoke about it.

When we started to try writing popular songs together he seemed very wholehearted about the whole thing. As a matter of fact, he <u>was wholehearted</u>. The same way a housewife is wholehearted about cleaning up the kitchen, but this doesn't mean she doesn't dream of being drunk at the Stork Club or playing opposite Errol Flynn, or doing something very noble like stirring pitchblende. She cleans the kitchen handsomely and skillfully and may even have a feeling of pride about how well she does it, but doesn't delude herself into believing that the whole accomplishment is anything more than a first-class kitchen cleaning.

I don't mean to say by this that Bill had any snob sense about Tin Pan Alley. He wanted to write songs. Big popular smashes. But he didn't kid himself into thinking that his musical life would end there. Now this is not an unusual kind of thinking for the young man already equipped technically for the so-called "serious" field. At the time Bill was not at all well educated musically, but he could already see his own path beyond such accomplishments as "In Love With The Memory Of You," "Waitin' For The Moon," etc.

Shortly after these and other songwriting attempts, Bill went to Europe to study music. When he came back, I asked him about Salzburg and he reported that it was wonderful. You sat down to dinner and automatically the waiter would ask "dark oder light?" Schuman had been reared on prohibition gin and had never tasted real German beer, or certainly not lots of it. He had had a fine time. We didn't discuss music, just beer and dames.

Musically Bill was already well beyond my depth and a little nearer to realizing the sounds that the little wiggling finger had tried to make.

After that, the Schuman weight began to be felt in musical circles. I heard some of the choral stuff from time to time and some orchestra stuff. I am too corny to appreciate all of it. My ear stops listening around Tschaikowsky. But I heard all the noise about his success and his growing importance and, of course, was very anxious to see him and take stock of the new Schuman. (I have been living in California for many years.)

I came to New York and we got together, talking mostly about old times – the fist fights, the musical comedy based on the life of Leonardo da Vinci we once almost wrote, the time we threw chocolate cake at each other at the home of some perfectly decent people we hardly knew, and stuff like that.

When Bill laughs ha-ha, it's ha-ha. There are no variations. It's just plain ha-ha and quite loud. He was in the middle of a big ha-ha. Then he stopped abruptly and informed me that any minute the bell would ring and someone would be coming to see him on some school business. (Bill was teaching at Sarah Lawrence College.) "I'm going to have to adopt my professional tone," he announced, "You will throw up when you hear it." I braced myself.

"I wring my hands piteously and bow a little and use small, ordinary words with great precision as if they were big ones. I am obsequious but with great authority. I am dignified, modest, reasonable yet severe and frighteningly polite every minute. It's phoney as hell."

"Why do you do it?" I asked. "They expect it of me," he explained. "It is a way for a college professor to be. I sort of enjoy it." To emphasize this, he slapped his wife's ass. Then the doorbell rang and the visitor came in. Schuman went into his act, sort of an American Roland Young. It was a fine job except that every once in a while I could almost hear the big ha-ha breaking through. When the visitor had gone, it did, quite audible. That was the first sound, just to clear the air and the second was one of Schuman's pet phrases. It's an expression which he saves as an important punctuation point. He has been using it after long confirmation speeches, tedious dinners and unsuccessful taxi encounters with young ladies. It consists of eight short words. "Stop picking your nose and pass the butter."

I have seen Bill once or twice since the Juilliard job. The ha-ha is still very loud and apparently no demands are made on him by the school to adopt the "professor" character.

But what you want, I guess, is detail about Schuman, the boy.

He once threw my shoes in the Central Park reservoir.

At eighteen he delivered a stirring lecture for my benefit, on the proper way to pace around a room while thinking. "Do not walk in circles," he advised. "Circles make you dizzy. Go to the Central Park Zoo. Watch the lion. Do not watch the black leopard. He is neurotic. But watch the lion. The lion paces all day long but always faces in one direction. Only the back of him paces. You'll notice that his steps form a figure eight pattern. He makes 45 degree turns and then swivels. His tail may get dizzy but never his head. He probably gets a lot of songs written."

Once when we were about twelve, I dared him to eat six peanut butter sandwiches without drinking anything. He did it.

So help me, mister, that's all I know about the wheelbarrow. I hope it can be of some use to you. Forgive me for taking so long.

> Best wishes,
> Frank Loesser

In 1933, Loesser decided to pursue songwriting full time.

1933: To Arthur Loesser[33]

Dear Arthur:

I think when I wrote you last, it was more than a year ago. Until now there hasn't been much good news about myself or my business . . . which accounts to some extent for the silence. At present, and for many months to come I expect to be busier than ever with business, and (8th wonder) making a living, or better, at it. So there, between

---

33 International Piano Archives, University of Maryland, Arthur Loesser Collection.

the economic darkness and dawn, goes a sort of concentrated letter ... which you can put in the Good Cheer file.

Enclosed you will find your check to mamma ... which I think is about the most vital evidence of our impending good fortune in business. To put it in words, Mama has been doing a little better than she expected with her lectures, and I have managed to gather in enough funds out of [the] song business to keep the roof on, and even <u>real</u> cream in the coffee. I never have said anything directly to you about how awfully swell I thought you have been to keep us going these years ... but I have been doing a lot of thinking about it. Now, the quicker I try to relieve you of the burden we must be, the better and more effectively I can say thanks.

And so I have gone back to the song business. Although I have been writing them five years or more, I have never stuck to the trade for more than a year at a time. Not because I got tired of it, but because every once in a while, some "money-making" idea comes up (Process-serving for example) which takes me off the track, in the hope that I can make a better living in it than with music. But in every month <u>off</u> Broadway, I lose a <u>year</u>'s worth of contacts which are of the greatest importance in this trade. I said "trade." It's no <u>art</u>. I found that out. It is all contact, salesmanship, handshaking etc. ... not a bit different from cloaks and suits or any other industry. This time I am a salesman and a handshaker ... (still a little too genteel for Broadway, but going Broadway fast) This will bring success. I know it, and amd [sic] going to stick to it.

Hopes, with a capital H, are of course coming thick and fast. A play I have adapted for the American stage (was a hit in Vienna) ... various songs, acts etc. Even a movie idea. One out of every ten of these MAY come near realization. The entire industry (entertainment) is improving. I had a talk with Mr. Bitner, Pres. of Leo Feist Inc.,[34] who showed me figures on 1933, for sale of educational music as well as <u>new</u> piano sales based on major jobbers reports. Educational music is up 30 percent over the year previous, and pianos are up ten percent

---

34 Edgar F. Bitner (c1877–1939), president of Leo Feist, Inc., a major publisher of popular songs.

(in number of pianos sold)... This means a lot to me and my popular songs. The more pianos sold, the more sheet music (popular), and the more educational music this year, the greater the piano sales next year. Popular songs are already at about one third of the gross figures for record high years (1924–5–6–)... which some day will make me a millionaire instead of a multi-millionaire.

I read marvellous accounts of Anne in your letters, as well as Jean's[35] and Aunt Helen's to mother. She must be an amazing thing. If she chortles at Snigglefritz,[36] I wonder what she would say to some of my lyrics, or some of anybody's lyrics, for that matter. Aunt Helen told mother that you might be able to bring her with you when you come this summer. I will cancel all dates.

Aunt Helen has been marvelous. Her interest in my songs etc. flatters me to death... She asked mother about them, when and by whom they are being sung. I gave mother only the barest information to write, because things don't always come through as planned. I'd much rather wait till I have a hit and then you can't avoid hearing the damn thing everytime you tune the radio or even walk in the street.

"I raised my hat"[37] is fairly popular here. A little too smart aleck... without the inspiration of "Did you ever see a dream walking?"[38] which is the current nationwide hit. Listen for it. "Big Bad wolf"[39] of course you have heard. Especially if you recall the Fledermaus score, which has been plugging it for years ... and that old German folk ditty about Schnapps.[40] But the words are cute. Jean wrote that Anne knows them by heart.

---

35 Arthur's wife, Jean Basset (dates unknown), and their daughter Anne Hollander (1930–2014), later a fashion historian.

36 Apparently slang, originally from Pennsylvania Dutch country, referring to a mischievous or talkative child and often used as a term of endearment.

37 Music by Franz Steininger, lyrics by Edward Pole. Numerous recordings 1933–1934; see https://lyricsplayground.com/alpha/songs/i/iraisedmyhat.html (including lyrics).

38 Music by Harry Revel, lyrics by Mack Gordon; written for Art Jarrett in the 1933 Paramount Pictures film *Sitting Pretty*.

39 'Who's Afraid of the Big Bad Wolf?' music by Frank Churchill with additional lyrics by Ann Ronell, from the 1933 Disney cartoon, *Three Little Pigs*.

40 Possibly 'Ein Prosit der Gemütlichkeit', a traditional Oktoberfest beer song.

For perfectly marvelous small orchestra entertainment, listen to Willard Robison[41] Monday evenings on WABC. (Columbia Broadcasting) He sings fairly well [...] and his orchestra (22 man, woodwinds all double) play the most amazing arrangement of obscure [...] songs, bayou melodies, backwoods music etc. ... also some standard material, all performed splendidly. Tell me what you think. Robison is a friend of mine (No relation to Louis and Paula, although he lives in Crestwood N.Y!)

Since out [sic] last talk on science I have read Book of the Damned[42] and loved it (not as literature). It gave me a very goofy idea for a play something like the Guild hit of 1925 "This World we Live In."[43] But it will be quite a time before I have the leisure to gamble my time writing it.

I suppose you hear from sister and Teddy[44] often. They are swell correspondents. Sister seems to like her job, and Teddy his pearl-diving or whatever it is.

Arthur, I will write you again when I get a chance to be social, or much sooner if I have some startling good news. In the meantime love to all of you. See you around Easter?

Frank.

(I forgot you liked signatures in pen and ink. sorry)

---

41 Willard Robison (1894–1968), singer, pianist and composer known in particular for music reflecting rural America. He appeared with his Deep River Orchestra on the radio show *The Deep River Hour* in the early 1930s. Robison's orchestrator was composer William Grant Still (1895–1978); Wayne D. Shirley, 'Religion in Rhythm: William Grant Still's Orchestrations for Willard Robison's *Deep River Hour*', *Black Music Research Journal* 19/1 (1999), 1–41.

42 Charles Fort's *The Book of the Damned* (New York, 1919) is generally considered the first on the topic of 'anomalistics' – UFOs, the existence of mythological creatures, curious weather patterns and other entities or events excluded from scientific study for their apparent lack of credibility. In its extensive dealing with paranormal phenomena, it foreshadows popular movies and television shows such as *The X Files*.

43 *The World We Live In* (also known as *Pictures from the Insects' Life*, *The Insect Play*, *The Life of Insects* and *The Insect Comedy*) was a satirical play by the Czech brothers Josef (1887–1945) and Karel (1890–1938) Čapek; it played in translation in the United States in 1922.

44 Grace Loesser's husband, Theodore Drachman.

(About Mrs. Marx ... you know the main facts. I'm really glad you and Jean were'nt [sic] visiting ... you wouldn't have had much fun. Mother was excited for a while, but everything is all right now ... in fact a little pleasanter than this fall, to have our own house to ourselves and Whoopee. I don't think we'll ever need another roomer ... but don't say this to mama. She is a born pessimist.)

Loesser had his first commercial successes in 1934: 'Junk Man', recorded by Benny Goodman, and 'I Wish I Were Twins', recorded by Fats Waller. And in 1935 he collaborated with composer Louis Herscher (1894–1975) on *Poetic Gems*, a series of thirteen songs inspired by the poems of Edgar A. Guest (1881–1959) that he later described to his attorneys:

1962: To his (unnamed) attorneys[45]

This collection of songs represents all my collaboration with Herscher. They were written at the request of a man named Pizor (spelling?) who seemed to be a film manufacturer on 9th Avenue. I seem to recall that they made a series of short scenic films based on Edgar Guest's poetry and Herscher and I were required to adapt Guest's subjects to song form. I remember that I did not use any of Guest's actual titles or poetic lines, but simply adapted his subjects. I believe the songs were used in the films mentioned, but there was also a reading of the original Guest poetry ... I simply sat down with Herscher and Herscher paid me in hand $5 cash for each completed work ... Somewhere in my gederum[46] I have the feeling that the $5 he gave me was out of the $100 they gave him, and in those years the gederum had a lot of wrinkles in it. My opinion of the series of pieces is as low as my caloric count was in those days.

In the mid 1930s, Loesser composed a number of stand-alone songs, some of them possibly intended for the stage, and in 1936,

---

45 Kimball and Nelson, *The Complete Lyrics of Frank Loesser*, 14.
46 Yiddish for 'intestines', so 'in my gut'.

together with one of his regular collaborators at the time, composer Irving Actman (1907–1967), he wrote *The Illustrators' Show*. Although it closed after only five performances (22–25 January 1936), *The Illustrators' Show* led to a six-month contract with Universal Studios, Hollywood, at $200 a week, beginning in April 1936.

27 April 1936: To Arthur Loesser

Dear brother Arthur. . . .

It looks as if the seven lean years have passed. I only hope there are as many fat ones ahead. All I know is that I'm good for my salary for the next twenty weeks . . . but there are options in my contract with this picture firm that may keep me here steadily for seven (count 'em) years, at an ever increasing wage.

The job is to write songs for the pictures this firm (Universal) produces. It involves some luck of course. The men at the head of this outfit have just bought it from the famous Carl Laemmle[47] and the entire program of the studio is reorganized . . . as far as production plans go.

I have seen all (or almost all) the "lots" of the big companies out here. They would interest you. My firm is situated on so great an expanse of real estate, that it has been made an incorporated city,[48] with its own police force and post office. There are some acres and acres, devoted to permanent exterior settings . . . facades of buildings . . . early Italian or Vermont Log Cabin. Saloon doorways . . . reproduction of Versailles palace, with fountain (Working) Model bridges, skyscrapers, entire jungle villages . . . and so forth.

I haven't been here long enough to inquire much into the technique of making pictures but the sound and camera machinery is impressive. I'll learn.

You know what the climate is around these parts. . . . I remember your having been here . . . well I am thriving on it. Two days after I arrived I had a tan.

---

47 Carl Laemmle (1867–1939), co-founder in 1912 of Universal Pictures.
48 Culver City.

I also have a car ... or rather a half interest in one with my new partner.[49] Brand new Plymouth Coupe. I had a driving lesson today. Will be tearing around Los Angeles (Red light district of course) with an arm around one Hoyden[50] (tight) and the other on the wheel (loose) in another 2 days.

That's what I imagine mother pictures, anyway. ... Although she hasn't been the worrier she used to be. I was going by plane, but at the last moment learned the planes were down from St. Louis east, and so took a train from New York. Got on the plane at St. Louis and the ride to the coast was marvelous ... it being my first, of course. Later I wrote mother about the plane (she had supposed I was taking the train all the way) ... and in her letter to me, she didn't seem to have been awfully shocked. Maybe mama is improving.

I'd love to see you and Jean and Anne. I suppose that's impossible for the next five or six months unless you people decided on another summer in the west like the one in Oregon a few years ago. It would be swell.

Anne must be quite a lady. Tell her I send my love ... and of course loads to Jean.

Frank

Write me Care: Music Dept. Universal Pictures, Universal City, California.

Loesser's work for Universal included songs for *The Postal Inspector*, *Yellowstone* and *The Man I Marry* (all 1936), *Three Smart Girls* (1937) and several Walter Lantz cartoons, including *Mysterious Crossing*, *Everybody Sing* and *A Meany, Miny, Moe* (all 1937). He subsequently worked for RKO Pictures, including 'Blame It on the Danube' for *Fight For Your Lady* (1937), and United Artists, for whom he wrote his first big hit, 'The Moon of Manakoora' for *The Hurricane* (1937).

The year before he moved to Hollywood, while still based in New York, Loesser had met the singer Lynn Garland (1918–1986, born

---

49 Irving Actman.
50 According to Merriam-Webster, 'A girl or woman of saucy, boisterous or care-free behaviour'.

Mary Alice Blankenbaker). After his move to California, they corresponded on a near-daily basis, about Loesser's work and their future plans.[51] Loesser proposed in September 1936 and they married on 19 October 1936.

May–July 1936: To Lynn Garland

William Powell and Carole Lombard are making a picture[52] on a sound stage across the back yard from our bungalow at the studio. Neither of them has a chin in real life . . .

The movie I saw last night was pretty bad, probably the fault of most of the company, notably Otto Kruger who takes too long to die, and makes very stagey love. Edith Barrett was swell though, and also a couple of others. Remember the guy in "Sweet Aloes" who looks like he was made of ice? The nasty tall man with the clipped speech like cubes popping out of a rubber tray? Well, he was in it too. Up to his neck he was in it . . .

Right now Irving [Actman] and I are in the throes, trying to knock off a hit out of a situation where the producer orders a certain title, the musical director orders a certain rhythm, the dance director orders a certain number of bars and the composers order a certain number of aspirins . . .

The first picture of ours to be released[53] is an utter stinker. The only redeeming feature is the orchestrations and recording of the music which we watched like hawks at every step. "Don't Let Me Love You" is in it at every possible moment, during bank robberies, flood scenes, dance hall sequences and a long shot of the Bronx Zoo. It is

---

51 Letters from Frank Loesser to Lynn Garland, both before and after their marriage, are known only from Susan Loesser's *A Most Remarkable Fella* (New York, 1993).

52 *My Man Godfrey*, directed by Gregory La Cava, was released on 6 September 1936.

53 *Postal Inspector* (Universal Pictures, 1936). The plot centres on postal inspectors who track down money stolen from a railroad car.

also sung by a guy and Pat Ellis very mournfully indeed, while they dance. God, why didn't I stay in the process-serving business?[54]

23 September 1936: To Lynn Garland

I've given up making specific plans because it's too hard to stick to them – I mean about WHEN I'll send for you – it depends on a lot of things that haven't happened yet, so I'm shutting up. Only be ready. Also be ready to be broke when you get out here.

3 October 1936: To Lynn Garland

Enclosed please find 150 bucks, for which please hurry and buy a railroad ticket (something like 73 dollars) and a lower berth (about 18) and a suitcase (cheap please) and food on the train (about 25 bucks) – and get the hell out here . . . Get on the train quick, because any day now I may be awfully busy – and right now I have the time to buy you a second-hand broken-down flivver,[55] and bring you to the offices where we can make some contracts for you – and get married (which takes time and travel) – and get you some clothes, and show you some scenery and friends – which would be impossible if you came too late. So kiss the folks chastely goodbye, darling, and take a chance on little Frankie please please please.

Lynn continued to spend much of her time in New York, trying to further her singing career, while Frank remained in Hollywood writing lyrics for films.

---

54 'Don't Let Me Love You' was cut from the film and registered for copyright only in 1957. Loesser's other songs for the film were 'Let's Have Bluebirds', sung by Patricia Ellis, and 'Hot Towel', sung by Patricia Ellis and Hattie McDaniel. Kimball and Nelson, *The Complete Lyrics of Frank Loesser*, 19.
55 A cheap car.

3 and 10 July 1937: To Lynn Loesser[56]

Getting off the lot we ran into Dave Dreyer,[57] who asked in his usually high tension hurry-up manner whether we have a continental type of waltz for Ida Lupino[58] and John Boles[59] – a melody that is easy enough for Lupino to yawp, and good enough to sound all right with Boles singing it. We said we would whip one up, which we proceeded to do this afternoon at Akst's[60] house. This is about it:

> If we should kiss
> While dancing like this
> Let's blame it on Vienna
>
> If muted strings
> Say heavenly things
> Let's blame it on Vienna
>
> If I get gay
> On too much Tokay
> And foolishly say:
> "Be Mine!"
>
> And if you answer yes
> Let's blame it on Vienna
> For making this night so divine!

I get home and call Akst. They don't like Vienna. It happens to take place in Budapest – and they want to settle on a song TOMORROW. So last night Akst and I worked – and worked and worked until three.

No results.

This morning, we met at seven. No results. The date at RKO is for nine thirty.

---

56 As given in Loesser, *A Most Remarkable Fella*, 29, two letters are conflated here.
57 Dave Dreyer (1894–1967), American composer of songs including 'Me and My Shadow'.
58 Ida Lupino (1918–1995), British actress and director.
59 John Boles (1895–1969), American actor.
60 Harry Akst (1894–1963), songwriter who also appeared in the film *42nd Street* (1933).

We go – ready to stall and play the tune. Al Lewis the director and some others including Dreyer hear the tune. For fun, I sing the old Vienna lyric which wasn't bad. They loved it! Only we're to change the locale from Vienna to the Danube. Half conscious from my lack of sleep and their lack of taste and brains, I make a few highly unsubtle changes to the Danube of all things and up we go to Briskin,[61] who okays the song, and that's that.[62]

August 1937 or 1939: To Lynn Loesser

Paul and I went to a movie last night: "Stand Up and Fight." Subtitle: For Your Money Back.

Yesterday we auditioned the Veronica Lake song and the producer and director took exception to part of it (the good part as usual) and I'm very low ... Yesterday Harold and I rewrote the Veronica Lake song for the shit-ass producer and director according to their ideas, putting in a few big words (one French) so they'd think it was smart and we hope we don't vomit at the demonstration this afternoon.

The [ASCAP[63]] meeting was the usual thing – Ira Gershwin fell asleep – Mack Gordon shouted louder than anybody, and Arthur Schwartz read a lot of legal stuff from a piece of paper. Arthur Freed raved about his own pictures. Johnny Mercer read a magazine, and Harold Arlen kept looking in the bar mirror, as if any minute his face would become bearable and then he'd start enjoying it.

I miss you like Grant took Richmond
I miss you as X is to Y
I miss you, I miss you, I that you, I this you
Oh hark, how the similes fly![64]

---

61 Samuel J. Briskin (1895–1968), American film producer.
62 'Blame It on the Danube' appeared in *Fight for the Lady* (RKO Pictures, released November 1937).
63 The performing rights and licensing organisation the American Society of Composers, Authors and Publishers, founded by Irving Berlin (1888–1989) and Victor Herbert (1859–1924) in 1914.
64 The texts given here, a conflation of several letters known only from Loesser, *A Most Remarkable Fella*, 34, are problematic. Although Susan Loesser dates them

9 September 1937: To Lynn Loesser

Now look: I listen to all the raised-eyebrow people who ask me how you are with the same disgust. It happens to me all the time ... The only thing that constitutes a real challenge from these idle people with their cocks in their hands is their attitude toward <u>why</u> we aren't together. The more they suspect, the more necessary it will become for you to <u>be somewhere</u> before you quit.[65] The <u>personal</u> reflections don't mean a thing, laugh them off, like I do. Only I'd just a little rather they didn't think we were damn fools to go through all this. So don't start trying to justify your position by sitting home or ducking dates with people you like. Justify it by, for Christ's sake, going to work.

P.S. Suggested shortcuts in dialog between you and our inquisitive friends:

"Aw go fuck yourself" (from *Barber of Seville*)

"Kindly shit in the lake" (Act 2, Scene 4, *Richard the Turd*)

"Kiss my ass" (Ibid)

"Piss on you" (from *30 Years Before the Mast*)

. . .

Don't sustain notes – any notes. I don't care if it's grand opera you're doing – beyond the point where they stop making sense, or beyond the safety limit of your wind or nervous system. Breathe your head off any time you want. Don't sing over-long phrases in one breath, because even a Kenny Baker[66] can't do it without making the next passage suffer from lack of control. It beautifies nothing except your own private opinion of your vocal prowess – which is not what the public wants. They want entertainment.

Remember to tell the story and let God take care of the tones.

August 1937, *Stand Up and Fight*, starring Wallace Beery and Robert Taylor, was not released until 6 January 1939. What is more, Loesser's songs for Veronica Lake, 'I've Got You' and 'Now You See It, Now You Don't', derive from the 1942 film *This Gun for Hire*; the composer of the songs was Jacques Press (1903–1985).

65 Here Loesser writes about Lynn's attempts to build a career in New York.

66 Kenny Baker (1912–1985), singer and actor. Baker was a featured singer on *The Jack Benny Program* during the 1930s.

Singers love to <u>vocalize</u> beyond the <u>sense</u> of a lyric – just like some ham actors. I wish there were an operatic Orson Welles. But that's expecting too much from trained singers. They are always so sure you want to hear their God damned <u>tones</u>.

While in Hollywood, Loesser continued to correspond with Arthur, mostly about family though occasionally touching on his film work.

23 September 1938: To Arthur and Jean Loesser[67]

Dear Arthur and Jean . . .

I got your letter and took my time settling with Phone Co. but finally got to it. Reason is I have been suffering from a sweet little item called arsenic poisoning. All over now, and no damage but a lot of bellyaches for many days.

The amt. I sent mama WAS small ($50) and that's on me. Since then have fixed things pretty well for her in New York.

We are sending for furniture from Chicago (Lynn's family stuff in storage) and will take a gorgeous house in Los Feliz Hills . . . much more alone and quiet and much more convenient to H'wood.

Hope you were'nt [sic] East during the storm. I haven't heard from mama . . . but that is just a routine worry . . . since I'm sure God would spare Yorkville (Quote Hitler)

I am up to my pretty pink pratt[68] in work. Campaigning now to get my name on the air every time they play a song of mine, also writing some new things which I hope will not include salt water catfish for Arthur's sake.

Will write at great length later. Expect three or four new ailments this year, as I have made a running start already with operations, streptococci, and now Arsenic.

If I were still the old F. Loesser I used to be I would close by saying "Hoping you are the same,"

---

67 International Piano Archives, University of Maryland, Arthur Loesser Collection.
68 'butt'.

But

Much Love
Frank.

25 October 1938: To Arthur Loesser[69]

Dear Arthur,

I am amazed to find myself with two free minutes in which to write. We have been doing some gradual moving to the new house. Write this down:

5432 Red Oak Drive
Los Feliz Hills
Los Angeles
Cal.
Phone Granite 5432 (yes, same as street addr.)

We will be there on or about Nov. 2nd.

I'm very glad to see what a swell response you got on your article. Right now any favorable (and lucid) comment on ASCAP is received very warmly by that some what embattled organization.[70]

No, don't tell Mills I'm your bro. because apparently he knows it. (I received a copy of his thank-you note to you, from his office, a few days before you sent me the selected raves from music biz.)

The Arsenic I got from lettuce, they say. It is very annoying, and quite painful but only lasts four or five days.

I am still A. Loesser's bro. in Hollywood. They say lovely things about you at all times . . . even people I'm sure you don't know well, who know you only by reputation.

---

69 International Piano Archives, University of Maryland, Arthur Loesser Collection.
70 During the 1930s, ASCAP was at loggerheads with radio stations, demanding that broadcasters pay fees based on stations' total income, rather than on the proportion of ASCAP music broadcast. In 1938, the Federal Trade Commission had notified ASCAP that payola – the practice of paying commercial radio stations to broadcast songs – was unethical.

I'm enclosing those letters you want back. Also a little clipping about Frank Loesser which might amuse you ... in that it <u>isn't true</u>. Must go now.

Love to Jean and Anne

Frank

Beginning in 1938, Loesser wrote lyrics or music (or both) for dozens of films, mostly for Paramount Pictures, and his work brought him in contact with many of Hollywood's leading composers and biggest stars: *Cocoanut Grove* (1938, with Burton Lane, 'Says My Heart', Loesser's first song to reach number 1 on the popular music chart);[71] *St Louis Blues* (1939, music by Matt Melneck and starring Dorothy Lamour); *Some Like It Hot* (1939, with Lane and Carmichael among others, starring Bob Hope);[72] the Marlene Dietrich–Jimmy Stewart vehicle *Destry Rides Again* (1939); Tyrone Power's *Johnny Apollo* (1940, with music by Lionel Newman); *Seventeen* (1940, including the first published song with both words and music by Loesser, 'Seventeen'); *A Song is Born* (1948, with music by Hoagy Carmichael including 'Heart and Soul', another number 1 hit recorded by Larry Clinton and his Orchestra with vocalist Bea Wain); and *Sis Hopkins* (exceptionally for Republic Pictures, with Jule Styne). *Spawn of the North*, with incidental music and underscoring by Dmitri Tiomkin, included Loesser and Lane's 'I Like Hump-Backed Salmon', which bandleader Skitch Henderson performed, in 1965, on the Johnny Carson Show, prompting a letter from Loesser:

24 September 1965: To Johnny Carson

Dear Mr. Carson:

You may tell Skitch Henderson that I thank him not at all for his cavalier remark the other night about the "legit" contributions from the audience in your "stump the band" stanza. I take very special

---

71 Kimball and Nelson, *The Complete Lyrics of Frank Loesser*, 33.
72 Unrelated to the classic 1959 comedy *Some Like It Hot* with Marilyn Monroe, Tony Curtis and Jack Lemmon.

umbrage at his lofty dismissal of a very fine contribution to musical literature called "I Like Humped-Backed Salmon." In addition to his outrageous taste in clothing, he is now displaying a profound ignorance of a gem among the great American compositions – a piece that is absolutely undying in its sheer loveliness.

For him to be seen and heard publicly dismissing "I Like Humped-Backed Salmon" as obscure, if not indeed some sort of hoax – seems to me to be an insult to the American public and its treasured sentiments.

I cannot write this letter of rebuke directly to Mr. Henderson as the morning mail might find him not properly dressed (in his opinion) for reading. Further, no doubt he would probably find my stationery to be not at room temperature and therefore not decently negotiable – and would forthwith toss the whole thing into his flowered chintz waste basket. Therefore I am addressing this to you in the hope that you will transmit the following information to him toward his cultural betterment: "I Like Humped-Backed Salmon," beloved by millions and ever on the lips of young and old alike, was first performed in a Paramount picture called "Spawn Of the North," starring George Raft, Henry Fonda and Dorothy Lamour, in 1938. Only shut-ins, prisoners, and a few feeble-minded missed seeing this great cinema classic. But nobody, absolutely nobody, failed to hear the enchanting sound of the song via radio, night clubs, organ grinders, and strolling minstrels.

I thank you in advance to transmitting this bit of elementary education to Mr. Henderson who cannot have been too young to go to the movies in 1938, and to the best of my knowledge was not confined to the hospital or jail – and therefore must have been one of the feeble-minded.

Very sincerely,
Frank Loesser

P.S. Oh. I forgot to tell you. I wrote the lyrics of "ILHBS."

Loesser's letters from Hollywood are evidence enough that composing for films was often a hit-or-miss proposition or a matter of luck. Hoagy Carmichael later recounted a story concerning the song 'Small Fry' from the 1938 Paramount film, *Sing You Sinners*:

He [Loesser] used so many jokes to keep me alive and happy – he said, 'let's write a song called "Small Fry"' – that sounded like him. Before he had reeled off a few stanzas, it was quite evident that he was the lyricist I hoped he would be. It only took us a day and a half to write the whole thing. The music department decided we should record it ourselves for the library. I can still hear myself being the papa singing my part and Frank singing in the high pitched voice of a 12 year-old kid. I think Frank really enjoyed this song . . . You've heard the expression in show business, 'Be there at the right place and the right time'? Frank's timing came up again the very same week. Wesley Ruggles made a picture using a 12 year-old boy. Somebody said, 'Take your record over to his office and see if he likes it and can use it.' Frank and I entered Ruggles' office that Saturday. There was a boy sitting there. Frank ran over and put the record on the Victrola. Ruggles listened, looked at the boy, listened to the record, back at the boy. The record never finished. He said, 'That's it, gentlemen. Meet Donald O'Connor. He, Bing Crosby and Fred MacMurray will sing your song in the picture.'[73]

At the same time, there was always the danger of being accused of plagiarism, a constant in songwriters' lives. In 1940, Loesser and Burton Lane's 'Dancing on a Dime' for *Johnny Apollo* was said by an unnamed source to have plagiarised the song 'Midnight on the Trail', recorded by Tommy Dorsey and his orchestra and released on 28 December 1938. Apparently nothing came of the accusation although the first four bars of the two songs are virtually identical.

73 Kimball and Nelson, *The Complete Lyrics of Frank Loesser*, 35.

11 June 1940: To Arthur Loesser[74]

Dear Arthur:

Enclosed you will find a copy of a brand new song of Burton Lane's and mine.[75] VERY CONFIDENTIALLY some doubt has been cast on the originality of the first four bars of the chorus, which I have marked. We are trying to protect ourselves by finding a piece of music written and published prior to 1938 which contains this phrase or a similar one. The similarity, from a <u>melodic</u> point of view, is naturally the most important; and if such a melody exists, with identical meter and harmony, it is that much more valuable as a protection against a possible lawsuit.

I am calling on you – with your phenomenal mental library and access to many an ancient volume of <u>forgotten tunes,</u> to see if you can dig up as many examples of music as you can. Dig up whatever you can and send it on to me; or at least information as to the title of the work, name of edition and number of bar or bars.

Nobody is suing us yet, but after recording this number in a picture we happened on a song published by one of the big popular firms in 1938, in which the opening three and one-half bars are identical with our opening. This job is more important than it may sound; so please help me out if you possibly can. If there is anybody you can assign to this job it's O.K. as long as he doesn't visit or gossip with any popular music publisher. Anyway, please try and help me out as <u>quickly as possible</u>.

Best love to you, Jean and Anne. Mama seems to be reasonably happy out here, although not as busy as she would like to be. Will enlarge on this subject in a letter of a more personal nature very soon. Right now I am copyright conscious.[76]

Your ever-loving brother,
[signed:] Frank

---

74 International Piano Archives, University of Maryland, Arthur Loesser Collection.
75 'Dancing on a Dime'.
76 'Dancing on a Dime' was copyrighted on 5 September 1940.

[an arrow from <u>forgotten tunes</u> points to the bottom right corner of the page where Loesser has handwritten:]

> Research, of course
> should include
> classical, literature,
> opera, everything!!
> F.

As part of his work for Paramount, in 1940, Loesser and Hoagy Carmichael travelled to Miami to write songs for the film *Mr. Bug Goes to Town*, an animated feature released in February 1942.

18–19 July 1940: To Lynn Loesser

They are really lazy down here. I mean mentally. The crew of artists, writers and idea men admit they accomplish about half a day's work compared to what they'd do in a day in California or New York. None of them like it down here, and there is a tendency to quit on their part, whenever the slightest personal annoyance comes up. That's why the bosses are nice guys. There isn't much in the way of replacement manpower down here.

Once in a while there is a bright spot. For instance last night we went to a place called the Carousel and had VEGETABLES with our roast beef. Of course they were frozen, but that's better than grits and gravy and fried potatoes.

1 November 1940: To J. M. Watermulder

Dear J. M. (I forgot your first name, but I have your initials)

Received the check for two bucks; a pleasant surprise to anybody from Broadway or Hollywood.

I know it has taken a long time to write you but I have been busy writing (again for Paramount), cheering Roosevelt and trying to find my draft number from a long, long list.

If you see Illava ask him if he remembers me, which he probably doesn't.

Drop me a line if you get a chance. Best regards to Westchester, its stately homes and phony building contracts.

[signed:] Frank Loesser

In early 1942, Loesser wrote the hit song 'I Don't Want to Walk Without You' for the film *Sweater Girl*. Shortly after, he was apparently visited by another songwriter and wrote: 'Irving Berlin came in today and spent a solid hour telling me that "Walk" is the best song he ever heard. I was flattered. He played and sang it over, bar by bar, explaining why it's the best song he ever heard. I was flattered like crazy, then. Maybe he'll take an ad in Variety about it.'[77] Much of Loesser's film work in the early 1940s, however, was for patriotic films which, because of the Second World War, were widely produced and distributed. These included the Bob Hope vehicle *Caught in the Draft* (1941, including 'Love Me as I Am', recorded by Frank Sinatra with Tommy Dorsey and his Orchestra), and *Kiss the Boys Goodbye* with Don Ameche and Mary Martin (1941) and *True to the Army* (1942).

In response to the Japanese attack on Pearl Harbor, on 7 December 1941, Loesser wrote 'Praise the Lord and Pass the Ammunition', one of the most popular Second World War songs: it sold more than 2.5 million recordings and more than 750,000 copies of the sheet music.[78] In his article 'My Brother Frank', Arthur Loesser wrote:

In August [1942] my mother showed me a letter from Frank explaining that he was writing a song on the alleged Pearl Harbor outburst . . . The nature of the tune reveals a great canniness. It refrains from modern, urban, musical slang; it avoids any suggestion that anyone might consider disreputable . . . jazzy, Jewish, Broadwayish, or night clubby. Instead the melody has an affinity for that of 'The Battle Hymn of the Republic'; it tastes like school, church, grandma, and biscuits; a master-stroke of diplomacy, aptness, and good business.

---

77 Kimball and Nelson, *The Complete Lyrics of Frank Loesser*, 86.
78 Ibid., 92.

Loesser first had the idea for 'Praise the Lord' in April 1942. And some years later, he was asked by Lockwood Doty of NBC to appear on a radio show about Navy chaplain Howell Forgy (1908–1972), who was credited with originating the phrase 'Praise the Lord and pass the ammunition'.

April 1942: To Lynn Loesser

I have a title – "Praise the Lord and Pass the Ammunition" – which is a quotation from a news story a few months ago – a sentence supposedly spoken by a brave Navy chaplain. Joe Lilley[79] and I are on it.

31 July 1951: To Lockwood Doty, NBC

My dear Mr. Doty:

In answer to your letter, I hasten to tell you that I couldn't volunteer any information in connection with a program dedicated to Howell Forgy and his alleged utterance of "Praise the Lord and pass the ammunition."

The fact is I don't quite believe he said it, although I believe it is possible. The Navy public relations people apparently selected chaplain Forgy[80] as the man who originally said the words. They did so in an officially datelined newspaper story more than a year after Pearl Harbor.[81] Before that time no Navy representative had come forward to identify the author, even though the song had been making a big noise since October 1942. Around the same time as the official Navy

---

79 Joseph J. Lilley (1913–1971), American composer and orchestrator.
80 Forgy was serving on the USS *New Orleans* when Pearl Harbor was attacked.
81 See the *New York Times*, 1 November 1942, 35: 'Honolulu, Oct. 31 (U.P.) – Lieutenant Howell M. Forgy, 220-pound chaplain aboard a heavy cruiser, said today he was the chaplain who originated the phrase, "Praise the Lord and pass the ammunition." ... [He] was at Pearl Harbor directing preparations for church services aboard his ship, which was moored to a dock, when general quarters were sounded as the Japanese attacked. He reported to his battle station. The power was off on a powder hoist, he said, and so Lieutenant Edwin Woodhead formed a line of sailors to pass the ammunition by hand to the deck. The chaplain moved along the line, encouraging the passers and repeating, "Praise the Lord and pass the ammunition" he said.'

2. Frank Loesser in his army uniform, c1944.

release, a book by Howell Forgy was published called, "And Pass the Ammunition." In it the chaplain very guardedly, obscurely and completely unconvincingly, refers to his connection with the phrase.[82]

If you want my story about where I heard the phrase, about who I think said it and about the whole matter of military, as well as religious denominational policies concerning it – you can have it. Except that you won't use it. Meanwhile, as I have told you, I can't subscribe by association on your program, to the Forgy story.

Many thanks, of course, for thinking of me. You must know that this letter is not intended in anyway [sic] to be a criticism of NBC or its activities.

With best wishes,

Sincerely,

---

82 Howell M. Forgy, *"And Pass the Ammunition"* (New York, 1944).

In the autumn of 1942, Loesser enrolled in the army. He was first posted to the army base at Santa Ana, California, as part of the Radio Productions Unit, producing recruitment shows, two live shows a day, five days a week. In 1943, he was transferred to the Special Services Division in New York, where he worked on the Blueprint Specials, musical revues created for performance by soldiers to boost morale; these were published as do-it-yourself kits including scripts, orchestrations, set and costume designs and choreography. Loesser's contributions included *About Face* and *Hi, Yank!*[83] He also wrote a number of stand-alone war songs, among them 'What Do You Do in the Infantry?' (1943), 'The Sad Bombardier' and 'One Little WAC' (both 1944) and, in early 1945, his second great wartime hit, 'Rodger Young', which he mentioned in an undated letter to lyricist Nat Halpern Jr and later described in a letter to David Ewen (see p. 199):

[Probably 1945]: To Nat Halpern

Dear Nat

big hurry. New Song. MAMMOTH SONG, called "Rodger Young" which I wrote for the Infantry, about one of its dead heroes. I had it all written when you were up here, but plans were just being laid. If Your song is a little late in going to press it is probably my fault for crowding up Miller's facilities with this new one. However "Reveille" will be coming along.

Thanks for the butts. If you can find any more I'll be very grateful for whatever you can send me. Here's some dough to cover it, as I don't want you to pay for them. This goes under the heading of bribery, and if you're sending anybody free cigarettes it might as well be a colonel or somebody who can really do you some good.

Don't catch no summer Clap, or snake bite, and keep in touch

best

[signed:] Frank

Frank Loesser

---

83 *About Face* was first given at Camp Shanks of the New York Port of Embarkation on 26 May 1944; *Hi, Yank!* first played at the War Department Theatre No. 5, Fort Dix, New Jersey, on 7 August 1944.

Shortly before his discharge in April 1945, Loesser was sent for basic training – one incident of which he reported to Lynn.

18 April 1945: To Lynn Loesser

One guy here is a really sad case. He was sent in because of a retching cough. He is <u>vomiting</u>. Only nothing comes out because he doesn't eat anything. He has tried to explain to <u>everybody</u> that he has, and always has had, a nervous stomach, and that's that. So they give him cough medicine and aspirin which irritates his stomach – which in turn makes him vomit – which is construed as a cough. I don't know how long he's been here (he was here when I arrived), and I shudder to think how long he'll stay on.

The army nurses and the student nurses are just like civilian ones. The only change in their behavior is their walk. It has become military. The ward boys are medical students of army age, deferred for the purpose and continuing their "study" by this experience, which consists of pushing wheel-hampers of dirty laundry and mopping up ward floors etc.

Saturday is inspection day, just like in the barracks. The hospital C.O. marches through and looks us over. We are standing at attention by our beds – we have remade our beds with nice new sheets, folded over exactly 4½ inches, and blanket folded twice on the long axis, with only the rounded edges showing. Also we have swept and mopped the ward floor, which is fucked up all week with big gray clots of wool from the hospital blankets which shed all the time. This shit has blown around the floor all week getting into everybody's lungs and keeping all the coughing and sneezing up to par. But on Saturday all is serene.

Yet the war also had a personal dimension for Loesser, a legacy of his family's German background. Although both his father and mother had immigrated to the United States, Julia Loesser's family – the Ehrlichs – at least partly remained in Germany. Julia's great-grandfather Josef had been married twice: most of his first wife's children came to the US, but his second wife's children remained in Germany, including Paul Ehrlich, Julia's half-brother. In 1941, Frank and Arthur Loesser attempted to secure Paul Ehrlich's safe passage to the United States through the National Council of Jewish Women (NCJW), a grassroots movement founded in 1893 that initially focused on educating Jewish women and helping immigrants become self-sufficient; during the Second World War, the NCJW was active in rescuing Jewish children and families, often routing them through Shanghai, which for a time was the only city or country to unconditionally accept Jewish refugees from Germany.[84]

20 May 1941: To Arthur Loesser[85]

Dear Arthur:

I have started on a brand new attempt to get visas for Paul Ehrlich and his family and establishing them over here. I am doing this through an organization called the "Council of Jewish Women" and have made out complete new affidavits. The Council office here informs me that it is very important to get additional affidavits from another reasonably prosperous member of the family. Will you please do this right away and help the cause? Contact Mrs. Joseph H. Gross at the "Council of Jewish Women" at 2010 E. 102 Street, Cleveland, Ohio. She will prepare your affidavit concerning your desire that the Ehrlichs come to this country and your intention of supporting them, should they need support.

These are the facts about Paul: He is the son of Richard Ehrlich, who is the brother of Julia E. Loesser. He was born December 27th, 1909 at Karlsbad, Czechoslovakia. His wife's name is Marie Ehrlich, her maiden name being Fuchs. She was born September 1st, 1913 at Granesau Czechoslovakia. They have an infant boy, born in February or March, 1941. He is a lawyer and she is a housewife. To the best of your knowledge they both read and write English.

You will probably be asked to get supporting affidavits from your bank and insurance companies, as well as certified copies of your last

---

84 See Bernard Wasserstein, *Secret War in Shanghai* (Boston, 1999).
85 International Piano Archives, University of Maryland, Arthur Loesser Collection.

income tax return. All of which seem to be very important in determining your capacity for supporting this family. I was told by Miss Berres [or Borres], at the Council office here, that our failure to get the Ehrlich's through, was due largely to the incompleteness of the statements which I sent several months ago – even though I complied with every request and followed every instruction made by Paul in his letters to me.

Don't forget to address all affidavits to the American Consul, Shanghai China. When all your papers are compiled properly ask Mrs. Gross to forward them to Miss Berres at the "Council of Jewish Women" in Los Angeles. Here they will be added to mine and sent to Shanghai as the strongest possible appeal we can make on the refugees' behalf.

I have already guaranteed payment of passage for them and secured a booking on a steamer, pending the granting of their visas.

Once more, let me urge you to rush.

My love to you and Jean and Anne and the Bassets.

I won't turn this letter into a family gathering, as I am looking forward to the pleasure when you arrive here in June.

> Love
>
> Frank

[handwritten:] Mama looks fine, but feels a little <u>hot</u> at the moment. I'm trying to make her take that Mexican trip this summer, but the conservative impulse which always drove her into wishing <u>me</u> a bank-teller or chain-store buyer – is strong upon her.

> love
>
> F.

Much of Loesser's surviving correspondence during the war years is addressed to Lynn, his brother Arthur or his mother, reporting not only on the war, but also his film work and domestic matters. At the same time, he kept up his professional and personal contacts, with the humorist Abe Burrows and his friend John Steinbeck. Loesser's text for *The Moon is Down*, based on Steinbeck's novel of the same name (New York, 1942), was eventually set by Arthur Schwartz.[86]

---

86 Arthur Schwartz (1900–1984), composer known in particular for the Broadway show *A Tree Grows in Brooklyn* (1951) and the film *The Band Wagon* (1953).

6 November 1941: To Lynn Loesser

Last night I got a <u>THRILL</u>! I went riding with Johnny Johnston[87] – at eight o'clock, after a Chinese dinner somewhere in the valley. We picked up his girlfriend and the three of us rode over the hills in the bright moonlight – in spots they use for locations – we couldn't even see telegraph poles or wire or anything – and live wild <u>deer</u> leaping around us from out of the trees. It was <u>beeoootiful</u>.

8 December 1941: To Lynn Loesser

Of course the <u>war</u> is preoccupying everybody, including <u>me</u>. I heard about it on the bridal [sic] path yesterday. A lot of soldiers on leave were riding. I got up on a trail on a mountain overlooking the whole section – and <u>watched</u> the new spread – and could see the soldiers turning their horses around and making for the stables.

12 March 1942: To Lynn Loesser

I didn't really write it,[88] Steinbeck did, all I did was to make it rhyme. I'll show it to Joe Lilley today and have him write the music – which he'll do beautifully. Then we'll produce it on a record, for baritone and 8 voices (mixed), organ, and sound effects. When the music is done, and I have a real idea of how the whole thing sounds, and I still like it, I'm going to mail the poem to JS to see what he thinks. I'm a little self-conscious about it – like first long pants – from Poppa, and too big in the waist . . .

18 April 1942: To Lynn Loesser

There are only a dozen singers in the country who could really do it well – Robeson, Keast, Tibbett, Rise Stevens, Marian Anderson[89] . . .

---

87 Johnny Johnston (1915–1996), singer and actor.
88 *The Moon is Down.*
89 Paul Robeson (1898–1976), singer and civil rights activist known for performing the role of Joe in the London production of Jerome Kern's *Show Boat* (1928), among many other important works and appearances; Paul Keast (1902–1979), concert

Anything less than <u>40</u> musicians in the orchestra will make it sound like whorehouse music ... Today we're finding out (we hope) how to get that god damned record made. It's as important to get the right sample as anything else in the whole set-up. Even Rise Stevens won't actually do it correctly, I'm sure ... I am organizing Dave Rose's Band, KHJ and its executives, Joe Lilley, Walter Scharf,[90] two copyists, a print-shop and various press representatives – all <u>free for nothing</u>, and correspondingly touchy and tough to handle – for that Saturday recording.

30 April 1942: To William Schuman[91]

There is a poem written by me and set to music by Arthur Schwartz. It was inspired by the book [*The Moon is Down*] and Steinbeck gave me permission to use the title. This piece of work is soon to be highly publicized by the government itself. Its ultimate function is to reach people of the conquered countries via short wave ...

It is an example, not of the form, but of the language that you and I discussed in our break-away plans for the great American oratorio and that dream about an opera. Am I in the right groove for you? If "The Moon Is Down" is successful, will it help my stock with those opera people?

18 October 1943: To Arthur Loesser[92]

From:
Loesser, Frank, PFC AAF

---

artist and Hollywood singer; Lawrence Tibbett (1896–1960), American opera singer; Risë Stevens (1913–2013), mezzo-soprano active at the Metropolitan Opera, New York, during the 1940s and 1950s; and Marian Anderson (1897–1993), singer, activist, and the first Black American to perform at the Metropolitan Opera.
90 David Rose (1910–1990), British-born American songwriter and bandleader; Walter Scharf (1910–2003), American television and film composer; KHJ Radio, based in Los Angeles, was originally a popular music broadcaster; it has broadcast Catholic religious programmes since 2014.
91 Kimball and Nelson, *The Complete Lyrics of Frank Loesser*, 93.
92 International Piano Archives, University of Maryland, Arthur Loesser Collection.

To:
Loesser, Arthur A. Capt. AUS

Re: Entrance into Armed forces as Commissioned officer

Remarks: Hooray.

That's the official way for me to address you on paper, that is . . . if I have permission from my First Sgt. However . . .

Dear Arthur,

I am really thrilled that you made it. I know you've been trying for at least two whole wars. I won't ask any questions about what your job consists of, but whenever you CAN tell me, I'd be terrifically [deliberate!] interested. Will you travel? Possibly out here?

Lynn and some of our friends heard the concert yesterday. They all loved it. I was in an automobile en route somewhere on business for the Army and there was no radio in the car, so I had to miss it.

I am still one of the Government's pampered wards. I don't report at camp except to sign the payroll and to pick up my rations and pay. I live at home (forty miles from camp) and do my work from there. The authorities have found that I accomplish it better at a distance. At present I am on loanout, so to speak, to the Treasury Department and will be starting soon to devise gay little phrases by which to snatch at your pocket during the Fourth Bond Drive, which is tentatively set for about the middle of January.

Write me from Minnesota, will you? I'd like to get your reactions to some of the things that go on at Army stations. Congratulations again, from Lynn and Florrie too.

Love

Frank

Jean!! Gosh, aren't you proud? Wonder what Anne thinks. Arthur is a Captain in Minnesota, I'm a Buck Private in California, and Mama Julia is secret operative X-9 in New York! Hitler has really accomplished some fantastic things with our little tribe. Drop us a line, huh?

love to all of you,

Frank and Lynn.

Before 3 January 1944 [Probably December 1943]:
To Julia Loesser[93]

Mama dear,

again I have neglected you. But maybe I will be seeing you soon and I'll make up for all the silence. As a matter of fact I will talk you blue in the face about world events, music business, Arthur, the Army, and your grandchild. But I'm not sure yet. As it stands there is a fair chance of my coming to New York late in January. We haven't told Florrie <u>anything</u> about such a move so put it in the back of your mind for the moment . . . and you'll be hearing from me about it.

What is new about Arthur. I'm very proud of him. Where do I write him?

Mrs. Goooooooootwilllllliggggggggg continues to send regards to you. I meet her in the hall occasionally. She smokes the goddamndest evilest smelling cigarettes. The smoke permeates the whole building and smells like marijuana. What kind of friends do you have?

How are your feet? And the cold? Have you a way of keeping warm at home?

I've just had four days of what might have been the flu . . . if I hadn't taken the pills the army gives out to ward off such evil germs. They are sulfa-soda and you have to drink gallons of water all day after taking them. But they stop the infection apparently. Really the army does wonderful work in preventive medicine.

It's a pretty thin Christmas this time. The stores seem to be sold out of everything, and people are having trouble finding things to buy for their friends. Maybe it's just as well.

---

93 International Piano Archives, University of Maryland, Arthur Loesser Collection. The dating of this letter derives from a pencil notation upper right '(PM from Julia to AL 3 Jan 44)'. It was apparently forwarded by Loesser's mother to Arthur Loesser and includes a handwritten postscript, presumably by Julia Loesser: 'P.S. A sp. Del-letter from Hollywood arrived this A.M. saying that FR. has been transferred to N. Y. City and will arrive here on January – J A N U A R Y 13th. Lynn will follow as soon as she can finish settling affairs in Hollywood. Fine, what? I am all excited'. If by 3 January Julia knew the date of Loesser's arrival in Hollywood, then his letter announcing his possible return must pre-date this. And his reference to a 'thin Christmas' suggests a date of December 1943.

We'll be celebrating quietly at home. Florrie will probably be cooking a dinner.

Merry Christmas Mama, and like I said, maybe soon I'll be with you.

love

Frank

P.S. we sent you a card with a giftie enclosed. This is to be SPENT, not put in the bank. Get something you NEED and think of us. Love

While it is unclear precisely when Loesser became acquainted with Abe Burrows (1910–1985), later the book writer for *Guys and Dolls* and *How to Succeed*, they were in regular, friendly contact from at least the early 1940s:

3 May 1944: To Abe Burrows

Dear Abe.

Pretty soon ASCAP. I am submitting our opus "You haven't got cheeks like Roses" to Para. which ought to mean five hundred bucks in the kick for you again, and a number TWO nod from Deems Taylor.[94] Wait and see.

Sorry not to have written before, but Lynn had to make a trip to the middle west where her grandmother had an accident (died a few days later) and being alone in NY with no little helpmeet and worrying about her bump[95] and what the train would do to it, I was too busy and in no mood to correspond. Now she is back and things are easier for me. I have been going up to Shanks to add stuff to the show,[96] which ought to produce about the end of May. Little Willie Stein the 42nd street Corporal wrote a nifty poem about Mort Lewis's two headed brother with the one cigar:

There was a young soldier named Lewis

---

94 'You Haven't Got Cheeks Like Roses', probably written in 1943, was one of Loesser's first collaborations with Burrows. The song was apparently a stand-alone.
95 Lynn was pregnant with their daughter Susan.
96 Presumably *About Face*, the first of Loesser's Blueprint Specials for the U.S. Army Special Forces.

Who only got laid on Shevoois
Each night he would yank it
All over his blanket
Now no-one would know it says U.S.

Funnier when Willie said it.

Lyons[97] continues to regard you as the genius of our time. Also me, but in a different way. They are good people, the Lyons. If you get a chance to drop him a note hello. One west 81 Street.

Have you moved out of Grayson's house. That's the little broad who was my secretary who once brought you a bottle of Booze at Las Palmas in the afternoon.

Have seen Zero and his girl, and also Sam Jaffe.[98] Sam is a sweet guy. Zero's girl is starting to get a bulging forehead like Zero. Can you screw your way into these physical troubles? Or is it just association? I had dinner with them a couple of weeks ago and he went bang bang with his finger and shot two oysterettes out of her fingers. Her timing is lousy but everybody in the restaurant laughed which was all Zero wanted.

Have you seen Hy Kraft. Did he get my letter and the script of Cafe Crown?[99] If you see him ask him, I never heard from him after that. Maybe he did not like my criticism of the play. Personally I screamed my head off but that doesn't mean it's another "Mutiny on the Bounty."

Seen DeLugg?[100] When is your child? Play "One Little Wac." Write me.

      Love
       Frank

---

97 Leonard Lyons (1906–1976), columnist for the *New York Post* and friend of Loesser's.
98 Zero Mostel (1915–1977), American actor and comedian known for his portrayal of Tevye in *Fiddler on the Roof* (1964) and as Max Bialystock in the film version of *The Producers* (1967); Sam Jaffe (1891–1984), American actor whose film credits include *The Asphalt Jungle* (1950) and *Ben-Hur* (1959).
99 Hyman Solomon Kraft (1899–1975), American writer and theatrical producer. His play *Cafe Crown* played for 140 performances in New York, 23 January–23 May 1942.
100 Milton Delugg (1918–2015), American composer and arranger.

20 May 1944: To Abe Burrows[101]

Dear Abe,

This is more than you deserve. I have to hear from Art Schwartz that you are okay. This is like Booker T. Washington charging up San Juan Hill.[102] Not the McCoy. So how are you? When does Ruth drop the new calf? Have you moved. Did you ever get my note addressed care of Young and Rubicam?[103] I have heard from Hy Kraft. A nice letter.

Allen called up and invited me to do a guest on his show, and said it was mainly so you would listen to something other than acetates of the Duffy show.[104] The thing will very probably be written for your benefit. I think it will be June 11th.

Will have news within a couple of weeks I think, about "You haven't got cheeks like roses." Will leave you know. I have had to hold up progress on the publication of your "type" songs for a while but the project is still very much on.

Lynn is now very obviously pregnant. The child applauded Benay Venuta[105] at the State a couple of weeks ago. Of course it was my material Benay was doing. Lyons keeps asking how you are. I don't tell him. Lundsay [sic] and Crouse[106] give you billing in their conversation as THE GREATEST LIVING AMERICAN which they got from me and Lyons. This is spreading around now so you better protect your

---

101 Abe Burrows papers, New York Public Library.

102 In 1898, Booker T. Washington delivered a controversial speech, his so-called 'Peace Jubilee Speech', arguing for the South to do away with racial prejudice on the basis of the battle at San Juan Hill, during the Spanish-American War, when both Black and white soldiers served in the trenches.

103 Young and Rubicam, an advertising agency founded in 1923 and now VMLY&R, a marketing and communications company.

104 Fred Allen (1894–1956), born John Florence Sullivan, known for the long-running radio programme *The Fred Allen Show* (1932–49). The Duffy show is *Duffy's Tavern*, a radio sitcom co-created and written by Abe Burrows, 1942–1951, that was adapted for television in 1954.

105 Benay Venuta (1910–1995), American actress and singer.

106 Howard Lindsay (1889–1968) and Russel Crouse (1893–1966), playwrights and librettists known for Cole Porter's *Anything Goes* (1934) and Rodgers and Hammerstein's *The Sound of Music* (1959), among many other works; they won the Pulitzer Prize for Drama in 1945 for their play, *State of the Union*.

future by writing a voluminous correspondence. Write one to a Mrs. Bixbie. This will positively make you.

But more important, Write ME

Love

Frank

29 May 1944: To Abe Burrows

Dear Abe,

Our letters crossed. Has Lynn made a deal with you about the car. She told me she would. Haven't had time to talk to her about it lately, but maybe she has already written you. New baby arriving soon? Leave us know. Today all the NY papers reviewed "About Face" and your name was among the credits just as if you had put pencil to paper. Very good reviews. I go on Fred Allen[107] the eleventh of June. If you are not waiting around a Maternity Hosp. try to listen. Saturday we are having our first shindig since your departure. Will try to get pictures of it by Gjon Mijhli, or is it ghdjoughnn mieldgjee.[108] It will be in your honor. Lindsay and Crouse speak of you as some sort of a God. God!

Now starting to write the second Army show. This won't be as involved. We have learned many things. One of them about George Kaufman.[109]

Love to all. More later.

Frank

---

107 Not to be confused with Steve Allen (1921–2000), co-creator and host of *The Tonight Show* from 1954; see the previous letter.

108 Gjon Mili (1904–1984), Albanian-American photographer.

109 George S. Kaufman, playwright, producer and director. Kaufman won the 1932 Pulitzer Prize for Drama for the George Gershwin musical *Of Thee I Sing* and for the 1937 play *You Can't Take It With You*; in 1951 he won the Tony Award for Best Director for Loesser's *Guys and Dolls*.

11 July 1944: To Abe Burrows (Telegram)

POSITIVELY STOP DOING THE SONGS FOR ANYBODY SKOLSKY[110]
SPILLED THE WHOLE PUNCH BUT TRY AND BREAK HIS COLUMN
LATER FOR A FAVOR JUST TRY LOVE=
    FRANK.

18 July 1945: To Abe Burrows

Dear Abe–

I'm kind of confused about what to do with your stuff. I'm pretty sure I can get a book printed. That's not hard. But maybe it's better to have a record album. Let me think. Meantime whatever you do, don't give anything away for nothing. If pictures want anything soak them hard, and be sure the songs are done the way you want. Also release only for a particular use, or else you'll wind up in a Matty Malende one-reel short. If you get a chance to use them yourself on radio appearance that's okay, but don't fuck-up with Ozzie Nelson.[111] Better you should be an exclusive parlor comic.

I will play some of the clean ones for a recording co. and see if we can get up an album of you doing them. May have to wait till production of records is heavier, but this would be the best idea

Love

[signed:] Frank

In 1946, the Loessers returned to California, where Frank continued to work not only for Paramount but other film companies as well, including MGM and United Artists. He considered exploiting some of his Blueprint Special songs, hoped that the Shubert Organization would want to produce the musical he was writing, *Where's Charley?*, and apparently turned down a request from William Saroyan to set his play *Jim Dandy*. Letters from this time are scarce.

---

110 Sidney Skolsky (1905–1983), Hollywood gossip columnist. It is not clear what Loesser refers to here.

111 Oswald George (Ozzie) Nelson (1906–1975), American actor, filmmaker and bandleader known in particular for his radio series *The Adventures of Ozzie and Harriet* (1944–1951) and its later television adaptation (1952–1966).

4 June 1946: To David Mann

Dear Dave:

Thanks for your letter. I would rather you didn't make any moves on the songs as they stand. This is for two reasons. Firstly, the titles were originally suggested by our two friends – the authors of the play – and are not completely ours. Also, we once made an agreement by which we cannot sell separate pieces of this show without the consent of the other two fellows. Besides all that, I don't think the songs are really number one calibre and I don't want them out now.

However, if you want to divorce any melodies, please feel free to do so. It will be perfectly okay as far as I'm concerned. However, I think you should check with the playwrights whose names escape me completely now. This is probably a psychological rebellion against all things military.

I took out with me a book about how to draw pictures – which belongs to you. I can still use it, but if you want it back let me know and I will rush it to you.

Best wishes,

14 June 1946: To Don Walker (Telegram)[112]

HARRY BRANDT[113] HAS ARRANGED FOR SCORE[114] TO BE PLAYED FOR SHUBERT ON MONDAY. A GOOD DEAL DEPENDS ON HIS REACTIONS. BRANDT HAS COMPLETELY DISENGAGED HIMSELF FROM PRODUCTION IN SOFARAS HIS NAME OR ANY FINANCES ARE CONCERNED. I AM NOW WORKING COMPLETELY ALONE WITHOUT FINANCIAL SUPPORT FROM MY FATHER.[115] THEREFORE SHUBERT'S REACTION IS VERY IMPORTANT. WILL WIRE YOU AS SOON AS I KNOW ANYTHING. REGARDS=
FRANK.

---

112 Don Walker papers, Library of Congress.
113 Harry Brandt (1897–1972), Broadway producer and theatre owner.
114 Possibly *Where's Charley?*, though the date seems too early.
115 The meaning of this passage is a mystery: Loesser's father had died in 1926.

Where's Charley? opened on 11 October 1948 at the St James Theatre after a mixed tryout in Philadelphia: the critic for *Life* magazine, for one, complained of an overly long and wordy first act. The show did not fare much better in the *New York Times*, where Brooks Atkinson lukewarmly described Loesser as a 'very interesting' composer. Nevertheless, *Where's Charley?* ran for a respectable 792 performances (until 9 September 1950) – aided in part by the prestige of its creative team including George Abbott as the book writer and George Balanchine as the choreographer, and in particular the acrobatic dancing and drag performance (as Charley's Aunt) of Ray Bolger.[116] And the show did reasonably well in the Donaldson Awards – an early alternative to the Tonys – finishing behind the powerhouses of Rodgers and Hammerstein's *South Pacific* and Cole Porter's *Kiss Me, Kate*.

There was no original cast album of the show due to an American Federation of Musicians recording ban – Weill and Lerner's *Love Life* is another major Broadway production of that year that suffered from having no recorded legacy – but Bolger recorded cover versions of the songs 'Once in Love with Amy' and 'Make a Miracle', which were released as a single by Decca on 15 February 1949. Loesser noted the impact of the record on sheet music sales and also anticipated success for Bolger's forthcoming film *Look for the Silver Lining*, which was released in June.

[late February 1949]: To Ray Bolger

Dear Ray –

I couldn't possibly say all that I meant in the wire about "Amy". It is simply colossal. More than that, I'm positive it will take the song itself out of the sales doldrums it has been in. Sheet music has shown signs of life since your record and even though there are a lot of live plugs

---

116 George Abbott (1887–1995), American theatre and film producer, screenwriter and director; he later wrote the books for and directed *The Pajama Game* (1954) and *Damn Yankees* (1955) by Loesser's mentees Richard Adler and Jerry Ross. George Balanchine (1904–1983), influential Georgian-American choreographer and co-founder of the New York City Ballet. Ray Bolger (1904–1987), American actor, singer, dancer and vaudevillian.

([Bing] Crosby etc.) <u>you</u> are doing the job single-handed. I hope it is as nice a feeling for you as it is for me – and I also hope you get rich on the proceeds!

Incidentally, while I'm standing here telling you how wonderful you are – I should add that I'm hearing sensational things about your Warner Brothers picture job. Maybe you are Mr. 1949. Anyway I'm very proud of you – very grateful – and more than a little sexy about you (see how far things can go?).

Have Paris wipe this letter down with acetone, as it is a little sticky – but

I mean it

Much love + no end of thanks

Frank

7 November 1948: To William Saroyan

Dear Bill:

I read "Jim Dandy"[117] on the train going home. Then I read it again very calmly one evening at my house just to be sure that it wasn't the Santa Fe road bed that was jostling me into a state of bewilderment. It wasn't the Santa Fe road bed.

What I am mostly bewildered about is why you would ever want it to be more of an opera than it is. It's all poetry and singing already and scenically very colorful. And I think the form is already perfect for what you want to say in the play. The only thing I can suggest would be for somebody (like maybe Copland.[118] <u>I'm</u> not smart enough) to score the entire thing and blend from the underscoring to the songs where the songs now occur. That way you'll get the most out of the rhymed dialogue as well as the general color and feeling of the whole play. Also, it will cost the producers a fortune for all those

---

117 William Saroyan's (1908–1981) *Jim Dandy* was written in 1941 for the National Theatre Conference and distributed to colleges across the United States. Set in the reading room of a public library, Saroyan described it as containing 'no characters . . . and no plot'.

118 Aaron Copland (1900–1990), renowned composer of *Fanfare for the Common Man* and *Lincoln Portrait* (both 1942) and *Appalachian Spring* (1944).

men in the pit, but, then again, that is why we are writers – to cost the producers a fortune.

Listen. Think of something for you and me about who struck John, who are the pearls, and does Sam get the girl? This kind of thing can still be a fine philosophical work.

Incidentally, "Be, Beget, And Begone" is a fine song title. I think you ought to write it out as a song. If you want to wait till I get to New York I will help you with it – that is providing I can be its publisher. I am a greedy man. The snow only says "Shovel!" to me. Write me. Meantime, my best to you and your good wife.

[signed:] Frank Loesser[119]

18 August 1949: To Arthur Loesser

Dear Arthur:

Must ask you to forgive the delay in answering your letter, but I have been up to you know where – in you know what. I think it would be just dandy if you accepted the challenge from that fancy magazine to write about your brother.[120] I would be very curious to see what you wrote but of course these people probably have no Hollywood circulation. (Maybe, if and when it gets published, you will send me a copy.) If they want a reasonably good authority regarding my so-called middle years or 'hitless hiatus', you might refer them to Billy Schuman whose copy or information I am sure would be acceptable in this seemingly obscurantist publication. I met Eric [sic] Leinsdorf[121] for the first time the other day and he described "Notes" almost exactly as you did. Incidentally, he reminds me in many ways of you. Some little physical mannerisms are almost identical with yours. However, he seems to be a much more self-conscious fellow.

---

119 In another letter, Saroyan also asked Loesser to compose his text 'The Guy in the Gutter and the Girl on the Walk.'

120 'My Brother Frank', published by Arthur Loesser in *Notes* 7/2 (March 1950), 217–39.

121 Erich Leinsdorf (1912–1993), Austrian conductor, at the time conductor of the Rochester Philharmonic; in 1962 he became music director of the Boston Symphony Orchestra.

Lynn, Susan and I, plus the helps, will probably be coming to New York around October and are likely to stay for three or four months. Will you and Jean be in New York for any of that time? It would be fun getting together, of course I am anxious to see Anne and be amazed that she is no longer a kid – and hear all about how she likes New York, which I am sure she does.

Mama has just come back from Cape Cod as you no doubt know, and I am phoning her today or tonight to see how she feels and gather tidbits about the Drachmans.

Did you know your old friend Norman Siegel[122] is now head of publicity for Paramount. Imagine the pleasure of not having to write anything any more.

Best – love

[signed:] Frank

Increasingly during the 1940s, Loesser wrote both the lyrics and the music to his songs,[123] and several for which he wrote the texts earned him Academy Award nominations, including 'Dolores' from *Las Vegas Nights* (Paramount, 1941), 'They're Either Too Young or Too Old' from *Thank Your Lucky Stars* (music by Arthur Schwartz, Paramount, 1943) and 'I Wish I Didn't Love You So' from *The Perils of Pauline* (Paramount, 1947). He eventually won an Oscar for 'Baby, It's Cold Outside' from *Neptune's Daughter* (Metro-Goldwyn-Mayer, 1949), where it was introduced by Esther Williams and Ricardo Montalbán, and by Betty Garrett and Red Skelton. According to Susan Loesser, 'Baby, It's Cold Outside' had been written in 1944 for performance with Lynn Loesser, as a party piece. In an unpublished

---

122 Norman Siegel (?–1961), publicity chief for Paramount Pictures and later editor of a screen magazine.

123 According to Leonard Lyons, it was director Edmund Goulding (1891–1959) who convinced Loesser to write both lyrics and music: '[Goulding] was the one who persuaded Frank Loesser, who then was only a lyricist, to write both words and music. "For three reasons," said Goulding. "(1) When you break an appointment with yourself, to work on a song, it's not as irritating. (2) You have exclusivity in failure. And (3) you don't have to split royalties with anyone."' (*Daily Defender*, 4 January 1960, 8). Since Loesser and Lyons were good friends, it may be that this anecdote derives from Loesser himself.

memoir, Lynn wrote, 'Well, the room just fell apart. I don't think either of us realized the impact of what we'd sung. We had to do it over and over again and we became instant parlor room stars. We got invited to all the best parties for years on the basis of "Baby." It was our ticket to caviar and truffles. Parties were built around our being the closing act.' When Loesser sold it to MGM, Lynn 'felt as betrayed as if I'd caught him in bed with another woman. I kept saying "Esther Williams and Ricardo Montalban!!!" He finally sat me down and said, "If I don't let go of 'Baby' I'll begin to think I can never write another song as good as I think this one is." '[124]

---

124 Loesser, *A Most Remarkable Fella*, 79–80.

CHAPTER TWO

1950–53
GUYS AND DOLLS TO HANS CHRISTIAN ANDERSEN

In 1949, Loesser made his one and only appearance in a film, as the gangster Hair-do Lempke in John Farrow's *Red, Hot and Blue* (Paramount Pictures), starring Betty Hutton and Victor Mature. Deriving its title from Cole Porter's 1936 musical of the same name, the film uses neither Porter's plot nor his songs but four songs by Loesser: 'I Wake Up in the Morning Feeling Fine', 'That's Loyalty', 'Hamlet' and '(Where Are You?) Now that I Need You'. The following year he and Lynn had a baby boy, John.

29 September 1950: To Abe and Carin Burrows
(Telegram)

IT'S A BOY THIS MORNING ST JOHN'S HOSPITAL, SANTA MONICA, EVERYTHING FINE LOVE
LYNN AND FRANK LOESSER

Abe Burrows – whom Loesser had known since at least the mid-1940s – was the book writer for Loesser's 1950 show, *Guys and Dolls*. He was brought in to provide a new book after Jo Swerling's original script was rejected, though Swerling retained credit with Burrows. No correspondence from the time survives documenting the genesis of the show although Loesser did make some comments

3. Frank Loesser as Hair-do Lempke on the set of the 1949
Paramount film *Red, Hot and Blue*.

about it in an article, 'Frank Loesser – Hit Parade Habitue', published
in the *New York Times* for 17 December:

> What counts is the basic situation . . . Take that number we have
> in the show – 'Sue Me', for instance. Sam Levene[1] sings it and he's
> playing the part of a guy who runs crap games and there's this

---

1 Sam Levene (1905–1980), Russian-American actor who starred as Nathan
Detroit in the original *Guys and Dolls*, both on Broadway and in London.

dame trying to reform him. Think of all the guys who've been in that spot where they just are what they are and there's nothing they can do about it. So all they can say to a dame when the going gets rough and she's got him cornered is: 'Sue me. Shoot bullets through me.' Similarly, a show, according to Loesser, had to have what he described as a 'provocative' song, as well as 'your big slob of a sophomoric ballad': 'Now here', Loesser said about 'If I Were a Bell', 'we have this quiet, conservative mission broad falling for a gambler when she gets a snoot full. But what she's saying is something she can take back. She's not committing herself. She wants to be able to change her mind. Already we've had the duet, "I'll Know", where the dame says she wants to marry a conservative guy and the gambler is saying love is just chemistry. The people in the duet are on two different levels. How are they going to get together? Everything's all set up for the big duet-ballad, "I've Never Been in Love Before." In "South Pacific" it was "Some Enchanted Evening." That Hammerstein. With two lines he can make T. S. Eliot look tired.' Loesser does let on how the original idea for a song – for example, 'Adelaide's Lament' – can change in the course of writing the book: 'Originally, it was figured that Adelaide should catch cold from a lack of clothes in a drafty cabaret' but Loesser then had the idea 'that maybe she could be a psychosomatic victim of love. That gave Vivian Blaine the number that is in the Ethel Merman tradition for humor and showmanship.'[2]

Guys and Dolls premiered at the 46th Street Theatre (now the Richard Rodgers Theatre) on 24 November and was an immediate success. Writing in the *New York Times* (3 December 1950), Brooks Atkinson raved that '. . . every now and then a perfectly-composed and swiftly-paced work of art comes out of the bedlam of Broadway . . ', while the *Brooklyn Daily Eagle* (25 November) described the score as

---

2 Vivian Blaine (1921–1995) played Miss Adelaide; her appearance in *Guys and Dolls* was her first Broadway lead role. The legendary Ethel Merman (1908–1984) starred in several of the great musicals from the 1930s to the 1960s, including Cole Porter's *Anything Goes* (1934), Irving Berlin's *Annie Get Your Gun* (1946) and Jule Styne's *Gypsy* (1959).

'superior'. Shortly after the show's premiere, Cole Porter wrote to Loesser: 'I saw your finished product in New York a few nights ago, and I congratulate you on your magnificent job.' Loesser, as was customary for him, kept a close eye on the production, even after the opening:

17 May 1951: To Abe Burrows

Dear Abe:

Here are some clippings that my secretary held out in case you want a look. . . . Now be a nice guy and go and see Guys & Dolls and fix up the actors who by this time, no doubt, are lousing everything up. Please.

[signed:] Frank

One of the musical's most successful elements were the designs by Jo Mielziner (1901–1976). After the Broadway opening, Loesser wrote to ask him to fulfil a promise:

18 December 1950: To Jo Mielziner

Dear Jo:

Now that we are all walking around with blue marks on our stomachs from taking bows, I have relaxed enough to remember a very kind promise you made me. You said I could have the original painting of the rainy street drop. I have a space reserved next to a pretty good Roualt. Okay?

Love,

In the late 1940s, Loesser formed his own music publishing company, Frank Music Corp. Intended in part to discover new young popular composers and lyricists, and in part to ensure Loesser had publishing control of his own works, Frank Music was instrumental in launching or furthering the careers of several successful songwriters and songwriting teams during the 1950s, including Meredith Willson (*The Music Man*, 1957) and Robert Wright and George Forrest (*Kismet*, 1953). Together with Music Theatre International, founded by Loesser in 1952 with orchestrator Don Walker, Frank Music was a major force in music publishing and licensing secondary theatrical rights. His most successful early promotion was the songwriting team Richard Adler (1921–2012) and Jerry Ross (1926–1955) – authors of *The Pajama Game* (1954, winner of the Tony for best musical) and *Damn Yankees* (1955, which also won the Tony for best musical) – whom Loesser initially promoted to Paramount Pictures and then to the producer John Murray Anderson, who commissioned them to write songs for his show *Almanac*.

1 August 1951: To Don Hartman, Paramount Pictures Corp

Dear Don:

Here are some examples of the work of Adler and Ross. You will note that one of the records is an already well established number ("The Strange Little Girl," recorded by Guy Lombardo).

The others, I think, show remarkable talent and great versatility. I have been interested in the boys for about six months now and their capacity for writing to order is really wonderful. I think this would be very important to you at the studio. The enclosed group of sample records represents only a small fraction of the stuff they have produced since I knew them. Before that time each had small, but far from negligible credits in the song writing field.

Ross and Adler are quite young (somewhere under thirty) and are more than passably personable. They talk good English and keep their nails clean. I think that this ought to be important to you as it pretty much assures you of a nice, pleasant relationship at the studio.

They are going to be a hit team. If you don't make use of this, I will continue to do so. However, if you want them it will be an easy thing for me to unhook them for service to you. If you like the sound of these records, I think it would be a brilliant idea for you to invest in round trip plane fares, etc., so that you can have a look at them out here for a few days and subscribe whole-heartedly to my good opinion of them, or I will never speak to you again.

Love,

1 December 1952: To John Murray Anderson[3]

My dear Mr. Anderson:

I am sorry we missed each other in the east. As far as my writing goes, I am afraid I won't be available for quite a while. However, as a music publisher I have access to no end of goodies. It is very possible that I will be able to put certain songs and the services of certain writers at your disposal, in the event that you plan a show.

With this in mind, I have asked my Professional Manager to contact you and arrange an audition for a team of writers of exceptional merit. Their names are, Richard Adler and Jerry Ross. Please try to make time to see and hear them, as I think such a meeting could benefit all of us.

Of course, you and I will be seeing each other upon my return to New York, which might possibly be in January. At that time, it will be more than interesting for me to get acquainted with you, as well as your project for the theatre. I must add at this point, that I have always had unbounded admiration for your accomplishments, and I look forward with pride and pleasure to my association with you.

Best wishes.

Cordially,

5 January 1953: To Adler and Ross

Dear Gents:

I have your long letter; also the cheese. Thanks for both. Cy Feuer[4] is out here and we will be discussing you fellows. I will be discussing

---

3 John Murray Anderson (1886–1954), screenwriter, theatre director, producer, songwriter and actor. He made his Broadway debut in 1919 as writer, director and producer of *The Greenwich Follies*; he later produced the *Ziegfeld Follies* of 1934, 1936 and 1943 as well as Billy Rose's *Jumbo*, 1935. The acting school he founded in New York in the 1920s included among its pupils Bette Davis and Lucille Ball.
4 Cy Feuer (Seymour Arnold Feuer, 1911–2006), theatre producer, had produced Loesser's *Where's Charley?* (1948) and *Guys and Dolls* (1950). Later he produced Cole Porter's *Can-Can* (1953) and *Silk Stockings* (1955), and Loesser's *How to Succeed in Business Without Really Trying* (1961).

you, also, with certain picture people, but this is only an outside chance at the moment.

Sorry you got dispossessed. There isn't much I can do about that from here.

More later.

Love,

Loesser's chief compositional activity at this time – from about mid-1950, even as he was putting the finishing touches to *Guys and Dolls* – was the film musical *Hans Christian Andersen*. Samuel Goldwyn had conceived the idea as early as 1936 and more than twenty screenwriters worked at various times on drafts of a screenplay; the final version was by Moss Hart.[5]

Directed by Charles 'King' Vidor, the film tells the story of the cobbler Hans Christian Andersen (played by Danny Kaye) who is asked to leave his hometown because his imaginative stories distract the local children from school. He moves to Copenhagen, where he falls in love with the ballerina Doro (played by Jeanmaire), for whom he writes 'The Little Mermaid'.[6] Doro, however, is already married and Andersen must be content writing popular children's stories.

5 November 1951: To Charles Vidor

Dear Charley:

Here's a blow-blow description of the tape recording I made and it represents the entire sequence of events as they belong in the

---

5 Moss Hart (1904–1961), who co-authored the Kurt Weill–Ira Gershwin *Lady in the Dark* (1941), later wrote the screenplay for *A Star is Born* (1954); he directed several Broadway musicals, including *My Fair Lady* (1956) and *Camelot* (1960).
6 Danny Kaye (1911–1987), actor, comedian, singer and dancer, was among the biggest Hollywood stars of the 1940s and 1950s; his filmography included, in addition to *Hans Christian Andersen*, *The Secret Life of Walter Mitty* (1947) and *White Christmas* (1954). Renée Marcelle 'Zizi' Jeanmaire (1924–2020) was a ballet dancer, singer and actress; active in Paris in the 1940s, she danced the title role in a 1949 London production of Roland Petit's *Carmen* and thereafter appeared in several Hollywood films, including *Anything Goes* (1956), with Bing Crosby.

story. However, I can make any changes you suggest, so don't hesitate to kick it around.

I have a total time of about two and a half minutes, but I have not allowed for any high jinks by Danny in the course of his part of the number. Personally, I think that whatever he does should be included in the time of the existing set-up.

Love,

Attached:
SHOE SONG

Tape record of entire sequence was made by the members of the "Guys and Dolls" National Company cast, Lydia Marcus, Dianna de Rosso and Alex Steinert,[7] at Mr. Loesser's house – Thursday, September 6th, 1951.

It was characteristic of Loesser to be deeply involved with any production he was associated with, whether on film or in the theatre, whether concerning the broad outlines and dramatic thrust of a plot or minute details of staging, costuming or facial expression. In the case of *Hans Christian Andersen*, his concerns included the basic structure of the plot, the motivations of the characters, the quality of the underscoring and the sound of the singers' voices.

25 March 1952: To Sam Goldwyn

Dear Sam:

This is what I submitted and what you apparently approved of a couple of months ago. It probably contains much more detail than is necessary or practical. Nevertheless, I believe it tells a completely understandable visual story of Hans' dream.

I think the essential story is that they are a happy couple preparing to get married, announcing to the world their great love for each other, getting married and finally being applauded by an admiring

---

7 Alex Steinert (1900–1982), composer and conductor. He sometimes transcribed songs for Cole Porter.

throng. This is essentially what Hans wishes for himself. He doesn't necessarily wish himself a red carpet or eight girls whose toes happen to be pointing in a certain way.

However, I think the audience must know that they are heading for a wedding. We should be able to know this by seeing the couple's reaction to church bells and church. I think a wedding gown that is obviously a wedding gown <u>and nothing else</u>, should be purchased. Also a suitable groom's outfit for Hans. Also the selection of the ring. The reason I put in such details as the cake, the carpet, the flowers, the dishes, etc. was to form some sort of an entourage to which the couple should sing their song. I believe the couple should enter the church after the song and come out, immediately, in such a way as to indicate clearly that they are married. From that point on, I don't think we can afford any rug rolling but should get to the "Mr. and Mrs. Andersen" line in the ensemble <u>as soon as possible</u>.

More important than anything else, in my mind, is that this is a dream that Mr. Andersen has about himself and the girl he loves. I think that where possible we should photograph the couple and not linger too long with the dancing tradesmen. We are interested in their function only as it applies to the happy couple. We are not interested in <u>their</u> private lives.

I never went to a movie to see anybody's feet, including Fred Astaire's or Gene Kelly's. What I want to know about my principals is what is on their minds. The best way to show this is through the attitude expressed by their faces. I want to be near enough the faces to see this – not every minute, but at times when it is necessary to know their intentions. If the medium of dancing is used for people to move from place to place I am delighted, but first and foremost I want to know <u>why</u> they are going from place to place.

In fairness to you I must concede that you have given considerable thought to all the above elements. I have not seen any rehearsals of the second fantasy, nor have I had a chance to rehearse the part where the song is sung. But I don't mind telling you that I am scared to death.

Love,

P.S. Remember it's <u>my</u> money.

14 July 1952: To Samuel Goldwyn

Dear Sam:

I agree with you that the sound must have been at least partly the fault of the theatre equipment as I heard many things much better in the projection room. Nevertheless, there are certain points where I think we could get greater clarity out of the singing. I think there is much too much orchestra presence in "No Two People." The lyrics are complicated and therefore the voices should be very much in the clear. The choral parts at the finish of the number, when they are singing "Mr. and Mrs. Hans Christian Andersen . . .," are indistinguishable. Therefore, it is not quite clear why the two principals repeat these words as they walk down the carpet.

The scoring[8] under the turning pages of the story book near the end . . . sounds much too much like end-title music and unless the whole tone of this music, as well as the volume, is reduced I feel there will be a lot of hat grabbing at this point. Although I think that the reprise finale is very good, I think that the choral singing of the words at the very end of "Hans Christian Andersen" is a disgrace. It is too fast, too short and too thin. If it can be redone in bigger dimensions and start immediately after we end "Thumbelina" going up the kite string, it can vastly improve the end of the picture. Right now it sounds like the end of a Porky Pig Cartoon.

The character of some of the individual voices in the market place I think is very damaging to the whole nature of the scene. I do not think this would be too hard to correct. Some of the people sound as if they were auditioning for opera instead of selling apples. Maybe this is not too important to you, but I am just mentioning it.

---

8 The orchestrations for *Hans Christian Andersen* were by Jerome Moross (1913–1983), later composer of the theme music for the television series *Wagon Train* (1959–1963); Sidney Cutner (1903–1971), later the orchestrator of *Around the World in 80 Days* (1956) with Leo Shuken (1906–1976), whose other orchestrating work included *Roman Holiday* (1953), Alfred Hitchcock's *Rear Window* (1954), *The Ten Commandments* (1956), *The Magnificent Seven* (1960) and *Breakfast at Tiffany's* (1961). Cutner and Shuken are uncredited in *Hans Christian Andersen*.

Transition from the end of "Copenhagen" to the newsboy is in three cuts. Actually it was intended that the newsboy's first note should be superimposed on the last note of "Copenhagen." Can these things be overlapped? It would help a great deal, in my opinion.

Likewise, there is a lack of flow between the end of the road scene and the long shot of the Copenhagen boat. Is there enough footage at the end of the reunion scene between Hans and Peter, so that you dissolve into the long shot of the boat?

I am purposely leaving out any suggestions about cuts as these things have to be talked out. I have some views on the subject which I would like to discuss with you, possibly later today or tomorrow.

Also I am not giving you my opinion of some of the details of the scoring. I know of some vast improvements that can be made, but this too requires discussion.

Will talk with you later today.

Sincerely,

Released on 25 November 1952 in New York (and on 19 December nationwide and in the UK), *Hans Christian Andersen* garnered widespread praise, in particular for Loesser's music and the dancing of Jeanmaire. Shortly before its premiere, Loesser was visited by Joe Csida, a staff writer for *Billboard*, who wrote: '. . . any real student of words and music will recognize the intense, coldly analytical thought, mated with warm human understanding, which Loesser put into every syllable, every sound, in each and every song, ballad and novelty, adult and kiddie. . . . This was true of the "Guys and Dolls" score, and I think you'll find it even truer of the "Hans Christian Andersen" collection.' Bosley Crowther, in the *New York Times*, described Loesser's score as 'bright and saucy', adding that the music 'injects more vitality into the whole show than does the syrupy script of Moss Hart'. *Hans Christian Andersen* was nominated for six Academy Awards: for best art direction, best cinematography, best costume design, best scoring, best sound recording and best song – 'Thumbelina' – only one of several songs in the film to have achieved widespread popularity, including 'The Inch Worm' and 'Wonderful Copenhagen'. In Denmark, the film was not released until 6 September 1953.

• • •

The success of Frank Music led to numerous approaches and proposals for musicals, many of which Loesser rejected, in part because he was already thinking about what in 1956 would become his next show, *The Most Happy Fella*, but more often for solid drama-turgical reasons that are telling of his theatrical aesthetic and his sense of what works, or does not work, in a musical.

7 November 1951: To George Abbott

Dear George:

I really don't know what I want to do, or once I know I want to do it – when I can do it. I have committed myself to practically exclusive activity for Goldwyn until April 1st.[9]

In the meantime, I think I am going to continue on a sort of opera[10] I have been preparing, slowly, for a long time. This one I expect to write by myself, until I find out it is a bad job and scream for help. I put it aside for the Goldwyn project, with the expectation of getting it on Broadway sometime in the spring of '53. (It will take a tremen-dous amount of music writing.) If I wish, I guess I can delay it even further, but it would have to be in favor of something very exciting.

I am not yet sure whether "Turn to the Right"[11] is this dish, although I share some of your enthusiasm. My feeling about this play is that it should be done on a frankly economical basis – physically reducible so that it can play anywhere at a profit. (I am thinking especially of stock and amateur uses, plus the road.) I think it should be written so that the casting of any number of companies is not a terrible problem, etc., etc.

---

9 For *Hans Christian Andersen*.
10 *The Most Happy Fella*.
11 Presumably a version of Winchell Smith and John E. Hazzard's 1916 play *Turn to the Right*. Winchell Smith (c1872–1933) wrote and produced more than two dozen plays and musicals between 1901 and 1930, mostly without any notable success. John Hazzard (1881–1935) was a composer and performer; his credits include the *Ziegfeld Follies of 1912* (additional music) and Jerome Kern's *Very Good Eddie* (1916), in which he performed and for which he contributed additional lyrics.

My reason for this is as follows: It is a cornball story and I think this should be capitalized on frankly. The Broadway lovers of effete entertainment are not going to welcome it as opposition to "The King and I" or "The Cocktail Party." It is not rich enough in novel characterizations to compete with "Guys and Dolls" or "Annie Get Your Gun."[12] I think it should be a frank tear-jerker with spots of unsubtle high jinks, so that it can play Rochester and Akron for money. It should have more hit songs than "Guys and Dolls" and "The King and I" and less finesse.

I have a conviction or at least a strong opinion that despite the jolly talk from Hollywood, picture theatres are going to continue to close. They will not convert easily to skating rinks or meat markets, but will be panting for live attractions. I note that this situation is already showing itself in Detroit. Naturally I know that there is a hesitancy to book a show out of town without a pre-established Broadway reputation, or without a name actor. Maybe there is a way to overcome this, assuming that it is not a great success in New York.

Not that I am making this assumption, I think it can also be a hit on Broadway, but I feel that its ultimate value will be in its standardization. If "Blossom Time"[13] did it maybe "Turn to the Right" can do it.

Now I am only theorizing and applying certain instincts which may be all cockeyed. My instinct is that the public will be hungry for live entertainment. Even their ball games are being watched at home and pretty soon all the horse races, fist fights, etc. You will note that the circus is still healthy and books its successful thirty-three weeks per year as usual. There is also Judy Garland at the Palace to consider, and the ice shows, etc.[14]

---

12 Richard Rodgers and Oscar Hammerstein II's *The King and I* (1951); T. S. Eliot's *The Cocktail Party* (1950); Irving Berlin's *Annie Get Your Gun* (1946).

13 An operetta based on music by Franz Schubert, Heinrich Berté and Sigmund Romberg that played at the Ambassador Theatre, New York, from 29 September 1921 to 27 January 1923, and at the Shubert and 44th Street theatres during May and June 1923. *Blossom Time* was the one notable success of composer Heinrich Berté (Heinrich Bettelheim, 1858–1924); it was revived in 1926, 1931, 1939 and 1943.

14 Judy Garland's twice-a-day vaudeville played at the recently refurbished Palace Theatre for nineteen weeks, beginning in October 1951.

I want to talk to you about all the theoretical things first, before we go into the business of whether we want to do this show or not. Is it likely that you will be out within the next few months? I know you said you could come out, but that was in the event we had a definite project. I mean, would you be vacationing here anyway? I would like to have some long talks with you about the whole musical comedy business and us.

I am sorry that you aren't going to London, but you know best. Please write.

Love,

18 December 1951: To Hume Cronyn[15]

Dear Hume:

This will have to be short. My feelings about "The Flying Yorkshireman"[16] are something like this: Although there is a warmth and possibly musical quality to the relations between Sam and his wife, I do not think there is a whole evening's worth of entertainment in it emotionally or sentimentally. It is a somewhat superior Maggie and Jiggs relationship,[17] which however sweet is primarily comic. To enjoy this couple we must, in a sense, patronize them and their antics.

As I suggested on the phone (and I am having it crossed-stitched and framed as a motto for my library wall) the people in a musical comedy have to <u>care</u> when they sing. You will note with what immense enthusiasm the pacing lions treat the subject of dames in "South Pacific." The effect was comedic but the delivery was ultra-serious. I think "Adelaide's Lament" works for the same reason. On the less funny side, "This Nearly Was Mine," sung by Pinza,[18] was as sincere an

---

15 The actor Hume Cronyn (1911–2003) was active on stage, in films and on television. He was nominated for an Academy Award for his performance as Paul Roeder in *The Seventh Cross* (Metro-Goldwyn-Mayer, 1944).
16 Eric Knight, *The Flying Yorkshireman* (New York, 1938), ten stories about Sam Small and other Yorkshiremen in America in the early twentieth century.
17 Maggie and Jiggs, the main characters in George McManus's comic strip *Bringing Up Father*, published between 1913 and 2000. Jiggs was an immigrant Irishman hod carrier who wins a million dollars in a sweepstake; Maggie was his wife.
18 Opera singer Ezio Pinza (1892–1957) had created the role of Emile in *South Pacific*.

expression of a torch situation as we have ever seen in the theatre. And this is the way it goes, I think, with almost any memorable vocal numbers.

Now Sam Small is not equipped as a character to care strongly about certain important things, for instance, sex. We can let him sing "Believe Me If All Those Endearing Young Charms"[19] and possibly dance a sentimental jig around the less than exotic figure of his wife. That is about as far as he can go on that score. He can't sing with any conviction "Yours Is My Heart Alone," "Night and Day," or "Bali Ha'i."[20] And the same goes, I think, for Mrs. Small.

We leave these assignments normally, to those characters with whom we choose to identify ourselves: the people who remain appetizing under palm trees or in bedrooms. They are the Alfred Drakes, the Mary Martins, the Ann Jeffries [sic], the Judy Garlands and the Robert Aldas.[21]

They are the ones who make us believe the slob words in the ballads and the cute words in the rhythm numbers. They can be damn fools, but only on a heroic basis. That is to say, the hero can volunteer to be a paratrooper and kill himself, and the heroine may set fire to the local draft board files to protect him from such a fate, but neither one of them can have a bumpy nose or a bald head or a too funny walk. A tragic example was "Texas' Little Darling,"[22] in which an otherwise personable young man played the part of the village idiot and then attempted to sing believable baritone solos. He was

---

19 A popular Irish song based on a text of the poet Thomas Moore (1779–1852).

20 'Yours Is My Heart Alone' from Franz Lehár's 1929 operetta *The Land of Smiles*; 'Night and Day' from Cole Porter's 1932 musical *Gay Divorce*; and 'Bali Ha'i' from Rodgers and Hammerstein's *South Pacific* (1949).

21 Alfred Drake (1914–1992) had appeared in Rodgers and Hammerstein's *Oklahoma!* (1943) and Cole Porter's *Kiss Me, Kate* (1948), among numerous other shows. The beloved Mary Martin (1913–1990) made her debut in 1938 in Cole Porter's *Leave It to Me!*; she subsequently starred in Rodgers and Hammerstein's *South Pacific* (1949) and *The Sound of Music* (1959) among others. Anne Jeffreys (1923–2017) appeared in numerous films and starred in the 1950s television series *Topper*. Robert Alda (1914–1986) played Sky Masterson in the original Broadway production of *Guys and Dolls*; he was a prolific film actor as well.

22 *Texas, Lil' Darlin'* (1949), music by Robert Emmett Dolan and lyrics by Johnny Mercer.

not appreciably romantic enough in the part to make his singing count, even though it was technically good and so were the songs.

Now the two young characters supplied in the original "Flying Yorkshireman" are not going to be any good at all, in my opinion. The girl seems to be a bloodless tool of her mother's whims, with no motive power of her own. I guess she is pretty and desirable but, deep down, people will know that she is only desirable to such a make-shift stock character as the boy friend reporter. I understand why Knight buried these two, but I don't think a musical comedy can afford it.

The number one problem I think is to supply two self-propelled, sex-worthy, ultra-musical characters whose paths join that of the Sam Smalls often enough to make it reasonable that the four of them should appear in the same play. This is no kid job for an author, because when I said the same play, I mean it. The paths would have to join in some philosophical sense in the same way that in "South Pacific" the two sets of love lives mingle in terms of an over-all socio-philosophical treatise. The wrong author will give you forty jokes for the old folks and ten song cues for the young ones and there will still be no reason for their walking into each other's scenes.

Did you ever see a picture called "The Miracle on 34th Street?"[23] Can you remember anything that happened between the young man and the young lady involved (sic)? If they had had twenty hit songs to sing you wouldn't have had any more fun with them. They just would have succeeded in wasting some of Edmund Gwenn's jolly time on the screen.

This play will be a good deal more trouble than "The Miracle on 34th Street." Sam Small is not a man with distinct motives. He is a man to whom things happen. He can't pull in other characters, they will have to push themselves in and all I can say is, God help them.

---

23 Released by 20th Century Fox in 1947, starring Maureen O'Hara (1920–2015) and John Payne (1912–1989) with Edmund Gwenn (1877–1959) as Kris Kringle. Ironically, Loesser's mentee Meredith Willson would later write a musical version under the title *Here's Love* (1963).

It is late at night and maybe I haven't said everything I mean and maybe I have said some things I don't mean . . . expect that I am going to sign this and mail it to you.

Let me know what you do. I'm interested but very wary.

Merry Christmas.

5 February 1952: To Kay Arnen[24]

Dear Kay:

This just a note to say thanks for coming over and singing for me. I knew I'd think you were wonderful so it was no surprise to me. However, this is no guarantee that:

a. I'll ever finish the show I have in mind.[25]
b. That I'll like it enough when I get finished with it.
c. That anybody else will like it enough even if I do like it.

Also, there is no way of being sure that I will manage to write anything that fits you: or for that matter that you will want to bother with when you hear it. In short, we are not making committments [sic] to each other. Of course, you know that I hope we will, but that's for later.

Meanwhile, best love and thanks to you again.

Sincerely,

Frank Loesser

26 February 1952: To Phil Silvers

Dear Phil:

Some time back I looked at "Room Service"[26] with the idea of a musical in mind and it wound up that I didn't think too much of it. However, I don't know your producers' plans and possibly they have,

---

24 Kay Arnen (Armenuhi Manoogian, 1915–2011), Armenian-American singer active in the 1940s and 1950s.

25 Presumably *The Most Happy Fella*.

26 The Allen Boretz and John Murray play *Room Service*, produced by George Abbott, ran at the Cort Theatre from 19 May 1937 to 16 July 1938; an unsuccessful revival played at the Playhouse Theatre from 6 to 18 April 1953.

along with you, thoughts on it that might turn me optimistic. I am coming to New York early in April and I can have a long talk about it.

I am sorry this has to be so short and no jokes, but I'm the new Sol Bornstein[27] these days.

Love,

1 December 1952: To Billy Rose

Dear Billy:

Count me out on the business we talked about. I have much too much mapped out for me already and can't even think about doing anything more for quite a while. Of course, thanks for thinking of me. Your whole idea sounds wonderful.

Love,

• • •

In addition to his compositional activity, his consideration of other properties suggested to him and his promotion and mentorship of other Broadway composers, Loesser was occupied with the day-to-day running of Frank Music. This involved rights issues; dealing (on his or others' behalf) with the performing rights organisation ASCAP (American Society of Composers, Authors and Publishers); managing recording contracts for his own works and his stable of composers; publicity; exploitation (commercialisation of works); and promoting the Frank Music catalogue. Almost always, his decisions were based not only on practicalities, but also on his aesthetics, whether related to dramatic conception or actual performance. Of particular importance is Loesser's letter to Bing Crosby's writer, William Morrow. As Loesser says, in late 1951 he undertook Frank Music's first large-scale publishing venture, and an endorsement by Bing Crosby – through performance – would be a significant boost for the company.

---

27 Saul H. Bornstein (1884–1957) co-founded the music publishing company Irving Berlin Inc. It became Bourne Inc. in 1944 when he parted ways with songwriter Berlin.

10 September 1951: To Irene Gladys Selznick

Dear Irene:

Here is a photostat of Morton's[28] ASCAP application. Also a carbon copy of my letter to Miss Rosenfeld, with which I assume she will comply as soon as possible.

Read the backside of the photostat carefully. Mr. Morton has had several partners in the writing or adapting of musical works. I think it amy [sic] be assumed that these people knew him well enough to know whether or not the writing of the work in question was in fact an arrangement of a piece of traditional music.

As I suggested on the phone, you might have an expert check over all the compositions Miss Rosenfeld sends you and see whether or not Melrose Bros. ever acquired anything resembling the composition in question prior to the time that Mr. Morton seems to have given his love and affection to Tempo Music. From the sound of the various titles, I would venture to say that Mr. Morton's early catalogue is ultra redundant with melodic phrases, harmonic patterns and general song structures which resemble each other closely and which collectively represent a type of music rather than a group of separate distinguishable compositions. I could be wrong.

You will note in the letter from the Society to Wolfe Gilbert[29] (enclosed) that the Tempo Music Company of Washington, is not a member of ASCAP. It would be a good idea to find out whether Morton, at the time of his assignment of the piece to Tempo, was or was not a member of ASCAP.

It is my opinion (sic) that you did not make a dramatic use of any music[30] and that had there been any rights of others used by you,

---

28 Jelly Roll Morton (born Ferdinand Joseph LaMothe, 1890–1941), jazz pianist and composer.

29 Louis Wolfe Gilbert (1886–1970), Russian-born American lyricist.

30 A reference to theatrical producer Irene Gladys Selznick's production of *A Streetcar Named Desire* (Ethel Barrymore Theatre, New York, 3 December 1947). Morton's estate pursued Selznick for using two Morton songs without permission. See https://www.pure.ed.ac.uk/ws/portalfiles/portal/15533807/Dramas_with_MusicAV.pdf. Selznick, a daughter of film producer Louis B. Mayer (1884–1957), was the wife of producer David O. Selznick (1902–1965).

they would fall into the category of "small rights" – at least that is my opinion from your description of the music which was played between scenes, etc. As I recall from your description, no lyrics were sung so that the music had no inherent narrative or dramatic content: that it did not accompany any specific dramatic action so as to clarify or heighten the meaning of a scene; that it did not describe any character or group of characters in the manner of a motif.

In "Madam Butterfly," a few bars of the "Star Spangled Banner" are used to indicate that Pinkerton is a chauvinist American. In "Guys and Dolls," "Home Sweet Home" is used instrumentally to indicate that the people are leaving the cafe not because there is a fire but because it is late and they are getting home. I think these are typical dramatic uses and from what you tell me and from what I remember from having seen the play, I do not see where you used any music dramatically in the technical sense of the word.

ASCAP seems to have acquired the right to bargain for Morton's small performance rights. If the theatres involved were not ASCAP licenses and ASCAP felt one of its members' works had been used without permission, then it would have a right to sue. I doubt whether Morton's heirs or agents have this right. If Morton, by virtue of his being an ASCAP member, did not include the right of small performance in his assignment to Tempo, then I assume it still belongs to ASCAP. You will note that apparently at the time he submitted his application to ASCAP, Morton did not claim. That was March 28, 1939, although he seems to have prepared the application more than a month earlier. Wouldn't it follow that if the works in question were "created" subsequent to his date of membership in ASCAP that he could no longer include in a publishing assignment rights already delivered to ASCAP? Especially if the publisher was not a member of this organization.

Have fun. I have gotten my morning exercise over this megillah. Show it to your lawyer who will think that I am a terrible fool, except that I am right.

Love,

7 January 1952: To William Morrow[31]

Dear Bill:

As per your request here is a run-down on some of the Frank Music Corporation's catalogue. The ones marked with an asterisk are the ones I think Bing has already performed at one time or another.[32]

SPRING WILL BE A LITTLE LATE THIS YEAR.
I think Bing knows this one although I don't think he has ever done it. The company is going to work on this almost right away and I think it might be a good idea from February through June.

HAVE I STAYED AWAY TOO LONG.
The company is starting to work on this right now. It is an old one that never got attention when it started, but sold an awful lot of copies despite the lack of important performances.

WHAT DO YOU DO IN THE INFANTRY. *
There is an Army Day coming up some time in the first half of this year. Maybe that is your cue. Bing started this one back in 1943 and it sounded just fine.

IN MY ARMS.
This is one from the last war, but there are some new, timely lyrics. I sang it for Columbia Records. After it Tito broke with Stalin. Also I broke with Columbia. Sample on request.

---

31 William S. Morrow (1907–1971), screenwriter and producer. Morrow worked as a writer for Bing Crosby's radio and television shows beginning in 1946; in 1957 and 1958 he scripted Frank Sinatra's second attempt at a variety and drama television series, *The Frank Sinatra Show*.
32 Of the songs mentioned here, the only ones to be recorded by Crosby were 'Spring Will Be a Little Late This Year' (stand-alone, 1943); 'What Do You Do in the Infantry' (stand-alone, 1943); 'If I Were a Bell' (*Guys and Dolls*, 1950); 'Baby, It's Cold Outside' (stand-alone, 1944, later used in the film *Neptune's Daughter*, 1949); 'I've Never Been in Love Before' and 'More I Cannot Wish You' (both *Guys and Dolls*, 1950); and 'The New Ashmolean' and 'Once in Love with Amy' (both *Where's Charley?*, 1948).

IF I WERE A BELL. *
Bing made a wonderful record of this with Patty Andrews. Some such arrangement might work when you get a girl guest.

BABY, IT'S COLD OUTSIDE.
Wait for a girl guest.

ON A SLOW BOAT TO CHINA. *
I think Bing did this with Peggy Lee. It may be ripe again for some such visit from a doll, although it is just as good as a single. When your time is short, remember this chorus can be done in sixty seconds flat or even less.

HOOP-DEE-DOO. *
No comment.

RODGER YOUNG.
Bing never did this, but it would be a beaut for Decoration Day. It is easy to learn and easy to make cuts in if you are short of time. This is a pet of mine and for many years I have restricted it so that the wrong ones would not be tempted to sing it. When you feel you owe the public a solemn one, please look it over.

WHAT ARE YOU DOING NEW YEAR'S EVE.
I am just making a note of this in passing. I will buzz you on this ahead of the fall term.

A BUSHEL AND A PECK.

I'VE NEVER BEEN IN LOVE BEFORE. *
Bing recorded this one, but I thought a little too slowly. However, that is none of my business. I think he should sing it.

MORE I CANNOT WISH YOU. *
Bing made the only record of this. The sentiment is, I think, appropriate for Valentine's Day or whenever Bing feels like issuing a blessing, if you know what I mean.

MY DARLING, MY DARLING.
Short and sweet and good for a single or double.

THE NEW ASHMOLEAN.
This is a good way to have fun with the orchestra. It requires some ensemble singing, I think.

ONCE IN LOVE WITH AMY.
I don't think Bing ever did this and I modestly submit that it is high time.

ORANGE COLORED SKY.

THE STRANGE LITTLE GIRL.

TENNESSEE WEDDING.
This is a new one which Norwood will be bringing you shortly. It is by Victor Missy and Dave Franklin.[33]

YOU'RE SO MUCH A PART OF ME.
This is a new one. It is by Adler and Ross. Norwood will be delivering it.

As you suggested, I am sending a carbon of this note to John Trotter[34] so he will see what an immense bill of goods I am trying to sell.

This is my first venture into big time music publishing and my organization needs as much support as I can possibly get for it. After all it is not such a painful catalogue. As a matter of fact, after I look it over it occurs to me that you people should have been requesting use of it all those years. Oh well, if Sol Bornstein can solicit business, so can I.

Sincerely,
Frank Loesser
President *
PS. * As Harry Ruby[35] once remarked, who said a jew couldn't be president?

---

33 Victor Mizzy (1916–2009) was a popular songwriter during the 1930s and composer for television in the 1960s (his credits include the themes for the sitcoms *Green Acres* and *The Addams Family*). Dave Franklin (1895–1970) was a songwriter best known as the composer of the theme song for the Looney Tunes cartoons. Norwood is unidentified.
34 John Scott Trotter (1908–1975), composer, arranger and orchestra leader known in particular for his work with Bing Crosby between 1937 and 1954.
35 Harry Ruby (1895–1974), American actor and composer. He is known for his scores to the Marx Brothers films *Animal Crackers* (1930), *Horse Feathers* (1932) and *Duck Soup* (1933), among other films and Broadway scores.

14 August 1952: (via secretary) to George Cates[36]

Dear Mr. Cates:

Mr. Loesser, as you probably know, had to return to New York. He, therefore, asked me to return your enclosed manuscript and to apologize for the delay. He also said to tell you "he had no talent at the moment" ... And that he would get in touch with you as soon as he returns.

Sincerely,

Secy. to Frank Loesser

1 Enc.

5 December 1952: To Alan Livingston[37]

Dear Alan:

When we talked on the phone Friday I forgot to mention that Herb Reis[38] had talked to me from the east, and he assured me that February 1st would be an okay release date for "I've Got a Letter."[39]

Frankly, he is trying to get Decca not to release the version they made. They may decide to put it out, but he has their assurance that it won't be until in February sometime.

This information, of course, is confidential. I hope that it gives you enough time to plan your recording of this song. I believe it can make a big hit record.

Lunch soon.

Best,

Frank Loesser

---

36 George Cates (1911–2002), conductor, songwriter and record executive known in particular for his work with bandleader Lawrence Welk.
37 Alan W. Livingston (1917–2009), producer at Capitol Records and from 1959 vice president in charge of programming at NBC.
38 Herb Reis (1910/11–1976), music publisher, founder of Herb Reis Music Corp.
39 By Richard Adler and Jerry Ross; a performance by singer Dolores Hawkins (1929–1987) was released by Decca in 1953.

In early January 1952, Loesser wrote to Richard Rodgers, wishing him luck with a Broadway revival of Rodgers and Hart's 1940 musical *Pal Joey*:

3 January 1952: Lynn and Frank Loesser to Richard Rodgers (Telegram)

ALL GOOD WISHES TO YOU TONIGHT – LYNN AND FRANK LOESSER

Pal Joey opened at the Broadhurst Theatre on 3 January 1952. As with many Broadway productions, the intersection of promotion, performance and direction represented a network of Broadway personalities – little on Broadway happened in a vacuum. In the case of the *Pal Joey* revival, the show was produced by Jule Styne, Loesser's friend and colleague from his Hollywood days; and the original orchestrations by Hans Spialek were supplemented with orchestrations by Don Walker, Loesser's partner in MTI. On 7 January, Rodgers wrote to Loesser, thanking him for his 'help and encouragement with the production', adding: 'Everything seemed to work so wonderfully the other opening night and I know that in the earlier days of its conception you had a great deal to do with encouraging Jule with the project.' To *Life* magazine's theatre editor Tom Prideaux, Loesser wrote to ask for a preview of an article about him called 'The Fine Art of the Hit Tune':

15 July 1952: To Tom Prideaux

Dear Tom:

I don't know what [journalist Ernest] Havemann wrote. He is a nice man, but I gave him a chance to murder me. Would it be real terrible to ask to get a look at what he wrote? Certain statistical things ought to be checked anyway. Please drop me a quick line on this. I will be out here at least another two weeks.

My very best.

Other correspondence from late 1952 includes letters to his friend, *New York Post* columnist Leonard Lyons, Abe Burrows and, as a humorous but at the same time detailed demonstration of his attention to detail generally, a certain 'Phyllis', presumably – given the subject of the letter – one of the Loesser's housekeepers (at the time, the Loessers were commuting regularly between New York and Beverly Hills).

3 December 1952: To Phyllis[40]

GOOD HOUSEKEEPING LETTER

Dear Phyllis:

Hurry!

Sometime, when you have uncle Otto's shows on so that you are good and strong, turn the far end table by the sofa so that the drawer faces front. This way you will not have to break your pretty pink ass getting paper napkins.

Please hustle the carpenter, in the event the book rack has not arrived. Also get him to loosen up the closet doors and put handles on the window.

Check with Plummer's and see if they have a new supply of our highball glasses, and get another half dozen.

Don't lock the bottom part of the corner cabinet, as the lock jams. I'd rather people stole booze.

Check with Shelley about the benches and see if you can rush them, as I may be coming back quickly. When you see him, give him back the brass tray-stand which is now in the bathroom.

In case you haven't thought of it or Herb didn't tell you, have a new pane of glass put in the little picture that was hanging on the door until I slammed it. After that, leave the picture on the piano.

---

40 Given the references to Plummer (a high-end housewares store at 734 Fifth Avenue founded in 1895, and declared bankrupt in 1962) and Martin's (a specialty apparel retailer founded not later than 1903 and based on Fulton Street in Brooklyn), Loesser writes concerning one of the family's New York or New York area residences. None of the other persons mentioned in the letter are known to the Loesser family.

See if Phil has time to put the big brass handle on the wine tub. Tell him it will have to be a through bolt rather than a wood screw. He will probably have to drill the hole a little bigger. As I recall, I left the brass handles (stolen from the Warwick) inside the record player.

If and when you get the laundry back from Martin's laundry (2 deliveries), put the boxes on top of the file cabinet in the closet. You will find my medicine chest is there now. If there is room for all these things that's real dandy, but if the laundry boxes take up too much room, move the medicine chest to the floor of the shower, for the moment. However, do not put it on the scale, because if I ever find out how much it weighs I'll stop carrying it.

Little bitsy items from you to Naomi:

Bring some moth balls and put in strategic spots in the closet. Not, however, in the pockets of clothes.

I am glad Phil has shown Naomi how to clear the filter. Do not shut down the air conditioner for the winter. I don't think it needs over-hauling yet.

The rug should be vacuumed thoroughly UNDER all the furniture. Arrange for some cooperation between Naomi and John for the heavy moving. Also the drapes should be vacuumed – without changing the eternal beauty of the lovely, lovely folds. This is no job for a schmuck, but I think Naomi is our girl, as she is no schmuck (crossed fingers).

The heat in the radiators should be all the way off at all times, except when the room is actually being used. Be sure it is off over night especially. If Reis brings a broad up there in the evenings he can generate his own heat.

The silver lighter and the black one are out of fuel. My brush pens are getting all cruddy by now because the ink is thickening up. If Don or anyone else wants to use them, okay. Otherwise, however, I suggest that you empty them back into the bottles and clean the pens out for future use. This applies to the color pens. The two that write black can stay as they are, in my desk drawer.

You see, I never left town.

And hurry.

Frank Music Corp.

146 WEST 54th STREET • PLAZA 7-6334 • NEW YORK 19, N. Y.

Little bitsy items from you to Naomi:

Bring some moth balls and put in strategic spots in the closet. Not, however, in the pockets of clothes.

I am glad Phil has shown Naomi how to clean the filter. Do not shut down the air conditioner for the winter. I don't think it needs overhauling yet.

The rug should be vacuumed thoroughly UNDER all the furniture. Arrange for some cooperation between Naomi and John for the heavy moving. Also the drapes should be vacummed - without changing the eternal beauty of the lovely, lovely folds. This is no job for a schmuck, but I think Naomi is our girl, as she is no schmuck (crossed fingers).

The heat in the radiators should be all the way off at all times, except when the room is actually being used. Be sure it is off over night especially. If Reis brings a broad up there in the evenings he can generate his own heat.

The silver lighter and the black one are out of fuel. My brush pens are getting all cruddy by now because the ink is thickening up. If Don or anyone else wants to use them, okay. Otherwise, however, I suggest that you empty them back into the bottles and clean the pens out for future use. This applies to the color pens. The two that write black can stay as they are, in my desk drawer.

You see, I never left town.

And hurry.

4. The second page of Frank Loesser's letter to 'Phyllis'.

1 December 1952: To Leonard Lyons

Dear Lennie:

I am sorry everything was so rushed in New York that we never got a chance to laugh it up. However, the next time will be a little less turbulent visit.

Item for you: Sam Goldwyn has a suite in the Sherry Netherland, from the window of which he can see the Paris theatre and the line of people in front of it. He tells me on the phone, that he spends a good deal of time at the window. Funny way to rent a hotel room. Ask him whether he contemplates taking a room at the Astor, so that he can look at the Criterion line.[41]

More later.

Love,

P.S. How did you like Lynn's and my MGM kiddie records? To me they sound like I am still in the Runyon[42] department.

5 January 1953: To Abe Burrows

Dear Abe:

Alex Gottlieb,[43] you wouldn't believe it, has written a play. It is called "Melinda" and might turn out to be a successful play, of its kind. That its kind is the most meretricious in the world I wouldn't deny and neither would you, but it might just possibly be a success. It needs a song. If anyone should write this song, <u>you</u> should. The Morris office is handling the property for Gottlieb. He seemed to agree with me that you are the kind of guy who could write the right piece for this and I think the Morris office will be after you to read the play, etc.

---

41 The Sherry-Netherland Hotel, built in 1927, is located at 781 5th Avenue, at 59th Street; the Paris movie theatre, opened in 1948, is a block away, at 4 West 58th Street. The Astor Theatre, at 1537 Broadway, at West 45th, opened in 1906; the Criterion Theatre, built by Oscar Hammerstein I in 1895, was at 1514 Broadway. At the time, it was showing *Hans Christian Andersen*.
42 That is, Damon Runyon. The allusion is a throwback to *Guys and Dolls*.
43 Alex Gottlieb (1906–1988). A play by him titled *Melinda* apparently does not survive.

Let me know what happens . . . Especially before you sign anything. I am probably going to the races tomorrow with Martin Gang[44] and we will discuss this whole immense project . . . especially the later one about getting you out of a lawsuit for having assigned all your royalties to Alex Gottlieb or his brother-in-law, Billy Rose, or something dreadful. Why I worry about you I don't know, as you are old enough to worry about <u>me</u>. Please worry about me.

Christmas was exhausting, but not New Years. Lynn and I went to sleep at 10:30 New Year's eve, both with colds.

Love to you and Carin.

Frank

An extensive correspondence from 1952 and 1953 with Shawnee Press – founded in 1939, dissolved in 2009, and for many years the largest educational music publisher in the world – documents Loesser's ongoing exploitation, through the publication of arrangements[45] and recordings of several works from his catalogue, as well as *Guys and Dolls* and *Hans Christian Andersen*. The correspondence is telling of his unsatisfactory earlier dealings with the Decca Record Company and revealing of an educational music publisher's view of their market and Loesser's reaction to that.

5 December 1952: To Herb Reis (Shawnee Press)

Dear Herb:

If Hilliard[46] wants standard material, here's some statistical information and a guide for this particular phase of our unfortunate relationship with the Decca Company:

---

44 Martin Gang (1901–1998), entertainment lawyer; his clients included George Burns, Bob Hope, Olivia de Havilland and Frank Sinatra. During the McCarthy era, he counselled clients approached by the House Un-American Activities Committee (HUAC) to confess to former communist connections and to name names.

45 In 1947 Shawnee Press had published a choral arrangement of Loesser's 'The New Ashmolean Marching Society'.

46 Bob Hilliard (1918–1971), lyricist.

"MY DARLING" – was made, grudgingly, by Decca with Mary and Peter Lind Hayes[47] at a time when they thought it would be nice to have bells ringing instead of an orchestra playing. Their choice of artists was typical of the Decca treatment of us. You have already observed how they didn't make a cast album, but spoiled it for themselves by issuing a single Ray Bolger record of "[Once in Love with] Amy." However, that is water under the bridge. It would, nevertheless, be desirable to get a decent version of "My Darling"; possibly Peggy Lee[48] and someone. Of course, it is not necessarily a duet. The main thing is that the tempo should be slow enough to allow the singer actually to <u>vocalize</u>. Expecting a record company to know this is, of course, sheer folly.

"RODGER YOUNG" – was made by Decca with Burl Ives[49] singing, a hillbilly jazz drummer making a party of the funeral and Dave Kapp[50] watching the clock to be sure he could complete seventeen sides in three hours. The record almost got me a dishonorable discharge from the army. As you know, we have a perennial sale of sheet music, quartet and choir versions of this song. It is about time a pop singer and group with enough balls, had a crack at it. There is no rule that says that a standard piece with such life to it (without the help of any decent records) couldn't clean up. Considering our friendly relationship with Waring,[51] he might be the man, although it might be as well to speak to him separately about this. Meanwhile, I would be just as happy if [arranger] Gordon Jenkins summoned up all his good taste and took a crack at it. You might warn Decca that we already have Nelson Eddy and John Charles Thomas,[52] in case they ever start thinking that way.

---

47 Mary Healy (1918–2015) and Peter Lind Hayes (1915–1998), vaudevillians and film and television actors, married in 1940.
48 Peggy Lee (1920–2002) had performed 'My Darling' on radio in 1952.
49 Burl Ives (1909–1995), singer and actor.
50 David Kapp (1905/6–1976), recording industry executive with Decca Records; in 1954 he founded the independent label Kapp Records.
51 Fred Waring (1900–1984), bandleader; he did not record 'Rodger Young'. Waring recorded some of the songs mentioned here including 'The Inch Worm' and 'Anywhere I Wander' on his 1958 album *All Through the Night* (Capitol Records) and 'Once in Love with Amy' on his *Broadway Cavalcade* (Capitol, also 1958).
52 Nelson Eddy (1901–1967), actor and singer; John Charles Thomas (1891–1960), opera singer.

"SPRING WILL BE A LITTLE LATE THIS YEAR" – ask them to play over their Percy Faith instrumental record of it.[53] The mood is right. I think it is a woman's song, but a pop woman who sings absolutely in tune. Do they have one?

"MOON OF MANAKOORA"[54] – hasn't been done in 4/4 time since Ray Noble and Tony Martin made a fine record of it.[55] That was fourteen years ago. The Four Aces[56] might do a splendid job of it. It is the same Loesser vintage as "Heart and Soul," in case you find Hilliard in a superstitious mood.

"NO TWO PEOPLE" – Louis Armstrong and a girl, as soon as they feel it won't insult darling Danny Kaye – to whom we owe so much.[57]

"ROSEANNA"[58] – from the Goldwyn picture of a similar name, is one of the best songs I ever wrote. I don't believe Decca made it. It would be nice to have their best ballad boy try it out. I am forwarding you an example of one of the records that was made a few years back. It's Freddy Martin, on Victor,[59] and of course the vocality is restricted to Mr. Martin's tempo. Today, I think this song is ideal for the Schreierei[60] division.

"HAVE I STAYED AWAY TOO LONG" – was an eminently successful song, with practically no records. Those that were made, I believe, were "all vocal" during a year when there was an orchestra ban. The Mills Brothers[61] couldn't get hurt with this, especially since it contains no more than the three or four chords they already know.

---

53 Percy Faith (1908–1976), bandleader and composer; he recorded 'Spring Will Be a Little Late This Year' for Decca in 1944.

54 From the United Artists film *The Hurricane* (1937).

55 Ray Noble (1903–1976), bandleader and composer; Tony Martin (1913–2012), singer and actor. Noble's recording of 'The Moon of Manakoora' was released by Brunswick Records in 1938.

56 A popular male quartet active 1949 to 1987.

57 Trumpeter, bandleader and one of the founding fathers of jazz, Louis Armstrong (1901–1971) apparently did not record 'No Two People'; the song was introduced in *Hans Christian Andersen* by Danny Kaye and Zizi Jeanmaire.

58 From the RKO film *Roseanna McCoy* (1949).

59 Bandleader and saxophonist Freddy Martin's (1906–1984) recording of 'Roseanna' was released on RCA Victor in 1949 (DJ-733).

60 German for 'screechy'.

61 The Mills Brothers (Donald, Herbert, Harry and John) were among the most popular vocal quartets from the late 1920s to the early 1980s.

Naturally, expecting Decca's country department to double up on this – would be wishful thinking. However, expecting them to leave it stranded with a minor country artist like Sam Glom and his Nashville Five,[62] would be more painfully realistic.

"I'VE NEVER BEEN IN LOVE BEFORE" – was made by Bing during his blue-green or crappy period as it is called. The tempo was much too slow, as if Bing were deliberately out to get Manny Klein and the boys some overtime.[63] As you know, the song is our best seller from the show. But that, of course, is because the people who buy the sheet music have heard some actor who put in five or ten minutes learning how to sing, from me.

"FUGUE FOR TINHORNS" – my new arrangement. I understand Gordon Jenkins[64] doesn't think it is right for him. A combination of two Decca men stars and one woman; such as Dick Haymes and some other guy, and Patty Andrews could do as good a job as the nice record that was made of "No Business Like Show Business."[65] It is inadvisable, however, to attempt to make this record without a real producer in the booth. Or is this asking too much?

I guess that's about all I can think of on the subject. You can show this letter to Hilliard if you like. Frankly, I don't think he will take much store in what I have suggested above, although I think he is trying to be a nice fellow. Fundamentally, we are both in the same business,

---

62 The Nashville Five were an obscure country music band; Sam Glom is unidentified.

63 Manny Klein (1908–1994), American jazz trumpeter. Bing Crosby's recording of 'I've Never Been in Love Before', coupled with 'If I Were a Bell', was released by Decca (27232) in 1950.

64 Gordon Hill Jenkins (1910–1984), American composer and arranger who worked with Johnny Cash, Frank Sinatra, Judy Garland and Nat King Cole, among others.

65 Richard Benjamin (Dick) Haymes (1918–1980), Argentinian singer, songwriter and actor; Patricia Marie Andrews (1918–2013), American singer and one of the popular Andrews Sisters (active 1925–1967). A recording of the 'Fugue for Tinhorns' by the Andrews Sisters was released by Decca in 1953. No recording of the 'Fugue for Tinhorns' by Dick Haymes is known although he recorded Loesser's 'I Wish I Didn't Love You So' (from the 1947 Paramount Pictures film *The Perils of Pauline*) for Decca in 1947. The Andrews Sisters recorded 'There's No Business Like Show Business' for Brunswick in 1947.

Jimmy and I. That is the <u>entertainment</u> business. But I don't think he quite believes that <u>I</u>'m in it.

Yours for,
[unsigned]
<u>D</u> oing
<u>E</u> verything
<u>C</u> olumbia
<u>C</u> asts
<u>A</u> side

9 December 1952: To Herb Reis

Dear Herb:

As long as we have no reaction from Decca, but we do have a contract with Fred Waring on choral arrangements, I think it behooves you to have a visit with Waring and discuss, very seriously, his recording of RODGER YOUNG. The existing records are very bad examples of the piece and Waring knows perfectly well what value this can be to him. He now has the right to print his own choral arrangements of it and I believe, in view of past and current history, he could make a record which we ourselves could do a great deal to help standardize.[66]

Waring brought your name up when I saw him out at Shawnee and said he would welcome suggestions from you on our catalogue; providing it was not just routine plugging, but well thought out programming for him on a prestige basis. In other words, Fred does not want to be used to make the sheet. I don't think that we would seem to be doing this with RODGER YOUNG. You might, for the sake of reference, deliver him the Nelson Eddy, green label, Columbia, 12" version of it[67] as well as some copies of the sheet music. Not that the Nelson Eddy record is a good example of how the piece should

---

66 Waring apparently did not record 'Rodger Young'.
67 Nelson Eddy's recording of 'Rodger Young' was released in 1949.

be performed, but it's still better than the John Charles Thomas or Burl Ives versions, which are really horrible in my opinion.[68]

Love and kisses,

P.S. Of course, in talking with Fred you will be bringing up the contents of the HANS CHRISTIAN ANDERSEN score. He has heard the music, but I think has performed only the duet. Maybe I'm wrong on this point. He might be amused with my version of THE UGLY DUCKLING and INCH WORM on the MGM kiddy records.[69] Frankly, I don't know which of the pieces he likes, if any, but I believe that with all the noise and prestige the picture is now making, he might see a way to program one of the above or WONDERFUL COPENHAGEN or THUMBELINA or something. You're in charge.

Shawnee Press released a number of arrangements of Loesser's songs, including 'Baby, It's Cold Outside', 'Luck Be a Lady' and 'More I Cannot Wish You' from *Guys and Dolls*, 'Hoop-Dee-Doo' and 'Wonderful Copenhagen' from *Hans Christian Andersen*, among others. Marjorie Farmer, wife of Shawnee Press co-founder Ernest Farmer, wrote to Loesser about some arrangements of his songs by Fred Waring. Waring suggested changing some of Loesser's lyrics 'for school use', in particular the lyrics to 'More I Cannot Wish You' from *Guys and Dolls*. Shawnee was worried, in particular, with the lines 'with the sheep's eye and the lickerish tooth and the strong arms to carry you away' – where, according to Farmer, 'the song becomes the song of an older person singing to a young girl'. She also questioned 'Anywhere I Wander' from *Hans Christian Andersen*, 'Once in Love with Amy' from *Where's Charley?*, 'A Bushel and a Peck' from *Guys and Dolls* and, in particular, 'Wonderful Copenhagen' from *Hans Christian Andersen*:

Neath her <u>tavern</u> light
On this merry night,
Let us <u>clink</u> and <u>drink one down</u>.

---

68 A recording of 'Rodger Young' by singer John Charles Thomas was released by RCA Victor in 1942; Burl Ives's recording was released by Decca in 1945.
69 Frank and Lynn Loesser released versions of these songs, with narration by Frank, on MGM's record label in 1952.

I have underlined the words that will raise eyebrows and close purses among our customers ... We are having a struggle with our editorial conscience about the publishability of "Fugue for Tinhorns." It is so cute! (But it is about – shudder – gambling.)

5 January 1953: To Marjorie Farmer

Dear Mrs. Farmer:

Thanks for your letter of December 30th. In answer to your question about "More I Cannot Wish You" I believe I would prefer to keep the original lyrics. The song's character is really built around the line you have in question. Also it is from a production and I think should remain memorable in terms of the scene in which it was performed. Before the next few years are over, there will have been a movie version of "Guys and Dolls"[70] and millions of people will have absorbed in their minds the scene in which the old man sings this song to his daughter. I think we all have a better chance to standardize the piece by keeping the words the way they are. I hope I have you convinced.

I would like to take a crack at changing the lyrics of the verses of "Anywhere I Wander," as you suggest. I believe I can take some of the animal intimacy out of them. Although I don't think the general intent of the song can be changed much since the chorus continually and unmistakably emphasizes a romantic theme. How much time do I have to deliver you a set of verses with a little more purity?[71]

In closing, let me thank you and your organization for all your help and courtesy.

Very truly

---

70 Released by MGM in 1955. However, 'More I Cannot Wish' was omitted.
71 'Anywhere I Wander' from *Hans Christian Andersen* (1952).

16 March 1953: To Marjorie Farmer

Dear Mrs. Farmer:

Thanks for your nice note. There have been some moralistic bone-dry beefs about those lines in "Wonderful Copenhagen," and for those non-alcoholics on radio, etc., I have substituted, with success, the following lines:

> With her harbor light
> That she wears at night
> Like a golden, golden crown.

I think they will do the trick.

While you are struggling with the "Fugue for Tinhorns" decision, please also consider that it is all right as the theatrical material, but there is difficulty in hearing all the lyrics no matter how well performed. Toward clarifying this, I am in the process of preparing a model arrangement which might be of some help. Can you wait? I'll be sending it on to you.

Answering your P.S., "Bloop Bleep" is on your list.

It has just occurred to me that I ought to suggest that you print the production sources under the song title on your editions. I hope this is possible. Identification of, let us say, "Anywhere I Wander" as being from "Hans Christian Andersen" might attract the users toward examining other pieces from the same production, such as, "Wonderful Copenhagen," etc. I hope this is feasible to print this way, or maybe you have already thought of all this. Please drop me a line about it.

Meanwhile, thank you for the progress you have indicated in your letter.

Cordially,

23 March 1953: To Marjorie Farmer

Dear Mrs. Farmer:

I forgot one tiny little detail in the corrected "Wonderful Copenhagen" lyrics I sent you, which read:

> With her harbor light
> That she wears at night
> Like a golden, golden crown.

The following line now reads:

To wonderful, wonderful Copenhagen

This should be changed to:

Oh, wonderful, wonderful Copenhagen

The original word "to" applied to the unmentionable custom of drinking, which is the only thing I have ever known to make group singing bearable ... but then I guess I'm un-American.

Best wishes.

• • •

In early 1953, Loesser wrote to one George Mercader of the now-defunct Business Administration Corporation – presumably on tax or business-expenses related matters – and while the exact purpose of this letter is unclear, it neatly sums up Loesser's activities in 1952 and 1953, filling in gaps where the documentary record is otherwise blank (including some of Frank and Lynn Loesser's business trips); gives a detailed representation of his involvement in all aspects of Frank Music; describes his promotion of *Hans Christian Andersen*; accounts for some of his income; and generally paints a picture of the extraordinary, non-stop frenzy of Loesser's professional activities.

3 March 1953: To George Mercader, Business Administration Corporation

Dear George:

I have before me a list of travel routes taken by Mrs. Loesser and/or myself during the past year. Since the list involves what may seem to be an unusual amount of travel, I am writing you the following analysis of the quite important business purposes involved. Before starting, however, let me point out to you that some of these trips were paid for not by myself, but by the Samuel Goldwyn organization and I am sure your records account for this.

As you know, for the last seven months of 1951, as well as the first three months of 1952, I worked on what is possibly the most important money making venture I have engaged in thus far. This was the writing, preparation and shooting of a motion picture called HANS CHRISTIAN ANDERSEN. My compensation for this work accounts to 10% of the net profits of this picture, which I have every reason to believe will be income-bearing for a long time.

When my work on the picture was drawing to a close, early in 1952, I realized that the responsibility for the promotion of it (especially its musical contents) would rest, to a great extent, on my shoulders. The motion picture had been designed especially to attract the European market and this was a territory with which I had no familiarity. Under the terms of my deal with the producer, I was responsible for the exploitation of the picture through its musical elements. So I decided to add this as a project to a number of others I had previously planned for England, France and Italy. I will describe in subsequent paragraphs the whole picture of my European activities including the ANDERSEN project.

On April 6th, I left for New York, where I stayed until April 18th, at which time I sailed for Europe. The intervening period in New York was spent in discussing foreign assignments of my music with my publishers, as well as discussing the various European projects with my managers, the Music Corporation of America, in New York. In addition it was at this time vital for me to approve certain changes in casting, as well as to re-rehearse my current Broadway production of GUYS AND DOLLS.[72]

Mrs. Loesser had left Los Angeles earlier, on April 3rd, for advance discussions in Chicago with Howard Miller, Fran Allison and Marty Hogan.[73] These are the leading musical exploitation media in Chicago and are vitally necessary to any such project. She went on to New York for the organization of the "Music Market," a business project of

---

72 *Guys and Dolls* ran on Broadway until 28 November 1953.

73 Howard Miller (1912–1994), actor and radio disc jockey at WIND, Chicago; according to an obituary in the *Chicago Tribune*, 13 November 1994, 'Time magazine called him "probably the nation's single biggest influence on record sales". The television and radio personality Frances Helen Allison (1907–1989) worked at NBC Chicago on *The Breakfast Club*, a popular radio show. Martin Hogan (dates unknown) was the general manager of radio station WCFL Chicago.

her own. At the same time she joined me in making and recording demonstrations of the ANDERSEN score for various disk jockey, radio and television program people. We sailed for Europe on April 18th.

In Paris we were joined by our Paris representative, Mr. David Stein, who put us in touch with Mr. Andre Sarrut,[74] who had been awaiting our arrival to discuss the translation and partial rewriting of an important cartoon subject he had made.[75] We had seen a print of the picture in the U.S.A. and Sarrut was anxious for me to come to a deal with him immediately, so that the picture could be corrected and under-scored in time for the Cannes Festival in the summer. We spent a great deal of time running and re-running parts of his picture and discussing a deal. However, in the end I could not conclude a deal with Sarrut, as I had to be in the United States in June to start the American exploitation of ANDERSEN. In addition to this activity, I covered as many of the theatrical productions as possible, to try to determine the castibility of a GUYS AND DOLLS company for France. Also at the time, I was considering the adaptation of three plays by Pagnol.[76] In this same theatrical coverage, I was trying to determine an imported casting for this project.

While I was engaged in these activities, Mrs. Loesser concerned herself with the review and acquisition of French melodies which had not yet been given out for translation in the United States. As you know, she has always been my editor, as well as musical demonstrator. She also acted in the capacity of agent for Harold Orenstein[77] in the sale of certain rights to compositions.

While in Paris, of course, we saw and were interviewed by the press, notably the European editions of the Herald Tribune, Variety, etc.

---

74 André Sarrut (1910–1977), producer and director, known for *Pardon My French* (United Artists, 1951).
75 *The Curious Adventures of Mr. Wonderbird* (L'Alliance Générale de Distribution Cinématographique, 1952), based in part on a Hans Christian Andersen story.
76 Marcel Pagnol (1895–1974), French writer and filmmaker.
77 Harold Orenstein (1904/5–1998), entertainment lawyer, from 1945 head of nonradio licensing for Broadcast Music Inc. and from the early 1950s copyright lawyer for Frank Loesser.

One of the projects involved conferences with Serge Glyxson, the reigning musical contractor and recorder in Paris. I anticipated (and still do) making certain recordings in Europe, as the rates are much cheaper there and the artists are becoming more acceptable to the American market.

Also I had arranged to meet John Steinbeck in Paris, and did so. At this meeting we concluded an agreement to do a new musical show together and this work is now in progress.[78] Our only opportunity for meeting during 1952 was at this time and place, as he continued to stay out of the United States for a long period afterwards.

A short trip was made to Rome for the purpose of setting-up personal exploitation of my words. Mrs. Loesser and I gave various demonstrations of the forthcoming score for the leading musical authorities there. This trip of a few days also included conference with Mr. Willie Wyler,[79] who was to shoot a picture and required certain musical material.[80]

In the final week of this trip we went to London, to hear the sound tracks of the Sarrut film, as well as to meet the press, for whom we performed the HANS CHRISTIAN ANDERSEN music together.

Also I had vital first conferences with my European publisher, Mr. Teddie [sic] Holmes of Chappell, Ltd.[81] These conferences were

---

78 Loesser's planned show with Steinbeck, *Cannery Row* (based on Steinbeck's 1945 novel of the same name), was never realized. On 16 October 1952, Steinbeck wrote to his friend and former college roommate Carlton Sheffield, 'I'm going to do a job that sounds very amusing. Frank Loesser and I are going to make a musical comedy of Cannery Row. It will be a madhouse but getting such a thing together should be great fun.' Elaine Anderson Steinbeck, ed., *Steinbeck. A Life in Letters* (New York, 1975), 459. Rodgers and Hammerstein later based the musical *Pipe Dream* (1955) on *Cannery Row*.
79 William Wyler (1902–1981), director and producer best known for *Roman Holiday* (1953) and *Ben-Hur* (1959). Wyler won three Academy Awards for best director, for *Mrs. Miniver* (1943), *The Best Years of Our Lives* (1947) and *Ben-Hur*.
80 Possibly *Roman Holiday*; Loesser was apparently not involved with the film.
81 Chappell & Co., founded in 1811 by Samuel Chappell (c1782–1834), was a leading music publisher; it was acquired in 1987 by the Warner Music Group (now Warner Chappell Music). Teddy Holmes (dates unknown), who had joined Chappell in 1917 as a junior shop assistant, founded Chappell Recorded Music (now part of Universal Music Group) in 1941.

concerned with both HANS CHRISTIAN ANDERSEN and the GUYS AND DOLLS London company.

Just a note of the entire European trip: HANS CHRISTIAN ANDERSEN has opened in London and the score is particularly successful. GUYS AND DOLLS is about to open in London this May and our trip accomplished tremendous advance good-will toward both of these products.[82]

We arrived back in New York on June 18th. Mrs. Loesser remained there a few days to discuss her European observations and results with Harold Orenstein. She returned to Los Angeles on June 24th.

I returned here July 4th to stay for a period of two days. This was for the purpose of seeing the first preview run of HANS CHRISTIAN ANDERSEN and make decisions and give approvals. (This trip was paid for by Samuel Goldwyn Productions, including my return trip to New York.)

In New York I had to make immediate decisions and give approvals on the entire publication and exploitation of the HANS CHRISTIAN ANDERSEN score. I returned to Los Angeles July 11th, having completed these details.

On August 13th, I again left for New York to start on the personal exploitation and promotion of the score. Mrs. Loesser joined me on September 6th, and we appeared on a number of radio and television programs; notably Kate Smith's, Tex and Jinx' and the Stork Club,[83] and an array of important New York disk jockeys.

Mrs. Loesser had also come to New York to perform some children's records for the MGM record company. She did this and was paid for it. At around the same time, Mrs. Loesser and I together made four recordings for the same MGM company. These were

---

82 *Hans Christian Andersen* was released in London on 19 December 1952; *Guys and Dolls* opened at the London Coliseum on 28 May 1953.
83 Kate Smith (1907–1986), singer, had several long-running radio shows on NBC, beginning in 1931. Tex and Jinx – husband and wife Tex McCrary (1910–2003) and Eugenia Lincoln 'Jinx' Falkenburg (1919–2003) – popularised talk radio in the 1940s and early 1950s. *The Stork Club* was a television series broadcast live from the Stork Club, New York (132 West 58th Street, 1929–1965); it featured celebrity guests who performed and were interviewed at tables.

pieces from the ANDERSEN picture. Compensation for each of us is 2½% of the retail selling price of each record sold.

October 3rd Mrs. Loesser finished her work with me in New York and returned to Los Angeles. However, later Samuel Goldwyn's office required her services for two concert appearances for the press; one in Boston and the other in Chicago. This travel was paid for by Samuel Goldwyn Productions. She returned from this trip on November 1st, and I remained in New York.

In New York I finished the radio and television exploitation. Also at this time Life Magazine, Newsweek, the New York Times, etc., all reported lavishly on me and the score. I made various visits to disk jockey and television programs and made a large number of tape recordings which were sent to out-of-town jockeys. I returned to Los Angeles November 26th.

I have examples of the printed publicity arrived at in advance of the crucial opening period of the picture. So far I have received $11,000.00 in song royalties from the publisher on this and there is approximately another $20,000.00 due and payable this August. The resulting increase in ASCAP royalties is not accurately predictable.

I have no way of computing my share of the profits of the picture at this time, but from every indication it is a huge financial success. Along with the major reference to HANS CHRISTIAN ANDERSEN, I always continue exploitation of the GUYS AND DOLLS subject and score. As you know, this project represents a gross weekly income (two theatrical companies operating) of between $3,000.00 and $4,000.00 a week. A third company will be in London in May and should add approximately $1,200.00 per week gross while it runs.

As you know, we have made it a policy not to engage a press agent or exploitation manager. My wife and I do all this work ourselves ... a perennial project which would normally cost a minimum fee of $15,000.00 a year, plus photographic, telegraphic, mailing and other expenses. We have succeeded over many years in effecting enormous publicity campaigns by spending money judiciously in the entertainment and maintenance of contact with all important elements of the press, radio, etc. This last year has been one involving the responsibility for pressure in this direction, since my most effective and profitable output to date is currently being offered the public. You have seen the impact we have caused in the newspaper and magazine world and you have heard the results on radio and seen them on television. If you have any further questions, please don't hesitate to ask me.

Sincerely, Frank

CHAPTER THREE

1953–54
A NEW PROJECT, ADLER AND ROSS,
AND RUNNING THE BUSINESS

Although Loesser had the idea as early as 1951 for the show that would eventually become *The Most Happy Fella*, it was not until 1953 that he and Lynn started thinking seriously about a production – with Lynn as producer, her first musical. In March 1953, she wrote to a film executive friend in Italy, Pilade Levi (1912–1973), who for a time was the general manager of Paramount Pictures' Rome office, asking for help casting the show. Some months later she contacted producer Leland Hayward (1902–1971) – who had recently produced or co-produced Rodgers and Hammerstein's *South Pacific* (1949), Irving Berlin's *Call Me Madam* (1950) and Harold Rome's *Wish You Were Here* (1952) – about the project, possibly to enlist him as co-producer; although Lynn Loesser's letter does not survive, Hayward sent her a telegram on 27 November: 'OF COURSE HAVE ALWAYS TIME FOR YOU. PROJECT SOUNDS VERY EXCITING.'

10 March 1953: Lynn Loesser to Pilade Levi

Dear Pilade:

I am in the process of acquiring the rights to a play[1] which I think will make an exciting musical, and which I intend to produce. Frank

---

1 Sidney Howard's (1891–1939) *They Knew What They Wanted* (1924), which ran on Broadway from 24 November 1924 to 14 November 1925 and won a Pulitzer Prize; it was revived in 1939, 1949 and 1976. A film version, starring Carole Lombard and Charles Laughton, was released in 1940 (RKO Radio Pictures).

has agreed to do the book and score. . . . In fact, he is very enthusiastic about it.

The leading man is a bit of a problem and will be hard to find. He
must be Italian, middle-aged, virile, without the glamour of Pinza,[2]
and a fine singer and actor, plus speak English. At this point it is not
important whether he be a bass, tenor or baritone as Frank will write
according to his voice.[3]

I am coming to Rome either April 28th, or May 7th (depending on
available transportation) to search for such a man. It will take months
to write this show, so if I find a man whose English is not too good, he
would have time to study.

I understand the opera is active all the year around in Italy, and I
feel the type of man I need would probably be in opera. However,
he doesn't have to be.

I need your help in this as I do not speak Italian and do not know
my way around the theatre or opera in Italy. I would be most grateful
if you could spare some time for me and arrange for me to contact
the proper people who can see to it that I get to hear all the male,
middle-aged singing talent available. I will only have about two weeks
in Rome, as I have to be in London by the 26th of May.

Please let me know <u>immediately</u> if you can help me – MCA[4] says
you can – And if you can, will you???!!

I hope you can, and will. And it will be wonderful to see you again.
– I'll even let you help me pack for London.

Best wishes always.

In late March, while Lynn was in Rome, Loesser accompanied
Richard Adler and Jerry Ross to California, where he introduced
them to representatives of the major studios as potential songwriters
for future film musicals. Of particular interest is the suggestion that

---

2vEzio Pinza (1892–1957), Italian operatic bass who had starred in Rodgers and
Hammerstein's *South Pacific* (1949).
3 The lead in *The Most Happy Fella* was eventually taken by American baritone
Robert Weede (1903–1972).
4 Music Corporation of America, a leading talent agency across music, television
and film.

they be considered for MGM's *The Sobbin' Women*, which became Gene de Paul (1919–1988) and Johnny Mercer's *Seven Brides for Seven Brothers* (1954). He also promoted them to MCA and Columbia Pictures. After their return to New York, Loesser kept Adler and Ross apprised of his meetings and progress on their behalf.

27 March 1953: To Fred Kohlmar,[5] Columbia Pictures

Dear Freddie:

Thanks so much for listening to Adler and Ross this morning. You certainly seemed to share my enthusiasm for them, and I am very grateful for your visit.

The three of us will be in New York as of this coming Wednesday morning. From then on I can be reached through my secretary at home here, or through the [Frank] Music Corporation.

Many, many thanks again.

Sincerely,

30 March 1953: To Jack Cummings,[6] MGM

Dear Jack:

Many thanks for your reception of Adler and Ross. I understand they are not quite right for "The Sobbin' Women," but that something on the more "youthful" side may come up. Of course, I couldn't be more delighted if that should happen.

Meanwhile, the boys and I are going to New York tomorrow and we can be reached at the above address.

Thanks again, and love to you and Betty.[7]

---

5 Fred Kohlmar (1905–1969), American film producer. Kohlmar later produced films of several musicals, including *Pal Joey* (1958) and *Bye Bye Birdie* (1963).

6 Jack Cummings (1905–1989), one of the major producers at MGM in the 1950s; his credits include the Frank Sinatra vehicle *It Happened in Brooklyn* (1949), with songs by Sammy Cahn and Jule Styne; Cole Porter's *Kiss Me Kate* (1953) and *Can-Can* (1960); and *Seven Brides for Seven Brothers* (1954).

7 Cummings was married to Betty Kern (1918–1996), daughter of famous composer Jerome Kern.

31 March 1953: To Dore Schary,[8] MGM

Dear Dore:

First all, many thanks for the time and attention you have given Adler and Ross.

Johnny Green[9] tells me that although [Jack] Cummings was very favourably impressed, he did not quite see them for the score of "The Sobbin' Women." Johnny [Mercer] added that Jack [Cummings] thought them quite capable of delivering a score for a "youth" type picture. I don't know exactly what that means, but I suspect it means that Debbie Reynolds[10] is in it. Anyway, Johnny added that you too were in favor of [a] future relationship with Adler and Ross and this, of course, makes them and me very happy.

We'll be leaving for New York tonight, but can be reached through the Music Corporation of America . . . sometimes referred to as Harry Friedman.[11]

Meanwhile, the three of us are very grateful for the nice warm interview.

Best.

31 March 1953: To Sol Siegel,[12]
Twentieth Century Fox

Dear Sol:

I can't tell you how grateful I am for your enthusiasm for Adler and Ross.

---

8 Dore Schary (1905–1980), also a producer and writer for MGM.
9 Johnny Green (1908–1989), composer, songwriter and music director at MGM 1949–1959.
10 Debbie Reynolds (1932–2016), actress. Loesser may be referring to her film *I Love Melvin* (1953) in which she plays an aspiring Hollywood star.
11 Harry Friedman (dates unknown), talent agent at Music Corporation of America, dealing in particular with MGM.
12 Sol Siegel (1903–1982), leading film producer at Twentieth Century Fox; his credits and projects included *Monkey Business* (1952), with Cary Grant, Ginger Rogers and Marilyn Monroe; Irving Berlin's *Call Me Madam* (1953); *Gentlemen Prefer Blondes* (1953); and Cole Porter's *High Society* (1956).

Freddie Kohlmar has already heard them and seems to have joined you and me in our high estimate of this composing team.

Again let me say how kind you were to give them your time and attention.

Best as always.

31 March 1953: To Aaron Rosenberg, Universal International Studios

Dear Aaron:[13]

You were most kind to give Adler and Ross such a generous amount of your time, but I do think you found it rewarding. I am very proud of them and very grateful for your attention.

Sincerely,

30 June 1953: To Adler and Ross

Dear Gents:

I take it you are busy writing. Well, so am I. However, I have been doing my missionary work on the Adler and Ross cause here in the west and wish to report that a big MCA meeting was held about you fellows just this morning. It appears that several things may be in the wind very shortly. Each of the MCA men is following not only the original leads among the people you met, but certain new opportunities that have just started showing their ugly little heads.

Be of good cheer . . . And write hits.

Love,

By November, Adler and Ross were developing their first Broadway book musical, *The Pajama Game*. George Abbott had already signed on as co-author of the book and director and was in touch with Loesser,

---

13 Aaron Rosenberg (1912–1979), an American football player and later a film producer.

5. Richard Adler and Jerry Ross, 1953.

suggesting he ask Michael Kidd to take on the choreography (in the event the choreography was by Bob Fosse). For his part, Loesser offered to audition songs for actor Van Johnson (1916–2008), who presumably was intended for the lead, Sid Sorokin, a role eventually taken by John Raitt. Clearly Loesser was the moving force behind *The Pajama Game* – not just its inception but also its personnel, including the performers, and its exploitation overseas. Adler and Ross were part of the Frank Music stable, and Loesser, in a gesture reminiscent of Tin Pan Alley, provided them with a piano and a place to work, in addition to promoting other possible projects for them – although this gesture was not without difficulties as Adler and Ross were seemingly emboldened by their successes to assert their independence.

24 November 1953: To George Abbott

Dear George:

Thanks for your letter. I'm glad that the boys [Adler and Ross] have at least made some kind of a start.

I telephoned Mike Kidd, as you suggested, and told him what I knew about the project. He seemed "interested" which, as you know, is a very tentative word among dance directors. Although he has had some conversations about a picture this spring he has, at the moment, no actual commitments; and suggested that your office approach the subject with him in the official manner through the Wm. Morris office[14] in New York, and forward what you have, to date, of a script.

Meanwhile, if you will <u>wire</u> me approval I will deliver the novel to him immediately. This might pique his interest. I think I can tell him what my bright hopes are about the score.

Of course, whenever you want me to demonstrate anything for Van Johnson I would be delighted. Please let me know.

Meanwhile, best love from Lynn and me.

18 February 1954: To Max M. Meth[15]

Dear Max:

Thanks for your letter, and forgive the delay in answering. I am purposely keeping away from all discussions, opinions or suggestions concerning musical direction of "Pajama Game." Producers and writers have a way of blaming an outside guy like me when they get unhappy in Philadelphia.[16] I remain the publisher of the music only.

I assume you are friendly with George Abbott and I suggest that you talk to him.

---

14 The William Morris Agency (now WME), a leading talent agency.
15 Max Meth (1900–1984), Austrian-American Broadway producer and conductor. Presumably he had written to Loesser to enquire about the music directorship for *The Pajama Game*.
16 That is, at out-of-town tryouts, if things go badly.

This is absolutely no negative reflection on your very high ability. I just don't want to put my foot in this department. I am sure you understand.

Best regards.

Sincerely,

6 July 1954: To Adler and Ross

Dear Gents:

Any new plans? How does BILLION DOLLAR BABY[17] appeal to you as a picture project? Please give me your views on this? Also any other ideas about theatre, new pop songs, etc., etc.

It is quieter here than New York, but no less busy.

Please write.

Love,

18 October 1954: To Joe E. Zerga[18]

Dear Joe:

In your letter of October 13th, you asked for my comments on the subject of the release of "The Pajama Game" songs in certain foreign countries. I can't agree with you that it is <u>extremely unlikely</u> the show will ever open in Sweden or France. To me it is <u>extremely likely.</u> However, I am not in charge of such things, nor in anyway an authority. The best I can do is protect the producer, writers and the foreign publishers.

I wish you would, however, drop a note to our Harold Orenstein asking him the same questions. He is much closer to the subject. He may be reached at our New York office.

Best wishes.

Sincerely,

Frank Loesser

---

17 *Billion Dollar Baby* opened on Broadway on 21 December 1945 and ran for a moderately successful 220 performances. The score was by Morton Gould, Betty Comden and Adolph Green.
18 Joseph E. Zerga (1924–?), record producer.

20 August 1954: To Harold Orenstein (Memo)

<u>Harold:</u>

Please have a secondhand piano picked out for the office. An upright, very good quality and not over $400.00.

Tell Nat to buy it as a present. Nat knew all about it – except that he wasn't listening the 15th time he was told, but I'm getting used to that.

I feel that Adler and Ross should not be the last word on the choice of a piano. Someone should be selected that will see we get one which will stay in tune a long time. Whoever does the selecting should be well aware of what the insides should look like, how well the felts are and how soon various parts will need replacement. Adler and Ross don't know these answers. It is possible that Adler's father does. Find someone.

FL

19 October 1954: To Harold Orenstein
(Internal Memo)

Answering your question re Adler and Ross piano room. Of course I am more than delighted to give every possible convenience to our writers and consider it proper that they should make headquarters with us. Nevertheless, the question came up at a time when, according to your reports, the writers, through their legal representatives, were asking what I consider preposterous suggestions about our future relationship. If anything resembling these proposals is to be taken seriously then we are dealing with two amnesia victims now behaving like fellow capitalists and I might add competitive ones. In this instance it would not seem suitable that we should humiliate with squatter's rights people with such delusions of grandeur. Frankly, I have terribly hurt feelings from the last proposal you quoted. Possibly they are just testing to see what the traffic will bear. I think such tactics would be foreign to the nature and feeling of our association. I understand and applaud their ambition and sincerely believe that their status with us should improve. In this direction I am more than anxious to give them a lift up, but if I am going to be the ladder itself then they should take a suite at the Waldorf. Let me add that I am too much of a ham to romance them at this point. I did all that when they had nothing. You will recall, Harold, that you and I have been begging them for a long time to get their own lawyers so that there would never be any question of my advantage over them as the result of their getting free advice from you. Now that they have finally taken the suggestion I want you to judge whether we are being bitten by our own teeth. If you feel that current negotiations are within the realm of sense and decency then by all means give them a welcome to all possible facilities.

11 November 1954: To Adler and Ross (Telegram)

UNDERSTAND LYNN LOVED THE NEW STUFF.[19] AFTER TWENTY YEARS STANDING INSPECTION BY OUR VICE PRESIDENT ALL I CAN SAY IS THAT IT MUST BE WONDERFUL. CONGRATULATIONS.
FRANK

16 December 1954: To Adler and Ross

Dear Gents:

I wish you a Merry Christmas and Happy New Year, etc., etc., as you well know.

Virginia O'Brien[20] called today to ask if she could submit FORTY-NINE ACRES as a possible recording for Capitol. I told her I would ask you. Apparently she has a manuscript which you gave her. This is perfectly all right with me, unless you have an idea of using it in some production in the near future. Please discuss this between yourselves and with Harold Orenstein. If the answer is yes, I will tell Virginia out here . . . With the proviso that if she fails to make it for Capitol she will not leave a manuscript or dub in their possession. Please advise.

Again, happy holidays. Think I'll be seeing you soon.

Love and kisses,

---

19 Presumably songs for their forthcoming *Damn Yankees* (1955).
20 Virginia Lee O'Brien (1919–2001), American actress and singer.

In addition to Adler and Ross, Loesser was at the same time promoting two other young writing teams: composer Moose Charlap (1928–1974) and lyricist Carolyn Leigh (1926–1983); and composer Hugh Martin (1914–2011) and lyricist Timothy Jack Gray (1927–2007). Charlap and Leigh were to write songs for a new adaptation of *Peter Pan* and Loesser worked behind the scenes to try to make sure they were hired by providing veteran producer Edwin Lester (1895–1990) with contractual language that would allow him flexibility if he needed to replace some of their work. In the event, Lester did bring in the more established composer Jule Styne and lyricists Adolph Green and Betty Comden to write some extra material. Martin and Gray had already written *Love from Judy* (1952), produced in London by Emile Littler (1903–1985); Martin is best remembered as the composer-lyricist of *Meet Me in St Louis* (MGM, 1944).

10 February 1954: To Edwin Lester

Dear Ed:

Here is a suggestion for an agreement between you and [Carolyn] Leigh and between you and [Moose] Charlap. Of course I observed the realistic not the legalistic in writing these. You will, of course forgive me for not being a master of contractual phraseology. I have trouble enough these days writing just plain lyrics.

Please give me a call and tell me your reactions.

Sincerely

17 February 1954: To Lee Eastman[21]

Dear Lee:

The enclosed is something I slapped together as a suggestion to Edwin Lester, after first having discussed certain points with him on the phone.

The idea, generally, is to protect the producer if in his judgment he finds the writer's product not satisfactory, and at the same time

---

21 Lee Eastman (1910–1991), veteran entertainment lawyer.

give him a deadline before which to decide that he will not require this protection. I am quite sure that the amounts of money involved are just about the limit possible that the producer can pay. Nevertheless, I feel it is just possible that a box office percentage deal for the eight summer weeks could be made if your client were willing to sacrifice a certain portion of the guarantee. I have not discussed this with Lester because my personal hunch is that you and your client will prefer guaranteed cash.

It may be assumed that the eight weeks out west will earn a total gross of possibly $400,000.00. Two percent would come to $8,000.00. I believe (but I am not sure) that the above was a mental reflection of Lester's in calculating his ability to pay the $4,000.000 guarantee to each of the writers.

Anticipating that some attempt might be made to have [Carolyn] Leigh collaborate with someone other than [Moose] Charlap, I put in some of the controls that you will note. Lester is quite agreeable on this point.

I am quite anxious that Leigh should continue to write with Charlap and feel he is capable of doing a very fine job. She seems at home with him as a collaborator and although I am sure she deserves partners with greater name value or experience, I would not like to see her exposed to some of the attendant work-habit, personality struggles, etc ... at a time when she is facing a deadline. I recall my own jump from Burton Lane to Hoagy Carmichael. It took entirely too long to get adjusted to new harmonic patterns, suddenly broken appointments and gentile companionship.

Lester <u>seems</u> to be planning to come to New York shortly. He will probably get in touch with you.

I would like your reflections on the enclosed as soon as possible.

Best regards.

15 March 1954: To Lee Eastman

Dear Lee:

I gather from Lavin that Walt Disney made an agreement with the Barrie[22] estate for all motion picture rights, but that the agreement

---

22 J. M. Barrie (1860–1937), Scottish writer of the original *Peter Pan*.

provides that the estate may make or have others make a live action motion picture after the release of the Disney version.[23]

Lavin gave me only this very brief digest of what he remembered about the contract and I am passing it on to you. I suggest that next time you are out here that you have a look at the details. Somewhere along the line it ought to be possible for the Barrie estate and the new song writers to have a salable picture property. Possibly a package with Mary Martin,[24] made in England and providing for the collection of American dollars in this hemisphere in favor of the Barrie estate, which is probably subsisting on gulls' eggs. You see how my mind works.

Sincerely,

12 April 1954: To Carolyn Leigh

Dear Carolyn:

This is the first opportunity I've had to tell you how pleased I am that you are making such wonderful progress not only in your career as a lyric writer, but also in the preparation of the score of PETER PAN.[25]

To say my feelings reflect those of Edwin Lester[26] would be putting it mildly. I do appreciate that as a writer whose performing rights were previously contracted to Broadcast Music, Inc., you find yourself in the position of "straying from the fold" and trading a possible loss of performing rights against the prestige of writing for Frank Music Corp.

In concluding [sic], I am looking forward to the day your present contractual obligations will be fully satisfied and you may become a member of ASCAP of which, as you know, both my company and I have always been members.

Sincerely,

---

23 The Disney cartoon version of *Peter Pan* was released in 1953.
24 Mary Martin (1913–1990), actress and star of *Peter Pan* on Broadway in 1954 and on NBC telecasts in 1955, 1956 and 1960.
25 *Peter Pan* played for 152 performances at the Winter Garden Theatre, 20 October 1954 to 25 February 1955.
26 Lester's credits include, in addition to *Peter Pan*, *Kismet* (1953) and *Gigi* (1973).

13 December 1954: To Harold Orenstein

Dear Harold:

Enclosed is a copy of Emile Littler's[27] letter (typed on both sides of the paper). Note that it is dated September 1954. Further observe that the play in question opened in London exactly two years previously and this is the first communication of any kind on the subject.

The Jack Gray referred to in paragraphs two and three on page one, was Hugh Martin's writing partner on the score in question. Today Hugh Martin told me that he was about to wire Howard Hoyt[28] instructions to show you the papers relating to his engagement as the writer of this score. Knowing Howard Hoyt, I assume there will be some delay unless you buzz him on it. It is for his client's good. I imagine Hoyt also represents Jack Gray, who is in New York, and care should be taken that Jack Gray does not create an example by compliance with what seems to be some absurd request in the enclosed Littler letter.

I have already recommended Larry Green as a good attorney for Hugh Martin. I don't think it would hurt to call Larry in on an analysis of this matter so that his services (free) will be recognized and appreciated a little later.

Love.

20 December 1954: To Harold Orenstein

Dear Harold:

By now you have absorbed the matter of Emile Littler and Hugh Martin. I believe that in the interest of securing a thoroughly valuable client for Larry Green, as well as a very valuable attorney for Hugh Martin, you might telephone Martin when he arrives in New York after January 9th. His telephone number will be JUdson 6-1884.

---

27 Emile Littler (see p. 116).
28 Howard Hoyt (dates unknown), story editor for MGM and later a theatrical and screen agent.

Martin, together with his present partner Ralph Blane,[29] contemplates writing the songs for a New York theatre musical to be entitled "Three Tigers for Tessie."[30] It seems that Blane made a commitment to Max Dreyfus[31] to give Max publication rights on his next two Broadway shows. I believe this started with "Three Wishes for Jamie."[32] Both words and music for this production were composed by Ralph Blane and, as I understand it, his commitment to Dreyfus did not in any way imply automatic assent by any collaborator. It therefore strikes me that Martin is in a free position to and certainly would have an equal voice with Blane in determining who is to publish. Both boys have expressed a desire to stick with our company.

Any service you may be able to give Martin, whether on the Littler matter or on any other problem might be, I believe, realistically appreciated.

Love,

In addition to younger artists, Loesser's ambitions for Frank Music also included recruiting established writers, such as his long-time friend Johnny Mercer, for the company. And he not only continued to exploit his own works, but also took advantage of the latest technology, the 12-inch long-playing record, which was then in its early days.[33]

---

29 Ralph Blane (1914–1994), composer and lyricist.
30 The musical went unproduced but several songs were used in the stage adaptation of *Meet Me in St Louis* (1989).
31 Max Dreyfus (1874–1964), president of music publishers Chappell and Co.
32 *Three Wishes for Jamie* ran for 152 performances, 21 March 1952 to 7 June 1952.
33 While the development of long-playing records began before the war, the first commercially viable LP recordings, either 10 or 12 inches, were not introduced until 1948. Even as late as 1952, 78rpm recordings still accounted for more than half of the vinyl recordings sold in the United States; by 1958 LPs accounted for 25% of record sales, 45rpm recordings represented more than 70% of sales and 78rpm recordings were largely extinct, representing only about 2% of sales.

1 February 1953: To Johnny Mercer

Dear Johnny:

I enjoyed our conversation. Please don't forget to send me as many demonstration records as you can find. I would like to get started.

Best.

18 August 1953: To Harold Orenstein

Dear Harold:

Enclosed is a letter from F. M. Scott[34] at Capitol. I will let you answer him directly. Frankly, I don't know what our policy is, but I think we ought to give them anything that Chappell gives them on the same kind of item.

In addition I am enclosing a letter from Walt Heebner[35] outlining a project on his transcriptions involving MORE I CANNOT WISH YOU.[36] Please make a price with him which is in keeping with our company dignity with relation to our precious show tunes, but also keeping in mind that Heebner, generally speaking, is a friend.

Love and kisses,

PS. Yes, your letter to Luisa Field re THE UGLY DUCKLING[37] was okay and has been mailed.

---

34 F. M. Scott III (dates unknown), record producer and head of artist repertoire at Capitol Records.
35 Walt Heebner (1917–2002), recording director at RCA Victor, pianist, composer and songwriter.
36 From *Guys and Dolls* (1950).
37 From *Hans Christian Andersen* (1952).

28 December 1953: To Mike Sukin[38]

Dear Mike:

Lieberson[39] and I had a conversation on the phone about the possibility of a Kostelanetz[40] album of some of my stuff. Of course this is very flattering and I am very happy about it. Lieberson asked me to send a list of my compositions which I considered most suitable for this purpose, and I have enclosed such a list for you to go over with him. There are twelve titles, but I imagine he will only need eight of them.

You will note that these songs are all published by us. Of course I have many more, but I thought these seemed to be the proper titles for this kind of interpretation. If Goddard has any feeling to the contrary, please ask him to phone or write me.

The enclosed list is not supposed to represent my "hit list," but I hate to stick Kostelanetz with such items as PRAISE THE LORD AND PASS THE AMMUNITION and even SLOW BOAT TO CHINA. Please keep track of this possible project with Lieberson. And if there is the remotest chance that I can discuss any of these things with Kostelanetz before hand, I will be most grateful. Many of the numbers listed have been mangled by previous interpretations and although Kostelanetz is a very rare and tasty guy, the pitfalls are still there. Go.

Love and kisses.

List:

LUCK BE A LADY
MORE I CANNOT WISH YOU
I'VE NEVER BEEN IN LOVE BEFORE
MY TIME OF DAY

---

38 Mike Sukin (dates unknown), was one of the managers at Frank Music.
39 Goddard Lieberson (1911–1977), president of Columbia Records (1956–1971) and veteran producer of cast albums including *My Fair Lady*.
40 Andre Kostelanetz (1901–1980), Russian-born American conductor and arranger. Kostelanetz recorded 'The Moon of Manakoora' in 1954 but not an album devoted entirely to Loesser; in the 1960s he recorded two songs from *How to Succeed in Business Without Really Trying*: 'I Believe in You' and 'Paris Original'.

PERNAMBUCO
MY DARLING MY DARLING

ANYWHERE I WANDER
WONDERFUL COPENHAGEN
THE INCH WORM

ROSEANNA

SPRING WILL BE A LITTLE LATE THIS YEAR

WHAT ARE YOU DOING NEW YEAR'S EVE41

8 January 1954: To Mike Sukin

Dear Mike:

Let me tell you a story. Judy Hicks[42] gets called on the phone by a recording artist, a friend of hers. He is looking for material to make on a small label. She looks through the bulletin and also the newly arrived deschons.[43] She finds a copy of "OLD SHOES,"[44] with <u>no note of any kind referring to the fact that this is positively an exclusive with Columbia – having been made by Frankie Laine.</u>[45]

This happened today. What happens tomorrow depends on how we manage our God damn business. I rest my case.

Guys and Dolls continued to loom large in Loesser's catalogue. Abe Burrows updated him on Washington, DC and London productions, reporting that the show had broken attendance records at the

---

41 'Luck Be a Lady', 'More I Cannot Wish You', 'I've Never Been in Love Before' and 'My Time of Day' from *Guys and Dolls* (1950); 'Pernambuco' and 'My Darling, My Darling' from *Where's Charley?* (1948); 'Anywhere I Wander', 'Wonderful Copenhagen' and 'The Inch Worm' from *Hans Christian Andersen* (1953); 'Roseanna' from the RKO/Samuel Goldwyn Film *Roseanna McCoy* (1948); and 'Spring Will Be a Little Late this Year' from the Universal Pictures Film *Christmas Holiday* (1944).
42 Judy Hicks (dates unknown), an executive at Frank Music.
43 A kind of onion-skin paper that allowed for the easy copying of music manuscripts.
44 Music and lyrics by Adler and Ross.
45 The singer and songwriter Frankie Laine (1913–2007) recorded 'Old Shoes' as the B-side of a 45rpm single in 1954.

Coliseum. He congratulated Loesser's mother, Julia, on her theatrical Astuteness: she was one of the backers of Cole Porter's *Can-Can*, then playing on Broadway and for which Burrows had written the book. And he pitched the idea of a musical based on Brock Williams's novel *The Earl of Chicago* (1937), which had been turned into a film by MGM in 1940; the story revolves around a Chicago gangster who inherits an English title.

Fans wrote to Loesser, asking for explanations of some of the text, including the line 'the sheep's eye and the lickerish tooth' referred to in 'More I Cannot Wish You', and colleagues kept in touch as well, including Moss Hart, screenwriter of *Hans Christian Andersen*, and Stubby Kaye (1918–1997), who created the role of Nicely-Nicely Johnson in *Guys and Dolls* and later reprised the role in the 1955 film version.

1 September 1953: Abe Burrows to Loesser

Dear Frank:

Oy it is hot in New York! Ninety-seven today. We're hiding in the house with the air conditioning.

Everything seems to be going well here otherwise. GUYS AND DOLLS is back from Washington and did very well before the heat and I'm sure it will do very well after. I've been watching the company and giving notes to Arthur Lewis about them. I think basically they are giving a very good show. Iva Withers[46] is amazingly good. She can fix a few things in her performance which we are working on. Her song delivery is great. I was there when the show reopened in New York and she did the "Cold" song[47] as well as it's ever been done. She lacks some of Vivian [Blaine]'s warmth and then you must remember she is married to a dancer and that is guaranteed to cool off any girl.

---

46 Iva Withers (1917–2014), Canadian-born actress and singer. She took the role of Miss Adelaide in the Washington production of *Guys and Dolls*; she had earlier been the understudy for the role of Laurey in Rodgers and Hammerstein's *Oklahoma!* (1943) and Julie in *Carousel* (1945).
47 'Adelaide's Lament'.

Your mother[48] still has a big hit in CAN-CAN – standees every night.

Of course, you've heard the wonderful reports of the show in London. We've broken the Coliseum record the last few weeks which, of course, means the London record. Everybody I speak to tells me it's going great there.

I got a note from Bernard Braden.[49] You must remember he was my friend who was in the television business. Nice guy. He writes and tells me that he has acquired the rights to "The Earl of Chicago,"[50] and he'd like to turn it into a musical over there and then maybe bring it over here. I don't know if you remember "The Earl of Chicago." It was made into a movie with Robert Montgomery.[51] It was a fascinating picture of a Chicago gangster who inherits a title and it's very believable as it's told. The gangster is a real no-good killing rat with a lot of charm. He has some funny experiences in England and is seated in the House of Lords but the big, fascinating part of the story to me is this: You may remember he gets stuck on a girl, the only real lady he ever meet [sic], and kills a guy who is trying to ruin her life. It's the only decent killing this guy ever commits. He is tried in the House of Lords by a jury of his peers and is convicted. He is executed in the Tower of London in one of the most thrilling moments I have ever known. The old family retainer puts the traditional robes on him and speaks of the other Lords of his line who faced this sort of thing like gentlemen, and this gangster rises to it and goes to his execution like a hero and you have a great scene which amounts, in a sense, to a happy ending.

I'm telling you this with the thought that you might be interested in this thing some time in the future when we are both through with our immediate projects. I thought maybe the idea of doing a musical in England might appeal to you. It kind of does to [me].

---

48 Burrows refers to the fact that Loesser's mother had invested in Cole Porter's *Can-Can* (1953).
49 Possibly Bernard Braden (1916–1993), Canadian-born British comedian, actor and presenter.
50 Brock Williams's novel *The Earl of Chicago* (1937) was turned into a film by MGM in 1940.
51 Robert Montgomery (1904–1981), American actor, producer and director.

Please think about this and please don't say anything about it to anyone. Just write me a note and let me know how it hits you.

I'm now engaged in a new project that I don't want to discuss because it's too unformed but I'm spending my working time on it.

Otherwise, things are very quiet. Both of my children came back from camp with their left arms in casts. Jimmy broke a cartilage in his elbow playing basketball and two days later Laurie tripped, fell and broke her left arm. Neither of the cases are serious. As a matter of fact, after we had gotten over the shock of Jimmy's injury and poor Laurie went and did the same thing, it kind of got amusing. Anyway, they are here, walking around with autographed casts and seem to be happy about the whole thing.

When are you coming to New York? Let me hear from you.

Carin sends her love to you, Lynn and the children, as do I.

Love,

7 February 1954: Stubby Kaye to Loesser

Dear Frank—

I am very well and hope that you and the Mrs. and Sue and John[52] are the same.

Guess you are still one of the busiest men in the world, so I'm not going to make this a lengthy letter.

Here is the news of doings at the Coliseum Theatre. Business has not been good and we are hoping it will pick up during March so that we can coast into the better show months of May, June, etc. Sam [Levene] is leaving Feb. 20. After all, his wife is pregnant and he wants to get her back to the States. His replacement is Sidney James,[53] a very good English movie actor, who played one of the two gangsters in the local production of "Kiss Me, Kate," so I guess the guy knows his way around. Helluva nice fellow and am sure he will be OK as Nathan, although I can see nobody but Sam in the part. He IS Nathan Detroit.

---

52 That is, Loesser's children.
53 Sid(ney) James (1913–1976), South African actor known for the *Carry On* film series.

126

Guess you've heard that John Silver[54] is now married and living in California. He will most likely look you up out there. Sure do miss the little mug.

Vivian [Blaine], Tom Pedi[55] and Lew Herbert[56] close here May 30, but my contract goes to July 28. How is your new project coming along? Is it ready yet?

Freezing cold here but thank God it is nice and dry. None of the usual English dampness, so it is very similar to New York weather, and I love it.

Cy [Feuer] is here with Arthur Lewis,[57] and both of them are in the hotel rooms with heavy colds. They should be leaving here this week for home.

Latest info around and about is that Bill Goetz[58] is going to do Guys & Dolls on the screen. I presume you know all about this and I'd like to know if you have any idea when he intends to start on it. I'd sure love to be in it, Frank, and anything you can do for me along those lines will be very deeply and sincerely appreciated, believe me.

Must go now, so take care and give my best to Lynne [sic] and the youngsters. I am,

Your oldest established permanent floating fat pal,[59]

Stubby

---

54 Johnny Silver (1918–1983), American actor who played Benny Southstreet in the original *Guys and Dolls*.

55 Tom Pedi (1913–1996), American actor who played Harry the Horse in the original *Guys and Dolls*.

56 Lew Herbert (dates unknown) played Big Jule in the original London production of *Guys and Dolls*.

57 Arthur Lewis (1916–2006), American producer, associate producer of *Guys and Dolls* on Broadway and in the West End of London. He worked with Feuer and Martin on several other productions.

58 William Goetz (1903–1969), film producer. Ultimately, Samuel Goldwyn produced the film.

59 A reference to 'The Oldest Established (Permanent Floating Crap Game in New York)' from *Guys and Dolls* (1950).

18 November 1953: To Mrs. John Courtney Long

My dear Mrs. Long:

Your letter has been forwarded to me. The phrase is "the sheep's eye – And the lickerish tooth." It should not be familiar as it is archaic and of British origin. "Casting sheep's eyes" of course you know. In the second part of the phrase, "lickerish" is an old English spelling of "lecherous" and this word combined with "tooth," in those times, meant having a sweet tooth in the covetous animal sense . . . That is to say, covetous for some tasty dish of the opposite sex. I believe there is a reference to this in the Oxford English Dictionary under "lecherous."

Thanks for asking, and for your kind words about the show.

Sincerely,

24 November 1953: To Moss Hart

Dear Moss:

I have just finished reading with great delight Brooks Atkinson's[60] review of the new production of "The Climate of Eden."[61] Besides telling you how happy I am that your play is being appreciated, I wanted to say hello to you and Kitty.[62] And, of course, love.

9 December 1953: Moss Hart to Loesser

Dear Frank:

What a thoughtful and considerate letter, and I was very pleased to have it. What a strange cup of tea you are, dear boy. You never call when you are in New York and it is almost impossible to get hold of you even when we are both in California and then this very sweet

---

60 Brooks Atkinson (1894–1984), theatre critic of the *New York Times*.
61 *The Climate of Eden* originally opened on Broadway on 6 November 1952 and played only twenty performances. An off-Broadway production opened to more success in October 1953 and ran for over six months.
62 Hart's wife Kitty Carlisle Hart (1910–2007), actress and singer.

and touching letter out of the blue. But then I suppose we are all a strange cup of tea more or less.

If by any chance you are passing through town, do give us a ring for a brief drink. I have much to talk to you about. Kitty is recovering and is much better day by day and joins me in sending you our fondest, always.

Sincerely,

[signed:] Moss

16 December 1953: To Moss Hart

Dear Moss:

The strangest cup of tea can still have sugar at the bottom of it. I recall now that during my long span of work with you on HCA[63] I didn't call my dear friend Abe Burrows; or for that matter, my mother.

I have been keeping track of Kitty's progress through friends here and of course I'm delighted that everything is going so well.

Lynn is in New York for a very brief business trip and you won't be hearing from her. But that doesn't mean that she does not join me in sending you and your family holiday greetings and much love.

Sincerely,

23 December 1953: Moss Hart to Loesser

Dear Frank:

Well, sir, all I can say is: "Scratch a composer and you find Voltaire." I loved your letter and this may be the beginning of a whole new Holmes-Laski correspondence.[64] If it is, I want you to know that I am choosing the role of Justice Holmes, since our ages are roughly comparable.

---

63 *Hans Christian Andersen.*
64 Hart refers to the correspondence of Associate Chief Justice of the Supreme Court Oliver Wendell Holmes Jr (1841–1935) and English economist and political theorist Harold J. Laski (1893–1950). The letters had been published in two volumes by Harvard University Press in 1953.

Your mother is a very astute woman. I did the first scene of a project play at the Omnibus Hour[65] last Sunday and went on to talk about it afterwards. Both the play and myself were superb. However, I doubt that I shall ever finish it.

I ask the same question of you – what are you up to?

Kitty joins me in sending you all fondest wishes for the New Year and a special Christmas kiss.

Always,

[signed:] Moss

Among other projects, including the development of *The Most Happy Fella*, Loesser worked with his friend, playwright Samuel Taylor (1912–2000) – best remembered for *Sabrina Fair* and *Vertigo* – on a possible musical adaptation of his hit play *The Happy Time*, with a score by a young songwriting team, Bob Allen and Al Stillman. Taylor backed out, but it would eventually become a musical with a score by Kander and Ebb in 1968. And Loesser continued to field requests for specially composed songs – including a Christmas song for department store Neiman-Marcus – as well as requests to publish songs by composers not, to this time at least, affiliated with Frank Music, or, conversely, to recruit new talent based on his own taste. One project that he considered was to write a television show sponsored by Bufferin.

5 October 1954: To Samuel Taylor

Dear Sam:

Along with this letter, my office will be delivering to you three acetate records. Before you play them, please absorb the following.

You will remember that when we laid out a sort of formula for a musical version of THE HAPPY TIME we discussed certain opening scenes. To refresh your memory they went something like this: We open on the stage of the vaudeville house. A "girlie" number is in

---

65 Series 2, Episode 11 of *Omnibus*, which was in five segments. Hart's was titled 'The Nature of the Beast'.

progress. It should be a non-vocal and non-acrobatic, but simply a fast dancing line in the small-time vaudeville tradition. We see what seems to be the <u>end</u> of a number only. Upon the exit of this act, the house manager comes out and delightedly announces a new acrobatic act which has recently played Keith's Omaha, "The Flying Goldfobs." The music now starts again in the pit and out come the Goldfobs, in typical acrobat outfits. Featured among them is Mignonette, dressed as a little boy in a sort of Fauntleroy outfit. In the course of the acrobatic action the little boy gets tossed around by the others. Then he comes forward and sings a song, CHIP OFF THE OLD FLIP and returns to the act and takes a terrible comedy pushing around from the group.

This develops into a mock argument and fight, at the climax of which the head of the troupe seems to be wringing Mignonette's neck, etc. A fiddle player in our pit starts yelling at him to stop. The people in the act pay no attention. Now the fiddle player, incensed and a little tipsy, comes up the ramp brandishing his fiddle. (Of course this is the combined character of Papa and Uncle.) There follows an argument on stage and, of course, Papa breaks the fiddle over the acrobat's head. Mignonette takes Papa's side of the battle and for her trouble gets fired by the acrobats. Papa likewise gets fired by the manager. The whole thing is knockabout style, with the house manager pleading with them to stop the disturbance, etc., and finally succeeding in having a fast curtain lowered on the proceedings.

Presently we are in "one" against a drop which represents the outskirts of a town. We learn that Papa is taking Mignonette home with him. Since he has caused her to lose her job he feels that he should give her some kind of employment and he is going to present her to his wife in the hope that she will be accepted as a maid. And since he is now an out-of-work musician, he can expect to be home a lot and therefore there is every reason that Mama will need domestic help. They discuss, of course, the fact that the acrobat troupe is not her own family. Soon she is singing the song BEE-OO-TEE-FUL.

Later on in the play, I am sure there is room for a very fine song called ALWAYS LEAVE THEM ASKING FOR MORE. This can be sung by Grandpapa to Bibi as a song of somewhat outrageously sophisticated advice to a young boy. Or it can be sung by Desmonde in establishing his character with the audience, and then repeated by the adoring Bibi, who has overheard it. For the men-folks in this play there seems to be many a chance to do this song.

The records were made by Robert Clary[66] and Gizelle McKenzie.[67] They are accompanied, in each case, by the composer of the music. Along with the records, the office has enclosed complete lyrics to follow in the event that you don't catch everything on the recording.

I purposely asked the writers not to get too exquisite in their analysis of the possible song content. I wanted you to hear their fundamentally very commercial side, as well as their ability to understand a theatrical assignment.

I am getting this off to you in a hurry and so I am sure you will find most of my plot description very inept, but I did want to give you some kind of a guide in case you forgot what we talked about.

Please give me your impressions as soon as you can. I'll be waiting eagerly by the phone.

Love to you and Susanne.

21 February 1955: To Bob Allen and Al Stillman[68]

Dear Bob and Al:

The Sam Taylor decision is finally in, and the answer alas is no.

Taylor and I are the closest of friends and for the past week that he has been here I have spent hour after hour trying to convince him that new writers can do the trick.

It turns out that Sam is afraid of his own lack of authority in the musical theatre. What he feels he has to have is a composer, or a team, with more musical comedy experience than he has. (This would be his first musical.) It was to no avail that I volunteered to sit in on

---

66 Robert Clary (1926–2022), a French film and television actor.
67 Gisele MacKenzie (1927–2003), Canadian-American singer and actress who regularly appeared on *Your Hit Parade*.
68 Presumably actor Robert Allen (1906–1998) and composer and lyricist Albert Stillman (1906–1979).

every bit of it and even take the reins as producer. Sam is just scared. And besides he doesn't feel that this should be done right away as there are certain playing values left in the original.

I told you this might happen and you gambled some time preparing songs. But all in all I don't feel it was too much of a waste or too bad an experience. Anyway thanks for trying and let's maybe try somewhere else when the time comes.

I will let you know through Mike [Sukin] about my next trip to New York and we will have a look at each other.

Thanks again.

Love,

8 March 1954: To Stanley Marcus[69]

Dear Stanley:

Thank you for your letter suggesting that I write you a Christmas song this year. I am afraid it will have to wait on my getting a really good idea for such a piece. This is going to be a tremendously busy year for me and there is no telling whether or not I will get the idea or have the time to execute it. But, in the words of Oscar Hammerstein, 2nd (Carousel, Act I, Scene III)[70] I'll try, by God! I'll try.

Thanks for asking me again.

Sincerely,

8 July 1954: To Stanley Marcus

Dear Stanley:

It looks as if I am not your boy for this year's Christmas song. That makes it two years in a row and I am afraid I have lost the spirit. I mean the Christmas spirit and not the idea of joining forces with you and your organization. I just can't seem to get a decent idea and I want

---

69 Stanley Marcus (1905–2002), president of Neiman-Marcus in Dallas. Loesser later included a reference to Neiman-Marcus in 'Big D' from *The Most Happy Fella* (1956).
70 Billy Bigelow's 'Soliloquy'.

you to know this now so that you have time to think of someone else if you haven't already.

I am coming to the end of a three year concentration on a musical version of "They Knew What They Wanted"[71] for Broadway and I guess this preoccupation is what has been making other writing efforts hard to accomplish. Please forgive me anyway for not coming through on your Christmas song. Maybe one of these years.

Thanks and best wishes.

Among other concerns for Frank Music, rights loomed large as an issue. Loesser was apparently often offered songs, the rights to which – or their previous use – were not clear.

15 April 1954: To Fred Spielman[72]

Dear Fred:

I have your second (impatient) note before me and have excused myself from everything important I am doing just to answer it. With regard to the two melodies which I received: The faster one is of no interest to me, as I once told you. The slower one is a strong possibility, providing you are in fact its owner. I know you wrote it, but I also have reason to believe that you have already sold all rights to a motion picture company. Neither my company nor I can undertake to pull this chestnut out of the fire.

I understand the piece was never used in any form by the producer. Therefore it seems to me that you could easily get all rights back. In that event, I would like to consider acquiring the tune and do something about it. But I do not propose to acquire part of the rights, exploit the piece on television, radio and records, thus making a hit out of it, and by this manner give the original producer-owner the privilege of capitalising on my effort without paying anything. I love music and also love money.

---

71 *The Most Happy Fella.*
72 Fred Spielman (1906–1997), composer.

In the matter of this last mentioned tune, I note that both Leo Robin[73] and Eden Ahbez[74] have attempted to supply lyrics. You informed me that Ahbez had relinquished his interests in the song. But what about Robin? These are all your problems and not mine.

Of course I am happy that you thought of me. But I can't undertake all the intricate untanglings. If you care to do them yourself, I would like to hear from you when the job is accomplished. I am pretty sure at that point I could get Wright and Forrest, or lyric writers of equal ability, to do a proper job.

For the time being, I am enclosing both manuscripts you sent me. Best wishes,

21 April 1954: To Harold Orenstein

Dear Harold:

I have already forwarded a record (78 rpm) entitled MISS X SINGS IN ARABIC AND HEBREW. It is labelled this way so as not to reveal Hannah Messinger's[75] name for the moment. These are the songs which she claims are old folk and traditional pieces.

First of all, will you check with your New York authority and satisfy yourself that these are <u>un</u>protected. Coincidentally, please determine your opinion of the merits of such recordings as entertainment.

What I have in mind is the following: Assuming these pieces to be available to us for publication (arranged) then Howard Hoyt should call Miss Messinger (her N.Y. address is 19 E. 65th St., Apt. 2E, c/o Ann Borthe) and have a look at her as a possible client. If her possibilities satisfy Hoyt, he should then take her and the records to various recording people, <u>at</u> <u>my</u> <u>direction</u>, for the purpose of creating a Hannah Messinger album with <u>our</u> material.

You will note that the production cost involves one lousy instrument. Possibly a flute would be added, but that is all. It has already

---

73 Leo Robin (1900–1984), lyricist. ('Diamonds are a Girl's Best Friend').

74 Eden Ahbez (1908–1995), songwriter ('Nature Boy').

75 Hana Messinger (dates unknown), Calypso singer. For a contemporaneous account see Gabriel Prevor, 'Accent on Calypso', *New York Sunday Mirror*, 5 May 1957, 3.

been indicated to me by recording executives that this kind of thing would be welcome. However, it is also possible that this kind of thing has already been done.

First and foremost I want to own this and a tremendous array of other material of this type which Miss Messinger knows. Unless we own and control these compositions I have no special interest in la Messinger. If Howard Hoyt, however, thinks she is going to [be] a [Marlene] Dietrich that's his business.

Love and kisses.

30 April 1954: To Harold Orenstein

Dear Harold:

Hana Messinger's phone number is Lehigh 52693 and her address is apartment 2B, 19 East 65th Street in New York.

I have a note from her in which she says she is waiting for Hoyt to call. When you see Hoyt on Monday please tell him to contact her immediately and arrange to examine her possibilities. If he has not already heard her records, please be sure he hears them.

Also remind him to contact Marion Harris, Jr. at No 1 Fifth Avenue. Otherwise, her address if [sic] 400 East 57th Street.

Your fellow police officer,

P.S. Two things: First, please thank Henry M. Katzman of BMI[76] for forwarding the very interesting book of Recorded Bridges, Moods and Interludes. I got a nice note from him as well. Second, I have forgotten to thank you for the legal dictionary. It has arrived and I know a tort from a tart already.

7 July 1954: To Herb Rosenthal

Dear Herb:

For what I think are some pretty cute reasons, I would like you to answer the following question. Is there a possibility that the company

---

76 Henry Manners Katzman (1912–2001), composer and co-founder of the performing rights organisation Broadcast Music Incorporated (BMI).

manufacturing Bufferin[77] would take major time on television? If so, but only if the possibility is very strong for a successful presentation of a package to them … I would like to write you an outline of an idea. This would be a dramatic not musical show and to my way of thinking should be quite inexpensive to produce. Please drop me a line on this immediately.

Thanks and best wishes

In 1950, Goddard Lieberson, president of Columbia Records, produced a long-play, studio-cast album of Rodgers and Hart's 1940 musical *Pal Joey* that led to a Broadway revival in 1952. The success of the *Pal Joey* album led Lieberson to consider revisiting other musicals that had not been given full original cast albums, and he wanted to record Loesser's *Where's Charley?*, which (as noted earlier) had played Broadway at a time of an American Federation of Musicians recording ban and was therefore not recorded. (Ultimately, Lieberson's potential *Where's Charley?* project came to nothing.)

13 July 1954: To Goddard Lieberson

Dear Goddard

Herewith is WE ARE A STORM. The demonstration record gives only a mild notion of what can be done orchestrally and vocally in order to create the necessary unrestricted sex emphasis with which to make a hit record. Your idea about Tony Bennett sounds good, assuming that [Percy] Faith[78] or somebody equally brilliant cooks up the proper storm in the background. I trust the judgment of your eastern musical directors more than those likely to be assigned to Nelson Eddy.

Don Walker is likely to call for the return of the material on WHERE'S CHARLEY since we need it for stock booking use. But be assured that it will be returned to you in time for a CHARLEY album.

---

77 A brand of pain relief medication.
78 Tony Bennett (1926–2023), jazz and pop singer; Percy Faith (1908–1976), Canadian-American bandleader and composer.

It was fun talking to you this morning. It would be more fun if the Frank Music Corp. was getting the following results:

<u>DORIS DAY</u> – "I'M NOT AT ALL IN LOVE." From the immensely profitable production PAJAMA GAME, which since having been awarded to Columbia has earned nothing but mortal enemies for the Frank Music Corp. among the other record companies.[79]

<u>JO STAFFORD</u>[80] – "TRUE LOVE GOES ON AND ON" and "LOSING YOU." Both sure popular smashes merely waiting for Jo's pristine early American treatment.

Love.

Although he was not often inclined to recommend artists for jobs, Loesser wrote a recommendation of the actor and songwriter Ross Bagdasarian (1919–1972) to John Patrick (1905–1995), author of the hit play *The Teahouse of the August Moon* (1953). Bagdasarian was a cousin of Loesser's friend William Saroyan.

21 July 1954: To John Patrick

Dear John:

It was nice talking to you. The fellow I was raving about is Ross Bagdasarian, actor, songwriter and mimic. As I told you, he has spent his youth picking grapes and observing and mimicing [sic] the speech and antics of every possible oriental type.

As an actor he is frequently busy in motion pictures, his latest being THE [sic] REAR WINDOW with Alfred Hitchcock. Theatrewise he has done a few things, none of them too important, including the pinball machine addict in the New York company of TIME OF YOUR LIFE.[81] He is now around 35 years of age.

---

79 A soundtrack of the film version of *Pajama Game*, featuring Doris Day (1922–2019), was released in 1957.
80 Jo Stafford (1917–2008), American singer.
81 Bagdasarian had played the role of a songwriter in Alfred Hitchcock's *Rear Window* (1954). William Saroyan's *The Time of Your Life* was written in 1939; Bagdasarian appeared in a short-lived 1955 run at the City Center, New York.

I guess I sound like an agent, but maybe all true enthusiasts are entitled to make noises like Louis Shurr.[82] Here's my final Louis Shurr noise: Bagdasarian may be reached through me.

Thanks to you and Bobbie Lewis[83] for any attention you can give this inspired notion for your road company.

My very best wishes.

Sincerely,

The increasing popularity of television in North America – the number of households with a set had risen from about 9 million in 1950 to 26 million in 1954[84] – meant an opportunity to exploit existing musicals and to write new musicals for the medium. On 28 March 1954, all four main networks simultaneously broadcast a two-hour salute to Rodgers and Hammerstein for the twenty-fifth anniversary of General Foods, showing the potential for more such events. Loesser came up with an idea for how his company could benefit from being involved in developing new television musicals.

22 July 1954: To Harold Orenstein

Dear Harold:

The following is a report and some reflections on a conversation I had with Hubbell Robinson,[85] national program director for CBS television. The conversation took place yesterday at my house and was started by me.

I told him that I believed that standard existing material for what are now called "spectacular television musical shows" would be exhausted in no time. No recent musical comedy Broadway successes would be available to television; nor would the really great standards,

---

82 Louis Schurr (?–1967), theatrical agent.
83 Robert Lewis (1909–1997), director of *Teahouse* and founder of the Actors Studio.
84 TV History, 'Number of TV Households in America: 1950–1978' (accessed 15 November 2014), http://www.tvhistory.tv/Annual_TV_Households_50-78.JPG.
85 Hubbell Robinson (1905–1974).

such as SHOW BOAT, OKLAHOMA and THE STUDENT PRINCE;[86] that the only readily available stuff would be the flops, the near flops and those shows which have really worn themselves out in the live stock and amateur field. Hubbell agreed readily and further subscribed to the idea that since something of a demand has been created for these one hour, or one-and-a-half hour shows that there would have to be a supply of original works. He added that he intended commissioning the writing of certain original musical <u>books</u> and had already indeed ordered the first.

I then proposed that CBS television, as the producers, should call on the Frank Music Corp. to supply the necessary song content. I pointed out to him that we have available a vast supply of already written material and also the services of many expert songwriters. I proposed that for an individual one hour original musical comedy contemplated, he should decide on a total budget to be paid for the delivery of the necessary words and music. The rights delivered would be <u>first television grand dramatic rights only</u>. (He seemed to want no more.) Having established the budget, he would then allocate part of it to be paid for disbursement by the Frank Corp. to writers as advance down payments against a full price to be paid after the use is made.

It would be left to the Frank Corp's discretion as to what works to submit. However, the producers could refuse numbers and demand substitutions, thus sacrificing whatever down payments had been involved and thus <u>possibly</u> add to the fixed budget. I say <u>possibly</u> because I believe it would be part of the Frank Corp's function to deliver songs to CBS <u>under</u> the budget whenever possible.

I did not indicate that we would deliver Hoagy Carmichael, or Cole Porter, or Johnny Mercer. Robinson knows that generally this top-rank type neither needs the money, nor wants to expose its wares in a one night stand. Robinson agreed that when his current writing commission has been delivered by the playwright, he would consult me and very possibly apply something like the above formula.

---

86 Kern and Hammerstein's *Show Boat* (1927); Rodgers and Hammerstein's *Oklahoma!* (1943); Romberg and Donnelly's *The Student Prince* (1925).

Now! The first purpose of an idea like this is to help market for money the works of writers without going to the same old heavily loaded Carlton-Geller-Miller axis. The secondary purpose, of course, would be for our organization to make money. So the following is a notion ....

Simultaneously with the signing of the SPA agreement with the Frank Music Corp., the writer signs a document with Frank Distributing Corp., giving the Distributing Corp. an exclusive agency to handle grand dramatic use of the title and all other rights specifically excluded in the SPA agreement. This would be a pure agency deal and the writer would pay Frank Distributing, let's say, 20%. Frank Distributing would be the organization dispursing [sic] advances from funds supplied by the producer. These advances, per song, would never be less than $250.00, <u>and would be accepted by the writers in exchange for a waiver of the $250.00 minimal royalty advance under the SPA contract</u>.

The above paragraph refers to acquisition of already written material. In instances where we <u>commission</u> a work to be written and delivered the minimal $250.00 is paid in advance, together with an agreement to sign the SPA form, waiving advances, after the producer has indicated acceptance of the material.

I wish, while sitting up in Cabrini Boulevard doing nothing (that will be the day), you would examine what is right and what is wrong about all the above. I mean in terms of <u>form</u>. As far as benefits are concerned it would be obvious that we will be acquiring copyrights and getting them performed at least once at no royalty expense and at the same time collecting commissions for the selling of dramatic licenses through the Distributing Corp. I would say that in the beginning Robinson <u>might</u> agree to a total song budget of $10,000.00 for 6 numbers . . . something like that. This would entitle the Distribution Corp. to $2,000.00 in commissions.

After the first performance on TV I believe it would be our function to create permanent collaboration agreements among all book and songwriters involved and to secure the proper agency for the product as a whole, so that the Distributing company can, in truth, represent the entire thing as well as its individual numbers. These properties, if titled wisely and expanded, might make valuable fodder for Music Theatre Inc. for later live stage uses.

I am not even murmuring about the possibility of picking up hit songs. But the possibility of picking up hit writers seems quite strong.

Please think all this over and give me your reactions very soon . . . preferably in a letter. Hubbell Robinson may be calling me within a couple of weeks.

> Schem-ingly
> The Loop hole

3 August 1954: To Nat Perrin[87]

Here is the Bud Freeman TV musical script called PATIENCE AND THE PANTHER GIRL. I don't know whether it is good or bad, adaptable, or even slightly usable.

What I think is very interesting is that there are people willing to write and submit this kind of special television material.

Please look it over and let me know. Thanks very much.

Regards.

In the late 1940s and early 1950s, the American entertainment industry operated under the threat of McCarthyism and blacklisting; the majority of Broadway artists were left-leaning, and many belonged to Actors' Equity or other unionized organizations such as the League of New York Theatres, which the House Un-American Activities Committee (HUAC) considered de facto to be communist. Not only were prominent Hollywood luminaries blacklisted – among them Orson Welles and Charlie Chaplin – but many of Loesser's friends and colleagues were called to testify at HUAC hearings, including William Saroyan and Abe Burrows. Loesser, though never called to testify, did not escape the 'Red Scare'.

---

87 Nat Perrin (1905–1998), screenwriter, producer and director. He was attached to the publicity department at Warner Bros. in the 1930s and subsequently produced films for Columbia Pictures and MGM; in the 1950s and 1960s he produced television shows including *The Red Skelton Hour*, *Death Valley Days* and *The Addams Family*.

28 June 1954: To George Mercader, Business
Administration Corporation

Dear George:

I have just returned from an extremely important business trip to the east. When I left here May 19th, I did so in such a terrible hurry that I had no opportunity to inform you or your office at the time of all my purposes in going. This letter will clarify for your information, what the whole trip was about.

On Tuesday, May 11th, there appeared in the early edition of the Los Angeles Examiner an alarming Un-American Activities story which seemed to refer to me in a manner that could have been quite damaging to me at this point in my career. The seeming reference to me, however, was deleted in later editions. Although quite alarmed I waited for several days without hearing any repercussions. My chief apprehension was that I stood in danger of having Samuel Goldwyn withdraw his bid to pay one million dollars for the picture rights to "Guys and Dolls." As you know, I own a 35% interest in this property and, as you also know, an otherwise firm offer in our industry can be withdrawn if the seller's name comes into disrepute. I was afraid that Goldwyn would take advantage of the existence of the above news-paper story in an attempt either to cancel or to reduce the price of the deal.

For a while there was apparently no commentary within the industry on the story mentioned above. Then on May 19th, in the Rambling Reporter column of the Hollywood Reporter which, as you know, is the most widely read daily trade organ in the motion picture industry, there appeared a direct reference to my good name on the same subject. Before the morning was over Louella Parsons[88] had tele-phoned both Sam Goldwyn and me. She bluntly asked Goldwyn whether he still intended going through with the record breaking purchase price of one million dollars for "Guys and Dolls" in the light of what he had read in the Hollywood Reporter. Goldwyn told her that he trusted fully in my loyalty and patriotism. When Parsons called

---

88 Louella Parsons (1881–1972), gossip columnist.

me she simply asked for some kind of comment, which I refused. Further, I succeeded in getting her to promise not to print anything on the subject for a few days and at the end of that time I told her I would satisfy her curiosity as to the truth of the Reporter's implications. She agreed. I quickly phoned Goldwyn to make an appointment for me in Washington with the Un-American Activities Committee so that I could ask them to clarify the situation with the press. Goldwyn telephoned Vice-President Nixon[89] who scored an appointment with congressman Velde[90] in Washington for the next day.

A few hours later I was on the plane to Washington and at 4:00 P.M. the next day I was in conference with congressman Velde, his attorney Mr. Taverner, and his research staff. In short order they satisfied me that there was no intention on the part of the committee to implicate me and further congressman Velde promised that he personally would release to the press a statement clearing my name. This was the most satisfaction I could get, but it involved new and intricate problems. Anticipating this release, I had to rush to New York in order to ward off the publishing of this correction in certain quarters. This may sound somewhat odd to you, but I think you must realize that the very mention of a man's name in connection with these matters, whether favorably or otherwise, still produces a memorable connection in the minds of readers. In other words, it was better not to make any "noise" at all in those portions of the press which had made no original reference to me.

For three consecutive weeks in New York I busied myself promoting the use of Velde's release in some quarters and discouraging it in others. Attached to this letter is a series of clippings and documents arranged chronologically. This will give you some idea of the entire history of this unfortunate incident, as well as some of the work accomplished by me.

---

89 Raphael I. Nixon (dates unknown), ex-FBI and Director of Research for the House Un-American Activities Committee.
90 Harold Himmel Velde (1910–1985), Congressman for Illinois's 18th district and chair of the House Un-American Activities Committee 1953–1955.

All during this period I had to visit with and in many cases argue with various members of the press. The following is a partial list of names of newspaper and magazine people contacted during my stay in New York:

Nat Goldstein[91] – New York Times
Leonard Lyons – New York Post
Emilie Coleman – News Week [Newsweek] Magazine
Joe Janoff – New York World Telegram
Tom Prideaux[92] – Life Magazine
Abel Green[93] – Variety

Bear in mind that all during this time I was receiving constant pressure from Samuel Goldwyn, the Music Corporation of America and Feuer and Martin (my partners in "Guys and Dolls") to clear things up so that the motion picture sale would not be impeded.

I did manage to clear things up shortly after the first week in June, making it possible for the Goldwyn deal to continue. After that time and until yesterday when I returned, I busied myself in New York City in resuming musical exploitation of my past product. Most of this effort was on renewing performances of the "Hans Christian Andersen" score as the picture had been re-released for the summer. I made some efforts to secure new recordings on my older works and the fruits of this will be very gratifying this fall. You may have noticed that my ASCAP income has diminished and requires a little more attention on my part toward getting more public performances of my songs. Also while in New York I gave auditions to upwards of 25 candidates for the cast of my new musical "They Knew What They Wanted."[94] I had planned on this activity for August, but since I had been forced east by my other problems I thought I would save the trouble and expense of a second trip.

---

91 Nat Goldstein (1908–1986), circulation editor of the *New York Times*.
92 Tom Prideaux (1908–1993), senior editor of *Life* magazine.
93 Abel Green (1900–1973), editor of *Variety* for over forty years.
94 *The Most Happy Fella.*

Your office will be getting hotel bills, entertainment bills, etc. during the period above described ... also certain cash-out-of-pocket vouchers from me. You will note on the Warwick Hotel an inordinate number of small room service charges. Because theatres were almost entirely unavailable I used my hotel suite for auditions as well as for conferences with recording people, television contracts, etc ... and did a brisk trade, as you can see, in coffee and whisky and lunches and dinners.

You will note the withdrawal of about $650.00 in cash from the hotel. About $480.00 of this was spent in outside entertainment, taxis, tips, etc. over this six week period.

If there are any further details I can furnish you concerning this trip, please do not hesitate to ask.

Sincerely,

A summary of this unfortunate episode – including comments by Loesser and Harold Velde's telegram to Loesser – appeared in *Variety* for 26 May 1954 (page 67):

Cause and Effect

Radio scripter Allen E. Sloane, testifying Jan. 13, 1954, before the House Committee on Un-American Activities chairmanned by Rep. Harold H. Velde (Ill.), had this to say:

"At any rate I was introduced to this young man and he was a songwriter. I should like to furnish his name off the record. He wrote a good many songs, popular ones, and collaborated with Duke Ellington on very, very popular songs. He, if not a Communist, followed closer to it than anybody could by outright joining the party ... Here was this person, a lyric writer who had been made known to me as a 'terrific guy.'[95] *He was a lyric writer of great impor-tance in the commercial world, and here am I, a radio writer of some skill and experience, and there was joined to us by this one Lan Adomian ... The person I spoke of was earning his living*

---

95 'Terrific guy' was previously explained by Sloane to be intra-Commie argot for a 100% Red.

writing lyrics for popular songs, such as 'Praise the Lord and Pass the Ammunition'..."

The following telegram from Congressman Velde was sent songsmith Frank Loesser (author of "Praise the Lord and Pass the Ammunition") to the Warwick Hotel, N. Y., May 21:

"Following release made today: 'Mr. Velde today stated that it has come to his Attention that through the recent release of testimony before the Committee, certain Los Angeles newspapers and Hollywood tradepapers had gathered the erroneous impression that some portions of this testimony related to Mr. Frank Loesser, prominent composer. Mr. Velde continued that a review of the testimony by Mr. Allan E. Sloane, released on Jan. 13, 1954, in the committee publication entitled, Entertainment Part I, disclosed that the unnamed musical composer referred to by Sloane was a person other than Frank Loesser, and that Loesser was not mentioned anywhere by Sloane. Mr. Loesser has not been mentioned in previous testimony before the Committee."

[*signed*] Harold H. Velde, Chairman.

When a Coast trade sheet (not Daily Variety) made a crack about Loesser and Abe Burrows' collaboration on "Guys and Dolls," and Louella Parsons phoned Samuel Goldwyn, who will produce the film, the chain-reaction was such that the songwriter took the situation in hand and journeyed to Washington. One, he never collaborated with Duke Ellington and "unfortunately I've never even had the pleasure of meeting him, as I told Raphael I. Nixon, director of research for the Committee," says Loesser. "Two, quite obviously Mr. Sloane's reference to 'earning his living writing lyrics for popular songs, such as "Praise the Lord and Pass the Ammunition" was a figure of speech, like somebody saying he wrote a beautiful ballad 'like Irving Berlin,' and Mr. Tavenner (Frank S. Tavenner Jr., counsel for the committee) was most charming in helping straighten out this confusion. Hence, the committee volunteered the wire sent me by Chairman Velde which I naturally appreciate."

CHAPTER FOUR

1954–56
DAMN YANKEES, THE *GUYS AND DOLLS* FILM AND *THE MOST HAPPY FELLA*

Arthur Loesser's *Men, Women and Pianos: A Social History* (New York: Simon & Schuster), which became a standard text on the history of the piano, was published in late 1954. Frank was proud of Arthur's achievement and actively promoted the book to his friends. Arthur hoped to visit Frank in California and while Loesser was uncertain of his travel plans – he apparently hoped to be further along with *The Most Happy Fella* and as a result to be in New York – Arthur did visit in the summer of 1955.

[?] November 1954: To Arthur Loesser (Telegram)

ENJOYING YOUR BOOK TREMENDOUSLY. CONGRATULATIONS AND LOVE.
    BROTHER FRANK.

15 November 1954: Arthur Loesser to Frank Loesser

Dear Frank, –
    Thank you very much for your encouraging wire. I feel most warmly touched to think that you would be willing to attack that heavy tome – called "forbidding-looking" by one of our most celebrated musicians – and take the trouble to tell me about it. I am deeply grateful.

On second thought it occurs to me that there may be a little reward for you in it; you may get a few smiles amidst the inevitable yawns, especially if you are persistent enough to get past the first section. Besides, you may feel a gleam of identification here and there at observing the congenital Loesser nimbleness with words, of which you and I are both exponents, in different phases. But sister, too, has it, as her correspondence proves.

I talked to Lynn briefly over the phone in New York a couple of weeks ago; short contact, but better than nothing. She reported to me about the alternations of exuberance and depression that you are undergoing in connection with your new opus.[1] I understand all too well. She said, substantially, that it was a musical show without spoken dialogue. O.K., O.K., – it's in the air these days; but I trust you are enough of a showman, politician, business man, and common-sensible human being to insist that the dirty word "opera" not be breathed, or even thought of, in connection with your production.[2] In the reign of the "common man," the more glitter the thing had once, the dirtier it is now. And I hope you will not discourage your fine talent for jingles and tunes. Tunes are the lasting pleasure of any musical theatre, no matter what else is in it. No Italian dictionary will ever make more out of the word "aria" than just "tune" or "melody." An aria is a tune for which you could get a high price if you could persuade people to dress up for it. The best of Rossini and Bizet, and yes, of Mozart and Verdi, is in the tunes. And the tunes of Handel, and Bellini still keep going long after the shows into which they were written have disappeared. All right, I'll shut up now, but maybe this subject may be in my next book, if I live long enough, and if S&S[3] remain indulgent.

It seems a shame that I always just miss you in N.Y. I am developing a strong hankering for California, but whether I can satisfy it next summer I don't know.

---

1 *The Most Happy Fella.*
2 Also see Loesser's letter to Arthur, 29 November 1954 (below).
3 Publisher Simon & Schuster.

Thanks again for your very kind attention.
With love
Brother
Arthur

[handwritten:] Very good review of my book in yesterday's N.Y. Times Book Review section, Nov. 14, done by an eminent English musicologist.

29 November 1954: To Arthur Loesser[4]

Arthur!

Thanks for your nice letter. It contained most of the points I try to make when giving basic orientation to my Company's junior writers – except of course that you <u>write</u> more effectively than I talk. Anyway I agree with <u>everything</u> you say and am trying to keep the thing so full of tunes, they won't <u>dare</u> call it an opera.

love
Frank

22 December 1954: Arthur Loesser to Frank Loesser

Dear Frank, –

Thanks very much indeed for the clipping with the review of my book in the L.A. Times. I would never have seen it if you hadn't sent it. The publishers get only one copy of everything from their clipping bureau, and I have to rely on kind friends or brothers.

Incidentally, will you please inform me a little more clearly about just what happened in connection with some kind of radio plug involving my book, with which you had something to do. Henry Simon wrote me that something was going on and that the firm of S&S had contributed some money; but exactly what occurred is dark to me. Will you enlighten?

---

4 The date of this letter derives from a notation on the upper right: 'PM [postmarked] Nov 29, 1954'.

Furthermore, they told me that you had ordered an extraordinary number of copies, for one individual. I trust this was enthusiasm mingled with family affection on your part; if so, it gives me a mighty warm, slightly inexpressible feeling, which I will therefore not express to you, but which you may be able to get through your internal radar. Anyway – thank you.

No real reports have come this way about your forthcoming opus;[5] and I won't conceal the fact that I am very curious about it, indeed. For when are you planning the opening? Or is it all hush-hush as yet?

When am I going to see you again? I expect to be in the West next summer, for about two weeks; but it will be up in the North, near Seattle. Anyway, if you should encourage me, and are home, I may blow myself to a flight in your direction at that time, say early or middle July.

Love to you all, and Christmas and New Year's greetings.

Bro.

Arthur

27 December 1954: To Arthur Loesser

Dear Arthur:

I hasten to answer your inquiries. First of all, I assume that the program you asked about in your letter was a TV show I was invited to appear on and which I was forced to turn down. I make it a policy not to appear on radio or television at all. Of course I would have loved helping to plug the book, but the moment I make an appearance all the wolves in disk jockey clothes descend on me to repeat same on entirely too many occasions. I am sorry I couldn't do this one. Or is this the one you are talking about?

Yes, I did order a few copies of the book and expect to order more. They make very fine Xmas presents for what may roughly be described as folks in our trade. So far I have given a copy to Andre

---

5 *The Most Happy Fella.*

Previn, Vernon Duke[6] and such people. Maybe they will learn what they are sitting in front of. It gives me no pain of forced fraternity to hand out this gem of a book. I guess like Papa said, you <u>are</u> a genius.

About your coming West. I only hope we are here. It is possible that by that time we might be East in advance of rehearsing my new show.[7] We will let you know our plans as they come through. Meanwhile, it is quite a job completing the writing of it and I find that to accomplish almost two hours of continuous music, one has got to steal miles of Puccini. Don't tell anybody.

Best love to you and Jean, and of course a very Happy New Year.

Frank

4 January 1955: To Arthur Loesser

Dear Arthur:

I am happily helping to exploit your book chain-letter style, as you can see from the enclosed note of thanks from Andre Previn.

Previn, in case you don't know, is the young musical genius at MGM – a fantastically good pianist, orchestrator and musical director.

Love,

19 August 1955: Arthur Loesser to Frank Loesser

Dear Frank, –

When I asked for the bill Wednesday morning at the Beverly Hills, the cashier told me there was none. I shrewdly suspected your fine conniving hand in that deal, and my only crumb of consolation is that I was fairly conservative in signing breakfast etc. checks. I enjoy very much accepting your hospitality, up to a point. After that it embarrasses me, because I can't rack my brains to think up any way in which I can effectively reciprocate. Anyway we had a wonderful week with you and yours. I enjoyed particularly chewing the fat, tit-bit by bit-tit,

---

6 André Previn (1929–2019), composer, pianist and conductor; Vernon Duke (1903–1969), composer known in particular for 'Taking a Chance on Love'.
7 *The Most Happy Fella*, which was finally produced only in 1956.

6. Arthur Loesser, 1949.

with you about music, words, and people, and was sorry there wasn't more.

The Las Vegas excursion was fine as an experience, and added still another cubit to my stature, thank you very much. Again I take my hat off, with a low deferential bow, to G's and D's[8] – authors, composer and performers – superb! As for L.V. as an institution, I remain snooty. That is substantially what I said in the piece I wrote about it for the Cleveland Press, to appear tomorrow. I'll send it on to you if you want it, and if the copy-desk hasn't maimed it too unrecognizably, after the well known space-economics of noose-peppers. But I don't think Mr. Kuller[9] will like it.

---

8 *Guys and Dolls.* The Las Vegas production at the Royal Nevada Hotel featured the original Broadway stars reprising their roles.
9 Sid Kuller (1910–1993), comedy writer, producer and composer/lyricist. Though nominally based in Hollywood, Kuller was also active in Las Vegas as a producer.

Excuse me for intruding a little tachlis,[10] or face-pidgin, or what-ever you call it. Do you remember a violinist named Sam Kuskin? He used to play second violin in the Stringwood Ensemble in the days when I was a member of that serious-minded group, while you were a teen-ager. Well, he has written me to say that he has had a tough time making a living this last year, and couldn't I help him get in touch with you with a view to your giving him a job with the orchestra in your forthcoming show. If he is as good now as he was then he must be an excellent player. Would you hear him? Or with whom ought he to get in touch, and how and when? I imagine it might be some months before you are ready to hire pit men. Let me know, however. Thanks.

Thanks thanks thanks – a regular tremolo of thanks. Love to you and Lynn, and a special brand of love to Mama. Friendly greetings to Betty Good[11] and to Bill Ellfeldt.[12] Also an appreciative snick of the thumb to Abe Burrows.

Maybe I can see you in N.Y. early in September.

And as they say in the musicians' union:

Fraternally yours,

Arthur

Adler and Ross's *Damn Yankees* was by this time in its final stages of preparation; it opened at the 46th Street Theatre on 5 May 1955. The cast included Robert Shafer as Joe Boyd, Stephen Douglass as Joe Hardy, Shannon Bolin as Meg Boyd, Gwen Verdon as Lola and Ray Watson as Mr. Applegate. Throughout this period Loesser regularly communicated with Adler and Ross about the show, typically – for him – addressing not only larger issues of dramaturgy but also very specific details in the texts and music of the songs. He notes, for instance, that critics might find 'Whatever Lola Wants' to be a rehash of 'Hernando's Hideaway' from Adler and Ross's previous show, *The*

---

10 The Yiddish word *tachlis* has several meanings, including 'end', 'purpose', or in this instance, apparently, 'seriousness'.

11 Betty Good was Loesser's long-time secretary.

12 William Ellfeldt (1906–1977) had been the choral director for the 1953 produc-tion of Wright and Forrest's *Kismet*.

Pajama Game. Strikingly, he addresses what he sees as a potential pitfall for authors: too great an attachment to their creations, at the expense of objectivity and dispassionately judging – and reacting to – an audience's response. As with other shows, Loesser is also concerned with exploitation and publication – the song 'Heart', in particular – especially as it might contribute to promoting the show before its opening.

A West End production of *The Pajama Game* opened at the London Coliseum on 13 October. Loesser sent good luck messages to several members of the production crew, the last of which, to Jerry Ross, is especially poignant: it hints at the lung disease (bronchiectasis) that brought about the composer's death at the age of twenty-nine just a month later.

10 February 1955: To Richard Adler and Jerry Ross

Dear Gents:

Like they say in the Congressional Record, this is an extension of remarks about the contents of your very fine score for "Damn Yankees." I have received what you loftily referred to as the integral coda of "A Man Doesn't Know." I have not yet gotten your instructions on the word "you've" in the line "whatever it is you've lost." I seem to recall that on the phone you both agreed that the word should be "he's." Possibly this is an oversight. I hope it is not a disagreement as I see no other evidence in the song for the use of the second person. If you agree on "he's," please wire. Ellfeldt has to repair all the copies for use.

I have also received the show version of "Goodbye, Old Girl." I personally prefer it to your "pop" version. This is a chemical kind of preference. I haven't got any really logical reasons, but "when you awaken I'll be gone" conjures up a domestic picture early in the scene. I think this is valuable to keep.

There are two other items, while we are on the subject of this song. Firstly, I don't think we should print "somethin'" and "squabblin'" without the "g's." I don't think that duplicating the style of your performers in the show by printing it that way is going to help sell a lot of the valuable legit and semi-legit people with monocles up their asses. If the requirements were as distinct as in Ol' Man River, I would understand the printed colloquialism.

My final remarks on this song is [sic] that I quarrel ever so slightly with the word "we" on the line "never even knew what we fought about." I think it should be "we'd." It would not have hurt a singer to make the effort of pronouncing the "d." On the other hand, I think you fellows should go down in history as pluperfect writers. Please wire if you agree.

Now, I have an over-all notion to get off my chest. I have an idea that you will be criticized in some quarters and possibly in important quarters for having repeated yourselves in a way which, to some minds, might seem obvious. I quote first, "Whatever Lola Wants" as being seemingly a paraphrase of "Hernando's Hideaway" and in the same score I find a piece called "Near to You" with the same kind of provocative, interrogative ending as in "Hey There." Now I do not propose for one instant that you should change these, but please be prepared for being attacked on this count. I don't believe the critics will notice, but the wise guys in Sardi's[13] may; however, they will never say it to your faces. You will forgive me for being over-fussy, but I am an anxious parent and don't want you typed too early in your careers.

One more defensive measure against critical concentration on the above, is that we get an early head of steam up on "Heart" and try to be sweeping the country around New York opening time. I think Mike [Sukin] will agree on this. If it works, you will be able to point with pride to a truly unassailable item in advance.

Dear Gents, remember this is a discussion and by no means a set of directions. If I were there with you, I would be talking in my softest and most awed manner about all this because I am, generally speaking, tremendously impressed with the "Damn Yankees" score. But I can't get there yet and I guess this letter will have to do. Please read it carefully and think carefully – and let me know what your thoughts are.

Love and kisses,

---

13 Restaurant at 234 West 44th Street, opened on 5 March 1927, a traditional hangout for Broadway personalities.

11 February 1955: To Adler and Ross

Dear Gents:

This is a supplementary letter to my letter of yesterday concerning the YANKEE score. Please read the other one first.

Since writing it I have received from Margie[14] the special songs (which I have not yet looked at) and the corrected copies of NEAR TO YOU.

Margie tells me that you have already changed "you've" to "he's," which answers the question in my other letter.

On the subject of NEAR TO YOU, Ellfeldt and I reviewed it and Bill noted that in some cases the symbols for the chords may not have been marked correctly. Please refer to this when you make your appointment with whoever is making the commercial piano part.

As a further reflection on the "HERNANDO–HEY THERE" discussion in my previous letter, we again have here a bit of minor mysterioso with some style resemblances to HERNANDO. Naturally, I understand that you are doing a Faust-line fantasy, but remember what I told you about the boys in Sardi's.

Please give me your answers on my questions in the other letter as quickly as you can.

Love and kisses,

23 February 1955: To Adler and Ross

Dear Gents:

Since talking and writing to you last I have reviewed the "special songs" you sent. There is no useful comment I can make on their specific content. Broadly, none of them seem to have much bite. Whether you agree now is not important, but the final judgment rests with you on those dreadful evenings to come in Philadelphia.[15] It will be up to you to judge laughs and other effects <u>objectively</u>. If

---

14 Marjory Gans (dates unknown) was a trusted employee of Frank Music who, though possibly known as a secretary, seems to have performed the duties of an office manager.
15 That is, during the out-of-town tryouts.

you indulge yourselves in appreciative giggling fits while the audience doesn't ... and then proceed to blame the performers' technique or the orchestration for this strange difference of opinion ... you will be wasting some precious time.

My suspicion is that FOR AN AUTOGRAPH doesn't do anything but indicate that Joe is now quite a celebrity. I don't know what George Abbott has added to your story, but I can't imagine any principal singing this song.[16] This suggests that the budget on this new hopeful Judy Garland stops at about $225.00 a week. It is rare that a $225 actress knows how to command attention with a single song, especially when we are not too interested in her as a character in the play. Of course I am guessing wildly, but couldn't this scene be danced? I think it is easier to find the new Dorothy Jarnac.[17] Let me know more about this if you feel like it.

THOSE WERE THE GOOD OLD DAYS reminds me of WAS I WAZIR in Kismet. The performance of this song was always brilliant, but the song was never good enough. Drop in the Ziegfeld[18] and listen again. It still stinks. I believe the Captain Hook character in PETER PAN has a solo of this kind. There are also some examples in the Gilbert and Sullivan operas. I have always felt that it was terribly difficult to express willful villainy in a first person song. Don't let the actor's rehearsal technique fool you. Watch the audience.

Incidentally, in passing let me suggest that Marie Antoinette was no longer a villain, but definitely a <u>victim</u> at guillotine time. Madame Defarge[19] would be more like it, except that nobody but you and I can remember who she is ... and sometimes <u>I</u> forget.

---

16 In the event, 'For an Autograph' was not included in the show. It was included in some out-of-town performances, possibly as a solo for Joe's wife.
17 Dorothy Jarnac (1916–1994), actress. Loesser's reference here is not clear although Jarnac also apparently worked as a choreographer with Hanya Holm (1893–1992) on John La Touche (1914–1956) and Jerome Moross's (1913–1983) *The Golden Apple* (1954).
18 That is, the Ziegfeld Theatre.
19 Leader of the tricoteuses, French revolutionaries, in Charles Dickens's *A Tale of Two Cities* (1859), known in particular for knitting beside the guillotine during executions.

Maybe what I am squawking about is just the prevalence of burnt flesh and ganglia. I understand the song, I appreciate the song, I think it is well written and I don't think it's funny. When you leave somebody up there for a minute and forty-five seconds with his mouth opening and closing, I believe you have informed the audience of your intention to be funny.

Well, I've gone and done it. I promised not to go into detail, but there you are. Please don't send me demos to try to prove something. Do the proving to yourselves. Maybe by that time I will be easy and will enjoy having been all wrong about the above.

One more note. I don't know who has been assigned to make your commercial copies, but be sure he understands your <u>intentions</u> in terms of harmony, as well as time values in the vocal line. If possible try to get this done before you are swallowed up in rehearsals.

Love and kisses,

1 March 1955: To Richard Adler

Dear Dick:

Thanks for your long letter. I hope you are right about most of the points. I still feel that Marie Antoinette didn't use a guillotine as an instrument of villainy. It was used <u>on her</u> by people historically regarded as humane saviors. This is of extreme importance when presenting an array of parallel images in a song.

Anyway, all of this is like algebra ... There's very little use for it in a grocery store, but it sharpens the mind for buying the right can of beans.

Love to you and Jerry.

3 March 1955: To Adler and Ross (Telegram)

PLEASE TRY VERY HARD TO GET FISHER[20] TO PERFORM PICKUP OF "HEART" ON LOW DOMINANT AS WRITTEN. NEVER MIND WHY BUT I SUDDENLY CONSIDER THIS VERY IMPORTANT TO

---

20 Eddie Fisher (1928–2010), singer and actor. His cover of 'Heart' reached no. 6 on the US charts.

YOU. IN FAVOR OF FINAL HIGH ENDING THERE MIGHT BE
TENDENCY TO SING PICKUP ON THE THIRD. THIS MATERIALLY
REDUCES VALUE OF ATTACK. YOU BOYS DIDN'T WRITE "I'M
BIDING MY TIME."[21]

    FINICKY LOESSER

14 March 1955: To Robert E. Griffith[22]

Dear Bobby:

I would be a false friend indeed if I were to let your letter of March
11th go unanswered for a single day, lest you might imagine I was
thinking over its suggestions.

I am afraid no thinking over is required. Frank Music Corp. has
never paid royalty to a theatrical producer. There was no intention on
our part even to consider it. Someday if a producer delivers us Cole
Porter we might consider it. In the instance at hand <u>we</u> delivered the
very expensively reared writers.

The Frank Music Corp. finds that it needs an extra two cents out of
every copy to put into <u>real</u> music exploitation. Sometimes we even
go over the two cents' worth and manage to lose money, but that's
our problem.

Of course if you want a piece of <u>our</u> gross we might arrange a
transaction by which we exchange it for a piece of <u>your</u> gross. It might
be a good plan for the future.

    Best love to you.

    Sincerely,

12 October 1955: To Richard Adler (Telegram)

HERE'S WISHING PAJAMA GAME GETS A BIG WELCOME. GOOD
LUCK.

    LYNN AND FRANK.

---

21 From George and Ira Gershwin's *Girl Crazy* (1930).

22 Robert E. Griffith (1907–1961), theatre producer. He produced Adler and
Ross's previous hit *The Pajama Game* and earlier in his career was stage manager
for Loesser's *Where's Charley?*

12 October 1955: To Robert Griffith (Telegram)

HERE'S WISHING PAJAMA GAME A HAPPY OPENING. IT IS
TOO MUCH TO EXPECT THE SAME FROM YOUR POCKETBOOK.
AS A CLOSE RELATIVE OF ONE OF YOUR INVESTORS[23] I
CANNOT SAY I EXACTLY APPROVE OF YOUR HAVING
MADE THE TRIP. NEVERTHELESS I NOTICE WITH SOME
SATISFACTION THAT IN YOUR INSULTING LETTERS YOU HAVE
THE SENSIBLE THRIFT TO USE WILLIAMSON[24] STATIONERY.
ANYWAY LOVE AND KISSES AND GOOD LUCK TO YOU AND
THE BOYS.
                    FRANK LOESSER

13 October 1955: To Jerry Ross (Telegram)

XX KNOW PAJAMA GAME WILL BE A BIG SUCCESS IN ENGLAND.
HOW CAN IT MISS. MORE IMPORTANT IS FOR YOU TO GET
WELL. WHEN IT IS POSSIBLE WE'D LIKE TO SEE YOU. LOVE AND
KISSES.
        LYNN AND FRANK

Throughout 1955, Loesser was also occupied with the Samuel
Goldwyn film of *Guys and Dolls* – which opened on 3 November
of that year – starring Marlon Brando as Sky Masterson, Jean
Simmons as Sister Sarah Brown, Frank Sinatra as Nathan Detroit and
Vivian Blaine as Miss Adelaide. The project was plagued with contractual, promotional and personnel problems: it can be surmised that
Sinatra was unhappy with Loesser's choice of music director, and
whereas the original Broadway cast album of the show had been
released by Decca, the film soundtrack would have to go to Capitol,
for whom Frank Sinatra recorded exclusively. Loesser also recognised

---

23 Loesser's mother, Julia.
24 Williamson was the publishing company of Rodgers and Hammerstein.

7. Frank Loesser and Marlon Brando rehearsing 'Luck Be a Lady'
from *Guys and Dolls*, 1955.

the need for the score to become current again – five years after its
Broadway debut – by having new recordings put out by the latest
popular musicians, among them Sammy Davis Jr, whom Loesser
contacted directly. Then, with the release of the film just a month away,
a change of date for a long-planned episode of *The Ed Sullivan Show*
on television upset the careful sequence of release dates Loesser and
his company had planned around the extra songs written specially for
the screen version of the musical, 'Pet Me Poppa', 'A Woman in Love'
and 'Adelaide'. Loesser also came up with a novel idea to promote the
singing debut of Hollywood star Marlon Brando – who had never
sung in a film before – through a special recording. But Brando got
cold feet, worried about his singing voice, and in the end, no special
promotion materialised and a soundtrack of the film was never
released.

12 January 1955: To Jack Entratter (telegram)[25]

WHEN YOU SEE [FRANK] SINATRA I WOULD LIKE HIM TO CALL ME AND QUOTE EXACTLY HIS CONVERSATION WITH GOLDWYN IN CONNECTION WITH MUSICAL DIRECTOR.[26]
FRANK LOESSER

14 March 1955: To Milton Rackmil[27]

Dear Milt:

As you know, Samuel Goldwyn has begun the filming of "Guys and Dolls." Of course he and I both want to see an album produced representing the picture version. In connection with this there seems to be a small obstacle which I will now describe to you.

Frank Sinatra is in Goldwyn's cast and, as you know, he has a long, firm deal with Capitol.[28] Further, he has expressed his personal affection for that company and there is no possibility that he would wish to record elsewhere. This puts Goldwyn and me in the position of being able to offer the album only to Capitol Records. I am by no means against this idea as Capitol seems to have done well with movie albums in the past.

But as you may have learned, the picture cast also includes Vivian Blaine, Stubby Kaye and Johnny Silver[29] all of whom performed in your original cast album of the Broadway show. I may be wrong, but I understand all of them signed agreements with you by which they are prohibited from performing the same numbers on phonograph records for a number of years.

---

25 Jack Entratter (1914–1971), an American business executive who at this time worked at the Sands Hotel and Casino in Las Vegas.
26 The musical director for *Guys and Dolls* was Irving Actman.
27 Milton Rackmil (1906–1992), a co-founder of Decca Records (in 1934), was at the time head of Universal Pictures.
28 Capitol Records, founded in 1942 by Johnny Mercer, songwriter and film producer Buddy DeSylva (1895–1950) and record store owner Glenn E. Wallichs (1910–1971).
29 Stubby Kaye played the role of Nicely-Nicely Johnson; Johnny Silver (1918–2003) was Benny Southstreet.

I am writing this letter to ask you and your company for a favor. I would like you to deliver to me, personally, a letter which releases the services of these people (or their movie sound tracks) for use by another company in connection with an album of the motion picture version.

I realize that I am asking you to do something which might <u>theoretically</u> reduce the value of your already established package. However, you must realize that you are in an advantageous position with the show album, since you may continue to merchandise it along with Goldwyn's enormous advance publicity on the title, possibly many months before the appearance of any new package. There will be new factors characterizing the picture version, including three additional songs by me ... and possibly some deletions from the original score.[30]

Please give me an answer on this as soon as you possibly can. I am depending, of course, on your appreciation of our wonderful business relationship in the past. I have no bargain of any kind to suggest, but can only assure you that my appreciation will show itself at every opportunity.

With many thanks.

Sincerely,

Frank Loesser

27 June 1955: To Howard Dietz[31]

Dear Howard:

You wanted me to remind you about the exploitation of "Guys and Dolls" by MGM Records. This is of the utmost importance and I hope there is some way that we can get a maximum of cooperation. This would include <u>single</u> sides by the company's best

---

30 For Loesser's new songs, see p. 162; five numbers from the original Broadway show were not included in the film: 'A Bushel and a Peck', 'I've Never Been in Love Before', 'My Time of Day', 'Marry the Man Today' and 'More I Cannot Wish You'.
31 Howard Dietz (1896–1983), lyricist and publicist, at the time vice president in charge of publicity for MGM.

performers ... Joni James,[32] Art Mooney,[33] Davey Rose,[34] etc., etc., I emphasise <u>single</u> sides because these are the ones performed by the jockeys with the proper announcements concerning the picture. It is a good deal harder to get LPs and EPs performed, although they are quite welcome and are certainly an exploitation asset.

When I speak of song exploitation I refer not only to new recordings of the three new songs in the picture, but also to new recordings of the score's original pieces. The other record companies in general are going to balk at making new versions or even reissuing those which came out at the time of our Broadway opening. Therefore, it is of vital importance that MGM Records gives us every possible help.

I imagine your Mr. Walker[35] is the one concerned here. If he will have an <u>early</u> discussion with my people in New York (he knows them) I believe we can help each other. My company has set a date of October first as the general release date for recordings of the new pieces. I believe Frank Walker and staff should hear these new pieces and should also review the old ones. This can be arranged with my New York office. <u>I</u> mean <u>right</u> <u>away</u>, if possible.

Thanks, and best wishes.

18 July 1955: To Howard Dietz

Dear Howard:

I hope this note will answer your request for specific suggestions regarding MGM Record Company's cooperation on "Guys and Dolls."

---

32 Joni James (1930–2022), American pop singer who had achieved six Top Ten hits in the previous four years; she released a recording of 'I've Never Been in Love Before' on her album *When I Fall in Love* (1955) and 'If I Were a Bell' on *Joni Sings Songs by Victor Young and Songs By Frank Loesser* (1956).
33 Art Mooney (1911–1993), American pop singer and band leader.
34 David Rose (1910–1990), British-born American arranger, songwriter, composer ('The Stripper'), and orchestra leader. He had performed a tribute to *Guys and Dolls* on *The Red Skelton Hour* in 1954.
35 Frank Buckley Walker (1889–1963) was a talent agent and co-founder of MGM Records.

In the first place it might be wise to remind Frank Walker that "I've Never Been in Love Before" and "A Bushel and a Peck" are not used in the picture. Further, that Billy Eckstine's "I'll Know" cannot possibly be considered of value to any of us (my opinion).[36] Among the <u>existing</u> records by the company this leaves "If I Were a Bell" recorded by Art Lund.[37] I don't know what interest MGM Records would have in producing and exploiting a record by this artist as I believe they have no present stake in him. Also I am quite sure that the public could not be awakened to any such interest.

I have the following suggestions to make:

1. Joni James record of "I'll Know"
2. Betty Madigan record of "Take Back Your Mink"
3. Betty Madigan record of "If I Were a Bell"
4. LeRoy Holmes or David Rose record of "My Time of Day"[38]

There are three new numbers on which my people will be approaching Frank Walker directly.

In all instances I feel comfortable in assuming that MGM Records, in addition to its function as a profit making organisation – is also in a sense a public relations instrument of MGM Pictures. I do not mean by this that they should go broke by virtue of having applied all possible resources toward the exploitation of the picture, but it is a matter of notable record that over a period of time nobody has ever done anything but profit through the recording of works of the Frank Music Corp.

In the past it has been assumed by many in the record business that a "production" song has little popular merit. My company has proved quite the opposite, as in the case of the complex and rangy "Stranger in Paradise," the weirdly modal "Unchained Melody," the

---

36 Billy Eckstine (1914–1993), American jazz and popular singer; he recorded 'I'll Know' for MGM Records in 1950.

37 Art Lund (1915–1990), American singer and television and stage actor; he recorded 'If I Were a Bell' for MGM Records in 1950.

38 Joni James recorded 'I'll Know' on her 1956 album *Joni Sings Songs by Victor Young and Songs by Frank Loesser* (MGM Records); recordings of 'Take Back Your Mink' and 'If I Were a Bell' by singer Betty Madigan (born 1928), and 'My Time of Day' by bandleaders LeRoy Holmes (1913–1986) or David Rose, are unknown.

highly special "Whatever Lola Wants," the preposterously constructed "Hey There" and that triumph of special effects "Hernando's Hideaway." These have all been smashes for the Frank Music Corp. It is nice to observe that most of them were recorded by the MGM Record company even though it had no official connection with the producers. There was none of the above mentioned mistrust of show and movie songs. Now that MGM Records is seemingly a close and willing ally of the "Guys and Dolls" project I feel, and I think maybe you feel, that it should break its behind in advancing and sustaining attention to the musical contents.

Among other things, MGM Records could certainly produce a brightly packaged EP selection of tunes from the picture, by David Rose or LeRoy Holmes. Incidentally, I note that the company has never made a record of the title song. Possibly Art Mooney could do a fine job on this.[39]

I believe these are enough suggestions with which to dismay Frank Walker. You will note that although I am speaking of my own works I have not lost any of my customary immodesty. Just wait until you hear me scream what I want from MGM Records from the Wright and Forrest score of "Kismet" which I publish. This note will seem to have been an obsequious murmur for help.

Anyway, this is what you wanted in writing. Am I unreasonable?

Love,

17 July 1955: To Sammy Davis Jr[40]

Dear Sammy:

Here is the music and a demonstration record of "Adelaide," which we went over the other day in Las Vegas. The demonstration was sung by me and if you are worried about <u>yourself</u> the sound of my voice will give you a rough idea of how badly the <u>Jews</u> are doing. However, I felt because the singing is so pathetic it has the kind of

---

39 Mooney apparently did not record 'Guys and Dolls'.
40 Sammy Davis Jr (1925–1990), iconic American singer, dancer, actor and comedian.

appeal that will melt you into either recording it for Decca as a single, or organizing a benefit for helpless old Frank Loesser.

Also enclosed to futz around with is a copy of "Luck Be A Lady." Both of these pieces are for October 1st release, in favor of the exploitation of "Guys and Dolls" and the further glorification of Samuel Goldwyn, who can't sing either.

So far you are the only guy who has been sent "Adelaide" and so of course I would appreciate hearing what happens.[41] I'm in the Beverly Hills phone book.

Thanks, and love to you. And my kindest regards to Morty.[42]

Sincerely,

Heavy smoker

29 July 1955: To Frank Walker

Dear Frank:

I believe that I can deliver Marlon Brando's services for a special kind of two-sided record in a fancy display sleeve. It occurs to me, and I believe it will to you, that a single by Brando displayed in stores might be of terrific interest to the public ... especially the young ones.

As you may know, the Capitol Record Company will be producing the "Guys and Dolls" original cast album of the picture. This is because of their contractual control of Sinatra. It is my belief that Goldwyn will request withholding of release of this album until at least after the first showing of the "Guys and Dolls" picture. I intend to support Goldwyn on this policy because I agree with him that Brando's singing should be introduced through the picture where the visual values are immense.

In the meantime, what I propose is this: One side of Brando sexily reciting the lyrics of "My Time of Day", from "Guys and Dolls" against a lush orchestra performance of the tune. The other side a mambo

---

41 Sammy Davis Jr recorded 'Adelaide', 'I'll Know', 'Luck Be a Lady' and 'Sit Down, You're Rockin' the Boat' for Decca on 18 August 1955.
42 Arranger and composer Morty Stevens (1929–1991).

style orchestration featuring Brando playing the bongos and occasionally shouting "ugh." In case you weren't aware of it, Brando is quite a competent drummer and exhibited himself doing same on the Ed Murrow program recently. The orchestration, of course, would be of a Frank Music Corp. Copyright, preferably something from "Guys and Dolls." This would be for release about September 1st, which would precede the Capitol album by possibly sixty days. I believe this could be packaged in a sleeve designed like the front page of a newspaper with headline type proclaiming BRANDO SPEAKS or BRANDO MAKES LOVE and on the other side BRANDO BONGOS.

This morning I described this project over the phone to Howard Dietz and he <u>seemed</u> to favor it. In discussing it with him, of course, I was pointing up the advantages in terms of picture promotion because of the advance date at which it could be released.

Nevertheless, I am directing this suggestion to you on the basis of my belief that it could be very valuable <u>commercially</u>.

Of course I am no authority on the record business as you are, but I do get ideas and maybe you can use this one. I wish you would give me your opinions and feelings about this as soon as possible.

Many thanks. And best wishes to you as always.

4 October 1955: To Samuel Goldwyn (Telegram)[43]

JUST LEARNED SULLIVAN SHOW ON "GUYS AND DOLLS" WILL BE BROADCAST OCTOBER NINTH. ORIGINALLY I MADE FIRM RELEASE DATE WITH ALL NETWORKS, RECORDING COMPANIES, ETC. OF OCTOBER FIFTEENTH BASED UPON SULLIVAN BROADCAST OCTOBER TWENTY-THIRD. I HAVE NEVER BEEN INFORMED OF THIS CHANGE AND SEE NO POSSIBLE WAY TO RELEASE PERFORMANCE OF THE NEW PIECES BEFORE OCTOBER

---

43 The telegram is quoted verbatim in a letter from Marjory Gans to talent agent Herman Citron (1922–2009), best known for his representation of director Alfred Hitchcock (1899–1980); the whereabouts of the original is unknown.

FIFTEENTH IN CASE ANY USE IS INTENDED. THIS WOULD DESTROY VERY VERY VERY VERY VALUABLE RECORDING PLANS. I MEAN VALUABLE TO YOU AND ME BOTH. PLEASE ADVISE. BEST REGARDS.

12 October 1955: To George Chasin (Telegram)[44]

AGAIN URGENTLY REQUEST YOU SIGN BRANDO FOR DECCA ALBUM. PLEASE CONTACT SONNY BURKE.[45] THIS IS NOT IMPORTANT MONEY BUT WELL TIMED IMPACT OF RECORD. THANKS
    FRANK LOESSER, CLIENT

13 October 1955: To George Chasin (Telegram)

AM TERRIBLY SHOCKED AND EMBARRASSED BY YOUR REPORT ON BRANDO'S SUDDEN DOUBT ABOUT PHONOGRAPH RECORDS OF HIS VOICE. FOR A LONG TIME I HAVE TAKEN FOR GRANTED THAT HE WAS SATISFIED WITH THE WAY HE SOUNDS. NOW I AM FACED WITH THE PROBLEM OF UNWINDING AN OTHERWISE BEAUTIFUL RELATIONSHIP WITH DECCA. I HOPE YOU CAN CONVINCE BRANDO THAT HE IS AS GOOD AS I THINK HE IS. I THINK WE ALL AGREE THIS IS NOT TO BE CONSIDERED A MONEY MAKING PROPOSITION BUT SIMPLY AN EXPLOITATION CHANNEL FOR THE PICTURE. PLEASE BARE [sic] IN MIND THAT GOLDWYN HAS A PERFECT RIGHT TO TRANSCRIBE BRANDO'S SINGING AND GIVE IT AWAY TO THOUSANDS OF RADIO STATIONS ANYWAY. THEREFORE IT WOULD APPEAR FOOLISH IN MY MIND TO RESIST THIS VERY GOOD ALBUM IDEA. TIME IS OF THE ESSENCE. LOVE AND KISSES.
    FRANK LOESSER, CLIENT, CLIENT, CLIENT

---

44 George Chasin (1906–1987), senior vice president of the record label MCA.
45 Joseph Francis 'Sonny' Burke (1914–1980), American arranger and bandleader.

18 October 1955: To Marlon Brandon (telegram)

IT WILL MEAN A LOT TO ME IF YOU CONSENT TO RECORD ALBUM DEAL. IF I THOUGHT RELEASE WOULD EMBARRASS YOU IN ANY WAY I WOULD NOT SUGGEST IT. BUT I FEEL THAT YOU WILL COME OFF TREMENDOUSLY. FOR A LONG TIME I HAVE BEEN ASSUMING THERE WOULD BE NO OBJECTIONS SINCE YOU NEVER MENTIONED ANY IN ALL OUR TIMES TOGETHER. NOW IT IS QUITE LATE IN THE DAY AND I AM MOST EMBARRASSED IN MY POSITION WITH THE RECORD COMPANY. PLEASE CONSIDER THIS OR I WILL HAVE YOU ARRESTED NEXT TIME YOU RING MY DOOR BELL IN THE MIDDLE OF THE NIGHT. LOVE LOVE LOVE AND THANKS.

    FRANK LOESSER THE MONSTER

Frank Music continued to expand in the mid-1950s. Loesser approached lyricists Betty Comden (1917–2006) and Adolph Green (1914–2002) – whose productions included *On the Town* (1944), *Wonderful Town* (1953) and *Peter Pan* (1954) – maintained contacts with old friends like Johnny Mercer, and was sure to remain on good terms with other Broadway composers, including Cole Porter when his and Porter's production interests collided, and Rodgers and Hammerstein on the opening of their musical *Pipe Dream*. (At one point, Loesser's name was associated with the show, which was based on the novel *Sweet Thursday* by his friend John Steinbeck.) Loesser was also concerned to maintain control over the use of his music – or at least, since his music was licensed by ASCAP, the circumstances relating to how and whether he would be credited.

25 March 1955: To Betty Comden and Adolph Green

Dear Betty and Adolph:

    Last night I had a talk with Jule Styne and from his conversation it appears that you all have started working together.[46] Jule didn't give

---

46 On *Bells Are Ringing* (1956).

me any absolute assurance that the team would want to come to Frank Music Corp., but he did seem amiable about it.

I will not press you further about McIntyre[47] until you tell me you have some practical plan for trying things out with him. Naturally I understand that you had a commitment with Jule and, of course, I think you three can be wonderful together. Especially with the Frank Music Corp. proving it to everybody.

Much love,

20 June 1955: To Johnny Mercer

Dear Johnny:

Just a note to tell you how crazy I am about "Something's Gotta Give."[48] It's a real pleasure to see carriage trade writers getting the hits.

Love,

18 October 1955: To Cole Porter

Dear Cole:

I have swiped something from you. Not a tune, but something maybe a lot more precious and I am writing in the hope that you will understand. Together with Lynn [Loesser] and Kermit Bloomgarden,[49] who are producing my show, I have succeeded in spiriting away from "Silk Stockings"[50] one Herb Greene.[51] Knowing how much you appreciate him, not only for his talent but his wonderful good will . . . I felt obliged to write you this note of apology. But I guess I need him

---

47 Possibly a reference to composer and pianist Mark McIntyre (1916–1970).
48 Written for Fred Astaire in the 1955 film *Daddy Long Legs*; it was nominated for the Academy Award for Best Song.
49 Kermit Bloomgarden (1904–1976), theatrical producer; his Broadway productions included *Death of a Salesman* (1949), *The Diary of Anne Frank* (1955) and Meredith Willson's *The Music Man* (1957).
50 Cole Porter's final Broadway musical, based on the film *Ninotchka*.
51 Herbert Greene (1921–1985), Broadway conductor and arranger. He had previously provided vocal direction and arrangements for Loesser's *Guys and Dolls*.

more than you do at this moment and I feel sure that you will understand.

Thanks, and as always my best.

30 November 1955: Lynn and Frank Loesser
to Rodgers & Hammerstein II (Telegram)

ALL THE BEST.   LOVE AND KISSES.
LYNN AND FRANK LOESSER

3 January 1956: To Irving Caesar[52]

Dear Irving:

It would have been easier to 'phone me, but as long as we are going on the record, I guess I'll have to answer by letter.

These are my facts: I was asked by North[53] whether or not I minded his using, as a score for the '56 circus, a collection of stuff written in the past by me. I told him that I not only did not mind, but that I could not stop him since he operates under an ASCAP license. Nevertheless I would not accept billing of my name unless the entire show was scored with compositions wholly or partially mine. That is the substance of our deal. There is no exchange of money. I did not advise him to do it, on the contrary he came to me and he gave me to believe that he, up to the time of his very flattering suggestion, had no obligation which would prohibit him from being so nice to me. I have never had any intention of writing anything new for the circus, nor have I volunteered to publish anyone else's circus music, including yours. Apparently you have been misinformed. If you had a prior agreement on the '56 circus with North, I have not been informed of such an agreement.

I am spelling out the cold facts as I know them without any senti-mental references to our long and valued friendship – in terrific haste,

---

52 Irving Caesar (1895–1996), lyricist. His songs included George Gershwin's 'Swanee' and Vincent Youmans's 'Tea for Two'.
53 Alex North (1910–1991), composer and arranger.

and, therefore, seemingly without warmth and understanding. You will have to write that between the lines. I am a notoriously bad letter writer and a remarkably good songwriter. I am so busy being the latter these days that I suppose this note to you suffers as a work of art. Please forgive me.

Best love as always.

Sincerely,

FRANK LOESSER

In early May, Loesser was approached by a young acquaintance, Stuart Ostrow (born 1932), who had studied music education at New York University and from 1952 served in the United States Air Force, asking for a job. Ostrow eventually became vice president and general manager of Frank Music, co-producing Meredith Willson's *The Music Man* (1957) and Loesser's *The Most Happy Fella* (1956), *Greenwillow* (1960) and *How to Succeed in Business Without Really Trying* (1961).[54]

4 May 1955: Stuart Ostrow to Frank Loesser

Dear Frank:-

I trust this letter finds you in the best of health. In reading the trades and the national publications, I am happy to see that your endeavors are working out so well. It is difficult for me, as a comparative newcomer in the business, to write with authority, in an attempt to sincerely express my feelings towards your success. However, I'm certain you will try to understand my desire to add a small bit of congratulations. If anything, it gives me a profound feeling of personal gratification in writing to you as a friend.

To be quite honest, Frank, I have hesitated to write you before in view of the feeling I might have generated, of looking for a job. With nine months more to serve in the military and the immense jittery jungle of Showbiz in front of me as my chosen career, naturally I am

---

54 Ostrow has published two autobiographies: *A Producer's Broadway Journey* (Westport, CT, 1995) and *Present at the Creation, Leaping in the Dark, and Going Against the Grain: 1776, Pippin, M. Butterfly, La Bete, and Other Broadway Adventures* (New York, 2005).

concerned. I will not minimize or attempt to disguise the fact that our limited association has meant a great deal to me. I respect you and your word to a great degree. After weighing pride against mostly ambition, I decided to quit wrestling with this angel and be honest with myself.

Sure, I'd give my left eye-ball to work with you. The only way to get a yes or no is to ask, so "serve a paper and sue me" . . . I'm asking. Can you use an ambitious man who wants to learn and work hard for you?

I have enclosed a resume that may lend some insight on what I have done, and more so, what I know I can do better.

Frank, let me be square with you on this, I sincerely hope that this will not appear as just another guy who wants to climb on the band-wagon thinking he can promote a good deal from an acquaintance. If this correspondence appears that way, I strongly suggest you forget it and if you feel, send back a hello or a recipe for Beverly-Hills matzoh-brei.[55]

I would really like to visit with you at your convenience and perhaps have dinner or a drink. Till le-chiem[56] time or when you have a chance to write. Kindest personal regards.

Respectfully,
[signed:] Stu
STUART OSTROW
A/1C USAF
Director of Productions
P.S. Give my best to Betty Good. She's a doll.

16 May 1955: To Stuart Ostrow

Dear Stu:

I have your interesting letter. I note that you use my name as a "reference." This is perfectly all right, but if called on by some

---

55 A traditional Passover breakfast dish consisting of matzo, eggs, applesauce and sour cream.
56 *L'chaim* ('to life'), the traditional Hebrew drinking toast.

prospective employer to report on you I would have to limit my observations to the fact that I know you, that you gave some good army programs, that you are a personable young man and so far have never stolen anything from me, or burned my house down. Maybe you should have asked me.

When you get closer to being released from the army, please get in touch.

Sincerely,

[unsigned:]

22 July 1955: To Stuart Ostrow

Dear Stu:

Pursuant to our talks, this will confirm that our company can and will hold the western exploitation job open for you providing that you can report for work preferably September 1st, but no later than October 1st, 1955, at the salary agreed on while you were here in Hollywood last week. Since our corporation adheres to the general practice of not giving contracts, my attorneys would not approve of my stating the amount in writing, as this might, in effect, constitute a written contract.

Although in my original presentation of the opportunity to you I referred to October 1st as an approximate starting date, I now find that it is urgent for you to report before that time. Preferably in early September.

We are obligated to start work on the new Rosalind Russell Paramount picture "The Girl Rush."[57] This will be followed by several months of continuous work on Samuel Goldwyn's "Guys and Dolls." Following that we will be concerned with an Alfred Hitchcock motion picture,[58] as well as one of the important Broadway shows.[59] It is vitally important that my firm be represented <u>continuously by the same man</u> in the western territory. Any change in personnel would

---

57 Paramount's *The Girl Rush* was released in September 1955.
58 Mark McIntyre's music for Hitchcock's *The Trouble with Harry* (1955).
59 Probably *Damn Yankees*.

act as a serious set-back because our clients would lose confidence in our company's operation. Therefore, we must make a permanent change as soon as possible. I cannot employ an interim executive.

Would you be good enough to advise me of your earliest available date. I realize that you must determine this through official application. The sooner you can fill the urgent need we have for your services, the more advantageous it would be.

Sincerely,

[unsigned]

Frank Loesser

Other business correspondence from the time included an exchange with music attorney Mike Sukin concerning the Cuban pianist Pérez Prado (1916–1989), who popularised the mambo in North America in the 1950s, and the singer Perry Como (1912–2001). *Cash Box* was the name of a trade magazine (1942–1996) similar to *Billboard* that published sales figures and other data related to the music industry. Loesser similarly fielded implicit or explicit requests to consider various properties (in the process demonstrating his broad knowledge of American popular culture – and humour), among them a correspondence with film producer Nancy W. Stern concerning a film version of *The Mouse That Roared*, a post-war parody of the US Marshall Plan that provided aid to defeated countries: the Duchy of Grand Fenwick, the smallest country in the world, declares war on the US, which it loses in less than a day with no casualties, after which the US rebuilds the country.

30 December 1954: To Mike Sukin (telegram)

NEW PEREZ PRADO VICTOR RECORD TITLED CHERRY PINK AND APPLEBLOSSOM WHITE WAS PICKED AS SLEEPER BY CASH BOX. TITLE VERY SIMILAR TO OURS NOW WAITING FOR [PERRY] COMO. NEED HONEST EXPRESSION FROM CARLTON[60]

---

60 Joe Carlton (dates unknown), head of Artists and Repertoire at the RCA record label.

IMMEDIATELY. WOULD NOT LIKE TO THINK HE WAS HOLDING DECISION KNOWING THAT NO ONE ELSE BUT VICTOR HAS HAD A CHANCE AT IT. FRANKLY THINK WE MUST ESTABLISH TIME LIMIT ON COMO. ANY QUESTIONS?

FRANK LOESSER

10 February 1955: To Nancy W. Stern

Dear Nancy:

I enjoyed "The Mouse That Roared"[61] very much. But I think there are some problems and they may be big ones. At this point in history I think it is very dangerous to futz around comedy-wise with the atomic bomb, international war or anything like it.

Don't know what Kaufman[62] did with "Silk Stockings" characterizing the Russian politicos, but I am willing to bet he didn't show any or if he did, he made them deadly serious and have long ago stopped accepting jokes about the war situation.

You and I know, of course, that the book is no joke, but it would come out that way as a musical. More importantly, this book is distinctly pacifistic in its intention and these thoughts, where they may exist today, can be eradicated from the public's mind overnight by one radio announcement.

I think you will recall how Bob Sherwood had to retire his great play called "There Shall Be No Night." He identified the Russians and Germans and the United States joined forces. When Russia and the United States joined forces, Sherwood and his <u>producer</u> and <u>investors</u> got a kick in the belly, and the play was without honor or income until 1946.[63]

---

61 A then-new novel by Irish-American writer Leonard Wibberley (1915–1983).
62 George S. Kaufman (1889–1961), who wrote the book for Cole Porter's *Silk Stockings*, a satire of Cold War relations between America and Russia.
63 Robert Sherwood's (1896–1955) *There Shall Be No Night*, which won the 1941 Pulitzer Prize for Drama, ran on Broadway from 29 April to 2 November 1940. It concerns a Finnish scientist who is reluctant to believe Russia would invade Finland – which Russia did, on 30 November 1939.

I don't know whether your letter was an invitation to me to work on this. If so, I must tell you that I have committed my time for almost the next two years. Why don't you and I watch current history and talk about this some other time? Or do you have to act on your option this minute?

Meantime, I would like to hear what you have gathered in the way of opinion from smarter people than me. There are some, you know!

Thanks for thinking of me and best wishes.

Sincerely,

3 March 1955: To Nancy W. Stern

Dear Nancy:

Thanks for your note. Maybe my emphasis was too one-sided. I certainly enjoyed the book and admire the writer very much for basing the whole story on two 1947 jokes. The first one that got around was the one where a small principality couldn't get Marshall Plan money because it had no Communists to fight. Whereupon it borrowed several dozen from France and then applied for American support.

The second joke that I heard around and about in that same year concerned itself with a discussion between two members of the Israel government. They were trying to find a way to make their country more prosperous. One suggested that they declare war on the US and naturally after they lost the US would rehabilitate the country as it did so beautifully with Japan. "But Morris," says the other, "suppose we win?"

The coincidence of these tidbits with the novel is not important because I don't believe anybody owns or controls the original stories, but they do give it a kind of topical flavor which might continually remind us of the facts of the story rather than the fantasy. I am sure that the Saturday Evening Post readers were not offended.

I am, of course, repeating myself on the dismal side of the ledger. On the other side, let me say once more that I thought it a very entertaining and picturesque piece and certainly adaptable for the musical stage. Is there a way that I can have a look at your adaptation before you and Howard do anything further about it? I take it Howard is doing the lyrics. Is he also doing the book?

Please keep in touch. And remember I am not knocking the idea, but just being cautious.

Best wishes always,

[unsigned]

16 May 1955: To Paul Hollister[64]

Dear Paul:

I have your letter suggesting a song. Apparently you are not aware that a long time ago I wrote an ode to my wife. It is entitled SHE IS ALWAYS ON THE HOPPER WHEN THE BELL RINGS and is sung frequently in our house, thus establishing a copyright.[65]

I will try to call you via Amanda and see how it works.

Much love from us.

7 June 1955: To Oliver B. Schwab[66]

Dear Mr. Schwab:

Thanks for letting me have a look at "Spin The Bottle." I am afraid I don't like it very well, although I am sure it has its good points. I am returning it herewith.

Incidentally, I feel I should tell you that I have a number about grape pickers in my musical adaptation of "They Knew What They Wanted."[67] It concerns itself with the money they will earn for picking grapes and is called "Fresno Beauties." It was written a couple of years ago. I wanted you to know this so you would understand I had not lifted a similar idea expressed on the first page of the "Spin The Bottle" outline.

Thanks again.

Sincerely,

---

64 Paul M. Hollister (1890–1970), advertising executive and author. His positions included vice president of CBS and national publicity director of RKO.
65 Apparently a joke; no song by Loesser, 'She Is Always on the Hopper', is known.
66 Identity uncertain, possibly Oliver B. Schwab (dates unknown), a lawyer in Beverly Hills who among other cases sometimes litigated copyright disputes.
67 *The Most Happy Fella.*

Two short notes to the literary agent Bertha Klausner show that Loesser was once connected to *The Last Resorts*, an adaptation of Cleveland Amory's book:

29 March 1956: To Bertha Klausner (Telegram)[68]

ONLY ONE BIT COMPLETED OF LAST RESORTS. PRODUCER MAILING ME IN A FEW DAYS. LOVE TO YOU + RICHARD.
FRANK LOESSER

11 April 1956: To Bertha Klausner

Dear Bertha:

Just received the following note from Bobby Griffith and Hal Prince[69] re "THE LAST RESORTS":

"We do not feel the script of THE LAST RESORTS is ready for appraisal at this time. Therefore, we will not be sending it to you."

As soon as I have further word from the boys, will get in touch with you.

Best to Richard and yourself.

Sincerely,

[unsigned]

FRANK LOESSER

After nearly five years in the works, *The Most Happy Fella* was by mid-1955 close to completion. Lynn Loesser finally decided on a co-producer, Kermit Bloomgarden, turning down Lawrence Langner (1890–1962) and Armina Marshall (1895–1991) of the Theatre Guild, who had been interested. Herb Greene was hired as music director and Joseph Anthony (1912–1993) as director. In a series of letters and

---

68 Bertha Klausner (1901–1998), a literary agent.
69 Robert E. Griffith and Harold Prince (1938–2019). With the legendary Harold Prince, Griffith co-produced Adler and Ross's *The Pajama Game* and *Damn Yankees* as well as the landmark *West Side Story*. Prince's other production credits include *Fiddler on the Roof* and *Cabaret*, as well as directing musicals by Stephen Sondheim and Andrew Lloyd Webber.

memos, Loesser detailed for Greene directions for promoting the score; and a little less than three weeks before the opening he sent Anthony remarkably detailed comments – typical for Loesser – on the staging, character motivation and dramaturgy of the production.

8 July 1955: Lynn Loesser to Lawrence Langner

Dear Mr. Langner:

After a great deal of thought, I have decided on Kermit Bloomgarden as my co-producer. The deciding factor for me was that he will be available exclusively for our show from October until we open, and I as a novice producer feel a great comfort in the security of undivided attention.

I am very flattered and grateful that you and your wonderful Theatre Guild wanted me and my "Treasure" with you. I hope we can be associated on another production in the future.

I am looking forward to visiting your exciting Stratford Theatre this summer and hope when I do, I'll have the pleasure of seeing you and your wife. I saw "The Meanest Man in the World"[70] on television and loved it. I hope some day I can be as good a producer as she is.

Thank you again for your interest.

Best wishes always,

11 January 1956: To Herb Greene

Dear Herb: Under separate cover, have just sent you a vast and impenetrable sea of crap which you will have to wade through in the interest of FMC.[71]

First, there is the master demo tape #2 of the production "THE MOST HAPPY FELLA." This includes 8 recorded numbers as described outside, and inside, and all over the box. These are the first 8 numbers from the production to be worked on by FMC.

---

70 Sidney Lumet's production of Joseph Julian and Augustin MacHugh's *The Meanest Man in the World* was broadcast on *The United States Steel Hour* on 6 July 1955. It was produced by the Theatre Guild.
71 Frank Music Corp.

In addition there are included one (1) 78' acetate each of these numbers for your convenience and for immediate listening These are also for your convenience in a very important current matter.

PLEASE NOTE THE WAY THEY ARE LABELLED. THESE LABELS HAVE BEEN TYPED ON THE BACK SIDE OF A REGULAR FMC LABEL AND UNTIL FURTHER NOTICE THIS IS THE ONLY WAY TO LABEL THESE EXCERPTS. THEY ARE NOT COMPOSITIONS, NUMBERS, OR SONGS, BUT I REPEAT EXCERPTS.

I suggest that before anything goes wrong, you ask Judy[72] to make a sample label by copying from each of these acetates so that identification of song titles with Act #, Scene # is a matter of permanent record for the future use of such labels. There will follow further compositions at a later date with similar instructions.

Only four of the above numbers (what we lovingly call 'the big four') are at present to be demonstrated to anyone anywhere except you and Judy, and Betty Good, if you feel like it.

The 'big four' are:

THE MOST HAPPY FELLA	- Feb. 15th release
JOEY, JOEY, JOEY	- April 1st release
SOMEBODY SOMEWHERE	- " " "
STANDING ON THE CORNER	- " " "

The additional four numbers are simply for your advance information and their release dates are possibly by May 15th. I do not suggest that without special orders from Mike [Sukin], that you demonstrate these for anyone.

Also, in another package, are 8 copies each of the black printed music of 'the big four.' They are for your immediate and most judicious use and I suggest that in delivering them you deliver one at a time until requested for more copies. Please ask for more copies well in advance of your needs as I prefer that you do not make duplicate skins in the west.

As Mike has probably told you, "THE MOST HAPPY FELLA" is your first and very immediate project, and I suggest that you play the

---

72 Judy Hicks (dates unknown), head of music at Frank Music.

very poor demo of this song for [Ross] Bagdasarian[73] in the hope that he will record it as a new Alfi & Harry record. I understand these two urchins have planned two new sides, but since our release date on "MOST HAPPY FELLA" is Feb. 15th, I suggest that they use the best of their already planned second sides and make "THE MOST HAPPY FELLA" the second side. Shortly I will have advised Bag of my wishes on "THE MOST HAPPY FELLA" and hope Liberty[74] concurs. It is vitally important to FMC to get this title across, and I can't think of a better performer than Bagdasarian (provided he rehearses and thinks clearly).

There is only one way to deliver physical properties connected with my show to A&R[75] men or record performers. It is as follows: The space provided for on the labels should be filled in wherever possible with the name of the A&R man, record executive, or specific performer to whom you hand it. Along with the manual or mailed delivery of such demos should go one of the form letters provided by me on my stationery, which I have also sent along to you. In these instances you are acting as personal representative for Frank Loesser and not as a FMC employee.

The fact of the matter is that these excerpts from my show are still my property and not as yet assigned to FMC. It also might interest you to know that none of these individual excerpts in themselves are copyrighted but that the entire production is a single copyright.

If you will study the letter, you will get a glimpse of my intentions, attached to each letter should be an example of the license form referred to. A supply of these is also included. There are six letters and six licenses and you will receive whatever extra supply you may require, providing you ask for them well in advance. Please tell Judy that in addressing the recipient she need not concern herself with the difference in typewriter type as that represented in the form letter.

---

73 Ross Bagdasarian (aka David Seville, 1919–1972), American singer and songwriter; he is best known for creating the band Alvin and the Chipmunks. In 1955, under the pseudonym Alfi & Harry, he recorded a novelty song, 'The Trouble with Harry', based on Alfred Hitchcock's film of the same name.
74 Liberty Records, for whom Bagdasarian recorded.
75 Artists & Repertoire.

She may date all such letters the actual date of delivery. The license forms need no filling in but are simply exhibits.

If anybody in the record industry questions your intentions in providing these letters and license forms along with music and demo records, you may hasten to assure them that receiving them does not imply any commitment on their part and that they should immediately refer all questions to their own legal departments with whom my attorney, Harold Orenstein, has been in touch or will be.

After you and Judy have digested everything in this letter, I invite you to call up with intelligent questions and then maybe I'll find out what I'm talking about. Suffice it to say I am never content unless I am pissing in an otherwise clear puddle.

Love,

FRANK LOESSER

P.S. Be sure to keep an accurate record of the date, place and delivery of demos and copies of the songs. If you simply play a demo for anyone and do not deliver any material to him or her, you have no obligation to fuss with all the above. Simply keep a notation.

15 April 1956: Notes to Joseph Anthony[76]

JOE ANTHONY from FRANK LOESSER – 4/15/56

The following for the First Scene is intended to give us a somewhat different ROSABELLA than previously. A great variety of minds who have seen our show seemed to agree that we are dealing with a virginal sort of ingenue. Consequently we believe the end of the First Act to be a rape scene. Also we give the girl very little chance to express herself positively but merely let her become the pawn of a plot. I think this scene, as re-written, succeeds in showing her to be a girl of like character of the other girls in her surroundings – typically defensive and some respects hard-shelled, but with a big soft spot which nothing and nobody has touched until this exact moment in her life.

I prefer not to see ROSABELLA at all until her entrance from up stage and the scene with the CASHIER. After the CASHIER shoos the

---

76 Joe Anthony (1912–1993), American stage director. These notes are written on half-sheets, like memos.

table cloth dancers out, I think he should walk down to ROSABELLA'S two tables.

Please discuss this with me as soon as possible.

JOE ANTHONY from FRANK LOESSER – 4/15/56

ROSABELLA should not take her cap and apron off but should appear waitress-like as long as possible in the first scene. Maybe you can find a much later spot for her to take the cap and apron off. It might belong with CLEO's putting on of her black coat.

JOE ANTHONY from FRANK LOESSER – 4/15/56

Scene 2, I believe we should start tension music with TONY's idea that when he watches JOE during the valigia monologue.[77] I think he should be pretty close to JOE and up stage of him and begin singing "Soon you gonna leave me" right though the valigia talk, passing JOE and walking down stage. JOE discontinues his monologue on hearing the first line and then gets up, as he does currently. When he sings the little duet passage with TONY it should be done laughingly and an audible laugh should continue out of it and be interrupted by "Ma, every morning."

JOE ANTHONY from FRANK LOESSER – 4/15/56

In scene 3 at the point where ROSABELLA has just said "Be sure and tell all your friends", I believe the whole idea of ROSABELLA being trapped by social pressure of Tony's sentimental community — could be expressed by the sudden return of at least a partial group of bacci[78] ball players, etc. Some of these could come from down right and therefore physically block any possible exit. As they enter they of course know her from her photograph and immediately trap her with smiling greetings. We then centralize and point out ROSABELLA's first helpless response because of her fundamental weakness for handsome and friendly faces and a few seconds later we hear the lady scream and we see TONY brought in.

---

77 A reference to the number 'Joey, Joey' and the ensuing dialogue between Joe and Tony.
78 *Recte*: bocce, an Italian bowling game.

JOE ANTHONY from FRANK LOESSER – 4/15/56

I am not sure of the following, but would like your opinion and possibly we could try it:

At the point where the crowd greets ROSABELLA most of them smiling or with out-stretched hands, the little girl (who has led some of them back) curtseying, the little boy bowing, etc., and the entire group babbling "How do you do" and "Oh, it's Rosabella" and "Isn't she pretty", etc., we see ROSABELLA helplessly nodding, trying to smile, and at the same time looking for a way to escape them, we freeze and cut off the babble and fix the people in their friendly welcoming attitudes as ROSABELLA now does "No home, no job" etc. changing "That old man" to "an old man." The scream of the woman can then break up the freeze and we see TONY being brought in.

Incidentally, in the above babble there is no reason why JOE cannot say "Hey folks this is Rosabella. She just arrived" and the little girl come in up stage saying "I told you she was here."

JOE ANTHONY from FRANK LOESSER – 4/15/56

I would like you to try the following in the sex part of Scene 3.

At the big clinch near the porch, she should not make a break but this should be the final assent. I think they should break apart slowly but just enough to look at the house and then very obviously start to exit up stage with topic A in mind. If she makes two escapes, as at present, it may be inferred that she is going to make 12 or 15 and keep it up all night. When and if he finally catches up to her, it may then be assumed that he is committing rape since her consent has been at the very best a wavering one and a tentative one.

JOE ANTHONY from FRANK LOESSER – 4/15/56

In the finale of the show, there may be a greater symbolic value in TONY's holding out the pin to ROSABELLA which she does not accept until "I want to get married." This gives TONY the opportunity to walk towards her in stages during "I don' no [sic] nothing" etc., and when she finally accepts the pin at the same time they go into the embrace. I think there is a greater symbolic significance.

CHAPTER FIVE

1956–58
THE MOST HAPPY FELLA AND
THE MUSIC MAN

With a week to go before the opening of *The Most Happy Fella* at the Imperial Theatre in New York on 3 May 1956, the playwright Samuel A. Taylor wrote to wish Loesser good luck ('I felt quite sure that the show would be a hit because – like me – you don't believe in failure. But much more important is the fact that you have done exactly, and with great flair, the thing you set out to do'). The show was greeted with mixed but largely positive reviews and ran until December 1957 for a 676-performance run, though it had stiff competition in Lerner and Loewe's blockbuster *My Fair Lady*, which had opened on 15 March. In the *Hollywood Reporter*, Leonard Hoffman admitted that *The Most Happy Fella* boasted 'an advance sale of half a million dollars, great word of mouth reports, and the cheers of an opening night audience' but countered that the show 'is like a huge, multi-tiered wedding cake. One slice might be enjoyable, but having eaten the whole cake, with its gaudy melange of dramatic and musical dressing, ranging all the way from tragic opera to musical comedy, only resulted for me in a case of severe indigestion.'[1] Other reviewers raved: Brooks Atkinson wrote in the *New York Times* that 'in its most serious moments "The Most Happy Fella" is a profoundly moving dramatic experience', adding that 'Broadway is used to heart.

---

1 Leonard Hoffman, 'The New York Play: *The Most Happy Fella*', *Hollywood Reporter* 139/32 (4 May 1956), 3–4.

Excerpt from Act I Scene II

Standing On The Corner

KERMIT BLOOMGARDEN and LYNN LOESSER
present
FRANK LOESSER'S MUSICAL

THE MOST HAPPY FELLA

starring ROBERT WEEDE

with JO SULLIVAN · ART LUND
SUSAN JOHNSON · SHORTY LONG
MONA PAULEE

based on SIDNEY HOWARD'S
"THEY KNEW WHAT THEY WANTED"

orchestra and choral direction by HERBERT GREENE
orchestrations by DON WALKER
choreography by DANIA KRUPSKA
costumes by MOTLEY
scenery and lighting by JO MIELZINER
directed by JOSEPH ANTHONY

from the score
SOMEBODY, SOMEWHERE
JOEY, JOEY, JOEY
STANDING ON THE CORNER
THE MOST HAPPY FELLA
DON'T CRY
BIG D
WARM ALL OVER
MY HEART IS SO FULL OF YOU

©-Copyright 1956 by FRANK LOESSER
FRANK MUSIC CORP.

8. Title page of the sheet music for 'Standing on the Corner'
from *The Most Happy Fella*, 1956.

It is not accustomed to evocations of the soul.'[2] Loesser's friends, the distinguished writers Noël Coward (1899–1973) and Harold Arlen (1905–1986), sent their congratulations after the opening.

3 May 1956: To Samuel Taylor (Telegram)

THANKS FOR YOUR NICE LETTER. WISH YOU WERE HERE HOLDING MY HAND. LOVE TO YOU AND SUZANNE.
FRANK LOESSER

9 May 1956: Noël Coward to Loesser (Telegram)

DEAR FRANK THANK YOU FOR A WONDERFUL EVENING A BEAUTIFUL SCORE AND LYRICS AND MUCH ENCHANTMENT=
=NOEL COWARD=

1 June 1956: Harold Arlen to Frank and Lynn Loesser

Dear Frank & Lynn:
Sweet thanks for the beautiful location. It is an exciting evening in the theatre.

My only criticism is that you overpowered us with too many goodies and a mite of restraint might have lessened the exhaustive pull. But again may I repeat, it is an evening to be remembered and it was good to sit and listen to a friend's work, who through the years has kept growing musically.

Love to you both,
[signed:] Harold

Unusually, the original cast album was recorded in a longer format, on two vinyl LPs, which required more than one recording day. Most of the score was included, rather than just highlights. *Variety* noted

2 Brooks Atkinson, 'Theatre: Loesser's Fine Music Drama', *New York Times*, 4 May 1956, 20.

the distinctive approach in a brief news item headed 'Editing is Loesser of 2 Evils on "Happy Fella"; 2 Dates for Long Score'.[3] While it may not have enjoyed the popular success of *Guys and Dolls*, *The Most Happy Fella* showed Loesser's sophistication as a composer of a three-act musical with a lot of music in it (articles of the time normally refer to the score as containing thirty-five songs). He sent a telegram to thank musical director Herb Greene and the orchestra for their great efforts.

25 June 1956: To Herb Greene (Telegram)

DEAR HERB: PLEASE IN MY BEHALF THANK NANO, FARBER, AND MACE FOR THEIR WIRES. AND THANK THE BOYS ON THE CUT LIST[4] FOR THEIR NICE CARD AND THANK THE BOYS FOR THE BOOZE. ALSO IN GENERAL THANK GOD FOR A GREAT ORCHESTRA. LOVE.
    FRANK LOESSER

And there was appreciation in *Variety* for one of Loesser's cleverest marketing innovations: 'In an offbeat promotion for the venture, Loesser gave key [disk] jockeys around the country a chance to buy a piece of the show. And many of them did invest, thus giving them a personal stake in spinning the tunes. Loesser also made the same offer to the artists & repertoire chiefs of the major disk companies . . . Whether that was any influence in Loesser getting unusually wide disk coverage on the "Fella" tunes from companies other than Columbia, which snagged the cast album, is undetermined, but the Loesser offer is certainly regarded as slick public relations.'[5] Loesser knew steps had to be taken to support both the box office and the commercial success of his score, attested to by communications to

---

3 Anon., 'Editing is Loesser of 2 Evils on "Happy Fella"; 2 Dates for Long Score', *Variety* 202/10 (9 May 1956), 41.
4 Each Broadway theatre had a minimum number of musicians that had to be hired; any above this number were on a 'cut list', which meant that they could be given notice after a certain point.
5 Anon., 'Loesser's "Most Happy Partners"', *Variety* 202/10 (9 May 1956), 41.

Bill Randle (1923–2004), the leading disc jockey in America in the 1950s, based in Cleveland, Ohio.

19 August 1956: To Bill Randle

Dear Bill:

This is a reminder about our theoretical project with the Doris Day recording of "Somebody, Somewhere."[6] I am sure you realize from the intensity of my conversation how important it is for me to learn that I am not a complete fool and have some commercial guts left in my career. Please let me know the extent of your contribution on this particular record, and my forces will be checking on the actual sale market in your area, as time goes on. I consider this a great favor, and it may turn out to be a valuable lesson. The worst it can do is to increase awareness in the Cleveland area of "The Most Happy Fella," in which I want you to be a proud investor.

Many thanks for a very nice time at breakfast the other day. I hope we can repeat it again soon, maybe without any schemes but just philosophical conversation.

Meanwhile, for letting me know what you are doing, you can reach me at Frank Music Corp., 119 West 57th Street, New York City, Columbus 5-7337.

Thanks again.

Very cordially,

FRANK LOESSER

In November, Loesser returned to give a new set of notes and suggestions to the director (Joe Anthony) and musical director (Herb Greene) of *The Most Happy Fella*. Maintaining a hit was not just a question of good marketing: the show itself had to continue to be polished.

---

6 Doris Day's recording of 'Somebody, Somewhere' from *The Most Happy Fella* was made on 24 February 1956 and released on 19 March, pre-dating the Broadway opening by several weeks. Day was accompanied by Frank DeVol and his orchestra.

1 November 1956: To Herb Greene

Dear Herb:

Here are a handful of notes extracted from a much more complex group of notes from me to Joe Anthony. These apply specifically to your department and so I extracted them. Any questions?

Love,
FRANK LOESSER

NOTES TO HERB GREENE: November 1st, 1956   FROM: Frank Loesser
The singing by Rosabella, Scene I, Act I, "genuine amethyst tie-pin," the word "tie-pin" is vocalized at too great a length. I'll illustrate shortly.

Jo Sullivan hangs on to the last syllable of "this young fella" and vocalizes the vowel "a" instead of simply intoning the syllable "uh." I'll illustrate.

The angry music under Shorty's two speeches to Joe after the accident is much too loud and I can never hear Shorty. Try and blast in the spaces.

"Cold and Dead" as slow as possible, as we have discussed.

In "Love and Kindness" the Doc is singing the word "the" stronger than the word "nurse." The register differential is the reason for this, but I believe he can, without too much strain, resume his mezza voce delivery of "the" and push the word "nurse."

The song "How Beautiful the Days" was put together so that it would be a concurrent expression of the phrase "how beautiful the days" by all members of the quartet. However great the difference in their various points of view. For this reason I wish you would have a brief conference with the contestants to the end that when this phrase occurs we have a well-balanced quartet delivery of it with [Robert] Weede carrying the basic tune a couple of decibels stronger than the others carry their parts, and upon completion of this gigantic effort, resume the dynamic differential required for identification of each individual. Know what I mean?

The Doc's delivery of "Folks! Folks!!" should actually interrupt the music and should rise above the sound of the music. Possibly you and

Kaldenberg can discuss this so that the cut off of the music occurs at a non-final musical point.

The Brakeman is yelling "All aboard" in the wrong place during "Tell Tony and Rosabella."

Loesser even managed to obtain some unusual exposure for the show when it was the subject of an episode of the popular Lucille Ball (1911–1990) television show *I Love Lucy* in March 1957. News of the episode was reported in *Variety*: 'The filmed stanza is being produced on the Coast, using settings representing various New York locales, including the Imperial Theatre, where the Frank Loesser-Sidney Howard tuner is playing.'[7] Loesser wrote to thank Ball's husband, actor Desi Arnaz (1917–1986), who was co-star of the show, playing Ricky Ricardo. And to the journalist Leonard Lyons (1906–1976) of the *New York Post* he actively promoted the publication of the piano-vocal score of *The Most Happy Fella*, which took a slightly unusual format, complementing the approach to the recording of the original cast album.

1 April 1957: To Desi Arnaz

Dear Desi:

I gave up an encounter with some extraordinary quiff[8] for the purpose of seeing "I Love Lucy" last Monday night. This is to tell you how immensely I enjoyed it and how grateful I am to you and all your people for a really wonderful as well as understanding plug for "The Most Happy Fella."

I didn't miss what I could have had that evening. As a matter of fact, I may permanently give up banging on Monday nights in favor of looking at you and Lucy. I hope you both feel flattered as I am a very sexy fellow.

Really and truly, thanks.

Love,

FRANK LOESSER

7 Anon., 'Legitimate: "Lucy" Will Plug "Fella" On TV Film From Coast', *Variety* 205/11 (13 February 1957), 91.
8 Slang for a promiscuous woman; Loesser is of course being humorous.

26 May 1957: To Leonard Lyons

Dear Lenny:

Here's the combination libretto and vocal score. Actually it has been in print and distributed since the last few weeks. Should I send Mr. Bright one? He seemed interested but I don't exactly know what he covers, or what he would say about it. Would you call me after you have looked it over? The point of this edition is that the script is readable in sequence for those that wish to read it as a play. As far as I know this has never been done with a musical show vocal score.

Love,

FRANK LOESSER

The Most Happy Fella was the longest, most complicated and most sophisticated musical Loesser would write, and its completion after several years of work was a significant milestone. But in private, Loesser had been facing challenges around his health.

18 February 1957: To Arthur Loesser

Dear Arthur –

I have had my throat cut again[9] – NOTHING SERIOUS – just the result of neglect on my part (SMOKING + TALKING) after the last job.[10] What I had was a recurrence of discrete (Oxford Engl. Dict. Pathol. Definition – sub-definition #c) polyps on the vocal cords.

I now have to shut up and smoke less.

I have your recent communication with clipping of some tardy but valuable columnist remarks about MHF.

Soon I'll be sending you a report from my mgr. at Music Theatre Inc – about his dealings with KARAMU[11] – not very complimentary to them as regards their management but nothing too serious –

---

9 The surgery – Loesser's third on his throat – was also briefly mentioned in Mike Connolly's column in The Hollywood Reporter on 20 February 1957, 2.
10 The Most Happy Fella.
11 Karamu House in Cleveland, Ohio is the oldest African American theatre in the United States, opening in 1915. Arthur's interest is unclear but may have been related to Karamu's music programme.

Cleveland – as witness the ALPINE VILLAGE[12] exploits – seems to be the home of copyright abuse.

Are you + Jean well? Since seeing you I had a lovely evening with Ann + John.

I'll be in Nassau with daughter Susan from Feb 19th to 27th and will miss your next visit here – but I'll be more in shape for discussing life, music, etymology etc. if I don't get myself hoarse too soon – so the next trip will be the one.

love

Frank

Not only was Loesser undergoing health problems, his marriage to Lynn had come to an end as well. His daughter Susan describes how his relationship with Jo Sullivan, the young star of *The Most Happy Fella*, blossomed during the show's tryouts: '[Lynn] would walk into a restaurant and [Frank and Jo] would be there at a table for two. She would try to reach him about a problem or a decision and he would be "unavailable". Everybody could see what was happening, and everybody was talking about it. But not with a whole lot of sympathy. After all, they said to each other, Lynn was almost asking for it, the way she acted, the way she drank.'[13] Frank and Lynn separated and the family moved into two residences in New York in the spring of 1956, after the opening of *The Most Happy Fella* in May. Subsequent correspondence describes Frank's new life with Sullivan, for example in travel plans. And domestic correspondence has

---

12 Cleveland's Alpine Village Theatrical Bar and Restaurant operated between 1935 and 1961. According to John Vacha, the venue put on an unauthorised production of *Guys and Dolls*: 'In 1951 the hot show on Broadway was Frank Loesser's *Guys and Dolls*, and [John L.] Price drew the assignment of pirating the show's plot and songs for the Alpine Village. "I paid to see the first and second acts six or seven times, but knew the second act better because I walked in so many times after intermission without paying," he later confessed. Given his intense exposure to the show, Price was bound to either love it or loathe it; happily, it became one of his perennial favorites. Loesser, hearing of the theft, wasn't at all happy, but his reported threats to bring suit were never carried through.' John Vacha, *The Music Went 'Round and Around: The Story of Musicarnival* (Kent, OH, and London, 2004), 8.

13 Loesser, *A Most Remarkable Fella*, 152.

survived more readily for this period, hinting at some of the everyday details of his life.

5 June 1957: To M. E. Ricketts (Telegram)

PLEASE PAY PAN-AMERICAN AIRWAYS IMMEDIATELY FOR TWO ROUND TRIP TICKETS NAMES OF FRANK LOESSER AND JO SULLIVAN FLIGHT 114 NEW YORK TO PARIS JUNE TENTH. FLIGHT 101 LONDON TO NEW YORK JULY SIXTH. HAVE THEM WIRE THEIR NEW YORK OFFICE IMMEDIATELY. AM ANXIOUS TO HAVE TICKETS IN MY HANDS. REGARDS.
    FRANK LOESSER

7 October 1957: To Rose Larson

Dear Rose:

Enclosed, is my check for $16.33 covering the balance you request for the electric bill.

On the question of the wagon, my man Harold is of the distinct impression that I paid the grocer for it. He has the grocer's adding-machine slip for the day he got it, and one item is $13.00 which he says could not possibly have been for anything else. I wonder whether you would check this with the grocer to satisfy yourself that we have already paid for it. I, myself, remember at the time that Harold told me he had bought one, and there was no indication that anyone else had paid for it, or intended to. I sincerely hope that you can straighten this out. Please let me know.

Kindest wishes.

Sincerely

FRANK LOESSER

By February 1958, the Loessers' divorce was being gossiped about inaccurately, as Frank wryly informed the talent agent Herman Citron, whose clients at MCA included Alfred Hitchcock. And at times Loesser had to communicate the separate relationship to business correspondents such as a young playwright, Robert Beihoff (dates unknown).

10 February 1958: To Herman Citron

Dear Herman:

Thanks for your alarming note. Just in case anybody should ask you, I am still married to Lynn Loesser (until sometime in March). Furthermore, I have no plans to get married, nor have I ever had any. Sometimes I wonder why the citizens of Hollywood don't read the gossip items with the same fish-eye they give to printed picture grosses.

But thanks for your good wishes anyway and I'll hoard them against that dim distant day when I might possibly once again wind up in the community property racket.

Love and kisses,

1 April 1958: To Robert Beihoff

Dear Mr. Beihoff:

My name is Frank. My ex-wife's name is Lynn. She is the producer. I am the writer. If you meant your letter of February 23rd for her, I'll forward it to her. If you meant it for me, I must tell you that I have three years work ahead of me already prescribed and can't even think about a new project now.

In my youth I was reading Captain Billy's Whizz-Bang[14] and not Labiche. If in the next while I get to read "La Voyage De Monsieur Perrichon"[15] and find out what we are discussing, I'll write you at least my reflections.

Thanks.

Sincerely,

The Polish-born American author David Ewen (1907–1985) was significant as one of the first serious writers to publish books on both classical music and Broadway composers. For example, he followed up *The Book of Modern Composers* (1942) and *Encyclopedia of the Opera* (1955) with a *Panoroma of American Popular Music* (1957)

---

14 A reference to a joke in Meredith Willson's *The Music Man*.
15 *Recte*: *Le Voyage de Monsieur Perrichon*, a French play from 1860 by Eugène Labiche and Édouard Martin.

and a *Complete Book of the American Musical Theater* (1958). He shared his draft of a section on Loesser for the latter book, and Frank responded with some comments.

19 November 1956: To David Ewen

Dear Mr. Ewen:

Thanks for sending me your unedited sections referring to me. A few comments, if you don't mind:

On page 38, you refer to the impression that the Rodger Young incident[16] had on me, etc. This is not particularly the case. Infantry officials expressed themselves as being somewhat miffed that no heroic Infantryman had been singled out and delivered to the public as a symbol as had various Air Force heroes, such as Colin Kelly. The Infantry approached me to write a song which would glorify "The Infantryman." This came at a time when many an Air Force mechanic or Quartermaster non-com was being deployed to Infantry (which means getting not only muddy but possibly shot at) in anticipation of the coming need for a huge ground force in Europe. The re-deployment process threatened to make many mothers, fathers and wives uncomfortable about what was in store for their loved one who had, to date, led a relatively safe life in the Army. The Infantry seemed to feel that this was the time to advertise the noble identity of the footsoldier with the rifle. They gave me the job of writing a song which would have this effect. In planning a song, I sent to Washington for a list of Infantrymen who had been posthumously awarded the Medal of Honor. I received a list of only about twelve names. Of these, eleven, however heroic the exploit of each – had singularly unheroic names, such as Janikowski, Gromet, Drla, etc. The twelfth was Rodger Young. He was singable. He made as good a sound as Nathan Hale, Daniel Boone, or Molly Malone. The rest was a matter of methodical research into the details of his very brave action. The song was completed about a week after I had read his name. Previously his valorous deed had

---

16 See Chapter 1 for more information on this song.

been celebrated by one stick of type in his hometown newspaper. The results you know. My attempt was to make a narrative form depicting an individual's life and <u>death</u> by reviewing the fundamental common concept of "Barbara Allen," "Dan McGrew," "Frankie and Johnnie," "Molly Malone," "Brennan on the Moor," "John Brown's Body," and countless others. I concluded that there must be, at least in our western world, a profound attractiveness in the recital of the events of a heroic or romantic individual's life, ending in a description of his or her death. In the most universal form we have the stories of Jesus and Joan of Arc, or more localized ones such as that of Lincoln. These stories, especially when translated into the poetry of song, have a way of living on and on. I was consciously aiming for a "standard" using a form that had seemed to work for many centuries. The detail of the poetic form itself resembles "Hiawatha" – not metrically, but in the repetition of the verb forms in an attempt at emphasis. All the above is written for the purpose of pointing out to you that I think I am more a purposeful craftsman than a wandering minstrel. You may not quote me directly on any of the above.

On page 332, you refer to the writing of "Jingle, Jangle, Jingle."[17] My intention was to write a jocular song, but not necessarily a satirical one. I don't think that it can be called a ballad. If it has any outstanding characteristic, it is that it is printed in two voice staves in canon form. This was the forerunner of the group of two voice pieces that I have become identified with, such as "Baby, It's Cold Outside," "Make a Miracle," "No Two People," "Happy to Make Your Acquaintance."

At the top of page 333, you seem to be referring to solo song efforts of mine. If this is the case, then "Hoop-Dee-Doo"[18] cannot be

---

17 '[I've Got Spurs That] Jingle, Jangle, Jingle' was written by composer Joseph J. Lilley (1913–1971) and Loesser in 1942. It appears in the film *The Forest Rangers* (1942) and was also recorded in a number 1 hit cover by bandleader Kay Kyser (1905–1985).

18 'Hoop-Dee-Doo' had music by Milton Delugg (1918–2015) and words by Loesser. It was published in 1950 and recorded by Perry Como and the Fontane Sisters in March of that year.

included since it is a collaboration with Milton Delugg. It is not quite accurate to say that since "Praise the Lord [and Pass the Ammunition]" I have been without a collaborator. Since then I have written an entire score with Arthur Schwartz[19] and a couple of pieces (not yet published) with Johnny Green. I have no fixed policy about collaboration.

On page 346, you hurt me, but not too deeply, by a reference to a couple of songs in the score of "Where's Charley?" Of course your opinion is involved, so I have no strong suggestion to make, except possibly to recall that "My Darling, My Darling" remained Number Two on the Hit Parade for many many weeks. Its failure to get to the Number One spot was occasioned by the fact that "On A Slow Boat to China"[20] insisted on holding the spot during the entire period.

Of course I don't want to alter your opinion in the slightest, but I take it that this book is to be read by the public. The individual reader would recognize "[Once in Love with] Amy" and "Darling" as more memorable titles than "What Do You Do in the Infantry," which you seem to make much of in an earlier paragraph. This latter was a minor item in my "war effort" compared to "They're Either Too Young or Too Old" or "In My Arms," both of which are reasonably recognizable titles.

I seem to be scolding. Don't believe a word of it. At the same time, consider that you have become the leading authority on composers and their lives and works. Not being as dead as Mozart, I am here in the interest of preserving your good reputation for accuracy. Many thanks for all your interest.

Very cordially,
FRANK LOESSER

---

19 Loesser and composer Schwartz wrote the score to the cavalcade film *Thank Your Lucky Stars* in 1943. The movie included the song 'They're Either Too Young or Too Old', which was nominated for an Academy Award.
20 Loesser seems to be defending his score for *Where's Charley?*, including the song 'My Darling, My Darling', on the basis that the latter was second on the Hit Parade only to another Loesser song, 'On a Slow Boat to China'.

P.S: I am about to listen to the Portnoff[21] record and will communicate separately on this.

P.P.S: On your carbon manuscript, I have indicated some corrections in song titles.

The years 1956 and 1957 showed Loesser's activities expanding across different areas of production and publishing, and rumours of his work appeared more regularly in the press following the opening of *The Most Happy Fella*. An article in *Variety* reported on Frank Music's '1957 expansion program' with not only a 'personnel reshuffle' – Stuart Ostrow was to move from the West Coast office to become executive assistant to the general manager Herb Eiseman – but also a widening focus: 'In the expansion blueprint are projected buildups for all of Frank's subsid operations. They are the recently formed Frank Productions, which will hold future legit musical scores and tv spec[ial] scores; Saunders Publications, a purchased catalog which is now holding most of Arthur Hamilton's songs; Empress Music, which contains the Bessie Smith catalog; Audubon Music, which holds foreign copyrights; Liberty Songs, firm jointly operated by Frank and Liberty Records; Globarry Music, recently established firm for arranger-composer Buddy Bregman copyrights, and Desilu Music, firm set up to hold tunes emanating from telepix produced by Desilu.'[22] Of note, there is an emphasis here on purchasing catalogues of music that did not emanate from the theatre: Arthur Hamilton (born 1926) was known for writing the pop hit 'Cry Me a River', Bessie Smith (1894–1937) was a blues singer, Buddy Bregman (1930–2017) was an arranger for recording artists including Ella Fitzgerald, and Desilu was the company of television stars Lucille Ball and Desi Arnaz. Loesser also signed up as 'General Music consultant', through Frank Productions, to the global marketing agency Young and Rubicam in the spring of 1957, thus making both the Frank Music back catalogue and its writers available to write jingles

---

21 Probably a reference to Russian-born composer Leo Portnoff (1875–1940).
22 Anon., 'Set Expansion Gait for Loesser Subsids', *Variety* 205/8 (23 January 1957), 43.

for any medium.[23] Typically smart, Loesser could see the commercial sense of looking beyond Broadway.

It is also noticeable that by this point, Loesser was increasingly passing on submissions to his staff for their advice or opinions, though he would still get involved in scrutinising them; he needed to delegate if he was to expand. Among his correspondents were actress Rosalind Russell (1907–1976, wife of producer Frederick Brisson, 1912–1984), who had submitted a song for Frank Music's consideration; the writer David Dachs (?–1980), who had written a musical, *Love from Sandy*, with his songwriter wife, Julie Mandel (born 1923); and Ted McMichael (1908–2001), a member of the Merry Macs vocal quartet.

29 June 1956: To Mrs. F. Brisson [Rosalind Russell]

Dear Ros:

Thanks for your little note, and also for the song you sent along. My professional staff and I will be going over the song very shortly, and should have an answer for you.

Give my very best to Freddie.

Sincerely,

17 July 1956: To David Dachs

Dear David:

I have finished reading "Love from Sandy" and I don't feel that I am overwhelmed. There are too many reasons to discuss in a letter. Nevertheless, don't let this dissuade you from marketing it, along with the songs, provided, of course, that you close no deal on Julie's end of it without Saunders Publications approval.

I will be interested to know what the TV people's reaction is. When I come back from the coast in early August, I'll call you and

---

23 June Bundy, 'Singing Commercial Dollars Cue Tin Pan Alley Respect', *Billboard* 69/20 (13 May 1957), 1, 34.

maybe you will have some news. At that time I can discuss in detail my feelings about the piece.

Sincerely,

7 August 1956: To Ted McMichael

Dear Ted:

Thanks so much for your letter. I am delighted about your ERA[24] recording deal and very interested in knowing who the group consists of outside of Jud and yourself.

I am forwarding your letter to our West Coast executive, Mr. Stuart Ostrow, suggesting that he get in touch with you. Stu is in charge of our motion picture, recording, and television relations in the West, but beyond his tremendous capabilities as a business representative, he also happens to be an experienced vocal arranger so that when you meet him you will all be speaking the same language. He will try to dig up the right things for your recordings and help you in any way he can.

My best to you all and thanks for your kind letter.

Sincerely,

FRANK LOESSER

Cc Stu Ostrow

He also continued to write humorous responses to letters from friends and acquaintances, including one to Richard Brazeau (1914–1968) of the Central Cranberry Company, Wisconsin Rapids. And though Loesser's businesses had expanded into different areas, Frank Music remained a key focus. He responded to the composer Bernie Wayne (1919–1993), whose prolific output included the standard 'Blue Velvet', about the possibility of joining the company's roster.

---

24 Era Records was an independent record label that opened in 1955. It was taken over in the 1970s by K-tel.

20 May 1957: To Richard Brazeau

Dear Dick:

I acknowledge with thanks your note of May 14th. May I observe here that any potential client who has time to read news magazines is probably not selling many cranberries. Therefore, I feel that you will welcome our special June offer:

We can deliver to you, upon your written order, a television jingle suitable for the exploitation of your product for a down-payment of $1.75, and a final payment of $2.00, plus 4 cents to cover postage, upon your receipt of the jingle or within thirty days thereafter.

In filling out our order blank, please note choice of composers. We have available now: Max Mozart, Sam Beethoven and Ed Scriabin. Among the poets we have under contract and available to you are: Ed Longfellow, and Solly Shakespeare. This latter member of our staff has been sick a while but I understand he is better and I think would be an ideal choice as lyric writer for the cranberry trade, as you know what a smash he has been with "Under the Greenwood Tree." Also, you will recall his candid commercial for Heinz' canned water chestnuts – "You blocks, you stones, you worse than senseless things."

However, take your choice and send it along with your $1.75 down-payment.

Sincerely,
FRANK LOESSER

15 August 1957: To Bernie Wayne

Dear Bernie:

Thanks for your note. I was tempted to phone you a few hours later and apologize for being such a captious critic. As usual I had my nerve with me. I guess that's the way I am.

Since our meeting I have played over your albums. You certainly are very inventive. Of course, by their very nature, albums demand a uniformity of <u>color</u> in the execution of the various numbers. Consequently, although very fine album examples, they are not very much of a clue as to what your dramatic potential is. Let's have another meeting this Fall.

Meanwhile, drop me a note telling me what the possibilities are for your becoming an ASCAP writer.

Best,

FRANK LOESSER

Complementing the publishing business, Music Theatre Incorporated[25] (MTI) was now firmly established, four years on from its creation by Loesser and orchestrator Don Walker in 1952.[26] As ever, Loesser was tenacious in his endeavours: he wrote to lyricist Alan Jay Lerner (1918–1986) and composer Frederick Loewe (1901–1988), to make a case for why they should turn to MTI for their current hit; rivalry did not seem to be a consideration. The letter shows remarkable foresight: the poor condition of the performance materials for musicals of that and earlier eras has posed incredible challenges for companies attempting to revive them.

19 September 1956: To Alan Jay Lerner and Frederick Loewe

Dear Gents:

This is just a reminder of my conversations with Fritz [Loewe] about "My Fair Lady" stock amateur representation. I know there is plenty of time before you will want to release the show for such purposes, but against the possibility that in a weak moment you go elsewhere (sheer folly) I urge you not to close anything before discussing Music Theatre Incorporated. You will note that this stationery is large enough for an extra paragraph devoted to extensive braggadocio about our company but modesty* impels me to quit at the customary 32 bars.

Love and kisses,

FRANK LOESSER

*(sic)

---

25 Later Music Theatre International.
26 For more information on the development of MTI, see Loesser, *A Most Remarkable Fella*, 228–9.

P.S. Important after-thought: You will probably soon be engaged in a lot of other matters. By the time stock and amateur rights become available you may find that nobody quite knows the exact content, sequence and manner of the score as it was performed opening night on Broadway. That is why <u>we</u> should <u>now</u> assure you perfect duplication for your National Company as well as your English Company. Otherwise bits of soft-boiled egg stain will appear on the viola parts, some 3rd trumpet player will have given way to an instinct for cartooning, and half of the choral parts, long since memorized, will have been just plain lost. At the gentle but firm hands of my partner in Music Theatre Inc., Mr. Don Walker, this sort of thing will never happen. An instance in which it did happen (and Mr. Walker had to do a huge research and reconstruction job) was in a not too old Cole Porter show[27] from which simply nothing was left but some sheet music.

A great time and money saving device is Mr. Walker's duplicating and library system, as well as music policing service. From the day that we become agents for your rights, Mr. Walker can quickly assure you that what is being played is actually on paper and not simply a product of the whim of your present conductor. I'll bet you now that part corrections are still in pencil and that the master score does not match the parts. Nor are the dynamic markings uniform. All this becomes a much greater expense to the authors at a later date when nobody remembers anything and all the original music people have been replaced. Of course, our organization advances the cost of this repair, preservation and policing service against royalties which may become due many years from now. We don't mind. We just want to keep you neat.

Well – that blew the whole page after all.

A further subject of occasional correspondence is the possibility of a stage production of *Hans Christian Andersen*, which could benefit Loesser doubly as writer and licensor through MTI. He was proud of his score and makes a case for why it would be a popular stage

---

27 Perhaps Loesser means *Kiss Me, Kate* (1948) or *Can-Can* (1953).

property for rentals by regional theatres and schools. After Loesser's death, the score was eventually used in professional stage productions with stars including Tommy Steele (London, 1974), Larry Kert (St Louis, 1981) and Michael Feinstein (St Louis, 1991).

14 October 1957: To James Mulvey, Samuel Goldwyn Productions

Dear Jim:

I have before me a copy of Harold Orenstein's October 8th letter to you concerning "Hans Christian Andersen." I am writing this not only in strong support of his suggestion, but if you will bear with me, with certain additional suggestions and requirements.

As you know, we have adapted a "free" subject. Any stranger may create a musical based on the life of Hans Christian Andersen if he so pleases. He may even use the exact title as that of the Goldwyn product without much fear of restraint by us. Now I take it that we do not want such a thing to happen, and I sincerely believe that we can fortify our unique position as THE musical adaptors by continuing to emphasize the identification of the subject with the score, which is indeed protected by us.

Toward this end I think it immensely valuable for us to create a stage version of what we have on film – for use in what we refer to as second class and amateur theatre. The principal producers of such entertainment are the summer theatre operators, schools and churches. A project similar to what I suggest has already been accomplished with "The Wizard of Oz" through the permission of M.G.M. about six years ago.[28] I feel positive that this has not damaged it. On the contrary, I am sure that this stage production has helped in making the score and story synonymous in the public's mind.

Now I do not arrive at this request idly. Only recently we have had two requests from schools for "Hans Christian Andersen" in the hope that such a version existed. I would like my company to be able to fill

---

28 In fact, the St Louis Muny adapted the MGM *Wizard of Oz* for the stage in 1942.

this order in a way by which your company would not only receive the benefits I have described above, but also a financial share of the income involved. Further I am sure that we could make arrangements by which we could retire booking of the stage version at any time during which re-release of the picture might make you feel that it was being competed with.

I wish you would consider this very carefully and then write me regarding your and Sam's[29] reaction.

My warmest good wishes as ever.

Sincerely,

Frank

Loesser wrote dozens of good luck telegrams over the years, but he was particularly attentive when his collaborators, past or present, or writers connected to one of his companies, were involved. For instance, Loesser acknowledged the first preview (31 October) and opening (1 December) of Jerome Lawrence (1915–2004) and Robert E. Lee's (1918–1994) play *Auntie Mame*, which starred Rosalind Russell (as Mame) and Polly Rowles (as Vera Charles). Loesser was never less than strategic in who he kept up with: Lawrence and Lee were writing the book for a musical for Vernon Duke (1903–1969), who intended to publish the score with Frank Music, and Russell's husband Frederick Brisson was a major Broadway producer.

31 October 1956: To Lawrence and Lee (Telegram)

EVERY GOOD WISH FOR TONIGHT. REGARDS.
FRANK LOESSER

31 October 1956: To Rosalind Russell (Telegram)

BEST OF EVERYTHING TONIGHT. LOVE.
FRANK LOESSER

---

29 Sam Goldwyn.

1 December 1956: To Polly Rowles
(Telegram)

THOUGHT YOU WERE WONDERFUL LAST NIGHT. WILL CALL
SOON. MUCH LOVE.
    FRANK LOESSER

1 December 1956: To Rosalind
Russell (Telegram)

LOVED YOU LOVED YOU LOVED YOU LAST NIGHT BUT LATE
DATE PREVENTED DRESSING ROOM COMPLIMENTS. REPEAT
LOVED YOU LOVED YOU LOVED YOU AND THE PLAY.
    FRANK LOESSER

An earlier note to Lee, whose play *Inherit the Wind* was about to open on Broadway for what would turn out to be a two-year run, reveals the name of the Duke-Lawrence-Lee musical – *Dilly* – which was ultimately unproduced.[30] The musical was based on Theodore Pratt's novel *Miss Dilly Says No* (1945). A later telegram to Lee appears to refer to casting Broadway star Mary Martin in the London production of *Auntie Mame*; Richard Halliday was Martin's husband and professional manager.

11 April 1955: To Robert E. Lee

Dear Bob:
    Thanks for your note. We will save the daily trade reviews.
    Basking, my ass, you'll be fixing up DILLY and it needs plenty.
    Good luck, again.
    Your conscience,

---

30 Duke's holograph scores for around thirty songs for the show are housed in his collection at the Library of Congress; Lawrence and Lee's working scripts are at Ohio State University.

20 August 1957: To Robert E. Lee (Telegram)

[RICHARD] HALLIDAY TURNED ME DOWN FLAT ON MARY [MARTIN]. PLEASE TELL ME WHAT OTHER STAR NOW PROPOSED FOR LONDON. I HAVE GOOD IDEA. LOVE.
    FRANK LOESSER

As for *Dilly*, an ongoing disagreement with the composer Vernon Duke came to a head.

17 January 1957: To Vernon Duke (Telegram)

=SIGN AND RETURN THOSE PAPERS YOU COSSACK. LOVE=
=FRANK LOESSER=

10 June 1957: To Herb Eiseman

Dear Herb:

On the eve of my departure, it is sad for us to learn that Vernon Duke is so very sick. It used to be a <u>grandeur</u> problem, and now it appears that the delusion is one concerning persecution. In a way it surprises me that his attack on us was sent registered mail and not nailed by hand to the front door of Frank Music Corp.[31] As in many classic attempts at "reformation" let us all see that he gets a much needed rest.

Sadly

In the new year, Loesser began work with composer, conductor, songwriter and personality Meredith Willson (1902–1984), whom he had known for at least fifteen years, since Willson had recorded Loesser's 'Praise the Lord and Pass the Ammunition' in 1942. It is well known that Loesser had encouraged Willson to write a Broadway musical, which became *The Music Man* (opening 19 December 1957),

---

31 A reference to Martin Luther's 95 Theses nailed to the door of the Wittenberg Castle Church, as 'reformation' in the following sentence makes clear.

one of the longest-running shows of the 1950s.[32] One of Loesser's newer companies, Frank Productions, was to be co-producer of the successful show with Kermit Bloomgarden (1904–1976), and over the next twelve years Loesser was deeply involved in the evolution of Willson's Broadway career, as well as close to the Willsons socially.

18 January 1957: To Harold Orenstein

KERMIT BLOOMGARDEN – "THE MUSIC MAN"

Bloomgarden has asked me to suggest a formula for Frank Productions Inc. association with his production of "THE MUSIC MAN."

I believe in exchange for our virtual co-producership and application of special energy and 'know how' in the preparation of this show for production, that we should ask for 10 percent of the general partnership's share of the show, plus a fee of $500 weekly for each running week while the show is produced by the producers. This would apply to try-out weeks, other first class companies, as well as Canadian and English companies.

Bloomgarden does not see how he can arrange for any prevailing author's share. Willson already has a script collaborator[33] who <u>apparently</u> has signed Willson all rights forever amen so that Willson appears presently as sole author-lyricist-composer. However, Bloomgarden expects to call in some established author to re-do the book and does not want to act in our behalf to secure our company a collaborative deal. Therefore, I suggest the weekly fee which we hope would be tantamount to a weekly average of one percent over a period of time. The 10 percent interest in the general partnership would net us $10,000 in the event of a $500,000 picture sale. (I quote this only as an example of the possible residual value of this deal).

The deal would be made only with the understanding that Willson had already established a complete assignment of all his music

---

32 Dominic McHugh, *The Big Parade: Meredith Willson's Musicals from 'The Music Man' to '1491'* (New York, 2021), 36.
33 Franklin Lacey (1917–1988), who is credited with Willson as co-author of the story of *The Music Man*.

publishing rights to a publisher of our choice. These rights would refer to songs, lyrics, music written for, intended for, and/or used in the production. Further, the producer would have to agree in a separate document with the publisher, that he would accept no interpolations or original writings by others unless all publishing rights in such material belonged to the publisher.

We would ask designation of the record company which would make the cast album and for approval of the dealing. We would ask for designation of the agency for stock and amateur rights, and Bloomgarden would have to secure the co-signatures of the authors along with himself, and further would agree to deliver from these authors signatures on representation for foreign productions other than Canada or England. I think we would want to designate the award of the souvenir program so that we could possibly factor its manufacture to create a proper type of income for one of our organizations.

Please discuss this with me.

24 February 1958: To Kermit Bloomgarden

Dear Kermit:

The following are some reflections and suggestions for you to consider in anticipating such a thing as a television deal on "MUSIC MAN":

Ordinarily, deals are made for single live television use at a time when such use will not destroy the box office economics of the original stage version, and usually do not take place until after the end of the first class run, or at least shortly before such a date. I believe quite strongly that single performance television rights should not be granted on this so-called "spectacular" form. It seems to me that there is a preferable kind of deal that can be made – one which would bear potentially larger incomes to the producers and possibly even larger guaranteed income. My thinking is this: The title as well as the nature of the story seems to me to be worth examination as a filmed series of half-hour musical chapters depicting the career of a pleasant con man named Harold Hill, who for possibly three years running

213

manages to cut a swath (humorously crooked, romantic, musical) on the American scene without ever finalizing or completely reforming his career by marrying anybody. This would feature someone of the same stature as Bob Preston,[34] plus a series of well-known young lady "victims," "allies," "seductresses," etc. – one lady to a program. There are cliff-hanger possibilities where Harold Hill must go to the altar if he does indeed escape from jail, or comedic finales such as used in the "I Love Lucy" formula, or musical hoopla finishes.

A deal could be made for such a series of productions now, taking advantage of the popularity of the title, and yet its filmed preparation would take considerable time so that the release of the first chapter need not be until possibly a year from now.

I frankly do not believe that such a sale would seriously damage the ultimate picture sale value of the original story (no character or story feature of which should be included in the TV series). The feature motion picture buyer will claim, of course, that the theatrical motion picture feature length values have been reduced, but I believe that in the end a very high price can be secured for this ultimate sale. At the moment we could possibly hit and run with a large cash sale from some sort of Sam Goldwyn – but neither he nor any other typical movie maker would make such a purchase without rigorous restrictions on TV uses.

Therefore, why not establish the serial TV use very soon. When the time comes for the so-called feature length motion picture sale, we may already have experienced a successful nation-wide pay TV system – at least for important features. These might very well compare gross-wide with theatrical movies and might be the preferable form of deal for an ultimate full length feature. It would therefore be wise in making a serial deal to have a control limiting the period of time in which it can be exhibited. This would protect more advantageously sales in the future.

Of course I realize I am speaking of a privilege and function of the authors when I speak of deals. Nevertheless, since we share in the

---

34 Actor Robert Preston (1918–1987) starred as Prof. Harold Hill in the original Broadway production of *The Music Man*.

benefits I think it behooves us to consider suggesting to Meredith Willson whatever opportunities we consider advantageous to all of us. I have merely sketched over roughly the principle of the idea. It may have several holes in it. Please have a meeting with me about this and if we agree on a policy we can then shoot the suggestion to Willson.

Best,

With *The Music Man* set in for a long and successful run, Willson started to sketch an idea for a sequel over the summer of 1958, tentatively called *The Son of the Music Man*. Loesser's reaction was lukewarm; sequels of Broadway musicals were unusual, and the most famous, the Gershwins' *Let 'Em Eat Cake* (1933), after the Pulitzer Prize-winning *Of Thee I Sing* (1931), was a flop. Loesser's manner to Willson is perhaps a little different from his approach to other writers of the Frank Music stable: he often goes to great lengths to make sure he is not misunderstood, and significantly invests a lot of effort in providing ideas for the promotion or development of Willson's career. He is also willing to follow Willson's wishes even when he disagrees with him. For example, he supported Willson's decision to turn down Sammy Davis Jr, one of the most commercially successful artists of the 1950s, when the singer requested to record 'Ya Got Trouble' from *The Music Man*, though it is fairly clear that Loesser himself would have granted the request.

6 August 1958: To Meredith Willson

Dear Meredith:

It might have seemed at our last meeting that I wasn't too enthusiastic, along with you, on the subject of your next show. On the other hand, it might have looked as though I were too enthusiastic, if you regard the way I grabbed the ball and tried to run with it.

I don't really know how I feel myself about the play or what there is of it at this point. That is because I have not been exposed to the idea for very long and it would be ridiculous of me to express any firm opinion on such short acquaintanceship. So this note is not to comment on the show itself, but rather to discuss your admitted and confessed "follow-up" purpose.

It seemed to me that you were sort of bent on typing yourself. I remember a conversation in which you told me that you felt equipped to write about "folks" and not much else. I thought that this was very modest of you as I believe you have an enormous scope. Nevertheless, let's agree to leave it at "folks." But do they have to be "folks" related to the music business or "folks who wind up in the finale with the band on stage and the hero conducting it"? "Pajama Game" is about "folks" and so is everybody in "Oklahoma!". I don't think the idiom has anything to do with the yarn.

What I am scared about is that you may be electing for yourself too narrow a path – one seemingly designed to fit the trimmings rather than one first designed and then trimmed. There is nothing against this unless it seems obvious that the author was following himself up.

I am sounding off here as your friend and admirer regardless of how many hits we publish. Being your friend and admirer, I guess I am entitled to be dead wrong too, and if I am, I guess you'll forgive me, but I had to tell you how I felt. Meanwhile, of course, as you go along we'll break our necks to help you in every way no matter what you do.

Love to you and Rini.[35]

Sincerely,

FRANK LOESSER

27 February 1959: To Sammy Davis Jr

Dear Sammy:

I had a plaintive talk with Meredith [Willson] on the phone about your request, describing it as favorably as possible. Nevertheless, he still says no, and we have to be guided by that. He regretted having to turn down what he described as a marvelous artist. However, I had to agree that if you performed "Trouble" we would be descended

---

35 Willson's second wife Rini (Ralina) Zarova (1912–1966), opera singer.

on by Betty Hutton, Dan Dailey, Dinah Shore, Jerry Lewis,[36] and all the others previously turned down cold, on using this song. Please understand.

I am giving [Stuart] Ostrow a copy of this note with the instruction to let you know specially when the time comes for permitting the use of this song outside the show.

I'll be seeing you at the Copa. Meanwhile, my love,

Frank Loesser

The drawn-out discussions of *The Happy Time*, and a possible musical by Samuel Taylor (see Chapter 3), continued throughout 1957 and 1958 and indicate the wider focus for Loesser on Frank Productions. A West Coast production of the play was produced at the Players' Ring in Santa Monica Boulevard in January 1958, showing the continued interest in the story generally.[37]

21 January 1957: Memo to Harold Orenstein

SAM TAYLOR

The problem with Sam Taylor is that if he becomes a stockholder in Frank Productions, Inc. he will be entitled to observe and/or complain about any activities of the corporation which do not suit him. Even with non-voting stock, his objective would be to amass later dividends and/or re-sale value of his stock at a time when a gain can be established for him. It is now not implicit in our concept of F.P.I. that we are attempting to amass a big distributable surplus. It is more likely that our efforts will be in the direction of expansion, public relations, acquisition for capital assets of all kinds, etc. I would not like any of our judgment and methods along these lines to be questioned by a minority stockholder. At the same time, our common interest with such a minority stockholder would be to sell along with

---

36 Betty Hutton (1921–2007), actress and singer; Dan Dailey (1915–1978), actor and dancer; Dinah Shore (1916–1994), singer and actress; Jerry Lewis (1926–2017), comedian nicknamed 'The King of Comedy'.
37 James Powers, 'Play Review: "The Happy Time"', *Hollywood Reporter* 148/9 (9 January 1958), 3.

him at a later date, all the stock in the company. It might be a slow process for Sam, and considering that I visualize offering him no more than 5 percent in the beginning, he might balk, however, I suggest offering him the purchase of this 5 percent at a very low cost, providing he is willing to act as an "executive editor" for the company for five years at no salary.

At the same time I propose that he, as an author and/or director, will give the company five years exclusivity as a producer of all his works alone, or in collaboration. The intention here is that as author he will have approval of our assignee producer (Feuer & Martin, Kermit Bloomgarden, etc.) and will profit as a stockholder out of our associate producer share. He has told me already that he can deliver the basic producing of the television spectacular of "Happy Time" to F.P.I. so that they can deliver the production at a profit to NBC. What I am worried about is the possible dissipation of the profits involved if they do not show up as dividends to him. Is there any variable expense system which would encourage this deal and which we could safely afford?

You see the picture. We produce "Happy Time" for $100,000 and deliver it to NBC for $135,000, thus pocketing a profit of $35,000. This sum might have come directly as ordinary income to Sam Taylor. Now he is only entitled to $1,750 out of it if and when it shows up as a dividend. Here is where an expense account system might do the trick. How it could be spelled out in a contract is a tough one to figure, but that is why I have you, dear Harold.

A further message to Taylor himself hints that he may have been offered the chance to adapt Scandinavian author Hilda Wernher's book *My Indian Family* (1943) into a musical (it eventually went to Pearl S. Buck and Charles L. Peck and became the show *Christine* in 1960).

7 March 1957: To Samuel Taylor (Telegram)

ARRIVING MARCH TWELFTH. WILL PHONE YOU. MEANWHILE WHAT ABOUT INDIAN FAMILY. PLEASE WIRE. LOVE.
FRANK LOESSER

11 March 1957: To Samuel Taylor (Telegram)

ARRIVING TOMORROW MORNING. PLEASE HOLD TOMORROW
NIGHT OPEN FOR ME. REGARDS.
FRANK LOESSER

5 August 1957: To Samuel Taylor

Dear Sam:

Thanks for the news outburst. I had been thinking about you with
great warmth, when in came the letter.

Look, if you want to work on "Happy Time" early next Spring,
that's the time for me. I assume you will adapt the play and I would
like to volunteer to be of some help unofficially. Officially, I want my
company to produce it. The main thing is that an outline gets written.
If you would stop gardening and sailing (which can only get your
script either dirty or wet) you could have a scenario-type outline in
my hands within a month.

As far as songwriters are concerned, I feel that you have a leaning
toward the <u>exquisite</u>. I would rather curve this in the direction of
<u>hairy-ass</u>. There is something wonderful about commercial writers
and something very sensitive too, as witness Irving Berlin's great
renunciation scene called "The Girl That I Marry," or Adler-Ross' plot
transition entitled "Hernando's Hideaway." I am scared of a lyric writer
who is such a language stickler and refiner that he can't be argued
into writing a hit; or the tune writer who knows all the Cesar Franck
chords and none of Walter Donaldson's. My specialty is dragging
them up to your knowledgeable sensitive but wholesome class. I can't
guarantee dragging anybody down from Cloud 9. I would like you to
trust me on this. You wrote a very solid, understandable, healthy,
robust, real, happy, funny play. I now submit the following envoi:

Bernstein effetely would broil it,
Blitzstein would mention the toilet,
As for Menotti,
He'd dot it with spotty
Allusions to God, which would spoil it.

Forrest and Wright would sound shrewish,
Arlen would paint it all bluish,
Further conjecture
That Harburg would lecture,
And Rome would compose it in Jewish.

Leave things to me*, like I said.
(Mozart's in hiding, not dead)

*me the boy producer.
Love,

18 April 1958: To Harold Orenstein

Dear Harold:

This is to bring you up-to-date about my conversations regarding "HAPPY TIME."

I spoke to Sam Taylor on the 'phone and he agrees that he would like to work with Milton Schafer.[38] It is very likely that they can work together starting in a couple of weeks and continue over the summer. Therefore, I believe it important to make a deal for Frank Productions, Inc. for the first-class rights to a musicalization. Toward this end, Sam Taylor said he would get in touch with Kay Brown's[39] office and that she, in turn, would be in touch with you. There would be a number of documents to look over, of course, including agreements by which Taylor adapted the basic published novel and by which Rodgers and Hammerstein acquired first-class production rights. Thereafter, the details of the motion picture sale, and finally a recent deal I understand has been made for a non-musical serialization for television.

Meanwhile – back at the ranch – I have started conversations in which I recommended Schafer for another musical now starting preparation. If these people accept him, it would mean immediate work, and therefore, might cancel out Taylor for the time being.

---

38 Milton Schafer (1920–2020), composer and pianist.
39 Katharine 'Kay' B. Brown Barrett (1902–1995), famous talent scout and agent.

Nevertheless, I feel that an effort should be made to make the "Happy Time" production deal anyway.

I'll see Taylor in San Francisco shortly and confirm that he has urged MCA to get in touch with you. I believe it politic that you should wait until they do so.

25 June 1958: To Samuel Taylor

Harold Orenstein gets the impression from Howard Reinheimer[40] that you and I were proposing a "co-production" to each other. This is not what I had in mind and I hope I did not give you such ideas in our ramblings on the subject.

What I have in mind is that Frank Productions, Inc., should acquire rights for a stage musical (plus whatever subsidiaries may still be acquired along with it) from you and your basic partner. Upon making this acquisition at satisfactory terms, Frank Productions, Inc. would want you for the adaptation in collaboration with composers-lyrists of your choice. Frank Productions, Inc., would want you to accept a minimal royalty (2%) as adaptor ... and in addition separately award any <u>designee</u> of yours a share of 3% of the net profits payable out of the producer's share. Under ordinary and normal circumstances this would amount to 10% of the producer's share.

The <u>designee</u> might be the Taylor Corp., some indigent aunt, a children's trust fund, or the Bide-a-Wee Home for Stray Cats. At any rate, the objective here would be to reduce the size of your personal gross income and allow some other growing institution to receive its own independent taxable income. The obligations of the <u>designee</u> would be microscopic and unimportant, but would simplify this transaction. It seems to me that the above was the objective in our discussions.

As a footnote observation on the above paragraph, let me point out that the use of your actual personal services as an active producer would be a waste of your time and talent.

---

40 Howard E. Reinheimer (1899–1970), lawyer specialising in copyright law, representing in particular playwrights, composers and producers.

Meanwhile, I gather that you and our boy Shafer are engaged in a tentative collaboration. This is fine with me assuming that we agree on the principle of the deal to be embarked on. On the other hand, if my concept of our plan is all wrong in your opinion . . . then expensive Shafer should certainly not go visiting in Maine nor forsake our other projects, including his editorship of our publishing company.

Fate finds me here in the West until about August 1. At the moment I am at Beverly Hills Hotel, but will be renting a house during July. I don't at the moment know the address or the telephone number, so I wish you would write me a note care of Harold Orenstein, 145 West 57th St., New York, with your reflections on this note. If we are in accord, then it would be important for you to have Kay Brown contact Orenstein for the purpose of making the basic agreement immediately.

If we are not in accord, I think it is important for you to let me know at once.

And now to less business like items. I am out here for an extra month to get what the gentiles refer to as repose. I have also heard from Talmudic scholars that when a Jew accomplishes repose, he also gets some work done. This is my objective. Anyway, I am taking a very pretty house and renting a car. By a strange coincidence, Jo [Sullivan] is also staying out West for the same period, unless we get mad at each other. If we don't get mad at each other and I also get repose, there will be great progress on "Greenwillow." But this is expecting too much, as it is predicted that I will be seen now and then at Chasens[41] with a small blonde . . . and that itself is a wholesome change from "21"[42] during July.

Please write immediately. Meanwhile, best love to Suzanne and the boys. . . . And as for you, let me suggest that this is no summer in which to break a leg, although come to think of it, the French* with their macabre greeting habits would argue to the contrary.

Love,

Frank Loesser

---

41 21 Club, a trendy restaurant in West Hollywood patronised by Hollywood luminaries. Established in 1936 at 9039 Beverly Boulevard, Chasen's closed in 1995.

42 Fashionable restaurant formerly located at 21 West 52nd Street, New York. Originally a speakeasy established in Greenwich Village in 1922, it moved to West 52nd Street in 1926; '21' closed permanently in 2020.

P.S. * you know, those odd singing people up in Canada.

Doug Whitney (dates unknown) was an agent at MCA in the 1940s and early 1950s until working as a producer for CBS television (from 1954) and moving to RKO as 'talent executive' in 1957. He also worked as a press agent. Whitney was good friends, and regularly corresponded, with Loesser, and it appears that he wanted to work for one of Loesser's companies though finally did not do so. During his time at CBS he proposed bringing together Loesser with Danny Kaye for a television project, and had suggested the operatic baritone Lawrence Tibbett (1896–1960) as the lead for *The Most Happy Fella* before Robert Weede was cast.

1 May 1957: To Doug Whitney

Dear Doug:

I know you will forgive me for my unsociable disappearance. First of all, you will do so because you are a sentimental Jew. Secondly, because I had no intention to jump down a hole, and you know it. And thirdly, and most important reason why you will forgive me, is that you are now a two-bit employee of a relatively E flat company and, therefore, very much in need of my good will. Let me hasten to point out here that my affection and regard for you are fully 100% of what they have always been. According to your letter, Screen Gems only thinks 60% of what RKO thought of you.[43] So you do well to kiss the hem of my garments.

Meanwhile, it continues to delight me that you are coming down in class commercially. After a comparative survey of the assortment of letterheads bearing various evil messages from you in the past, I can only deduce that soon you will be ready to work for one of my companies. At the moment, of course, I must take it for granted that you are still fooling people into paying you a living wage, and so I will

---

43 Whitney had moved from RKO to Screen Gems – the television subsidiary of Columbia Pictures – in April 1957.

have to wait for your ultimate peonage within the dark vastnesses of my empire.

Meanwhile, of course (although there isn't a buck in it) you have my very warm affection, thanks, and at the moment – apologies.

Love,

1 June 1957: To Doug Whitney

Dear Doug:

I got your obsequious letter. I suppose the advent of summer has softened you and you are molting. Your note contained hardly an insult, and by the time I got to the second paragraph, I distinctly felt your warm breath on my ass. Anyway, it arrived in the afternoon only a few hours after I had had a very pleasant meeting with our friend Henry White, which resulted in a date with him for tomorrow morning. I think this will answer your queries.

I am glad you are well and happy. So am I. I think I will be going to Europe within a couple of weeks long enough to bite into a real snail.

Love to the Ragtime School Teacher.

Love and kisses,

FRANK LOESSER

30 September 1957: To Doug Whitney

Dear Doug:

Characteristically, your letter of September 20th arrived in the envelope, which I enclose in order to rub your nose in a mess for your own exquisite penury. How a man of your E-flat caliber can hope to convince anyone to consider selling him a house in Beverly Hills – is beyond my imagination – one which is notable for its fertility as well as its charity. Nevertheless, I have forwarded your question to the accountants now in charge of my ex-wife's affairs.

Note also that I have paid the United States Post Office six cents in your behalf, and that should the marshall appear at your door it can only be in the nature of your failure some years back to play the clap doctor.

Give the Rag Time school teacher my deepest sympathy.

24 February 1958: To Doug Whitney

Dear Doug:

Sylvia[44] is here and I have talked to her but not about that subject, except to ask her who the manager was. The answer, Abe Lastfogel.[45] The other young man is simply a public relations representative.

The approach will be delicate but I will try for an opening, and as you know Sylvia has a very difficult opening.

Love,

11 March 1958: To Doug Whitney

Dear Doug:

A hurried note answering your March 3rd letter – to assure you that I have not taken unto myself a wife, nor have I any special plans to. If I want a broker for the purpose, I would not engage a Hollywood trade paper.

Possibly I might be west for "The Most Happy Fella" at the Philharmonic – but wait and see. Meanwhile,

Love,

1 April 1958: To Doug Whitney

Dear Doug:

Answering your letter and megilleh[46] of March 28th, I think it is your longest written work since your clandestine literature on the walls of the Boy's Room at P.S. [Public School] 165 in the early 20's.

Seriously, I was once approached on an all-[Black] version of "Camille" by a Hollywood author whose name I forget now. He had a whole script which I read and didn't especially like. It does not seem to conflict as it takes place in the West Indies, and as I recall, has the

---

44 Sylvia Fine (1913–1991), lyricist. She was married to the movie star Danny Kaye, for whom she wrote much of her material.
45 Abe Lastfogel (1898–1984), president of the William Morris Agency.
46 Literally, the Book of Esther, but colloquially a long, often complicated, story.

bum lung[47] element and other "Camille" trappings much more distinctly.

Anyway, for what my thinking is let me think about this.

Love,

29 September 1958: To Doug Whitney

Dear Doug:

Thanks for your September 23rd letter. Also, I am abreast of your communications with dear Allen Whitehead.[48]

I write this to greet you with the usual caloric intensity, and also to point out your next-to-last sentence in paragraph three of your letter and to go on record with the remark that there is no way for anyone to represent Frank Productions Inc. without being employed exclusively by it. I don't have the cabbage with which to steal you and your intrepid services from Frank Cooper Associates Agency, so we'll have to wait until you are fool enough to work for us.

Meanwhile, you are invited to price any or all of our goodies, as well as those represented by Music Theatre Incorporated, Frank Music Corp., Saunders Publications, Inc., Empress Music Inc., Carmichael Music Publications, Inc., Andrew Music Corp., Audubon Music Inc., Desilu Music Corp., Liberty Songs, Inc., Annavic Music Corp., Messina Music Corp., Globarry Music Inc., Sanga Music, Inc., Simon-Jackson, Inc., Loubarry Music Inc., Luther Music Inc., Frank Music Co., Ltd., Frank Music Company of Canada, Ltd., Edizione Frank Music, Frank Music (Latin America) Corp.

Since Marge is doing the dirty work in preparing this answer to you, I'll let her thank you for your best wishes. As for Jo and the kids, I add their greetings to mine both to you and the Rag Time schoolteacher.

Fondly,

---

47 I.e. tuberculosis.
48 Allen Whitehead (1919–2008), president of Loesser's Music Theatre International (MTI). He was responsible for the dramatic rights to *Guys and Dolls*, *The Music Man*, *West Side Story* and *Fiddler on the Roof* among other works.

There had been conflict between Loesser and Frank Sinatra during the filming of *Guys and Dolls*. Sinatra hired two private vehicles to take thirty people, including Whitney, to see Judy Garland perform in Las Vegas, and during the journey Whitney spoke with the singer about the incident against Loesser's wishes, even trying to persuade Sinatra to perform some of Loesser's work.

20 October 1958: To Doug Whitney

Dear Doug:

It seems like I had better clear things up for the record. This is with reference to your report on a conversation with Frank Sinatra in your letter of October 6th. I know you are an actively good friend with nothing but the kindest intentions, but that very sincere and much appreciated fact might still not prevent you from over-shooting the field.

There has never been any wishful or purposeful suggestion on my part that I would like Sinatra to sing anything of mine or my company's. In illustrating to you how well we two successes got along <u>without</u> each other, I once pointed out that Sinatra's total performances of my stuff in the last ten years consisted of his singing a ballad of mine which was Number One on the Hit Parade in 1947, and, therefore, a "must" in his work on that program. I pointed out that between that year and the time of the "Guys and Dolls" picture when we disagreed on how to write a certain tune, there had been a total vacuum which apparently had done both of us no harm. This was not by any remote consideration a pitch. In the ten years prior, Bing Crosby and I had gotten along (albeit with no conflict) on very much the same frequency of contact, and you will note that neither of us seem to languish for need of the other. All this was an observation and never intended to be a pitch, or a rebuke, or a tale of woe. So for Christ's sake don't sell something that doesn't want to be sold. My only pitch is: WHAT IS SINATRA MAD ABOUT?

When we had our discussion about the notes in one of my songs, we came to a choice of the following conclusions: Either he couldn't sing the notes, or didn't want to sing the notes. In either case, I recall our understanding each other well enough. Then a few weeks later I heard from quite a number of people that he had a fresh and violent mad on. This I tried to ask him about a few times, including one evening at a party and he mumbled something about having to take a lady home. That was the end of that and to this day I can't imagine what it is all about.

Maybe I refused to marry his sister; or said something derogatory about Jack Entratter; or maybe he just plain resents anybody who doesn't feel like being a stooge. It is all a mystery to me, and although I am not losing any sleep about it, it would please me to know what his squawk was or is. Outside of that, I haven't the remotest reason for hustling his good will and would hate to think that anything you had to say seemed to be representing me or my company in this way. Maybe for your own comfort you should just drop the whole subject forever.

Love,

In the summer of 1956, Loesser began work on his next musical: *Dream People* (sometimes referred to as *The Purple People*), a collaboration with the playwright Garson Kanin (1912–1999) based on the latter's unproduced play *A Touch of the Moon*. Kanin and Loesser had communicated their plans to write a musical together as early as 1954: the *New York Times* had announced on 25 June that 'The idea for the Kanin-Loesser show is already mapped out. According to Mr. Loesser, the theme was thrashed out by both of them during a series of strolls in London and Paris.'[49] Between September 1956 and the summer of 1957 at least eleven songs and a script were written for this show,[50] and it is clear that Loesser was seriously committed to it: during this period he regularly turned down projects that would eventually make it to Broadway by other writers. (For example, a

---

49 Sam Zolotow, 'New Musical Duo Is Mapping Plans', *New York Times*, 25 June 1954, 16.
50 For the extant song texts see Kimball and Nelson, *The Complete Lyrics of Frank Loesser*, 197–200. For a brief discussion of the show, see Thomas L. Riis, *Frank Loesser* (New Haven, 2008), 193–4.

letter of 1 July 1957 from Jo Mielziner[51] proposes a collaboration on a musical version of Elmer Rice's (unrelated) play *Dream Girl*, to which a handwritten note at the top reveals he phoned to say 'no'.) Susan Loesser reveals that the plot was 'about two people who, never having met, imagine each other in elaborate and delicious daydreams while living their mundane lives until they actually come face to face one day and really fall in love.'[52] Kanin and Loesser were serious in their efforts about the show and were approached by producer David Merrick (1911–2000) about it, but by 1959 it had fallen behind other projects that each was pursuing separately, and they abandoned it.

18 February 1957: To Garson Kanin

Dear Gar:

I have your letter. I will probably not be able to join you in Chicago in March but would like to be sure that you will be in New York starting April. Meanwhile I will use March for shutting up and letting my throat get better, and going on a necessary ten day trip to the coast. But please give me some picture of April and thereafter.

As you must know, David Merrick called me about our show and I asked him to wait. Until I have a long talk with you, I would not like to discuss the producer element. I think this conversation must wait until April. The most important thing is that we should be able to collaborate at close range for most of about 90 days starting April 1st. I am afraid this would have to be mostly in New York.

I am leaving for Nassau tomorrow morning and will stay one week, arriving in New York in time to root in your opening. Please write me immediately so that your letter will be waiting for me on my return.

And lissann.

Love,

---

51 Jo Mielziner (1901–1976), prominent theatrical scenic designer; among other productions, he designed Rodgers and Hammerstein's *Carousel* (1945), *South Pacific* (1949) and *The King and I* (1951), Loesser's *Guys and Dolls* (1950), Jule Styne's *Gypsy* (1959), Tennessee Williams's *A Streetcar Named Desire* (1947) and Arthur Miller's *Death of a Salesman* (1949).
52 Loesser, *A Most Remarkable Fella*, 176.

12 July 1957: To Garson Kanin

Dear Gar:

Thanks for your germ[53] regarding Dan Dailey. I think it is a little too early to decide such things.

– which brings us to a consideration of our present differences. The Morris office in representing you seems to want to limit my production date to October '58 latest. Since I would like to be a good writer and caster rather than a fast one, I have asked for a year beyond that time. I can see your point of view if you feel that you don't want other projects to intervene and delay our show. This is not my intention. What I do want is ample time to consider and re-consider what I wrote yesterday and rewrite it tomorrow without feeling the old cold pistol at the back of my neck. Why don't we settle for May '59 as an outside date?

Point number two is the question of your personal privilege to invest in the show. Of course I would welcome such a thing if the show takes that form. Not only welcome it, but strenuously invite it as a matter of selfish interest on my part. However, it is just possible that I might seek a total investment from somebody in the aluminum business or somebody with a TV network. In that event, the existence of a commitment either with you or my own dear Mother (a perennial investor in the musical theatre) might very well become an obstacle. I would like to agree that if the show takes the ordinary limited partnership form with a variety of investors, that I will certainly give you the right to invest. I suggest that your representatives make a proper wording of this. It would be stupid of me not to have you as a betting rooter if I possibly could.

The third difference of opinion is a serious one and one which I consider involves a moral question. The Wm. Morris office are insisting on receiving a commission of the producer's share pro rated in accordance with the Author's share of the subsidiary income. According to Orenstein, the Wm. Morris office claims that their clients always support them. Now it is all very well that a client should wish

---

53 I.e. the germ of an idea.

his agent good luck and easy living, but I do not propose that the Morris office should get one plugged nickel from the producer. The producer is not its client. The producer does not wish the services of the Morris office in selling anything. The producer did not meet the writer through the Morris office, or by virtue of any of the Morris office efforts. The Morris office can accept whatever it wants from Garson Kanin. That is none of the producer's business.

In the same mail in which I got your most recent note, there arrived a letter from Abe Lastfogel suggesting our using an actress client [Jeannie Carson]. I want to take this and other suggestions seriously. I want to be a Morris office customer. I do not in any respect want to be a Morris office client. I believe they will insist on what I consider a scavenger bite unless and until you tell them not to. I wish, for the sake of decency, that you would. And, since I am attacking the writing job at the moment not only heroically but beautifully, I wish you would do so right away.

Let me point out for a finish that the Morris office's commission of the producer's share of the subsidiary rights does not improve your take at all but reduces further the commission of the active agent who is licensing the subsidiary rights. Please let me know.

Meanwhile, love, love, love to you and Ruth.

27 January 1958: To Garson Kanin

Dear Gar:

Here it is. Read it, weep, and cable your comments. If we are still speaking, telephone me, REgent 7-2173.

Love,

4 March 1959: To Garson Kanin

Dear Gar:

My last recollection of you is when we said goodbye after a meeting at your house, looking very much like the gold-dust twins as we vowed eternal collaboration or something like that. You were the one who, after that happy meeting, was to call me within the next few days breathless with exciting new contributions to "Touch of the Moon." I knew that you were up to your navel in arguments from the editors of your new book; concern over your brother's imminent play; sudden urgency to adjust your 1958 income by means of a quick and lurid motion picture sale; conjecture about buying a new piano; the electric excitement of a visit from [Hollywood producer] Ray Stark; and among these other things, a surge in the recurrent qualm about what the hell to do with our project.

On leaving, I did some thinking about our past meetings and I decided to take literally your suggestion that you would be in touch with me and to leave you alone to all your other troubles until you felt like it.

Well sir, plenty of time has gone by during which I have been forced to decide to continue another project which I had previously preferred to abandon till our job was done. I told you before about this one. It's called "Greenwillow." Anyway, that's what I am now loaded with and, by virtue of bold commitments to partners, collaborators, and the faith of a proud and anxious mother comfortably set up on the East side, I'm moving forward with this, anticipating production next fall or winter.

I have to assume that either you have tried and failed to make some new golden geetis[54] out of our show – or else you have abandoned interest in it in favor of the many other things you get called on to think about. Or maybe both.

Now there looms on the horizon the day marking the end of the period in which Frank Productions, Inc. was entitled to the privilege of producing a version of your original idea without further writing contribution from you. You will recall this agreement, arrived at laboriously between the William Morris office and my good counselor, Harold Orenstein. It is now but a few hopeless little weeks before that handsome thick bundle of papers loses all purpose and legal effect. Now I am not a man who cries at the waste of ceiling wax [sic] and ribbon. Nor do the files at City Hall, crammed with unconsummated marriage licenses, bring to me any special sense of need for fulfil-

---

54 Slang for 'money'.

ment. I didn't even mind what happened to the Versailles Treaty, and I found myself able to shrug off with ease the tragic lapse of Mabel Normand's contract with Mack Sennett.[55] But the idea of "Touch of the Moon" fills me with such possessive nachis[56] as never came near hardening the arteries of Milton Berle's[57] mother. It would be an understatement for me to say that I love it. I am afflicted with it.

Sure. Maybe I did it wrong the first time, but then you'll remember that when I wrote "Praise the Lord and Pass the Ammunition" the war insisted on continuing for three long years afterward. It was not until I had written "Rodger Young" that the contestants came to their senses. Writing takes time, patience, and never-abating self-criticism and examination. What I would like is for you and T.F.T. (I think that was the name of your spurious and transparent organization) to give me an extension of 18 months after the termination now imminent – so that I can continue in my love affair with it, in the hope that you will be very proud of me finally. Assuming that my present show will get on sometime before the end of this year, this would give me till the following autumn to become the first Jewish Crown Prince of Fantasy, having already mastered in turn the subjects of eccentric Oxonians and Broadway gamblers.

I'm writing you this request rather than phoning. This way I will have forced on you less of that compulsive sense of obligation that makes you call me dear and feed me lunch. Of course, if you want to go walking and talk about it with me, all you have to do is let me know. Otherwise, tell Lefkowitz[58] to tell Orenstein what the news is. But while either piece of business machinery starts turning, maybe you and Ruth would feel like spending some time with my girl and me, eating sensibly and walking briskly to some theater where we can

---

55 A reference to the falling out between silent-film star Mabel Normand (1893–1930) and her lover, producer Mack Sennett (1880–1960). Their tumultuous relationship was fictionalised in Jerry Herman's 1974 Broadway musical *Mack & Mabel*.

56 Yiddish for 'joy'.

57 Milton Berle (Mendel Berlinger, 1908–2002), comedian and early television personality.

58 Nat Lefkowitz (1905–1983), co-chairman of the William Morris agency.

have an aloof view of some third party's show and decide smugly that we're glad never to have touched it with a 10-foot pole. We can do that first and then walk briskly to eat sensibly. Or maybe first walk briskly and then eat sensibly after the show. Or it doesn't have to be in three acts but simply sit around in one room and discuss which year was the best Doctor Pepper, or what's happening with your new jazz book, or is Loehmann's Brooklyn further than Loehmann's Bronx if you live in the East forties.[59] Anyway, I'd love to see you if you have time. It's always gratifying because I know that you adore and admire me. That's why I miss you.

Loesser's final letter to Kanin mentions *Greenwillow*, another musical that he worked on, and completed, after *The Most Happy Fella*. The show was an adaptation of the recent (1956) novel of the same name by B. J. Chute (1913–1987). The *New York Times* first reported on the project on 22 September 1957, though Loesser had agreed to write the score for a production by actor-producer Robert A. Willey (1920–2009) four months earlier: ' "Greenwillow," in case you have not heard, is currently in its eighth printing; it has been a choice of the Book-of-the-Month Club, The Literary Guild, Best in Books, and when it first appeared Orville Prescott hailed it in this newspaper as "an utterly enchanting novel . . . will be cherished by thousands of readers for years to come." It has also been described as "an isolated village on the banks of the Meander, beyond the boundaries of time, which has no geographical locations except perhaps in the hearts of all of us." It will be solely up to Mr. Loesser to capture this flavor, for, as with "The Most Happy Fella," he will write the book as well as compose the score and the lyrics. To round out the details for the moment: Mr. Loesser also will be associated in the production through his firm, Frank Productions, Inc.'[60] The *Times* article hints at the unusual, mystical atmosphere of *Greenwillow*, something which it

---

59 Loehmann's was a chain of cut-price department stores, first established in Brooklyn in 1921; the Bronx branch opened in 1930. Loehmann's filed for bankruptcy in 2014 and closed for business in 2018.

60 Lewis Funke, 'Gossip of the Rialto: Frank Loesser Adds "Greenwillow" to his Busy Schedule', *New York Times*, 22 September 1957, 133.

had in common with *Dream People*. Chute's novel is about how the men of the Briggs family are cursed with wanderlust, whereby they must leave their wives and children behind, much to the chagrin of the hero, Gideon, who wishes to stay put.

The peculiarity of the material would ultimately be its undoing. After working on it on his own for a while Loesser eventually collaborated on the book with Lesser Samuels (1894–1980), screenwriter of the Oscar-nominated films *No Way Out* (1950) and *Ace in the Hole* (1951), but they never quite got it right. Nevertheless, at the beginning of the process Chute was excited by the idea of her novel becoming a musical and wrote to Loesser to express her excitement:

22 May 1957: B. J. Chute to Frank Loesser

Dear Frank Loesser,

I have been sitting here, with typewriter poised, trying to think of some way of expressing the great pleasure I feel in knowing "Greenwillow" is to have your very special gifts in its translation from book to stage.

I have an awed appreciation of what is required to put a musical production on Broadway in terms of energy, imagination, talent, courage, wilfulness and possibly a touch of moon-madness, and I find myself extremely fortunate in being associated with you and Bob Willey.

In hope you will have great satisfaction in the production in the most professional and profound sense of the satisfaction of the craftsman. In the words of a well-known songwriter, "More I cannot wish you."

Yours,

[signed:] Joy C.

In this busy period of working on both *Dream People* and *Greenwillow* alternately, Loesser regularly declined invitations to write songs for other projects: his brother Arthur, for example, seems to have passed on his details to a charity that wanted him to write a song for them; to his friend Louis Stone (1914–1958), a talent chief at

CBS television, he was robust in rejecting two ideas; and to Phyllis Cerf (1916–2006), New York socialite and the wife of Random House founder Bennett Cerf (1898–1971), he was similarly firm.

8 August 1957: To Douglas Mueller

Dear Mr. Mueller:

Thank you so much for your painstaking letter, but I am sure that I can't do the job you suggest. Therefore, I feel that a trip on your part to meet with me should be discouraged.

Really and truly, although I well understand your very good purposes – I cannot address myself to a piece of work which is not my very, very best. My very very best takes more time and thought than I can possibly afford for quite a long while to come. At the moment I am digging out of the not always reliable muse what I hope will be a successful Broadway show. If it is successful, it will give me the usual huge gross personal income in 1958. In reliance on this, I expect to make the customary large (deductible) charitable donations. I can't do anything now which would deprive me of the privilege of doing so. I know the above may sound like a specious beg-off, but let me assure you that my donations next year will have a calculably larger effect than any grouping of words and music I may put together toward that end – especially if I hurry and I worry. Please forgive me for being such a self-disciplinarian.

Arthur told me you were going to be in touch and I thank you for thinking of me. But I can't accept.

Very sincerely,

8 August 1957: To Louis T. Stone

Dear Lou:

I have done my homework. Frankly, I don't give a damn about either subject and don't think I can be made to give a damn.

Millay[61] is a better lyric writer than I am, and being a jealous fellow, I don't propose to garnish her immortality.

The story by Lord tells me nothing about anything. I have not read the Titanic book and cannot do so for a long time.[62]

I am busy travelling back and forth from Fire Island at great hazard to life and limb.

Yours for gentler drivers,

29 August 1957: To Phyllis Cerf

Dear Phyllis:

I would really love to do one of those books, especially the one suggested by Ceisel, but my conscience won't let me. I just have too much work piled up. So it is painful for me to have to say no.

Thanks for thinking of me. And much love to you and Bennett.

The particularity of Loesser's dealings with star performers in granting permissions to promote certain songs is highlighted in a letter to pop singer Frankie Laine (1913–2007). And although Frank Productions had now provided a new method by which Loesser could be involved in making money from musicals, he was not the only Broadway composer who was doing so. An exchange with Jule Styne – an old friend and colleague from Hollywood – shows the composer's desire to produce Loesser's work in the future.

25 March 1957: To Frankie Laine,
Desert Inn Hotel, Las Vegas

Dear Frankie:

---

61 Poet Edna St Vincent Millay (1892–1950) was winner of the 1923 Pulitzer Prize for Poetry for her 'Ballad of the Harp-Weaver'.
62 Walter Lord (1917–2002), author of *A Night to Remember* (New York, 1955), an account of the sinking of the RMS *Titanic*. Coincidentally, the captain of the SS *Californian*, the ship nearest to the *Titanic* when it sank, was also named Lord (Stanley Phillip Lord, 1877–1962, no relation to Walter Lord).

Enclosed are two piano part copies and a demo of "WARM AND WILLING." This letter will serve as permission from me for you to perform this song in cafes and in theatres until such a time as I revoke the permission in writing. It is our understanding that you will not perform this composition, or any part of it, in a recording of any kind on the radio or television or as part of the contents of any production, play, show, or review in which you may appear. In other words, it may become part of the Frankie Laine act in clubs and theatres.

Sorry to make this so formal and sticky, but I have a very rough lawyer (thank God!) who hits me with a baseball bat every time I don't act like him.

I had a wonderful time with you and Nan,[63] maybe we'll get together soon. Let me know if you do anything with "WARM AND WILLING" and whether you get arrested or not.

Love,

22 April 1957: Jule Styne to Frank Loesser

Dear Frank:

Although it's a long way off, I would again like to remind you that when it comes to producing your next play, I would appreciate being in the running. Since, for the first time in your life, you are <u>indebted</u> to me, I feel I can ask for a very big favor.

In all seriousness, I would very much like to produce your next play. Warmest personal regards.

Love,

Jule

1 May 1957: To Jule Styne

Dear Jule:

Here's the 22 bucks I owe you. The fact that we are now even does not diminish at all my obligation to consider you strongly as a

---

63 Laine's wife, actress Nan Grey (1918–1993).

producer. Let me here quote the profound words of Jule Styne as follows: "I am a great producer."

I find myself living by this incontrovertible statement of positive fact. The awareness of this illuminates my every move and thought. It is gospel. It is the undying truth. The theatre is a cathedral dedicated to the goodness, the wisdom, the flawless perfection of Jule Styne. I know you listen to my prayers and I trust in your everlasting kindness.

In short, Yes, Jule, I take very seriously your recent statement to me.

Love, love, love, love love,

(and thanks for the loan)

Letters to the songwriters Harry Ruby (of 'A Kiss to Build a Dream On' fame; 1895–1974) and Sunny Skylar (known for writing 'Besame Mucho'; 1913–2009) partly concern copyright regarding the titles of a song by Loesser ('Standing on the Corner') and another by Frank Music writers Adler and Ross (reference unclear). Loesser had several years earlier defended himself in court over the origin of the title 'A Bushel and a Peck'[64] and such legal cases were and are common in the realm of commercial music.

29 August 1957: To Harry Ruby

Dear Harry:

I know I owe you a response to your note of a long long time ago. And must ask you to forgive me for taking so long.

It now occurs to me that the World Series is very likely to be played in New York this year. Therefore, I can assume that you will be on hand for a period.

I wish you would phone me if and when you get here in the interest of satisfying yourself about the "standing on the corner" title. Also, if you like, in the interest of pleasing me very much with your always good company.

Meanwhile, please forgive the delay.

---

64 Anon., 'Loesser Sued by Trio On "Bushel" Writing', *Variety* (13 December 1950), 57.

Love,

FRANK LOESSER

P.S: My phone number at the office is C01umbus 5-7337. My private home number is Regent 7-2173 – or Marge Gans at the office will know where to find me.

17 October 1957: To Sunny Skylar

Dear Sunny:

Thanks for being so thoughtful as to tell me about your song title. I'll file your letter against the time that Dick Adler has a squark – and flash it on him.

Meanwhile, my fond regards.

Sincerely,

FRANK LOESSER

A letter to the arranger and orchestrator Jack Mason (1906–1965) is of interest because of Loesser's comment on writing vs. business. And two letters to composer Jay Livingston (1915–2001) and lyricist Ray Evans (1915–2007), whose hit songs included the Oscar-winning 'Que Sera Sera' and the Christmas standard 'Silver Bells', show his interest in the Broadway musical *Oh, Captain!* (1958), for which they were nominated for a Tony Award.

24 February 1958: To Jack Mason

Dear Jack:

Thanks for your letter. I am taking the liberty of having Herb Eiseman, my general manager, call you and discuss some of the things you mention. Subsequently, I hope you and I have a meeting, but at the present moment I am loaded with the problem of being a writer, which is more tedious and more confining than that of being a business man.

Thanks and best wishes.

Sincerely,

11 September 1957: To Jay Livingston and Ray Evans

Dear Gents:

In addition to wishing you the best of luck with "Captain's Paradise,"[65] maybe I can actually help to bring you some.

I would like to suggest your using the good services of Sam Farber as musical director. I do not hesitate to assure you that I think he is of enormous value to any musical show. He conducted "Guys and Dolls" for me and did it exceedingly well. At present he is giving me the same admirable service on "The Most Happy Fella." It must be apparent to you that this covers quite a range of musical understanding and control.

So if you are now thinking about choosing a musical director, be sure to think about Sam Farber.

My warmest regards.

Sincerely,

20 January 1958: To Jay Livingston and Ray Evans, "Oh, Captain," Shubert Theatre, Philadelphia (Telegram)

JUST ARRIVED FROM EUROPE TO LEARN FROM MANY FRIENDS HOW WONDERFUL YOU ARE DOING IN PHILLY. DON'T WORRY I AM NOT ASKING FOR OPENING NIGHT SEATS. JUST DELIGHTED TO SEE TWO TALENTS JOINING THE BROADWAY RANKS. SINCERELY.

FRANK LOESSER

---

65 *Oh, Captain!* was based on the 1953 British film *Captain's Paradise*, starring Alec Guinness.

CHAPTER SIX

1958–60
THE MOST HAPPY FELLA IN LONDON
AND *GREENWILLOW*

*T*he *Most Happy Fella* continued to do well on Broadway; it was named Best Musical in the Drama Critics Circle awards in April 1957. And in its wake, Loesser's activities under the banner of Frank Productions expanded considerably in the final years of the decade, with new projects regularly announced in the press. In May 1957 he made public his purchase of the rights to *When in Rome* by Charles Peck Jr (1921–1996), a stage musical to involve the beloved 1930s Hollywood team Nelson Eddy (1901–1967) and Jeanette MacDonald (1903–1965) and a score by Frank Music writers Norman Gimbel (1927–2018) and Moose Charlap (1928–1974);[1] a year later, he announced he would produce a musical version of the 1946 film *Specter of the Rose* by its original screenwriter Ben Hecht (1894–1964), book writer John Martin (identity unknown), composer Lyn Murray (1909–1989) and lyricist Lenny Adelson (1924–1972), as well as co-producing Leonard Sillman's (1908–1982) *New Faces* revue, which was to contain six numbers by a young Jerry Herman (1931–2019) from the Greenwich Village revue *Nightcap* (1958).[2]

---

1 The involvement of MacDonald and Eddy was announced in *The Hollywood Reporter* in the article 'Rambling Reporter', 145/7 (4 June 1957), 2.
2 Sam Zolotow, '"Specter of Rose" Coming to Stage', *New York Times*, 23 May 1958, 28.

There is a general sense of Loesser's reach expanding into new areas, and his involvement in the success of *The Music Man* proves how perceptive his ideas could be. Yet at heart he remained a writer, and knew that this must continue to be his key focus. *The Most Happy Fella* continued to absorb his time: the *New York Times* reported that in the spring of 1958 he 'made a trip to San Francisco. His object at this late date was to rewrite and direct a scene in the successful musical that would be acceptable to the Baptist owners of Los Angeles' Philharmonic Auditorium', where the show was to play for five weeks.[3] In February 1959, a short run was staged at City Center in New York, directed by Dania Krupska (1921–2011), who had been nominated for a Tony Award for her choreography of the original Broadway production.[4] And preparations were under way for a London production, following the success of the 1953 British staging of *Guys and Dolls*. It was front-page news in the London-based *The Stage* when Loesser visited England in June 1957 to organise the production.[5] Correspondence from this period reveals some of the challenges of producing Broadway shows in other countries: the British censor (the Lord Chamberlain) had to approve each text that appeared on the stage, and there were rules about allowing non-British artists to conduct and act in British productions.

The London production was produced by Hugh 'Binkie' Beaumont (1908–1973), one of the most successful theatrical producers of the twentieth century; in 1958 alone, he oversaw the original London productions of *My Fair Lady* and *West Side Story*. Loesser's anxieties about casting the British version of *Most Happy Fella* were also reported on the front page of *The Stage* in March 1960: in a column titled 'FRANK LOESSER FINDS IT HARD TO GET THE SINGERS HE WANTS' it was said that he 'has encountered difficulties in finding singers with voices robust enough to meet the requirements of his score ... Mr. Loesser feels that the average British singer underestimates himself,

---

3 Ibid.
4 Sam Zolotow, 'Warners in Deal for "Tall Story"', *New York Times*, 16 January 1959, 35.
5 Anon., 'Most Happy Fella', *The Stage* 3975 (June 1957), 1.

and is much too "drawing-room" in his approach. This, he imagines, is because he is far more likely to get his experience in a theatre no larger than the Savoy.[6]

27 February 1958: The Lord Chamberlain's Office, St James's Palace, London, to Bernard Gordon, General Manager of *The Most Happy Fella* in London

Dear Sir,

"The Most Happy Fella"

I am desired by the Lord Chamberlain to write to you regarding the above Play and to ask for an undertaking that on page 115 the word "Jesus" will be changed to "Gee".

Yours faithfully,

Assistant Comptroller

3 March 1958: To Hugh Beaumont

My dear Mr. Beaumont:

It comes to my attention (quite alarmingly) that I might not be allowed to bring a conductor to England for the run of "The Most Happy Fella:" I understand that this is the result of a musician's union regulation, and, of course, I realize that the union must have its reasons for this prohibition. Nevertheless, I hope that the ruling applies only to ordinary musical comedies, revues, etc. In this instance, as you well know, we are dealing with a full-blown operatic production. For many sound business reasons, my producers and I avoided the use of the word "opera" in all our advertising and public relations. Nevertheless, a glance at the New York newspaper reviews, as well as the barrage of the articles and feature commentaries by long-haired musicologists – would indicate without question that we have a true operatic work to deal with. The majority of the cast (including the leading part) were recruited from the operatic ranks, and the orchestra was

---

6 Anon., 'Frank Loesser Finds It Hard to Get the Singers He Wants', *The Stage*, 4116 (3 March 1960), 1.

and still is of a quality and dimension (31 to 36 men) in keeping with the nature of the piece.

As you know, the score is enormously complex and cannot be directed by anyone, however talented, who has not made a long-standing acquaintanceship with it and meticulous study of it. The conductor now in charge replaced the original one only after three consecutive months of constant attendance and observation of the show, all the while making a personal study of it along with his predecessor, the company librarian, individuals in the cast and myself. And this was a man already fully qualified as an experienced and able operatic conductor.

My point here is to insist that you make every effort to convince the union there that we should be allowed to bring along a man so qualified – very possibly the one I refer to above, if he can be released from his duties here. I would want him for at least a long enough period in which to train his British successor.

I don't think I would object if, after a very short time, the British conductor were to take the matinees. Possibly this could begin with the first London week. It happens that the show is so exhausting for its conductor, that the original New York conductor could only handle the six evening performances and was forced to hand over the stick to his assistant for the two matinees.

In discussing this, you might also point out that we intend to employ many more playing musicians than ordinarily are used in a typical musical comedy. It is not my intention here to urge any special comfortable advantage for myself. I do sincerely believe that I am asking for something without which we might risk artistic failure.

In closing, I ask you to secure and answer for this request as soon as you possibly can. If the answer is favorable, I will have to rush to get an agreement from one of the three qualified men who have conducted over here, each of whom may be planning other projects. If the answer is unfavorable, frankly, I don't know what we can do.

Urgently,
FRANK LOESSER

12 March 1958: To Hugh Beaumont

Dear Binkie:

I would like you to give me complete information immediately concerning the number of non-English people who will be allowed to act on the stage in "The Most Happy Fella." I am speaking not only of the possible roster of Americans, but also possibly Italians who are not British subjects.

My question has nothing to do with <u>expense</u> to the production. Naturally, I want to keep expenses down as much as possible, but I must now explore the possibility of certain parts which may not be fillable by English people. First, there is the "Rosabella" part. I understand you have communicated with Jo Sullivan and that her agent will be in touch with you. In addition, however, I am thinking of Art Lund[7] (Joey) as a possibility. I think he will be finished with his American assignment in time. Both he and Jo Sullivan give their final performance in California on June 28th, and it is my private and unofficial belief that the tour will end there. The way I read the ouija board at the moment, Lund would come cheaper than Hockridge.[8] Then there is the part of "Herman"[9] to consider. I haven't the foggiest idea of who can fill the bill in London and, therefore, would want at least to inquire about the man now playing it here. From all I can learn, he is quite inexpensive.

Although there may be even more requirements, let's leave it at these three now. They all know their parts thoroughly and could be invited by [the] B.B.C. to give a sort of three person presentation of what is to come, singing a song each, etc. along with Te Wiata, about the first week of July. There's the possibility that [the] B.B.C. would be

---

7 Ultimately, Art Lund reprised his role as Joey in the London production of *Most Happy Fella* but Jo Sullivan was replaced as Rosabella by Helena Scott (dates unknown) and Robert Weede as Tony by New Zealand Maori bass-baritone Inia Te Wiata (1915–1971).

8 Edmund Hockridge (1919–2009) was a Canadian actor who had starred as Sky in the London production of *Guys and Dolls*, among other British productions of Broadway musicals in this period.

9 In the end, American actor Jack DeLeon (1924–2006) reprised the role of Herman, which he had played in a brief run of the show at City Center in 1959.

glad to pay their fares instead of our doing so. See what I mean? Maybe this is visionary, but first of all please inform me as to the government restrictions on non-English performers. We are a piece of Americana everywhere as typical as "Guys and Dolls" was. As you may recall, the entire principal cast of "Guys and Dolls" in London were Americans.[10]

I await your answer to this question, as well as my other question of recent date. Meanwhile,

Love,

Two years later, Loesser's frustrations with Equity rules around using non-British citizens continued to fester:

7 June 1960: To Hugh Beaumont

Dear Binkie,

The British Equity's decision about Rico Froehlich[11] comes as a serious blow to me. I speak as an author-composer who now must face the very strong probability of a reduction in his stature and esteem (such as it is) as a result of a new interpretation in public of his writing. Aside from your artistic concern and regard for me and my work, I am sure that you are also aware of the resultant possible financial benefits, and I feel it only fair to point out that unless the quality of all the elements of THE MOST HAPPY FELLA is maintained—that we will not run for anywhere near as many weeks or months as we had anticipated.

I think that the length of our run should be of equal interest to British Equity as it is to you and me – assuming that they are truly concerned with the continuity of employment for an <u>unusually large company of British</u> performers at a rather generous rate of pay. I am sure that you have been able to point all this out to British Equity, but

---

10 In fact, Sarah Brown was played in London by British actress Lizbeth Webb (1926–2013).
11 Rico Froehlich (1919–1976) played Pasquale in the original Broadway production of *Most Happy Fella*. Thanks to his grandson Rico for confirming his dates.

I am not quite certain whether you yourself understand the basis of my insistence on Rico Froehlich.

Froehlich was engaged by me for the original company in New York and he played the entire run in New York plus the entire tour engagement. There is only one other person who has been qualified enough to play it under first-class circumstances, and he is likewise an American. When I engaged Froehlich I promptly rewrote various elements of the part to fit his most unusual personality. Here we come to a discussion from the point of view of his effectiveness on the stage. The pure "musical" expert will, of course, tell you that the musical part can be delivered technically by others. He will even tell you that it can be done better by others. This is quite true, and we have at least two or three English people in our present company who can execute the notes. It is also quite true that a typical Scarpia can negotiate the notes required for Germonde [sic],[12] and vice versa. But rarely, if ever, is such a performance convincing.

In making the play short and concise enough for theatrical use (the original writing having required four hours to perform) the arrival of Froehlich, as well as the lady who played Marie,[13] made it possible for me to condense their originally long and tedious parts into quick and definite characterisations by way of very telling intermittent short appearances. Here, in England, we were fortunate to find an English lady who could give us this economy of characterisation as did the one in New York.

But in the case of the Pasquale part, I assure you there was not one among all the candidates auditioned who could deliver anywhere near the required quality. In securing Rico Froehlich I had to convince him to give notice to a Broadway production with which he was then quite well employed. That is how important he was and is to us, and that accounts for your and my personal support and encouragement of his visit.

---

12 Loesser is referring to the roles of Scarpia in Puccini's *Tosca* (1900) and Germont in Verdi's *La traviata* (1853).
13 Mona Paulee (1912–1995) played Marie in the original Broadway production. She was replaced by Nina Verushka (dates unknown) in the London production.

Let me dwell a little longer on the very special characteristics of Froehlich. Firstly, his voice. It has neither great range or great beauty, but it characterises him immediately as a boor and a bully. Ordinarily such use of the vocal equipment is devastating to the voice of a baritone or bass-baritone. It is in some respects a manner of <u>shouting</u> which comes naturally to Froehlich and does not damage or tire him in any way. This same production when practised by Wiata or the other low voices among our male singers – absolutely invites laryngitis or serious muscular and blood-vessel damage. This has already happened to Wiata who required a careful recovery as you know. In my opinion, it happened as a result of just this practise where unfortunately we require it (the phrase "shut up Marie" which must be shouted over ensemble and orchestral sounds from up stage: the expression of towering rage spoken in the confession scene etc.) out of enthusiasm and a not too judicious use of his energy, Wiata has been missing from too many performances, as you know. Froehlich's special equipment would never feel this strain. Now to another element of the latter's unique quality. He is as expert a dancer as most of our dancing group, and as you have seen, his movements are those of a cat-like martinet and he has absolutely no trouble with the required physical direction of the part. Eskow[14] will tell you that Froehlich keeps up a continuous directing and policing process with the other two members of the trio while on stage – hardly noticeable but of enormous value in keeping up the energy and symmetry of the group's business. Ken Alwyn[15] will tell you that the Trio at some vital points depends on hand signals from Rico, rather than baton conducting which at the moment they cannot observe. All this because of his notable special talents and experience in the part. Finally, there is the value of Rico's knowledge of the Italian language and pronunciation. It is a very rewarding asset since this character alone on stage introduces us speechwise to the entire manner and

---

14 American director Jerome Eskow (1923–2009) was the director of the London production of *The Most Happy Fella*.
15 British conductor Kenneth Alwyn (1925–2020) was the musical director of the production.

quality in a very short capsule (Abbondanza) so that there is auto-matic recognition and appreciation of the very economical capsules which follow. No one ever need say "now who is that guy again?" as he reappears.

Now Binkie, as you know, I am always most careful and I think considerate when planning for over here. You will recall that I asked for absolutely no Americans in the WHERE'S CHARLEY Company, even though there were many able American veterans whose employment might have supported my confidence in the produc-tion. Further, you will recall that I visited here two years ago and audi-tioned English people to play the part of Tony in THE MOST HAPPY FELLA. At these auditions, I found Wiata whom I subsequently brought to New York for a month and back at my own expense so that he could observe the part then being played expertly by Robert Weedy [sic] so that he could get American Equity's permission to perform on Broadway (through Mr. Weedy's courtesy) and so having satisfied me, as well as a New York audience, that he was capable of doing the part, that I could expect to engage him. All these things have been accomplished. I did not choose to demand an American in this role, although there were already many highly competent American possibilities. All this for the sake of complying wherever possible with the wishes of British Equity. I am only too pleased to continue to look for British talent for the shows I expect to do here, and it appears now that I will be doing several – hopefully in collab-oration with your office. It is to my advantage to know and appreciate as many British performers as I possibly can. Certainly, even in terms of economics involving transatlantic transportation etc., this is obvi-ously advantageous, but even beyond that I assure you I have no chauvinist American notions.

By the above observations I do not wish to express the opinion that there exists no possible successor to Froehlich. I would like to keep looking for him and toward this end I have already arranged for my return on June 27th and extended my stay through the month of July so that we can continue to beat the bushes for a British Pasquale. But considering the likelihood that he won't easily or soon be found, I am terribly frightened over the deadline now facing us. Please remember that we will already have lost a veteran in Farnworth[16] who is now to be substituted by a tenor less strong and less experienced. If there is no Froehlich at this time, a severe reduction in style and energy will be felt. Also recall that in November we lose Libbi Staiger,[17] and by the end of August we will have to do without the directorial maintenance and upkeep for which we are now paying Gerry Eskow. I know you and I would not like to see our run shortened considerably by negative word-of-mouth. We can pay for advertising and we can dry clean the costumes, and we can even ask Frank Loesser to take a cut in royalty, but we cannot artificially produce expert talent on the stage. Therefore, we now risk closing much earlier than we had hoped. Is this of no interest to British Equity? The personnel engaged on stage is of a much greater number than used on Broadway or anywhere in America, as is the number of musicians etc. It would be unfortunate if along about Christmas time we had to post a closing notice to the hard-working English employees.

I suggest I have been rambling, but I wanted to give you my point of view before leaving London. Can you possibly convey any of the sense of this to the people at British Equity? I hope you can.

Sincerely,

Susan Loesser reports on Frank's marriage to Jo Sullivan on 29 April 1959: 'They were both uneasy about their decision, and it took them some time to settle in comfortably together. "We didn't get along the first year at all," Jo told me. "I think we were both worried that we had made a terrible mistake. He was writing Greenwillow, and I would spend hours at the movies just to get out, because he was such a pain in the ass." '[18] The wedding was briefly mentioned in the *New York Times*: 'The ceremony was performed by Judge Stanley H.

---

16 American actor Ralph Farnworth (?1922–1994) played Giuseppe in the original London production, having performed smaller parts including the Bus Driver in the Broadway production.
17 American actress Libi Staiger (1928–2019) played Cleo in the original London production. She was married to Jerome Eskow, the production's director.
18 Loesser, *A Most Remarkable Fella*, 194.

Fuld of the State Court of Appeals in his private chambers at 36 West Forty-fourth Street.'[19] It was a low-key affair as Loesser explained to record producer Simon Rady (1909–1965).

14 May 1959: To Simon Rady

Dear Sy:

There were no fiddles at the nuptials or believe me, we would have called you first. Venuti[20] does not have the real connubial tone. This was a quickie by a judge with a tin ear.

Thanks for your good wishes.

Loesser's nephew Ted Drachman, who later became a professional lyricist – his musicals include *Narnia* (1985), an adaptation of *The Lion, The Witch and The Wardrobe* – was the son of his sister Grace (1907–1986). Loesser was fond of him and in the fall of 1959 he began a humorous correspondence with Drachman. Typically inventive, Loesser made himself out to be 'Dillinger C. Peck', President of the 'Rotten Kid Klub', and it became a long-standing joke between him and Drachman over the next few years. Dillinger is a reference to American gangster John Dillinger (1903–1934).

8 September 1959: To Teddy Drachman (Canaan, NY) concerning the Rotten Kid Klub

Dear Mr. Drachman:

Your application has been received and you are at this moment being considered for membership. Of course, we are grateful for your interest in joining this unworthy group, but our only apprehension is over the possibility that there may be remaining in you a few gangly shreds of worthiness. As you know, there are very strict

---

19 Anon., 'Loesser Weds Jo Sullivan', *New York Times*, 30 April 1959, 36.
20 Loesser is probably referring to the Joe Venuti (1903–1978) Orchestra, which accompanied singers including Bing Crosby, whose Roxbury label Rady was in charge of.

regulations governing this organization, and anyone not thoroughly rotten is of course, disqualified from membership.

Therefore, please find the enclosed questionnaire which will give us some idea about your fundamental depravity. Please fill out and return as tardily as possible. We do not admire promptness or neatness.

Most sincerely,
Dillinger C. Peck,
President

DCP: qq

QUESTIONNAIRE
For First-Time Applicants
(Answer each question "yes" or "no." Save your
fresh remarks for dinner time at home)

a. When your mother drives up in the car with 12 sacks of heavy groceries to bring into the house, do you at least open the car door for her?
   (if the answer to question (a) is "no," do not answer question (b))
b. Do you succeed in mashing her thumb when closing the door?
   (if (b) is unanswered by virtue of the ground rules, then you may answer the following:)
c. Do you stand gaping at the sky in search of migrant sea fowl?
d. Do you pick your nose?
e. Do you wait to do so during dinner?
f. Do you know a joke about two Irishmen that get off a trolley?
g. Do you keep telling it when your father is very tired?
h. Do you incinerate the papers when requested by either parent?
   (if the answer to (h) is no, do not answer question (i))
i. Do you include among the papers the Herald Tribune, just brought home and not yet read by your tired father?
j. Do you object to bathing?

For First-Time Applicants

(Answer each question "yes" or "no". Save your
fresh remarks for dinner time at home)

a. When your mother drives up in the car with 12 sacks of
    heavy groceries to bring into the house, do you at
    least open the car door for her?...................... Yes......
    No. ✓....

    (if the answer to question (a) is "no", do
    not answer question (b))

b. Do you succeed in mashing her thumb when closing the
    door?... Yes ✓ *
    No......

    (if (b) is unanswered by virtue of the
    ground rules, then you may answer the following:)

c. Do you stand gaping at the sky in search of migrant
    sea fowl?.. Yes ✓....
    No......

d. Do you pick your nose?.....⊟ 7.ee .y. ✓.............. Yes ✓....
    No......

e. Do you wait to do so during dinner? ✎ of... 4......... Yes ✓....
    No......

f. Do you know a joke about two Irishmen that get off a
    trolley? N.o. b.ut reasonable for Sample............ No ✓....
    Yes......

g. Do you keep telling it when your father is very tired?. Yes ✓....
    No......

h. Do you incinerate the papers when requested by either
    parent? when threatened............................. Yes ✓....
    No......

    (if the answer to (h) is no, do not answer
    question (I)

i. Do you include among the papers the Herald Tribune,
    just brought home and not yet read by your tired father? Yes ✓....
    No......

j. Do you object to bathing? hesitechly.................. Yes ✓...
    No......

k. Does the weight of family opinion ever overcome this
    objection?..bodily only.............................. Yes ✓....
    No......

    (if the answer to (k) is "yes", you may
    answer question (l)

l. Do you do so at a time calculated to use up all the
    remaining hot water?.................................. Yes ✓....
    No......

✳ the reason I am answering both is that I mash
her thumb in the screendoor!

9. Frank Loesser, Rotten Kid Klub questionnaire, 8 September 1959.

k. Does the weight of family opinion ever overcome this objection?

(if the answer to (k) is "yes," you may answer question (l))

l. Do you do so at a time calculated to use up all the remaining hot water?

m. Have you an older sister who is something of a dancer?

(if the answer to (m) is "no," do not answer question (n))

n. Have you ever tried tripping her as she comes down stairs?

o. Have you told that joke about the two Irishmen who get off the trolley in the last 5 minutes?

p. More than three times in the last 5 minutes?

q. Less than three times in the last 5 minutes?

r. Have the last 5 minutes given you great pleasure?

s. Have the last 5 minutes given your family great pleasure?

Signed:

7 October 1959: To Teddy Drachman re:
Rotten Kid Klub

Dear Kid:

Congratulations! You have been accepted as a full fledged member and we welcome you to our midst. Herewith is our official emblem, the meat hook, which you are now entitled to wear you know where.

The Klub had planned an early autumn picnic for last Sunday morning, but every single member was too lazy a slob to get up for it and nobody came. We all consider it quite a success and we are sorry you weren't there.

You will, however, be eligible to join us in our Halloween frolic. Here, you will learn, that we differ from other organizations in that we wear no makeup or costume whatsoever, and we play "trick or trick."

Once again, our heartiest welcome. Shortly, we will be sending you volume I of our own publication, "How To Produce and Maintain Anxiety in Others." It will come post paid in a regular book mailing carton. Please be sure to soak the whole thing carefully in a pail of

255

water overnight before opening. Meanwhile, do not let the ticking bother you. For new members we have enclosed a beetle who has been trained to turn pages.

EVOE![21]

Dillinger C. Peck

19 November 1959: To Teddy Drachman

Dear Kid:

For Thanksgiving try sulking. Then suddenly ask questions about the cranberries. Nothing pointed. Just enough for everybody to wonder how long your mother has had them in the freezer.

Yours for more poisonous

current events,

Dillinger C. Peck

The announcement of a new show, *Let's Go Steady*, on 5 June 1958 suggested Loesser might act as co-producer, noting that his 'interest stems from the fact that he regards Charles Strouse and Lee Adams, who will compose the music and lyrics, as the brightest talents to come forth in years'.[22] The show would become the award-winning *Bye Bye Birdie* (1960) and, although Loesser was not involved in the end, an internal letter reveals his thinking about the project. Edward Padula (1916–2001) directed Lerner and Loewe's early musical *The Day Before Spring* (1945) but subsequently worked as a stage manager until his debut as a Broadway producer with *Bye Bye Birdie*. The book for that show was eventually written by Michael Stewart (1924–1987) but Loesser's letter mentions Warren Miller, possibly the novelist (1921–1966) of *The Bright Young Things* (1958) and *The Cool World* (1959), and an unknown writer, Raphael Milian. Hillard Elkins (1929–2010) was a major agent in the 1950s who became a Broadway producer with a later hit Strouse and Adams musical, *Golden Boy* (1964).

---

21 An archaic expression meaning a Bacchic frenzy.
22 Louis Calta, 'Loesser Shows Interest', *New York Times*, 5 June 1958, 39.

17 April 1958: To Harold Orenstein

I have recently had exploritory [sic] talks with producer, Edward Padula. He is preparing for Broadway production, a musical now entitled, "GOING STEADY." Previously, Padula had brought to the attention of [Frank Music executive] Herb Eiseman a partially completed score of this piece, composers of which are Buddy Strouse and Lee Adams. The playwrights are Warren Miller and Raphael Milian, who seem to have collaborated on this script as an original. Subsequent to Eiseman's rather enthusiastic reception of the partial score, I heard it and was also given some idea of the story content – the script of which is almost ready, and will be sent to me in Los Angeles. In our meeting, Padula did not claim any rights or privileges or shares of interest in the publishing and allied rights, but simply was acting in concert with his writers in selecting a music publisher. Hillard Elkins entered the discussions as agent for the two composers. I volunteered that FHC would like to publish the score and Elkins indicated that his writers would require an advance of $5,000 against their royalty. In saying so, he admitted that he thought this was high. I heartily agreed and then, rather than try any further bargaining, both of us agreed to table these discussions and suspend any further negotiations with other publishers until such a time as I have finished reading the script and returned to New York.

Meanwhile, I opened discussions with Padula with regard to FPI collaboration as associate producer. He seemed to welcome my suggestion that FPI would bend its typical efforts for a 20% share of the general partnership (assuming that the general partnership would be due at least 50% of the net profits). One of the obligations I suggested FPI could assume was that of delivering limited partnership investments of a total of $60,000, which is ⅕ of the $300,000 anticipated for production. I further suggested that if smaller limited partnership investment were secured, that the 20% FPI interests would be reduced proportionately. No provision in our loose conversation about the possibility that a total limited partnership investment would be made in one piece by a network, advertiser, or some such organization. I told him that under no circumstances, however, would FPI require more than the 20%.

Padula also said that if he did accept some such deal as the above, that he would not mind FPI's purchasing its proprietary share for some token amount. I suggested this to avoid unfavorable interpretation in the event of a resale of the interest for capital gains purposes. I did not tell him what I thought the token amount would be, but I believe that $500.00 would be proper.

The associated producership billing would be similar to that with MUSIC MAN, except that FPI would control the emergence and billing of other contributors in the general partnership. The discussions on both publishing and producing levels will not continue until we have examined the script, as well as the proposed budget and production dates.

Nevertheless, I wanted to acquaint you with my conversations to date since I will be gone for two weeks, and upon my return will have to be reminded of what the hell I was talking about.

F.L.

On 29 January 1959, a column in the *New York Times* announced that 'Frank Productions, Inc. . . . is extending its scope. Mr. Loesser has established a new department and placed Lesser Samuels in charge as editorial consultant. His duties will include the discovery of plots suitable for processing into musical comedies.'[23] (Samuels had previously worked with Loesser on the book of *The Most Happy Fella*.) This appointment reflects the increasing focus on business discussions around producing musicals by other writers, whether *Bye Bye Birdie*, a possible adaptation of the 1940 MGM film *The Shop Around the Corner* (which eventually became Bock and Harnick's *She Loves Me* in 1963, but not under the auspices of Frank Productions), an adaptation of the 1934 film *Viva Villa!* that became Matt Dubey (1928–1998) and Harold Karr's (1921–1968) flop *We Take the Town*

---

23 Sam Zolotow, '"Raisin in the Sun" Sets Back Opening', *New York Times*, 29 January 1959, 19.

(1962),[24] or *The Merry Partners*, a musical about the stage partnership of nineteenth-century song and dance men Edward Harrigan (1844–1911) and Tony Hart (1855–1891), which only reached the stage as the flop *Harrigan 'n Hart* in 1985. J. Fred Coots (1897–1985) is best remembered as the composer of 'Santa Claus is Comin' to Town' (1934).

5 February 1959: To Harold Orenstein

Dear Harold:

In view of the surprising answer from MGM, in which they insist on owning publication and album rights, I believe it important for us at this time to confirm that this is indeed a policy already in practice and intended for future practice. First of all, we could afford to be mortally wounded if we had been made exceptions. Possibly this might lead to certain re-formation of MGM's proposals.

Nevertheless, the chances are that they will be firm on the above matter. More importantly, I believe Stu Ostrow should not waste his time with certain producers and song writers if MGM indeed holds to the above policy generally. At this moment, he is spending precious time with Max Liebman,[25] who seems to have acquired from MGM the rights to a Broadway musicalization of "Shop Around the Corner." Except for their sudden non-availability, Wright and Forrest would have been selected as the result of mutual approval and wild praise by both Liebman and Ostrow. This is a situation in which Ostrow has in good faith accepted Liebman's assertion that his contract with MGM does not involve the above type of limitation. Currently also I understand Dubey and Karr, plus some producer, have succeeded in getting musical stage rights to "Viva Villa" from M.G.M. Suppose Stu were to spend precious time, whiskey and a battery of blandishments in an effort to land this score – only to learn that it was not available.

---

24 *We Take the Town* was a star vehicle for Robert Preston of *The Music Man* fame.
25 Max Liebman (1902–1981) was the producer of a number of theatrical revues as well as the variety TV series *Your Show of Shows* (1950–54).

The above are just two examples. There may be many others in the making or in the wind or already arrived at. I think it is now important for us to do some detective work and find out under exactly what terms these works were acquired by prospective Broadway producers. I believe Stu could possibly wheedle a copy of the contract out of Liebman. Or possibly you have some acquaintanceship with Liebman's lawyer. We should know where the stone walls are and not rely on heresay [sic]. If we find they do not exist and that we have been handled with comparative disfavor, that would be an important fact to find out.

Every day someone suggests a play or property for Broadway musical treatment. A great many of these continue to be works at one time produced by MGM and subject to their ownership. It would help us hang up quick if we knew that there were uniformly stone walls about all such. In that way you could practice more law, Stu could pull harder on Mitch Miller's[26] beard, and I could get more unencumbered gems written every day. I leave you with the following quotation from Hollywood: Sic Transit Gloria Swanson.[27]

F.L.

P.S. Please discuss this with Stu.

16 February 1959: To J. Fred Coots

Dear Fred:

Answering your note and clipping concerning a Feuer and Martin production of "The Merry Partners," I don't believe that this is anything but a whim like many an announced title. But I will be speaking to them presently and find out.

Best wishes,

Frank Loesser

As part of the public widening of Frank Productions' remit, Loesser was frequently approached with ideas for songs, topics for

---

26 Mitch Miller (1911–2010) was the head of artists and repertoire at Columbia Records.

27 Gloria Swanson (1899–1983), the star of *Sunset Boulevard* (1950). Her film career declined precipitously thereafter; hence 'Sic Transit Gloria Swanson'.

musicals, or suggestions for songwriters to hire. He was diligent in offering his views, opinions and advice in writing, though he often preferred to speak in person instead. Warren Steibel (1925–2002) is best remembered as the producer of the long-running television programme *Firing Line* (1966–1999); his business partner was opera composer Leonard Kastle (1929–2011) who later wrote and directed the cult movie *The Honeymoon Killers* (1970), which Steibel produced. At the time of Loesser's letter, Kastle was a conductor and assistant musical director for NBC Television Opera Theater, and his short opera *The Swing* was broadcast under his direction in 1956. John J. ('Jack') Wildberg (1902–1959) was co-producer of several revivals of *Porgy and Bess* and *One Touch of Venus* (1943) with Cheryl Crawford (1902–1986). No information has been found about *Mr. Thornton and the Love Tree* but even without context Loesser's analysis of the script provides an insight into his views on musicals.

14 April 1958: To Warren Steibel

Dear Mr. Steibel:

Thank you for your suggestion about Mr. Kastle but I, too, am leaving town and would not be able to see him until the Fall, at the earliest.

A reflection on your next-to-last paragraph. I believe that all music is <u>serious</u> when approached seriously. The publisher's approach is no less <u>serious</u> than the composer's. The <u>seriousness</u> of the publisher may be measured in how much time, effort and cash he spends in trying to prove that the composer never should have been with Ricordi in the first place.

If Mr. Kastle feels like it, I will be glad to make a date sometime this Fall.

Sincerely,

19 January 1959: To Jack Wildberg

Dear Jack:

After reading the screen play "Mr. Thornton and the Love Tree," here is my gratuitous, narrow-minded, pompous and totally unalterable conviction. Taking it as a bare story and not as a lengthy and inexpert screen play, the number one problem in my mind is the presentation of Thornton as an engaging character. I guess this character existed some time in the Scott-Fitzgerald period, and probably enjoyed a fleeting attractiveness as did flagpole sitters and goldfish swallowers. I'm fairly certain that Americans today would not appreciate him as written. He is fighting for stakes which are mere dollars. This does not entitle him to much emotional expression, especially in song. He is irredeemable. Nothing he <u>wants</u> finds any emotional sympathy in the audience. If his mother had pneumonia, or he was in the throes of a great love for an unattainable woman, or if his wooden leg were holding him back from enlisting in the Bulgarian Navy to save the country, I would understand in each instance, such wonderful and violent outbursts as "Mammy," "Yours is My Heart Alone," or "The Star Bulgarianed Banner." But all he has to say or sing in the beginning is "Money Money Money," which may be interesting but not attractive considering that we are asking the audience to pay attention to this man for three solid hours. This does not bar him from wanting money, but I believe that something should redeem him long before 50 pages have been consumed. It can be a whopper. It can be a horrible mistake, like being stuck on an obviously wrong girl; or he may have ambitions to become famous as an acrobat or a politician or a lawyer. Toward any of the ends which propel him, he can of course use his aunt's money. Nevertheless, I feel he must have a need or a wish or a want that is emotionally understandable.

It seems to me that in terms of the present story his morbid allergy to dogs should be highly dramatized and illustrated in advance – and not simply reported on in two passing lines. We then find understandable a chemical horror at the very thought of the dog and not simply a rather cavalier neglect of it. Subsequently, I feel that Harriet can emerge as a valuable character and not just a juiceless professional virgin, but letting her function as dog psychoanalyst rather than leave that part to a casual player. In fulfilling this function she, of course, reveals to Thornton several interesting facts about his own personality and finally releases him from his terrifying allergy. This can provide some decent comedy scenes between our two principals, and not stuffy and phony ones. It seems to me that if a good-looking young lady wanted to train me how to pet a dog – breaking me in on her own comfortable person from ear scratching to belly tickling – that I would submit to the experiment rather willingly. If you were watching, I think it might give you some laughs. Especially when one of the rules was that for every groping privilege on the girl I had to pay the same compliment to the dog.

We are dealing with a simple and very old story. That is the regeneration of a man at the hands of a pretty young lady. If her resistance to his love-making is overcome by the Horatio Alger[28] stunt of his tackling her court case, she is simply a stuffy moralist. I believe his redemption has got to come out of a capacity for love. This way we are telling one solid story.

I'm now tired of being so pompous and will quit. Please call me if you want me to knock this some more. Meanwhile, thanks for letting me see it.

Best wishes,
Frank Loesser

George Abbott – book writer and director of *Where's Charley?* – corresponded with Loesser about the musical *Whoop-Up*, which opened on Broadway on 22 December 1958 and ran for only fifty-six performances. The book was by Feuer and Martin – the producers of Loesser's *Guys and Dolls* – and the score by Charlap and Gimbel; it was published by Frank Music. French movie star and crooner Maurice Chevalier (1888–1972) recorded a cover of the song 'Nobody Throw Those Bull'. American actor Fess Parker (1924–2010) was especially known for portraying the title character in the ABC television series *Davy Crockett*, produced by Walt Disney, from 1954 to 1955. At the time of his correspondence with Loesser, Parker was under contract to Paramount. Shamus Locke (1924–2003) was the co-producer, with Lynn Loesser, of Frank Music writers Wright and Forrest's *The Love Doctor* based on Molière. The musical had already

---

28 Author Horatio Alger's (1832–1899) novels often promote the rewards of good deeds.

folded in America after tryouts in Detroit and Cleveland (September–November 1957) under the title *The Carefree Heart*, with a cast including comedian Jack Carter (1922–2015) and Broadway actress Susan Johnson (1927–2003), who had played Cleo in *The Most Happy Fella*. It was now preparing for a 1959 opening in Manchester, UK, in August 1959 with a new cast headed by British character actor Ian Carmichael (1920–2010). Loesser offers Locke detailed suggestions about how best to secure a beneficial record contract. And to American composer Harold Spina's (1906–1997) request for assistance on an idea for a musical play, Loesser has a direct response. It's striking that he is so focused on the book and not just on the score. Loesser had previously acted as lyricist to Spina for the Paramount Film *True to the Army* (1942).

19 February 1959: To George Abbott

Dear George:

Herewith are selected songs by Charlap and Gimbel from the late lamented "Whoop Up." As I told you, I felt that the laments were much more expressed for the book, casting, etc. than for the actual song literature. As you can well imagine, Messrs. Feuer and Martin (known affectionately as Fang and Claw) dictated both subject and language level to the two song writers. I think Charlap and Gimbel show up very well considering this.

Please play this record (33 ⅓ r.p.m.) and observe for one thing the use of patois French in the Chevalier recording. The wordage and its accent is the invention of the composers, not Chevalier. Also, notice the capacity for duet writing in "Flattery" and the ability reflected in "Sorry For Myself?" to express personal pathos at least to the extent supplied by a totally unmoving book.

After playing this, if you feel like meeting with Charlap and Gimbel, of course I can arrange it. However, if as a result you feel like meeting with Cole Porter, I won't threaten to excommunicate you, but I may resign my position as Pope.

Regardless of the above suggestion and their outcome, I wish you would continue to keep me up to date with the book, just so I know.

I love to know. Everything but rhumba dancing. Popes are not allowed.

Love,

5 June 1959: To Fess Parker

Dear Fess:

Thanks for your note. We certainly enjoyed seeing you. Johnny[29] especially is still reeling. I wish it had been a longer visit. At the risk of sounding queer, I promise that I'll keep my beans warm for you.

About my suggestion concerning music and music rights, what I had in mind was the following: Since you are bargaining for compensation for your services as an actor in motion picture and TV films, you might find from time to time that you can agree to a salary or other reward that is a little smaller than you expected – if in return, the maker of the film will contract exclusively with your music publishing company to provide songs, as well as complete music background, signature and titles themes, etc., for such films. The film company would, of course, pay the composers, vocalists, musicians and arrangers for their work, but your music company would be given world publishing and allied rights in these compositions. Upon the public performance of these films on TV in the U.S. and in both theatres and TV elsewhere, your music company would then get its cash reward through the various performance societies with which it is affiliated all over the world. I don't know whether your music firm is BMI or ASCAP. Either way, it would get certain incomes from the above sources. Also, if your music company wanted to make the effort exploiting any separate pieces or even entire scores, it would control the printing and sale of various editions, as well as the licensing of mechanical rights. Here it would be wise to acquire from the film company the right to license for phonograph records and albums the actual music track of the films produced. At times, this sort of thing has become very lucrative for the publisher, and without any

---

29 Loesser's son, John (born 1950).

overwhelming effort. That depends on the power and importance of the motion picture and, again of course, its quality.

The above is a very loose description of what you might possibly ask for when somebody with a camera wants to make a living by shooting pictures of you. I believe you ought to get a more specific and detailed outline of such planning from your own lawyer. If you decide on the course I have described, and want help from any of my resources in foreign countries, I would be very glad to put you in touch with the right people in my outfit. At present, Frank affiliates include our own companies in England, Italy, Argentina and Canada. Soon we expect to add an autonomous operation in Germany. This means that we could, if it pleased you, safeguard your collection and other interests in these places.

My God! I sound like a business man! As you well know, I am a bean-cooking yachtsman who likes to write songs. But you asked for all this megilleh.

Best from Jo and me.

7 July 1959: To Shamus Locke

Dear Shamus:

I imagine that about this time some discussion must be going on about an original cast album for your show. I don't know who is entitled to negotiate or sign such an agreement, but I take it that you will be very much interested and therefore let me hasten to suggest some restrictions valuable to you as well as to the writers.

First of all, the exclusivity of such an album should be limited to the English production and cast, and nothing should prohibit members of the same cast (stars or otherwise) who later might appear in the Broadway version of this same show – from participating in a BROADWAY original cast album. Very often in their contracts record companies like to put too great a restriction on the participants. In this instance, you and Lynn and the writers will be very much concerned with an eventual Broadway version and it would be sad if one or more of the performers were not permitted legally to deliver similar services in America for an American record company and for the benefit of the production.

In connection with this, also note that a total restriction should be put on the recording company against distribution of records or masters in countries other than England. I note that here in New York we will soon have a theatre production of "At The Drop of a Hat." Long ago the English recordings were distributed here and sold in the stores. In consequence, a great number of first-nighters and many more in the early months will be too familiar with the material to bother to applaud – having already had years of access to the very faithful LP made in England and exported. You may well see how an ultimate BROADWAY cast album would seem an unattractive bargain in the face of already established competition with a foreign record already on sale and possibly well known.

I don't know anything about comparative income values between English and American LP's, but I would be willing to bet that our interested population here and its buying power predict an enormous balance in favor of American versions. As I understand it, the retail price of show LP's in England is almost prohibitive and in terms of gross sale there has been nothing resembling "Oklahoma!," "Guys and Dolls," "South Pacific," etc. I could be wrong, but in view of your and the writers' parallel interest in an ultimate American production and all its benefits, please consider the above cautions or, if you are not the one entitled to negotiate or close – pass them on to the proper party or parties.

I have a "safely arrived" cable from Lynn so I know she is all right. I have no doubt that you are and jolly well _expect_ the writers to be. Good luck to you all with the show.

Cordially,

3 August 1959: To Harold Spina

Dear Harold:

I have your note and various brochures addressed to me on flamboyant two-color stationery entitled "Glorioso Productions." I take it the production still features the immortal punch line (and I call it immortal because it has lived continuously in my memory since Sid Silvers[30] first quoted it to me in 1215 A.D.) – "on to Moskowitz." Whether or not this doubtful gem is still in the script, I am of course interested in your emergence into the legitimate musical field without benefit of historical federal court adjudication. I must reserve an expression of the extent of such interest until I see a script. Hearing a dub of the songs would only confirm my already established approval of anything you compose. What I would like to see is a script. I have learned in, lo, these many years that the play's the thing. This was Hamlet's shorthand for what he really meant. What he really meant was "the play's a motherfucker to accomplish." Let me see it.

Also, let me see your smiling face, play or no play, sometime soon. I don't wander through Laguna often enough to count on running into you by accident. Anyway, it was a great pleasant thing the last time.

Love to you and the family.

Frank Loesser

While Loesser was increasingly becoming the oracle for all things related to musicals and popular music, he was the first to admit that the culture was changing, in response to Ted McMichael of The Merry Macs vocal quartet. And if it seems that Loesser's activities were always successful, it is also the case that he sometimes lost writers from his stable. In the case of composer Hoagy Carmichael (1899–1981), with whom Loesser had written the hit 'Heart and Soul' (1938), correspondence suggests that the composer was negotiating for greater freedom rather than being obliged to publish all his songs through Frank Music. By the late 1950s most of Carmichael's considerable successes were behind him; it must have been difficult for Loesser to promote his new work. The composer had a law degree, which may explain his focus on the details of his contractual relationship with Frank Music.

---

30 Sid Silvers (1901–1976), comedian, actor and writer.

14 September 1959: To Ted McMichael

Dear Ted:

Thanks for your long note of September 6th. I hope we have been able to send you something you can use. Meanwhile, I am at a loss for a word of advice even though it's very flattering to be asked for it. As a matter of fact, almost all the problems you express in your letter have been and still are parallel to my own in the past years. It seems that the public taste can't be anticipated by "old-timers" like you and me any more. It used to be that we could call the turn both on compositions as well as their recordings. Now I guess this is no longer as easy and I notice that the business of predicting public acceptance is in the hands of somewhat younger people. It is hard to say whether or not they resemble what we were 15 years ago or earlier. I knew what to do with "Jingle Jangle" then and so did you, but I wouldn't know the first thing about it if it were at this time a fresh piece.

Of course, <u>quality writing</u> has a little longer life than <u>quality performance</u>. Therefore, sometimes a piece can become "standard," but seldom does a performance weather change in taste, methods of arrangement, recording etc. What has become obvious to me is that the torrent of new pieces on records have been mostly effective but quite easy to forget after 6 months or so. This very fact seems to be the reason why lately so many pop recording artists have tried to use hits again; a much greater proportion against current new material than was heard 15 or 20 years ago. I believe that until the level of current writing comes up a notch that interesting new expressions of old standards will have a better chance in the market. Is it possible for you to record such pieces? Or do the record companies prefer you do the odds and ends you so painfully describe? You seem to describe a somewhat oppressive situation which I don't really understand.

Answering some of your specific questions – I couldn't possibly write a 30 minute show of "sell" material, even if I had the time, because I no longer have that kind of talent. Also, I am up to my neck in finishing a new Broadway show – an industry to which I escaped partly out of fear of competing with "Kookie – Lend Me Your Comb."[31]

About management I have no idea who is good, but if something occurs to me for you to investigate, I'll be glad to suggest. Meanwhile, let me think about you seriously and see if I can come up with an idea. Can you send me an 8x10 print of the group?

In closing, let me once more admit my own ignorance and weakness about the present day music business. If I knew how, I'd be the first person to wave the magic wand over the Merry Macs.

Yours as ever,

7 May 1959: To Hoagy Carmichael

Dear Hoagy:

Forgive me for the long delay in answering your letter of the 22nd. I am not even answering it with this one, but simply apologising for making you wait. You can appreciate how occupied I've been. Number one, I just got married. Jo Sullivan. I don't remember whether you ever met her. Anyway, I did, and look what happened! Secondly, Harold [Orenstein] has been in Europe until yesterday. And thirdly, I have been trying to finish writing a show that won't write easily [*Greenwillow*].

Anyway, rest assured that we won't have any difficulty and very soon I will be able to suggest a total agreement with your already made suggestions, or something very close to it. Sincerely, I don't mean to hold anything up and, as you know, I certainly would not want to be any kind of a villain with you. Hold tight, and I'll get back to you very soon.

Love,

5 June 1959: To Hoagy Carmichael

Dear Hoagy:

I blush, but our last communications came right in the middle of an enormous exercise in bigamy on my part. I not only got married to

---

31 Song by Irving Taylor (1914–1983) based on the character Kookie from the television show *77 Sunset Strip*.

Jo Sullivan (as predicted by [the music journalist] Radie Harris in 1911), but simultaneously became wedded to collaborators and producers on a Broadway show. Being a man of conscience, you can understand what a time I've been having keeping these two marriages compatible. That's my excuse for taking this time to answer your last. I do remember getting off a short note to you asking you to wait, so I don't feel too badly about the delay.

My legal department reminds me that everyone all around, including yourself, had already approved a re-arrangement of our doings together, one which involved the turning over of 50% of the Carmichael stock immediately rather than waiting for the long period prescribed in our original contract – and leaving you free in every respect, while leaving us with whatever material was now assigned to the company. I believe that this was actually suggested by you and I feel that it is probably the best course. In your note you suggest some compensation to us for our efforts and I feel I wouldn't want you to write us a check of any kind. I think such a course would stigmatise our relationship which I take great pride in (and pleasure), even though so far it has not been enormously profitable. In adopting the "adjustment" I have tried to recollect above – you will have absolute freedom of action and we will have some remnants with which to try to prove to you as time goes by that we are indeed Carmichael-minded. I know you too long and admire you too much to let anything of yours sit there. Also, I would like in the future to be able to set up such things as television musicals for your consideration, and have a door marked "Carmichael Music" for you to pop in, at least on a single project of such kind.

So I hope that we can settle things in the manner originally decided on. My legal department tells me that they have already prepared an agreement along these lines. Shall I have them shoot it to you fast? Let me know immediately. If you feel otherwise, (and I hope you don't) tell me right away. I'm just as anxious as you for mutual contentment.

Love,

24 June 1959: To Hoagy Carmichael

Dear Hoagy:

Thanks for your note. I won't be able to answer at great length in this present one to you, but it makes me happy to get things settled and I wanted to say so.

Your letter accepts our proposed contract whereby we obtain 50% stock proprietorship in Carmichael Publications now, instead of waiting seven years. Therefore, with some sadness, I acknowledge the fact that you are now free to do what you please with all your new unpublished material to come. Naturally, we would like to see whatever you write before any other publisher does, but that will be up to you.

As to your current suggestion about Frank Music activation of any of your new songs, and the pre-arrangement of a 50-50 share at some later time – I feel that we would be drawing a diagram at this moment of something that doesn't exist. I think we ought to avoid any such formal arrangement now and wait until you offer us something and at that time we can arrive at a suitable deal based upon our enthusiasm for each other's work, and based on a clear analysis and estimate of the values to each of us on that particular work.

As far as Nacio Herb Brown[32] is concerned, please let me think about what you propose for a week or so. Meanwhile, I can get this off to you in a hurry and very shortly I will have some kind of answer on your suggestion about a Carmichael Music contribution to Brown's fees. At that time, your opinion of his services and value to you will be enriched by another week's experience. I don't want to hold up this present communication to you.

I take it that contracts formalizing the main content of this letter have already gone out to you. If they have not, I will see that they are enclosed herewith.

Speaking of "enclosed herewith," I'm so busy I've just overtaken and swallowed myself. I can now eat a hot dog and burp lyrics. This is possibly from doing exemplary dance steps for my producers in the

---

32 Ignacio Herbert (Nacio Herb) Brown (1896–1964), best known for the songs (from various earlier projects) that formed the score of the movie *Singin' in the Rain* (1952).

absence of a choreographer. These steps are prompted by the fact that I don't have time to pee, but I AM going to get a show on this winter. This is partly determination and partly because I don't have the strength to shoot myself. I wish we were back in the days when the ex-wives suggested usable song titles and we had all year long to steal money from Paramount.

Love,

Frank Loesser

Now approaching his fiftieth birthday, Loesser was a well-established figure in the community by the end of the decade. Four notes to friends and colleagues illustrate the many calls on his attention. Russel Crouse, playwright (*Life with Father*, 1939) and book writer (*Anything Goes*, 1934), requested a charitable donation from Loesser. A close friend, Larry Adler (1914–2001) was a famous harmonica player often falsely credited with giving Loesser the idea for the song 'Rodger Young'.[33] Composer Albert Hague (1920–2001) was the writer of musicals including *Plain and Fancy* (1955) and *Redhead* (1959), winner of the Tony Award for Best Musical; Loesser had just been to see the latter at the time of writing to the composer. Alexander Cohen (1920–2000) was one of the most prolific theatrical producers of his generation. Loesser's letter includes a startling list of the companies with which he was now associated (nor is it comprehensive – Music Theatre Inc. is missing).

5 May 1958: To Russel Crouse

Dear Buck:

Here's enough money to cover the cost of supporting one small Jew for a duration of nine seconds on the basketball court at the "Y." At his election, he may instead get new laces for his sneakers – or buy some undelinquent girl a coca-cola. Anyway –

Love and kisses,

Encl.

Check for $10.00 to YMCA

---

33 See Chapters 1 and 2; also Loesser, *The Most Remarkable Fella*, 51.

4 December 1958: To Larry Adler

Dear Larry:

In answer to paragraph 1: I don't know anything about the "Village Gate" but will probably be there a half hour before you go on for the first time – just to shush people.

Answer to your second paragraph: Yes, I am interested in whatever you write, even if it's a score for a Max Bygraves picture.

Answering No. 3: I believe I can recommend a good accompanist, at least, I can suggest one for you to audition. [Pencil annotation: Abba Bogin[34]] But, that will have to wait till you get here. Since this is December 4, I take it your arrival is imminent, which is why this is such a hurried note, in answer to yours.

I'm glad you didn't get a look at "Where's Charlie" [sic] as you would have hated it with renewed vigor.

Love to you and the family.

15 June 1959: To Albert Hague

Dear Albert:

I finally caught up with you at the 46th Street Theatre and oh, my, what a wonderful evening I had. You and Dorothy and the others have done a terrific job and at this point I want to apologize for underestimating Kiley's[35] talents. When he sang in "Kismet" he didn't have one-tenth of what he is showing in your theatre. It was a most exciting surprise to me. Of course, I needn't tell you what wonders Verdon[36]

---

34 Max Bygraves (1922–2012), comedian. Abba Bogin (1925–2011), conductor and arranger.

35 Richard Kiley (1922–1999), actor and singer. In addition to *Kismet* (Robert Wright and George Forrest, 1953) he also appeared as Don Quixote in *Man of La Mancha* (1965) among many other stage shows and films.

36 Gwen Verdon (1925–2000), star actress and dancer, winner of the Tony for her performances in Adler and Ross's *Damn Yankees* (1955), *New Girl in Town* (Bob Merrill (1921–1998) and George Abbott, 1957) and *Redhead* (Albert Hague, 1959).

does, but then Dorothy[37] and you supplied most of them, and so, congratulations.

Sorry that I hadn't seen it earlier, but as of Friday night it was still plenty fresh enough for me.

Love, and thanks to you and Dorothy.

Sincerely,

18 June 1959: To Alexander H. Cohen

Dear Alex:

I take it you are the Alexander Cohen who sent me the case of O'Keefe beer. I haven't tried it yet, but I'm sure that it will do the same thing to my bladder as all other brands. I'm very grateful for the ease with which I perform the above function – ever since my first painful fright after a weekend with a lady named Hortense on the wrong side of Albany, New York. So I am therefore very grateful to you for the beer. Also curious to know why you think it's going to have great meaning in show business. You know it can't possibly have without:

Frank Productions, Inc.
Frank Music Corp.
Frank Management Corp.
Frank Distributing
Audubon Music Inc.
Empress Music Inc.
Saunders Publications, Inc.
Desilu Music Corp.
Carmichael Music Publishing Inc.
Liberty Songs Inc.
Union Record Co.
Andrew Music Corp.
Luther Music Inc.

---

37 Dorothy Fields (1904–1974), lyricist of more than 400 Broadway songs including 'The Way You Look Tonight' and 'A Fine Romance' (both from the Fred Astaire–Ginger Rogers film *Swing Time,* 1936) and 'Big Spender' (*Sweet Charity,* 1966).

Simon Jackson Inc.
Annavic Music Corp.
Messina Music Corp.

Frank Loesser

Loesser was concerned with all aspects of the business: it was not just a case of offering advice via letters but providing the right ambience at his headquarters. He instructed that the offices of Frank Productions be redecorated, apparently in line with a recent overhaul of those of Music Theatre Inc.

15 June 1959: To Allen Whitehead
(Frank Productions Inc.)

Dear Allen:

In connection with our so-far very effective socio-industrial relations efforts, please do not hesitate in using your imagination toward making our new office an attractive show-place. There is an increasing flow of important visitors to our headquarters and, as we discussed, we should take advantage of any effect of <u>graciousness</u> we can produce in our very high-rent office suite. Virtually all Broadway producers, veterans and new-comers alike – sit in dingy, badly lighted and dismally furnished little offices with rumpled clippings and type-writers and dirty window panes painfully in evidence. The vast majority of such colleagues are located on streets much better known for less dignified and older pursuits – prostitution, hot-dogs, delica-tessens, and cut-price shoe stores.

You will recall how profound was the result of the manner in which you organized the Music Theatre Inc. premises and personnel. Please go even further in this instance. Of course, I know you will be cautious about expenditures, but there may be various occasions on which it will be a good investment to loosen up. The curtains look fine and the air-conditioners do a thoroughly comfortable job. Please observe carefully the furnishings and how they could improve, both as to comfort and design. Also, will you see that we get better than the normal cleaning service and window washing.

Very possibly soon we may want to talk about some cocktail party here, and come that afternoon there should be no more tables with legs that fold, or secretaries with the same inclination.

23 June 1959: To Stanley Smilow

Dear Mr. Smilow:

Just a note to tell you how pleased I am with your design and decoration of my company's headquarters. Not only do my staff and I enjoy the comfort, beauty and practicability so excellently combined by you, but I relish telling you that many of our visitors and conferees compliment us frequently on the graciousness of the Music Theatre, Inc. surrounds. This quality is in itself an enormous asset in our socio-industrial efforts, and along with Mr. Whitehead and the others, I send you my warmest thanks and admiration.

Sincerely,

Frank Loesser

By 1959, *Greenwillow* was substantially written and Loesser started to build a production team. Hollywood veteran Leo McCarey (1898–1969) – whose work included *The Awful Truth* (1937), *Going My Way* (1944), and *An Affair to Remember* (1957) – was initially considered for the director, but George Roy Hill (1921–2002), later famous for directing *Butch Cassidy and the Sundance Kid* (1969) and *The Sting* (1973), was hired. On 4 September 1959, the *New York Times* confirmed that *Greenwillow* would open the following February. At last, Loesser's next show was in sight and, as ever, he wanted to explore new ideas in its production. Loesser had read an article in the *New York Times* on 1 November, titled 'Company Buying Psychiatric Help', in which it was reported that a new Division of Psychiatric Services had been opened at Mount Sinai Hospital to 'explore a new concept in the care, treatment and prevention of mental upsets' in the work-place. The article continued: 'Developed and directed by Dr. Milton

R. Sapirstein, staff neurologist and psychiatrist, the division has two principal functions. One is to provide psychiatric services to corporate employees along the lines of general medical services furnished by company medical departments. The other is to conduct research on a variety of psychiatric problems as they affect industry and the health of workers.' The article added that mental health was costing businesses 'billions of dollars' due to absence, accidents and reduced productivity.[38] Loesser was curious, and made a suggestion for how his company could get involved:

30 June 1959: To Leo McCarey

Dear Leo:

After a whole lot of deep thinking, all of us (the producers and myself) have made a decision about the direction of the show. Before you read about it in a trade paper I felt, after our discussions and your enthusiasm and ours about the possibility of your joining us, that I ought to let you know personally.

One of the most important things that has happened is that the book more and more emphasizes the relationship between the two ministers in "Greenwillow," and that, although totally unrelated to "Going My Way," might seem to smack of motif repetition if in any way connected with you. This, of course, would not be very good for either of us. Maybe I'm splitting hairs, but I know at this point that I could not afford to tackle another Runyon[39] kind of story for fear that comparisons would easily be made not quite favoring the new one.

Anyway, I wanted you to know and thank you for your interest and to tell you that I sincerely hope we can work on something together some day. Preferably from scratch. Meanwhile, of course, my kindest regards.

Sincerely,

---

38 Morris Kaplan, 'Company Buying Psychiatric Help', *New York Times*, 1 November 1959, 124.

39 Damon Runyon (1880–1946), author whose short stories, in particular 'The Idyll of Miss Sarah Brown', were the inspiration for Loesser's *Guys and Dolls*.

13 November 1959: To Dr. Milton Sapirstein

Dear Dr. Sapirstein:

I have read with great interest the New York Times story about your leadership of the Mt. Sinai Psychiatry Department, in its apparently effective handling of office and industrial groups. I would like to explore with you the possible value to all concerned in my forthcoming show "Greenwillow."

Here I refer to a special collaborative process among sixty people for a duration of 8 to 10 weeks covering the time of preparation, rehearsal, road tryout and opening of a new show. In my experience this process is one which can be counted on to include a high monkey-wrench frequency. The simple differences of opinion, the emergence of violent jealousies, sudden apathetic drops in energy and attention, misfiring business decisions, and seemingly too frequent health failures, laryngitis, colds and physical accidents.

The above, obviously, are impediments to the overall purpose of the collaboration. But we are dealing here not with the ordinary office or factory control system of command from the high down to the low. We are dealing with a cockamamie collection of people, each of whose lives is dedicated to the idea that he or she is a very special, self-propelled and highly luminous individual. All our heads have the built in lumps and bumps that made us go into this business in the first place. Or maybe I'm painting this nutty picture for you out of one of the tendencies I am trying to describe. Anyway, we are not the Amalgamated Blueprint Corporation with sixty clerks.

I am sure you have a great deal of advance information or suspicion along these lines. At any rate, maybe you and your staff have enough curiosity to think about a deal by which you could work with our project. You yourself as a consultant in the writing of "Greenwillow" have a head start. The point would be to avoid some of the hazards I have just tried to describe – or if they persist, to use your expert knowledge in ending them or rendering them harmless.

Of course, I know that this would be an experiment, but certainly so is a new show, and so is psychiatry itself. Notice that I am not here representing the Greenwillow Company, but my own production company, which is a substantial partner in the enterprise. I would not like to introduce this subject until I have gone over it with you, so that I have a way of reporting the cost, the technique of your work, etc., and tested to some reasonable extent the acceptability of this plan to the individuals involved – from the frenetic producers down to the irritated seamstress in the basement who has an incurable ulcer because she "sewed the waist correctly in the first place, but it's the leading lady's fault for getting fat, and she can't sing good anyway, so I'm not coming to work. . . ." The group, of course, includes me.

Please phone me when you have absorbed this.

> Best regards,
> Frank Loesser

5 January 1960: To Milton R. Sapirstein

Dear Milton:

As I've already told you informally, my own suggestion about psychiatric care of a theatrical company blew up in my face. My group has reasons, some of them good, why they would rather not subscribe to the idea.

One of the chief arguments is the oyster-pearl argument. That is, that artistic or creative people kindle their sparks out of pressure, discomfort, hostility, ultra-competitiveness and other itches . . . and that a state of calm or self-satisfaction rarely delivers pearls from anything but a hack who should have been fired for eating so regularly, sleeping so well, and loving everybody. I must admit there is some merit in this argument. At the same time, I argued against it because of its too specific "first-aid" approach, and tried to point out that your staff would not just be sitting there with iodine and splints in case of a fist fight in the alley, but would be much more subtly concerned with warding off the impulse toward the first blow. This argument was countered by the suggestion that a new rabbi is hardly ever trusted, and that this effort would be of very short duration and that there would be no time for the company to develop a true reliance or trust – probably nothing but a self-conscious and frightened awareness of the stranger.

As the man said as he wearily laid down the twelve bottles of Cutty-Sark – I rest my case.

Sorry to trouble you. Probably will again.

Best,

In January 1960, *Greenwillow* was in rehearsal, due to play at Philadelphia's Shubert Theatre for the first two weeks of February. Its cast was headed by Anthony Perkins (1932–1992), on the brink of stardom thanks to his role in Hitchcock's *Psycho* (1960), which started filming just weeks before rehearsals started for *Greenwillow*; Pert Kelton (1907–1968), fresh from her appearance as Mrs. Paroo in *The Music Man* on Broadway, appeared alongside him. The production team was headed by the (previously mentioned) director George Roy Hill, who was hired over Loesser's preference for Moss Hart because he had directed Perkins in *Look Homeward, Angel* (1957),[40] and choreographer Joe Layton (1931–1994), who had worked on *The Sound of Music* (1959), then still running on Broadway. But it's apparent from a set of notes from Loesser to Hill that the show was in trouble.

29 January 1960: To George Roy Hill

The following notes are based on a look at the show at Thursday night's run-through and can't help but be pretty much the same as will be obtained from the Philadelphia opening night. I am not here going to discuss the obvious murder to the play by the lighting formula I saw, as I understand that is under radical repair. But the time has come to paint in black and white and not fuzzy grays. It seems incredible that the only clean delivery of words on the stage comes from a singer who is not supposed to know how to act. There are no great shadowy subtleties in this play or its lyrics – certainly not in its lollipop scenery and costumes. Why they should have to be in the playing of it I don't know. Certainly it is hard enough to play a drawing

---

40 Barney Lefferts, 'He Sings in "Greenwillow"', *New York Times*, 28 February 1960, X3.

room piece to 400 seats with faces turned upstage. In our show, we have speaking and singing voices with neither enough decibels nor timbre to do anything but come down and yell. Here the subtlety is the director's, but not ostensibly the actors'.

I believe every effort should be made to justify and qualify the delivery of the script and the songs head-on. This involves certain conventions, like the tall boy standing behind the short girl so we can see and hear both. Sure we wince. We also wince at C major and 32-bar songs, but with an inner pride in doing them better than Julie Styne. There is something wonderful about corn and it should not be overlooked. I have not made this a field day for musical gymnastics or quarter tone coloratura passages. Where such conceits have occurred to me, I have volunteered to throw them out before anybody else nudged me into it ("Buzz-A-Buzz"). I am now volunteering to throw out "Yes Moss" in favor of a better and shorter idea – as well as "Tangle" which I will discuss later in these notes.

Among the other conceits that have to be rooted out are those side issues that blow the very point that is involved. The montage (God forgive me for ever using that word – it has screwed us out of too much time. The entire play happens to be a montage) . . . Like I was saying, the montage is full of such conceits. It is not to any good point that we illustrate how ladies gossip and men try to stop them. Certainly, if there is gossip, it should not be away from the presence of those gossiped about. Also, the sweeping up game, which escapes me in terms of our purpose in showing a continuing courtship. I have a plan for the montage which I think we should discuss, so I'll drop the subject here.

But there are other conceits which become harmful diversions. Included are Maidy's not knowing when to kneel in "He Did Good." If the song does not say itself, I will be glad to take it out. But first it should try to say it well.

SPECIFICS

1. Jabez shirt: The misfit idea is a conceit. I'd like to see him as bare-ass as the law allows, so we get something out of "Looks

like little Jabez," especially if he is two steps up and knocks. We will discuss dressmaking any time. I didn't think I'd have to.

2. Jabez sniffing: Could not be discerned by anyone. It succeeds in tilting his head back as if he'd been hung. Much more important is the forward purpose.

3. The pace of the villagers in the opening scene should be leisurely. The music can be controlled to accompany this. There is no possible way to get better excitement out of opening than with the falling scenery. We want to throw in excitement of Riddleweed and therefore it should be against an existing sweetness and calm and not an attempt to walk four steps to the bar. We have no bombastic overture and no rip-roaring activity to open with, and any attempt at pace only promises something it will not deliver.

4. Jabez' knock on door (music cut-off – Maidy speech).

5. Lapp's hat and manner of wearing it.

6. Music cue on discovery of Riddleweed. Physical and strong. "Heavens to Habbakuk!" is what draws attention of crowd, not Gramma's private reaction.

7. Dramatic mystical light change for riddleweed.

8. Riddleweed number should be insistent, climactic, ritual. Almost trancelike and yet predicted by Gramma's delivery of information. Present tone is still Brooklyn washer-woman, with no sense of real mystery expressed.

9. Riddleweed – If a re-routining of the first scene permits (as of plan at present being suggested) – there is no reason why Gideon and Dorrie cannot take part in the ritual. Gideon may very well be the youngling who nearly trod on it. Separating Gideon and Dorrie – on either side of Gramma – keeps them visible but not communicating.

10. "Push to the west, etc." should be more doggerel. Gideon should say entire couplet, not just finish it, with characteristic elbows over head in ritualistic style.

11. Delivery of first "Nesting Dove" in fast 4/4 time doggerel.

12. If Maidy and Emma say "The boy takes it hard, etc" they should be in crowd reacting to Gideon's cross, or in some way be

connected with this reaction. At present they are not. Consider giving Maidy and Emma a part in the "far past hell" dialogue. They are more valuable characters and more realistic performers. This might make the connection and gives them only two steps more center.

13. Second "Nesting Dove" somehow not ritual. Can Joe find a way for the girl to plant her feet so the porch does not rock her off?

14. Tangle: Has to be done expertly or not at all. This is difficult in the face of the fact that we have engaged no experts on stage. Even when it is done brilliantly and with wonderful precision, it is a terrible piece of robbery. It works for all the world like the verse of a big homecoming song and then gets truncated by a hug and a joke. In this same scene, we are forced into this same sort of thing by the call, which promises to be a song and isn't. I do not wish to rob the customers twice in the same 10 minutes. If we can review part of the December script (third draft) and maybe improve it and play it with the same kind of action now in Tangle, we may be improving ourselves and get more pace than we now have.

15. Gideon's occasion to whistle while upbraiding his father should follow the script. I think there are 3 occasions. This is the beginning of Amos' remorse. Amos is playing swashbuckler when he should be on his way to penitence. He is commending Lapp to "pray him."

16. "How I'd wish to see him dead" is superfluous and should be substituted by a line of scornful doubt as to whether the devil's hand will ever get off his father's throat. This gives him a shocking surprise to see his father kneeling – and he really has something actively dramatic to react to. I'll discuss this with Lesser.

17. I still do not like "Naturally" and would like to put something else in there. Also for Lesser and me to discuss. It should still be one or two words only, and should be expressed after a solid beat following – not during – whatever response "Is he gone" gets.

18. Gideon's hooking on to Amos' singing at the start of the first MOH[41] chorus is a whole lot of caboose-riding. I need field glasses and a hearing aid to find out where the squeak is coming from. My eye has to shift from Martha and Amos and finally I've found Gideon and I've lost all sense of satisfied commentary on what he sees. I feel he should be directly up of them, encourage their physical union, and be seen reacting way in advance to his father's new-found proclivity for home cooking and wife-screwing. If he wants to drag Micah over with him, I don't care. I don't care where anybody drags Micah. The entire above process should be observed and appreciated by the ensemble. They should be seen leaning in or actually coming forward. They should be totally attentive and appreciative when father and son go into the cook's tour, starting with "Crickets in the grass." Their avid happiness over the reunion should make all their "welcome singing" come out of them at the peak of their interest, not simply at an Abba Bogin downbeat. At present, they are all marble-eyed and flat-footed and thinking of their insurance.

19. The recital of the call should find Amos intensely isolated light wise. During the recital, Gideon should be as dark as possible. During "Such is the curse … etc", we should sneak back to general lighting and at the same time, blow up Gideon for "Then knowing that ..."
We have prepared a slightly different finish for this scene and Dorrie's exit. Whatever happens, the puny half chorus of MOH should not be a befuddled search for exits but a very very very concentrated attention on the subject of Gideon giving romantic chase off stage. This is, again, a matter of leaning in and working with Amos and his point of view.
Gideon's off stage calls of "Dorrie" should be big and loud enough to bring the entire ensemble forward even though only one asks "What's that." The others are acting out the same question and then in answer. Amos indicates something

---

41 Song, 'The Music of Home'.

distanceward. This takes eye fixation, and the only way to produce it is to order it by the numbers.

20. We have prepared new dialogue for scene 3. It is intended to give Gideon a forward, self-assertive continuity of action and speech. It should be played with a kind of impatience by Gideon, and I think with much less leisure than previous versions. The description of the swing does not let Gideon savor the image, but simply passes it on to the girl. This is an unnecessary failure and can easily be fixed by a prescribed timing. That is, of course, if he is within 6 miles of Dorrie's apparently leprous body.

A review of the Philadelphia preview offered few concerns: 'Although Frank Loesser's beguiling score is easily the feature of the show, the book that he and Lesser Samuels have concocted from B. G. [sic] Chute's novel is way above average, with warmth, intelligence and understanding. The score is undoubtedly one of Loesser's best. Virtually every song is a delight . . . "Greenwillow" can stand cutting in the first act, but after that it's just about right as is, with the proviso that the Dickensian flavor will be boxoffice.'[42] Yet other reviewers in Philadelphia were less enthusiastic, and on 17 February it was announced that the Broadway opening had 'been delayed for about five days so that more polishing can be done on it', with several New York previews added.[43] And *Greenwillow* became the stuff of jokes: in the *Hollywood Reporter*, Radie Harris gleefully related in her 'Broadway Ballyhoo' column that 'After seeing "Greenwillow" in Philly, Anita Loos quipped, "This makes 'Sound of Music' sexier than 'Diamond Lil'!"'[44]

---

42 Waters, 'Legitimate: Shows Out of Town', *Variety* 217/10 (3 February 1960), 70.
43 Louis Calta, 'Musical Postponed', *New York Times*, 17 February 1960, 31.
44 Radie Harris, 'Broadway Ballyhoo', *Hollywood Reporter* 158/49 (18 February 1960), 4. Anita Loos was known for writing the witty novel *Gentlemen Prefer Blondes* (1925). Rodgers and Hammerstein's *The Sound of Music* was often dismissed as saccharine; here, Loos is comparing it favourably to the racy Mae West play *Diamond Lil* (1928) as the ultimate put-down of *Greenwillow*.

Nonetheless, the show proceeded to New York. In a preview in the *New York Times*, Anthony Perkins said: 'As for the songs, Loesser had told me that the only time a song should occur is when the emotion has become so intense that it's no longer sufficient to explain it in speech. I try to bear that in mind. When I'm doing a number, I try to remember that it's a moment so intense I can't speak it.'[45] And Loesser tried to plug the show's score through cover versions by popular singers: for example, Rosemary Clooney (1928–2002) made a single of 'Summertime Love', Bing Crosby recorded 'The Music of Home' and Della Reese (1931–2017) covered 'Faraway Boy'. The latter was picked as one of the 'strongest releases of the week' by *Billboard*.[46] Among the opening night telegrams was one from Meredith Willson ('GO GET 'EM KID'). And Loesser thanked George Marek of RCA Victor, the record company that was to record the original cast album of *Greenwillow*.

10 March 1960: To George Marek
(NB RCA Victor) (Telegram)

THANKS FOR ALL YOUR GREAT CONFIDENCE AND CO-OPERATION. VERY SINCERELY
   FRANK LOESSER

In his typical style Loesser focused on improving and fixing details. An exchange with the show's musical director and orchestrator reveals his usual sense of humour.

15 March 1960: To Abba Bogin and Don Walker

This is a bet.
   With Abba Bogin and Don Walker.
   As Follows:

---

45 Lefferts, 'He Sings in "Greenwillow"'.
46 Anon., *Billboard* 72 (29 February 1960), 57.

I hereby proclaim to Jew and Gentile alike that the second half of bar 6 of "The Music Of Home"[47] is being played wrong. It should be harmonized as a tonic major exactly one full tone higher than the key in which the piece is being played. I refer specifically to that measure which accompanies very badly (and as far as the album is concerned, permanently badly) the immortal word ANGEL – even more specifically the syllable GEL. Terrifically specifically I reiterate and embellish as follows:

That if the song is being performed in D Major, then the chord on GEL has got to be E Major. Just to push a point, I give you another example. If the song is being played in B Flat, the chord should be C Major. Further, I insist that in the album we are playing a cockamamie G 7th, instead of a C Major (in a B Flat chorus).

28 March 1960: To Abba Bogin

Dear Abba,

Your Carta arrived and it sure was Magna. I will not subscribe to one bit of it and you can come and get me here at Runnymede. Meanwhile a group of my masked henchmen have been inquiring about who did the typing and who paid the bill for the photostat of the score.

Further, Sandra Klein who seems to have notarized the untutored series of x's which distinguish your signature – happens to be one of my ladies in waiting and has already sworn the notarization to be a forgery, probably executed by Emery Davis in his own defense.

You are advised in addition, that Donald Walker who has been misharmonizing me during my entire reign is already scheduled for the gallows or possibly, through my leniency, a life sentence in the Tower with no pencil sharpener. Lastly, I wish to remark on the mendicant and mercenary baseness of the final suggestion in your document. The wish to be engaged to re-record is deep in the hearts of all you scoundrels. It means nearly fifty golden guineas per slovenly session for each contributor, and I know well the scheming tithe you

---

47 Handwritten annotation: a song from *Greenwillow*.

exact from these vassals of yours. You have already robbed one of my precious provinces of time and energy in the preparation of your enormous self-incriminating Megilleh (to coin a suitably base phrase). In this suicidal waste of time there is no doubt that you have neglected to rehearse understudies or to resume your archive work among my deathless and harmonically impeccable manuscripts.

Fie on you

Frank

P.S. As a matter of fact, fie double sharp.

P.P.S. That particular spot in the album still smells from Herring.

c.c. Pope John XXIII

Greenwillow was not a success, and the New York critics made it clear that there were serious problems. John Chapman of the *New York Daily News* summarised it best, saying that *Greenwillow* 'is filled with songs, robust, lilting, or charming; its company is one of the best, from Anthony Perkins to a captivating small boy whom I cannot identify from the program; the airy, flying Peter Larkin sets create a lovely dream world. But I'll be blessed if I can tell you what it's about.'[48] Leonard Hoffman added in the *Hollywood Reporter*: ' "Greenwillow" has a book as slim as a reed and about as straight.'[49]

B. J. Chute, who wrote the novel on which the musical was based, continued to believe it could be improved. But Loesser was the first to admit it was not good enough and his ultimate response made it clear he thought it was a lost cause. *Greenwillow* was his first flop as a Broadway writer and he was ready to move on.

27 May 1960: B. J. Chute to Frank Loesser

Dear Frank,

Thank you for your letter. What a nice person you are!

---

48 John Chapman, 'Music Good, but Lack of Plot Vexes Critic', *Chicago Daily Tribune*, 9 March 1960, B1.
49 Leonard Hoffman, 'The New York Play: Greenwillow', *Hollywood Reporter* 159/13 (9 March 1960), 3.

I am not as sure as you seem to be that apologies are in order, however. There is your music for one thing, and you know how I feel about that. There is also the fact that the production was loved by two such disparate beings as Marianne Moore and Tennessee Williams.[50] There is also the high spirit with which the cast has been playing it; you would be proud of them, I know I am.

I know what I think is wrong with it. I expect you have just as definite opinions. But so much is so good and has given such very real delight to so many people that I shall retain a hope that the willow tree will get a future opportunity to turn green again, with perhaps some changes in leaves and branches. It is much better than you think it is, you know. Mr. Atkinson is not so young as Mr. Tynan[51] and brighter in many ways. (I had a note from Mr. A., by the by – "My wife and I were thoroughly delighted with your novel, and we were also thoroughly delighted with the transcription on the stage. I do hope it succeeds. I'm sure there is a grateful audience for this sort of play, though probably not the familiar Broadway gang." It didn't, and there wasn't, but still the man is not exactly an innocent.)

Well, enough of that. I hope you are having the best of all possible journeys. I have settled down, snarling, in Chapter IX of my current novel, and I only hope I have staggered ahead to Chapter X by the time you come back to New York. Please do let us plan to get together then – knowing you has been one of the good things that happened to me too, and I can return your appreciated compliment.

My love to Jo, and to you. And please tell Jo that, long before "Greenwillow" closed, "Faraway Boy" was getting excellent applause.

[signed:] Joy.

---

50 Marianne Moore (1887–1972), poet and critic, nominated for the Noble Prize in Literature in 1968. Tennessee Williams (1911–1983), playwright best known for *The Glass Menagerie* (1944), *A Streetcar Named Desire* (1947) and *Cat on a Hot Tin Roof* (1955).
51 Brooks Atkinson and Kenneth Tynan (1927–1980), critics.

5 September 1960: B. J. Chute to Frank Loesser

Dear Frank,

I promised to write down for you a few phrases that I would hope could be changed in the "Greenwillow" script before it is used in summer stock or anywhere else. So here they are.

I-5-34   Birdsong: "Would those be popovers I smell?"

         Dorrie: "Warming in my kitchen."
A popover is made of egg, milk and flour, and, unlike ginger cake, has no fragrance while baking. Also it is served hot the moment it comes out of the oven and would <u>not</u> be "warming in the oven" to be eaten later.

II-4-24 – Dorrie: "I've to hurry and mix my sugar muffins for the morning."
Muffins are <u>not</u> "set" the night before, not even English muffins which are made with yeast. The kind of muffin most people are familiar with is made with shortening, egg, milk, sugar, flour and served <u>fresh</u> from the oven. (Later on, Birdsong asks Jabez if he smells these sugar muffins at the distance of the Briggs' house away, and Jabez says he does. Which is impossible.)

I tried very hard and many times to get these lines of Dorrie's changed before the opening, and not for culinary reasons but because they undermine the audience's belief in her. Dorrie is presented as a good cook. You know she is, in the novel, because all the details bear it out. In the stage version everyone goes around saying she is a good cook, but the minute Dorrie herself opens her mouth, she says she is doing things that would be inconceivable, even to a very bad cook. The willingness of an audience to make-believe depends on the contact and trust between the audience and the stage. If Dorrie talks like a stage character pretending to be a cook, then the kitchen itself is papier mache and laths, and by just so much Greenwillow ceases to be a real village of the imagination and becomes a fake instead.

The same point can be illustrated with a line of Clara's. II-3-14 – "Suppose we all tippytoe out for biscuit and broth." More than one drama critic picked up this line, and I think the reason is that it has the same sort of untruthfulness that shows in Dorrie's lines about her cooking. Farm women like Clara do not use babytalk. And no farm woman, or any woman in her senses, would serve broth to guests. Broth is for invalids. She would serve tea or something of that sort. If she had broth in the house, it would be a small quantity for her husband, and could not be divided among the dozen people she had there.

There are a good many other lines in the script that, to me, carry this same quality of basic untruthfulness. (Gramma's phrase about the "cherub nose" on I-1-5 jars on me, for instance) but I don't know how far you want me to go along with this. I would like very much to talk over the whole script with you from this point of view. My own feeling is that a series of relatively minor changes would increase tremendously the willingness-to-believe of the audience and make the script much more nearly worthy of your beautiful, beautiful score.

It was good to talk to you the other day and good to have you back in New York. Give my love to Jo.

And to you.

[signed:] Joy

12 September 1960: To B. J. Chute

Dear Joy:

Thanks for your notes. I wish that your list accounted for all that's the matter with the show.

When we get to repair time, we will be calling you for suggestions to substitute for our bungled bakery.

Love,

CHAPTER SEVEN

1960–61
MAINTAINING THE BUSINESS

Following the success of *The Music Man*, Meredith Willson took some time before choosing his next project. By June 1959 he had committed to provide the score for *The Unsinkable Molly Brown*, to a book by Richard Morris (1924–1996) and with direction by Dore Schary (1905–1980), former executive of MGM, and choreography by Peter Gennaro (1919–2000).[1] The show recounts the exploits of the famous survivor of the *Titanic*, starting with her family life in the Midwest. As with *The Music Man*, Loesser took a keen interest in Willson's new musical, offering comments and suggestions. Some of their exchanges about *Molly Brown* were humorous, others full of detailed advice.

Willson finished most of the score by February 1960; compared to his first Broadway outing, *Molly Brown* was a troubled production, as Loesser's letter of 27 September 1960 reveals. A review of the Philadelphia tryout summarised: 'The critical reception for [Willson's] new musical at the Shubert was mixed.'[2] And in a speech delivered to the company of the show on opening night, Schary acknowledged that 'There have been bruises, and cuts and bloodshed – literally and figuratively.'[3] On Broadway the reviews were as mixed as they had

---

1 See McHugh, *The Big Parade*, 131.
2 *Philadelphia Daily News*, 29 September 1960; quoted in McHugh, *The Big Parade*, 160.
3 Quoted in McHugh, *The Big Parade*, 161.

been in Philadelphia: the *Daily News* review noted 'lapses in this big offering' while the *World-Telegram & Sun*'s reviewer said that 'the show doesn't meet its own possibilities or the standards of the old Music Man master'.[4]

Nonetheless, Loesser was encouraging to Willson throughout, writing in one letter that 'I think you are very close to having a big one which will work', and overcame a tense exchange about an audit of Willson's earnings through Frank Music which Willson had unexpectedly ordered (Stuart Ostrow oversaw the relationship between the company and the composer). The two men's lives were intertwined, socially and professionally, and Loesser's respect and affection for Willson is apparent, but there were occasional conflicts between them on business matters.

4 January 1960: To Meredith Willson[5]

Dear Meredith:

Having nothing to do these days, I found myself thinking of you during the eleven minute cab ride to work this morning. I have written you a deathless piece of dramaturgy which you may have for nothing if you don't tell anybody.

(The white tie and tailed German virtuoso is playing Chopin softly at the piano, having usurped the bench. Mrs. McGloin and Molly are downstage.)

MOLLY

What's his name again?

MRS. MCGLOIN

Winkelbauer.

MOLLY (impressed)

Mr. Winkelbauer plays real good.

---

4 Reviews quoted in Steven Suskin, *Opening Night on Broadway* (New York, 1990), 684–5.

5 Meredith Willson papers, Great American Songbook Foundation.

MRS. MCGLOIN

Not Mr. Winkelbauer.

MOLLY

Oh. Professor Winkelbauer.

MRS. MCGLOIN (loftily)

No, Mrs. Brown. Just Winkelbauer. You see, my dear, on the continent the really superb artist is known simply by his last name. Paderewski. Puccini.

MOLLY

Dillinger. (?) (the one of that period)

MRS. MCGLOIN (witheringly)

Obviously you don't understand culture. Winkelbauer is a celebrity.
(Molly looks back at the pianist as if to confirm this puzzling phenom-enon, then looks back with slowly growing irritation)

MRS. MCGLOIN (cont'd)

Winkelbauer has class, or as we say in Berlin, klahss. He's the toast of all the European crowned heads. Why, my dear, he played before the Kaiser.

MOLLY (having had it)

Well, if he has so much klahss, why didn't he let the Kaiser play first?
Love,

28 February 1960: To Stu Ostrow

A note in answer to your February 25th memorandum about the meeting with Meredith and the Morris[6] office: It may have been over-generous of you to suggest any form of business association with Meredith. Judging from your note, I have no doubt that they will try to take advantage of the way you volunteered to put your suggestions.

Maybe I don't gather exactly what the conversation was, but I believe this: That if we form a corporation with a writer, we must have

---

6 The William Morris agency, which represented Willson.

a long and firm period during which all his writings are delivered to the company. If he really is interested as a partner in such an enterprise, he would not want to do anything else. Such a firm writer contract only serves to protect the writer against the ravages caused by attorneys and minor executives in movie companies, etc., always bent on sweeping into their pot values that they don't have coming, and that they cannot always handle effectively. This is an old story which can be summed up in one word – MONTA.[7]

Of course, FMC[8] would advance all necessary costs for the operation of the "company" and thus put all the financial risk on our side. At the same time, we would be building a perpetual interest for Meredith in addition to the interest represented by writer royalties. In this connection, I believe it is only fair that we should get both periods of copyright, and that this grant should be confirmed by Rini.[9] I say this because we are not dealing here at arm's length with an ordinary writer, but with someone who, if truly interested as a partner, would want as much value as possible to flow into the corporation – and for the longest possible period. I think Meredith's exclusive writer contract with his own company should be for at least ten years. A man doesn't build himself a new house and then immediately plan to escape from it. Our hope, of course, is to share valuable dividends with Meredith over the years, and at the same time build a solid equity from him as a stockholder in a worthwhile enterprise.

I don't think Meredith finds much fault with the way we operate our music business. At the same time, being human, he might easily be attracted by the tempting sounds of what seem to be truly competitive offers from other publishing houses. These flirtations always go on after a man has hit successfully under somebody else's aegis. That's when Al & Dicks becomes a bargain basement. I don't

---

7 Rudi Monta (dates unknown) was a legal executive at MGM and an expert in international copyright. See for example Rudolf Monta, 'The Concept of "Copyright" Versus the "Droit D'Auteur", *32 Southern California Law Review* (1959), 177.
8 Frank Music Corp.
9 Rini Zarova Willson (1912–1966) was a Russian soprano and Willson's second wife. A close supporter of his work, she would sing his songs to his accompaniment when Willson made occasional concert or television appearances.

have any wish to compete with the wild ante-raisers. I don't believe you wish to either, but I have a feeling in the gederum[10] that once a form of company structure between Meredith and ourselves is expressed in a memorandum – that the Morris office will carry it directly to three or four other music publishers to get the ante raised and take bows with their client for being clever. I don't think they are in a position to make the proper evaluations where they are most important. First and foremost, is our built-in love and respect for Meredith and our understanding of the writer's true interest – the same of his career and the maintenance of his professional dignity. I believe we are the only publishing house whose very first song writer was possibly the most difficult-to-handle man in the industry. This fellow (I think his name was Loesser) was well served on all points and although the experience might have cost the company a few pennies, it actually earned the company many, many dollars. At last report Loesser has refused all offers for any of his stock in it, seems to be eating well on his royalties, and hasn't had his reputation at all damaged.

To get to my point: I wish it were possible for Meredith to be represented by someone a little more familiar with his insides, his sensitivities – and above all, his real best interests. Does he have a personal lawyer? Or someone he customarily asks for guidance? It seems to me at one time this was Abe Meyer[11] of MCA. At least Meredith used to talk about him with a great glow, even though Abe was not his official agent. Maybe Meredith prefers his present representatives and won't have it any other way. If that is the case, I believe that he should at least be knowledgeably represented. This would not allay the fear expressed above, but would at least save you some of the embarrassment of teaching people our business.

Love,

---

10 Yiddish for the bowels or intestines; effectively, 'a gut feeling'.
11 Abe Meyer (1901–1969) wrote more than two dozen film scores before becoming an agent at MCA (Music Corp. of America).

10 March 1960: To Meredith Willson (telegram)

AFTER OUR CONVERSATION TODAY I LEARNED THAT THERE WAS A RELENTLESS AUDIT NOW IN PROGRESS CONCERNING YOUR ROYALTY ACCOUNTS WITH US. I SINCERELY BELIEVE THAT YOU SHOULD SATISFY YOURSELF THAT WE ARE HONEST BEFORE EVEN CONSIDERING A PUBLICATION DEAL WITH OUR COMPANY NO MATTER WHAT THE TERMS MAY BE. I HAVE SO ADVISED OSTROW WHO IS AT THE MOMENT BEING ASKED BY THE MORRIS OFFICE FOR AN IMMEDIATE PROPOSAL. IN ALL FAIRNESS TO YOU I HAVE SUGGESTED TO OSTROW TO PROPOSE NOTHING UNTIL YOU ARE SATISFIED THAT YOU HAVE NOT BEEN ROBBED. WHATEVER THE TECHNIQUES OF A DEAL, YOU WOULD NOT WANT TO DO BUSINESS WITH QUESTIONABLE PRINCIPLES.

YOU AND I ARE STILL PEOPLE AND NOT MACHINES. I ASSUME WE RESPECT EACH OTHER'S TALENT AND ABILITY AND HOPE TO WORK TOGETHER ON THAT BASIS. FROM ALL I CAN GATHER YOUR REPRESENTATIVES OBSERVE NONE OF THIS MUTUAL RESPECT NOR DO THEY SEEM TO WANT TO LEAVE ROOM FOR THE LUXURY OF HEARTFELT SUPPORT ON BOTH SIDES. IT COST ME SEVERAL HOURS OF TIME AND SEVERAL LIGHT YEARS OF EMBARRASSMENT TO SPEAK IN YOUR BEHALF TO SAMMY DAVIS, JR. ABOUT OMITTING TROUBLE.[12] I DIDN'T HAVE TO DO IT UNDER ANY CONTRACT I HAVE EVER READ. I DO NOT EXPECT IN THE FUTURE ANY AGREEMENT WHICH MAKES ME STINGY ABOUT THESE THINGS. NOR ABOUT THREATENING LITIGATION IN YOUR BEHALF AGAINST OLD FRIENDS WITH NO PROFIT IN VIEW BUT THE PLEASURE OF PRESERVING YOUR DIGNITY. I THINK MY COMPANY IS ENTITLED TO THE FUN OF AN UPHILL CLIMB IN YOUR BEHALF IF ON YOUR SECOND VISIT TO BROADWAY YOU GET A BARRAGE OF GREENWILLOW NOTICES. I WOULD LIKE TO BE ABLE TO AFFORD THAT FUN BOTH IN SPIRIT AND IN TERMS OF POSSIBLE ECONOMIC REWARD.

---

12 See Loesser's letter of 27 February 1959 in Chapter 5.

IF AND WHEN OSTROW PROPOSES A DEAL TO YOUR AGENTS, THEY WILL HAVE TO BE ABLE TO READ INTO IT THE INGREDIENTS WHICH CANNOT BE GUARANTEED IN WRITING OR IN FIGURES. OTHERWISE WE ARE SURE THEY WILL TURN US DOWN. WE ARE NOT ERRAND BOYS NOR PERCENTAGE PLAYERS. WE LOVE YOU DEARLY AND WANT ROOM TO EXERCISE THIS AFFECTION. OTHERWISE WE CAN CONTINUE WITHOUT TOO MUCH STRUGGLE TO PUBLISH YOUR DEAR FRIEND

FRANK LOESSER

27 September 1960: To Meredith Willson

Dear Meredith:

Last night I tried to make it fast, because I knew you wanted to get away, having been beamed at by all and sundry and having beamed back in return, probably with interest if I know you.

Anyway, to clarify what I said, it's like this: If each of us (you, [Dore] Schary, [Peter] Genarro, [Stu] Ostrow, Rini [Willson], Green,[13] [Allen] Whitehead, and Seymour Funk the usher) – were to write down a hundred critical comments about the opening last night, we would almost surely find after comparison that about 75% of the comments had been identical and that there were such obvious fixings indicated, that it would only be a waste of time to discuss them. It could be taken for granted that they would get done by you and Dory and the production people. The other 25% would very likely vary, some being suggestions which might be valuable good news to you, and others being outrageously impossible because all kinds of idiots squirm into the audience and the sidelines.

So this idiot wants to come see the show again if invited. If that happened at all, I don't doubt that it would be after some days of concentration by you and yours on the first important repairs. At that point, if asked to discuss anything, I would like to be invited for same by Schary and Morris as well as you. This is because I will very likely

---

13 Herbert Greene, the musical director. Allen Whitehead, executive at Music Theatre Inc.

want to talk about more than just songwriting technique. Also it is because special conversations with special people in special corners sometimes get wilted or lost by the aloof treatment of others who prefer their own special conversations. I have done this myself.

I think you are very close to having a big one which will work. If I can help, please please holler.

Love,

20 October 1960: To Meredith Willson

Dear Meredith:

Here are my notes the morning after seeing a greatly improved "Molly Brown" on October 19:

First of all, unless there is some very serious physical breakdown, I feel that Tammy Grimes[14] is very much your girl. Even without the advantage (?) of the almost Marcel Marceau[15] palor [sic], she is a distinguished person on the stage, and I believe in general has a very good sense of the part. Dickens in a novel would have called a boy chimney-sweep Tammy Grimes, and the character would have been full of color and long memorable. Mostly out of a kind of sympathy. Your Tammy has this quality built in and I find it missing only when I have to look at her at emotional points (laughing, crying, fighting or making love) in <u>profile</u> for too long a stretch. I believe there are ways in which she can communicate with others on the stage (by "advance reference") and still reach me out there. Then I will know the full value of some of her intentions, reactions, etc. even though many are on a characteristic dead-pan basis. Example: Johnny tells her that the extra room is for her father. At this point, she reacts word-wise quite well, but in advance I do not see the face which is now shining up with the realization that Johnny is indeed a good and worthy man. She has got her nose pointed west and I'm south. I miss the very fundamental of acting, which has to do with reaction to the speeches of others. It

---

14 Tammy Grimes (1934–2016), actress and singer. She took the role of Molly Tobin in Willson's *The Unsinkable Molly Brown*.
15 Marcel Marceau (1923–2007), French mime artist who typically performed in stark white makeup.

then validates the answer. This is one of the most touching dialogues in the play and I think should be protected in the way I describe. The above, of course, is only an example of what I am talking about. I believe a great majority of such <u>almosts</u> occur while she is singing, not so much while she is talking.

Now for some details:

You asked me about the overture. I liked it very much, except for one thing which I mentioned to Herb [Greene]. The phrasing of the unison brass opening could be just as arresting if the first three notes remain as they are (a retarded introduction to the fundamental down beat of "Ain't Down Yet"), but then are followed by a faster, more fluid and graceful telling of the song-phrases, rather than continuing in the marked slow tempo of a military funeral. By this I mean that it just takes too long being pompous. I could be wrong. If I heard it my way, I might vomit. So I'll let you try a new reading, and you vomit if you feel like it.

<u>Act.I. Scene 1.</u> Somehow I'd like to hear our girl predict orally her ultimate queenly status in the face of her brothers' mockery. There is to me hardly any value in her affectionate farewells to them. I would rather see and hear a "You'll see" attitude on her part as the boys linger at the fence observing her regal walk and letting me in the audience hear the girl predict glamor and riches, etc. for herself. If the boys now exit howling derision, our girl has the proper spur for deciding then and there to leave home and seek opportunities at least equal to those of her brothers. This involves decision, electric action, running into the house for the red mackinaw, springing the news on her father all the while, and providing us with a tense and determined departure. A departure spurred by the very competi- tive nature of the entire scene. Remember that you are presenting a girl who throughout the play is going to be saying "I'll show them." Relaxing into a fond farewell and then having to pop back into her natural arrogance, may be something of a strain on the actress and something of a pace-loser for the scene. She can still do her solo walk after the boys leave and then break out of it, having hit upon her <u>electric</u> decision, then <u>rushing</u> to her father to announce it.

Act.I. Scene 2. You told me what changes are intended for this scene so I won't comment on it except to say that I'm planning a musical on the life of Khruschev and may be able to use that bear outfit. Frank Productions, Inc. will put in a bid shortly.

Act 1. Scene 3. The "Belly Up" piano transposition has improved enormously. Congratulations!

As for "Belly Up" when in full bloom – I find a certain amount of vocal power missing. Are you favoring Tammy Grimes' keys by any chance? If so, might it not be wise to give the ensemble its richest and most gratifying key and reduce our heroine's vocal contributions – at the same time increasing her physical ones. I take it that she is supposed to be acting out an invitation to the customers to gather at the bar. Well sir, I notice that Christmas Morgan's business of pouring drinking is not visible because of the bodies in front of the bar. Could not our heroine be standing atop doing some lavish pouring business and handing the stuff down? If I were a customer that's what I'd put tips in the hat for at the end of the number. What I am saying here is based on the assumption that the key is now in Tammy's favor. If it is the best possible now for the ensemble, can you make that ensemble any larger? I mean among valuable singers. They don't seem to have to dress for quite a while. Of course, my discussions of physical changes in this number are academic in the event that you don't have time to fool with it.

One more note on this number is that in my opinion your orchestrator-arranger is modulation-happy in the dancing portions at the expense of the good old tune. Personally, I can't get enough of it myself, and don't like to hear it as written by Cesar Franck, but by Meredith Willson.

Act 1. Scene 4. I guess you meant the trio of country boys around our lover to be expert barber-shoppers, and I further guess that they didn't work out well musically. My feeling is that a sincere approach to love-making by a boy to a girl can never be conducted in the presence of anyone else. I think you should throw them off the stage and leave the boy and girl to play the scene. I see the physical direction as being one by which Johnny continually, during his song, blocks our girl's progress. This does not have to be navel to navel, and they don't even have to touch. It is really plaintive and tender. He is demanding attention and the manner and attitude of a threatened mugging. I further suggest that you can make better capital out of the scream for "Sheriff." No charge for the following extension of your song (see manuscript attached).

Act I. Scene 5. No comment except the one I made about Tammy's disclosure of her feelings at certain points, which have nothing to do with acting, but just visibility of same.

Act 1. Scene 6. I have a big holler about this one and I must admit it's a theoretical one because it could work out not as good as you already have. I'm talking about the end result after both are properly verbally dismayed with the news of the burnt money. Molly is being presented in this play as the indomitable, unsinkable go-getter. Yet you insist on having her beat and down and screaming on the bed while Johnny becomes the indomitable one in the new quest for riches. Okay, Okay, you've heard all this before and you have your reasons for wanting to leave it, but let me suggest a combination. Molly is on the bed kicking and screaming and Johnny is making his speech about the silver calling to him. But don't quit here. Have him stride off in the direction of his new mining prospect (preferably a cross from stage right to stage left). As he leaves the stage, have him start to repeat some other exhortation to the mountains to render him rich, and let him exit, continuing to make such noises off stage. Now have the damp-eyed Molly lift her head out of bed and with characteristic courage let her rise from her temporary defeat shouting "Wait, Johnny! Wait for me! I'm going with you! I ain't down yet! Johnny! Johnny! . . ." (This has brought her to the living-room section of the house). She now grabs a large pick-axe which has been hidden from view till now and brandishes it as she makes for the door, still calling to him. Now she crosses in his direction very bravely shouting the immortal line "I'm going with you, Johnny! Remember, a family that digs together, frigs together." And she goes off stage after him to the tumultuous applause of those who like dirty words. (Of course, I don't mean for you to accept these speeches, but I am very sure that this principle is valuable to the play. Otherwise why have the whole scene at all, which retards the whole story progress. Here in all honesty we have a chance to give an example of Molly's capacity for self-revival which is the keynote of the whole character and the whole play. Like the man said as he set down the twelve bottles of Cutty Sark, "I rest my case.")

Scene 7. You have described some of your intentions here and so I won't go into anything about it or the proposed Denver street scene. As you have reported, there is something of a talent problem here. But beyond that, there is a question of leading from a description of the Browns' mansion and then opening on the glamorous McGloin home. One moment of hesitancy as to impression is sometimes costly against the next fifteen moments of valid and important storytelling. In other words, if I think for five seconds that I am looking at Molly's place and not someone else's, I find myself busy fighting the impression of garishness which was predicted. Because I find Mrs. McGloin's place quite elegant and far from outrageous. While puzzling this, I am likely to neglect some key speech. Let me say in passing that the same principle applies in reference to Browns Palace Hotel. I suppose here you are dealing with true and honest American history. I don't think it is worth it if three customers get the mild impression that it is either the same thing as the Brown family's mansion, or that Molly and Johnny have actually bought a hotel and named it after themselves. Or have they?

As to the content of the scene: In "Beautiful People" Tammy runs the risk of seeming sarcastic rather than honestly overwhelmed. Part of this is the nature of the lyrics. Part of it is also due to a certain lack of innocence in her playing of it. Is it not possible to protect this in the following manner: Her raucous entrance is enough to develop a stony, unresponsive silence among the guests. As she begins her song, they adopt a disdainful freeze, but in the proper groupings for her to move among them. Now if she takes her husband by the arm and uses the lyrics to show Denver noblesse to him, there is less chance for a wrong impression of her real state of wonder. Her ignorance and shocking choice of language can still be reacted to at the proper occasions by the surrounding ensembles. Using the auditorium as the fourth wall, she can work down stage describing things to her husband while each shocked reaction in the rear turns another group of haughty backs to her recital. She now arrives at "Here we are to stay." On the next beat, she and her husband turn around. Johnny of course is aware of the frigidity of the reception and says something about it there, while Molly sails into the one pleasant face (providing you change his hair) of the priest – and the scene goes on. But we have delivered Molly at her most articulate and most audible by keeping her well down stage almost all of the time with her nose overhanging Herb Greene, but not so near as to overshoot the mikes. At the moment, some of the possible impact is missing. More important is the danger of interpretation I have described.

On the subject of "Are You Sure," I feel that there is a great deal of unnecessary lateral motion by our girl. Also I feel that the reaction to her penetrating lyrical questions should begin with a grudging compliance during the singing of the number as the chemically growing recital of her inquisition. If I were a member of the ensemble and found myself being thus queried, I would develop a shamed face and a reach for my wallet without waiting for the 64th bar. Okay, maybe the ladies' stockings can be a little later than the men's wallets, but the concentrated mechanism of the hat-passing, etc. gave no growth of involvement among those people being appealed to. You and I have been through this before with much success. You with "Trouble"; me with "Sit Down You're Rocking the Boat." I'm sure that any good staging of "Down With Burgundy"[16] has this same ingredient of growth. In the instance of "Are You Sure" we are dealing with a not particularly commanding voice as such, and I think that every effort should be made to compensate for this weakness by again making use of a great deal of the appeal in the direction of the fourth wall, and by the delivery of a growing and climactic compliance by the ensemble, who relent, come forward, and donate. It is relatively easy for Molly to back in among them momentarily and draw them forward, rather than to play laterally, which is real nice for the stage hands who didn't buy tickets.

---

16 Apparently a reference to 'Song of the Vagabonds' from Friml's *The Vagabond King* (1925).

Scene 9. Not much to say about this scene except for the timing of the curtain during the polka. I wish you would experiment with the idea of a curtain which starts a little earlier – let's say at the outset of the very well-earned applause – but with a slower speed. When the audience sees an act curtain begin to fall, it will sustain its applause once it has volunteered same. But if the audience is applauding only the magic of the happy polka, it will then have to make a new, lame start in appreciation of the entire act. See what I mean?

Honest to God, this is all I have time for today. It has taken most of it and I will have to resume concerning the second act as soon as humanly possible. Meanwhile I want to rush this off to you.

In the meantime, here are some notes for the first scene of the third act:

MEREDITH

Well, have you read it?

DORE

Yes, and here it is five in the morning and I say let's charge the music company for wasting our time.

RINI

Coffee, anyone?

MEREDITH

Wait a minute, Dore. The company is half mine.

DORE

That's what they told me at MGM. We both ran into schmuck partners. What does Loesser know about anything. He's only another writer like us.

MEREDITH

No, no. He's a former writer.

DORE

You're God-damned right. I saw "Greenwillow." If he knows so much now, how is it he didn't know so much then?

MEREDITH

He's an observer.

RINI

Vodka, anyone?

DORE

Ha, ha. Neutral observer, innocent by-stander, the wayfaring stranger, wandering Jew.

MEREDITH

Not neutral. He is simply trying to protect an enormous investment. Not Capitol Records' money, but his own cash, hard-earned in the publishing business

DORE

My grand-uncle David, may he rest in peace, used to sit around the back of the candy store in Newark and say wonderful clever things, for which he was known far and wide and he died a celebrated pundit at least well-known up to maybe the Raritan River.[17] His most famous saying was in answer to a neighbor's assertion that the world was round. It was short and to the point the way he said it, and I quote – "Horse shit." Well, sir, the phrase caught on like wild-fire.

RINI

Horse shit, anyone?

MEREDITH

Well, since you're so intense about it, I won't defend him any more. Frankly, I agree with you . . .

DORE

Now you're talking honest. That is, for a gentile.

MEREDITH

Which relieves me of the trouble of reading his notes.

---

17 The Raritan River, in New Jersey, empties into Raritan Bay between New York and New Jersey.

DORE

You mean you haven't yet?

MEREDITH

Of course not. I'm not a masochist gentile. There are no lion bites on me.

DORE

I could kill myself.

MEREDITH

There's plenty of time after we open.

DORE

I'm feeling chilly. I guess it's from exposure to the views of strangers.

RINI

Oh, you poor dear, until after we open – Should I light a fire?

DORE

If you please.

MEREDITH

(handing Rini the notes)
And throw this in. It will make a cheery blaze and keep us all warm.
(Business by Rini. The fire roars)

MEREDITH

Rini dear. Was there any mail today from New York?

RINI

No, my darling.

MEREDITH

That's strange. Very strange. Odd place, Philadelphia.

ALL

(unison singing as Herb Greene arrives to conduct)
Dolce Far Niente.[18]

---

18 One of the ballads in *The Unsinkable Molly Brown*; literally, 'the sweetness of doing nothing'.

The often intense back and forth between Loesser and writers such as Willson was different from the everyday experience of running his companies. The contrast between his artist and business lives was by now regularly referenced in the press. In 1960 Leonard Lyons's column for the *Chicago Daily Defender* reported a frivolous anecdote about *The Most Happy Fella*, no doubt fed to him by Loesser, who was a friend: 'Loesser is a rare combination of gifted artist and practical businessman. He was assured that, as soon as the ads appeared in Philadelphia, ticket-buyers who came to the box office formed a line that went around the corner. Loesser asked: "How far is the box office from the corner?"'[19] A window into the running of Frank Productions can be glimpsed in his correspondence with one of his employees, Mona Etkin, who took care of everything from written support for MTI executive Allen Whitehead to purchasing stationery; writer and director Joshua Logan (1908–1988) was one of the beneficiaries of Loesser's enthusiasm for, and purchase of, multi-coloured ballpoint pens, which Loesser often used to draw elaborate doodles.

31 March 1960: To Mona Etkin, Frank Productions Inc.

Dear Mona,

Thanks for your March 28 note, and the news that I own $10,000 worth of fractions gives me a rare pleasure in the gederum. Please call Blatas[20] and tell him to be sure and look us up immediately he arrives. Also tell Mrs. Leonard Lyons she has a pair for the 21st opening[21] if she can stand it.

You did not include orange in the shipment of ball point pens and this leaves me in an awkward position with Seurat and the others.

---

19 Leonard Lyons, 'Lyons Dens', *Chicago Daily Defender*, 27 January 1960, 11.
20 Arbit Blatas (1908–1999), Lithuanian-born artist and sculptor.
21 This appears to be a reference to the opening of *The Most Happy Fella* in London, which matches that date. Sylvia Schonberger (1910–2001) was Leonard Lyons's wife.

Twenty lashes. Also, don't threaten to come here. Take care of [Allen] Whitehead and [Paul] Hollister[22] and all the decent Americans.

Love,

7 April 1961: To Joshua Logan

Dear Josh:

You too can now be a ball-pointillist. It is very good for the soul. I know it stops me from screaming and ranting for hours on end. It also stops me from writing. Somehow the color orange is missing but I think it was Blend, seventh son of Shem, second son of Noah, who wisely said "Futz thee with red and yellow and there shall be orange throughout the land." After the flood this man was said to have settled in California, and to this very day there are Jews and oranges all over the state.

Having exhausted you at our last meeting, I am giving you a rest from me for a little while. But soon I will call, unless you call sooner, for a new exploring date.

Meanwhile, of course, have all the scenic designs executed in ball point.

Love,

(enclosed: 2 complete sets colored pens)

27 April 1960: To Mona Etkin

Dear Mona,

This letter once again makes an honest woman of you. So get up off the couch, wipe the chocolate marshmallow from off your chin and type several exact copies of the enclosed itineraries. There are two: one is for Jo and me and Mama too. Anyway, one set should stay in the office for you and Allen [Whitehead], another set must go immediately to my Mother, a further set to Harold Orenstein's office, a set to Stuart Ostrow and lastly, but very importantly, a set to Lynn Loesser. All this has got to be done last Tuesday, if not sooner.

---

22 Paul M. Hollister; see letter of 16 May 1955 in Chapter 4.

You'd love it here. 3d. worth of candy is enough to make you vomit.

Hurry – God damn it.

Love,

Frank

31 May 1960: To Mona Etkin

Dear Mona,

I have returned to London having had three nice weeks in and around Rome, armed with a dictionary and a grammar with which to augment my knowledge of the Italian language. It is amazing how much Italian I knew already, some of it from my experience with musical notations and dynamic directions (traditionally in Italian), but most of it from my very early life on the streets of West Manhattan then populated at least by half with the scum of Sicily, Calabria and, at the best, Naples. From my playmates, the children of shoe repairers, icemen, grocery clerks and barbers, I quickly learned every filthy word there is or that can be invented in the Southern Italian dialect.

So with great facility I find my miserable little mind applying most of these unappetizing epithets to you, my dear Mona. I will not bore you with the Italian version, but let me suggest that you are of animal ancestry, that you have had affairs with all your uncles, that whom you kiss becomes a dwarf and that your Mother wears army shoes. This all because you send me a wad of bills and other notices and advices to ensure me of a fine vacation. I return them herewith, including notes about what to do with them.

In the future, please forward no bills of any kind. Wolman[23] is to receive all ordinary ones directly. This includes apartment rent, insurance premiums, electricity and gas bills (after being examined for reasonable normalcy under the circumstances). Those bills run up by authority of Eva (dry cleaning etc.) should be OK'd by Eva and then given directly to Wolman. Wolman is prepared in advance to issue cheques on certain of these items. Those for which he is not prepared

---

23 Martin Wolman (dates unknown), Loesser's accountant.

are to be paid by Cyd Cheiman[24] on my behalf. She, in turn, will keep track of things and ask me for reimbursement on my return.

Discuss all this with Wolman so that everybody has his or her notions straight.

There is one tiny argument in my mind against suggesting that you now shoot yourself. It is really a weak argument, but then, as you well know, I have always championed little puny things and tried to make them grow into giants of convincing strength. Somehow, therefore, I cling to the insistent little notion that some day you are going to stop necking with Whitehead, buy your own candy and fly right, so I have not ordered your execution.

But God damn it, give me clear news like the Hans Christian Andersen income report (for which I thank you), news that Hollister is in good health, or even tell me a joke. But do not give me no problems.

Love,

Although Loesser did not ultimately co-produce *Bye Bye Birdie*, he remained in contact with its writers, Strouse and Adams. They were interested in writing a musical version of the 1940 play *The Male Animal* by James Thurber (1894–1961) and Elliott Nugent (1896–1980), a political work about free speech that was made into a film starring Henry Fonda (1905–1982) in 1942. A discussion between Loesser and Strouse and Adams led to a stern communication from Loesser to his colleagues about the principles of their business: he was concerned less with the idea of the musical itself than with how Frank Music had handled the suggestion. This ability to see the bigger picture – even if he was not always right in his judgements – is what made Loesser a formidable figurehead for his companies. Reference is made to a successful new recording of "If I Were a Bell" by Sarah Vaughan and Joe Williams accompanied by Count Basie and his Orchestra.

---

24 Cheiman was office manager of Frank Music.

24 August 1960: To Harold Orenstein, Stu Ostrow and
Allen Whitehead

Subject: Charles Strouse & Lee Adams

The following is a report on a meeting with Strouse and Adams, who came to my house yesterday afternoon (the 23rd). The visit was my response to Strouse's suggestion on the phone a few days previous that he would like to "get together" with me.

THE CONTENTS OF THIS REPORT ARE FOR THE INFOR-MATION OF THOSE ADDRESSED AND UNDER NO CIRCUMSTANCES SHOULD ANY PART OF THIS SUBJECT BE DISCUSSED WITH STROUSE, ADAMS, OR THEIR REPRESENTATIVES.

Shortly after their arrival, they made it clear that they wished to discuss the subject of "The Male Animal." I had known of their consideration of this title as a theatrical musical possibility. I will not at this point go into any discussion about how they arrived at this thinking, but they made it plain that they would like to consider it a possibility and that, toward that end, they hoped that Frank Productions would acquire it and propose to produce it – with them as composers.

We exchanged various artistic opinions about the merit of the play and its possible musicalization. I had to be truthful in saying that I was not totally convinced that this would make a good musical at the same time pointing out that I had not yet given it too much analytical and constructive thought.

At this point I was forced to express a policy of Frank Productions, Inc. as far as Broadway shows are concerned. That if we thought well of a show's possibilities, we would acquire the right to produce it, pump ourselves full of serious intentions to produce it, and then offer writers (such as themselves) a deal to do the job. At that moment we were, as an organization:

a. not in control of the property in any respect;
b. not aware of what it would cost to get such control, and what oppressive limitations might already exist;
c. not aware that it could indeed be acquired at all;
d. not convinced that it was something worth doing, even if we could combine the services of Mozart, Ibsen, Mary Pickford,

Douglas Fairbanks, George S. Kaufman, and Rodney Gromit, the best prop man obtainable.[25]

I hastened to assure them that as their friends, and believers in their immortal talents, we would be glad to help them in any way we could – to acquire for themselves, any property they had a whim about. I added here that they would probably not call on us for such a friendly gesture since they were now pretty well heeled and could pay their own investigators, attorneys and other manipulators in their behalf.

I added that I was by no means dismissing this subject, but felt that I would like US to study the play over and decide as an organization that we wanted to produce it as a musical.

They said that would be fine.

But at this very moment, less than a day later, their own representatives may have already started trying to acquire the property for them. If this is carried through, and they proceed to adapt, musicalize, etc., they are free to auction off the little bauble to ANY producer and ANY music publisher, without one hang of vestigial "loyalty" to any of the Frank organizations.

Yet, a spit-ball was thrown at them from our organization. A spit-ball unsupported by any proprietorship or confirmed intention by the company. I submit to all of you that any such process is dangerous to us. WE SHOULD DECIDE WHAT WE WANT TO PRODUCE AND THEN CAST THE WRITERS. IF THE WRITERS COME IN HAVING ORIGINATED THE BRIGHT IDEA, THEN WE HAVE THE OPTION TO SAY YES OR NO. THAT WILL VERY LIKELY HAPPEN WHEN WE HAVE ENOUGH CREDITS TO BE CONSIDERED THE NEW JED HARRIS,[26] THE IRRESISTIBLE BULLS-EYE HITTER TO WHOM EVERYBODY RUSHES TO GET HIS OR HER IDEA PRODUCED.

---

25 Composer Wolfgang Amadeus Mozart (1756–1791); playwright Henrik Ibsen (1828–1906); actors Mary Pickford (1892–1979) and Douglas Fairbanks (1883–1939); playwright and director George S. Kaufman (1889–1961). Rodney Gromit was Loesser's joke.
26 Producer-director Jed Harris (1900–1979) was known for hit Broadway plays including *Our Town* (1938).

WE ARE NOT YET THAT. WE ARE NOT YET EVEN GRIFFITH &
PRINCE.[27] WE ARE NOT YET EVEN GRIFFITH AND SCHWARTZ –
A NAME WHICH I JUST INVENTED TO ILLUSTRATE OUR LOW
LEVEL OF CREATIVITY AT THE MOMENT.

Our function should be to <u>own</u> – and then dangle what we own. I
suggest that we all have a meeting and discuss all opinions concerning
this expressed policy. Maybe I'm wrong, but I would like somebody
to prove it.

Now back to the rest of the discussion with Strouse & Adams. I
volunteered that they should now think seriously about a permanent
home for their works as far as publishing rights are concerned. I
pointed out that the producer is at best a pro tem associate whose
interests are rarely parallel with those of the writers. I explained that
in general, the producer works for profit on the investment. The
writer just wants to run at capacity and take royalties from the gross.
I pointed out that the producer lasts as long as his capacity to produce
remains technically effective (as of the usual 21-75 performance
formula) and after that he remains a receiver of certain residual benefits and is no longer effective in the prolongation of the life, profit, or
reputation of the original production or any of its by-products. I then
pointed out that the life-long partnership – the completely parallel
association – is the one between publisher and writer.

Earlier in the afternoon, I had played for them the new recording
of "If I Were A Bell" – which they enjoyed immensely. I had told them
how well it was doing, and how gratifying it was that this was produced
on purpose some years after its debut in a Broadway show. Now I
made reference to this incident earlier in the afternoon, pointing out
what the publisher's true function is, and using as examples our other
accomplishments, such as the emergence of "Til There Was You," a
good year after the opening of the show,[28] "Baubles, Bangles and

---

27 Robert E. Griffith (1907–1961) and Hal Prince (1928–2019) produced hit
musicals including *The Pajama Game* and *Fiorello!*.
28 Probably Anita Bryant's (born 1940) recording of the hit song from Meredith
Willson's *The Music Man*, which reached No. 30 on *Billboard*'s Hot 100 in 1959.

Beads" a good 2 years after its show,[29] "Slow Boat To China,"[30] Number 1 for the second time in England 11 years after its original success. They agreed that this was very good publishing indeed, and made other remarks commenting glowingly on our way of doing things. I then invited them to make a home with our music publishing organization. A life-time home, like Kern with Max Dreyfus.[31] I told them how, because of my non-meteoric movie-bound rise, I had left a wake of un-organizable copyrights controlled in various quarters, at various prices, in various degrees of innocuous desuetude. I pointed out that they now had pretty much of a chance to consolidate their valuables of the future – without the awful pressure of having to make a living out of it through guaranteed advances, etc. etc. (They had told me that the "[Bye Bye] Birdie" picture rights are being sold for $850,000 against 10% of the world gross, so I felt no qualms in assuring them that it would be a long, long time before they would have to consider the value of a weekly $200 advance from a music publisher.)

They nodded pleasantly at all this. At the same time they insisted that they were thinking of us as producers, etc. etc. I told them that we would not want a long-term publishing association with 2 writers without making continual efforts to present them with every possible opportunity in shows, television, movies, etc. I told them that a permanent publishing association would insure such an effort without any production contract (quoting the current case of Wright & Forrest). I added here that we were being very careful to appear as associate producers so that we could do business with any Broadway producer without being considered competitors by any of them. Like Technicolor.[32] I assured them that despite anything, we would

---

29 Possibly the Dick Hyman Trio's version of 1955, though Loesser could be referring to several other covers that came out in the wake of the MGM film version of the Broadway musical *Kismet* (1953).

30 Emile Ford and the Checkmates released a hit version of Loesser's 'Slow Boat to China' in 1959.

31 Composer Jerome Kern (1885–1945) and his publisher Max Dreyfus (1874–1964) of Chappell & Co.

32 Loesser refers to the fact that the Technicolor cameras and process were used across film studios rather than just one.

1. Frank Loesser, 'Birthday Greetings for his Mother', c1915. Loesser's childhood notes to his mother were both affectionate and sassy. On one occasion he wrote: 'Dear mother, you said I was late. But you are very much mistaken. I was very early. Amen.'

2. Souvenir programme for Frank Loesser's army musical *Skirts: An All-American Musical Adventure in 15 Scenes*, 1944. As well as writing songs for patriotic films and shows, in response to the Japanese attack on Pearl Harbor, on 7 December 1941, Loesser wrote 'Praise the Lord and Pass the Ammunition', one of the most popular Second World War songs: it sold more than 2.5 million recordings and more than 750,000 copies of the sheet music.

3. Frank Loesser, George Abbott and Ray Bolger having fun during the production of *Where's Charley?*, 1948. Loesser's Broadway debut was a success, thanks especially to the song 'Once in Love with Amy', but because of a musicians' union strike there was no original cast album, an omission that has undermined the show's legacy.

4. Ray Bolger in *Where's Charley?*, 1948. *Where's Charley?* ran for a respectable 792 performances. In addition to 'Once in Love with Amy' critics were wild about Ray Bolger's acrobatic dancing and drag performance as Charley's Aunt. Loesser wrote to him jokingly: 'I'm very proud of you – very grateful – and more than a little sexy about you (see how far things can go?).'

5. Vivian Blaine and Sam Levene (as Miss Adelaide and Nathan Detroit) in the original Broadway production of *Guys and Dolls*, 1950. The *New York Times* raved that 'every now and then a perfectly-composed and swiftly-paced work of art comes out of the bedlam of Broadway', while the great songwriter Cole Porter wrote to Loesser: 'I saw your finished product in New York a few nights ago, and I congratulate you on your magnificent job.'

6. The Crapshooters ('Luck Be a Lady') in the original production of *Guys and Dolls*, 1950. Loesser particularly admired the designs of Jo Mielziner for the show, writing to ask a favour: 'Now that we are all walking around with blue marks on our stomachs from taking bows, I have relaxed enough to remember a very kind promise you made me. You said I could have the original painting of the rainy street drop. I have a space reserved next to a pretty good Roualt. Okay?'

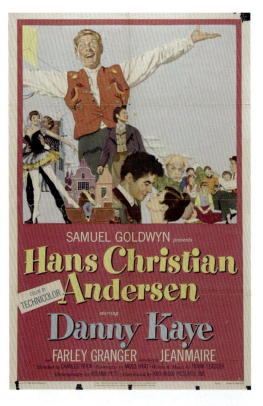

7. Original poster for *Hans Christian Andersen*, 1952. Loesser was keen that the film not just act as a vehicle for star Danny Kaye's dancing ability but that it should focus on the psychology of the story. He wrote to the film's producer: 'I never went to a movie to see anybody's feet, including Fred Astaire's or Gene Kelly's. What I want to know about my principals is what is on their minds.'

8. Frank and Lynn Loesser, early 1950s. Frank and Lynn got together in the 1930s when Frank's career was taking off in Hollywood, and they corresponded almost daily. Lynn was a professional singer and Frank wrote 'Baby, It's Cold Outside' for them to perform as a party piece, which they did on many occasions in the 1940s until Frank sold it to MGM for the film *Neptune's Daughter*. When Lynn found out he had sold the song, she said she 'felt as betrayed as if I'd caught him in bed with another woman'.

9. Frank and Susan Loesser, early 1940s. Frank was close to his eldest daughter Susan, who went on to write *The Most Remarkable Fella*, an insightful memoir of her father's life and work.

10. Advertisement for Glacierware shakers, tumblers and coolers found among Frank Loesser's papers. One of Loesser's quirks was to come up with business ideas for devices and gadgets of all kinds. He wrote to the company Aldco in 1965 to report that 'At present I am using the pitcher cooler for <u>vodka martini</u>. This I keep in the deep freeze along with the capsule, as well as martini glasses, and serve myself and others from it, keeping a pitcher pretty well filled in reserve all the time.'

11. Frank Loesser to Arthur Loesser, 18 February 1957. Arthur was Frank's older brother and when their father died, Arthur offered financial assistance to Frank and his mother.

12. The first page of Frank Loesser's letter to John Steinbeck's dog Angel. The Loessers and Steinbecks were close friends and this letter is typical of the lengths Loesser would go to in expressing affection through a humorous communication.

DEAR ANGEL

MEETING YOU AGAIN LAST NIGHT WAS A FINE EXPERIENCE AS ALWAYS, BUT, AS ALWAYS, IT LEFT ME WITH THE FEELING OF SOMETHING UN-SAID AND UN-SOLVED...(AT FIRST, ANYWAY.)

(MEMBERS OF MY BREED CHARACTERISTICALLY WANT THINGS SAID AND SOLVED, AND I AM NO EXCEPTION. LIKE OTHER PEOPLE I GET LITTLE SATISFACTION OUT OF THE SIMPLE SPIRIT AND SMELL OF SOMETHING — BUT AT ONCE PROCEED TO BOMBARD IT WITH NOTIONS ABOUT CAUSE AND EFFECT. THIS HUMAN PROCESS HAS MANY NAMES — DRAMA, MATHEMATICS, RECIPE, RESEARCH, LOGIC, AND WORRY. YOU DOGS ARE SMART ENOUGH TO KNOW THAT WORRY IS SOMETHING YOU DO TO A BONE, AND LET IT GO AT THAT. EVEN PAVLOV COULDN'T DO ANY MORE THAN PROVE THAT YOUR BRAIN IS IN YOUR GUT ———— SOMETHING

13. Frank Loesser, Jo Sullivan (later Jo Loesser), Herbert Greene, Robert Weede and Morley Meredith rehearsing *The Most Happy Fella*, 1956. The musical was co-produced by Loesser's first wife, Lynn, but he fell in love with the show's young star Jo Sullivan during the course of its Broadway run, leading to his divorce from Lynn.

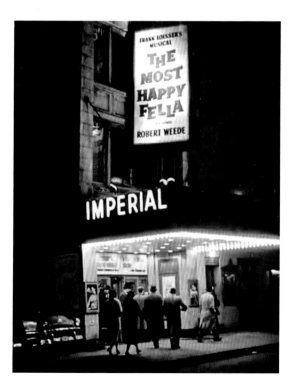

14. Imperial Theatre marquee for the premiere of *The Most Happy Fella*, 1956. The *New York Times* commented: 'in its most serious moments "The Most Happy Fella" is a profoundly moving dramatic experience', adding that 'Broadway is used to heart. It is not accustomed to evocations of the soul.'

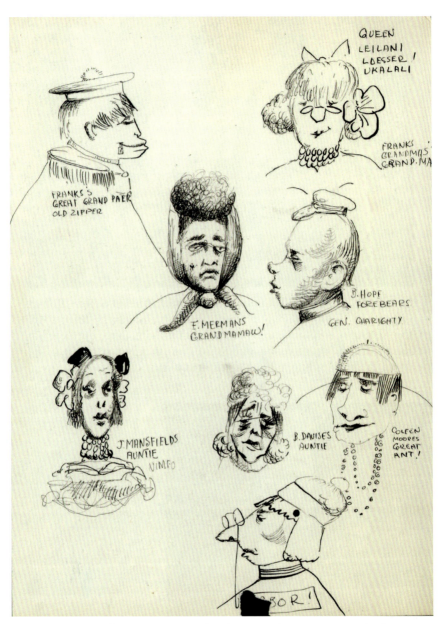

15. Frank Loesser's caricatures, undated. Loesser's creativity reached in many directions, including drawing doodles and caricatures, dozens of which have been saved among his papers. Whether through song or visual art, Loesser had the ability to capture others' personalities with insight and a comedic eye.

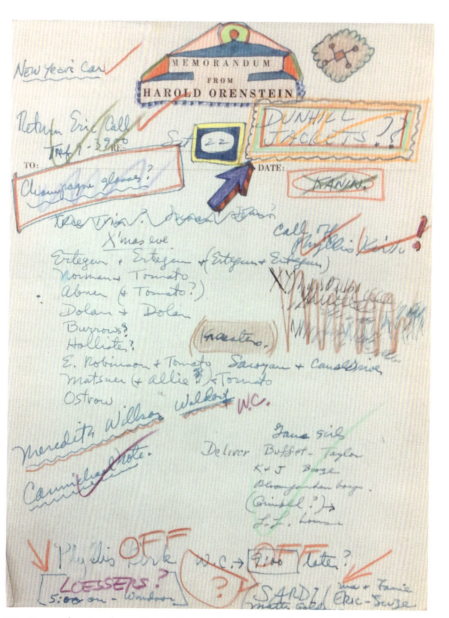

16. Page of notes from Frank Loesser's papers indicating plans around the holiday season; undated but probably late 1950s.

17. Anthony Perkins and company in *Greenwillow*, 1960. *Greenwillow* coincided with production of Hitchcock's *Psycho*, the film for which Perkins is best remembered. Perkins recalled, 'Loesser had told me that the only time a song should occur is when the emotion has become so intense that it's no longer sufficient to explain it in speech. I try to bear that in mind. When I'm doing a number, I try to remember that it's a moment so intense I can't speak it.'

18. Loesser and Robert Morse in rehearsals for *How to Succeed in Business Without Really Trying*, 1961. When Morse left the show in 1963, Loesser wrote to him: 'Thank you, thank you, thank you, thank you, thank you for two wonderful years. . . . Please know that I am very grateful to you for being Finch and for being a very fine fellow even without the great talent.'

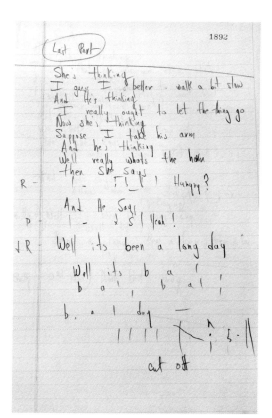

19. Working manuscript of the text for 'Been a Long Day' from *How to Succeed in Business Without Really Trying*, 1961. Loesser notates the rhythms around the lyrics to work out how the words and music will fit together.

20. Autograph draft for 'Been a Long Day' from *How to Succeed in Business Without Really Trying*. Loesser dated the page Christmas Eve 1960, showing that he working intensively on it over the holiday season in anticipation of its premiere in 1961.

21. Rudy Vallee as J. B. Biggley in *How to Succeed in Business Without Really Trying*, 1961. Vallee was a veteran from an earlier era of entertainment, an ideal foil for the youthful zaniness of the lead, Robert Morse.

22. Bob Fosse rehearsing a number for *Pleasures and Palaces*, 1965. Loesser's last completed stage musical, *Pleasures and Palaces* opened and closed in Detroit, never to reach Broadway after devastating reviews. In a telegram to Cy Feuer, who had produced Loesser's two hits and was about to open another show in Detroit, Loesser joked 'DON'T SKID ON MY BLOOD'.

continue to comb the world's ideas for show material to present to them. I added that, of course, any consummation of such a deal would have to include an agreement on the publication of the involved score. We could not risk bidding against other publishers at an auction of some kind, after having made our effort as producers.

Once more here, I pointed out that no one quite knows who Morey Riskin[33] [sic] is and that a revival of "Of Thee I Sing" has failed on Broadway, but that however vague the present recollection of that Pulitzer Prize winner, there is hardly anyone who does not recognize "Love Is Sweeping the Country," "Mine," "Who Cares," etc. The Gershwins are well celebrated (and well heeled) through the insistent longevity of their individual numbers. Same thing with Cole Porter. The show "Anything Goes" is absolutely unproduceable today, but try and avoid hearing "I Get a Kick Out of You," "You're the Top," etc. (the music, as well as the jingle of coin from ASCAP).

I am also being almost as long-winded as I was at our meeting, and I am being that purposely so that you can all gather the nature of the attempted sell. So I will go on. Following the above events, I launched into a self-servingly high appraisal of our function as publishers, to which the boys should enthusiastically agree. But there was still a hesitancy about making an alliance, so I decided on what you may all consider a bold step, and made the suggestion that it was by no means impossible to consider the opening of a firm whose profits they could somehow share. I described loosely the kind of arrangement (with no figures or percentages of any kind expressed) in which the writer's proportion of interest in profits grows in proportion with the accumulation of continuous years of exclusive employment with his own corporation. Here both boys beamed a little and said they felt highly flattered, and that could I please have a meeting with them and their lawyer on this subject. I said that sounded fine and they said they would call me for such an appointment early next week.

Having been carefully reared by Harold Orenstein, I knew that if they were to bring their lawyer, that I should be sure to bring mine.

---

33 Morrie Ryskind (1895–1985) was the co-writer of the Gershwins' *Of Thee I Sing* (1931), the first musical to win a Pulitzer Prize.

Now, the lawyer representing Stouse [sic] and Adams is a lady named Bella Linden[34] (spelling?) who is with the John Shulman[35] office (I believe she is a partner).

Now, if, because of her very busy schedule she happens to be available at dawn Thursday only, it would be fool-hearty [sic] of me to call Harold Orenstein for the session because I know he doesn't get up that early. But possibly Harold wants to suggest and enlist some other attorney for the purposes of the meeting so that he can sleep. On the other hand, he may think it proper to stretch a point and get up early and appear himself.

In principle, I am for closing some kind of long-term publishing deal with the boys. First, of course, I would like to hear all the pros and cons expressed by the people to whom this is addressed. Assuming for the moment that we wind up _pro_, and that we arrange for the lawyer meeting, we are still up against a strong possibility of an Al & Dick gambit. That is to say, we will propose a brilliant formula recited verbatim to one of our competitors and they will start an auction by promising both boys a trip to the moon and a penny more per copy in addition. Just in the nick of time a second competitor will promise them an extra 2 cents and a trip to Grossinger's,[36] which is more practical. We always run this risk no matter how nice our friends are, or how grateful for our solicitude, the use of our pianos, the use of our valuable counsel, lunch money and, for all I know, our better looking secretaries.

But few, if any, of our publisher competitors can say to the writers, "We intend to buy the musical rights to 'Green Grow the Lilacs.'[37] It will be called 'Oklahoma!' We predict it will have 8 hits and you are invited to write them."

---

34 Bella Linden (?1923–2013) was a prominent arts attorney in New York.
35 Attorney John Shulman (?1895–1974), counsel for the Song Writers Protective Association and Authors League of America.
36 A famous resort hotel in New York's Catskill Mountains, the largest of the so-called 'Borscht Belt' hotels. Founded in the early 1900s, Grossinger's closed in 1986.
37 Lynn Riggs's play _Green Grow the Lilacs_ (1931) became Rodgers and Hammerstein's hit musical _Oklahoma!_ (1943).

Now, gentlemen, how can we come up with this kind of <u>live</u> bait? Is it or is it not "The Male Animal"? I would like to be convinced in some way that this should be a musical. If not this, what? Or does anyone believe that we can solemnly declare our intention to produce a piece attractive to the writers – and later change our minds after all the papers are signed?

Don't answer that last one in writing.

Somebody call me for a meeting.

FL.

Loesser remained a kind of oracle for many other writers who were working on a new musical. American writer Sidney Sheldon (1917–2007) was prolific across Broadway, Hollywood and television; he had drafted a musical about Joe Uwanawich (1889–1963), 'King of the Gypsies', called Big Tene Uwanawich in the script. At the time of his correspondence with Loesser, Sheldon's Tony Award-winning musical *Redhead* had just closed on Broadway. Ervin Drake (1919–2015) was the writer of hit songs such as 'I Believe' and 'It Was a Very Good Year'. He would later write the musicals *What Makes Sammy Run?* (1964) and *Her First Roman* (1968). Loesser's comment about 'feelings rather than opinions' is revealing: he tended to have strong feelings about ideas – sometimes unreliable ones, as in his lack of enthusiasm for a musical about P. T. Barnum. Both the stage musical *Barnum* (1980) and the film *The Greatest Showman* (2017) have shown that the idea had legs. Loesser's response to Florette Henri (?–1985), a historian of racial bias in the USA, whose books included *Bitter Victory: A History of Black Soldiers in World War I* (1970), indicates that she proposed a musical based on a novel by Henry James (1843–1916).

31 March 1960: To Sidney Sheldon

Dear Sidney:

In your March 25th note you ask for my feelings about "King of New York."[38] I am glad you asked for feelings instead of opinions

---

38 A copy of Sheldon's unproduced play script, dated February 1961, was listed on eBay: https://www.ebay.com/itm/115787473605.

because I find the former guiding my decisions more strongly than the latter. The composer of the other show is an old friend. I was the first publisher privileged to hear the score. I think at that time he was aware that it had not made an enormous impression on me or Stu Ostrow, and I think he may have been a little wounded. It would trouble me to go into what he surely would consider competition with his piece. Oh, I know I am supposed to be some sort of an iron business man, and I regret having to cast a shadow of doubt in your mind about this myth. But while Drake (the composer) still has any kind of hope or prayer to get produced, I think I had better stay out of the gypsy business.

In any event, it would be impossible for me to do any new kind of work for quite a long while. I expect to disappear for most of the summer, and between sunbaths and sips of pernaud [sic] and aloof views at other people's theatrical offerings – reflect on all the reasons why I did such a dopey job on *Greenwillow* – letting the book sit there in rugged shreds hoping to illuminate it effectively with the ditties. I think this will result in confirming for me a principle I forgot to stick to last time. In short, it is: IT SELDOM DOES ANY GOOD TO PUT A PINK SEQUINED BALL GOWN ON A YOUNG LADY WHO HASN'T BATHED. This is something I thought (and told you about to some extent) after a first look at your early gypsy draft. If it is still the same play, I can't help thinking that it isn't ready for songs. This does not mean that it is too early for the <u>selection</u> of a collaborating composer, but the work of bathing the young lady is still yours. Ah, here we are in the realm of opinion which I thought I was going to avoid. So the operative answer to your note has got to be <u>no</u>. At least for now. Let me call you in the autumn and see how things stand about this or anything else. I don't want to lose you.

Best as always,

27 April 1960: To Allen Whitehead

I am returning the statistical summary on P.T. BARNUM. Frankly, I don't consider that there is even the value of a finder's fee in this type of suggestion. I can spitball you fifty names in as many minutes –

names whose biographies might, if properly exaggerated, illuminated and musicalised, become good shows. If the author of the BARNUM notes wants in any way to be the author of a BARNUM play, he damn well ought to write you something of a play.

In the last couple of years, the colourful biography has popped up in the musical trade – notably "Fiorello," "Sunrise at Campobello," and now in the writing stage Our Very Own "Unsinkable Mrs. Brown," and "Pancho Villa."[39] But they all take some writing sweat before they are worth anything. Otherwise, you and I can toss names at each other starting with Eve, dashing through Lydia Pinkham, Madame de Staal [sic], the Smith Brothers and Herbert Hoover,[40] and finishing an idle hour with "The Great Ostrow" (an action musical with six plots going at once). Or, maybe, it would be "The Life and Very Long Letters of Frank Loesser."

Tempus fugit –

or maybe just plain –

fugit.

31 May 1960: To Florette Henri

Dear Florette,

You have no idea how happy I was to hear from you. You see, in our day, I knew a Florette – that was you – and I knew a Fleurette – that was Fleurette Klingenstein. In all the years between (34 to be almost exact) I have never been able to remember who spelt it which way, and now at last I know. A great weight has been lifted from my mind and I thank you.

Of course, with the exception of the detail of the spelling, I remember you quite well and affectionately as the girl who was born

---

39 Bock and Harnick's *Fiorello!* (1958) was a musical about New York mayor Fiorello La Guardia; Dore Schary's play *Sunset at Campobello* (1960) was about President Franklin Delano Roosevelt's struggle with polio; Mexican general Pancho Villa (1878–1923) became the subject of the flop musical *We Take the Town* (1962). **40** Lydia Pinkham (1819–1883), inventor of a tonic for menstrual and menopausal pain; Madame de Staël (1766–1817), a woman of letters who survived the French Revolution and was exiled by Napoleon twice; William Wallace Smith I (1830–1913) and Andrew Smith (1836–1895), inventors of the cough drop; Herbert Hoover (1874–1964), 31st President of the United States.

in a caul, lived in the Jewish half-mile (West side), introduced me to Irving Hoffman, knew all the lyrics of the Bastard King of England,[41] and never harmed me in any way. Now, there is a whole bundle of authority, and so I cannot lightly toss away your suggestion about a Henry James story – even though you cleverly fail to tell me its title.

I am travelling. Your letter was forwarded to me in Italy and I am answering it in London. In a few days, I will be some other place. And a few weeks after that some other place again. I will not return to New York until September. How would you like to write me a short note mentioning your home 'phone number? And how about writing same around September 15 to me at 983 Park Avenue, New York City. Then I will 'phone you back and you will tell me more. Meanwhile, thanks for thinking of me. And thanks more than anything for clearing things once and for all about Florette. Fleurette was a rich East side girl whose parents pretended not to be Jewish, and who taught me how to inhale. I cough a good deal now.

Best –

The expansion of Frank Music into Europe led Loesser to hire a representative in Germany – Ralph Maria Siegel (1911–1972), a German composer, songwriter and publisher, who translated Loesser's 'Baby, It's Cold Outside' as 'Baby, Es Regnet Doch!' in 1950.

31 May 1960: To Harold Orenstein

Dear Harold,

I have copies of correspondence between you and Ralph Maria Siegel, and don't even pretend to understand it.

---

41 Irwin (not Irving) Hoffman (1924–2018), conductor. 'The Bastard King of England' is a bawdy English folksong variously attributed to Rudyard Kipling, Alfred, Lord Tennyson, Charles Dickens and Walt Whitman. The first verse runs: 'Oh, the minstrels sing of an English King of many long years ago / Who ruled his land with an iron hand though his mind was weak and low. / He loved to shag the royal stag that roamed the royal wood, / But better yet to lie in bed and pull the royal pud. / His only outer garment was a dirty undershirt / That managed to hide the royal pride but couldn't hide the dirt.'

I do feel, however, that our object should not be to predict separation or dissolution, but rather to make continuity the thing to be expected. If we believe that Siegel is a young man, a successful business man and an artistic talent – then we must expect a long association with him, and we must be sure to make a reasonably pleasant appraisal of future benefits. This does not mean that you are to forget the possibility of termination, but we should make every effort to secure Siegel's goodwill during the entire length of each term or extension of the contract.

I see where your reply to Siegel of May 26th already follows this thinking. I have no way to evaluate the details themselves, and so I leave the decision in your hands.

Love,

Letters to friends in this period include communications with American actress Libi Staiger (1928–2019), who played Cleo in the London production of *The Most Happy Fella* (1960), which was directed by her husband Jerome ('Jerry') Eskow; Paramount Films executive Pilade Levi; future attorney Douglas Lyons, son of journalist Leonard Lyons, on the occasion of his bar mitzvah; Robert Weede, who was due to appear in a brief revival of *The Most Happy Fella* in Phoenix; Lillian Ross (1918–2017), a veteran staff writer at *The New Yorker*; American impresario Julius Monk (1912–1995), who produced an annual revue at the venue Upstairs at the Downstairs, on West 56th Street, including (at the time of Loesser's letter) *7 Come 11* (1961); and lyricist E. Y. Harburg (1896–1981), best remembered for his work on *The Wizard of Oz* (1939), who had just written *The Happiest Girl in the World* (1961), based on Aristophanes' *Lysistrata* and using the music of Offenbach, for Broadway.

29 September 1960: To Libi Staiger

Dear Libi:

The waistcoat (as they say) arrived and, as you predicted, fits me fine. I am not allergic to cotton seam bindings, simply to the piss-poor-pederast-piety of our friends the British. This leaves nothing to say except thank you, thank you, thank you.

I spoke to Jerry on the phone yesterday and he reported being well and reasonably happy, considering.

Love from Jo and me and thanks again.

31 October 1960: To Pilade Levi

Dear Levis:

(This salutation sounds like an expensive pair of blue jeans.) Nevertheless, I wanted to say hello. I have lost your last letter somewhere, but remember your saying that you have moved and so I am addressing this to the Paramount office because now I don't know your new address.

Last night we ran our 8 mm. color film of parts of our trip[42] and the most exciting feature was entirely too many feet of the stuff showing Ah-Mo fetching sticks out of the Mediterranean of Circeo.[43] Also, of course we ran the Buckingham Palace stuff, and all the while were thinking fondly of you.

Soon Jo is going to visit her family in the back woods of St. Louis. She will be gone a little over a week and in this time I expect to get a whole lot of writing done. Abe Burrows and I are at it again with a new show,[44] and are trying to finish it so we can open some time in the late spring.

We haven't found a new place to live. Houses in this city are very hard to find, even for billionaires, which we aren't. Now we are looking at apartments, but nothing wonderful has happened yet.

A very famous Broadway director, José Quintero,[45] is now in Rome making a movie. It isn't for Paramount, but don't let that stop you from getting in touch with him because I think you will enjoy each other and possibly you can be of some help in your cordial process

---

42 The Loessers' trip to Rome, Italy.
43 The Circeo coast of Italy, a national park.
44 *How to Succeed in Business Without Really Trying.*
45 Panamanian director José Quintero (1924–1999) was known for a series of productions of the plays of Eugene O'Neill in New York in the 1950s. The film Loesser refers to was *The Roman Spring of Mrs. Stone* (1961) with Vivien Leigh and Warren Beatty. It was Quintero's only theatrically released movie.

of orientation. He has been staying at the Ingleterre Hotel and is doing some commuting to London.

When are you two coming over? We miss you.

Love,

4 November 1960: To Pilade Levi

Dear Pilade:

I forgot to mention in my last note that we have received a lovely oil painting from your friend Bracciola, the waiter in Nino's. Please be sure to extend our thanks and appreciation when you go in there. I can't write him a letter in Italian because I don't know enough. At least no more than molto bene, grazie, and ciao. Please repeat these three little gems to Bracciola in our behalf, and tell him that if he runs out of ball points I will send him some more through you.

Meantime, our best love to you and Carol.

As ever,

15 November 1960: To Douglas Lyons

Dear Douglas:

I want to tell you what joy my mother and I got out of seeing you become a full-fledged member of the Jewish community. It is something to be proud of.

You can feel proud as well, to be a member of the Lyons family. This is a rare and wonderful advantage and I got inexpressable [sic] pleasure in seeing you all together. I'm only sorry that my wife could not possibly be there as she had been called away for urgent family matters out-of-town.

Although being a Jew and being a Lyons is practically all the equipment you need for a good life, we Loessers thought we would add a tiny drop to the blessing bucket, in the form of a gift which we ordered from Hammecher-Schlemmer.[46] I was abashed to receive a

---

46 A catalogue retailer.

notice the other day that it could not yet be delivered to you, but they assure me it will arrive shortly.

Again, our warmest wishes for a brilliant future.

Very sincerely,

31 January 1961: To Robert Weede

Dear Bob:

My brood had to rush out with me after the performance Sunday or I would have shown you in what good shape our girl[47] is, but you can imagine since she has me for a husband.

About the Phoenix thing, I had no idea about this booking but am really delighted that you are going to do it. Do you recall a member of our original company named Alan Gilbert?[48] He now lives in Phoenix due to his young daughter's health problem and I am sure he would be valuable in the cast. I think you will recall that he was at first the baritone member of the "Standing on the Corner" group. Later I got very good reports on his execution of Tony (!) in a summer company. If possible I would like to see him understudy you and at the same time possibly play Pasquale – or maybe the cashier-postman.

Will we get a look at you before Phoenix? I hope so, although I am snowed under with Feuer and Martin, and Abe Burrows,[49] which is quite a blanket of precipitation to start with. However I will call you and see if we can squeeze in a drink or a sandwich. Jo sends her fondest love. Mine too of course.

Loud is good

---

47 Jo Sullivan Loesser, who appeared opposite Weede in the Broadway production of *Most Happy Fella*.
48 Alan Gilbert (dates unknown) appeared in the ensembles of several Broadway productions, including as Clem in *The Most Happy Fella*. He can be heard as a member of the quartet singing 'Standing on the Corner' on the original cast album.
49 A reference to *How to Succeed in Business Without Really Trying*.

6 February 1961: To Lillian Ross

Dear Lillian:

Thank you for the tear sheets. I enjoyed the stories tremendously. When is the big fat novel? Which I will want to adapt as a musical of course. Hurry. Jo and I will holler about some sort of evening conclave shortly unless the pressure of the new musical is really too much. I would like you to meet her – she is your height and just as feisty.

Love,

29 March 1961: To Julius Monk

Dear Julius:

Jo and I want to thank you for your hospitality last night and of course for the remarkable entertainment.

I think the trio are quite attractive and talented and I'll be in shortly to see them prove it. Meanwhile, thanks again and our warmest regards,

28 April 1961: To Yip Harburg

Dear Yip:

My family and I went to see "Happiest Girl"[50] last night and had a simply wonderful time with every part of it. I almost missed the second act opening because I took so much intermission time exclaiming to see Lee Guber[51] about the company, the scenery, the orchestra, and especially about you.

Thanks for a wonderful evening.

Frank

[handwritten notation:] Such praises from a knowing colleague deter me from the alcohol league

---

50 *The Happiest Girl*, with lyrics by 'Yip' Harburg (1896–1981) and based on music by Jacques Offenbach (1818–1880), played at the Martin Beck Theatre, New York, 3 April-24 June 1961.
51 Lee Gruber (1920–1988), theatrical producer.

Josef Marais (1905–1978) was a South African folk singer who performed as a duo with his Dutch wife Miranda (1912–1986) for more than thirty years. They made a number of recordings for labels including Decca and, as their songs became more popular, they were covered by major American artists including Doris Day and Jo Stafford. Loesser knew Josef and Miranda socially but some of their correspondence reveals negotiations towards Frank Music's acquisition of the Marais publisher, Fideree Music Corp. This was announced in *Billboard* on 27 January 1962 after a lengthy period of negotiation: *Billboard* noted that the acquisition included over 150 songs and added that it 'portends a greater emphasis by Frank on folk music'.[52] *Folk Song Jamboree* was a songbook published by Ballantine Books on 1 January 1960, credited to Marais and Miranda with illustrations by Barbara Remington (1929–2020), best known for her cover illustrations of the first paperback editions of *The Hobbit* and *The Lord of the Rings*. The book included words and music for 'songs from many lands'.

27 December 1960: To Josef and Miranda Marais

Dear friends:

Jo and I simply love the Folk Song Jamboree. It is put together perfectly as is everything you two do.

When are you coming East? I hope sometime in the New Year so we can have a look and maybe a listen at each other again. Meanwhile, our thanks for your thoughtfulness and our warmest good wishes –

And love,

24 January 1961: To Mr. and Mrs. Josef Marais

Dear Josef and Miranda:

Thank you for your note. Glad you're here. Jo and I will try to call you. I'm pretty snowed under with work on a new show as well as the weather. Will you be giving a concert here? Anything my outfit can do?

Love,

---

52 Anon., 'Frank Acquires Fideree Music', *Billboard* 74/4 (27 January 1962), 10.

13 March 1961: To Stuart Ostrow

Dear Stu:

Attached is a note from Josef Marais together with a hair-raising document between himself and Howie Richmond.[53]

My receipt of these arises from a conversation with Marais about six weeks ago. In the course of this he allowed that he might want to make a change from his present publishing arrangements. At this point I told him that I would not want to interfere with any association he might have with others. At this point he assured me he had a contract which was terminable on short notice. I asked him to let me see it, and here it is.

Although executed on catchall stationery including collectively the names of seven music firms – the signature of Howard Richmond is not accounted for by any indication of his directorial position with any of these. To my alarmed and innocent eye the contract implies an enormous amount of trust on Marais' part, in the character and activities of Howard Richmond. I have no idea whether or not other documents have been signed pursuant to paragraphs 5 and 6 notably.

Anyway, Josef Marais seems available to the fold, and I believe our firm could afford to make a deal much more generous to his. On the one hand we might be inviting another one of those time-consuming and costly co-publishing deals. On the other hand Marais is a sensational jingle man who knows how to handle primitive tunes and lyrics and is himself something of a recognizable name in the musical field. We might do worse than to put him on the Jean Thomas list of eyebrow-raising quotations. After reading the enclosed contract, please discuss this with Harold and Sam and get back to me with a recommendation for further conversation with Marais, or for a polite begoff.

---

53 Howard Richmond (1918–2012) was the head of the Richard Organization, a large (umbrella) music publishing organisation.

25 October 1961: To Josef Marais

Dear Josef:

I suppose by now you have read my hurried wire. Since sending it, I am told by Milt Kramer that your lawyer has been back in touch with him. I was really upset to hear that we were unable to close a deal. Apparently, the arrangements bringing Fideree with us on a simple, straightforward basis as originally discussed by you and Ostrow fell by the wayside when Bernard Reich[54] moved into the picture. He made request after request which Kramer (Ostrow's successor) acceded to, knowing I was personally very anxious to make this deal.

Finally, however, Kramer tells me that the deal became one which would be financially impractical and he felt that it was so far away from the original terms (which are really the only sound ones on which to make such a deal) that he had to call the whole thing off.

I'm personally very chagrined by the whole thing, but I'm afraid to overrule his judgment; he may fire me.

As you know, I'm now coming (slowly) out of the enormous mess of getting a show on. But it has been a happy and most successful mess, so I can't complain.

Jo sends her love, with mine, to you and Miranda – and with it my fond hope that we can still do something with our deal.

Love, anyway,

3 November 1961: To Josef Marais

Dear Josef:

Thanks for your letter explaining your innocence of the lawyer doings. At least you undoubtedly got something written and something sung during the time of the "negotiations" and that is as it should be.

Anyway, Milt Kramer knows the story to date now and will be in touch. However, he agrees with my reflection that here we are the Number One prestige and success publishers in the music industry

---

54 Bernard Reich (1914–2006), entertainment attorney.

and still seem to be "auditioning." At least I gather that from the way Milt describes your lawyer's concept of an agreement.

Milt will be in touch with you also about your Ballantine Pocket Book question and I'm sure something can be worked out.

Jo and I are still knee-deep in house straightenings, but on your next trip to New York you and Miranda won't see any signs of the current confusion, and the house will be nice enough for a visit from you which we will insist on.

Love as always,

3 October 1962: To Mr. and Mrs. Josef Marais

Dear Josef and Miranda:

Thank you for your note. Jo is writing you separately and will report on her own roly-poly condition.

Would you mind if I wrote a parody to "John Ferrera" which goes, "Stay in the middle of the bed, Jo Loesser, Jody with the great big bump." Or would you sue me?

Milt keeps me in touch with progress as to your record deals, etc., so I'm up to date on that. The news here is that Meredith Willson is recovering nicely out there. If you see him or talk to him, give him a gentle pat on the gut and my best love.

Of course, love to you both,

Frank Loesser

P.S. Notice I am using your stationery. It gives me great nachis.

Other business correspondence was more straightforward. Although many of Frank Music's successes were a result of its nurturing of younger or newer songwriters, the company's stable included lyricist Otto Harbach (1873–1963), veteran of hundreds of songs including 'Smoke Gets in Your Eyes'. Leslie Kettle (dates unknown) ran the London branch of Frank Music through Chappell; Loesser's letter to him refers to Leslie Bricusse (1931–2021), who would later become famous for his collaborations with Anthony Newley (1931–1999) ('Feeling Good' and *Willy Wonka and the Chocolate*

Factory, 1971) as well as for writing words and music to the film *Doctor Dolittle* (1967). He had been working with Canadian-British actress Beatrice Lillie (1894–1989) for several years since her discovery of him, and his orchestrations appeared on her Decca EP *What's New with Bea Lillie?* (1961). It's unclear which project Loesser proposed to director-choreographer Jerome Robbins (1918–1998) but perhaps he already had Sam Spewack's play *Once There Was a Russian* (which had flopped on Broadway in 1961) in his sights for his next musical: he would go on to adapt it into *Pleasures and Palaces* (1965) with the other major director-choreographer of the era, Bob Fosse (1927–1987), instead. Sol Meyer (1913–1964) was a Hollywood lyricist whose work appeared in more than forty films.

9 November 1960: To Otto Harbach

Dear Otto:

I have just finished listening to your song, "Slowly" and I hasten to tell you how very much I like it. I have already telephoned Harold Solomon to give him these sentiments, but I especially wanted to thank you for giving our publishing company such a beautiful song.[55]

It is not only gratifying to have such fine literature to publish; it is also an honor to have your name under our banner.

The last time we saw each other, if you will recall, was at the Press Club in Washington. Or, was it in Henry Morgenthau's[56] office in the interest of bond-selling? At any rate, it was much too long ago and I think it is time we met again over a cup of coffee. I will try to call you very soon.

With fond good wishes,

---

55 The song 'Slowly' was included on the album *Deep Velvet* (1964) by George Shearing with Quintet and Woodwinds Choir. Harold Solomon (dates unknown) wrote a number of popular songs including the Dinah Washington piece 'The Kissing Way Home' and 'Stranger in Mexico' for Steve Lawrence.

56 Henry Morgenthau (1891–1967) was United States Secretary of the Treasury during Franklin D. Roosevelt's administration. He oversaw the War Bond programme during the Second World War, raising $49 billion towards the war effort. See https://home.treasury.gov/about/history/prior-secretaries/henry-morgenthau-jr-1934-1945.

14 November 1960: To Leslie Kettle,
Holland Park, London

Dear Leslie:

Greetings.

Who is Leslie Bricusse, alleged to be assisting Beatrice Lillie in the construction of some sort of show for New York, as per the enclosed cutting in yesterday's New York Times? Please see if you can get me a complete rundown on Bricusse's career, and as much as possible on the Beatrice Lillie subject, intended dates, etc.

Be sure to see if you can inquire as to what musical or lyrical material has been acquired or optioned, and I suggest that where you can – plan for publishing rights acquisition in favor of Frank Music U.S.A. – since this country seems to be the first point of presentation. Note the underlining of the word plan. At this moment, other of our forces are at work on this entire subject. For the moment, it is best just to be snuggly with whatever writer-contributors you can find and tell them something may be in the wind and not to dispose of publishing rights, etc. until they hear from mysterious old you. Don't, however, reveal that Frank Productions is making the inquiries.

Thanks, and best love to you and the family.

27 February 1961: To Jerome Robbins

Dear Jerry,

I'm really sorry you don't think enough of the project. Anyway thanks for giving it thought. And now please remember not to mention the subject to anyone as it will be a long time before I do anything about it and so want to keep the whole thing quiet.

Best as always,

6 March 1961: To Sol Meyer

Dear Sol:

Thanks for your note. The people to call about the tithe – are Martin Wolman, MU 9-8686. He will account to you. That's why they call him an accountant.

This way you can write me poetry untainted by business considerations.

With a certain amount of dread I consider your emergence as a full general partner. I don't even know of what, but the whole idea gives me pause. Next thing you know you will be dunning me on embossed stationery from a classier address. Please get after Wolman on Topic A, and give me a phone call sometime about a drink or a nosh.

[note at bottom: envelope marked "Not A Bit Personal"]

Arthur Laurents's (1917–2011) works include the books for the musicals *West Side Story* (1957) and *Gypsy* (1959) as well as the play *The Time of the Cuckoo* (1952), which ran for 263 performances and was turned into the movie *Summertime* (1955) starring Katharine Hepburn (1907–2003). In 1965 Laurents wrote a musical adaptation of *Cuckoo* with music by Richard Rodgers (1902–1979) and Stephen Sondheim (1930–2021), *Do I Hear a Waltz?*, which received mixed reviews and was a commercial flop at just 220 performances. Yet as early as 1961, the songwriting team of Jack Lawrence (1912–2009) and Stan Freeman (1920–2001) had already pitched a version of their own, for which they drafted a score. Although not remembered as Broadway writers – their *I Had a Ball* (1964) later became a moderately successful star vehicle for comedian Buddy Hackett (1924–2003) – Lawrence is notable for writing the lyrics to the famous Disney numbers 'Never Smile at a Crocodile' and 'Once Upon a Dream', and Freeman was a prominent arranger for artists including Frank Sinatra and Peggy Lee. Loesser saw potential in the project and tried to promote the idea to Laurents, tantalising him with starry names such as Judy Garland (1922–1969) and Jerome Robbins, but it was not to be.

3 February 1961: To Jack Lawrence and Stan Freeman

Dear Jack and Stan:

As I gather it, Harold Freedman[57] selected me as one of the people whose opinion he would consider valuable in appraising

---

57 Harold Freedman (1935–1961), head of the theatre department of Brandt & Brandt, a literary agency in New York City (now Brandt & Hochman).

your work on "Time of the Cuckoo." Being thus flattered I felt impelled to hear the work and hasten to tell you that I had a wonderful time on both occasions when I listened. It gives me genuine nachis to be able to report that I love the work so far. It is imaginative and tuneful and has a point of view – something which is rare in a collection of arbitrarily-arrived-at pieces aimed at application to a final musical play adaptation.

I believe it is important for Arthur Laurents to hear what you have done. Even if it did not spark him into volunteering to write the adaptation himself (which is what I hope) it certainly ought to encourage him to give you the permission necessary for finishing the work.

Whether or not all of the numbers you presented will remain parts of the score is a question which will of course be decided by the nature of the adaptation. I don't think that part is important. I am confident that if you can arrive at the present pieces with no musical-play formula to follow that there is no doubt that you can very beautifully execute the ultimate score.

You are free to quote what I have to say here to anyone, but especially to Harold Freedman and Arthur Laurents. Thanks for the treat.

Sincerely,

13 March 1961: Interoffice communication to Allen Whitehead

Dear Allen:

Subject: Jack Lawrence & Stan Freeman

I don't know what progress has been on the songs the above writers played for us a while back, but I suppose that if they had concluded some sort of acquisition deal of "Time of the Cuckoo," that I would have heard about it.

Now in the meantime, something real nutty has occurred to me. The songs, as all of us here agree, are very well written and quite valuable for New York stage production. As I recollect listening at least four of the songs could apply absolutely beautifully to the Sol Rees project which we've been sitting on. The songwriters very wisely wrote on broad song-subjects – even though they may have been inspired by reading "Time of the Cuckoo," and in consequence if you look over the Sol Rees thing you will see how beautifully alot [sic] of their writing can be made to apply, even though there is not even a remote resemblance between the subjects, characters, or locales of the two pieces.

Briefly, what I have in mind is that you and Stu should invite Lawrence and Freeman to play over their things again and see if you agree. In the event you do, (and they do not make a satisfactory arrangement with Arthur Laurents soon) then maybe we ought to invite them into a collaboration on the other piece which is ours and ready to go any time. We might have a brilliant and quick head start. Certainly this is a very worthwhile composing team. Please give me your reflections as soon as possible.

Love,

28 June 1961: To Arthur Laurents

Dear Arthur,

If you note the passage of water under our bridge it is because my outfit told the prospective composers to make their own decisions about how they wanted to be heard. Since then I understand that their lawyer has been in touch with your representatives and something is being worked out. Meanwhile, this is to repeat that my outfit would dearly love to produce a musical version of "Time of the Cuckoo" and that we think that this team of composers has the right feel and ability for it. As to other elements of the project, much depends on you since our intention is to give you the greatest possible array of controls as basic author. Further, we would be more than thrilled at the idea of your becoming active adaptor as well. That would give you even greater authority in the production.

In the meantime, it would be idle for us to suggest a "package" such as JUDY GARLAND – CESARE SIEPI – JERRY ROBBINS. Approaching any of such people couldn't produce any practical results until we could show them something of a musical play with exemplary songs and a prospective date of production. They might all express extreme "interest" but I don't believe any proposal now would result in firm understandings. I wouldn't mind approaching important people on the subject, getting a nod and reporting same, but such report would only be of value to someone like Sam Zolotow[58] who has empty space to fill with still more empty space.

I suspect I am at the bottom of the page. I do not want to damage your writing hand on a sharp staple. It is too precious.

My very best,

Another famous show with which Loesser was peripherally involved was *The Fantasticks* (1960), an off-Broadway musical that ran for a record-breaking forty-two years and is remembered for the song 'Try to Remember'. The music was by Harvey Schmidt (1929–2018) and the book and lyrics by Tom Jones (1928–2023; not to be confused with the Welsh singer of the same name). Loesser sensed the show's potential – and posterity has proved him to be right – but his audacious attempt to persuade Chappell & Co. executive Louis Dreyfus (1877–1967) to relinquish the publishing rights was unsuccessful. Louis was head of the London branch of Chappell; his brother Max Dreyfus (1874–1964) was president of the American office. Loesser had a business interest in the show through Music Theatre Inc.

21 November 1960: To Tom Jones

Dear Tom:

Thanks for your note. All right, be cautious, but I beg you and your partner and your agent and your unborn children, to deliver at least the musical and lyrical contents of your NTA[59] show to some publisher, any ASCAP publisher – before committing these works as part of the contents of a TV or any other production.

I am not going to plague you with an explanation of why, but it's like polio shots, circumcision or baptism, all of which make you more comfortable later on and are well worth the small pain involved.

If your agent wants to call me about this, I will explain more fully.

---

58 Possibly Maurice Zolotow (1898–1993), theatre reporter for the *New York Times*.
59 National Telefilm Associates.

Best

7 February 1961: To Louis Dreyfus

Dear Louis:

At the risk of boring you (and here I bow to the champions in this division, including Prince Littler, Binkie Beaumont, Ernest Martin,[60] etc.) I am writing this note to express a wish of mine. This wish is based on "nachis" which is a word used frequently among us in the lower Jewish stratum for expressing affectionate and sympathetic love. Sometimes it gets contaminated with commercial cupidity. I can't say that I am entirely insensitive to the proddings of this latter element, but far stronger than all other motivating factors is my chemical affection for the score of "The Fantasticks."

As I have told you one of my companies (and I have more companies than there are demi-quavers in a scherzo) controls the licensing of productions of "The Fantasticks" in all parts of the world. As a matter of fact, our rights go beyond that. At the moment we are in touch with government scientists in an effort to launch a moon rocket containing a company of nine actors who will perform the play on the moon at the earliest scientific opportunity. In other words we not only have world rights, we have out-of-this-world rights.

Toward making this play a long-living standard musical, we have to consider the efficacy and general impact of the score. Thus far there has been no gigantic public recognition of the pieces from "The Fantasticks." I do not wish to imply here that no effort has been made. It is simply that no note-worthy effect has been produced. The score therefore seems to be of small value in enticing public attention to productions of the play – and I would like my publishing company to set its teeth vigorously into such a project.

In short, dear Louis, I would like to acquire United States and world publishing and allied rights to the score. I feel that if this matter

---

60 Hugh 'Binkie' Beaumont (1908–1973), British theatre manager and producer. American producer Ernest Martin (1919–1995) worked with Loesser on *Guys and Dolls* and *How to Succeed in Business Without Really Trying*; he later produced films of Kander and Ebb's *Cabaret* (1972) and Marvin Hamlisch's *A Chorus Line* (1985).

were entirely in your hands there would be no difficulty in coming to some sort of terms for acquisition. I say this because your English company and mine are constantly in a position to benefit each other and there has been a fruitful history of give-and-take between us but here we are discussing a property of your brother Max. Frankly I don't know how to approach him on this subject because I am sure he is not accustomed to such an approach from me, nor can I believe there is any cash basis on which he would consider this attractive; nor do he and I know each other well enough for me to volunteer a direct discussion at this point.

So you, Louis, are elected. (You see you don't have to be a Roman Catholic to be elected.) The job is this: speak to Max about the broad advantages to be derived from the suggested assignment. The following will give you and him something of a picture:

My organization is actively in the stage production business – on Broadway, off-Broadway, in foreign countries and if necessary the moon as predicted above. Thus far we have been the successful co-producers of "Most Happy Fella," "Music Man," and "Boy Friend"[61] (Cherry Lane production), the unsuccessful co-producers of "Greenwillow," the fairly successful co-producers of "Most Happy Fella" in London, the prospective co-producers of "The Fantasticks" in London, the prospective co-producers of "Anastasia" (Wright & Forrest), "Viva Villa," "Peg O' My Heart,"[62] and my current opus with Abe Burrows. I believe you have already subscribed a resounding approval of our judgment and sense of enterprise by your co-financing of some of the English ventures.

Now your brother Max is not directly in the production business although he is held in the highest possible regard by those in it. However vast the esteem may be for his judgment as a publisher, there is still the enormous fact that Burton Lane has not accomplished a Broadway show since I'd hate to tell you when. Likewise Ira Gershwin.

---

61 Sandy Wilson's *The Boy Friend* (1954), which marked the Broadway debut of Julie Andrews (born 1935).
62 Presumably a reworking of the musical *Peg O' My Heart* that ran on Broadway from 20 December 1912 to May 1914.

If Yip Harburg makes it with his current effort it will be the first in a long time, and limping from its Public Domain personality. Now that's where Frank Productions Inc. rears its head. We would like to – in fact intend to – invite these people and others under the Chappell banner to consider working on certain productions. I should think this would be of some value to Max who no doubt would relish the receipt of some new contributions to his catalogue from able and valuable writers. Few of these are self-starters and have to be <u>handed</u> a production, plus playwright collaboration, plus producer confidence.

The people of my publishing company have been instructed – on pain of death – not to attempt the making of any siren-like sounds toward spiriting writers away from their natural publishing habitat. We wouldn't want it done to us. We would hate to wake up in the morning to find Meredith Willson absent, Wright & Forrest else-where, and Frank Loesser shouting defiance from the protective arms of Buddy Morris or Lou Levy.[63] Max will recall that the very moment he wanted Marc Blitzstein,[64] all he had to do was write me a letter enclosing a check for five hundred dollars (advance paid Marc) and Marc was his. Conversely Max gave us no trouble at all in delivering one of Marc Bucci's works.[65] Today there is no outstanding "bargain" to offer. The only possibility is that one of my companies (the fifteenth to the left) is the legal licensor of the publishing rights of John Hollander who is at present collaborating with Jerry Moross on an imminent Broadway show.[66] I understand Moross is under contract to Chappell. I see no reason why Hollander can not join him as a

---

63 Edwin H. 'Buddy' Morris (1906–1996) and Lou Levy (1928–2001), publishers of American popular music.
64 Marc Blitzstein (1905–1964), American composer and lyricist best known for his musical *The Cradle Will Rock* (1937).
65 Frank Music published Mark Bucci's (1924–2002) *Tale for a Deaf Ear* (1958) and 'Sweet Betsy' (1961) from his opera *Pike*.
66 John Hollander (1923–2013) was a poet and literary critic who wrote the lyrics to an unproduced musical *Underworld* with music by Jerome Moross (1913–1983) and a book by Ben Hecht (1894–1964) and noted television documentary maker Ted Yates (1930–1967). He was married to Anne Loesser (1930–2014), daughter of Frank's brother Arthur.

collaborator at Chappell even though it is conceivable that a less understanding instinct could lead us to ask for Moross to join Hollander in publishing with the Frank company.

As our productivity increases, there may be more and more of such situations. We have every intention of making them fruitful for Chappell whenever we can. I hope Max can see value in this. Of course it is largely a matter of good faith and good will. I am sure that it is apparent to you that neither Max nor I have been without either instinct. Especially toward each other.

I don't know what more I can tell you except to convey some of these thoughts to Max. You are accustomed to some of my seemingly bullish approaches and can understand them because you know me rather well. I would not want Max to mistake my enthusiasm about "The Fantasticks" score for some sort of startling lunatic avarice. I leave it to you to be my interpreter. I believe you know that I am not a fourflusher or a doublecrosser. After all, to quote a Chappell copyright, you've grown accustomed to my face.

10. Frank Loesser performing at Camp Hiawatha for
Girls, Kezar Falls, Maine, 1950s.

Love,

Loesser took every opportunity to show off his love of language and sense of humour. He would take the trouble to write a letter as a joke for no other reason than to amuse himself. And when he was asked to write formal letters, he would sometimes write spoof versions and send them separately, such as in a series of letters of recommendations for his former Frank Music colleague Stuart Ostrow, now an independent producer; Leonard Sillman (1908–1982), producer of the *New Faces* revue series with which Loesser was briefly connected; and director/stage manager Lawrence Kasha (1933–1990), who acted as casting director for Loesser's next musical, *How to Succeed in Business Without Really Trying*.

22 March 1961: To L. J. Phillips-Wood, Dolson Co., offering a character reference for Stu Ostrow as a tenant

Gentlemen:

Answering your request for my reference regarding Mr. Stuart Ostrow, I hasten to assure you that you could not find a prospective tenant more desirable.

That is, if you want to get rid of all the other tenants quickly. I imagine this is a good plan for your building which you have been trying to turn cooperative for a long time and which would require the cancellation of the leases of those people not content with the cooperative plan. If there is one man in this world who can produce hordes of discontented people out of thin air – it is Mr. Ostrow. At present he is in my employ and I can assure you that he has everyone very unhappy.

Let me fill you in on the details. First of all, a young Jew with a Southern wife and a noisy kid is possibly the most perfect hazard you could wish for. Incidentally, the noises the kid makes are about wanting a dog and there is no doubt that she will soon have her way with her overpaid and spendthrift father. He will of course go to the Kramer Kennels and secure the most vicious Doberman-Pinscher obtainable. You can't blame him for his shopping choice as he and Mr. Kramer are old buddies. If you wish to observe the result of a prior sale you will note with some satisfaction that 55 East End Avenue now features one-legged elevator men and an assortment of hysterical maids.

But back to Mr. Ostrow himself. He is an ambitious young man, somewhat fortified in his pursuits by a definite tendency to steal. He limits this activity of course to certain valuable items. He has, for instance, planned building a Southern mansion to present to his daughter upon her marriage some years from now. Toward this end he has been very persistent in acquiring used building materials in order to give the proposed mansion the proper air of antiquity and gentle decay. It is said that Vyse Avenue in the Bronx doesn't have a brick on it any more, as these were removed one at a time during Mr. Ostrow's adolescence by way of his overcoat pocket – an item thoughtfully supplied by his father who is to this day perhaps the crookedest haberdasher in the Bronx. I have had a special interest in observing the Ostrow career at 55 East End Avenue as my mother also lives there, and so I have not failed to notice that the paneling in the hallways has mysteriously disappeared recently, and the entire building has been nibbled away from the roof through the eleventh floor except for certain perishables like tar paper and window shades. One notable evidence of his patriotism and respect for the Federal Government is the fact that the mail chutes still protrude and are intact. I am secure in my conviction that Mr. Ostrow accords me the same respect and consideration that he gives the government, and am pleased to notice that my mother has not been removed. Although from time to time Mr. Ostrow seems to be appraising her as if she would indeed make a fine lamp for his daughter's mansion. But this again is probably just an example of filial devotion and over-anxiety on my part.

I suggest a relatively short lease but with no too-oppressive clauses. I cannot afford to have him in hand-cuffs as he must sign my company checks from time to time.

You understand.

Sincerely,

8 May 1962: Recommendation of Leonard
Sillman as a tenant for an apartment on East
47th Street, New York

Gentlemen:

As an old and satisfied tenant of yours I feel it fair to answer the above request with great candor. You asked me for information as to the responsibility and desirability of one Leonard Sillman, who has applied for space in one of your buildings.

I hasten to assure you that he is absolutely <u>responsible</u> as well as <u>desirable</u>. Firstly, he is <u>responsible</u> for the utter collapse and failure of a series of Broadway revues doggedly titled "New Faces."[67] Secondly, he is <u>desirable</u>. To elves, rich old ladies, sometimes John Gielgud,[68] his maid Ruth, and a Central Park squirrel named Fred who discovered him in what might be termed a fruitful search for nuts. Frankly, I tingle for him a little myself.

Well, there you have the picture of his responsibility and desirability.

Golly! I can just see the goings on in that nice corner store of yours. Well, good luck.

Sincerely, Frank Loesser

[An alternative, marked 'actually sent', reads:]

In answer to the above request, I consider Leonard Sillman a highly desirable tenant. I have known him both as a business colleague and associate, and as a personal friend for many years, and find him completely responsible and a man of honor and dignity.

Sincerely,

[Enclosed:]
Dear Leonard:

---

67 *New Faces of 1934*, with a book by Leonard Sillman, ran for four months at the Fulton Theatre, New York, from 15 March to July 1934. Subsequent iterations were staged by Sillman in 1936, 1943, 1952, 1956, 1962 and 1968.
68 John Gielgud (1904–2000), English actor and theatre director.

I thought you ought to see what I sent your prospective landlord. Ever since winning part of a Pulitzer Prize[69] I simply have to be honest.

Love,

27 August 1962: To Jerome Robbins, letter of recommendation for Larry Kasha

Dear Jerry:

I have word that you are considering the idea of having Larry Kasha assist you with a forthcoming show. This note is to put in a very willing and enthusiastic word about him. His work as stage manager for "How To" seemed to me to be notable for its intelligence, accuracy, and minimal capacity for confusion and blowup. Further, I have watched him directing replacement rehearsals, and got great satisfaction from observing the process as well as the results. Further, he is on record for the direction of two of my shows ("Guys & Dolls" and "The Most Happy Fella") for the big theatre in Toronto, and although I saw neither one of them, the reports I get from many corners are all in praise of our friend. He seems to relish the idea of working with you, and I feel confident that you will not be disappointed.

With fond wishes,

Sincerely,

Also enclosed but marked "dummy sent to Kasha":
Dear Jerry:

There is a man named Larry Kasha who claims he has a chance to work for you in some capacity. I don't know how often you need a shoe shine, or a container of coffee, but I'd say that Mr. Kasha's limitations have been expressed right there. On second thought, there is some doubt about whether you would get the right change with the container of coffee, and how much would wind up on your lap because of Kasha's tendency to twitch suddenly. Now I don't mean to

---

69 Loesser's recent musical, *How to Succeed in Business Without Really Trying* (1961), won the Pulitzer Prize.

be inconsiderate about another man's infirmity, but in this instance the twitch is congenital and to the best of my knowledge and information comes from a long family history of venereal disease. And therein lies a real hazard, as the man would not hesitate to use your john – and I needn't tell you what a risk you would be taking.

There is a redeeming thing about an association with Kasha, which I feel obliged to report here. He is good luck. I remember distinctly crossing a road in central North Dakota with Kasha by my side, and reaching the other side without having been struck down by the traffic. This indicated to me that his presence lent a charm against the dangers of jay walking, and it is safe to assume that if Kasha is within the same four theater walls as you, that your hair will not turn green and your teeth will not fall out.

One note of warning however: I don't know whether you are including any livestock in your cast, but it is fair to warn you that poor Larry has a thing about dogs, cats and parrots, which if gratified by virtue of some devious lurking backstage, renders the poor animals a little lethargic in their execution of the next few days' performances. I don't know exactly what goes on, but there is a whole chapter in Krafft-Ebing's Psychopathia Sexualis book devoted to the aberrated career of one L. K., which mercifully fails to identify our friend too positively.

One last thing. He has a recurrent amnesia, which on the face of it may seem ominous, but regard for a moment the possibility that if you engage him, it is likely that he may forget to show up for work altogether – and this can be a blessing to you.

Well, I guess that's the rundown on Kasha. I am enclosing a 10-foot pole with which not to touch him.

Your sincere friend,

CHAPTER EIGHT

1961–62
HOW TO SUCCEED IN BUSINESS WITHOUT REALLY TRYING

Greenwillow may have been a huge disappointment, but Loesser knocked it out of the park with his next Broadway musical. *How to Succeed in Business Without Really Trying* reunited him with book writer Abe Burrows and producers Cy Feuer and Ernie Martin, the team behind *Guys and Dolls*. The new show would become his longest-running on Broadway – 1,417 performances to *Guys and Dolls'* 1,200 – and, in addition to winning seven Tony Awards, it won the 1962 Pulitzer Prize for Drama.

Feuer and Martin first announced they had acquired the rights to Shepherd Mead's book *How to Succeed in Business Without Really Trying* in late March 1960. It had already been turned into a play by television writers Jack Weinstock (1907–1969) and Willie Gilbert (1916–1980), who had previously collaborated on shows such as *Howdy Doody* and written material for Jackie Gleason (1916–1987), but their version had gone unproduced. The announcement of Feuer and Martin's purchase also mentioned that they hoped to interest Loesser in another of their current projects, *Cafe Crown*, which went on to be a three-performance dud in the hands of other writers in 1964; surprisingly, Loesser is not mentioned in reference to *How to Succeed*.[1]

---

1 Sam Zolotow, 'Musical Planned by Feuer, Martin', *New York Times*, 25 March 1960, 20.

By the end of June it was revealed in *Variety* that Loesser was 'working on a new musical' in Paris,[2] but it was not until 16 October that the *New York Times* could report that he and Burrows had signed up to work together on *How to Succeed* specifically. Lewis Funke reported: '"H.T.S.I.B.W.R.T.," to be sure, will be based on a book of similar name by Shepherd Mead, a satirical account of a somewhat ineffective young man who stumbles up the ladder of success. Its theatrical incarnation is in the hands of Abe Burrows who, with Jack Weinstock and Willie Gilbert, is working on the final draft. Entrusted with the music and the lyrics is Frank Loesser, and, if you are not hung over or beset by morning cobwebs, you already will have registered the fact that the enterprise brings together practically the same creative and managerial team that gave us "Guys and Dolls."'[3]

Initially announced for a May 1961 opening, the show was deferred to October 1961. An interesting casting combination brought together musical comedy actor Robert Morse (1931–2022), who had recently appeared in the Broadway musical *Take Me Along* (1959), with veteran crooner Rudy Vallée (1901–1986). The show opened in Philadelphia for a pre-Broadway tryout on 4 September 1961 and *Variety*'s reviewer wrote: 'A realistic appraisal of its assets would report that "How to Succeed" opened in a strong technical position and should move on to long-term gains on the Broadway boards . . . Frank Loesser has pulled out every stop in his extensive musical holdings, even working in an electric shaver for a washroom male chorus. It's a continuously clever fusion of words and upper case music that is nearly irresistible.'[4] In the *Evening Bulletin*, Ernest Scheier said that the show 'suggests a mixture of Moliere and the Marx Brothers. A good natured, tuneful, colorful assault on conformity and the easy ethics of the business world . . .'[5]

The reviews on Broadway were equally enthusiastic, and the show went on to become another hit for Loesser. Correspondence reveals

2 'Chatter: London', *Variety* 219 (29 June 1960), 78.
3 Lewis Funke, 'News of the Rialto: Musical Reunion', *New York Times*, 16 October 1960, X1.
4 Jerry Gaghan, 'Shows Out of Town', *Variety* 234 (6 September 1961), 54.
5 Quoted in *Back Stage* 2/32 (8 September 1961), 15.

that there were some backstage tensions along the way with Feuer and Martin, and Loesser's now finely-tuned business sense came to the fore, whether in negotiations over the film rights or the contracting of the musical director Elliot Lawrence (1925–2021). To one old friend he was able to accede to a request: Groucho Marx wanted copies of the sheet music and was sent them. To another, there was a firm 'no': Loesser could not allow Bing Crosby to record one of the show's songs and thereby allow its jokes to be widely known to people who had not yet seen the show. This time, Loesser didn't want the songs to be sung too widely or, he felt, it would spoil the impact of the Broadway production.

And the commercial impact of *How to Succeed* was indeed well handled. It enjoyed global success: before it had even ended its run on Broadway – which brought in over $10 million at the box office – the show had been seen in the UK, Australia, France, Japan, Denmark, Sweden, Brazil and Israel.[6]

16 January 1961: To Harold Orenstein

Dear Harold,

Abe phoned me last night. He informed me that he would not continue on the show beyond twenty-four hours from now unless everything about the cast album were resolved to my satisfaction. He had just finished a conversation with Cy Feuer. Feuer indicated that the move was now <u>mine</u> to answer the proposal expressed in a letter from Irving Cohen[7] to Feuer & Martin a couple of days ago!

We are <u>aware</u> of that letter, if you want to call it that. No signature appears on our copy. Nor was there a letter of transmittal. Forgetting all that technical observation in which you trained me so thoroughly – I <u>cannot</u> subscribe to the idea. It is obvious that if the producers had the power to disapprove, they could exercise any control or

---

6 Sam Zolotow, ' "Fade Out-Fade In" May Be Reopened', *New York Times*, 25 January 1965, 24.
7 Irving Cohen (dates unknown), lawyer.

decision they pleased whether to the writers' advantage or not. Especially if we should approach [record label] R.C.A. Victor.

Feuer and Martin have already predicted that they would disapprove the above company.

Therefore I would be forced to visit with the others – let's say Columbia, Capitol, MGM, Decca, etc.

Now we have already been informed by F & M and indeed put on rigid official notice by RCA Victor that some "contract" of the past still exists, is in force and is applicable to the present proposed show, if produced by them.

There is no doubt but that this information about F & M's legal obligation will be distributed forcefully among members of the recording industry – and in consequence there will be no company – big or small – which in fear of injunction, lawsuit, etc. will want to undertake the manufacturing of the album. This had already been demonstrated in a very wary conversation volunteered the other day by one of the major companies to Stu Ostow.

17 May 1961: To Abe Burrows

Dear Abe,

Since we have already been approached regarding a pre-production motion picture sale of "How To etc." I think I had better tell you here of certain conditions which I would have to insist on seeing in any motion picture agreement. From our conversations lately you seem to favor the idea of a pre-production deal, and so do Feuer & Martin, apparently. So in going along with you three in examining any possible offers, I want to give you an idea of what special demands of mine (mostly about music etc.) would have to be satisfied – so that if the time came for an objection by me to closing a sale regardless of money price, you as well as the producers would then have known in advance about this hazard, and I won't have surprised anybody.

While the attached general list of special terms of mine may seem formidable at first reading, a quick review of the "Guys and Dolls" agreement will reassure you that not much new has been added. I have presented them here quite loosely and the language is not intended to be contract language. Also, without being able to anticipate the demands of the buyer I cannot call the attached list complete. But it does express pretty much of the safeguard schedule I will need.

I am sending a copy of this note and the attached stuff to Feuer & Martin. I think they too should know in advance what kind of obstacles there might be to closing a sale. I don't want to be called names later.

Love

Frank

cc: Feuer & Martin, Frank Music Corp., Frank Productions, Harold Orenstein

14 July 1961: Memo to Allen Arrow[8]

It is probably my fault for not having examined until now the nature of the documents by which I employ musical personnel. I refer here to the proposed one already signed by Elliot Lawrence. Let me put my intentions into my own English without reference to the legal language that may find its way into an ultimate document:

> I understand and acknowledge and approve (or promise to do so) your employment in my behalf by Feuer and Marin as musical director of "HTSIBWRT."
>
> We understand, you and I, that your work in this respect is not of the "creative variety." That is to say you are to help me in the execution of playable piano versions of my compositions which I deliver to you in writing but in a form not always suitable for piano accompaniment. Further, it is understood that your function is to teach certain vocal performances, attend to the selection of instrumentalists, conduct orchestral rehearsals and corrections and ultimately conduct the performing orchestra and show.

---

8 Allen Arrow (1928–2016) was an attorney for Frank Music.

It is possible that among all your typical duties as musical director you may have occasion to suggest alterations or even additions to my written material. The fact that you may do so and that these things are accepted and used is not by any reckoning to mean that you are one of the creators of the material in the show and that automatically any such changes or additions will become my property. For this here's a dollar.

No matter how much editorial help of this kind you may give me, and no matter how effective its use in the show may be, you will not receive any credit of any kind except that the <u>musical</u> <u>direction</u> is by you. If, by any chance, the orchestrator's work shall be handed out by him to you under some private sub-contract – this will be of no concern or importance to me and the sole billing for orchestration that I will acknowledge or approve is that of the orchestrator. You will receive billing as musical director on all printed editions of the score or parts of the score published in which other such credits appear (producer, choreographer, author, scenic designer). Otherwise, as in the case of editions printed at [a] later date as standard ones, or included in folio or collections, the answer is no.

I will cause your billing to appear on the front cover of the original cast phonograph album but I cannot guarantee that it will appear on the labels. Tough titty, I am not the record manufacturer and have not asked for this for myself to the best of my recollection.

This expresses pretty much the way I consider the relationship between Elliot and myself. The document as printed looks for all the world to widows, innocent children, and various knockers as if I hired people to write for me.

I think I ought to have another look at his employment contract with the producers – if I ever did see it. Talk to me.

Love,

4 August 1961: To Cy Feuer and Ernest Martin

Dear Cy and Ernie:

In the span of the last ten months, as you know, I have written various pieces, intending them as possibilities for the production of "How To Succeed In Business Without Really Trying," and ultimately deleting them from the score. The following is a partial list:

Bless This Day
I'm An Organization Man
I'm A Company Man
Long Long Lashes
Reaction to Hedy
Clandestine
White Collar World
Marvellous Mind
Business Man's Shuffle

In general, although not always, I choose to make application for "unpublished" copyright only on songs which appear certain to remain as parts of a musical comedy score. In each instance the songs in the above list have not been registered in this manner, and therefore I am writing you this letter and enclosing with it examples of the music and lyric content of the pieces mentioned. Because there is no "official" record of their existence at intervals since last November, the enclosed examples of music and lyrics will come to your attention now, and remain in your files against a later time when I may possibly wish to call on you to recollect and identify them. Sometimes I leave material unused for quite long periods of years, and on occasion have been challenged as to the priority of existence.

9 August 1961: To Cy Feuer

Dear Cy:

Last night I went home feeling very sorry for myself, and this morning I woke up feeling even worse. I tried to write a few things and they all sounded like "Gloomy Sunday". This is not a good day for me, and I am not sure about tomorrow. What happened is, yesterday I got my feelings badly hurt.

Now you are not accustomed to catching me in this mood because, as you know, it is my practice to avoid imposing such a terrible cruelty on other people. So I skip this mother-in-law phase of behavior almost always, and simply get mad and shout when I am offended. As you have learned in our many, many years of experience together, this inflicts much less tyranny and pain on other people than going around with a quivering lip.

It gives them an immediate sense of right in themselves, rather than guilt. So regarding my behavior, however noisy it is at times, I think I can take justifiable pride in not having inflicted the ultimate and most damaging of psychological assaults on my various wives, children and fellow workers.

Last night I asked [Rudy] Vallee to my office without Elliot [Lawrence] or anybody, and simply asked him if he minded singing out some notes for me. That is all. No criticism, no advice, no nothing. Upon which Vallee expressed great apprehension and discomfort about "being told what to do," about my rigid attitude, about lack of "lee-way" in performance, and after that reminded me (justifiably I think) that he, too, had some authority about singing songs. When you walked into the room we were at the height of it, and you know what conversation followed.

You will recall that you volunteered in that conversation that you were the one who first remarked that you preferred certain lines sung as written, rather than spoken. Vallee seemed to get no significance from your expression of Independent opinion, and did not seem to realize that I may not be the only pistol he imagines to be limiting him in some way.

I have to tell you that I believe this is your fault. You already hinted a few days ago that Rudy "may be convinced that FL is the sole possible question-asker or critic of his performances." I believe that you put this in his mind some time earlier when negotiating with him and made me the villain who demanded that he sing a few grudging notes in the theatre. If this were not the case, I cannot imagine Rudy coming in with this enormous and readily expressed apprehension about everything I suggest to him.

So I will leave it to you to make him comfortable. While you are exercising what I hope will be the proper judgment, I am going to stay out of the way so that I don't get him nervous. At the same time, I do not know any way to forgive him for taking advantage of me last night, and in the future when I am shattered as I am now, but simply behave as I actually feel, and that is hurt, insulted, and quite useless.

Of course, I will be around when I feel better, to see what I think of Bobby Fosse's stagings, etc. I promise you I will not get into an argument about anything in that department. I am now saving my precious adrenal gland against the time it wants to do some sanguine and creative work. Meantime, I am in a defeated and deflated sulk because of my shocked belief that I have been put on a spot by you, and then thoroughly pounced on and upbraided by our actor. Sincerely, I don't know how to get out of this depressed mood. They don't print Kleenex with staff lines. See you later.

Undated notes to performers in *How to Succeed*: presumably autumn 1961 during rehearsals

[to Charles Nelson Reilly (1931–2007), played Bud Frump:] Prepare for vocal delivery of "Coffee Break." I know some of the notes are low for you and you have to arrange your gut to negotiate them. Tough titty.

[to Bonnie Scott (born 1941), played Rosemary Pilkington:] "What female kind of trap can I spurring" cannot be understood and is not attractive. "Spring" is one syllable. And the way your face looks right before you sing this line is one of the most important things to remember.

[to Claudette Sutherland (born 1939), played Smitty:] Could I see some dark and light transition between "land of carbon paper" and "land of flowered chintz"? The first is "oh, this old every-day shit-house at peon's wages," and the second visualizes vast and comfortable suburban glory. That was the purpose for my putting the word "this" in front of "land of carbon paper" – so you could kind of disdain it.

[to Robert Morse, played J. Pierpont Finch:] We NEED you to sing out loud with the girls at the end of "Long Day." You have already played "helplessly trapped" when the girls grabbed you by the armpits, and by the time you are called on to sing, you should be resigned to the idea of going to a nice dinner with this tomato. Whether or not you should continue to play "helplessly trapped" is possibly a matter of your own instinct, but if you don't sing, and sing the right notes, and sing them loud, I'm bringing you up on charges. I have a Diners Club card, and can charge anything.

A line from one of the show's songs, 'A Secretary is Not a Toy', reads: 'And when you put her to use, / Observe, when you put her to use, / That you don't find the name "Lionel" on her caboose.' The word 'Lionel' refers to the Lionel Corp, a toy manufacturer that operated from 1900 to 1969 before becoming a holding company. Between 1959 and 1963 the company was owned by Roy M. Cohn (1927–1986), notorious at the time for being Senator Joseph McCarthy's chief counsel. His time with the Lionel Corp was unsuccessful and he oversaw significant losses.

25 October 1961: To Roy M. Cohn, The Lionel Corporation

Dear Mr Cohn:

Thank you so much for the impressive gift. My boy of course will enjoy the trains immensely, but he will have to push <u>me</u> out of the room first.

I am delighted that you liked our show. The name Lionel does not need any further immortalization, but it was fun making the reference. My thanks again.

Sincerely,

15 February 1962: To Groucho Marx

Dear Groucho:

I had thought there was no such thing as a sheet music buyer anywhere. You turn out to be the <u>one</u>! So my company was not prepared for you. However, I have asked our production department to rush you a photostat of the version which will ultimately be printed in the piano vocal score of the entire production. When that gets into print, I will rush you one of the first copies. In the meantime, stand by for the ms. with symbols. You will have to be satisfied with guitar symbols as we are not allowed to send phallic ones through the mail.

Glad you liked the show. Sorry I didn't see you here. When do you come again? Next time let me know. I want you to meet Jo Loesser, the pocket Valkyrie.

Love,

15 February 1962: To Groucho Marx

Dear Groucho:

Here is a copy of "Rosemary" prepared specially for you. There are two restrictions. One, that you don't play it or sing it anywhere in public without asking us. And the other is that you play the right chords. There is a charge of 17¢ per wrong chord, and we track people down everywhere. We will have a man listening at your living-room window.

Best, as always,

P.S. The entire vocal score should be in print within a couple of months and I'll send one along.

28 March 1962: To Bing Crosby (telegram)

DEAR BING. I SIMPLY HAVE TO ADD MY NIX ON COFFEE BREAK. I NEVER THOUGHT THE DAY WOULD COME WHEN I WOULD BE FORCED TO TURN DOWN AN OLD AND VALUED FRIEND BUT THE SHOW DEPENDS HEAVILY ON THE COMEDY NOVELTY OF

MOST OF THE SONGS RATHER THAN ON THE MELODIC. THAT IS WHY THE GREAT MAJORITY OF MY NUMBERS ARE NOT EVEN IN PRINT. THE PRODUCERS BURROWS AND I AGREED ON THIS POLICY A LONG TIME AGO EVEN AT THE EXPENSE OF LOSING PREDICTABLY FINE TELEVISION PERFORMANCES. IF IT GIVES YOU ANY COMFORT WE HAVE ALREADY TURNED DOWN DINAH SHORE AND OTHERS ON COFFEE. IF YOU EVER CAME EAST TO STAR IN A BROADWAY MUSICAL FOR ME YOU WOULD QUICKLY SUBSCRIBE TO THE ABOVE POINT OF VIEW. WHY DON'T YOU.
REGRETS AND LOVE
    FRANK LOESSER

1962 [not dated any more precisely]:
Memo to Bert Siegelson[9]

SUBJECT: Gary McFarland[10] Jazz Album "How to Succeed"
   I have just finished listening to the Gary McFarland jazz album of "How To" and want to say thanks. Also pass my compliments along to Gary McFarland. I am not, as you know, a devotee of this kind of treatment, but the McFarland job is singularly tasty and ingenious. Especially in the handling of ostinati. [. . .]
        Best,

16 August 1963: To the How to Succeed Company, Her Majesty's Theatre, Melbourne, Australia (telegram)

BEST OF LUCK TO ALL TONIGHT
    FRANK LOESSER

---

9 Bert Siegelson (dates unknown) was 'national promotion director' at Frank Music.
10 Gary McFarland (1933–1971) was a prominent arranger of orchestral jazz for the Verve label during the 1960s. His *The Jazz Version of "How to Succeed in Business without Really Trying"* was his first album as a main artist.

10 October 1963: To Robert Morse

Dear Bobby:

This is to ask you to forgive me for not being at your closing night and not kissing you goodbye. I guess it wasn't in the cards for me to be in town. Anyway, here's what I would have said; Thank you, thank you, thank you, thank you, thank you, thank you for two wonderful years. Maybe we will have more things to do together (my office has been talking to your agent about a TV "Where's Charley"). But whether or not anything new happens between us, please know that I am very grateful to you for being Finch and for being a very fine fellow even without the great talent.

Sincerely,

10 February 1964: To the How to Succeed Company, Theatre de Paris, Paris, France (telegram)

BEST WISHES TONIGHT
FRANK LOESSER

Guys and Dolls also required Loesser's continued attention, now more than a decade after its Broadway premiere. He still received letters about the meaning of the term 'lickerish tooth' (see letter from 18 November 1953 in Chapter 3 for an earlier query about this) and was even asked if it could be replaced by another idea in a 1961 revival by producer Edwin Lester's (1895–1990) Los Angeles Civic Light Opera starring Dan Dailey (1915–1978) and Janis Paige (1922–2024).

Alan Livingston (1917–2009) was president of Capitol Records. He had written to Loesser about a possible re-recording of the original cast album of *Guys and Dolls* in stereo – Cole Porter's *Kiss Me, Kate* had received similar treatment after the roll-out of stereo technology – but was concerned about the imposition of a 30c licence fee, which would have made the project unaffordable for Capitol (Decca released the original mono version). In fact, no such deal had been reached, but there were longer-term tensions about *Guys and Dolls* between Decca and Capitol, as Loesser revealed in a private note to Frank Music Vice President Milton Kramer.

14 June 1961: To Robert H. Anders, Birmingham, Michigan

Dear Mr. Anders:

In answer to your letter of June 7th:

"Sheep's eye" is just as you suspect, descriptive of amorous longing. I suppose the exact expression is "making sheep's eyes at –." The color and sound of this was enough for me to hope that this passage of the song would describe the imagined lover's almost pitiable adoration of the girl. Now we come to "–lickerish tooth." I decided that the sense of sheep's eye was a little too weak, however sympathetic, and did not truthfully reflect Grandfather Arvide's rooting interest in our leading man, Sky Masterson. At the point in the play where this song is sung both Arvide and the audience would already know a great deal about Masterson's resolute and forward character. Therefore sheep's eye was not enough. So I consulted Roget (grudgingly, because usually I know more than he does) to find that "covetous" (which was the key meaning in my mind) could be described as "lecherous." I then looked up lecherous for variations less appalling in sound to the modern ear. This I did by way of the Oxford English Dictionary (the big twelve volume one) and found to my great delight – two archaic spellings: one was licorice (somehow combining the literal sense of "sweet tooth" with the fundamental meaning of the word) – and the other "lickerish" which had a much more satisfying adjective-suffix. In the exemplary material on these words I found "lickerish tooth" which fitted neatly with the notes in hand, and even more neatly with my sense of what the old man's mischief should sound like in the scene.

I correct myself. It was not the old man originally but the elder brother of the young lady Roseanna McCoy, heroine and title character of a Sam Goldwyn movie.[11] It was for a scene in which she sits

---

11 *Roseanna McCoy* (1949) was produced by Samuel Goldwyn and starred Farley Granger.

beside her brother in the seat of a wagon. She is 16 and she is being taken to her first fair. Through the song her brother is wishing her good fortune in the heart. In the picture, of course, she meets young Hatfield. This delays the heart's good fortune for several reels. Sam Goldwyn neither liked nor understood the song and asked me for another. This turned out to be "Roseanna" which gained certain broad popular approval and was quite right for the picture. I held on to the original and found quite proper use for it in "Guys and Dolls." The emotional purposes were parallel. After that, several leftovers from "Guys and Dolls" went into "The Most Happy Fella." At present I am preparing a new show for Broadway[12] which no doubt will contain leftovers from "The Most Happy Fella." It goes like that.

Thanks for asking.

20 July 1961: To Ed Lester

Dear Ed:

This is a hurried but definite answer. We are about to go in[to] rehearsal with a new one.

Please leave the billing as per contract.

"Lickerish tooth" stays. The song is valuable because of its provocative quality. Three-quarters of your seats can't hear the lyrics anyway. Nine-tenths don't know what a crap game is. Don't take off the shin guards yet.

As an experiment for this particular production only, you may try "And go store them at Magnin's for somebody else" instead of the "hollanderize" line. That ought to satisfy you and your provincials.

Abe is in Cape Cod resting from severe cuts in our script and won't be back for a few days. At that time I will ask him your question about "stabbed by a Studebaker" and he or I will give you the answer on that one.

I don't know what Abe's answer to you was about switching from Havana to some other place, but have you thought about "Costa Rica," which seems to be advertising lately as a resort place?

---

12 *How to Succeed.*

If all this sounds abrupt, that's because I am up to here with the present frenzy. I could fill in a lot of quite logical reasons for the above array of dicta, but there is just no time. You understand.

Sincerely,

5 December 1961: To Alan W. Livingston

Dear Alan:

Answering your letter of November 28, it is true that I did know that a new "Guys and Dolls" album of the kind you describe had been contemplated by Sy Rady,[13] presumably to be produced by him for your company. I had no understanding of any kind with him. Certainly not for a 30c license fee. Further, I am quite sure that no one else in my employ made such an offer or any kind of offer.

I think my point of view is best expressed in a letter I wrote to Sy Rady on October 12, 1959 – a copy of which I must insist on boring you with now. Along with this, I am enclosing correspondence with Rady leading up to my final letter, to which there was never any further reply. There was, however, a telegram to Stuart Ostrow which related to "Kismet," informing him that all plans were off. Also enclosed is a copy of a note to me from Harold Orenstein, who represents us legally. Please read all of these and you will have the attitude of my company and myself in a somewhat wordy nutshell. The correspondence happened at that moment to refer to "Kismet" as well as "Guys and Dolls," but the same principle applies to both.

I hope you will understand. If a new and attractive way of making records is established at a time, let us say, when "The Music Man" album artists are free to re-record elsewhere under the Equity rulings – I don't believe you or your company will turn handsprings over any collaboration by us, overt or otherwise, with another recording company. Fortunately for your peace of mind in that respect, such a thing is not likely to happen.

Toward the end of your note you tell me what you consider to be your present alternatives. I am not equipped to predict what kind of a

---

13 Sy Rady (dates unknown), record producer.

case Decca would have if they chose to claim that you were competing unfairly with them – regardless of the omission of certain numbers. Nor do I know how offended all the authors, producers, investors, in the original "Guys and Dolls" production, would feel about an unlicensed use of what can be considered a dramatico-musical subsidiary right in the original play. Of course, the publishing company would have to accept the statutory royalty per number on the basis of the compulsory license provision. But in accepting it, we would not be acknowledging in any way a special grouping or casting of these numbers.

Again I beg you to understand. Sometimes my company seems rigid in the application of business principle. Maybe that is because our president (that's me) doesn't need every last penny there is. Or maybe it is a nobler thing. At any rate, we are proud of our record for dealing scrupulously.

My best to you as always.

5 December 1961: To Milt Kramer

Subject: "Guys and Dolls" – Capitol Records

I don't think you were with the company when we made the "Guys and Dolls" picture, but the most important reason there was never any album of the sound track, was that Capitol records would not let go of Sinatra, and the original play performers (Vivian Blaine, etc) were still bound by the Decca deal. This is possible, casual ammunition for whatever discussions you may get into out west.

The lyric 'lickerish tooth' is not the only dental reference in Loesser's correspondence. He appears to have consulted two dentists in 1961: Robert Sloan and Ivan Prince, the latter a dental surgeon at Mount Sinai Hospital in New York.

12 June 1961: To Dr. Robert Sloan

Dear Dr Sloan:

The whole business of the work on my teeth has been deferred for a while because of jury duty, preparing Broadway show, bringing up small son, moving to new house, and general super occupation. I will bring the matter up again when all this business is over.

Meanwhile please bill me immediately for the visit.

Sincerely,

30 October 1961: To Milt Kramer

I guess everybody has a right to try to compose songs. This time it is my dentist. His name is Ivan Prince, and he wants to submit some, possibly one called "The Drill is Gone," or another entitled "Have Gun, Will Travel," or even "Getting Periodontal Over You."

Anyway, I am putting him in touch with you as a change from mid-western housewives.

On 29 June 1960 Loesser celebrated his fiftieth birthday and the date was acknowledged by the media. An article in *Billboard* reported: 'Broadway, radio stations, TV stations and other areas of the entertainment business are saluting Frank Loesser this week on the occasion of the composer's 50th birthday Wednesday, June 29. "The Garry Moore Show" will salute Loesser by devoting the entire segment of "That Wonderful Year" on his Tuesday (28) TV show to the cleffer,[14] and radio Station WNTA paid tribute to Loesser via a 10-hour musical program.'[15] Ironically, Loesser was in London with *The Most Happy Fella* at the time and missed the tributes. Among those offering personal birthday wishes was composer Richard Rodgers, whose own birthday was 28 June. Rodgers would later write a special introduction to the published *Frank Loesser Songbook* (Simon & Schuster) in 1971.

29 June 1960: To Richard Rodgers (telegram)

GOSH WE NEVER KNEW. FONDEST WISHES.
JO AND FRANK LOESSER

---

14 A slang term used in *Variety* meaning songwriter.
15 Anon., 'Show Business Offers Loesser Birthday Bows', *Billboard* 72/26 (27 June 1960), 4.

11. Frank Loesser and Abe Burrows at the premiere of
How to Succeed in Business Without Really Trying.

With the opening of *How to Succeed* around the corner, Loesser
started to look for new production ventures. Russel Crouse was hot
property in the summer of 1961, when Loesser corresponded with
him: he and his regular writing partner Howard Lindsay wrote the
book for *The Sound of Music*, which won the Tony Award for Best
Musical in 1960. Loesser cleverly tried to woo Crouse with an open
offer rather than touting only one property to him and, as so often,
his witty prose comes into play to endear himself.

10 July 1961: To Russel Crouse

Dear Buck:

I don't know whether I envy you your life as a summer
vacationist because I am still, along with others like Nunnally

Johnson[16] – allergic to the sight of green and the buzzing of bees. Nunnally once said that if he had twenty acres of meadow he would promptly have it paved. Anyway, I do envy your capacity for getting away from it all and I charge it in part to a well-controlled and businesslike youth. Since I can't tell when you're coming back to civilization from your well-earned bucolic frolic, I can only guess when we'll have that date.

In the meantime, give the following some thought between juleps. Did the other press agents get mad at you when you turned real writer, or did Frank Loesser have a squawk in the middle of flirtings with you about writing a musical – because you had gone and bought the Hudson Theatre and had become a virtual Shubert?[17]

Some cowardly gamblers like to invest in A. T. & T. Me, I like to invest in and run my own businesses so I can take all the blame. I have been doing this since before you and I met and the thing has grown so that lots of people come to be published and produced and agented by my pet octopus. Many of them say "Could you get us together with Lindsay and Crouse?". If my staff and I think it's a good idea, we try to introduce the idea to you. When we do this I am usually the spokesman because I know you better than my people do, but I'm representing my outfit just as if it were the Hudson Theatre.

Meanwhile, when I do have an idea for collaboration with you and Howard and me, I bring it up (did same some time back with "Peg O' My Heart" which didn't get either of you excited). Maybe it's your turn now. Although I have thought about a number of ideas and some proposals, I am in the clear after the present one with Abe.

Now here's what will happen:

---

16 Nunnally Johnson (1897–1977), screenwriter, director and producer. His writing and producing credits include *The Grapes of Wrath* (1940) and *The Three Faces of Eve* (1957).
17 The Hudson Theatre, 139–141 West 44th Street, built 1902–3, was purchased by Russel Crouse in 1944; the Shubert Organization, first established in Syracuse, New York, during the 1880s, was the dominant force among New York theatres during the first half of the twentieth century.

You

How about a musical based on the life of Irving Lazar,[18]

Me

Good idea but can we get rights?

You

I think for one percent plus ten percent.

Me

That means you and Howard and I could kick around maybe nine percent for ourselves, and give the balance between that and, let's say, fourteen percent for direction, choreography, etc.

You

Sounds okay, but while we're at it why don't we produce the thing? We have Leland Hayward[19] and you have your company and those two could do the crummy work subject to our enormous, persistent and totally rigid dictation – and grab off whatever we pleased out of their interests.

Me

Of course! Neither of those two worthy institutions could resist a package like you and Howard and me, plus Dooley Goldfarb in the lead and a fine choreographer like Pegleg Bates!

You

Hell man, we're in business! We can even dictate our own royalty cuts and never have the temerity to refuse. It would be bad business.

---

18 Irving Lazar (1907–1993), lawyer and talent agent. His clients included Richard Nixon, Lauren Bacall, Humphrey Bogart, Cary Grant and Ernest Hemingway, among others.
19 Leland Hayward (1902–1971), agent and theatrical producer. His producing credits included Rodgers and Hammerstein's *The Sound of Music* and Jule Styne's *Gypsy* (both 1959).

Me

Ah, you've got a good head on your shoulders. You should be in business.

You

Always have been you dumb bastard, just like you and Howard [Lindsay] and Swifty Morgan.[20] By the way, if we feel good about what we write I've got a neat way of stealing that theatre from Feuer and Martin. I happen to know they're in a very weak cash position.

Me

Where did you hear that?

You

From Howard.

Me

Boy! That Tim ain't going to inherit just a plain old lot of leftover dialogue.

Etc.

Call me when you get back to town and we'll write the rest of the above scene. But don't make no false moves, kid, because my company has already got it copyrighted and any additional material will ipso facto be an unlicensed adaptation. So watch what you say because I get my feelings hurt even though I don't look it.

Love to you and Annie and the children,

21 July 1961: To Russel Crouse

Dear Buck:

I love you, too, and you needn't tear this up.

---

20 A conman, immortalised by Damon Runyon as the 'Lemon-Drop Kid'.

I stay in New York until about September 1, when I go to Philadelphia for five weeks. Phone number here is REgent 7-2173 (home) or CIrcle 7-4388 (office). In Philadelphia it is the Warwick Hotel. I will have some time there while Burrows and Feuer yell at each other. So I will hear from you in either town.

Meanwhile, what in the world is Annisquam?[21] It sounds like apprehension about the rear end – which, I recall, was a widespread Indian problem after us boys got here.

Love,

Business correspondence from 1961–62 is typically diverse. Director-producer Harold Prince had asked to use a fragment of "Hey, There" for background music for a scene in the play *Take Her, She's Mine* (1961) by Henry (1911–1992) and Phoebe Ephron (1914–1971); the song comes from *The Pajama Game*, which was published by Frank Music, and there was some tension about Prince's request. A note to Leonard Sillman, of the *New Faces* revues, points to Loesser's generosity. Of particular interest is Loesser's letter in response to a series of questions from the *Saturday Review*, in which he shared some of his favourite song lyrics and views on the rules of musical comedy.

16 November 1961: To Harold Prince

Dear Hal:

Answering yours of November 15th, we make it a practice to get acknowledgment when delivering something of value – that it is indeed <u>valuable</u> – and that this value can be measured and given a price. Sometimes we only want $1.00. The important thing is to protect the writer and the legitimate producer by being able to flash a document in the face of some not so legitimate producer who wishes to claim that these things are always understood to be free for grabs.

---

21 Annisquam, Massachusetts, a town established in 1631, the name deriving from Algonquian meaning 'top of the rock'. Crouse lived there.

Let us suppose that Kismet Bloomergirl,[22] a notoriously tasteless producer, wishes to make what might turn out to be damaging use of one of our pieces. Further, we are aware that his play is written by a known Communist, and will be attacked as an infringement, raided by the police. Beyond that, with our knowledge and assurance that the fragment will be sung out of tune with the wrong words. In an instance of this kind, we would like the privilege of insisting that we always make contracts for such things. We would not like Mr. Bloomergirl to say "Hell man, I happen to know that Hal Prince took it for nothing."

Now we think Hal Prince is a tasteful, considerate and reasonable producer and so don't even question the manner of use he wants to make. I am sure that this has not come up in any of your discussions with our Mr. [Milton] Kramer. He knows better. He would not ask Cartier if one of their emeralds were real. I don't know what he asked for, but I am sure it was under $10.00.

As to the reflections in your second paragraph, let me suggest to you that possibly Frank Music did not make as much out of "The Pajama Game" as Hal Prince, even though FMC financed it for the last $5,000 it desperately needed when already on the road. The careers that Adler and Ross got from it were part of a very expensive pre-paid design by the Frank Music Corp.

Your last sentence is absolutely correct. I had not known that any of this was going on. Now I know.

Yours for neatness, clarity, sound information, precise agreements, and less volatile correspondence.

Sincerely

Frank

Frank Loesser

*PRESIDENT

* Who said a Jew couldn't be president?

---

22 A reference to Kermit Bloomgarden, producer of *The Most Happy Fella* and *The Music Man*.

20 November 1961: To Leonard Sillman

Dear Leonard:

The repayment of a small loan is an old old gambit. That is how you fool people into turning over a whole lot more on the next touch – but that one you disappear with into the interior of China never to cough up. So I don't thank you at all for the return of the $300, as now you're clearly an honest and thoughtful man in my opinion, and theoretically trustworthy. Some day my carefully built belief in you will get me stiffed. Frankly, I don't know what to do now.

See you soon.

Love,

28 November 1961: To Henry Hewes of the *Saturday Review*

Dear Mr. Hewes:

At last an answer to your questionnaire:

I was born June 29, 1910 in New York City. That seems to be all you want for the Best Plays Series. And now onward in favor of the Saturday Review.

[Q: Three lyrics and three tunes by writers other than yourself, which you most admire.]

Three lyrics are:

- The section of "Trial by Jury" (W.S. Gilbert) in which the judge sings "In the reign of James the Second ..." through the ensemble response "Oh man of learning."
- "Just One of Those Things" – Cole Porter [from *Jubilee*, 1935]
- "Blues in the Night" – Johnny Mercer [music by Harold Arlen, 1941]

Three tunes are:

- The aria by which the daughter cops a plea with the father in "Gianni Schicchi." I don't know whether it has a name. ['O mio babbino caro']
- "All the Things You Are" – Jerome Kern [from *Very Warm for May*, 1939]

- Chopsticks – (Composer unknown. Variationists too numerous to mention.)[23]

[Q: Favorite single lyric and single tune of your own you feel happiest about.]

Answer to question #2: I think among my own works my favorite single lyric is "Inch Worm" (it happens to be double. Is that all right?), and my pet tune is "Roseanna" (not well known).

[Q: How do you feel the requirements for today's musical comedies differ from those at the time you began your career?]

Answer to question #3: I have never been aware of any array of "requirements." When I started in the theatre (1948) there was already such a broad variety of styles welcomed in the musical theatre (Show Boat – Pins and Needles – Lady in the Dark – Three Penny Opera – Pal Joey)[24] that I could not visualize any distinct set of rules. I agreed to do a musical version of "Charley's Aunt" ("Where's Charley?", my first) because it was a challenge. So many of my colleagues thought that such farce could not be musicalized with any success. I think the fundamental requisit was a piece of "news." Such a piece of news was made when Rex Harrison appeared as a singing star. News was made at the first exhibition of superior flying apparatus in "Peter Pan." News was made by the first use of ultra violet lighting. News exploded when a chorus girl named Joan McCracken popped up in "Oklahoma!".[25] I think that is the perennial sine qua non, and I don't think it ever

---

23 'Chopsticks' was written by the British composer Euphemia Allen under the pseudonym Arthur de Lulli. Borodin, Rimsky-Korsakov and Liszt are among the famous composers to have written variations on the piece.

24 Loesser is listing several musicals with contrasting generic markers: Kern and Hammerstein's book musical *Show Boat* (1927); Harold Rome's political revue *Pins and Needles* (1937); the musical *Lady in the Dark* (1941) with book by Moss Hart, music by Kurt Weill and lyrics by Ira Gershwin; Brecht's play *The Threepenny Opera* (1928) with music by Kurt Weill; and Rodgers and Hart's musical comedy *Pal Joey* (1940).

25 Rex Harrison (1908–1990) was known as the star of plays and dramas before appearing as Henry Higgins in *My Fair Lady*. Joan McCracken (1917–1961) appeared as Sylvie ('The Girl Who Falls Down') in the original production of *Oklahoma!*

changes. Realistically, all explicit requirements are made by Actor's Equity, the musicians union and the SEC[26] and such people.

[Q: Do you believe that formally trained singers generally tend to deliver lyrics less comprehensively to an audience hearing them for the first time than song and dance performers, like [George M.] Cohan,[27] and if so is there any way that the training of musical comedy singers can be revised to improve this situation?]

Answer to question #4: Yes, I believe that formally trained singers generally tend to deliver lyrics less comprehensively to audiences hearing them for the first time, than do the Cohans, the Rex Harrisons, the Hustons[28] and the [Ethel] Mermans. There is a way to revise the training. Send them to me before they ever so much as meet a so-called singing teacher.

Thanks for asking.

Sincerely,

Internal correspondence is also typically diverse. Edgar Guest (1881–1959) was a writer whose series of 'Poetic Gems' were produced as short films in 1935. Loesser provided the lyrics for various songs in the series, to music by Lou Herscher (1894–1974). These songs were written early in Loesser's career, and his letter on the subject shows how comparatively casual he was about rights and ownership of his work in those earlier days.

A humorous internal memo to Milton Kramer discusses the composer and lyricist Sylvia Fine (1913–1991), wife of Danny Kaye (of Loesser's *Hans Christian Andersen*) – and incidentally makes reference to Loesser's ongoing dental problems – while another memo, to Allen Whitehead, Milt Kramer and Mona Lipp, describes his reaction to the script of a play that had been sent to him. Drawing on references to the Crucifixion and other imagery, Loesser humorously,

---

26 The Securities Exchange Commission.

27 George M. Cohan (1878–1942), composer, actor, singer and playwright known for the songs 'You're a Grand Old Flag' and the First World War song 'Over There', among others.

28 Walter Huston (1884–1950), Canadian actor and singer.

and with no intention to offend, plays on his Jewish cultural heritage, a common feature of his letters when, as president of Frank Music, for example, he sometimes signs off 'Who said a Jew couldn't be president?'.

10 January 1962: To Harold Orenstein
and Allen Arrow

Subject: Lou Herscher

Attached please find voluminous self-serving literature from one Lou Herscher, as well as copies of a printed edition of "Get Under The Sun." I had not known this edition existed, but only recall that this composition was included in a folio called "Poetic Gems" which, you will recall, was contained in my bound volumes of regular publications (Circa 1934).

This collection of songs represents all my collaborations with Herscher. They were written at the request of a man named Pizor (spelling?)[29] who seemed to be a film manufacturer on 9th Avenue. I seem to recall that they made a series of short scenic films based on Edgar Guest's poetry and Herscher and I were required to adapt Guest's subjects to song form. I seem to remember that I did not use any of Guest's actual titles or poetic lines, but simply adapted his subjects. I believe the songs were used in the films mentioned, but that there was also a reading of the original Guest poetry. Technically, I did not consider that I was adapting or arranging. I certainly never acquired any right to do so, and I don't know whether the film-makers acquired such a right.

I do not recall clearly how the publishing rights got into the hands of Mills Music Inc. (maybe you do), nor do I recollect any contract with the movie makers. I simply sat down with Herscher and Herscher paid me in hand $5 cash for each completed work. What he got I don't know. Nevertheless, presently we were published in folio form by Mills Music Inc.

---

29 William M. Pizor (1890–1959) was a film producer and distributor.

23 April 1962: To Milton Kramer

Dear Milt:

Thanks for your information. Please continue hinting Reign of Terror.

Sylvia Fine is an old and treacherous friend. I believe she is in town now. At least we were invited to some stranger's party for her the other day here. My last business discussion with her started with a rebuke. She didn't want to discuss business (I forget the subject now) with Stu Ostrow and thought she and I were old enough chums to make it direct. I had to remind her that she was the Ostrow of Danny Kaye. This conversation did not leave any specially inimical feelings. Since then she has bugged me for tickets, etc.

You wouldn't think, from the above, that I like her, but I do. It is just difficult. She thinks she is both me and Ostrow. Look out she doesn't think she is you. Or Pepper.

I miscalculated a crown moulding this morning and I am mad. Goodbye.

Frank Loesser

4 June 1962: To Allen Whitehead,
Milt Kramer, Mona Lipp

Dear People:

We come to the subject of loyalty, and I mean the kind of loyalty by which the Christian church has, for lo these many years, honored and participated in the martyrdom of its leader. Your leader, recently re-equipped with powerful bifocals, has just finished reading a script entitled "Wet Paint," and begs to inform you that the experience drove a nail through each of his hands and both of his ankles. As an experienced martyr he feels justified in insisting that you share the burden of this cross. Being out of apostles, he has to deliver this edict himself, freely and immodestly admitting huskily through a rakish thorn crown, that he would enjoy everybody having a big sip of gall along with him. Somehow the nails wouldn't hurt so much, so you buggers will be obliged to read every word of the above-mentioned work of art. And I mean right away, as I am bleeding profusely and need comfort. The comfort of knowing that in your monkish cells you are experiencing at least a little of the supreme torture inflicted on me.

Yes, it is true that this Judas was an old friend of mine and not yours. Nevertheless, you joined the faith and you are stuck with it. I simply will <u>not</u> undergo this alone. So seek out your monkish cells, and immediately! I would like written reports from each of you if you are still able to lift the pencil. And watch out that I don't ask you to listen to a demonstration of the score – an eventuality which my messianic power can produce with one phone call. Suffer with me, you dirty fucks!

Your Leader,

Jonathan Schiller (dates unknown), music director of the regional radio station WPRO, wrote to Loesser to propose writing a book about him, an idea that he firmly rejected. But Loesser's response is useful for providing insight into his early theatrical experiences, including the first musical he saw downtown: the *Grand Street Follies*, a revue that ran in 1922 and then annually from 1924 to 1929. The book and lyrics were by Agnes Morgan (1879–1976) with music for several editions by Lily Hyland (?1885–1962). Cecil Lean (1878–1935) and Cleo Mayfield (1898–1954) were a married theatrical couple, whose Broadway credits include *The Blushing Bride* at the 44th Street Theatre in 1922.

9 April 1962: To Jonathan Schiller

Dear Mr Schiller:

Thank you for the kind words. Incidentally, strangely enough the "Grand Street Follies" was the first downtown New York musical show that I ever saw. I had been bundled up at tenderer years and taken to "Hansel and Gretel" at the Irving Place Theatre, and in my very early teens had sneaked off to see a Saturday matinee of something with Cecil Lean and Cleo Mayfield at Shubert's Riviera. But that had been uptown and near home. "Grand Street Follies" was my baptism and I left the place in a state of great wonder at someone named Albert Carroll,[30] which gives you an idea about how young and impressionable I was.

As for your question about me as a subject for any sort of book or story or play, I would not think well of the idea at all. Please, I beg you, dismiss this idea from your thoughts.

But thanks anyway,
Frank Loesser

A letter to Nat Halpern Jr (1921–2013), a lyricist known to Loesser through his time in the army, refers to a song '(Will You Be Waiting for Me) After That Last Reveille?' with words by Halpern and music by a Pat M. Carlone (dates unknown), registered for copyright on 18 July 1945. And correspondence with Groucho Marx refers to the latter's autobiography *Groucho and Me* (New York, 1959).

18 June 1962: To Nat Halpern Jr

Dear Nat:

I have a copy of "After That Last Reveille," forwarded by you. My offhand opinion is that this, being a war subject, would be of very little value now to the public. However, if your purpose is to retrieve it from its present owners, I will try and help. Let me know. Our firms wouldn't be especially interested in acquiring this piece.

I was amused at that copy of an old letter of mine. God knows what others I wrote you and what scandalous words I used. Maybe you are planning to get the government down on me for misusing the mails. In that event, I will now be cautious and refrain from saying Fuck in this and subsequent ones.

Carefully,

---

30 Albert Carroll (1898–1970), actor. The revue *Grand Street Follies*, with choreography by Albert Carroll, played at the Neighborhood Playhouse, New York, from 20 May to 30 November 1924.

12 June 1962: To Groucho Marx

Dear Groucho:

Just in case I never told you before, I am enjoying your book tremendously. I am not done yet as I read it by degrees, but I assure you, my dear <u>real</u> writer, with enormous relish.

Love to Enid and Melinda. No love to you because I am a boy and it wouldn't look nice.

Oh, what the hell, love,

11 July 1962: To Groucho Marx

Dear Groucho:

Thanks for your note and the good news that you will be out of the provinces and among the civilized sometime in August. Please have someone who can write copy down our private phone number. Here it is:

RHinelander 4-4431.

Then, when you get to New York, find someone who can read and then find someone who can dial, and we will get together. Maybe if you put Melinda to all the above tasks you can deduct her trip.

As to your book: I have been using it on Jo's pregnant belly to see how strongly the baby is kicking. It must be very lightweight literature indeed, because it got kicked out of the window a couple of weeks ago. Although now well into her 6th month, Jo hasn't been able to budge "War and Peace," which I haven't finished either.

Anyway, Jo joins me in sending you and yours love, and we both look forward to some sitting around with you before you make a damn fool of yourself on the TONIGHT show, after which we can't afford to be seen with you.

Best,

P.S. On the level, can I do anything for you in advance of your arrival. Holler.

Frank Productions had been developing the musical *Viva Villa!* since at least February 1959. Matt Dubey and Harold Karr had written the score for the Ethel Merman vehicle *Happy Hunting* in 1956 and they anticipated *Viva Villa!*, now called *We Take the Town*, as their follow-up. It told the story of Pancho Villa, the Mexican 'Robin Hood', and was to star Robert Preston, of *The Music Man* fame, with a book by Felice Sauer, who had been Dubey and Karr's agent. Best known for his stagings of successful non-musical plays, Theodore Mann (1924–2012) was set to produce. But Mann and Frank Productions decided to withdraw from the project after many months of work, leaving it to Loesser's former colleague Stuart Ostrow to bring it to the stage. It closed in Philadelphia in March 1962, before reaching Broadway, perhaps justifying Frank Productions' decision to withdraw.[31] Sol Siegel (1903–1982) was vice president of MGM, the studio that had made the original film on which the show was based.

12 July 1961: To Matt Dubey, Harold Karr and Felice Sauer

Dear People:

I'm sorry about "Viva" not working out. As you have observed, I didn't spend much time with you people on the subject but it's because I can't help thinking like a writer and therefore did not want to inflict any barrage of so-called creative notions on you. But this does not mean that I have not been watching very carefully the developments of the last year. Now, if God or somebody else were to ask me for a report, the best I would be able to say was that there had been a disagreement with the writers' convictions about the way the play should be written and that it therefore followed that the writers had to prevail; that this is a point of morality much older and deeper than anything printed in any basic minimum agreements. An artist cannot remain an artist while creating something he has no wish to create.

---

31 See https://www.onstageblog.com/columns/2016/1/7/when-robert-preston-played-pancho-villa, for a personal memoir of the show's history.

So you might consider our divorce as a compliment to yourselves. At any rate you have the complete freedom you started with. I know the feeling and it keeps me in good health.

Even though I do agree with Allen and Ted on a majority of things – I more than ever feel that this can be a wonderful show and a big hit. So don't lose it, and God bless you.

And thanks for giving us a crack at it.

Sincerely,

12 July 1961: To Sol Siegel

Dear Sol:

By this time your company has no doubt learned that Frank Productions Inc. together with Theodore Mann have decided to abandon their attempt to produce a stage musical version of "Viva Villa."

I don't know whether this news has come to your attention, but since you were elected to give the final okay on this deal and promptly selected your old pal me to give your assurance of good will and vigorous intentions – I thought I'd better drop you this note to tell you of my regrets.

It seems that my company could not see eye to eye with the writers on various aspects of the show's structure and technique. All of us tried very hard to subscribe to the writers' efforts but could not do so and still remain within the boundaries of what we consider our good judgment. Now this is not an unusual situation. You well know how many shows (especially musicals) are optioned and then abandoned, but I feel badly about not having been able to come through for you this time. I still think the property has an enormous potential as a Broadway musical. We are the second set of producers who have tried and then let go and I sincerely hope that the third (if there is one) does the trick.

Meanwhile, my warmest regards and thanks. I would love to see you next time you come to New York.

Sincerely,

Helen Meinardi Stearns (1909–1997) wrote songs including 'April in My Heart' with Hoagy Carmichael. She approached Loesser with the idea of writing a musical version of the play *Man, Beast and Virtue* (1919) by Luigi Pirandello (1867–1936) that was turned into a film in 1953 starring Orson Welles. Loesser went to some lengths to obtain a copy of the play from the future writer and academic Masolino D'Amico (born 1939), a translator of English-language works into Italian; his mother Suso Cecchi D'Amico (1914–2010) was an Italian screenwriter for directors including Zeffirelli and Visconti, hence the reference to mutual friend Pilade Levi.

5 June 1961: To Masolino D'Amico

Dear Masolino:

First of all, Jo and I send you our fond greetings. Also some to pass along to the Levis.

There is a favor I would like to ask you. I am looking for the printed edition of a play by Pirandello which does not seem to be available over here. The play is called in English something like "Man, Beast and Virtue." It was produced in the French language in Paris several years ago, and that's all I know about it. It is certainly not known at all here. A printed edition of it in Italian would be of enormous help to me if you can find one. Of course if this is too much of a burden on your time and patience, please don't attempt it. But if this is easy enough I would appreciate your dropping me a line and letting me know that you have it, and then we will arrange to send it to me in such a manner that both of us can avoid a day's wait in the rain at an airport (remember the shower heads?).

Thanks.

Love,

5 December 1961: To Masolino D'Amico

Dear Masolino:

Thanks for your card and please forgive me for not acknowledging that I had received the Italian play you sent. I thought I had let you know how quickly it had arrived.

I have not yet had it translated. There is someone here who thinks it might become a musical comedy in the English language. That was my purpose in sending for it.

I hope you are well and happy and that your English is flawless. I don't want Pilade to get the impression that he is the only Yankee in Rome.

Jo sends fond greetings along with mine.

[handwritten addition:]
P.S. a thought just occurred to me! Would YOU like to translate it? If yes, tell me what your fee would be and how long it would take.

Best,
Frank

11 December 1961: To Helen Meinardi Stearns

Dear Helen:

I can't tell what I think before I read a translation. I have recently asked someone for one, and don't know how long it will be before he finishes. So if you are in a real big rush, don't worry about me. If you can wait, of course, I might join you in your enthusiasm for it and we could go to work.

Maybe it would help me if meantime you would write me a brief outline of the plot as you recollect it. That would give me a big start in my being able to estimate the whole thing.

Best,
Frank Loesser

22 January 1962: To Helen M. Stearns

Dear Helen:

Reviewing your outline of the Italian play, I find that it is not my dish – I mean me as a writer. As a producing organization, it might be of interest to us after seeing some development along musical lines in English. But this prospect is not a very likely one, as I learned just two days ago that another New York producer is at present in the act of acquiring rights in the original play from the Pirandello estate. For what exact purpose I don't know, but in a short time I will be able to find out what his intentions are, if that interests you.

When will you return to New York? Please call me then.

Best,

Frank Loesser

P.S. And love to Hoagy [Carmichael] if you see him.

2 February 1962: To Masolino D'Amico

Dear Masolino:

The English version of the play has arrived and I thank you very much for it.

Pilade made his lightning trip here. Most of the time he was swallowed up in his responsibilities to the great God Paramount.

I will be reading the play shortly. Actually, I am doing this in someone else's interest. I myself do not believe I want to produce it. I will return it to you as soon as I have finished it. Many thanks again, and love from Jo and me.

Charles Lederer (1910–1976) was a major Hollywood screenwriter whose work included *The Front Page* (1931), *His Girl Friday* (1940) and *Gentlemen Prefer Blondes* (1953). He was associated with Loesser due to their work on the Betty Hutton film *Red, Hot and Blue!* (1949), for which Loesser wrote four songs and Lederer the screenplay. They were also tangentially associated through the stage musical *Kismet* (1953), for which Lederer not only co-wrote the book but also acted as producer along with Edwin Lester; Frank Music published Wright and Forrest's songs. Loesser and Lederer met during the latter's trip to New York in April 1962, and Loesser provided his friend with tickets to *How to Succeed*.

5 March 1962: To Charles Lederer

Dear Charlie:

Just because we were once practically engaged, there is no reason for you to hide the fundamental truth. That curly headed janitor was

Ed Lester and I hear you are consorting with him again. So he did mean something to you after all. You had better come to New York quickly and make a clean breast of things. I'm not going to nestle in your inter-mammary sinus if I find it messy.

Let me know when you are on the way, and make it soon. Please.
Love,

12 March 1962: To Charles Lederer

Dear Charlie:

I take seriously your promise to show up here. All you have to do is tell me when. Hurry. Even if I didn't miss you, I'd still want to talk to you about something. Never mind what. Just hurry is all.

Love,

20 March 1962: To Charles Lederer

Dear Charlie:

Well?

When?

Anxiously, abruptly, but with love,

26 March 1962: To Charles Lederer

Dear Charlie:

I have your letter which tells me you are arriving around the 6th. Also, I have a phone call from Orenstein telling me that you will be here on the 5th. I guess that is the latest message and that is it.

What seems to confirm it in an ugly way is your piteous request for a pair of seats for the night of April 5th – a sniveling plea directed to an eminently honorable attorney in good standing with the bar association and marked as a good risk among the bar association and briefcase dealers. It is now a matter of indelible record (I'm sure Beverly Hills is fluttering with carbon copies) that you have involved this upright gentleman in some sort of conspiracy to join in and support the illicitly priced theatre ticket racket. I have volunteered, therefore, to take this unsavory task out of sweet Harold's hands and into my own slightly soiled pair and wander through dark garbage-littered alleys in search of some stir-bum who has two greasy tickets at 7 golden guineas each. If I get caught, it won't be the first time and my sentence in prison will hardly be noticed among the thousands and thousands of ASCAP members who go up every year for larceny and mayhem. I just don't want it to happen to Harold.

So you may assume that you will have two seats waiting for the evening of the 5th. You could have asked me in the first place.

Love,

23 April 1962: To Charles Lederer

Dear Charlie:

Although I lamented your illness here, it did give me a chance to reacquaint myself with your marvelous son! Except for one minor fracas, which I won by hollering, I enjoyed every minute of him immensely and I know my son John did. They both seemed to have forgotten their old friendship as five-year-olds. That is just as well, because Danny would have missed finding John hilariously funny, and John would have missed the sweet music of Danny's mirth at every one of his jokes.

I can tell you are now well if only by the news that you are up to some malicious mischief. I had intended asking you for a formula by which to get even with a certain crooked landlord. Please let me lay my problem at your feet when you come next – and maybe you can find me a way to punish this rotter.

And bring Annie.[32] Annie is good for your inner ear, and if she isn't good for yours, she certainly is for mine, or my inner anything. I dare you to leave her on top of the Empire State with me!

Tell us when you are coming. Meantime, Jo and I send love.

British writer Wolf Mankowitz (1924–1998) wrote the novel *A Kid for Two Farthings* (1953), and the screenplay for its 1955 film

---

32 Lederer's wife, actress Ann Shirley (1918–1993).

adaptation, based on his experiences of growing up in the Jewish community in London's East End. In the story, a small boy named Joe buys a kid (goat), believing it to be a young unicorn that will be able to grant any wish. In 1962 Mankowitz started communicating with Loesser on a possible musical adaptation of the story, with a score by Monty Norman (1928–2022) and perhaps some contributions from Loesser. Norman had previously written the scores for Mankowitz's musicals *Expresso Bongo* (1958) and *Make Me an Offer* (1959), and is best-remembered for writing the James Bond Theme; Mankowitz contributed to an early draft of the first Bond film, *Dr. No*.

The original novel *A Kid for Two Farthings* had been generally well received. In London, *The Times* reviewer said that it combined 'an affecting tenderness with sharply funny observation'.[33] The same publication's review of the 1955 film called it 'a sentimental artist's sketch-book. The feel, the look, the atmosphere of the East End are translated on to the screen . . . yet, as a whole, *A Kid for Two Farthings* is something both of a puzzle and a disappointment', going on to critique the 'handling of Jonathan Ashmore, as the six-year-old Joe'.[34]

Interestingly, Loesser ultimately raised concerns about the casting of the boy, and whether the story could really be successful in the theatre, towards the end of the extensive back and forth between him and Mankowitz. For a time, Loesser seemed interested in being a co-writer of sorts on the show, and shared various reflections and ideas with Mankowitz: the correspondence is highly revealing of his thinking of how musical theatre works. But once he started to involve other members of his organisation in discussing the possible musical, he seemed to step back, and the show never happened. In 1996 an unrelated musical adaptation of the book was produced at London's Bridewell Theatre, with music by Mankowitz's contemporary, Cyril Ornadel (1924–2011).

---

33 Anon., 'New Fiction', *The Times*, 16 September 1953, 10.
34 Anon., 'Sir Carol Reed's "A Kid for Two Farthings"', *The Times*, 11 May 1955, 7.

28 March 1962: To Wolf Mankowitz

Dear Wolf:

I'm sorry we didn't have a chance to meet on that hurry-up Friday. I tried you at the hotel but something or someone had spirited you away in the afternoon.

About "A Kid for Two Farthings," your mention of the title rang only a faint bell, I confess. It turns out that, although my office had read the story some time back, and advised me to do the same, I had lost track of the subject in favor of my then enormous preoccupation with my Broadway show. After that I guess your story was one of the loose strings I forgot to pick up.

But now since your reminder, I have read it – and with great great delight. It is really a warm and delicious story! I am told that the picture version preserves all this special genius of yours and I will shortly ask to have the film run for me.

In answer to your question, of course it could make a Broadway musical. But there are a number of cautions that come to my mind. Exactly what they are I will save against the day you come back to these shores. Please phone me as soon as you can after arriving and we will make a date to talk over the potential plusses and minuses about the Broadway possibilities. Also, maybe about any number of other subjects you may wish to broach. If we are having enough fun, we can even extend the scope of our conversation to include whiskey, broads, the common market, Binkie Beaumont, or anything you wish. In short, I look forward to seeing you.

Thanks again for the pleasure "A Kid for Two Farthings" gave me.

    Best,

    Frank Loesser

3 May 1962: To Wolf Mankowitz

Dear Wolf:

Forgive the delay but I have been juggling and weighing ideas in an effort to give you what I hope will be a reasonably valuable survey of the possibilities for "A Kid For Two Farthings" as a Broadway musical.

As you may have heard, I have a knowledgeable and sometimes brilliant staff, but I have not consulted any of these, although all have read your novel and some have seen the movie. I have avoided comparing notes and opinions with these people because my thoughts at this moment are largely concerned with writing, stylizing, composing, etc. and are therefore in my private province as a writer and none of their goddam business. So for the moment, what I am writing you is not the consummate expression of my company, but simply my own, with the prospect that I may become (with your permission) one of its collaborators. Naturally, my production outfit will have a number of valuable opinions about the manner and timing of production, the casting, the budget, etc. etc. etc., but I think it is better that you and I know pretty clearly what ought to be WRITTEN before anything else happens. Whether or not I am the right collaborator or songwriter, I can't tell yet, but as I said, I am approaching the subject as if I indeed were.

I have told you some nice things about the story in my recent letter. Now here are some considerations to watch carefully:

Firstly, as in most attempts to dramatize such writers as Dickens, Runyon, Mark Twain, there is a difficulty involved in removing the "presence" of the author. Let me compliment you here by comparing you with the three gents I mention above. The insinuation of your own canny but warm observation, your own gentle but truthful philosophy, does the same thing for the narrative in hand as do the pens of the three relatively immortal gents above for their stories. Facing squarely the narrative content of your talent, I believe we must confess that it is something of a soap opera. But there is a magic that makes it vastly superior to such fodder. In my mind a very important question is HOW DO WE RETAIN ITS CHARMS WITHOUT THE "PRESENCE" OF WOLF MANKOWITZ?

Offhand, I believe it cowardly and often fatal to insert as a character in such a play the ubiquitous "observer" or "author's agent," who sits in the audience's world, and turns from his telescope in every other scene to explain Mars amusingly to his fellow creatures. On the other hand, if one can accomplish such a purpose without, as George Kaufman used to say, getting caught at it, there is no reason for not trying.

Now I note that many of your most charming moments in the novel arrive when you make the reader aware of the child's innocent and wonder-filled point of view. Do you think this can be accomplished through his communication with others? Or with the unicorn? Or in the use of the convention of song soliloquy? Or a combination of all of these?

<u>Solo songs belted or whimpered at the audience should not happen too frequently of an evening, especially by a child.</u> There is often a professionalism and artificiality about such performances (and such writing) that robs an otherwise well-acted part of its charm. Witness what I consider a somewhat disgraceful gratuity by the darling young man who played "Oliver!" over there. I think it was called "Where is Love." I seem to recollect that it was an unwelcome song recital in the middle of something else. Did you ever see "Gypsy?" In it, the 12-year old young lady sings what is intended to be a plaintive philosophy to a little wooly lamb. It seemed to me to be over-articulate, self-conscious, and put there as some sort of rhinestone. I don't believe that it helped the part or the play, but rather reduced both. However, in both the instances I quote, the writing may have been more at fault than the idea itself of doing a number.

But everything I have pointed a warning finger about rests on the assumption that you would want to key the play to the boy's viewpoint, and since that may not be the case, I will let this part of the discussion rest here.

Now as to idiom: New York theatre has been exposed in the last six or seven years to a barrage of the "Jewish" in a variety of forms and levels. In the straight drama and comedy field, we have had "The Fifth Season," "The Cold Wind and the Warm," etc. Among the musicals there are "Milk and Honey," "I Can Get It For You Wholesale," "A Family Affair," all presently or recently on Broadway.[35] It is my feeling

---

35 *The Fifth Season* (1953): play by Sylvia Regan, 654 performances. *The Cold Wind and the Warm* (1958): play by S. N. Behrman, 120 performances. *Milk and Honey* (1961): musical by Jerry Herman (music and lyrics) and Don Appell (book), 543 performances. *I Can Get it for You Wholesale* (1962): musical by Harold Rome (music and lyrics) and Jerome Weidman (book), 300 performances. *A Family Affair* (1962): musical by John Kander, James Goldman and William Goldman (music, lyrics and book), 65 performances.

that the audiences have already experienced enough of this language and intonation and general climate, to be near the boring point. Nevertheless, I submit that if an unfamiliar version of the "Jewish" is presented, that it has every chance to be greeted warmly by both critic and ticket buyer. One of the delicious Jewish things not yet experienced by the New York public, is the cockney Jew. I hope I use the word "cockney" properly here. I mean the London Jew who sells goods in the Portobello Road or operates a tailor shop, and whose accent to the American ear is really more London than it is Jewish. His thinking, however, is very Jewish – and that subtlety is, I think, a perennial thing of wonder (witness "Jacobowsky").[36] Can you preserve this London quality so that the Jewish part of it will not seem to be a purposeful emphasis? I believe that would be very important. Something tells me that, for the New York theatre, any overt insistence on the "Jewish" is no longer the welcome novelty it was when a daring young man named Frank Loesser wrote "Sue me, all right already, I'm just a no-goodnik" (1950) from which all the Lindy diners (Isow's[37] to you) got an <u>unexpected</u> nachis.

Now as to general construction. Your story engages the reader's sympathy in turn; with the little boy and the possible fate of his pet and his dream world – then with the understandable indignation of the romantic but ringless young lady and the helplessness of her suitor under the pressure of a ring-respecting society. Then with the efforts in everyone's behalf by the saint-like tailor, etc. etc. etc. My feeling is that a musical play which followed this form exactly, would <u>appear</u> to be too whimsically episodic. Something tells me that the boy and girl story should be the prevailing one. That is to say, the one first proposed as a concrete problem and then bobbing up to the surface at convenient intervals to illustrate its development. Now I know what I've just said sounds like "commercial" thinking, and maybe in fact it is. What it does do, however, is protect the play from

---

36 *Jacobowsky and the Colonel* (1944): play by S. N. Behrman, 417 performances.
37 Isow's was a restaurant based at Brewer St in London that sold Jewish dishes as part of its menu. It was a popular destination for performers due to its proximity to London's West End theatreland.

becoming trapped with too much of an old man's philosophy which only develops an <u>active</u> purpose (the pressing machine) toward the very <u>end</u> of the story – or with the musings of a small child whose "wish" is granted very early in the play and whose aims are not well defined thereafter.

You will note that I speak of <u>specific</u> and expressible aims, hopes, wishes, endeavors, purposes and plottings. Please recollect that in most good musicals, a huge amount of singing time is devoted to the expressions of want, a need, a resolve, a purpose or a prayer. As a refresher, I submit the following offhand list of titles or lines:

"Someone to Watch Over Me" [from *Oh, Kay!* (1926) by George and Ira Gershwin]

"Somebody, Somewhere" [from Loesser's *The Most Happy Fella*]

"The Man I Love" [by George and Ira Gershwin; dropped from *Lady, Be Good* (1924)]

"Some Day My Prince Will Come" [from *Snow White and the Seven Dwarfs* (1937); by Larry Morey and Frank Churchill]

"I'll Know" [from Loesser's *Guys and Dolls*]

"I Want to Get Married" ['I Don' Know Notin' About You' from Loesser's *The Most Happy Fella*][38]

These above are only a few examples of "girl hopes to meet ideal boy as yet unknown to her." Now follows a list of some which express a plea for relief from stinking circumstances:

"Ol' Man River" (Let me go 'way from the Mississippi) [from Kern and Hammerstein's *Show Boat* (1927)]

"Why Was I Born" [from Kern and Hammerstein's *Sweet Adeline* (1929)]

"Sons of toil and danger,

Will you let a stranger. . .?" (Burgundy) ['Song of the Vagabonds' by Rudi Friml, William H. Post and Brian Hooker from *The Vagabond King* (1925)]

"Adelaide's Lament" [from Loesser's *Guys and Dolls*]

---

38 Theoretically, Loesser could mean the song 'I Wanna Get Married' from *Follow the Girls* (1944) by Dan Shapiro, Milton Pascal and Phil Charig, but this seems too obscure a reference for the context.

"Officer Krupky [Krupke]" [from Bernstein and Sondheim's *West Side Story* (1957)]

"If we only had a lousy little grand, we could be a
millionaire" (Guys and Dolls)

"Wouldn't it be loverly" [from Lerner and Loewe's *My Fair Lady* (1956)]

etc.etc.

Then, of course, there are other typical wishes and wants that comprise an enormous amount of effective song literature. Yearning for the lost, dead or stolen loved one; songs of resolve or purpose like the "Carousel" soliloquy, or "7 ½ Cents," or that long one note thing in "Rigoletto" where the buffoon swears revenge . . .[39]

Please observe how clearly these songs point up the emotional tuggings of the play, at the same time helping, in many instances, to introduce characters and their motives. They express nothing <u>final</u> like a flat declaration of love, or a simple report such as "It's Been A Real Nice Clambake."[40] What they help do is ask us to root for the fulfillment and therefore to keep the subsequent actions or events rewarding and meaningful.

Well, sir, it has taken me three sittings, many days apart, to finish dictating this diatribe which may mark the end of our professional friendship on the basis of its seeming positiveness alone. Actually, I am not positive at all. I have many, many theories, some of which contradict much that I have written above. I am not married to any one of them. What I did want to do was give you some kind of notion of what I would consider the thinking modus for a show of this kind. So if you disagree on any point, please hurry and write, and in turn I will comment upon your comments. This process, however long-distance, actually constitutes a preliminary collaboration, and if we disagree violently, we can't reach out and pummel or throttle each other. That is a rare convenience among co-writers.

Best,

---

39 *Carousel* by Rodgers and Hammerstein (1945); 'Seven-and-a-Half Cents' from Adler and Ross's *The Pajama Game*; the title character's curse ('Ah, la maledizione!') from Verdi's *Rigoletto*.
40 'This Was a Real Nice Clambake' from Rodgers and Hammerstein's *Carousel*.

8 May 1962: To Wolf Mankowitz (telegram)

I AM PREPARING A LONG AND PROBABLY POMPOUS ANALYSIS OF FARTHINGS STORY FOR MUSICAL STOP PLEASE GIVE ME ANOTHER WEEK AT IT.
      BEST REGARDS
      FRANK LOESSER

6 June 1962: To Wolf Mankowitz

Dear Wolf:

I had prepared a seemingly knowledgeable and certainly thorough analysis of "Kid For Two Farthings" – to forward to you in answer to your request for my feelings about it as a Broadway musical. Toward the end of this piece of work I re-read your note to me and must tell you that one suggestion gave me pause. That is the question of musical collaboration.

You seem to include me as a prospective composer-lyricist of this piece. Now all other things being equal, I might relish this sort of thing, but I have been told that originally "Kid For Two Farthings" was presented to this office (not to me) by Monty Norman, and that the assumption in these parts was that if it should be produced as a musical Monty intended to be its composer. This of course seemed perfectly natural to Allen Whitehead and others in charge of productions here and had I known about it, my impression would have been the same – since you and he have collaborated in this way before and with success.

Am I to infer now that you do not intend to collaborate with him? Or that he is one of several choices and that I might be another? I must ask this question as there might be some embarrassment here if I should, in a manner of speaking, step into Monty's shoes without his first being aware of his non-relationship with the project.

Please inform me on this as soon as you can. Frankly I would welcome Norman as the show's composer. As a matter of fact, I think I could help him to no little degree as an editor towards satisfying the Broadway market. Also, if it pleased you, I would enjoy collaborating on the book instead of the score.

In my analysis, which I will forward very shortly, I concentrate on the various cautions to be observed. Please do not consider this an over-all negative impression. It is simply a conscientiously arrived at compilation of danger signals. In general I do sincerely believe that the story can be produced as a Broadway stage musical if done with warmth and affection and a proper regard for the present day audience temperament.

But please answer the question about Monty. It would help me to know how you stand both in terms of your wishes as well as your actual commitments on the subject.

My God. I write more and more like a businessman. I wish you were around the corner at the Plaza again so I wouldn't have to write stuffy letters, and we could talk and drink the whole thing out. Oh well.

Best,
Frank Loesser

20 June 1962: To Wolf Mankowitz [only surviving page of a larger letter]

What I have been discussing (interminably) here, is the establishment and preservation of a state of tension, anxiety, fond hopefulness, among the members of the audience – about the play's outcome. Recall if you will, a good motion picture called "The Quiet Man"[41] which succeeded in making one subject work for approximately ten reels of film. Boy and girl love each other, but the mores in which the girl has enormous pride, dictate that she should not marry without a dowry. The dowry being withheld by her elder brother, she feels herself unfit to marry the man she loves. Her lover, having been exposed to another kind of culture – in which the very opposite thinking obtains (decent young men don't marry for money) – therefore abhors the principle upon which the girl, who loves him dearly, nevertheless steadfastly refuses his hand.

---

41 *The Quiet Man* (1952) was directed by John Ford. A musical version, titled *Donnybrook!*, had opened and closed in a couple of months in 1961.

Now, are we not dealing with the same thing here. Our girl's society cannot take seriously her declaration about being "engaged" because there is no ring. The little gold symbol is more realistic in their minds than the state of blissful affection between the two people. The girl, being a true member of this society, fully understands the other girls' disdain, and disdains herself along with them. Her resistance to the boy becomes painfully understandable to us. Therefore, when we see public prowess and fame heaped upon the boy, and we see how she accepts this equally crappy status symbol, we are mightily rewarded by her "change of heart."

I feel that the paths of plot which lead to the boy's desperate decision to fight someone twice his size, and to win, and to marry the lady – can be established early and, as I said before, become the prevailing aim and direction of at least the bulk of the play. This does not mean that other elements have to be abandoned. Nor does it imply that there cannot be one or two other sustained side plots, seemingly unrelated, which converge toward the end of the story with the main plot line to aid and abet, or possibly at times to attempt to frustrate the final consummation.

I am aware that I sound like a mechanic in the approach to this – and a longwinded one at that – but I do believe that the structure of a show, especially a musical where the time for talk is short, is very important to establish before the writers find themselves bogged down in a sea of whimsy, philosophy, empty melody, inconclusive scene endings, and curtains that create no breathless or even provocative demand for the following scene.

21 June 1962: To Wolf Mankowitz

Dear Wolf:

I have yours of June 14th, and I am forwarding this reply to Barbados as well as to London, in the absence of any information about the itinerary of such wealthy travelers as yourself.

I am happy that you have clarified your position about Monty, along with it flattering me mightily. It is possible that I might want to collaborate on the songs with Monty, as well as on the play with you, but I suggest we don't broach this subject to Monty at the moment.

The most important thing now is that you should see some sense in the comments I have enclosed with this letter. It may be tortuous reading, but that is the way I write, very often overstating a perfectly obvious case.

The next most important thing is that no commitments of any kind should be made on this project beyond those covering the relationship between Monty and you and me and Frank Productions, Inc. In that connection, I suggest that we go <u>slowly</u> toward visualizing a London production. I am counting here on my original assumption that you wanted this to originate on Broadway. If so, I believe it would be idle to come to any conclusion with Jack Hylton[42] at the present time. I know and admire him, but I think we are a little early for an understanding in that direction. Likewise, I am mad about Bud Flanagan,[43] although I have never seen him play a part, but simply romp with his gang.

If you are in London at the moment, please say hello to those of my friends you may meet, and if you are in Barbados, where I am acquainted with no one, then simply congratulate your tan and pleasure-bent self.

Best,

18 July 1962: To Wolf Mankowitz

Dear Wolf:

It is now past July 11th and therefore I address you with confidence at your London headquarters.

I am not quite prepared to make the opening feint in round two. Firstly, I want to have a look at the film, and toward that end my company will have a screening of it late next week, and my minions and I will look at it with much interest.

Shortly after that, I hope to be able to send you a sort of preliminary outline for a possible two-act musical. By this, I mean a skeleton scenario indicating the sequence of events to be seen and heard on

---

42 Jack Hylton (1892–1965), English composer, bandleader and impresario.
43 Bud Flanagan (1896–1968), English vaudevillian.

396

the stage. So please wait for my communication, and after that the next punch is yours.

In the meantime, have you spoken to Monty about the possibility of my ubiquitous collaboration? I wish that you would do so shortly, so that I may be assured that such an option is available to me on the writing of lyrics and music. The terms of such an arrangement need not be discussed at this point, but I would like to be certain that Monty has no objection to this prospect.

As to your question about a working schedule, I believe it best that we don't try to create one until we reach some kind of agreement on musical play outline. I assume that Monty is now quite involved with "Scobie Prilt"[44] and that you (at least according to the New York papers) are busy with Mr. Charles Dickens. Add to that the superfluous suggestion that I am at present as busy as the proverbial one-armed-paper-hanger-with-the-hives. I think you'll agree that we have at least a few months in which to toy purposefully with the subject.

I will write after seeing the film. Meantime, along with my great admiration, my warmest good wishes.

27 July 1962: To Wolf Mankowitz

Dear Wolf:

Last night the staff and I ran the film of "A Kid For Two Farthings," and all of us enjoyed it immensely.

But there loom this morning, after a meeting among us, certain cautions about producing this for the New York stage. Firstly, there is a hard and fast Equity rule here to the effect that a child must have attained the age of 7 before being allowed to appear (this rule applies to children of American or any other nationality). Well sir, our 7-year olds have difficulty, generally speaking, in mustering up the look of innocence. Firstly, one has to find them stunted enough to

---

44 A science fiction spoof musical *Scobie Prilt* by Monty Norman and Julian More, directed by Peter Brook, ran for seven performances at the New Theatre, Oxford, in 1963.

appear younger, and that is difficult because we have developed a system of big family incomes and powerful but cheap pablum, air-conditioning, Vic Tanny,[45] all of which seem to be producing young things who, at 6, are capable of mugging one in Central Park, armed with only a sharp lollypop stick. Occasionally, of course, we find a darling little thing who is just right. But his just-rightness seems to disappear in the few months between final casting and Broadway opening. He has grown 6-inches and has a distinct mustache and the wardrobe alterations would make even Kandinsky[46] lose faith.

But let's say we have found this little putz-puller, and given him enough cigarettes to have some reasonable assurance that he will remain little. The question is now: How can we make him heartwarmingly operative as your camera did? In our theatres big enough to house a musical, distance does not land enchantment to this view. Mostly we have to substitute a speech or lyrics for what a film shows us in a tiny flash to be an attitude of breathless and angelical beady-eyed open faith. Now here is how the substitute goes:

Mommy, Mommy, Mommy
When is daddy coming home?
Tuck me in and kiss me quick
For I'm a fatherless gnome,
A fatherless, fatherless, fatherless –
Gnome

And we are all likely to vomit all over the theatre foyer while rushing out.

Now as to animals (other than goldfish, or small lice that gather under a cheap actor's collar): Of course a young goat is manageable, but only to an extent, and if too long or too often in evidence in the course of a play, is likely to corrupt one scene or another with badly timed bleatings, or random calling cards. Here I am comparing the

---

45 Vic Tanny (1912–1985), American bodybuilder and pioneer of health club franchises.
46 A character in *A Kid for Two Farthings* – the neighbour who has told Joe about the mythical powers of unicorns.

stage possibilities with those so well and plentifully used in the film. I don't think anywhere nearly so much frisky, romping goat can be used, but that emphasis on its existence and importance would have to be written in another way.

Showing a realistic boxing or wrestling match on the stage has always presented enormous problems. I have never seen them surmounted. It does work when we are making a travesty of the action. But here, there are real stakes involved, emotionally, on everyone's part, and we believe that the writing will have to somehow present and protect this element of the play very skillfully.

Now to even more fundamental problems. If the ultimate musical version is going to be <u>less</u> of a heartwarmer than the film, we don't believe there is much point in doing it. Can the <u>care</u> expressed by Kandinsky, the mother, and others, deliver to the audience a similar feeling about the boy – so that if he is not the perfectly darling little creature all on his own (by virtue of some incapacity of his or some stagecraft shortcomings), we may still get all the needed sentimental enjoyment? After all, in its present version, the story says once there was a little boy who observed that everybody wanted something, including himself; then heard about unicorns; then found one; then, assuming that he now had magical powers, proceeded to instruct the unicorn to grant all his friends' wishes. All the wishes were promptly granted. Now, although we elders know that there were several coincidences, the boy felt that he and his unicorn had been responsible. So I feel we cannot escape the fact that the boy motivates the tale (coincidences notwithstanding). Therefore, in addition to the casting and technical hazards, there is also the enormous artistic one of sustaining interest and sympathy. We all thought you did marvelously in the picture, but also observe that it took enormous footage of closeup shots on the boy. Bringing him forward in that way occurs to us to be the big stage problem.

Question: Have you ever given any thought to a technique in this direction? Allen Whitehead recollects that Monty was going to discuss with him some notions about musical comedy form, but it appears he never got around to it.

Well, my dear fellow, as you now see, I have artfully avoided any responsibility in the matter of positive suggestions. What you have here is a dreary recital of prohibitions, injunctions, traffic regulations, etc., but they are not intended to be negative, but just possibly sign-posts along the forward route.

If you agree that the hazards outlined are indeed hazards, the next move would be for you to send over some sort of broad outline of a sequence of events that would skirt at least the important dangers expressed here. Of course, if you do not agree, please give us your contrary views. It is possible that we are being over-cautious. Your dice.

Warmest regards,

4 September 1962: To Wolf Mankowitz

Dear Wolf:

Thanks for your most recent note. I still await a copy of the film script. Meanwhile, be assured that we (both potential producers and potential writer) understand, and always have understood, that this is about a little boy.

While Whitehead is digesting the business information (not yet received) can you hurry along that film script so that I can design a stage musical? My memory of the film is not good enough, and having the script to refer to will help insure against some error of omission.

Best as always,

18 September 1962: To Wolf Mankowitz

Dear Mr. Mankowitz:

In Mr. Loesser's behalf I acknowledge with thanks receipt of the precious file copy of "A Kid For Two Farthings," forwarded by your admirable secretary Jacqueline Johns. I have brought my secretarial equipment here directly outside the steel door of the bank vault to which Mr. Loesser has retired for the purpose of reading and making notes on the immortal document. Just a few minutes ago, he tapped out a message on the concrete wall. I have since decoded it, and find it to be one of cheer directed to you and of complete assurance that all is safe and sound, although he does find it difficult breathing in there. Mr. Loesser does not quite trust the armed guards outside. One of them, I will admit, has eyes that are much too close together, but the other one I rather like. Unfortunately, I can't leave my spot.

There will be further word from Mr. Loesser after he and the manuscript have emerged and have been thoroughly sprayed for moths and other destructive elements (sometimes he spills coffee).

Wearily but loyally,

Mona Lipp

Secretary to

Frank Loesser

(Pro. Tem. Custodian of Portland Vases, Relics

Of the True Cross, Hope Diamonds, etc. etc. etc.)[47]

Loesser's enthusiasm for the next generation of writers is often impressive. Stephen Sondheim (1930–2021) was clearly pleased by the older writer's response to his score for *A Funny Thing Happened on the Way to the Forum*, which opened on Broadway on 8 May 1962 and ran for 964 performances ('Your letter is the best thing that's happened to me since "Forum" opened,' Sondheim replied). Sondheim had previously written lyrics to Leonard Bernstein's music for *West Side Story* (1957) and to Jule Styne's for *Gypsy* (1959) but *Forum* marked his debut as both composer and lyricist; he must have been delighted that Loesser refers to him as a composer in his letter, and they enjoyed a casual friendship. In return, Sondheim afforded more praise to Loesser than most of the other classic Broadway lyricists that he writes about in his two published editions of lyrics:

Loesser, along with his predecessors Dorothy Fields and Irving Berlin, was a master of conversational lyrics, though with a

---

47 The Portland Vase, currently housed at the British Museum, is a Roman glass vase dating to the first decades AD. The exceptionally large Hope Diamond, discovered in India in the seventeenth century, is housed at the Smithsonian Institution, Washington (National Museum of Natural History).

difference: he tailored his lyrics to the individual characters at hand . . . When they were characters he could understand instinctively, urban or raffish or both, as in *Guys and Dolls* and *How to Succeed in Business Without Really Trying*, Loesser was able to perform the rare trick of sounding modestly conversational and brilliantly dextrous at the same time . . .

Loesser was one of the very few lyricists who were genuinely funny. The lyrics of Gershwin and Hart received appreciative smiles and sometimes even chuckles, but not the kind of hearty laughter that songs like 'Adelaide's Lament' got . . .

Most impressive to me are the ideas behind Loesser's songs. The concepts of 'Make a Miracle' from *Where's Charley?* and 'Fugue for Tinhorns' from *Guys and Dolls*, among many others, are so strong that the lyrics need not be brilliant in execution: they can ride on their notions alone and bring the house down. Which they did, and still do.[48]

31 May 1962: To Stephen Sondheim

Dear Steve:

I saw your show last night and simply loved every minute of it. But especially the score, which I <u>know</u> you arrived at not only with the expected talent, but also with much valuable thought. I mean thought in favor of the play. No meretricious anachronisms, no tell-tale cheap Roseland rhythms, and at the same time, no crappy attempts at "period." Plus a lot of other things that I felt and I smelled, all of which tell me once more that you are awfully good at what you do. Sometimes even a composer's working partners, to say nothing of the critics, fail to dig every level and facet of what he is doing. But I know, and I wanted you to know I know. So there.

Best as always,

---

48 Stephen Sondheim, *Finishing the Hat* (New York and London, 2010), 6.

16 July 1962: To Stephen Sondheim

Dear Steve:

It was nice the other afternoon, and I hope we talk again soon. Next time, I will drink large, long gulps of some beverage I love so that you can get a word in.

This is to remind you about letting me see all the paper stuff we talked about. You have my promise that no one else will get the tiniest look, and that I'll return them very quickly.

Secondly, let me remind you of my glowing remarks about Martin Wolman, an example of whose business return envelope I left for you to ponder. While pondering, please consider that this man and his company act as tax attorneys and accountants not only for me and for Ed Sullivan, but also the American Shakespeare Festival, Wright and Forrest, Merle Jones (President of CBS Radio Operations), Roger Price, Mel Brooks, etc. etc.[49] Wolman has given me an immeasurable amount of comfort, both in terms of profit and saved money, but even more importantly to my peace of mind, in taking care of such routine annoyances as bill-paying, tax-calculating, form-preparing, etc. I fell into his lap many years ago, and don't expect to fall out ever.

If you like, I will introduce you to him, and will even pay for the lunch. Wolman will probably get up and applaud the appetizer in tribute to the deductibility of the occasion. Please phone me.

Fondly,

---

49 Ed Sullivan (1901–1974), television host; Merle Jones (?1906–1976), president of CBS Television-Station Division; Roger Price (1918–1990), American humourist who created *Droodles* and *Mad Libs*; Mel Brooks (born 1926), writer-director of films including *The Producers* (1967).

CHAPTER NINE

1961–64
LOESSER AND MEREDITH WILLSON

No group of correspondence better illustrates one of Loesser's relationships than his letters to and about Meredith Willson. The fact that so many of these letters have survived may give a disproportionate view of the importance of the relationship, but it appears that the pair had an unusual bond. On the one hand, Loesser was genuinely affectionate towards Willson, and had enormous respect for his talent: even when complaining about his professional behaviour, Loesser wrote to his Frank Music colleagues that 'I am quite fond of him and probably his most sensitive admirer'. The Loessers and Willsons socialised and the two songwriters regularly corresponded on everyday family and health matters. On the other hand, Willson was a key figure in the development of Loesser's organisation: Frank Productions had co-produced *The Music Man* and Frank Music had published it (as well as *The Unsinkable Molly Brown*).

The Loesser–Willson relationship was complex. From Loesser's perspective, there seems an ability and willingness to be both friends and colleagues, and he periodically becomes frustrated or upset about the personal implications when Willson expresses a business concern: this tends particularly to be the case when Willson feels he is being exploited or not well treated by Loesser's organisations, a suggestion that Loesser cannot understand because he regards Willson as a friend whom he would only ever treat with favour and courtesy in professional contexts.

12. Meredith Willson, 1957.

Then, too, there are other fragile aspects to the relationship. Loesser was eight years Willson's junior but was a much more accomplished businessman and, arguably, more successful songwriter than Willson, notwithstanding the extraordinary success of *The Music Man* and a few standards such as 'It's Beginning to Look Like Christmas'. Willson in his turn was a remarkably versatile musician, writing Academy Award-nominated film scores and two symphonies and achieving success on radio, television, stage and screen.

Thus, when Loesser wrote the extraordinary, extraordinarily long letter from June 1964 – the original is fifty-eight pages of handwritten words and images – reproduced in this chapter, it was the climax of tensions that had been brewing for several years between the pair. Willson's reaction is undocumented, but Loesser's insightful analysis of his older friend's career to date must have come across as brutally honest, even though it's clear that it was inspired by care and passion. This chapter covers the period of development, production and reception of Willson's third musical, *Here's Love*, through to the broadcast of three television specials hosted by Willson in June 1964, the second of which provoked Loesser's long epistle on Willson's career management.

• • •

On 29 November 1961 it was widely reported in the press that Willson's next musical would be an adaptation of the beloved holiday movie *Miracle on 34th Street* (1947). The *Hollywood Reporter* revealed: 'Next triple activity by Meredith Willson for Broadway will be to write book, music and lyrics for The Stuart Co.'s stage version of "Miracle on 34th Street," according to Stuart Ostrow, head of the producing company. Working title given by Willson to his legit musical adaptation of the film is "The Wonderful Plan." '[1] Later called *Here's Love*, the musical updated the plot from the 1940s to the present day (1963 by the time the show was staged) and made a significant change to the lead character of Fred Gaily, who is here lacking in the gentle romantic charm of the equivalent character played in the movie by actor John Payne. The story still concerns the identity of a man called Kris Kringle, who is hired by Macy's department store to play Santa Claus in their annual Christmas campaign; he claims to be the real Santa Claus and has to win over the hearts and minds of Macy's employee Doris and her young daughter Susan, neither of whom believes in Father Christmas. Willson worked hard on the adaptation from November 1961 through to the end of 1962 and many further changes were made before its opening to mixed reviews on Broadway in October 1963. Loesser's letters of this period refer to Willson's wife Rini, a retired soprano; to a Christmas gift of a set of the Dodd, Mead

---

1 Anon., ' "Miracle on 34th Street" Legit Next for Willson', *Hollywood Reporter* 167/50 (29 November 1961), 2.

& Co.'s annual 'Best Plays' volume of play texts; and to Stuart Ostrow, formerly of Frank Music and now the producer of *Here's Love*.

5 December 1961: To Meredith Willson

Dear Meredith:

We are sending you and Rini a bulky something for Christmas. There are parts missing and the wheels won't go around until you get those parts and it is very complicated. The whole bundle is being sent direct from the plant that makes it and it doesn't contain a card.

So just in case you think it is neatly wrapped firewood, or a collection of old celestes – here's what it IS: It is a collection of the Best Plays Series all the way back to the nineties – except that certain volumes in the 1940's are presently out of print and these will arrive separately later (that's what the publisher assures me). I guess you'll have to find room for this mass of information. But don't get rid of Rini.

Anyway, we wish you both a very merry Christmas. Also, we wish you were here more often. Too many of our friends have the wrong twang.

Love love love,
Jo & Frank

9 April 1962: To Meredith Willson

Dear Mer:

Apparently Dodd is doddering and Mead has gone stark, staring mead. They sent me the two books they owed you to complete the Best Plays set. Fortunately, I have a courier – Milt Kramer, who is coming west shortly and will bring along the missing volumes with my continued fond wishes.

I am phoning Stu [Ostrow] in the next day or so just to see how he feels. He should have the right effervescence of spirit to go with all his plans. As for you, I leave you to commune with Santa Claus, confident that you are bubbling joyously over the work. I hope Kramer comes back with glowing tales about the richness of the score, etc.

Love as always,

On 15 October 1962 the *Hollywood Reporter* published a short column titled 'Meredith Willson Home'. It revealed that the composer 'had returned to his Brentwood home from St. John's Hospital, Santa Monica, to recuperate from surgery from an inflamed appendix and correction of an adhesion. The "Music Man" will resume his work on book, words and music for his next Broadway play as soon as doctors permit him.'[2]

1 October 1962: To Meredith Willson (Telegram)

RELIEVED TO HEAR YOUR BASS NOTES ALREADY SUCCESSFULLY EDITED AFTER LAST NIGHT'S ALARMING NEWS STOP I'M IN TOUCH WITH STU FOR CONSTANT NEWS OF YOU STOP IF FATHER GUNN IS STILL AT THE HOSPITAL YOU'LL FIND HIM A DELIGHTFUL FELLOW STOP GOOD HEALTH AND LOVE TO YOU
FRANK LOESSER

On 14 January 1963 Milton Kramer distributed a production schedule of *Here's Love* to the Frank Music staff. Rehearsals were due to commence 20 June; the opening was to be in Detroit on 29 July, until 24 August; a Washington DC tryout was to play from 26 August to 14 September.[3] In the event, an extra stop was added in Philadelphia (15–28 September) and the New York opening was delayed to 3 October. Tensions had now begun between Loesser's office, particularly his attorney Harold Orenstein, and Willson's representatives, led by Martin Gang, and would continue through fractious correspondence over the course of 1963 in which Loesser would voice his frustrations about being cut out of negotiations for the use of Willson's compositions, including in the movie version of *The Unsinkable Molly Brown*, which was released by MGM in 1964; MGM also owned the rights to their movie *Miracle on 34th Street*, hence the importance of these relationships for Willson's current projects.

---

2 Anon., 'Meredith Willson Home', *Hollywood Reporter* 172/23 (15 October 1962), 2.
3 Memo from Milton Kramer, 14 January 1963, Frank Loesser Enterprises.

The value of Loesser's understanding is apparent from an inter-vention about the song 'It's Beginning to Look Like Christmas', which Willson had written a decade earlier but planned to use in *Here's Love*. Willson wanted to buy the rights for his song for the Loesser-Willson company Frank-Rinimer so that they would have full control over it for the new show, but Loesser recognised from experience that this would only be worth it if the song were actually used in the end (it was): scores of musicals are often changed and cut on their way to Broadway. In between business letters, and a stressful exchange about the termination of Frank-Rinimer, Loesser provided his usual comments on the evolving script of *Here's Love*, familiar from the period of the genesis of *The Unsinkable Molly Brown*.

23 January 1963: To Meredith Willson

Dear Meredith:

Stu [Ostrow] sounded buoyant when he called me yesterday to give me an idea of your rehearsal and production dates in New York, so this is to let you know that I'm excited too and look forward to your emerging out of the provinces once more. I expect to be around, ready and willing on anything you may need. But I have a feeling, since that last song recital, that you won't be needing much.

From a review of the interminable correspondence between your attorney and my attorney, I note with great relief that Harold Orenstein has written to Martin Gang telling him to send the MOLLY BROWN synchronization consent for signature. They have had a long hassle, those two – over something that really and truly you and I should talk about quietly sometime when there is no pressure. Certainly you and I are not out to scalp or betray each other, but somehow the lyrics of legal-contractual correspondence always seem to cast a light on the respective clients, making one of them Captain Hook and the other Jesse James. I don't believe these roles suit us in the slightest.

But as I said – maybe sometime shortly after your show opens we can sit down and discuss, for the sake of a calm future, what our inten-tions are. After that it ought to be simple enough for the lawyers to spell it out understandingly in their own special (and expensive) language.

As always, HERE'S LOVE* to you and Rini and I look forward to seeing you in the early summer.

* oops: Infringement.

22 March 1963 (Manchester) / 25 March 1963
(Transcribed London): To Meredith Willson

Dear Meredith,

In my sporadic hotel-room time between rehearsals and performances here in Manchester, I have been doing a lot of strenuous thinking about our session of last Sunday – and have distilled a strange nagging conviction. Like this:

The little girl's mother[4] should make her pitch to have KRIS defended in court <u>out of pure emotional urgency</u> – NOT BECAUSE SHE IS TEACHING SUSAN A LESSON. That means that prior to the scene in the judge's chamber (with the MARINE behind the door) there <u>has to be</u> a scene (maybe in the same set in advance of the judge's entrance), in which MOTHER capitulates <u>sentimentally</u> about the fact that there might very well <u>BE</u> A SANTA CLAUS.

I suggest this because I think the MOTHER'S present capitulation comes much too late. We want to see a nice decent <u>Rootable-for</u> heroine earlier than the last ten minutes of the play. Otherwise she may not be redeemable.

Please observe that you have already equipped her for capitulation in the song-statement she makes at the end of the first act.

Now then: Can you create a sudden interesting captivating NEW EVENT which drives our heroine into changing her point of view? I believe you can write one which proves to the MOTHER the efficacy and —dity[5] of APPLIED SUPERSTITION. Say that to yourself again before laughing. APPLIED SUPERSTITION.

---

4 The little girl is Susan; her mother is Doris.
5 Word cannot be transcribed due to a staple.

I have to talk theoretically this way because after a once-over-lightly I can't remember the exact sequence of events in the present play. So please stick with me on this basis. In dealing with the Mother we are dealing with a SCROOGE. You'll recall that the event in his life was his series of dreams. His resultant enlightenment made him change his tune in time for Christmas – AND THE END OF HIS DREAMS <u>QUICKLY CATAPULTED HIM INTO HIS FINAL KINDLY ACTIONS.</u>

From trying to recollect your reading, I have the impression that in the second act you have dropped Mrs. Bieler (was that the name of the maid?). Could she pop up again handily? Has she always had this <u>laughable</u> habit of stopping in the middle of her dusting to wish on the moon for the return of her long wandering and lost husband? And hasn't he now indeed returned to her early in the second act? And isn't he the Loch Ness Monster nobody but a dizzy child would believe in? But is Mrs. Bieler a dizzy child? NO! and neither is our heroine! And if a crazy impossible Enoch Arden[6] miracle can happen from being wished and believed in – WELL? OFF TO COURT AND DON'T SPARE THE HORSES!

Yes, dear Meredith, I am giving it to you real wild – for a not very mysterious reason. The reason is that I'm not smart enough to think of anything specific that would make this theory work.

But I <u>am</u> convinced of the theory. Of course I haven't taken into regard how this fits the present design of the show, or how much time it would take up.

When I get back to N.Y. I'll phone you in California and let's discuss this. Is there a way you can leave a script for me in New York? I'll call Stu and ask, when I get back.

Meantime thanks for the other day's exciting recital and here's love to you and Rini.

Frank

---

6 A reference to Alfred, Lord Tennyson's poem of the same name in which the fisherman Enoch Arden returns home after being lost at sea for eleven and a half years.

15 April 1963: To Meredith Willson

Dear Meredith:

I called Stu almost the moment I got back from England, and he obliged by sending me the March 30th script. Immediately I made some of my picky little notes in pencil, but the pressure of work made it impossible to transcribe them till now. So here goes.

1-3-14: Will the audience get the significance of the "Adeste Fideles"[7] treatment? Remember that the bearded gentleman's suggestion was two scenes ago (1-1-6). Please look back at 1-1-6, and see if the bearded gentleman can refer to it as "a real carol like 'Come All Ye Faithful'" – and even hum a tiny bit of it.

1-4-15: My presumption was that Shellhammer was still leading the band. His presence in this "vantage point" scene somehow seems to me to need an alibi, like:

Shellhammer

(sweating and puffing on arrival whilst taking off his regalia)

The regular drum major showed up finally, but I was great while I lasted, wasn't I?

(Doris is occupied with her binoculars)

Inspired, wasn't I?

Doris

I guess so. He's the best Santa Claus we ever had.

etc. etc. etc.

1-5: Nagging question: What are we to conclude about Susan's falling for the Santa Claus idea. Did she? Or does she just like Fred Gaily? Shouldn't she give some indication, however slight, of having enjoyed the parade?

1-11-53: Next to last speech on page, Shellhammer says "That must be Kringle" when he hears a knock at the door. Considering Doris' dismay at having fired Kringle, why should we immediately presume that they can still catch him ("He may be still changing

---

7 The opening number of *Here's Love* included a section of the Christmas carol 'Adeste Fidelis' but Loesser appears to be referring to a separate use of the piece.

clothes")? Isn't it funnier and quicker to think that the knock at the door may be Mr. Macy, ready to fire them?

1-11-55: Shouldn't the last reaction belong to Doris rather than Shellhammer? After all, she has made a lyric contribution to the singing of the song, and deserves to catch herself self-consciously and straighten herself out from having been caught in this sentimentality. It is, after all, the beginning of an important story capitulation. If you think this is too early, I don't see why she contributes to the happy lyrics.

1-13-58: The scene immediately prior to this does not seem provocative enough to Doris. Not enough to throw an ultimatum as she does when she says "Leave my daughter alone." Would it not help in the previous scene (1-12) to extend Susan's final remarks so that she reports to Mrs. Beeler that she has a <u>date</u> <u>with</u> <u>Fred</u>, to which Mrs. Beeler replies that such a date would get her mother very angry.

1-19-79: Doesn't Kris seem vindictive in insisting on reporting Sawyer?

2-2 and 2-3: First of all, I believe that 2-3 should precede 2-2. Here's how I see it: Susan should visit Kris as you have written, and wheedle his promise of a present. When he satisfies her on this subject, she in turn promises that she will get him a present. And she thinks she knows what he wants. As a matter of fact, it is something he needs and she's going to give it to him. It is just as difficult to find as a house and a cow, but she is going to do it. He asks her what it is, and she says "a lawyer."

Now go back to what used to be 2-2 but is now 2-3. Here Susan should be the prime motivator in favor of her mother. Now when we get to the present 2-2-8, it is Susan who prompts Doris into saying "Fred Gaily," and we can get a big emotional punch out of her exiting with her mother, and for the first time in her life, being able to say "Gee, thanks <u>MOM</u>," which affects Doris in a wondrous way before their exit.

2-4-14: Do I take it that the alter ego voice comes over a loudspeaker? If so, it seems to be injecting a new style into the play heretofore not experienced. Is there any way to predict this style

413

when we are dealing with Fred in soliloquy? Some evidence of this technique would be helpful somewhere in the first act, so as to give us a constant style. I wouldn't know where offhand.

2-7-38: Is this corridor a different corridor from the corridor indicated in 2-6-33, the scene immediately preceding? If it is the same corridor, couldn't the song ending 2-6 be a bridge somehow indicating lapse of time so that it can remain the same and still be understandable as having skipped to December 24?

2-9-44: I suggest a prior judicious use of the Marine's Hymn theme all through the play when it can underscore Fred momentarily. Especially in circumstances requiring his determination (observe his exit with Susan in 1-2-10 where the theme could blend for a few bars with the parade music now in mid-crescendo. The scoring would be intended here to supply an intrepid tone to his resolve to teach Susan how to be a little girl. Again in 1-13-59, in the pause after Doris says "is that clear?," this Marine Hymn scoring will support your direction of Fred as being "thoroughly in hand." Again, what you call Fred's Machiavellian exit as he tiptoes out of the judge's chamber after his eavesdropping scene – could have an impressive Marine Hymn theme. Now go to 2-9-44 in which Fred makes an exit for "Just a fast phone call." I think we have now come to believe it as general underscoring to any of his <u>determined</u> movements or purposes. What I am trying to support and make a big thing out of, is the enormous Marine Hymn underscoring that can be used at the entrance of the emergency Marine mailmen on 2-9-50. Do you dig me, Meredith?)

I have purposely avoided discussing the songs themselves, in this my latest opinionated opinion. I am thinking of structure and clarity of character writing. I understand Bert has a tape, and I'll get with him shortly if you want to hear some more crap from me about numbers. But offhand, on looking over the rundown in the back of the script, it seems to be that you might be overweighted on the subject of Christmas and its concomitant hooplah. Please observe that, although technically the Macy Parade music is not specifically Christmas-y, it predicts Christmas and absorbs light hearted juvenile interest in that manner. It is followed by the favorite of all Christmas songs, "Adeste

Fideles." Shortly thereafter, the expression of peace on earth, good will to men (which is a Christmas-y chestnut in this context), appears voluminously in "Here's Love." Shortly thereafter comes "Pine Cones and Holly Berries," and one song later we are back to a reprise of it, and then once more we are in the <u>related</u> Tinker Bell area with "You Never Can Tell." That's all in the first act. Immediately on embarking on Act Two, we go into "If Santa Claus Was Crazy," followed by "Pine Cones and Holly Berries," both relentlessly pushing the Christmas subject. Skip only one song and we are face to face with "That Man Over There," which hits the subject on the nose, and then "Fa La La Fa," which is a related feint. Shortly we have the next to the last song in the piece, which turns out to be a reprise of "That Man Over There." I think this whole subject is something to examine carefully. Not that they are not artfully devised and placed, but I don't know how this diet will sit with the critics, who are notoriously unaware of purpose when it comes to numbers, or of the technique of their insertion. Couple this possible over-supply on the subject with your proposed "toys coming to life" spectacle[8] this entire thing has been the butt of many a sophisticated joke since "Coppelia" – and you might get some unflattering response from Taubman, Kerr and the rest.[9] I say you might. On the other hand, they might eat it up. But just for fun, look back at "The Music Man" where the prime object and discussion was about boy's bands – a subject to which you related "Trouble," "76 Trombones," and as I recollect at this moment, that's about all. A well-distributed bunch of other songs talked about Gary, Indiana, Lida Rose, the librarian, "Till There Was You," etc. etc. etc. The present line-up may be laboring Christmasiana just a little too much. Then again maybe not. But think about it.

When are you coming here again? Please write me all your dates. Also, of course, whatever reaction to the above remarks.

Love as always,

---

8 The show featured a ballet near the end of the first act in which the toys in Macy's come to life, a showcase for choreographer Michael Kidd.

9 *Coppélia* is a popular ballet by Delibes. The plot focuses on the attraction of a young man to a lifelike doll; his lover dresses as the doll in order to show him his folly. Howard Taubman (1907–1996) and Walter Kerr (1913–1996) were major theatre critics.

1 May 1963: To Milton Kramer

Subject: "IT'S BEGINNING TO LOOK A LOT LIKE CHRISTMAS"

I have glanced at my copy of yours of April 30th to Harold Orenstein with reference to "It's Beginning To Look a Lot Like Christmas." Some sneaking thing tells me that any deal Frank-Rinimer makes as to acquisition of publishing rights in this song, should be in total reliance on its actual ultimate inclusion in the score of "Here's Love" or dramatic contents of the piece, as <u>intended</u>. Certainly none of us, including Meredith Willson, can be sure of all the final contents <u>produced</u>. Whatever the terms turn out to be, is it possible that they can be made on a "no performance-no deal" basis?

5 June 1963: To Milt Kramer and Harold Orenstein

As you both are aware, I have been suffering a continual personal unhappiness over the way the Frank-Rinimer enterprise fails to make the proper, dignified and profitable use of its privileges and rights under the contract. This feeling of mine (which I swallowed at the time) began when Stu Ostrow showed me the proposed papers in which his name appeared. In substance, Stu Ostrow was named as Meredith Willson's designated employee of Frank-Rinimer. In showing the clause to me, Stu was apologetic, but said that Meredith had insisted on it, and I allowed that it was perfectly all right with me. What wasn't all right with me was the implication that Meredith did not quite wish to trust Frank Music in its functions without Stu. Nevertheless, I accepted this idea if it were to give Meredith any comfort.

As you know, a much more serious rankle came into being as a result of the "Molly Brown" motion picture sale, and the subsequent demand for the delivery of synchronization rights. You both know what a blow it was to me personally, to have to knuckle under and deliver the rights, even though along with you I felt that, had we been party to the original negotiation by Meredith's representatives, we could have rescued a great deal more for the publishing enterprise without affecting the amount of cash involved in the overall sale of the play. Since that time, I cannot say I relish the thought of our appearing on the one hand as controllers of rights in the individual songs, and on the other hand unable to negotiate for a license requested by (for instance) United Artists for the use of the song and title "I Ain't Down Yet" in a big Doris Day feature. I quote this impromptu as an example of any number of egg-on-the-face positions we may be obliged to take.

Recently, I have been invited once more to walk in and bite into an empty pie plate. I refer to the present situation with Columbia Records. Apparently, Stu Ostrow completed a cast album deal for "Here's Love." This was done without our knowledge and I have it on good authority that an unusually handsome "artists" percentage was awarded. I understand that Stu accepted Meredith's agreement that he would "cause the mechanical rights to be delivered" – and Columbia in turn accepted Stu Ostrow's promise to make his "best efforts" to see that such was done. Neither the writer nor the producer seem to recollect that Frank-Rinimer had bought quite expensively its right to negotiate for the highest and most effective terms in its favor as to mechanical rights. Judging from the reports I get from you (Kramer) about your "negotiations" for these mechanical rights with Columbia, that firm has the impression that we are now the dogs who are allowed to crawl under the table and pick up the scraps – the banquet having already been devoured. Columbia _must_ have this impression, if it is willing to rely on Meredith's "cause to be delivered" and Stu's "best efforts."

You will note that I refer to _myself_ in most instances above. I think you are aware that I am a very proud (maybe foolishly) man – mostly over having emancipated myself from the ranks of under-the-table mongrels. There is personal prestige involved here, and I feel that this prestige has already lost ground (in [lawyer Rudi] Monta's office at MGM where up till now I have always been an admirable gladiator; and at Columbia Records, who in the past have come to honor and respect my position).

None of this delusion of grandeur in a sea of barracudas has anything to do with dollars or profit. As you both know, my last cast album deal with Victor was a soft touch for them, because I felt like compensating them for their profitless effort on "Greenwillow."[10] I think you are both aware that I could have marched off with a lot bigger bundle elsewhere. I enjoy giving gifts, but I enjoy even more the freedom of choice as to whether or not I want to do so.

To sum it up, no matter how many corporations, attorneys, executives and agents stand between me and people I deal with, I still have to be me, with my own big fat head.

The above history and array of egocentric revelations is what I recited to Meredith Willson at a long meeting this morning at his hotel. It was very painful for me, as I am quite fond of him and probably his most sensitive admirer.

I summed up my story by telling Meredith that I definitely wanted to dissolve Frank-Rinimer.

I told him I had seen copies of the letter from Martin Gang, suggesting a form by which he should instruct various representatives of his to confer with Frank-Rinimer on all pertinent subjects. Although I know this is contrary to your (Harold) agreement with Martin Gang. I firmly advised him not to sign any such thing. Further, I told him I believed in his exercise of autonomy in any possible quarter: I told him that I believed that whatever the most important function to him (motion picture, sale, etc.) it should carry with it the publisher considerations if he so chose. I told him that if he wished to make arbitrary decisions about pre-release personal performances of his pieces, he should be free to do so. I told him if he wished to overweight or underweight either end of a cast album deal (artist vs. mechanical royalties), he should be privileged to do so. BUT I ALSO TOLD HIM THAT UNDER ANY SUCH CIRCUMSTANCES HE COULD NOT DO SO IN PARTNERSHIP OR ANY KIND OF COLLABORATION WITH ME OR ANY OF MY COMPANIES.

I was not just making noise. I truly believe that Meredith has earned the right to call the turn the way he pleases, whether by himself or through those who do his bidding. It is just that I, too, have

---

10 Loesser had given the cast album rights for *How to Succeed* to RCA Victor in acknowledgement of their willingness to record *Greenwillow*, a flop.

also earned the same right to swing it, and neither one of us should be schleppers[11] – in fact or even in appearance.

It seems that Meredith has made a pre-sale of motion picture rights in "Here's Love." I asked him point-blank what the synchronization limitations would be on individual numbers, upon the consummation of the sale to Twentieth-Century Fox. Understandably, he didn't recollect. But I proposed to him that it was 99% sure that the effect of the already prescribed sale terms would be to diminish Frank-Rinimer's capacity to deal in at least the later motion picture uses of the individual songs, if not indeed television to some extent: and almost certainly the sound track album.

It is difficult for me to describe all of Meredith's reactions as we went along. He is an old friend and I am not accustomed to this kind of discussion with him. But generally, I think at first he was surprised at my proposal. Then later, as we exchanged philosophies on the subject (both quite reasonable), he began to understand my feelings and also began to understand that these dilemmas so debasing to me might very easily continue – not through anybody's mean, rotten intentions, but simply because of the way the cookie crumbles at the "point of sale." I think we agreed that we are both dogs and neither of us wants to be a tail.

Meredith's natural concern was how long would a divorce take, and how smoothly could the operation change hands. Naturally, he does not want to get out of stride in the exploitation plans for the score, and I assured him that at least for the time being, the firm would continue to operate full blast, as if no divorce were being planned. This with one possible exception: that I would no doubt advise you (Kramer) to suspend all further talks with Columbia Records. Here I pointed out to Meredith that if the project were entirely his, or his with a new publisher-partner or publisher-agent, that I would prefer, for the sake of my own blessed ego, to let HIM conclude a mechanical license, rather than accept one which did not fully satisfy us.

---

11 Literally, a person who carries or drags something, though colloquially a schlepper can mean a bum, or someone who is stupid or clumsy.

As noted above, this is an absolutely confidential communication. When you have both digested this information, please phone me and be ready for a meeting between just us. The chances are it will fall on Harold's shoulders to get in touch with Meredith's representatives and start some sort of simple annulment agreement. Meredith agreed that it would be perfectly all right for Harold to address Martin Gang on this subject. But in the interest of speed and unanimous understanding, I am going to ask Meredith whether there is anyone else (Morris office?) who should join with Gang and Orenstein so that there is no time lag involved in coast-to-coast confirmations, etc.

Firstly, though, the three of us should meet to try to estimate the time for readjustment, so that we do not in any way impede the progress of the printing, demo-making, etc. – even though we are not to be its final publishers.

Please both phone as soon as you have read this.

Frank Loesser

6 June 1963: To Meredith Willson

Dear Meredith:

The enclosed is my memo rushed to Orenstein and Kramer yesterday. I know it describes my feelings, although an expensive head-shrinker would probably call this a superficial description, a referred rationale implying a long forgotten infantile lust for my grandmother. Anyway, the main thing at the moment, is that I hope it accurately reports our conversation yesterday.

Please observe that there is an afterthought expressed at the end of my note to the colleagues about your letting me know exactly what people I can count on to represent you and your wishes in meeting with Harold. For the sake of avoiding delay, I wouldn't want – let's say – Nat Lefkowitz and Martin Gang to consider this entire matter separately and at different times. That might conceivably keep a lot of papers bucking back and forth, to no one's benefit.

I will phone you tomorrow for your instructions on this. Meantime, in thinking back to your diagramatic description of the relative size and importance of your various elements of output and ownership – I am more and more impressed by what good sense you make, and how lousy you draw. But a man who can write novels and hit musicals, play the flute, lead the band, invent the talking people, and marry a reliable soprano who can travel – doesn't have to draw so good.

Here's love,

10 June 1963: To Meredith Willson

Dear Mer:

I have your note of Thursday and wish to state that your handwriting makes the second paragraph of the Rosetta Stone a thing of crystal clarity. Nevertheless, by virtue of previous practice in understanding your <u>drawing</u>, I managed to decipher your message and wish to report that I love you.

One thing about the "arbitration" correspondence. None of this was arrived at under the pressure of any difficulty between our companies. The MGM sync rights had been delivered grudgingly by my company through H.O.[12] – and only at my personal request that we give in so as to facilitate your movie deal (this was "Molly Brown"). Anyway, it was all over and done when Harold and Martin Gang began a correspondence for the sake of clarifying this sort of difference between them as to interpretation of our contract – against such a time in the future when the same situation might come up again. They continued to differ in a friendly way (I was given the correspondence to read) and it was I who suggested an arbitration IN TIME OF PEACE so that both sides could see eye to eye on this sort of thing in the future. The best I can learn is that Nat Lefkowitz stepped in, advising both sides strongly against such arbitration. But the point is, that there was no battle going on and it seemed like a well-chosen interim in which to ask a third party for an interpretation to which both of us would subscribe for the future. I don't know how all of it was explained to you, or what happens to your special taste buds at the sound of the word "arbitration." I know I'm peculiar about

---

12 Harold Orenstein.

hearing the word "heartstrings" in a lyric. I see bleeding ganglia before my eyes and hate hate hate it – but really it is a harmless word overused by poets, and certainly not intended to provoke some special allergy of mine.

I gather that our representatives are in touch with each other these moments. I just hope they dig each other as well as you and I do.

How was Cedric[13] and the city of Dallas? Now that you are back on the firing line, I wonder whether you would have time to look at the sound-light thing that Stu and the director saw. I hope you get a chance to look. If not for this, maybe some other some time.

Here's love,

FL

15 July 1963: To Harold Orenstein

Dear Harold:

Following your talk with me, I have received a copy of the memo from Martin Gang to you dated July 12. I will have to be reasonably brief as I am trying to write something that does me a lot of good (my musical) and not Meredith Willson.

Make note of Martin Gang's first, second, and third paragraph to you. In proposing to reiterate the essence of personal agreement between Meredith and me, Martin seems to refer to the essential agreement as a <u>supplemental one</u>. I understand his caution, but I wish you would adjust the co-legal sights so that all of us once more understand clearly that caution was already thrown to the winds by Meredith when he proposed that I would be the last word on his agreement concerning, or in any way affecting music or lyrics, etc.

I think all parties and representatives must bear in mind that my object is to gain and preserve the very best status, safety, and earnings for the properties administered by the FRANK-RINIMER properties.

---

13 Cedric Willson (1900–1975), Meredith's older brother.

Is there then, a way to express the limited way in which my approvals are to be exercised? If this formula was carefully expressed, I would never have the right to make broad, arbitrary, or even a tiny self serving prohibition upon Meredith's wishes. Even then, let us say there should arise some dispute. Is it possible to name a third party as "arbitrator" under these circumstances? Upon the application of such arbitration, this party could immediately limit debate, comment, etc., to the area circumscribed by the personal approval agreement. As Martin puts it, this third party would have to be impartial, fair-minded and knowledgeable. His knowledgeability, may I add, would have to include the area of song copyright, its longevity and its variety of earning opportunity. Above all the "arbitrator" would have to be someone who understood that RINIMER has <u>one</u> lifetime partner on a 50-50 profit sharing basis, and that is FRANK.

I would not care at all to follow Martin's suggestion about a termination formula. This entire expression of enormous good faith on Meredith's part was made in an effort to <u>avoid</u> termination.

Let me add one personal footnote: I would like to volunteer here, that my knowledge of the difference between a cart and a horse was shown pretty clearly when I insisted (against your judgment) upon giving in to MGM in the matter of free delivery of synchronization rights in the "Molly Brown" sale. I hope not to have to do it again. It is my personal belief that the sale need not have taken place in such a hurry. It was true that offers were not pouring in. But I neglected to make any sale. Especially since, as I recall, Meredith was not necessarily inclined to be thoughtful and loving to any of his co-beneficiaries at that time. All these things are a matter of judgment, and I think I will be adding mine from time to time. Sometimes possibly in an effort to curb the urgency to make a fast sale. Here I would be doing nothing less than I do for myself, and it is with some pride that I note that each successive offer for motion picture rights to "The Most Happy Fella" has been substantially larger. Maybe I am waiting for the new Caruso. Maybe Meredith should have waited for the new Judy Garland. Maybe Irving Berlin was very smart during his later and not-so-freshly-productive years to have been able to make a motion picture sale – and a whopper – out of the simple fact that he was still entitled to deal with the title, words, and music of "Alexander's Ragtime Band" – or in conclusion, Mr. Bones,[14] – which would you rather be free to deal in all your life, "Knickerbocker Holiday" or "September Song"?[15]

You tell me Mickey Rudin[16] will be there this week. Please add the above notes to your discussion with him. If you feel like it, I have no objection to you showing him this entire letter.

Thanks and love,

On 7 July 1963 Lewis Funke of the *New York Times* reported that Meredith Willson had an idea for a new musical to follow *Here's Love*:

Charity begins at home and sometimes, too, ideas for musicals. Here is Meredith Willson this morning making up his mind that the next show he writes will deal with the life of his Russian-born wife and how he courted her ... Mr. Willson will do the music, lyrics and book ... The working title is "My Darling," sentimental to be sure, but unusable for Broadway because it already is the name of a popular song.

What makes Mr. Willson think he has the ingredients for his biographical–autobiographical notion? This is the way he tells it. In the days of the Russian upheaval, the Mrs. Willson-to-be was sent to Mexico from Leningrad (or St. Petersburg) by her parents, whom she never saw again. She had talent, early recognized, and as she grew older she entered the professional ranks of the theater as actress and singer.

---

14 A reference to a line from Irving Berlin's minstrel number in *Ziegfeld Follies of 1919*, reused on screen in *White Christmas* (1954).
15 Irving Berlin's hit song 'Alexander's Ragtime Band' (1911). The 1938 film of the same name is unlikely to be what Loesser had in mind; instead, the later movies *White Christmas* (1954) and *There's No Business Like Show Business* (1954) both feature songs from Berlin's back catalogue. 'September Song' is a hit number from Kurt Weill and Maxwell Anderson's rarely revived musical *Knickerbocker Holiday* (1938).
16 Milton A. 'Mickey' Rudin (1920–1999) was a famous entertainment lawyer with clients including Frank Sinatra.

In 1936 she arrived in San Francisco with a troupe performing "Mistress of the Inn." She was the comedian, and the role was changed somewhat to enable her also to sing. A scout for the National Broadcasting Company heard her and asked her to perform for his musical director. The musical director, too busy to attend the audition, heard her by remote control and hired her. The musical director later met her – the musical director being Meredith Willson.[17]

15 July 1963: To Mona Lipp

Dear Mona:

Thanks for warding off Selma Tamber.[18] I have heard nothing yet.

I have made note of the new Lipp address and phone number.

I note with some alarm your report on Willson's next musical [pen annotation:] and subject. Do we have a spare Anastasia[19] to play Rini?

Love

On 30 July *Here's Love* had its world premiere in Detroit. A review in *Variety* began by saying it was 'headed for success' but added a surprising caveat: 'its chances for success hinge mainly on elements which [Meredith] Willson inherited from other creative artists. Willson's music and lyrics, plus casting errors, are the principal obstacles to achievement of his third hit, following "The Music Man" and "Unsinkable Molly Brown".[20] No wonder Willson was considering taking on a lengthy television series, which he would present, as a departure from his work for the stage; no wonder, too, that he clarified his formal relationship with Loesser so that he would have support and advice on his existing activities. The suggestion for the

---

17 Lewis Funke, 'Meredith Willson Plans New Musical', *New York Times*, 7 July 1963, X1.
18 Selma Tamber (1907–1991), producer and manager.
19 A reference to Wright and Forrest's current project, *Anya*, based on the (Russian) Anastasia legend.
20 Tew., 'Shows Out of Town: Here's Love', *Variety* 231/10 (31 July 1963), 104.

series had come from the advertising and production agency Benton and Bowles, and the show would last for six months.

Sensing that *Here's Love* required further work before Broadway, Loesser was anxious that Willson not agree to a big television project before it opened in New York. He visited the Washington, DC tryout in September to provide further advice, and was so busy that he failed to greet the production's star, Hollywood veteran Janis Paige (1922–2024), familiar from the film *Silk Stockings* (1957).

As the months went on, tensions once more emerged in the relationships between Loesser, Willson and their representatives, and a big meeting was scheduled in January 1964 to thrash out how they would work together in the future, including the future of the Frank-Rinimer company.

24 July 1963: To Meredith Willson

Dear Meredith:

First of all, happy Detroit!

Kramer tells me on the phone that you sang some new goodies to him. Also let me report that the thing I hear most abundantly on Muzak from coast to coast, in airports, elevators, men's rooms and restaurants – is of all things – "Lida Rose."[21] It gives me special pleasure.

The other day I had a wonderful meeting with Martin Gang. On the subject of the personal agreement between you and me, Martin and I are in what seems to be perfect accord. Through him, as well as through copies of "deal" correspondence between Lefkowitz and Orenstein – I gather that there is some TV series being thought about, with you at the helm. Putting aside all "deal" details, the idea of such a thing for you – to be decided on now – is quite frightening. Martin Gang had the same impression, and just this morning on the phone, Kramer expressed a worry on his own about your important productivity and its possible diminution. Diminution is a legal word. Diminution from one to ten, is what it sounds like when you say it fast.

---

21 From Meredith Willson's *The Music Man*.

Anyway, being totally ignorant of what the TV thing is, who brought it up, how it involves you and your talents – I can only express the vague uneasiness I have described.

I know you are not going to stop in mid work to explain it to me, but you're the only one I would want to hear it from since I can't trust anyone else to give me a true picture of your artistic, career and public relations purposes.

Question: Can the whole TV subject be hung-up until after your New York opening? Or have you already given a nod as to your availability? Have you been invited to do this? Or are you being sold? If the latter is the case, would it hurt to keep the whole thing very loose and tentative until "Here's Love" opens?

Again, I beg you to understand that I am reporting a hunch of mine. I haven't anything else to go by.

Just now I have a short greeting from Stu, suggesting that maybe I can come to Detroit. Answering him through you, I will try like mad to get there – if not, certainly Washington.

Please give thanks and love to Stu, also of course to you. None to them fat-ass stage mothers.[22]

13 September 1963: To Janis Paige

Dear Janis:

I guess you're aware that I saw your show Wednesday night last in Washington. My first purpose in writing this note is to apologize for not saying hello, but the time was terribly short and I had to rush to a late late meeting with Meredith and Stu.

But saying hello isn't all. What I wanted to tell you now is how marvelously I thought you did the part. And I mean marvelously. I guess I used up plenty of conference time later exclaiming about this to the writer and director. Truly, I was enormously impressed, and even carried away. And remember, I am familiar with the script and

---

22 The cast of *Here's Love* featured a number of children, hence the presence of several 'stage mothers' in Willson's vicinity.

songs of this show in all its phases since the very beginning and so there were no great literary surprises for me. Janice [sic], you really dood it. I never really visualized the Doris character until I saw and heard you and in every department you gave me great pleasure. Thanks and of course my wishes for a huge success. I will be coming to Philadelphia to rave some more.

   Fondly,

10 October 1963: To Meredith Willson

Dear Meredith:

  This is to clarify my thinking about the whole proposal by Benton and Bowles – for a "Meredith Willson" show. We didn't have much time to gas over either your thinking or mine on the whole subject, even though we walked up Fifth Avenue quite slowly – so I want to repeat a few things and possibly make clearer what my general point of view is.

  What we witnessed was a very well organized agency-to-sponsor pitch through which client was to appreciate and to refresh his recollection of the importance of one Meredith Willson. All this with the aim that they should subscribe to the agency thinking and "buy" the idea. From all I could gather they proposed a rather magnificent full hour show which would be performed weekly – and that in this show Meredith Willson would be the central personality. You will recall that aside from the official prospectus, the agency man (at the moment I forget his name) implied that you would have complete command and control of the goings on.

  I was quick to tell you, as we walked away, that I considered the proposed plan as an invitation to slavery. Knowing you as I do, I'm sure that you would not allow your name to be applied to anything you did not have total control over. And with you, control is an infinite, fussy and highly personal matter. You are not as cool as Ed Sullivan, who is hardly comparable to you as an artist. And yet he experiences a full week's work before each of his shows, simply for the sake of coming off smoothly between the imported juggling act and the celebrated football hero, and then again between the football hero and the emergence of Maria Callas or whatever. He has a simple job compared to the one proposed for you and still he has to sweat all week. And so I shuddered and still do, at what your twenty-six successive weeks (no doubt with options for more) would be like if you accepted the job as described.

Now I'm aware that the agency man made it clear to you that the actual show format could differ from what he proposed – subject to your wishes. Yet it seemed evident that they did want something BIG. You yourself remarked on the incapacity of the home town television screen for making massive stage personnel or giant scenic stuff effective. Yet my feeling is that bigness may be the very heart of what the agency is trying to sell – and my fear is that it would be too much for you, and not very gratifying in the long run. But in all fairness, it might be a good idea if the Morris office inquired at Benton and Bowles whether they wish to present any variables in the "Meredith Willson" scheme. Possibly they have one more comfortable for you and still within the range of bigness they seem to be approaching the client with.

Let's look at the whole idea of a "Meredith Willson" show in a purely theoretical manner for the moment; such a show should succeed in creating and sustaining a proper and indelible impression of you. Looking back recall to mind Hoagy Carmichael's Sherman's March to the Sea.[23] The shortest possible line has been drawn between the person and his work. I believe that any public appearance of yours should help shorten that line for you. Right now Meredith Willson's "Music Man" is pretty much established. Nevertheless, it may not turn out to be your finest work or your longest lasting. If we had stopped too early with Kern, it would have to be Jerry Kern's "They Didn't Believe Me"[24] or with Carmichael it might have been Carmichael's "Washboard Blues" or with Sherman it

---

23 Carmichael appeared in the TV show *Laramie* (1959), about the Sherman brothers, whose father Matt was accused of aiding the Confederates during the American Civil War.
24 Jerome Kern's 'They Didn't Believe Me' was his earliest hit (1914) but was superseded by various more famous songs. Similarly, Carmichael's 'Washboard Blues' was one of his early hits, from 1925.

might have been <u>Sherman's</u> 1859 address to the volunteers. Now in connection with this I'm not merely discussing song composition or show writing. Examine, if you please, a colleague's accomplishment called the Waring Blendor.[25] Or look at Dr. Spock, who is better known at Womrath's than he is at any hospital.[26] To put the whole thing more bluntly, I believe whatever you undertake publicly should be clearly of your own invention, embodying your own personality and real talents – and not making use simply of your already established importance. A clear and lasting picture of you should be drawn. Major Bowes[27] did it for himself – and lately Mitch Miller[28] showed up as something unique enough. But I'm not quite sure about the difference between Jack Paar, Johnny Carson, Steve Allen, or any of the other desk sitters and visitor welcomers.[29] I think that if they all keep it up they will be one mashed and vague memory. But there is only one Meredith Willson and he should get more luminous as himself, rather than somehow get lost in the hopper.

The above must not be considered as some complete damnation of the Benton and Bowles idea to present you. Rather I would like you to think of it as the basis by which the Morris office can inquire about a format more specifically Willson-like and more related to your actual creativity. Please make time to talk to me about this kind of thing on your next trip to New York.

Here's love,

---

25 Bandleader Fred Waring (1900–1984) also promoted a kitchen blender called the Waring Blendor, launched in 1938.

26 Dr Benjamin McLane Spock (1903–1998) was the author of the book *Baby and Child Care* (1946), one of the best-selling books of the twentieth century. Loesser is joking that Spock is better known in bookstores like Womrath's than for his clinical work as a paediatrician.

27 Edward Bowes (1874–1946) was a radio personality known for the long-running *Major Bowes Amateur Hour* (1935–1952).

28 Conductor and producer Mitch Miller (1911–2010) was at that time enjoying enormous success with his own television show, *Sing Along with Mitch* (1961–1964), on NBC.

29 Jack Paar (1918–2004), Johnny Carson (1925–2005) and Steve Allen (1921–2000) were hosts of the late-night NBC talk show, *The Tonight Show*.

10 October 1963: To Meredith Willson

Dear Meredith:

About our last conversation regarding our personal contract. A lot of time has gone by since your decision to play completely into my devil hands – and although Martin Gang's office long ago gave it its blessing, there still seemed to be some cautions emanating from the director of the Morris office. You told me you had made it very clear to them that you wanted to give me complete approval of every last thing, and promised to tell them again like it was Lenny about the rabbits.[30] I can understand all their trepidations but what they don't dig is the fact that I'm the real Rini. Please tell them again.

Of course the Gang office will want to iron out with Orenstein the method for handling total, stolid, immovable, stubborn, beady-eyed disagreement between you and me. But I understand that this sort of formula is well on its way between the lawyers. While you are once more telling the Morris office who you love, I will be checking into the progress on technique for avoiding stalemates.

Here's love,

P.S. It occurs to me that Martin has been sending the Morris office carbons of his communications to you on this subject. What then seems to happen is that Nat Lefkowitz – regarding these carbons as invitations to make criticisms and objections – then phones Orenstein for further consultation. My impression is that Gang's forwarding of these carbons is intended as a business courtesy and nothing more – and I think this is quite proper except that it then behooves Lefkowitz to get in touch with you, and tell you whatever he considers the potential pitfalls to be. After listening carefully, it is then your privilege to tell him that you know that there are plenty of dangerous possibilities – but that your entire object was to take the chance. If you and I didn't truly trust one another, you wouldn't even give me balcony seats.

---

30 Lennie in Steinbeck's *Of Mice and Men*. He is intellectually disabled and is fixated on petting rabbits, so much so that he accidentally kills them.

29 October 1963: To Meredith Wilson

Dear Meredith:

We are waltzing around and around – to an orchestration which once again is getting thick with cautious outcries and enharmonic inner voices which threaten the pure sweet quality of the original tune.

That original tune was whistled by you and it was based on personal faith and trust in me. Before accepting, I warned you over and over again about the possible dangers of putting so much "power" into my hands. In response, you said you trusted me, and that was that. So I agreed to take the enormous array of responsibilities – the most important being a <u>moral</u> one.

In thinking about it later, I became less frightened about the job that was supposed to lie ahead. After all, you were merely returning a compliment. <u>I</u> had already expressed trust and faith within the company agreement. Nowhere were you obliged to write big hits, or even write anything at all. Expenses? My side would gladly advance them. Go along with your whims about sharing something that was already mine ("Music Man") to have and to hold? Of course!

Now back to our waltz. I feel that I, and I alone was and am entitled to warn you about my possible villainy. I do not believe these considerations should be within the province of your agents and lawyers or mine – except for erecting one technique for arbitration, and another against the event of my absence or non-existence. On the question of will Frank Loesser rob, cheat, discriminate against, or neglect Meredith Wilson – I think they should all keep very quiet.

Now I have in hand a copy of Martin's October 25th memo to Harold. I regret to tell you that I find Martin full of misapprehensions and inclined to suggest harmonic impurities in our waltz. In your speech to me about "even buying a cement company" I couldn't detect the sound of any kazoo parts.

Now I also have in hand the carbon of Martin Gang's letter to Nat Lefkowitz – which you sent me for my personal information. It says that you had come to a final conclusion and had asked Gang to communicate it, and that your position is that you made a deal with

Frank Loesser and that if you had the decision to make at this time you would make the same one. Later in this memo, however, Martin quotes you as feeling that the October 25th memo sets forth the basic arrangements you made with me. My darling Meredith, I submit that it doesn't at all. I want everything you told me you would give me, and I expect you to trust me to be a nice fellow, as well as an able one, just like I trust you to write smashes. Please please think about this. If you have changed your mind I would like to hear it from <u>you</u>.

And remember I love you, even though there isn't a nickel in it.

> Frank Loesser

P.S. What is this noise about your leaving the Morris office and changing to another agency? If it isn't so, there certainly should be no such hints. In their way they have worked very hard for you.

30 October 1963: To Meredith Willson (Telegram)

PLEASE DISREGARD POSTSCRIPT OF MY LETTER OF OCTOBER 29TH. I MADE MISTAKEN INFERENCE AS A RESULT OF HEARING DISCUSSIONS WHICH TURNED OUT NOT TO BE ABOUT YOU AND MORRIS. UNDERSTAND YOU WILL BE IN NEW YORK SOON. WILL EXPLAIN MY ERROR THEN.

> LOVE,
> FRANK LOESSER

11 November 1963: To Martin Gang

Dear Martin:

As a result of our phone conversation last Friday, I intended to ask Harold to prepare some sort of wording for clauses covering future agreements to be made by Meredith (in connection with motion picture rights of Broadway shows). Nevertheless, I have changed my mind about asking him this – but decided rather to abide the event of our four-way meeting – at which we can include this subject. There may be reasons why a rigid wording should not be subscribed to in advance.

Also, I believe that Meredith and you and Harold and I will have to begin deciding things on a much broader basis. The main purpose of this meeting will be to clear the air with regard to interpretation of the Rinimer-Frank contract. I am sure that this will be an easy matter if all four of us sit together. After that, I see no reason why Meredith's "Handshake proposal" should not be the simplest way to do things. So I urge the end-of-the-month meeting. I understand that Meredith and Rini will be coming in to perform on "The Ed Sullivan Show," and I am given to understand that this should be early in December.[31] For the sake of everybody concerned, please join him here. Keep in mind that as I told you, I would have to be away from New York from November 25th through Monday, December 2nd. I'm free for a meeting or meetings before or after this period. With thanks,

Sincerely,

11 December 1963: To Martin Gang

Dear Martin:

I understand from Meredith that the third week in January will be convenient for you and himself and therefore I will make it so for me. How about Monday 20th? There are, in my mind three basic agenda items. Firstly, a definition of Meredith's personal relationship with me and a system for consultation at the very very beginning, where they count. Secondly, a review of the Rinimer-Frank relationship for the purpose of establishing the same interpretation on both sides and rewording the document to make that meeting-of-the-minds clear. Thirdly, Meredith and I should have a meeting by ourselves to discuss the future in terms of artistic endeavor, career imagery, etc. The first two subjects should be discussed among four people: yourself, Meredith, Harold and me. I will serve coffee. When all is agreed, I will serve booze.

Please check this with Meredith, and both of you confirm the date of January 20th. Possibly, in order to discuss everything very thoroughly we will require a total of three successive days. I would like to allow for that anyway.

Fondest regards,

---

31 No evidence of such an appearance has been found.

For Christmas 1963 Willson sent Loesser a supply of his favourite snack: Corn Nuts. Introduced to the United States by Albert Holloway in 1936, they consist of roasted corn kernels. The company was owned by the Holloway family until 1998.

27 December 1963: To Meredith Willson

Dear Sir:

In one of Mr. Loesser's relatively lucid moments before we pumped him out, he requested that we forward to you his thanks for your Christmas gift. As you know, his is a serious addiction. Frankly, we have a much easier time with the heroin and marijuana patients. With Mr. Loesser it is a seasonal yet very violent addiction, and it seems to overpower him at this time of year. He was fortunate to come under our care, as the state allows only one Corn Nuts patient to a floor, and we had an opening. (This opening had been made in the brick wall of the ward by previous Corn Nuts patients who persisted in batting their heads against it.)

As matters now stand, your friend Frank is still shrieking piteously for more Corn Nuts, but the physical symptoms have subsided a little, and we don't think we'll have to have him here much longer than January 20th. That is, providing some well-meaning crony doesn't hoist another bucket of the stuff to his window.

As you well know, there are pushers all over, and authorities seem to agree that they acquire the stuff in Southern California somewhere. Realizing that you are a resident of that area, as well as a well-wisher of Frank Loesser's, we take the liberty here of asking whether you can shed any light on the actual source. Possibly you have been offered a shot of Corn Nuts by some furtive stranger in the night. If you can recollect any incident that will shed some light on this traffic in possibly the world's most habit-forming drug, we would be pleased if you would report to your local FBI, who will then add to our (and the rest of the medical world's) array of evidence against the culprits.

Mr. Loesser shows some curious withdrawal symptoms in about the second week of treatment. He doesn't want to eat any more Corn

Nuts, but likes to walk around in it barefoot. It gives him a sort of a harmless comfort, and toward indulging him in this way we keep a small supply of the stuff for trampling purposes. Our only problem is keeping the fact of this special supply and its whereabouts from the knowledge of our orderlies. Let me confess here that our orderlies are in many respects disorderly orderlies, and are given to sneaking some of the Corn Nuts even after it has been thoroughly crunched by the feet of people like Mr. Loesser. To be quite candid, I myself like the taste of it and happen to prefer the pre-trampled kind. It may be pleasant for you to learn that I consider Mr. Loesser's feet the cleanest I've ever had here at the Hospital. But that's possibly because he licks his toes very carefully after every "withdrawal mambo," as we archly call it.

Well, I'll have to close now, although I have enjoyed this chat, and I'm sure you will be glad to have heard through me of Mr. Loesser's gratitude for your Christmas gift, whatever it was. My haste in closing is occasioned by the sound of a scurry in the next office. Apparently the orderlies have unlocked the Corn Nuts bin and I'm not going to be the one that's left out. I've been here 37 years as a specialist in this field, and I've had my share every time. Don't be alarmed, I'm a very cautious and reasonable man, and don't overdo it to the point of addiction. Goodbye now.

Sincerely,
Blimpton (Fats) Goober
Social Service Division

Here's Love opened on Broadway on 3 October 1963 to decidedly mixed reviews. Critics tended to acknowledge that it was an audience pleaser but had deep flaws. *Variety*'s reviewer remarked: 'Willson isn't a master of dramatic structure and dialog, and "Here's Love" wobbles and staggers disconcertingly at times as promising situations are bungled and potential laughs are lost in the faulty writing and producer Stuart Ostrow's inept staging. Willson's songs are astonishingly so-whattish, without a real audience-stampeder in the lot. As usual with the composer, the lively tunes tend to be better than the slower ones. In the case of the lyrics, the straight numbers are better than the mediocre attempts at clever patter.'[32] This critique seems a little harsh, and others were deeply critical too (in the *New York Herald Tribune* Walter Kerr said that it required editing and 'a sense of style'), but it reflects the show's difficult journey to Broadway: producer Ostrow had to replace the original director Norman Jewison,[33] and he and Willson did their best to keep the ship afloat during a difficult rehearsal and tryout period. The show only ran one season, but it covered its costs.

2 January 1964: To Meredith Willson

Dear Meredith:

I had a nice long chat with Walter Kerr New Year's Eve, some of it about you and your show. Remind me to report to you on this when we see each other late this month. Meanwhile, did you ever get my buttery letter?

Love,

In January 1964 Willson showed some interest in allowing a reprint of his 1938 textbook *What Every Young Musician Should Know* (New York: Robbins Music Corp.). Subtitled 'A Concise and Modern Volume Revealing the Inside of Radio Musical Technique', it aimed to supplement the numerous books available on harmony and counterpoint with a practical guide to contemporary music making. In the foreword, he explained some of the questions he aimed to answer: 'How can you make a printed arrangement sound like a special? What are some simple rules for segueing from one chorus to another? With the modern instrumentation consisting so largely of brass, how can the strings be used most effectively to blend with saxophones, trumpets and trombones? How do you write a drum part? What are the signs used in a radio studio? What are the definitions of

---

32 Hobe., 'Shows on Broadway: Here's Love,' *Variety* 232/7 (9 October 1963), 54.
33 Norman Jewison (1926–2024), Canadian film director and producer known for *The Russians are Coming, the Russians are Coming* (1966), *The Thomas Crown Affair* (1968), *Fiddler on the Roof* (1971) and *Jesus Christ Superstar* (1973), among others.

some of the new musical terms which have been born in the popular orchestras of the day?'

23 January 1964: To Meredith Willson

Dear Meredith:

About the subject of that textbook of yours published by Robbins (at least I think you said Robbins).

Apparently, you indicated to them your willingness to assign the renewal period to them, and also to rewrite and augment. Although any new writing contribution on your part at this date would be a technical violation of your contract with your own publishing house, I can see where this would be permissible. I realize that there would be no point in being too rigid about prohibiting your re-polishing of an old brass doorknob.

On the other hand, from what you tell me, in the twenty odd years since the first publication of this instruction book, or whatever it is – there has been no success at all in its marketing. For this reason I am led to believe that Robbins is making use of a perfectly honest and proper opportunism in seeking a new fresh edition which would bear the name Meredith Willson at a time when that name carries many times more importance, popularity and authority than it did many years ago at the birth of the first edition. Further, according to what you told me, you seemed to have in mind broadening the scope and potential market for this piece of work so that it would appeal to a far greater population of buyers than could have been imagined to exist in the thirties.

So altogether it appears that an almost wholly new work may come into existence – and the idea is that you should do all the writing, editing, re-titling, etc. Also I recall that there were no guarantees or royalties offered in advance or any fees for your services.

Now I don't think that there is anything radically <u>wrong</u> with any of the above. Also, I hasten to tell you that I do not like to hear about discontinuity of relationship between publisher and writer who have behaved in good faith – just because of a law that separates the copyright life into two periods. Nevertheless, since our outfit is permanently and pointedly and sanguinely (is there such a word?) in the Meredith Willson business, I suggest that the following arrangement of things would be quite fair:

You do the job as described loosely above, ask for no advance royalties, bonuses or fees but limit the length of time of the publishing license to a period of five, seven, or at the most ten years; also limit the territory to the United States and Canada. Also, just for luck, you might reserve your exclusive right to perform and demonstrate the contents of the work via any of the media (recordings, motion pictures, television, radio and live lecture or concerts). I say this because the prose writing is likely, as usual, to be an extension of your own unique personality just as your various non-musical books have been. I would not like to see it made available for performance by Leonard Bernstein, or either Damrosch,[34] or some profession we haven't heard about yet.

Like I said, we are in the Meredith Willson business in depth. The object finally, of course, would be for you to assign the work to your own worthy company after Robbins' period has expired. Robbins will have had ample time to prove itself a great promotion and sales organization or otherwise. If so it will have gotten sufficiently rich and proud. If not, the big red ballroom will have been forward passed to your own company with a happy flourish, and perhaps a sigh of relief.

If you like what I am talking about at all, I suggest that you ask your agents to bring it up with Robbins – after first conferring with our Milton Kramer about his thoughts as well as his collaboration in expressing the details of the final deal. If, on the other hand, you don't like what I'm saying, please phone me. I'm not lonesome, it's just that I adore your voice.

Here's love,

---

34 Conductor Frank Damrosch (1859–1937) founded the New York Institute of Musical Art, which became Juilliard. His brother Walter (1852–1950) was a more distinguished conductor, whose work included over forty years at the helm of the New York Symphony Orchestra. Their father Leopold (1832–1885) was also a major conductor.

29 January 1964: To Meredith Willson

Dear Meredith:

Enclosed please find a roll of music tape left over by Mozart after "The Marriage of Figaro." He made so few mistakes he had this 600 inches remaining in his desk drawer. As a matter of fact, research reveals that the small quantity he did indeed use, was to cover up his billing on the original cast album so that people would think Goddard Lieberson[35] had done the whole thing out of his own head. Mozart was a generous and modest man. Finding both these qualities in you, we feel that you alone should be the heir to this little treasure. Also, we are sure you know the technique of applying this stuff. Being an ex-flautist you are sure to have a constant supply of saliva to apply to the backside. Not just anybody's backside. The tape, the tape! Pay attention!

As you may know, Mozart is no longer with the firm, and so we expect all our marvels from you.

Here's love,

Broido and Loesser

Token-of-Esteem division

By April 1964, with *Here's Love* coming towards the end of its run (25 July), Willson revived the idea of television shows. However, he seems to have been persuaded to be more modest in his ambitions: instead of twenty-six episodes, he would appear in just three specials for *Texaco Star Parade* on CBS-TV. Each would feature a mixture of talk and performances, focusing partly on Willson's work and partly on variety show-style guest performances of standards by other writers. The first special aired on 10 June and included Meredith and Rini, Robert Preston, actor-singer Sergio Franchi (1926–1990), recording artist Caterina Valente (born 1931) and the Young Americans (thirty-six young choristers). *Variety* said 'the result was an agreeable if not altogether buoyant hour for the family trade',

---

35 Goddard Lieberson (1911–1977) was president of Columbia Records and producer of cast albums including *My Fair Lady*.

adding in criticism: 'The less eupeptic moments were supplied by the Music Man himself. He simply shucked the corn a little too diligently, and by the third or fourth repetition of "viewer dear," the just-folks aura tended to hang there like a pall.'[36] The second special was broadcast on 28 June and featured Debbie Reynolds (1932–2016) in promotion of the new film of *The Unsinkable Molly Brown*, alongside actor-comedian Phil Harris (1904–1995), country singer Molly Bee (1939–2009) and the barbershop quartet The Sidewinders. This time, a different *Variety* reviewer was more enthusiastic: 'Refreshing is the word – and that goes both for Willson's easy, on-the-cob style of hostmanship and for the rich nostalgic flavor of the presentation itself.'[37]

A month later, on 28 July, the third special aired and included young singers Jack Jones (born 1938) and Vicki Carr (born 1940). A review noted a change of direction in the show: 'This was less an "and then I wrote" stanza than the others, which was probably why it came closer to being a run-of-the-mill video musicale. That spell of yesteryear's smalltown America that Willson can create so well, and which had been the distinctive ingredient of the two earlier shows (not to exclude his stage musicals), was written out of the script. This time the accent was contemporary, with Willson citing today's youth as the best generation ever, illustrating that theme with such currently hot singers as Jack Jones and Vicki Carr and underscoring it with marching and calisthenic performances by the U.S. Marines at Camp Pendleton.'[38] Loesser explained at length to Willson why he felt this was not a good direction for his career, and by August 1964 the pair were planning to meet up to discuss future plans.

13 April 1964: To Meredith Willson

Dear Meredith:

I have looked over the copy of the Mark Twain narration you left with me before your departure. Since that moment I hear[d] from

---

36 'Television Reviews: The Star Parade', *Variety* 235/3 (10 June 1964), 30.
37 'Tele Follow-Up Comment', *Variety* 235/7 (8 July 1964), 29.
38 'Tele Follow-Up', *Variety* 235/11 (5 August 1964), 40.

Milt Kramer that you have decided not to take this narrating job, and so whatever I have to say here is of no great importance. At the same time, I think it is only fair to tell you that I see nothing at all wrong with the writing. Let me add, though, that it may not be anywhere near perfect for recital <u>by yourself</u> – whereas it might be quite fine for Deems Taylor or maybe Hugh Downs.[39]

Generally speaking, I feel that whatever emanates from your colorful kisser should not only have been invented by you – but should appear to be occuring to you at the moment. So there's your assignment for the next fifty years.

I might as well report to you in this letter that this noon I received a mimeographed copy of a proposed contract between Rinimer and Texaco. This was forwarded by the William Morris Office. I will be taking it home tonight for studying and will make whatever remarks I have to make (along with those by Milt Kramer) as quickly as I have been able to digest what's in it. Milt did not receive a copy, so he will have to share mine and will no doubt have had a look at it by tomorrow.

I got your Sunday message and I knew there would be no point in phoning you back. Thank you for the reassurance, which made me sleep more soundly last night, knowing that Milt would have the new manuscript in his hands by today.

Dolce Far Plenty,[40]

12 May 1964: To Meredith Willson (Telegram)

DEAR MEREDITH MUSIC THEATRE AND MORRIS OFFICE HAVE ONLY ONE POINT OF DISAGREEMENT ON "HERE'S LOVE." WITHOUT EVEN TELLING YOU WHAT IT IS I AM HEREBY REQUESTING YOU TO INSTRUCT MORRIS TO GIVE IN ON THIS LAST ITEM. I EXPECT YOU WILL COMPLY SIMPLY OUT OF FAITH IN ME AND MY NOTIONS ABOUT WHAT IS FAIR. I AM ASKING

---

39 Deems Taylor (1885–1966), composer, critic and radio personality. Hugh Downs (1921–2020), radio and television broadcaster.

40 A reference to the song 'Dolce far niente' from *The Unsinkable Molly Brown*.

YOU TO DECIDE IN FAVOR OF THE AGENCY WHICH PAYS CASH IN ADVANCE AS OPPOSED TO THE ONE WHICH DOES NOT. THE TWO OFFICES HAVE PUT IN ENTIRELY TOO MUCH TIME ON THIS. ESPECIALLY THE ONE WHICH WILL BE CHARGED WITH DOING THE HARD WORK AND THEN PAYING OVER A SHARE OF COMMISSIONS TO THE OTHER. PLEASE JUST TRUST ME ON THIS. REMEMBER MY REACTION TO BEING THE GARBAGE CAN LAST SUMMER. I DON'T WANT THE FEELING TO COME BACK AND NEITHER DO YOU.
> LOVE,
> FRANK LOESSER

4 June 1964: To Meredith Willson (Telegram)

HERE'S LOVE AND GOOD LUCK
> FRANK LOESSER

(Date not specified; probably 5 June 1964): From Jo and Frank Loesser to Meredith Willson (Telegram)

WE LOVED YOU LAST NIGHT AND WE STILL DO THIS MORNING.
> JO AND FRANK

(Date not specified): To Meredith Willson (Telegram)

MY DARLING MEREDITH, I AM IN THE MIDDLE OF A THOUSAND PAGE HAND WRITTEN LETTER TO YOU AND HAVE TO CONTINUE IT IN THE COUNTRY. MEANWHILE THIS IS TO TELL YOU HOW MUCH I ENJOYED THE SECOND SHOW. PLEASE WAIT FOR LETTER.
> LOVE TO YOU AND RINI,
> FRANK

Undated, handwritten (c. 30 June 1964):
To Meredith Willson[41]

Dear Meredith–

This will be a sort of (accordion-pleated) ∧(hahaha!) compilation of my thoughts about the Willson career – past, present + future – now that I have seen the second instalment of The Texaco show.

I wish to tell you, first of all, that I liked it much better than I had the first program. I don't know all the reasons why, but one is that you seemed to be more AT HOME in it. Strangely enough, however, this time Rini seemed less intime [sic] – but I think that was because of a heavier and more formal vocal assignment – and WOW! How she sang! I mean "For the Gloaming" [sic].[42] She sure gloamed – and that was plenty rewarding! I just sort of wished that the spot had been arrived at more intimately. Your choice of the barbershop group was marvelous. I have NEVER heard better – and that includes the Buffalo Bills.[43] Finally a negative comment: The home town set ceased to be a home town set by virtue – in part – of the kind of NIGHT lighting. I don't mind the formalized architecture but I wished they had been accomplished by Grandma Moses or Thomas Benton.[44] MY FRIEND WILLSON DOES NOT RENT FROM CHARLES ADAMS' AUNT. On the other hand I'm not sure it's all my friend Willson – because there is an established style duality – that is, the dinner jacket and the beautiful-people-of-Dowra [Iowa?] playing and Rini by Balenciaga[?] ∧(as opposed to the following elements). I guess you are following a

---

41 The occasional word in this long and complex handwritten letter has been replaced with a [?] due to Loesser's handwriting being difficult to read at times. With the exception of '[AND THERE ARE ELKS EVERYWHERE]' every set of square brackets indicates a point of uncertainty or missed word. ∧ symbols refer to text added in afterwards (in brackets). Loesser's illustrations have been included in place. The layout of the original letter has been maintained to the greatest extent a word processor generally allows.
42 'In the Gloaming', a British song from 1877 by Annie Fortescue Harrison (1848–1944) with words adapted from a poem by Meta Orred (?1846–1925).
43 The Buffalo Bills were the barbershop quartet in *The Music Man*.
44 Grandma Moses (1860–1961), American folk artist; Thomas Benton (1889–1975), American painter, part of the Regionalist art movement.

sort of policy – but I can't guess what the policy IS. That will be something for you to tell me about some time.

And now for the third and last program. I have an idea of what you have planned but if you follow the same general format, you will once again be handing forth examples of your musical literature of the past – neatly and modestly (and Rini's assistance there is always immensely valuable) – but I suggest that a third show will be all it can stand. You can perform "Peony Bush"[45] but you can't take big hit-parade bows for it. There remains "You and I"[46] and "Beginning to look a lot like X'mas"[47] and maybe one or two other applause-fetching titles, and we've had it. I refer here only to "instant-recall" literature. It is obvious to me that you could go on for a long long series with demonstration of the "Talking People"[48] or Tchaikowsky's 4th Symphony analysis, or quotation out of "Fedalia"[49] etc etc etc.

BUT the name Meredith Willson is indelibly related to the word "BY" which precedes it. You accomplished this in an amazingly short time, and quite late in your career. Your earlier writings were not so closely related to your name for two reasons: You were best known as a musical director and your writing contributions were relatively sparse. The same, you will recall, applied to Victor Young,[50] ^(Ray Noble)[51] and some others. But now, by virtue of your amazing talent for associating yourself with your works, the public thinks in terms of:

BY MEREDITH WILLSON

[Hoagy] Carmichael and [Johnny] Mercer and only a few others have had this knack. But it requires a consistently growing body of works to support it.

I believe it is now time for you to attend to this growth. For this reason I'm happy to hear about your interest in a new writing project.

---

45 One of Willson's earlier songs, recorded by Danny Kaye in 1949.

46 Willson's first hit song, published in 1941.

47 Willson's 'It's Beginning to Look Like Christmas', recorded by Bing Crosby in 1951 and then recycled in *Here's Love* over a decade later.

48 The Talking People were a vocal group invented by Willson to speak in pitched rhythms for the advertisements in one of his radio shows.

49 *Who Did What to Fedalia?* (1952), Willson's only novel.

50 Victor Young (1900–1956), American film composer and songwriter.

51 Ray Noble (1903–1978), English bandleader, composer and arranger.

I mean the "AMERICANA SPECTACLE." A sort of digest of this plan was forwarded by Sol Shapiro[52] of Wm Morris to me – with the message that it was "self explanatory." I told you just now that I applaud your <u>INTEREST</u> but I hasten to add you may be making a pact with the devil. I'm not considering here the business details (although as expressed they give me what a large corned beef sandwich gives me – PAUSE!).

Let's consider the following: It is proposed that MW supply an original "piece" for a "spectacular" show to be performed ^(chiefly) in <u>huge</u> out door circumstances. The "book" or "scenario" is to be supplied and supervised by others. It is to follow a "format similar to those developed . . . for their California, Oregon and Kansas stories."[53]

Can it be that they are approaching the same Meredith Willson who saw fit to snatch "The Music Man" wholly from the talons of Feuer + Martin after allowing them a time-limit in which to produce it? (in strict accordance with a list of reserved approvals by MW)?[54]

Is this the same Meredith Willson who did <u>not</u> choose to write the "Further adventures of My Fair Lady" or "Four Penny Opera"?[55]

Can this be the same MW who never wrote anything resembling what somebody else had written previously?

THERE HAS TO BE (IN MY BOOK) a really excellent reason why MW should not

THINK OF IT <u>ALL</u>

WRITE IT <u>ALL</u>

AND DANGLE IT <u>ALL</u>.

Buyers, partners, investors, consumers, agents, assistants, will appear as if by magic

AT <u>YOUR</u> TERMS.

---

52 One of Willson's agents at William Morris.
53 Willson had served as musical director of *The California Story* at the Hollywood Bowl in 1950; *The Oregon Story* in 1959; and *The Kansas Story* in 1961.
54 In 1955 Feuer and Martin withdrew as producers of *The Music Man*, to be replaced by Kermit Bloomgarden.
55 Loesser is pointing out that Willson did not start his Broadway career by copying the work of others but rather created an original, *The Music Man*.

You can tell now that I don't like the sound of the proposal I have heard.

But now I address you as a fellow writer, with the following <u>artistic</u> calculation: If I were invited to do such a job I would somehow know in my belly-button that I was being called on to UNDERSCORE A GREAT DEAL OF MAMMOTH <u>EYE</u>-ACTION. I COULD PREDICT THAT <u>SOME</u> OF MY STUFF COULD BE EFFECTIVE INSTRUMENTALLY (THE VERY BROAD STUFF LIKE THE SLAVE MARCH IN AIDA) BUT WHERE WOULD I TURN TO FOR ANY KIND OF ATTENTION TO LYRICS – ESPECIALLY THOSE MAKING PREVAIL MY TRADE-MARKS IN SYLLABIFICATION AND RHYTHM NUANCE. BIG STAND-UP CHORUSES? MAYBE <u>ONCE</u> AN EVENING. TWO LOVERS STANDING THERE WITH A HAUNTING BALLAD? <u>ONCE</u> AN EVENING, WITH THE MAGIC WATERS UPSTAGING THEM AND THEIR SONG, ALONG WITH TWENTY HIGHLY CHARACTERISTICALLY GYRATING MERMAIDS. YOUR BIG BIG CHANCE WILL INDEED COME WHEN THE WAGONS FORM A CIRCLE IN DEFENSE AGAINST THE INDIANS – AND THERE BEGINS A FIREWORKS DISPLAY FROM BETWEEN WHEEL-SPOKES – REPRESENTING EARLY AMERICAN RIFLE-FIRE. YOUR JOB WILL BE TO SCORE THIS – AND SOME AMIABLE PARTNER IN THE ENTERPRISE WILL SUGGEST THAT THE MORE OF IT SOUNDS LIKE "LIGHT CAVALRY"[56] IN COUNTERPOINT WITH "LAND OF THE SKY BLUE WATER"[57] – THE MORE EVERYBODY WILL LIKE IT.

NO MATTER WHAT, NOBODY IS GOING TO FAVOR YOU BY AIMING FOR SMALLER GROSSES IN THEATRES NOT SUSCEPTIBLE TO CONTRIBUTIONS BY RAINFALL OR PASSING FIRE TRUCKS. EVEN THE WIND WILL BE AGAINST YOU AT TIMES.

AND AS FOR THE SCORE? WHERE IS "TROUBLE" AND "LIDA ROSE" AND "I'LL NEVER SAY NO" AND "HERE'S LOVE" AND – YES! "76 TROMBONES" THE ENTIRE MAGIC OF WHOSE LYRIC WILL HAVE EVERYBODY STRAINING TO HEAR FOR A SECOND, AND

---

56 Franz von Suppé's *Light Cavalry Overture* (1866).
57 Charles Wakefield Cadman's song 'From the Land of the Sky-Blue Water' (1909).

THEN NOT BOTHERING. THE TUNE ALONE WOULD STAND BY ITSELF IN A CERTAIN WAY BUT NOT IMPORTANTLY DEFINED.

AND THE AUDIENCE? WHERE? DES MOINES? GOOD! BUT DOES PHILADELPHIA KNOW ABOUT THAT? NO, BECAUSE ROBIN HOOD DELL DIDN'T PLAY THE SHOW. LOS ANGELES KNOWS, AND SAN FRANCISCO HAS HAD TO BEAR LIFE WITHOUT IT.

EVER HEAR OF THE WORLD'S FAIR? THE GOLDEN FLEECE? THE TAJ MAHAL? LINDY'S? THEY ARE, EACH OF THEM,

SOME PLACE

AND PEOPLE FLOCK THERE AND PRONOUNCE THEM WONDROUS. AFTER THAT, SOME OF THEM TRAVEL WELL – LIKE MICHELANGELO'S PIETÀ.

THIS DOESN'T MEAN THAT THERE AREN'T ICE SHOWS, RODEOS, ETC WHICH SKIP AROUND – BUT THEIR FORMAT + CONTENT IS SPECIFICALLY

NON ORIGINAL

NOW MY DARLING (RINI SOLD ME A HALF INTEREST IN THAT)[58] – I HAVE NEVER KNOWN YOU TO WRITE ANYTHING – THAT WASN'T THE RESULT OF A BEST EFFORT.

ON THE CERTAINTY!! THAT THIS HAS NOT CHANGED AND THAT A WONDERFUL "BOOK" OR SCENARIO OR SEQUEL OF STAGED EVENTS – CAN, BY SOME MIRACLE – BE MADE TO FIT THE AIMS OF THE PRODUCER – THEN WHY NOT SIT IT DOWN IN SOME

SHRINE

AND LET PEOPLE FLOCK. MAYBE NIGHT AFTER NIGHT

FOR YEARS

THEN PUT IT ON THE ROAD. BY THAT TIME, EVEN YOUR OVERTURE WILL BE APPLAUDED (EVER HEAR OF PEOPLE TAKING TOO MUCH GLUCOSE
OR

DEXTROSE

WELL, I SEE BY THE PAGE NUMBER THAT I'M OVERLOADED WITH

VERBOSE

---

58 A reference to Willson's idea to write a musical about his wife Rini.

BUT I GUESS YOU HAVE MANAGED TO LIVE WITH THAT.)
ONWARD:

REFERRING TO MY LAST SUGGESTION ABOUT WHAT TO
DO WITH YOUR <u>BEST</u> – I DON'T LIMIT SHRINE SITES TO
<u>BROADWAY</u>. HOW ABOUT MOTION PICTURES WHICH GLOW
SIMULTANEOUSLY IN THOUSANDS OF BRANCH SHRINES ALL
OVER THE WORLD – TO A POINT WHERE THEY HAVE GOT THE
CATHOLIC CHURCH BEAT FOR ATTENDANCE AND ATTENTION??

NOW THEN: IS IT POSSIBLE THAT YOU DON'T WANT TO
BUCK THE CRITICS? (AT LEAST SOME OF THEM)

ARE YOU NOT OBJECTIVE ENOUGH TO MAYBE REALIZE
THAT <u>YOU</u> GOT KNOCKED BECAUSE <u>YOU</u> WERE THE BIGGEST
TARGET?

I BELIEVE THEY <u>SHOULD HAVE</u> KNOCKED YOU FOR SOME
CASTING THAT DUMPED YOUR INTENTIONS. YOU WOULD
HAVE AGREED. I <u>KNOW</u> YOU WOULD. BUT THESE FELLOWS
HAVE TWENTY JUMPY MINUTES TO TYPE UP THEIR REVIEWS IN.
THE RESULT (BOX OFFICE) WOULD HAVE BEEN THE SAME OR A
GOOD DEAL WORSE IF THEY HAD POINTED THEIR FINGERS A
LITTLE MORE ACCURATELY. BUT YOU WOULD HAVE BEEN
MUCH LESS ANNOYED. MATTER OF FACT YOU WOULD HAVE
GOTTEN SOME WRY PLEASURE OUT OF HAVING HAD
CONFIRMED SOME OF YOUR OWN REASONS FOR CHAGRIN
ON THE ROAD BEFORE N.Y.

WHEN I WENT TO WAR WITH KERR ON YOUR BEHALF[59]
(ALTHOUGH WITH MY OWN SET OF COMPLAINTS, NOT
YOURS) HE CAME UP WITH WHAT I THOUGHT WAS A LAME
RATIONALE ATTEMPTING TO JUSTIFY CERTAIN COMMENTS.
NEVERTHELESS I NOTICED THAT EVERYTHING HE SAID IN THE
COURSE OF THE CONVERSATION WENT LIKE THIS: "WELL, <u>HE</u>
DID so and so, which I thought inferior to <u>HIS</u> so and so —— you see
<u>HE</u> has a knack for so, but this time I thought blah blah — unworthy
of <u>HIM</u>.

---

59 A reference to Loesser's conversation with Walter Kerr about the latter's review
of *Here's Love*.

Well sir, I have never heard a succession of GOD PRONOUNS so religiously intoned, and all with audible CAPITAL AITCHES!

YEA, O CREATOR YOU MADE EDEN AND IT WAS GOOD, BUT YOU HAVE GOT TO TAKE THE RAP FOR THE JOHNSTOWN FLOOD.[60] YOU ARE TOO BIG, O LORD, FOR PIOUS LITTLE ME, WHO KNOWS YOU MADE THE WATERS, TO GO LOOK FOR SOME ICEBERG TO BLAME FOR THE TITANIC SINKING. FOR PIOUS LITTLE ME WHO KNOWS YOU DID ALL THE CASTING OF NOAH'S ARK, IT IS IMPOSSIBLE TO PUT THE FINGER ON ONE LOUSY MRS. O'LEARY'S COW.[61]

All right, church is out. But please observe that Kerr joins me as an APOSTLE, however critical.

Also note this: my purpose in challenging some of Kerr's own writing was a TACTICAL one – not unlike Stengel's[62] approach when he differs with a plate umpire. HE DIFFERS LOUDLY, OUTRAGEOUSLY AND LONG – AND (KNOWING HE'S GOT THE ROOMAR TV LENS ON HIM) WITH GESTURES. Now Casey knows the decision is not going to be changed. BUT HE ALSO KNOWS THAT AS A RESULT OF A SORT OF OBLIGATION-SENSE, OR SHAME, OR WHATEVER HE HAS PRODUCED IN THE UMPIRE'S MIND – VERY SHORTLY – MAYBE ON THE VERY NEXT PITCH, THAT UMPIRE IS GOING TO CALL ONE IN FAVOR OF CASEY'S BATTER.

Allow me to add here, that like Stengel – I walked away from the discussion looking HURT. I am a lousy actor but by good fortune the back of my dinner jacket has a hurt look after long dinners on Windsor chairs. THE BACK OF THE COLLAR PEEKS OUT AS IF FROM THE GRASP OF A LARGE MEAN BOUNCER; AN ASSORTMENT OF CREASES FOLLOW, GIVING EVIDENCE OF A HABITUAL SQUIRMING AND CRINGING – AND THROUGH IT ALL LOOM

---

60 A reference to the well-known flood of Johnstown, Pennsylvania, on 31 May 1889, when the South Fork Dam on the Little Conemaugh River failed.
61 The cow belonging to Catherine O'Leary that was blamed for starting the Great Fire of Chicago of 1871.
62 Casey Stengel (1890–1975), a baseball player and manager known for his regular disagreements with umpires, in particular during his years in charge of the New York Yankees (1948–1960) and the New York Mets (1962–1965).

PITEOUS BUMPS WHICH DESCRIBE THE POSITION OF MY CHEAP SUSPENDERS. ALL IN ALL, THE IMAGE IS NOT UNLIKE THE UNNECESSARILY DROOPY BACK OF CASEY'S BASEBALL PANTS. IF ONLY FOR <u>YOUR</u> SAKE I AM NOT GOING TO LET MY WIFE OR MY TAILOR CHANGE ONE BIT OF THIS.

Ever hear of a fellow named Rome? Harold Rome.[63] Sure, because he's a colleague, etc. But he cuts no enormous ice. Many a <u>new</u> Broadway contributor (including you and me) has pressed him in terms of REPUTE – since he started trying, around 1932. Out of more than a dozen Broadway attempts to date, this man has had absolutely NO REAL HIT SHOW! He has now been (as far as I recall) food enough for thought among the critics, to be the FOCUS for PRAISE or BLAME. Somehow he has never engaged (or suffered) this distinction.

Nevertheless, the composite song – distillate, is <u>in his favor</u>. He can entertain at the Elks'[64] if he so chooses, with a medley from his Broadway career, including

"FRANKLIN D. ROOSEVELT JONES" [1938]
"SOUTH AMERICA, TAKE IT AWAY" [1946]
"WISH YOU WERE HERE" [1952]

Plus two or three other reasonably memorable pieces.
[AND THERE ARE ELKS EVERYWHERE]

This entitles our friend to a sort of comfort in being the standard semi-reluctant 9th choice composer on Broadway. It may be that he is bitter about not being M.W. or F.L. – we can't afford conjecture on that within this discussion. The fact that seems to loom up – is that he can quote a relatively formidable

BODY OF WORKS.

Like I said:

BODY OF WORKS.

Know what a circle is? The fine didactic words of Euclid escape me (and they have every right) but anyway it is impossible to inscribe a

---

63 Harold Rome (1908–1993), songwriter of numerous shows including *Pins and Needles* (1937) and *Fanny* (1954).
64 American fraternal order founded in 1868.

circle without the use of some sort of mechanism. You need a pair of compasses – or a set of trammel points – or you might have to trace your pencil around an old Andrews Sisters record. One way or the other, the perfect circle cannot be executed free-hand. To err here and there is human – and so lives intended as circles often seem lumpy and poorly planned.

Permit me this <u>rare</u> moment of <u>humility</u>. I am not a machine. I am human and fallible – but join me in this concession that I have at least

COME FULL-

-HOURGLASS.

BODY OF WORKS

Not clear?

Okay

BODY OF WORKS

More specifically-:

BODY OF MEMORABLE AND APPRECIABLE WORKS.

(Oh my God, I have the feeling that I will be much longer at this – yet, I owe you this whole story and you owe me the reading of it at least once through.)

Now look. The following is the ^(full) body of your works ^(NOT) as qualified above. I refer to WRITINGS, not performances or arrangements.

    (A) "MAY THE GLB and KY"[65]

    (B) "YOU AND I"

    (C) "BEGINNING TO L a LLX"[66]

    (D) "PICCOLO etc"[67]

    (E) "FEDALIA"

    (F) Another book – the title escapes me.[68]

---

65 'May the Good Lord Bless and Keep You', 1950 song.
66 'It's Beginning to Look Like Christmas'.
67 *And There I Stood With My Piccolo*, 1948 memoir.
68 *Eggs I Have Laid*, Willson's second memoir.

(G) An assortment of songs written as pops, or special material
(army, civic, etc)

(H) "THE MUSIC MAN" in its entirety
    (I)   including "SEVENTY SIX TROMBONES"
    (J)   "TILL THERE WAS YOU"
    (K)   "TROUBLE"
    (L)   a lump of other elements.

(M) "UNSINKABLE MOLLY BROWN" in its entirety
including (N) its lump of elements

(O) "HERE'S LOVE"
including (P) its lump of elements
                    PERIOD
(I am sure I have left something out, but equally sure that they are not
(at this moment) publicly memorable or appreciable.)

Voila! ("The voila has a duller tone than the fiddle but is indispens-
able in blending the delivery of really kosher divisi passages.
Incidentally it should be noted here that a quartet divisi against
itself cannot stand. 'Quartet' is actually a misnomer. It is somewhat
less than two pints and should properly be called a FIFTH. Generally,
fine composers avoid parallel FIFTHS, except in the case of Vodka,
which may be placed on any bar in parallel fifths (except on election
day). In such instances the composer is referred to as a de-
composer.")

                               – Rimsky Corsetcover[69]

Second Voila – et suivez >

Here is an <u>analysis</u> of the body of works. Before you read it, recollect
that I am not a fair-weather kiss-ass. Sometimes on rainy days I beat
my wife just to prove that point.

---

69 Rimsky-Korsakov.

I WILL REFER NOW TO THE LIST OF ITEMS ON PAGE #22

(A) Important song. Limited because of original identification or "signature" nowhere near as ubiquitous as "Begin the Beguine"[70] – but recognized and welcome. Evidence of some publisher neglect, but this may be intentional.

(B) Once big big Big. Much decline. Not nearly as healthy a standard as I believe it should be. Compare with "September Song."[71] Today's* eighteen year olds may have to be re-exposed.

(C) Fairly hardy perennial (personal). Performance frequency less than "Winter Wonderland"[72] and some others.

(D, E, F) Books, mostly of essays NOT widely read or otherwise celebrated as far as I know, at this time.*

(G) no elements at this moment* thrilling (or even touching) anybody's ears.

(H) a great big important Broadway hit, successful movie and promising stage perennial. However NOT, BY REPUTE AS YET*, IN THE LEAGUE WITH "SHOW BOAT" "MY FAIR LADY" "PORGY AND BESS"

(I) SMASH SONG, well established in the public ear. Predictably long life. A big credit.

(J) DITTO, BUT maybe not as distinguished a piece. Not in as unique a form (for our time)

(K) Unique, indelible etc !! Amazing impact considering the small number of people who have heard it more than once. It will preserve itself with some judicious care in withholding [?] rather than pushing it.

(L) Time will tell when and how "Lida Rose" or "Gary Ind." or others will join the big song titles. Right now* I regret that they belong in a lump.

(M) Half a Broadway Hit Show. Sorry, but I said: Half. May be quoted as an accomplishment without shame. But right now*

---

70 A hit song by Cole Porter from his show *Jubilee* (1935).
71 Weill and Anderson's standard from *Knickerbocker Holiday*.
72 Felix Bernard and Richard Bernhard Smith's winter classic (1934).

it cannot afford too much milking as a source of bow-taking.
The MOVIE may improve its position – briefly.*

(N) Right now* no really outstanding elements, but I'd say some
buds have begun to bud.

(O) <u>Half</u> a Broadway hit at the very best. Still running? Yes. <u>But</u> as
if from the Sheriff. BUT I think a surprisingly big after-life will
be possible. Better than "Unsinkable."

(P) No significant noises now.*

* The asterisks – if you will look back – all follow references to the
PRESENT TIME. And the capacity for matters to CHANGE, is implicit.

Now then, add everything up. You are already in better shape
than our friend Rome.

But your list figures to be roughly 1/6 as impressive as F.L.'s

And 1/10 as impressive as Noel Coward's

And 1/20 as glorious as Cole Porter's

On the face of this – it seems to be merely a cruelly contrived
quantitative analysis. It is not. First of all I picked three people who
write ^(both) words and music of their songs. Had I added Harry
Warren or Dick Rodgers, your fraction would have gotten littler.
Secondly I picked words + music fellows who write <u>show music</u> almost
exclusively. That excluded Irving Berlin. Thirdly I selected writers with
varying degrees of accomplishment in other writing departments:

COLE Porter – can't write anything but songs. Has hardly ever <u>read</u>
the plays he sticks them in.

FRANK LOESSER – some experience as a librettist, with some success.
Some screenplays, radio programs etc.

NOEL COWARD – A master playwright and novelist, with or without
songs.

Fourthly, I tried to show a variety of talents in <u>performance</u> and other
public relations boosters:

COLE Porter – Always preferred to let it go at having his name in the papers – except where it concerned his social (now professional) life which he is (or at least was) pretty proud of having. Performs little and un-impressively. Has no concert, lecture or other act.

FRANK LOESSER has been a first-rate public relations manager for himself, jumping from TYRO to JUNIOR DEAN in a few years on very little material. Has and still can perform, carefully avoiding invitations to play any <u>actual</u> piano. For the last ten years he has taken pains to avoid interviews, guest slots, or even private party routines. He will no doubt resume an accurate and relentless campaign on himself at a later date. He is NOT modest.

Noel Coward – a great entertainer, actor, etc. Gives marvellous and generous interviews. The color of his entire career image can be described by the word <u>SNOB</u>. But he makes it a comforting thing – and carefully <u>insults</u> only those who deserve it, and they are [??] invariably NOT <u>you</u>. It's a sort of miracle. But it has worked. At least in America and England.

Well sir, these are a group of your fellow travelers. Which one do you most resemble in terms of your operative assets?

I think NOEL COWARD

NOEL COWARD

NOEL COWARD

Not a soul in the whole world thinks

NOEL COWARD

means: a person who is leery of spending money on Christmas presents. They just somehow have learned to KNOW WHO and WHAT is

← ——————— NOEL COWARD

At this moment (at least in the U.S.) everybody knows who and what is

← ——————— MEREDITH WILLSON

But in 1966 or 1967

MEREDITH WILLSON

will still be

MEREDITH WILLSON

instead of

MEREDITH WILLSON

Compare type sizes and boldness

Unless something
HAPPENS IN-BETWEEN. SOMETHING THAT
CAN ADD A LAUREL.
(That is, if he chooses to present himself in concert tours, interviews, TV programs etc. in order to find out.)

Whether or not you smell it, let me advise you that we are touring the perimeter of another HOURGLASS – and may even negotiate a detour bump roughly describing the outlines of
ROBIN HOOD'S BARN[73]
[I think the expression is of central Indiana origin – along with "snatch him bald-headed" but if you ever want to claim it for Mason City, I promise not to give you away]

At any rate, I do not propose to discuss the nature of
LAUREL RESTING
The LAUREL is to the best of my recollection – a RHOTODENDRON [sic] – with succulent leaves and pliable stems – and is admirably suited for the forming of small wreaths to fit the narrowest or the fattest of heads.

The LAUREL WREATH is an award given to, and worn by – somebody judged to have given value or pleasure to a multitude of others.

To REST ON ONE'S LAURELS – carries the implication (to me) that sooner or later the CROWN becomes a pillow.

Back to Botany: It cannot be expected – that however admirably a laurel leaf holds its water – it will remain indefinitely pliable, green and comfortable. The fact is that sooner or later it becomes DRY, HARD and UN-COMFORTABLE

– and sitting on a bunch of it soon makes a sensitive butt feel as if it were on the receiving end of a cat-o' June-tail treatment. The discomfort (to a normal healthy butt) is never at all relieved by the knowledge that the dry laurel treatment has been self-inflicted.

The technique by which this pain is produced – is a subtle one. If the butt really RESTS TOTALLY INERT there is CONTACT INDEED,

---

73 I.e. all around the countryside, referring to Robin Hood's fields and pastures.

BUT NO FRICTION, and consequently very little TRIGGER FOR
IRRITATION

THE PAIN ORIGINATES

IN

LATERAL SQUIRMING

which I, Picasso, will now attempt to illustrate:

And what is wrong with this ULTRA REPRESENTATIONAL WORK
OF ART?
NOTHING!
EXCEPT THAT IT IS

OUT OF BALANCE
FOR LACK OF
MORE AND GREENER
LAURELS.

I have already told you about my doubts as to laurel sources – in the traveling extravaganza business.

I now wish to discuss the multiplicity of rewards for the writer whose stuff came in through the carriage entrance – albeit thru a gauntlet of critics as well.

Ever hear of a fellow named Gershwin? Why do they fumble and search thru every last shred of what he wrote, looking to perform something in a class with "Embraceable you" etc? (I am speaking of responsible program makers, performers, recording stars and their managers and musical directors and advisors.)

Because from the very beginning he stuck to the same class of medium for his stuff.

BROADWAY

MOVIES

CONCERT

OPERA

The carriage trade goes to them. The carriage trade does not go, or even listen to, or know about:

LAURENCE WELK[74]

GRAND OL' OPRY

COUNTY FAIRS

LEON AND EDDIE'S[75]

ROSELAND DANCE HALL[76]

SHLUMP'S BARGAIN ROCK + ROLL RECORD SHOP

GUY LOMBARDO[77] – COMMODORE HOTEL[78]

---

74 Lawrence Welk (1903–1992), accordionist and television host.
75 A famous nightclub and restaurant on West 52nd St in New York City.
76 The Roseland Ballroom, also on West 52nd St, which opened in 1956 and closed in 2013.
77 Guy Lombardo, bandleader (1902–1977).
78 Now the Hyatt Grand Central over Grand Central Station.

While a good percentage of this second (arbitrary) composite audience does indeed leak into the ranks of the <u>first</u>, I believe each of these composites attend MOVIES with equal gusto – but I'm not sure if they're the same movies.

Incidentally – by "carriage trade" I don't refer to people with more dough, or of special importance in the business world, or in political life.

I mean people who by virtue of special education, or leaning, or taste – somehow compose the corps of
INFLUENCE MAKERS.

Many have money, but many don't. Most live in the big cities. Of these cities NYC is fullest of them – most have gone to school, maybe college, many work in the WORLD of IDEAS (somebody once called it that).

TRANSLATE to people → Sec'y to architects,
lawyers, painters, school teachers . . .

I don't have to continue because you said it all in one section of "ASK NOT"
<u>INFLUENCE MAKERS</u>
That includes many many many people who are themselves
<u>IN SHOW BUSINESS</u>
WHY THESE PEOPLE HAVE COME TO BELIEVE, BROADLY AS A GROUP, THAT LIVE NEW YORK THEATRE IS THE <u>CLASSY</u> MEDIUM, I HAVE NEVER FOUND OUT. I HAPPEN NOT TO AGREE AT ALL, BUT THEY HAVE GOT ME LICKED.

I CAN'T BEAT THE FACT THAT WHEN I RETURNED TO NEW YORK WITH WHAT I THOUGHT WERE GREEN LAURELS UNDER MY ASS FOR: "PRAISE THE LORD AND PASS THE AMM[UNITION]" THEY JUST ABOUT <u>FORGAVE</u> ME FOR IT, IF THEY ACKNOWLEDGED ITS EXISTENCE AT ALL. YES, THAT ONE AND "I D[ON'T] W[ANNA] W[ALK] WITHOUT YOU BABY" AND SOME OTHER PLAIN POP SMASHES.

<u>BUT</u> MY PASSPORT TO
THE CARRIAGE TRADE
WAS A PARTY SONG

460

called
"BABY ITS [sic] COLD OUTSIDE"
which my then wife and I proceed to dine out on.

Eventually by way of a society that included Leonard Lyons, Bennet Cerf, Geo Kaufman, Albert Jacken, Vincent Sardi, Eleanor Roosevelt, Lindsay + Crouse,[79] various newspaper people, raconteurs, psychiatrists from the right avenue as well as the wrong; Army generals, diplomats who could read and write; actors, directors etc etc
— I WAS <u>IN</u>
—and what they all dearly cherished was the short journey – the <u>inside-news</u>. That they did not have to share with the grocery man or the maid.

Abe Burrows went thru the same thing (no credit for years of great Radio writing + direction) – just the funny parlor songs.

It would have happened to you, had you come in with "Trouble" still in MS. "MAY THE G L B + K Y" would not have been acknowledged.

Back to history: I MADE MY CONTRIBUTION TO "WHERE'S CHARLEY" A FEW YEARS LATER AND THE WHOLE THING, EXCEPT FOR [RAY] BOLGER, GOT MURDERED BY THE CRITICS, MY STUFF WAS CALLED "INFERIOR ROMBERG"[80]
BUT THE SNOB ARMY – WHO HAD LONG BEFORE MADE A CULT OF BOLGER – SUSTAINED THE SHOW – AND IT RAN FOR TWO YEARS. <u>REMEMBER</u> AMONG THAT ARMY ARE
THE CRITICS THEMSELVES.
THEY PAID ATTENTION WHEN ONE COLUMNIST QUOTED DICK RODGERS AS SAYING "WHERE'S CHARLEY" IS WHERE TO GO TO HEAR THE SEASON'S GOOD TUNES.

---

79 Albert Jacken (dates unknown); Vincent Sardi, American restaurateur (1915–2007); Eleanor Roosevelt (1884–1962), former First Lady. The other names in this list have previously been identified.
80 Sigmund Romberg (1887–1951), Broadway and Hollywood composer, mainly of operetta including *The Student Prince* (1924) and *The Desert Song* (1926).

"MY DARLING, MY DARLING" HAD ALREADY MADE NO #2 ON THE HIT PARADE AND SO BECAME UNIMPORTANT TO THESE PEOPLE. THEIR INFLUENCE CHOSE TO GO IN FAVOR OF "ONCE IN LOVE WITH AMY"

THE CRITICS SOON RE-VISITED THE SHOW AND PRINTED REVISED ESTIMATES – SOME APOLOGETIC. BENNY GOODMAN (A ^(SNOB) MEMBER) CHOSE TO LIKE "THE NEW ASHMOLEAN" AND PRIVATELY CONVINCED JOHNNY MERCER TO RECORD IT. MANY OTHER NICE THINGS HAPPENED.

TODAY "AMY" AND "ASHMOLEAN" ARE THE SONGS FROM THAT SHOW WHICH SUSTAIN THEMSELVES. "MY DARLING, MY DARLING" IS AN EX POP HIT, NOT PERFORMED MUCH OR HELD IN HIGH REGARD.

I AM REPORTING ON AN ORDINARY BROADWAY PROCESS, WHICH DOES NOT REQUIRE THAT WRITERS FORM PERSONAL ACQUAINTANCESHIPS WITH THE COGNOSCENTI. THE WRITER SIMPLY HAS TO WRITE FOR BROADWAY – PREFERABLY WITH-OUT TOO MUCH PRESS-AGENTRY.

(I have not meant to say here that "ORDINARY" refers to the rescue process of an entire show. That IS rare*. But the process of score presentation is common.
* "Roberta"
* "Wish You Were Here"
* "Charley")

A case history:
CIRCA 1934
COLE PORTER IS ALREADY "COLE PORTER" BUT NOT SUPER LUMINOUS.
HE WRITES A BROADWAY SHOW (REVIEW) CALLED "JUBILEE"
IT RUNS A COUPLE OF WEEKS + CLOSES
THERE HAS BEEN NO SPECIALLY VALIANT PUBLISHER EFFORT
NO SONG SUCCESSES.
COLE MUST REST ON PREVIOUS LAURELS

1940+[81]

MABEL MERCER[82] (FROM THE CULT) DOES NOT WISH TO SING A REPERTOIRE EVEN REMOTELY SIMILAR TO THOSE OF

{ LADY BAND SINGERS
VAUDE STARS (Sophie Tucker)
RADIO SINGERS (Vaughn De [Leath])
RECORDING ARTISTS (Kate Smith)[83]

SHE WORKS AT TONY'S, A LATE UN-POP SPOT, FREQUENTED BY A SEGMENT OF THE CULT. SHE HAS NEVER HAD A RADIO PROGRAM OR A VAUDE TOUR OR A HIT RECORD

SHE IS JUST OBSCURE OLD MABEL MERCER

BUT HER CUSTOMERS DON'T LISTEN TO KAY KYSER.[84] THEY ARE PEOPLE OF SPECIAL OPINIONS AND TASTES WHO WOULDN'T BE CAUGHT DEAD ENDING ON THE TONIC.

MABEL'S PIANIST IS ONE OF THE EARLY PUBLIC WEED SMOKERS.

TONY'S is NOT BLINSTRUBS[85] or the HOLLYWOOD PALLADIUM.[86]

MABEL MERCER HAS GOT TO LEAF THRU ALL KINDS OF OBSCURE LITERATURE SO THAT HER MUSIC WILL NOT BE ANYBODY ELSE'S. OTHERWISE TONY'S WILL BE TRYING TO COMPETE WITH "LEON + EDDIE'S" WHICH WOULD KILL IT AND HER. ACTUALLY SHE IS APPLYING HER OWN HONEST TASTE.

THIS SUITS THE RARIFIED SELECTIVITY OF HER AUDIENCE. THEY LIKE TO BE APPROACHED AS INTELLECTUALS AND SO MABEL FLATTERS THEM WITH SONGS THAT ARE MAUDLIN ENOUGH – BUT WHOSE LYRICS TEND

---

81 In fact, Artie Shaw's version of 'Begin the Beguine' was recorded in 1938, and the song featured heavily in the successful movie *The Broadway Melody of 1940*.
82 Mabel Mercer (1900–1984), cabaret singer.
83 Sophie Tucker (1887–1966), vaudeville star; Vaughn De Leath (1894–1943), early radio crooner; Kate Smith (1907–1986), radio singer.
84 Kay Kyser (1905–1985), bandleader.
85 A club in Boston.
86 An art deco theatre with a large dance floor on Sunset Boulevard.

(or sometimes pretend) to be articulate.

MABEL DIGS AND FINDS:

   "BEGIN THE BEGUINE"

A TAPEWORM OF IRREGULAR FORM CONTAINING NOT IMMEDIATELY MEMORABLE MELODIC VARIATIONS,

WITH A NOT STRAIGHT-FORWARD LYRIC AT FIRST HEARING

AND A RANGE THAT SHE CAN'T REALLY NEGOTIATE.

ONE NIGHT SHE PERFORMS
   "BEGIN THE BEGUINE"
TO A TYPICAL AUDIENCE OF NINE WHICH INCLUDES TWO BUD BOYS LEAVING SEVEN
AND AMONG THE SEVEN SITS
          ARTIE SHAW[87]
A SELF-STYLED INTELLECTUAL WHO HAS LUNCHED THAT VERY DAY WITH CHARLIE CHAPLIN SO THAT BOTH COULD AIR THEIR POLYSYLLABLES.

          ARTIE SHAW!
     ARTIE HEARS AND APPRECIATES
       "Begin the Beguine"
HE COMES AGAIN THE NEXT NIGHT AND THE NEXT, TO REASSURE HIMSELF, AND TO CONFIRM IN HIS MIND THAT
          BENNY GOODMAN[88]
would NOT play it.

ARTIE SHAW MAKES THAT IMMENSE RECORDING

LATER, IN APPRECIATION OF HIS "SUPERIORS" IN SONG TASTE, SOMEBODY HEYWOOD OR HEYWARD[89] MAKES THE RECORD VERSION WITH THE REBELLIOUS OSTINATO.

---

87 Artie Shaw (1910–2004), bandleader and clarinettist.
88 Benny Goodman (1909–1986), bandleader and clarinettist.
89 Pianist Eddie Heywood (1915–1989) recorded it in 1944.

MEANWHILE THE CULT HAS BUSTED ITS SEAMS AND
OVERFLOWED TO A POINT WHERE YOU CAN HEAR "B, The B."
ON MUSAK AND IN ROSELAND – AND EVEN CARMEN
LOMBARDO[90] CAN'T HURT IT ANY MORE!
And Cole Porter need not have regretted "Jubilee"

AND NOT ONE OF THESE INFLUENCES ON THE AMERICAN EAR
EVER SAW OR HEARD OF
"JUBILEE"

But Mabel Mercer knew where to dig, and rummage and pore,
and examine.
NOTE THAT SHE DID NOT ELECT
TO REVIVE
"CRYIN' FOR THE CAROLINES."[91]

AT THIS MOMENT, MABEL OR SOMEONE IN HER SPECIAL
AND USEFUL CLASS (MAYBE BOBBY SHORT[92])→
IS RUMMAGING THROUGH
"MOLLY BROWN"
FOR ALL WE KNOW.

I DOUBT VERY MUCH IF ANYBODY OF ANY INFLUENCE IS
LOOKING THRU OLD WALTER DONALDSON.[93]

LONG AGO,
THE REASON I OPENED THE KIND OF PUBLISHING HOUSE
THAT I DID – WAS THAT I KNOW ABOUT THE
POTENTIAL AFTER-LIFE OF BROADWAY MUSIC.
I TOLD YOU THAT TWENTY-ONE YEARS AGO, IN
HOLLYWOOD. IT HAPPENED THAT YOU RANKED ME IN THE

---

90 Carmen Lombardo (1903–1971), saxophonist and singer for his brother Guy
Lombardo's orchestra.
91 A long-forgotten song by Harry Warren, Joe Young and Sam Lewis.
92 Bobby Short (1924–2005), cabaret singer and pianist.
93 Walter Donaldson (1893–1947), songwriter.

ARMY AT THAT TIME – BUT THAT DIDN'T PREVENT YOU FROM LISTENING, AND NOW YOU HAVE BEEN LISTENING AGAIN. THANK YOU.

BROADWAY
IS THE
PLACE TO
FLOP

IN THE RODEO BUSINESS YOU GET KILLED FOR GOOD.

CONCERTS ARE FINE, BUT THEY ARE ONLY MOBILE
LAUREL-RESTING.
CIRCUSES AND FAIRS AND ICE SHOWS ETC. CALL ON MUSIC AS AN APPENDAGE AND DO MUCH BETTER WITH OLD STUFF THAN NEW.

BROADWAY
IS
THE
PLACE
IN WHICH TO ADD
TO YOUR BODY OF
LONG-LIVING
WORKS
WHETHER OR NOT
YOU
HIT
OR
MISS.

<u>NOW WAIT!</u>
If you were to create a wholly new convention that is not Broadway – like

PUNCH + JUDY
Or

OBER AMMERGAN PASSION PLAY
I, for one would say
Go, Go, Go, Go, Go!

↓

But I have yet to hear about any such thing. It's a cinch that nobody but yourself will arrive at such a brand new idea. Not me, not Wlm Morris office, or Stu Ostrow – or Milt Kramer or your brother Cedric.

By the way – I am very much taken with your brother Cedric. Do you two keep in touch with each other? I have a brother Arthur who I very much cherish. He has what he calls a food <u>attic</u>. He says that when people ask him how he knows so much (sanskrit for "carbonator" or the name of Glinka's first wife, the latitude of Guam, or the cube root of seventeen, and all) <u>attic</u> means a well organized and retentive store house of memories in his head. I <u>mentioned</u> your name to him about twenty years ago and he said "Oh yes! Two L's."

Well, I have closed up the other him – slam now – Robin Hood's Barn and all – with intersection into the first, plus tangents toward limbo.

Ever hear of Hungarian people? Those of my acquaintance have all seemed to be loaded with a capacity for being funny – I mean for saying funny things that come from their own native culture and language. Charley Vidor was a delightful man who once said

"I WAS AS CONFUSED AS A FART IN A WICKER CHAIR."

I have a Hungarian manicurist named Margaret who told me a good one. It's a gesture used (by Hungarians) to signify ennui or enduring somebody's endless old familiar tale.

Here it is →

HAND PLACED ABOUT WAIST-HIGH <u>PALM</u> <u>DOWN</u> IN FRONT + CENTER OF BODY. HOLD FOR ½ second

THEN, <u>WITHOUT</u> <u>CHANGING</u> <u>HEIGHT</u> OR CENTRAL
POSITION, TURN <u>PALM UP</u>

This is the Hungarian way (says Margaret) of saying "Oh sure, sure
sure; when I was a little boy – so high –
    (FIRST POSITION)

"I had a beard this long!"

    SECOND POSITION)

– and my darling man, you are well entitled to use it on me, lavishly – for this MEGILLEH (that is fanatic spelling for a long Hebrew document).

    ALORS: Le Re-cap:

(A) From what I have read about it, I'm not crazy about you doing that touring show. [I have not considered guaranteed <u>money</u> and how much you need or want it.]

(B) If you feel stung about certain discomforts of the last Broadway bout – ACCEPTING CHALLENGES IN AN EASIER LEAGUE, OR OTHERWISE "KEEPING BUSY" CAN BE DANGEROUSLY HABIT-FORMING, and therefore →

(C) I believe you ought to direct your thoughts to Broadway or maybe movies (Giants only, like "Gigi")[94] → which media are (in my opinion) most likely to add to your –

(D) —body of works – which (in my opinion, again) constitute

MEREDITH WILLSON

not the entertainer

not the travelling husband

not the giver of interviews

or the philosophical fraud of the military march

or the leading citizen of Mason City

but

MEREDITH WILLSON

who can do all those other things while his brilliant brain and electrically creative spirit are resting.

    RESTING FROM WHAT?

    I will close now, in the sincere belief that you know my feelings about you and your work – that you know this lecture comes out of my deep affection and regard, even though I say things snotty very often – and I over-state many a case.

---

94 *Gigi* (1958) was an Academy Award-winning musical by Lerner and Loewe, written in the wake of *My Fair Lady* (1956) and adding to their prestige.

Don't answer this, except to tell me you got it.

Prepare, rather, for a visit here sometime this summer or early fall. I would like two solid days of talk with you. Then you can spring all your answers, rebuttals, agreements and any variety of tangential suggestions.

OKAY? LET ME KNOW.

> Love
> Frank

17 July 1964: To Meredith Willson (Telegram)

WISHING YOU MAGNIFICENCE TONIGHT

FRANK LOESSER

5 August 1964: To Meredith Willson

Dear Meredith:

This is one of my two days in town this week and most of it has been spent at a place where they take x-ray pictures. They say I am photogenic but a little too Jewish for leading roles. To be serious, I feel fine and my visits to the docs are for the purpose of finding out whether I'm entitled to feel fine.

I received a whole bunch of photographs of correspondence from a Mr. Shapiro[95] at the Morris office. These letters relate to negotiations on the outdoor thing and indicate that you have already agreed to go ahead with this project. I asked Kramer for further information and he told me that you had a great deal of material ready and suitable for this, and it would not be an enormous strain on your creative fountain. That is good news, since I also learned from Milt that inquiries have been made concerning a possibility of your adapting a Tarkington[96] work for musical theatre. Do you want me to read it? If so, of course I will in time for whatever discussions you'd like at our next meeting.

---

95 Probably George Shapiro (1931–2022) of William Morris.
96 Booth Tarkington (1869–1946), novelist.

Now about that meeting. We seem to have predicted mid-August, but since then I learn that you will be coming through in early September on your way to Europe. Can you possibly come through New York a little more slowly than first planned so that we can have a day to ourselves before you skip over the ocean? That would obviate an August trip. Okay? Let me know in a letter or tell Milt [Kramer] in your next conversation on the phone, and he'll tell me.

As Milt must have told you I missed the third show [i.e. *Texaco Star Parade*] because of absolutely no TV reception at all in my corner of Long Island. But Milt will be setting up a running of it for me. Milt also reported to me that the West Coast opening of "HERE'S LOVE"[97] was sensational, and that you were delighted with the way the show went – and so was the capacity audience on Tuesday night. A few days ago I got a thoughtful note from Stu about this company closing in New York.

Love to you and Rini,

---

97 *Here's Love* opened in Los Angeles on 3 August.

CHAPTER TEN

1962–63
FAMILY, FRIENDS AND BUSINESS

Frank and Jo Loesser had their first child, Hannah, in October 1962. Loesser wrote to Arthur about her and other family or mundane matters – including a recommendation for razor blades and how best to keep them sharp – and to one of his accountants about a new maid the Loessers had hired. It is from this time, too, that letters survive documenting Loesser's interest in art – he was himself a habitual doodler and amateur artist – and in particular his curiosity about the paintings of Japanese artist Fumiko Matsuda (1929–?), a subject that he pursued as late as 1966. The Loessers' domestic affairs included travelling to California, sometimes for business, and in 1963, during one stay there – when they rented a house from Regis Philbin[1] – the Loessers apparently did considerable damage to the property. Frank Loesser deputised his secretary, Betty Good, to resolve the matter and make restitution.

Late October or early November 1962:
To Susan Loesser[2]

The baby[3] is wonderful and fat. She greeted the Steinbecks yesterday all dressed up in a pink thing with real booties and stared them down

---

1 Regis Philbin (1931–2020), television presenter and talk show host.
2 Loesser, *A Most Remarkable Fella*, 217.
3 Hannah Loesser (1962–2007), who became an artist.

like good babies do. Today Jo and I are going to wheel her in a carriage briefly and be very proud.

2 November 1962: To Arthur Loesser

Dear Arthur:

Little did I know, when I first saw daylight, that I had been born the brother of the world's leading literate authority on pianos. But I guess there was a good reason for God's will in this matter, because here I am wanting to know something about the Yamaha piano. I feel reasonably sure that you will know more even than the Nippon Gakki Co. Ltd. of Hamamatsu, Japan[4] on this subject. It is my experience that in 1920 you knew more than Jules Verne about rocket space craft,[5] and more about zoology than Horowitz.[6] Anyway, I depend on you, dear brother, to tell me what you know about this instrument (am enclosing their brochure). I need a piano for my work downtown and am being asked to consider one of this make. Shortly I understand there will be one available for me to try, but with my tendency in the direction of woodwork, I will probably fondle the case and holler hooray and buy it, without having learned about how quickly it goes out of tune, or it dries up or develops a hostile action. Anyway, please tell me what you know.

Love,

6 February 1963: To Arthur Loesser

Dear Arthur:

Again so many thanks for the hospitality, the conversation, and the very nice new friends I met. No news at this moment about the exact time of my next Cleveland quickie – but meanwhile, here are

---

4 Founded in 1887 in Nagoya as an importer of classical guitars, Nippon Gakki is now part of the Yamaha Corporation.
5 Jules Verne (1828–1905), author of *From Earth to the Moon* (1865), *Journey to the Centre of the Earth* (1864) and *Twenty Thousand Leagues Under the Sea* (1869), among other works.
6 Norman H. Horowitz (1915–2005), geneticist, famous for his experiments to determine if life exists on Mars.

the stainless steel blades I told you about. I tried one out and got eight shaves out of it, but they are supposed to do better than that for people not quite as wasteful as myself. Do NOT wipe them clean, but simply hold the loosened razor under the water faucet, and the goop will come off the blade satisfactorily. My scientifically more experienced friends tell me that wiping these blades is bad for them, as it alters the special surface adjacent to the edge. You see, there are specialists in everything.

Anyway, thanks again. I will be writing to Jean separately.

Love,

15 April 1963: To Arthur Loesser

Dear Arthur:

Thanks for thinking about those little scotch bottles. You are right to hold on tight till your next trip here. Meantime, Allen Whitehead tells me he has, or shortly will send you some more of those razor blades.

From the description in your letter, I guess Jean and you made Europe a little too fast this time. As a place to live, Rome has always seemed to me to be a vast loitering yard. No one who is anyone wants to eat dinner before 11 at night, and no restaurant who is any restaurant wants to serve it before that hour. Jean would be furious.

Mama was over for dinner yesterday (Easter Sunday) and ate well and spoke well and dandled the baby well, but seems still to be a trifle weak from her illness.

I just possibly may be going to London for a week at the end of May or the beginning of June. You might shoot me the Hollanders' address and phone there. Meantime, best love. [handwritten:] – from Jo too.

[typewritten:] P.S. I am enclosing a note to my secretary from William Ricketts.[7] She had sent him a copy of your book[8] in my

---

7 M. E. Ricketts (c1881–1972), at the time chairman of music publisher Chappell & Co.
8 *Men, Women and Pianos.*

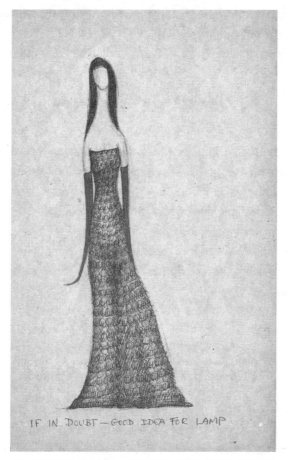

IF IN DOUBT – GOOD IDEA FOR LAMP

13. 'IF IN DOUBT – GOOD IDEA FOR LAMP',
undated doodle by Frank Loesser.

behalf. Ricketts is a co-director with Dreyfus[9] of the huge Chappell empire. He is one of the cutest men I know, well in his 80's, a formidable authority on early Georgian silver – the creator of the "His Master's Voice" symbol for Victor in the late 1890's – originally a railroad mechanic, and subsequently a leading authority on the mechanics of piano building. Also, he is an important British cattle

---

9 Max Dreyfus (1874–1964), president of Chappell & Co. Together with his brother Louis (1877–1967), he acquired a share of music publisher T. B. Harms, which was acquired by Chappell Music in 1926. Harms and Chappell were major publishers of the *Great American Songbook*.

breeder, as well as a professional grower of flowers. Any questions, Leonardo?[10] You ought to meet him.

Frank

9 July 1963: To Bob Goldberg

Dear Bob:

We have engaged Louise Maxey Sadler starting Monday July 8th, as general maid. Her gross salary should be $65.00 weekly. Her Social Security number is 311-20-5885, and her address is care of Loesser, 705 Pacific Coast Highway, Santa Monica, California.

Please super-immediately prepare her first week's salary check so that it will arrive here before the end of the current week.

This about fills out the domestic-studio business complement of employees.

Thanks.

Sincerely,

21 November 1962: To Fumiko Matsuda

Miss Fumiko Matsuda
Ibiza,
Baleares,
Spain.

Dear Madam:

I am a very great admirer of your paintings, and have recently bought one from FAR Galleries in New York City. It seems to be the last they have of yours, and they tell me they do not expect any more of your work. Are you by any chance represented by some other gallery in New York? Also, do you have a representative in London or Paris? I will be in London shortly, and would be very much interested in seeing more of your very impressive work.

Sincerely,

---

10 That is, polymathic, like Leonardo da Vinci.

15 May 1964: To John Schlesinger[11]

Dear John:

It starts this way. I am walking by a gallery on Madison Avenue one day, two years ago, and I see a picture in the window I like very much. I walk in and learn from the proprietor of the gallery (an old friend) that the picture is for sale for $1500. Upon hearing him quote this price, I throw myself to the gallery floor in a fit of righteous indignation, bellowing like a wounded seal. Also I rend my garments like a wounded Jew. Also I threaten to take my framing and restoring business elsewhere in the future. Finally, I seize the proprietor and actually throttle him. With what must be close to his dying gasp he announces that the price is still $1500.

So much for my ineffectual exercise in Oriental trading. The upshot is that when I go some weeks later to attempt to buy the picture, I learn that someone else had bought it. After that I ask to see some other works by this painter and am shown a couple and I develop a great fondness for this person's work.

She is a she. A Japanese she, named Fumiko Matsuda.

Several months pass. Or maybe more than a year. I inquire at this Madison Avenue gallery whether or not they have received any more of these paintings. They tell me no, but show me a few pictures of hers as yet unsold. I inquire as to her whereabouts, and as to her present representation. My Madison Avenue dealer professes ignorance. Apparently there has been a tiff or disagreement of some kind between Matsuda and this gallery. They volunteer no information. They are rotten, these art dealers.

Nothing daunted, I get in touch with my London office to find out whether this Japanese lady artist has ever had a show in England or the Continent. Shortly, it turns out that the Jeffress Galleries in London know something. They have shown her, and are pleased to report that she may be located as follows: [provides address in Ibiza]

Armed with this information I cable her, asking her where I may see more of her paintings. She replies by cable as follows:

---

11 Yacht owner (1950s–70s) John Schlesinger, other details unknown.

THANK LETTER PLEASE VISIT RICHARD
JABLOW 400 MADISON AVENUE NEW YORK
17 REGARD FUMIKO MATSUDA IBIZA

Feverishly I run down Richard Jablow – who turns out to be an attorney who represents many of my friends in various areas of show business.[12] He invites me to visit his office, which invitation I accept. I arrive at his office and he spreads out before me about fifty canvases which have been taken off stretchers and rolled up. He is acting as her sales agent and has a price list. Among those pictures he shows me is the one of the boy astride the bulls – the picture you seemed to admire at my house.[13] I but [sic] it, plus another. Then I ask Jablow how it is he, an attorney at law, forty stories up in a skyscraper, holds – and offers for sale – these pictures. He replies that he is acting as a sort of custodian, that there has been some sort of legal dispute, etc. Does he know the lady? He has merely met her. Oh. Then Jablow volunteers: "She is thirty years old and quite beautiful."

Being a red-blooded two-fisted American youth I respond to this description, summoning to work my sense of adventure. A thirty year old Japanese beauty who lives and paints in the Balearic Islands, has had some sort of trouble, has fled, and has left some sort of management of her American affairs in the hands of an attorney. The sweet thing shows a rare combination of attitudes in her work. She has a precision which never loses a profound affection. She probably scrubs whiting on her sneakers regularly twice a week – and still loves the way they smell inside. She shuts drawers compulsively when she finds them left open – and yet cares about the treasures inside the drawers. She is a sort of horny spartan – etc.

I indulge myself in these musings, until I bring myself up short with the realization that I am not a single man and therefore not entitled to know whether she likes the way the inside of _my_ sneakers smell. Also,

---

12 Richard B. Jablow (c.1926–1975) represented numerous literary and musical clients.
13 Matsuda's 'Nude Male Riding Bulls' from Loesser's estate was sold by Capsule Gallery on 17 October 2019; see https://www.bidsquare.com/online-auctions/capsule/fumiko-matsuda---nude-male-riding-bulls-1512486 (accessed 17 September 2023).

I'm not entitled to a furtive excursion into the Mediterranean to meet her. Not even for the purpose of watching her paint. Certainly not for the fun of undressing her. I am no longer John Wayne, because I married a violent little soprano.

Then I come across you. You with the yacht enormous enough to ignore small craft warnings. You with a schedule which probably brings you to the Majorca section of the Mediterranean pretty soon.

So, my dear fellow, I schenk[14] you the adventure I have tried to describe. I present you with all the excitement I have conjured up and can make no use of. I have absorbed Callas and can't go backstage to offer her my body.

So I pass on to you the glorious opportunity of being rewarded or disappointed or something in between. At the very worst, she may sell you some pictures cheap.

All I want from you is a series of reports, for my vicarious enjoyment.

With affection

11 January 1966: To Arthur Loesser

Dear Arthur:

Here's the letter I spoke to you about on the phone. My question is:

Does the lady[15] mean that she has indeed "decided to send" and can it thus be presumed that she has or will act upon this decision?

Since talking to you it has occurred to me that I don't know how long this lady has lived in Spanish-speaking territory. For all I know it might be a great portion of her life. In that event she might be accustomed to mental Spanish-to-English translation.

Anyway I feel that the phrase "I decided to" is the key. It is possible that she meant "I decided to ask to." Observe how she leaves out structural parts of sentences elsewhere.

---

14 German for 'give' or as is now common, 'gift'.
15 Japanese artist Fumiko Matsuda, as the next letter makes clear.

Please give this some study, and let me know what you think. And Please return the lady's letter. Your dice.

Love,

12 January 1966: To Arthur Loesser

Dear Arthur:

Last night I forwarded the Japanese painter's letter to you. This morning there came in the mail a customs notice indicating that the pictures[16] had indeed arrived at Kennedy Airport. Apparently the lady really meant "I decided." Also, her way of doing things may be innocent but certainly there is no evidence of any polite Oriental circumspection or hesitancy as of the present writing. I have to send someone through a now celebrated traffic jam all the way to Long Island in order to pay a wad of duty on something I didn't ask for.

Please read the lady's name carefully. On the face of it we may agree that it does indeed have a Japanese ring to it. Nevertheless she may not be Japanese at all, considering my recital of the facts above. Also, in researching this I have discovered a remarkable piece of information: FUMIKO MATSUDA in Esperanto means do not smoke in bed.

So do not bother your busy head about this any longer, but simply mail the letter back to me quickly. I will need her letter as some sort of affidavit as to evaluation.

Do you think Duveen[17] started this way. It seems too difficult.

Thanks and love,

---

16 Loesser also purchased Matsuda's 'Two Female Figures, a Young Girl and an Older Woman'. The painting, from Loesser's estate, was sold by Capsule Gallery Auction on 17 October 2019, in the same sale as 'Nude Male Riding Bulls'; see https://www.bidsquare.com/online-auctions/capsule/fumiko-matsuda---two-fe-male-figures-a-young-girl-and-an-older-woman-1512485 (accessed 17 September 2023).

17 Joseph Duveen (1869–1939), British art dealer.

18 September 1963: To Betty Good (Telegram)

ACKNOWLEDGING YOUR PHONE CALL I SUBSEQUENTLY RECEIVED CARBON OF TAIT'S COMMUNICATION TO YOU REGARDING DAMAGE OF PHILBIN PROPERTY. PLEASE WIRE PHILBIN FOR WRITTEN CONFIRMATION THAT TAIT IS HER OFFICIAL EXCLUSIVE REPRESENTATIVE IN THIS MATTER. . . .

24 September 1963: To Betty Good

Dear Betty:

Enclosed is my check for $409.87, reimbursing you for your payment of the car rental. For purposes of accuracy I would like you to re-deposit this in the $2,000 account I left with you. Also, if I have overlooked any withdrawals for that account you have made in the past, I wish you would remind me so that I can reimburse those amounts. The point here is to use the $2,000 account for Philbin purposes only.

Love,

Frank Loesser

P.S. For your information, I have a received a letter from Oliver Schwab[18] and turned him down on his suggestion that I should be the composer-lyricist for his client's (Ed Simmons)[19] prospective musical-ization of "Front Page."[20] However, I invited him to discuss other people with our company and got a second letter back which suggested that Simmons might indeed call [Milt] Kramer or [Allen] Whitehead. I'm telling you all this because there are some little notes in the file giving evidence of Mr. Simmons' personal contact with you.

---

18 Attorney (dates unknown).
19 Ed Simmons (1919–1998), screenwriter for Dean Martin and Jerry Lewis on *The Colgate Comedy Hour* television show.
20 *The Front Page*, Broadway comedy by Ben Hecht (1894–1964) and Charles MacArthur (1895–1956).

30 September 1963: To Betty Good

Dear Betty:

This is to acknowledge receipt, on September 27th, of the copy of the letter from Mrs. Philbin to you, dated September 25th. I have examined the list contained therein and I wish to state my position with reference thereto:

With respect to the missing items, I disclaim liability in toto. As you will recall, you were informed by Mrs. Philbin that she had insurance on all of the household effects. Her word was taken for this, without requiring her to exhibit her policy. Furthermore, the Tait inventory originally furnished to you contained evaluations which we presumed were for the purposes of such insurance. It would have seemed proper, therefore, for Mrs. Philbin to report such losses as she seems to indicate to her insurance company. You and I (and certainly Mrs. Philbin as well) know that many keys to her house were held by persons other than ourselves, and without our permission. You will recall that one of these was held by a pool-man who mysteriously disappeared for a period of about nine days after we took possession and another key was held by a gardener who likewise did not report for the last three weeks of our stay. I pass over the fact that their services were made part of the lease in the first instance. I'm certain, too, that Mrs. Philbin was aware when she rented the property to us that:

  A. There was a gaping hole in the side wall leading to adjoining property which was her obligation to seal up and

  B. That the wall between the property and the public beach was easily vaulted by anyone wishing to retrieve a volley-ball – a circumstance which regrettably prevailed all summer; the special knowledge of Mrs. Philbin and not within our own, prior to taking possession

I have pointed out A and B above because I refuse to believe that Mrs. Philbin is accusing us or our help or our infant child of making off with her household effects.

I have examined the list of items said to have been damaged, broken and soiled as well as the estimated cost of repair. You will recall with what meticulous care you and the help and Mrs. Loesser and I, or our guests, put aside for final candid exhibit to Mrs. Philbin every single thing broken or damaged by us. Under the circumstances, we leave it to your good judgment as to what the actual cost of replacement or repair for these items will be and agree that you may deduct same from the $2000 deposited for you before returning the balance to us. We are indeed fortunate that you were on the premises daily (to observe how many household items were not in perfect condition at the outset) and we trust that you will exercise your recollection as well as your judgement in this matter.

Very sincerely,

18 October 1963: To Betty Good

Dear Betty:

I send you hugs and kisses from Jo and me for your recent accomplishment. If the bank has cashed your check to Mrs. Quagmire that seems to be the end of that. We love you and we thank you. More later.

Love,

Frank Loesser

P.S. Possibly, by now you may have a letter from Mrs. Quagmire saying she has accepted the check as part payment, subject to further squawk. But that is only a possibility. If anything like that happens, be sure to tell Harold right away. Meantime I'll keep him up to date on our present happy correspondence.

11 November 1963: To Betty Good

Dear Betty:

I'm up to here with everything, and that's why I left it to Allen Whitehead to ask you to dump all the stored goods on us. I appreciate your help. Also, congratulations on reducing the B. of S.M[21] to a

---

21 Loesser's reference here is unclear.

state of reasonableness. How would you like to be Dean Rusk[22] for a living?

Love from Jo and me,

3 December 1963: To Betty Good

Dear Betty:

Honest to God, this is my first chance to say thank you, thank you, thank you for forwarding all the western muck.

We have your note acknowledging how beautiful our children are photographically, and I guess we agree.

Oh. I realize at this moment that I haven't even said my thanks for your management of the final and very economical settlement with "that creature." My only excuse is that I have had a gum operation, a finger operation, and a desk continually piled high with crappy detail. You know this situation only too well, so I know you will forgive me. We have been down to Missouri for the four Thanksgiving days, visiting Jo's folks who are delightful company – and it turned out to be a real rest for me. Not so much for Jo, who was busy managing and displaying Hannah to all and sundry. I had a lot of fun, and have decided that Missouri is alright after all. And that includes your part of it.

I'm glad your health is back. Keep it that way, because I may holler at you to help me out – like with doing forty push-ups, or calling on some crazy lady to rent another house for us.

According to your instructions, I have kissed Hannah on the nose and it made me at that instant many degrees happier and one small booger richer. Infant ones are not salty. Anyway, it's better than burped milk up your sleeve. Forgive me again for taking so long to write.

Love, love, love,

Cultivating properties from both friends and colleagues, including Johnny Mercer (1909–1976) and Ira Gershwin (1896–

---

22 Dean Rusk (1909–1994), US Secretary of State 1961–69.

1983), or considering and often rejecting approaches from song-writers, among them Donald Kahn (1918–2008, best known for his 1956 song 'A Beautiful Friendship'), was a significant part of Loesser's activity at Frank Music. As usual, both his approaches to and his rejections of potential collaborators offer some insight into what he thought made a successful theatrical song. Nor was Loesser stinting in his advice to colleagues, among them lyricist Arnold Horwitt (1918–1977), about the role a producer plays in mounting a show or what role he himself would play and why. And he was generous in his support of colleagues, among them the singers Josef Marais and Miranda.

18 June 1962: To Johnny Mercer

Dear Johnny:

It was nice seeing Ginger[23] again, if only briefly. Or maybe she hasn't mentioned that I ran into her and Matty Malneck[24] at a funny show where we all laughed. I learned that you people were leaving for the coast a matter of hours after that evening, and so I decided not to try to make a rush date with you. But I do want to talk to you, about writing more for Broadway, and about publishing. I don't think there is much point in writing or phoning about such matters, and so I wonder if there is any way for us to have a meeting. I mean soon.

There is going to be a new Loesser this year[25] and so I am inclined to stay close to New York and dance attendance on my bride, the pocket Valkyrie with the lump in front, so can you possibly come to New York for the purposes I have described quite broadly above? If so, my outfit would be delighted to pay for your round-trip fare, as well as for a few days' appropriately lavish expenses. I am sure you are in no need of such encouragement, what with all the millions you

---

23 Johnny Mercer's wife Elizabeth (née Meltazer), known as Ginger (1909–1994).
24 Matthew Michael ('Matty') Malneck (1903–1981), American jazz violinist and songwriter.
25 Hannah Loesser.

have salted away out of royalties on "Work Work Working on the Chain Gang"[26] – but I guess I am expressing my earnestness in wanting to talk with you.

Please accept. Any time after the 15th of July will be fine.

I forgot to mention that it is not mere cupidity which prompts the writing of this note (I made all the loot there is on "Fidgety Joe"[27]), but that I would get enormous pleasure out of an association in the interest of Mercer and his works. You are one of our most brilliant talents, and I believe that you owe yourself some sparkling company here. Maybe I have a way to help such things happen.

And if we don't arrive at anything staggeringly businesslike, we can always sit around and knock Peter Tinturin.[28]

Please let me know. Fondest to you and Ginger.

Sincerely,

27 July 1962: To Johnny Mercer

Dear Johnny:

Thanks for your answer. A day after I sent my letter off to you I read about the Alaskan show and I had a feeling that I would not be hearing from you immediately, so I understood.

I'm glad you like my interest, which is an understatement. I am frothing at the possibilities – although there are no pin-pointed specific ones in mind until I have had a chance to talk it over with you. So I look forward to your arrival. A month or so from now, as you put it, would be fine. Please let me know.

Best,

---

26 Possibly 'Chain Gang' by Sol Quasha and Herb Yakus (1955).
27 Written for the 1939 Paramount Pictures release *Man About Town*.
28 Peter Tinturin (1910–2007), Russian-American film composer; his credits include *Outside of Paradise* (Republic Pictures, 1938) and *Double Deal* (George Randol Productions, 1939).

19 July 1962: To Ira Gershwin

Dear Ira:

I'm afraid you have confirmed my suspicion that I had become a collector's item, and it's a very uncomfortable feeling.[29] Nevertheless, I welcome the pleasure of hearing from you.

Now, about the London Times. How did it ever slip in front of your racing form? And once there, how did it ever tempt you into negotiating its front page? There are better things, like, for instance, coming east. Do you ever? Will you ever? It would be nice to see you again.

Till then, barring some not-likely need for me to be in California – thanks, and love to you and Lee.[30]

Fondly,

27 September 1962: To Ira Gershwin

Dear Ira:

I wonder whether you would like to write lyrics for a Broadway show? Not, of course, simply for the sake of plunging into another one, but there is a project taking form now on a theme which my instinct tells me would tickle your fancy (if I were Groucho or Harry Ruby, at this point I would remark that a dark corner backstage at a Broadway show featuring a lot of pretty broads – is the best place for a writer to get his fancy tickled. But my sober and mature suggestion above is not to be considered a suggestive suggestion, but let us just suggest that it is a seriously suggested suggestion).

At this point, I am not permitted to reveal all, except that a well-appreciated and valuable composer has agreed to do the job, and wants to collaborate with a man of great talent, a man well-informed and seasoned, amiable yet earnest, jocular yet profound.

---

29 Gershwin had sent Loesser a copy of the London *Times* from 12 July 1962, which contained the following note in the Personal column: ' "WHERE'S CHARLEY?": Substantial premium offered for recorded songs from operetta by Frank Loesser.'

30 Ira Gershwin's wife Leonore ('Lee', 1900–1991).

On reviewing this bill of particulars, I thought immediately of you, but did not shoot the idea at the composer, feeling I would rather ask you first whether you felt like writing. The composer wishes to publish with my firm (honest, however arrogant, effective without too much ostensibly vulgar push, and with a president who happens to be both sincere and Jewish). If you chose to tackle the job, would you have any objection to going along with him to these quarters?

One more thing: If it interests you, I believe a great deal of the early work on this project can be accomplished in the West, even though the ultimate hegira[31] and encampment must eventually follow. But maybe by this time you owe yourself a deductible Eastern visit.

Please write me on this. Not, of course, on the possible merits of this particular proposal, but on the subject of your harnessability at all for Broadway.[32] Meanwhile, my fondest to you and Lee.

Sincerely,

27 June 1962: To Donald Kahn[33]

Dear Donald:

I have played over your array of demonstration pieces. I am afraid that although I find many of them attractive, they do not seem to be particularly theatrical.

I suppose I ought to give you a definition which may differ from someone else's. Generally, I feel that most theatrical music requires a violence, or a dynamism, or an expressiveness, which seems to be lacking in the pieces you sent. The fox trot and the waltz, etc., as they occur in the context of a present day musical comedy, are in themselves pure by-product. Witness Perry Como's highly successful version of "Some Enchanted Evening"[34] – a placid, energy-less, uncon-

---

31 A migration, derived from Mohammed's *hegira* from Mecca to Medina in 622.
32 Nothing came of Loesser's suggestion.
33 Donald Kahn was the son of lyricist Gus Kahn (1886–1941) whose credits include 'I'll See You in My Dreams,' 'It Had to Be You,' 'Yes Sir, That's My Baby,' 'Makin' Whoopee' and 'Dream a Little Dream of Me'.
34 Perry Como's recording of 'Some Enchanted Evening' was released by RCA Victor in 1949.

vinced recital. It would have sounded like tse-tse fly juice if it had turned up in the original cast album. On the other hand, Pinza, though not as "popular" among the vast hordes, was enormously effective as THE PERSON IN A DRAMA EMOTIONALLY INVOLVED IN WHAT HE WAS SINGING AND VERY MUCH CONVINCED OF HIMSELF IN THE PART.[35] The piece was written with this effect in mind primarily.

Now your collection of pieces doesn't seem to include this essential intention. Maybe that is difficult without a play and without lyrics, yet I had expected more tunes that bore some of the instinct to dramatize.

All the above doesn't imply that you are not equipped somehow for writing musical comedy scores. Nevertheless, you are not 19, nor do you live in New York where things happen and people set fire to each other. The best suggestion that comes to my mind, is that you get together with a dramatist who has your respect, as well as a drama-minded lyricist, and try a collaboration aimed for the Broadway stage. Seeing what you have done (and I mean done, not an outline and a collection of song phrases) my outfit and I would like very much to have a look and a listen in the hope of agreeing with you and thus becoming your producer-publisher.

Meanwhile, thanks for asking. Do you want the record back? Drop me a note.[36]

Fond greetings,

10 January 1963: To Arnold Horwitt[37]

Dear Arnold:

Anticipating that you will shortly have made an agreement on the amount of royalty you want from your producer for supplying the

---

35 Ezio Pinza had created the role of Emile de Becque in Rodgers and Hammerstein's *South Pacific* (1949).

36 In the end, Kahn did not produce a Broadway show.

37 Arnold Horwitt, lyricist. His Broadway credits include *Make Mine Manhattan* (1948) and *Two's Company* (1952); he also worked in television.

lyrics,[38] I will try to clarify in this note the thoughts and suggestions I spoke to you about briefly. This would take into concern other elements of your agreement with the producers. Of course, your attorney is well aware of the privileges which should remain yours (and your partners') as members of the Dramatists Guild. Nevertheless in recent years there have been some accepted practices which seem to be taken for granted as <u>producer</u> privileges. Just in the event that such subjects might be overlooked, I would like to remind you of certain values which could possibly be vitiated by being placed out of the writers' control.

I must presume that the producer has or will have acquired a basic work in behalf of the collaborators jointly and that, upon the performance of the collaborators' obligations under the production contract, the entire musico-dramatic property will be owned jointly by those collaborators. (This of course, subject to whatever shares they may have contracted to pay the producer and the basic writer out of subsequent income from various other productions, performances, etc. in all media.)

These other media may very well include the customary "original Broadway cast album." It would make me comfortable to know that you and your songwriting collaborator reserve to yourselves the right to negotiate for and dispose of this "subsidiary" right – and that the producer does not appear by some sudden and special magic as a "collaborator" or "author" in any respect.

In short, I think it is fundamentally wrong that the producer should be allowed to make or even negotiate the deal for the cast album. Why? Because it has become evident that many a producer, armed (with or without actual consent of the writers) with the privilege of disposing of the cast album, does so in exchange for the delivery by the record company of limited partnership investment. Almost always in such instances, the bargain ends there. The producer has not been inclined to demand any more than minimal "artist royalty," minimal mechanical royalty, and quite often, no

---

38 It is uncertain which lyrics Loesser refers to here. Horwitt's final Broadway production was several years earlier, *The Girls Against the Boys* (1959).

supporting single records, jazz albums, symphonic treatments of the score, specific advertising and sales promotion of these items, etc. etc. etc.

Now the items listed immediately above are of direct interest and sometimes enormous value to the song writers. On the other hand, the profits to be derived from a producing partnership closed via record company contribution, are of absolutely no interest to the writer with nothing in his hand but a Dramatists Guild contract. He's on the gross, buddy boy. In agreeing to go with a producer, he assumes that the producer's capacity for raising money is what makes him a producer.

As your prospective publisher, I beg you to stand fast in the above matter and some others, which we ought to discuss before you close. This same prayer goes out to your partner by way of a carbon copy of this note, with my apologies for butting in. Just remember that no publisher can have any strength if he isn't given it by the writers.

You want it plainer? How can I fish out a Harry Belafonte single of your ballad, if RCA and your producer are already in bed together?

If you care to invite any discussion between your lawyer and myself I'd be glad to hear from him. Meanwhile, as the man said, wearily setting down the twelve bottles of Cutty Sark, I rest my case.

11 June 1963: To Milton Kramer

I have in hand your memo attached to correspondence from Josef Marais. You asked the question about a use of THE CRICKETS.[39] THE CRICKETS is a pet of mine, and so is Josef Marais. Nevertheless, Josef makes an exceedingly wrong guess in his expressed assumption that he need not ask Frank Music for a film use of the piece. I think in

---

39 'The Crickets' appeared on Marais and Miranda's 1955 LP *Marais and Miranda in Person* (Decca DL9027). Marais began performing with the Dutch singer Rosa de Miranda in 1945.

the nicest way possible he should be advised that a request for license, describing the use, should be forwarded by the picture maker to Frank Music. Naturally, our wish will be to grant such a license if Josef wants it. Nevertheless, Josef must not usurp the function of the publisher licensor – especially for legal and copyright reasons, but more practically important is that his enthusiasm for using one of his own works in a film can only serve to drive the license price down, rather than up. His artistic choice should be honored and applauded by his producer, but the acquisition of rights should be made from strangers. That's us. We were entertaining at that very moment an insecticide tie-up for national television by which THE CRICKETS might earn a tidy sum for publisher and writer both. Or possibly we were considering an African musical in which it would be featured along with other Marais stuff. Shucks: We had no idea what Marais was suggesting out West there. But hold on. If this is more worthwhile for Marais, possibly we can forget the other deals, at least temporarily. Josef should learn to say "I wrote it all right, but it's not mine to deal in. For that I have a respectable and reasonable publisher. Please call him." You may feel free to quote me to Josef. Or use your own eloquent hyperbole.

In the summer of 1963 Loesser travelled to Las Vegas, hoping to arrange a production of *The Most Happy Fella* as a follow-up to an earlier production there of *Guys and Dolls* (while in Las Vegas he also apparently renewed contacts with several performers there, including comedian Milton Berle). He pursued possible business opportunities in England, and corresponded with both Ben Starr and Garson Kanin concerning potential properties. Loesser's attention to details concerning the promotion of his works, the cultivation of new collaborators and properties, business and personal expenses and financial situation – all in the context of his view that letters were stylish narratives with polished prose, often akin to short stories – is apparent in his letter to lawyer Martin Wolman. And he continued to cultivate Marais and Miranda, as late as 1965.

19 July 1963: To Allen Whitehead

Dear Allen:

This is to advise you briefly about my Las Vegas trip.

I took along Trinz from the Sammy Lewis[40] office, and can report that I have been quite convincing about another run of "Guys and Dolls" and possibly one for "MHF" within a year.[41]

Charlie Rich[42] was very cordial (he marked my room bill "complimentary" and I didn't have to pay). On the other hand he was adamantly against continuing "Guys and Dolls" at the Dunes. A great part of his opinion seems to be based on Betty Grable's[43] mercurial attitude. At any rate, he could not be convinced to move back the Kingston Trio[44] and continue my show.

My opinion about Jaques [sic] Foti[45] is that he will not do at all to play the part of Boumin.

As you suggested, I sidled up to Harry Bloomfield and he confirmed the fact that he is to be the New York representative of the Riviera Hotel in Las Vegas. He and I spent a few hours together very sympathetically, and he said he would contact you shortly in New York about "Where's Charley?" and some others. Among other politenesses, I told him I would try to get him seats for "How" opening night here.[46]

I spoke to Stubby Kaye who says he will be available for my present piece of writing – although he hasn't any notion of what it is

---

40 Sammy Lewis (dates unknown), entertainments manager of the New Frontier Hotel in Las Vegas.

41 *Guys and Dolls* opened at the Royal Nevada, Las Vegas, on 7 September 1955. It starred Vivian Blaine (Miss Adelaide), Robert Alda (Sky Masterson) and Sam Levene (Nathan Detroit), reprising their roles from the original Broadway production. *The Most Happy Fella* was apparently not performed in Las Vegas.

42 Charlie Rich (dates unknown) owned the Dunes Hotel in Las Vegas.

43 Betty Grable (1916–1973), American actress and singer. Grable had wanted to appear as Miss Adelaide in the 1955 film of *Guys and Dolls*, a role taken by the original Miss Adelaide, Vivian Blaine. Beginning about that time, Grable performed in a singing act at several Las Vegas hotels.

44 The Kingston Trio (Dave Guard (1934–1991), Bob Shane (1934–2020) and Nick Reynolds (1933–2008)), a popular folk music group.

45 Jacques Foti (1924–2018), Hungarian-American actor, composer and singer.

46 Presumably a planned production of *How to Succeed in Business Without Really Trying*.

about. He once told me he wanted to do Herman in "MHF," but subsequently turned the part down in favor of Lil [sic] Abner.[47]

So much for Las Vegas.

Monday and Tuesday I will spend in San Francisco rehearsing changes for Los Angeles, as well as general refresher work.

I also hope to see Peter Lind Hayes[48] up there. Is there any factual information on "The Guardsman"?[49]

More later.

29 July 1963: To Mona Lipp

Dear Mona:

Answering the Leonard Sillman[50] questions, I am really and truly – as you well know – up to my neck. I haven't been able to read the re-write of the Ben Starr script.[51] I am so far behind with my writing that I don't know when I can get to it. Even though it may have been improved, I have turned this show down twice for production before and the whole subject cannot take precedence now. I am sure Leonard will understand.

Love,

26 August 1963: To Milton Kramer

Dear Milt:

I'm returning herewith your cryptic memo, on which I have jotted my comments. It was only after this that I found a piece of correspondence relating to it. Now it dawns on me that "Julie and Carol" refers

---

47 *Li'l Abner*, with music by Gene de Paul (1919–1988) and lyrics by Johnny Mercer, ran at the St James Theatre, New York, 15 November 1956 to 12 July 1958.
48 Peter Lind Hayes (1915–1998), American vaudeville, film and television actor.
49 Presumably a reference to Hungarian playwright Ferenc Molnár's (1878–1952) *The Guardsman*, which played at the Garrick and Booth theatres, New York, 13 October 1924 to 6 June 1925. Molnár's play *Liliom* (1909) was the basis for Rodgers and Hammerstein's *Carousel* (1945).
50 Leonard Sillman (1908–1982), Broadway producer.
51 Ben Starr (1921–2104), playwright. Possibly Loesser's reference is to *The Family Way*, which played on Broadway at the Lyceum Theatre for only five performances, 13–16 January 1965.

to Julie Newmark [sic] and Carol Lawrence.[52] I had no way of relating the intimate first name cutism with the facts of the case.

I have not yet come to think of Bing Crosby as Bing. As it turned out there was another Bing. Two others. Herman Bing (who is dead) a fair comic – and Rudolph Bing who lives at the Metropolitan Opera.[53] I am glad to say that I have never been confused by thinking of "Bing" as someone's entire name. I am inclined to go further. I even say Garbo who? Or sometimes, who Garbo? Just to be sure. There is only one exception to this: "Frankie" really does mean something all by itself. It may surprise you to know that it doesn't mean someone named Sinatra. It is me, the little old whine maker.

Now to the point. We have lovely memo forms with a line dedicated to the subject of the memo. When I read in this allotted space JULIE AND CAROL AT CARNEGIE HALL[54] it comes to my mind to answer this bit of news with a shrug and the added remark that somebody must have given them tickets. This is how this sort of thing hits my mind. Like the rabbit scene has to be reborn in to Lennie's skull[55] – certain images have to be revived in mine. Now on complete re-examination of both the blue and white pieces of paper covering this subject (both of which I return herewith) I can tell you that I have not only mastered total recall of the existence of a TV film performance by two harpies in chaps – but also of the remarkable fact that I nodded okay to your suggestion to allow performances outside the USA. This was at least a couple of months ago and I thought the subject was dismissed. Well, we have covered it again and I must say it makes life on the hospital bed a busy adventure.

Love and kisses.

---

52 Julie Newmar (born 1933), American actress, dancer and singer; she won the Tony for best featured actress for her role as Katrin Sveg in the 1958 production of Leslie Stevens's *The Marriage-Go-Round*. Carol Lawrence (born 1932), American actress and singer; she played Maria in the original Broadway production of Leonard Bernstein's *West Side Story* (1957). In fact, Loesser is referring to Julie Andrews and Carol Burnett; see below.
53 Herman Bing (1889–1947), German-American actor; Rudolph Bing (1902–1997), general manager of the Metropolitan Opera, New York, 1950–1972.
54 *Julie and Carol at Carnegie Hall*, a 1962 musical comedy television special starring Julie Andrews (born 1935) and Carol Burnett (born 1933), broadcast on CBS.
55 A reference to the plot of *Of Mice and Men* (1937) by Loesser's friend John Steinbeck.

3 August 1962: To Sidney Kornheiser[56] (E. H. Morris)

Dear Sidney:

This will confirm my permission for the cockney parody lyrics as forwarded to me along with a copy of Teddy Holmes'[57] letter to you of July 25.

This permission on my part, as I told you, is granted providing Teddy Holmes secures from this group of record companies (Pye) a concurrently released record by an artist honestly deemed to be of "commercial" standing – of a composition written by me and published by Morris Ltd.[58] As was discussed, this could be "Anywhere I Wander," "My Darling, My Darling," "I've Never Been In Love Before," or something else. Of course, Teddy Holmes knows the latest possibilities as to compositions and artists over there, and so he ought to do the choosing, and let us know what has been promised in return before permission on the parody becomes effective.

As you know, "Baby, It's Cold Outside" never gained much vogue in England, and I have been hesitant about allowing a comedy distortion (however entertaining and successful) to make more noise than the original. That is my reason for asking for a compensating <u>commercial</u> factor as described above.

My suspicious mind suggests the possibility that this parody has already been recorded by the artists, and although that is not an unusual situation, it is nonetheless a technical error which might call for a practical apology.

Lastly, I notice that Teddy indicates that the authors of the parody material will be assigned to "us." I take it he means Morris Ltd., and I insist that the assignment is made directly to Frank Loesser, as are all foreign translations, show orchestrations, etc. I don't mind if you forward a copy of this entire letter to Teddy, who understands me

---

56 Sidney Kornheiser (dates unknown), theatrical agent and at the time part agent of the publishing firm Burke and Van Heusen, Inc.
57 Teddy Holmes (dates unknown), director of Chappell Music.
58 Now part of Chappell Music.

quite well. You might also reassure him that I do indeed know Joyce Blair, who was in the original "Guys & Dolls" company in London.[59]

It was nice talking to you after so long, dear Sidney, and I close with my love. Usually I close with a bang, but the doctor says I'm getting too old for that sort of thing.

29 August 1962: To Ben Starr

Caro Mio Ben:[60]

You have been saluted with a song title created some centuries ago by one of my monks. He did not at all mean "my darling Ben" or anything like it, as he went with girls [. . .] Anyway, I answer your note of August 25th – a self-serving document if I ever read one. I appreciate, of course, your instinct to recite glowingly the various opportunities you have found to make a pact with the devil. Further, I realize, after all this time you have been stuck in the mire of you-know-what, which piles up directly behind and below a talking horse – that you are full of an urgency to pop out into what you think of as a place of brilliant light which also smells sweet.

In the case of "The Big Inch" (which you now choose to call it in an attempt to baffle many a fallible memory), don't be too sure that the emergence of this play on Broadway wouldn't land you in a darker shit-house than you are already in.[61]

These words of mine come with difficulty. Same thing when I felt compelled to instruct Abraham to knock his little boy off. Later they (some Lutheran group) said it had been a "test." Actually, I disliked the little rotter and wanted him out of my realm. The real reason that he was spared, was that Abraham was a proud and talented enough father to rewrite the boy quickly. It was an exhausting process for

---

59 Joyce Blair (1932–2006), English actress and dancer; she sang the minor role of Mimi in the 1953 London production of *Guys and Dolls*.
60 A play on the title of the famous aria 'Caro mio ben' by Tommaso Giordani (1733–1806).
61 Possibly Loesser refers here to a proposed play based on the history of the Big Inch Pipeline, a wartime emergency oil pipeline built 1942–1944 extending from Longview, Texas, to Norris City, Illinois.

poor old Abe, but he straightened the kid out and I was glad to accept a substitute sacrifice – a tired lamb who, although a member in good standing of the Dramatists Guild, had been incurably persistent in attempting to market the same old bundle of uncombed wool, time after time. Here in New York this is known as Lamb's Club Lassitude.[62] You will note that today they don't even have a member who can spell, and those of them who still whimper of a belief in me are just showing off.

You will note that in my management of the universe I play fair. Having created rain, I announce it with thunder and lightning and presently everyone gets wet. I would be a cruel God indeed if I were to thunder and lighten and promptly drop iron stove lids on people. This would be not only murderous – but worse than that, deceptive. I rain rain and I snow snow – with minor variations such as mean wind velocity, temperature, and a variety of artful metamorphic cloud formation just to keep things interesting. But generally speaking, my stuff is as advertised. Stones don't talk while women do. Leopards have spots and peonies have perfume. Among the four examples you couldn't possibly mistake one for the other. Further, I have ordained that fornication brings pleasure. Anybody who gets a headache from it has a self induced headache. Usually from a lingering sense of guilt about not having written as well as he should have.

And now. As your most powerful sponsor toward an ultimate sainthood, I give you every possible moment of heartfelt attention and concern. Nevertheless, having thus far decided that your peony smells like a leopard, I cannot now impose upon another of my subjects even the slightest suspicion that I believe your peony does indeed smell like a peony. If I send him rain it has to be good old blessed rain, and if I send him stove lids it is because it is only after I have told him accurately what was going to fall. I hope you will recollect in passing that I warned everybody about the flood. It was only Noah who listened. I had not remarked "See the nice water now rising

---

62 The Lambs Club (currently at 3 West 51st Street, New York), established in 1874 and the oldest professional theatrical organisation in the United States, is a private social club for supporters of the arts.

above your navel! Take a dip! Stick around a while in the valley! When it's up to here gurgle me a psalm."

To put it briefly (and I never have), I cannot be the agent for the sale of something I have not, in spirit, bought. That is called "unloading" – and if I were prone to such a practice, I would be Irving Lazar[63] in no time – and nobody prays to him.

But, you say in your letter ". . . I'm sounding you out when the play has a certain warmth . . ." Am I to infer that this certain warmth now glows out of a newly amended script? If so, I would like to read any new version. Remember that I would much rather buy it than sell it. So give me what news there is, hopefully about how to avoid the growingly ugly image of segregation conflict in the south. This subject today bids fair to spoil an otherwise funny, bouncy, imaginative play journalistically referred to as the Political Scene. It certainly frigs up a relatively defenseless fifteen hundred seat comedy like yours.

I admit a sense of lost dignity as I re-read my approach to you directly above. I seem to be wheedling, imploring, urging you on an almost Morris Office basis. I hasten to assure you that I have not asked for some adjustment for the sake of an ultimate "sale." If you believe in me as your God, you cannot help but believe in yourself as one who needs no prodding into perfecting himself in my image. You may consider that I have called upon your conscience, and that's all.

Well, I must go now and tend my bruises. Spinning through space these days on my rounds, I get jostled by the strangest objects. Whatever they are, I guess I have to accept them as my work and therefore my responsibility. I wish there really were a devil so I could honestly lay off some of the blame for everything that happens. But he, too, would be my creation and again the fault would be all mine. Oh shit.

Blessings.

Frank Loesser

P.S. Speaking of blame, I am not such a fool as to bar my saints, apostles and disciples here at the office from joining me in my various

---

63 Irving Paul Lazar (1907–1993), talent agent for both film stars and authors; his clients included Cary Grant, Cole Porter, Ernest Hemingway, Humphrey Bogart and Loesser's friend William Saroyan.

judgments, opinions and acts. So you may consider that this letter is from the entire holy phalanx. We are one. So yell on [Milton] Kramer.

20 November 1962: To Garson Kanin[64]

Dear Gar:

Just to clarify my response to you in our telephone conversation:

The subject of "Born Yesterday"[65] has, for a long time, intrigued me as to its musical possibilities. But in thinking about this, I have invariably concluded that it ought to be a "serious" work. What I mean by "serious" is exactly what you meant when you wrote the original. I do not think that the comedic innocence and ignorance of the leading lady, or the fact of official banquets, balls, luncheons, egg-rollings, gymkhanas,[66] parades or other such gay gatherings should influence the musicalization of this piece in any <u>major</u> way. That would be the tendency of the average picture-maker, or the average adaptor for Broadway, and I am, thank God, neither.

What I think is that you have written a master work which comments pointedly on our time, just as "What Makes Sammy Run" does, and just as "Death of a Salesman" does.[67] It is a giant, and should remain one, and above everything else, should not rely on certain conveniences (the girl happens to be pretty and witty; the newspaperman happens to be young and good-looking; the sub-rosa plot can easily be hatched at a table during a fan dance at the Capitol Casino, or that a tryst can find convenient locale in one of the more bizarre corners of the Smithsonian Institute; the senators taking rhumba lessons; Harry has choreographed flashback dreams of his

---

64 Garson Kanin (1912–1999), American writer and film and theatrical director.
65 Kanin's play *Born Yesterday*, premiered on Broadway in 1946; a film version was released in 1950. Partly a Pygmalion story – junk dealer Harry Brock hires a journalist to tutor his mistress Billie Dawn – it also deals with Brock's attempt to bribe a congressman.
66 Originally an Anglo-Indian expression that generally refers to social and sporting clubs.
67 *What Makes Sammy Run*, a novel by Budd Schulberg (1914–2009) published in 1941; Arthur Miller's (1915–2005) play *Death of a Salesman* debuted on Broadway in 1949.

slugging childhood; etc. etc. etc. etc. etc.). Such things are easy but they are a barrel of shit if their "entertainment" value is taken as the REASON for musicalizing.

What I am trying to say is, the giant should stay a giant, and help emotionalize itself by being sung at the right times. That is what "Carmen" is, and also what "Show Boat" is, and also "West Side Story," and also "Carousel." You see what I am driving at.

To suggest that some special specialty talent, or proven popular approval in advance about some actor or actress is going to help a piece of this kind – is, in my opinion, to piss in the wind. When I think about a play in terms of musicalizing it, the first thing I do is look for avenues for emotional explosion on the part of the main characters – based on their original delineation. I refuse to invent as a sine-qua-non the fact that our girl was once a fan dancer, or a car-hop, or a prostitute, or a Roxy usher – or anything else that will give her a characteristic "bit" or "number" which [has] nothing to do with her thoughts about her sweet father wanting her to have a hot lunch.

Please don't think for a moment that I would overlook any chance to use entertaining diversions, juggling, tap-dancing, magic, Think-A-Drink Hoffman at a senate reception,[68] the Gaudschmidt [sic] Brothers[69] walking the girl's poodles, Willie West and McGinty redoing the White House portico,[70] the Washington Cloakroom Ballet by Jerry Robbins,[71] or Fink's Mules[72] picturesquely activating the traditional Democratic Party emblem, etc. etc. etc. – but first and foremost, I have got to believe the singing of the principal people, and that singing has got to take place mostly under emotional duress, just like "One Fine Day," or the "Carousel" soliloquy, or "Luck Be a

---

68 Charles Hoffman (dates unknown), known as 'Think-A-Drink Hoffman', was a vaudevillian whose act included a bar and cocktail shakers that he used to create any drink an audience asked for.

69 The Goldschmidt family were prominent German-British bankers.

70 A comedy trio from Lancashire, England.

71 Presumably a made-up ballet Loesser credits to American choreographer and dancer Jerome Robbins (1918–1998).

72 An animal vaudeville act popular in the 1910s and 1920s.

Lady Tonight," or "Hey There," or "Standing on the Corner," or "The Man I Love."[73]

Am I breaking through? I don't believe in pre-casting a musicalization of this, but simply in respecting its enormous values and translating them into the larger-than-life, more poignant, more colorful, more everything world of the musical as I see it. In short, trained seals can't do a thing for "Hamlet." And Jack Paar's Nielson[74] can't remotely help him play Lincoln.

What I really keep saying is that you have a wonderful play, and that its sights should not be lowered, but I think you will have to learn to feel my medium, rather than just respect it or admire it or wonder at it, or get rich with it. Toward this end, leave us shortly take a walk. I suggest that we do this before winter really sets in. Under 32 degrees I start writing "Boheme" all over again, and neither of us has any right to touch it.

Love and kisses to you and to Ruth.

Sincerely,

14 January 1963: To Milton Berle[75]

Dear Milton:

Once more a big hooray for what a brilliant job you have done with the act at the Desert Inn. I have recently finished yelling an unrhymed paean to you into the ear of Nat Lefkowitz,[76] and I think it only fair that you should get at least the echo of my very sincere tribute to your genius. Really, Milt, you are a master and I salute you.

---

73 'One Fine Day', Cio-Cio-San's aria from Puccini's *Madama Butterfly* (1904); Billy Bigelow's soliloquy from Rodgers and Hammerstein's *Carousel* (1945); 'Luck Be a Lady' from Loesser's *Guys and Dolls* (1950); 'Hey There' from Adler and Ross's *The Pajama Game* (1954); 'Standing on the Corner' from Loesser's *The Most Happy Fella* (1956); and George Gershwin's 'The Man I Love', written for but deleted from *Lady, Be Good* (1924) and then put into *Strike Up the Band* (1927).

74 Possibly a reference to the Nielsen TV ratings that measure the viewing figures for television programmes.

75 Milton Berle (Mendel Berlinger, 1908–2002), comedian.

76 Nat Lefkowitz (1905–1983), talent agent executive and co-chairman of the William Morris Agency.

As a producer, as a director, as a performer, as a writer, and of course, as a person. Without being a person you couldn't be any of the other things, and I'm glad and proud that I know you.

Love,

17 January 1963: To Martin Wolman

Dear Martin:

Happy New Year. I send you this wish without any security or faith, that the new year will turn out at all that way – in view of the new tax regulations which you have been kind enough to describe and send to me. I mean specifically those involving "business" entertainment expense, meals and travel.

Your firm has had the kindness to send to me a sample form carefully designed to allow me to conform to the new regulations in reporting on the above type of expense. I have been staring at this blank document all day in desperate puzzlement about how to fill it out in terms of what happened last night. I will shortly describe the events of last night and those leading up to it and then ask you to judge from this quite accurate novelette – how I can apply it effectively and precisely in the filling out of the form you have so carefully prepared.

THE NOVELETTE

During the year 1960 or 1961 I suggested to a friend of mine, Arbit Blatas,[77] that I knew of his old and solid friendship with Marcel Marceau.[78] I had a very important business purpose in wanting to meet and discuss things with Marceau, who is a valuable star and a very shy and sensitive artist. Blatas half-heartedly agreed to introduce me, because he himself had a theatrical project in mind to present to Marceau and did not relish the idea of mine superseding it. Nevertheless, I succeeded in convincing Blatas that my project was sounder and the process of convincing him cost me several rounds of

---

77 Arbit Blatas (1908–1999), Lithuanian artist.
78 Marcel Marceau (1923–2007), French mime artist.

drinks, lunches, etc. – the expense of which I am quite sure appeared justifiably as deductible in my reports in those years. Blatas did indeed introduce me to Marceau at that time, but it was not seeming that we fellow artists should plunge into a business meeting without first knowing each other. I forget the details but I am quite sure that if you look back you will find it as one or possibly two of the items in those years – tagged as generative business expense.

Now Blatas is not fundamentally a business connection at all. He is a painter, well esteemed – nevertheless not really in my business. On the other hand, he did agree to act gratis as a sort of agent. Consequently, I felt in those good old days that it was perfectly sound for me to apply those items of expense, which added to my powers of persuasion and resulted in my first meeting with Marceau. I am not so sure about <u>these bad old days</u>.

The proposal I had (and still have) for Marceau was that he should tour a mime version of the musical "WHERE'S CHARLEY?", possibly his own adaptation, plus my adaptation of my own music. I represent the majority royalty income from this work, and am entitled by the other authors to negotiate and deal for it.

After the seemingly frivolous meeting I mentioned above, Marceau left the country and did not reappear in these parts until the first of this year. I wanted to bring up the "WHERE'S CHARLEY?" subject this time, but since there had been a lapse of years since the original meeting, I felt inclined to call upon Blatas to help me again. Marceau is currently appearing at the New York City Center.[79] I could not, in all respect for proper salesmanship, arrange a date with Marceau at the risk of having to tell him I had not seen his show. I believe even the United States Government can understand that.

Therefore, a few days ago, I purchased four seats for his show at the City Center. They were for myself and my wife (who as you know, is theatrically famous, decorative and authoritative), Blatas and his girlfriend (without whom he will not make any kind of date). I paid

---

79 Marceau began a four-week engagement at the City Center beginning 1 January 1963; see the *New York Times*, 3 January 1963, 5.

cash for the tickets and, alas, have no receipt, although I do indeed have the stubs which indicate the price paid (about $20.00).

Blatas had made an after-theatre supper appointment with Marceau for the five of us, and we were to pick him up back stage and take him to the Plaza Hotel.

Mrs. Loesser and I called a taxi at about 8:00 P.M. and drove to Blatas' address to pick him and his friend up. Thence to the theatre. That was approximately $1.40. We attended the show. Then we went to Marceau's dressing room and told him he was wonderful (I don't expect to include as deductible items the cost of liniment for over-applauded palms, or bills for laryngitis prescriptions upon having delivered lengthy and loud paeans to Marceau). But in the dressing room Marceau had lots of company and was delayed in getting dressed and joining us. Meanwhile, our taxi waited. Finally, I squired the ladies to the Plaza, and sent the same taxi back to wait for Marceau and Blatas, who eventually joined us in the same taxi. The total taxi bill was $2.50.

Now we are at the Plaza (Oak Room). The headwaiter had been kind enough to hold our table (reserved by my secretary earlier) and this kind act predicted my delivery of a large tip at the end of the evening. For business reasons I should pre-purchase the good will of any maitre d'. The five of us embarked on the usual convivialities. Marceau, Blatas and his girlfriend all ordered heavy dinners. This is not a surprise since most artists (especially theatrical ones) like to do their big eating after the day's labors are over. Mrs. Loesser and I kept them company with more drinks.

Shortly after our orders were in, a coffee cup was placed on the space next to mine in anticipation of a table hop from Leonard Lyons, the famous columnist. As you know, he is of tremendous importance to anyone like me, and I couldn't very well tell him to go away. Nor could I tell him that I insist he talk business to me. What he wants is cozy, quotable commentaries and other kinds of column news.

Well sir, he got it. But I want it to go on record here that it cost me a cup of coffee.

No sooner had our orders been served, than there appeared hovering over our table two very vastly valued colleagues. One is

Harry Kurnitz,[80] with whom I have been friendly for years (I believe he is probably the best motion picture and theatre light comedy author around). The other was Paddy Chayefsky,[81] the famous playwright, who has cost me many a sandwich and many a drink and many a wasted hour – in my efforts to make him let me musicalize his famous movie "Marty," possibly for Danny Kaye. Here opportunity knocked. It not only knocked, but it lingered. The Oak Room didn't seem to have many available good tables and further, I suspect that Kurnitz and Chayevsky were already bored with each other at this point in the evening. At any rate, these two business opportunities HAD to be asked to join us. And that is what happened. They were so happy! Leonard Lyons was so cozy! Blatas was so jocular! Indeed, it turned out that Marceau and I never had a chance in the world to even embark on the notion of a business conference on this occasion.

At nearly two in the morning, we closed the place. I signed a check for which I will be billed early in February. It amounted to something like $60.00. In addition to that, I gave the headwaiter $15.00 and then paid another $1.50 taxi bill. This figure is a little more than it takes for us to get home since we dropped off two of our friends and one of those routes was an out-of-the-way one.

The business result of the meeting was not remotely discernable. I promised to call Marceau shortly to arrange a new date. I expect to do so and I expect that it will involve further expenses (although this time I am confident that I will not need Blatas). Further, I have confidence now that I will acquire the rights to "Marty," since I laughed at all Chayevsky's jokes and didn't once bother him with business. Incidentally, the chance meeting with Kurnitz gave me a possible inside track into certain businesses of Noel Coward, with whom he is now collaborating. Frankly, I think he was disposed to bring up the subject more out of a tendency to enjoy my wife's company than

---

80 Harry Kurnitz (1908–1968), playwright, novelist and screenwriter of *The Thin Man Goes Home* (MGM, 1945) and *Witness for the Prosecution* (United Artists, 1957), among others.
81 Paddy Chayefsky (1923–1981), American playwright, novelist and screenwriter; he received three Academy Awards, for the romantic comedy *Marty* (United Artists, 1955), *The Hospital* (United Artists, 1971) and *Network* (MGM, 1976).

mine. I believe he has eyes for her, which is a good reason for his having visited our table, but of course I can't prove that to you.

Now suppose this supper gathering had taken place somewhere other than the Plaza, where I happen to have a charge account. There would have been a total of about $100 paid out of my pocket. I would have no proof that I had wined and dined anyone; I could not with any honesty report a single bit of business discussion; the theatre stubs would only prove that I had <u>been entertained</u>, which I don't imagine is a deductible item.

Once more to Leonard Lyons: As I have told you, he is an extremely valued connection. He has four sons and I have attended each of their Bar Mitzvahs, as well as the eldest's wedding. In each instance I am quite sure that I have given the boys gifts which cost me far in excess of $25.00. There are undoubtedly to be three more weddings, and I know that I <u>want</u> to lavish gifts on each occasion. All for the express purpose of keeping cozy with Leonard Lyons, who appreciates such things, and can thus be counted on to continue his favorable expressions about me and my work in his broadly syndicated column, as well as orally among a host of influential and valuable people in my field. Lyons personally introduced me to Walter Winchell,[82] Lindsay and Crouse, Moss Hart, Harold Rome, Greta Garbo, Mrs. F.D.R., Billy Rose, and countless other people who, in one way or another, have positively influenced my work and benefits since. As I told you above, I will want to continue with the gift giving, but under the new rules I will have to appear niggardly. I suggest that you recollect that in twenty-five years I have never paid a publicity man or press agent any kind of fee or salary for such services. I prefer to spend time and money on my own direct contacts, and I don't think that I have done badly with this policy. If I am now radically limited in my behavior as a spender who casts his bread great distances out on the water, I am very much afraid about my future.

The other night I took my wife to see and hear Sergio Franchi[83] at the Waldorf. Since the newspaper strike, business is bad and Franchi

---

82 Walter Winchell (1897–1972), gossip columnist and radio news commentator.
83 Sergio Franchi (1926–1990), Italian-American singer and actor.

was ever so glad that we came. We asked him to our table and didn't talk one damn word of business. I make better than one hundred such visits in the average year. Just to let the performer, who is fundamentally responsible for my basic income (see facts on the continual increase in public performance income from ASCAP between 1934 and the present time. It goes roughly from $200 annually to about $60,000 in 1962).

Also, I cover a great many night clubs and theatres for the purpose of casting. I cannot select an actor or singer or musician by looking at his X-rays, or a chart of his height and weight.

What do I do about all this in 1963, and possibly thereafter? Should I stay home, or should I continue with my increasingly successful career in the manner to which it is accustomed? Either way, it appears that I will sooner or later go broke.

Love and kisses,

Frank Loesser

P.S. This letter has taken most of a business day to write. I could have been writing a song. I guess I'm not supposed to be in that business any more – what with all the tax crap keeping me so preoccupied.

7 March 1963: To Marcel de Miranda[84]

My dear Marcel:

I have in hand your musical message delivered in person last evening by your very reliable folks. I marvel at your accurate memory of that obscure old cantata of mine. I can't say I have equal enthusiasm for your qualities as a lyric writer, but I do indeed get the message!

Please by all means get in touch with me when you are in or near New York. But first inquire from Josef and Miranda about where I am because it might just be California, and that might be nearer to you.

Again, my profound thanks.

Sincerely,

---

84 Marcel de Miranda (dates unknown), son of Josef Marais and Miranda.

2 January 1964: To the ASCAP
Popular Awards Panel

Gentlemen:

I'd like to add my support to the request for a special award made by Josef Marais in accordance with the terms of Section VI of the Writer's Distribution Formula. Let me begin by suggesting that Josef Marais is in the fullest sense a writer of (and here I quote the terms of Section VI): "... works having a unique prestige value for which adequate compensation would not otherwise be received by such writers; ... works that are performed substantially in media not surveyed by the Society."

Josef Marais, together with Miranda Marais, have been over the past twenty years full time writers and performers of folk-inspired music. All of this music is licensed by ASCAP.

It cannot be denied that the activity of Josef Marais over this long period has been in great measure responsible for some of the vogue and success of "folk-style" material in the ASCAP catalogue.

Josef Marais and Miranda have toured the length and breadth of not only this continent but much of the world, performing in concert halls, auditoriums, colleges, universities, high schools – in short whenever and wherever an audience can be accumulated. They have brought their music (ASCAP licensed) to the far corners of the country and developed an enthusiastic and knowledgeable audience, numbering in the many thousands.

As we know, the distribution formula of ASCAP is not particularly well-suited to evaluate properly this type of performance, and Josef Marais has, I believe, not received ASCAP revenue commensurate with his influence and <u>lasting</u> importance.

An additional indignity: Mr. Marais himself is forced to pay fees to ASCAP in most of the concert halls in which he performs. These fees are not excessive, ranging from $5.00 to $20.00 each, but over the past twenty years they surely have totaled several thousands of dollars. This presents an odd paradox at best: an ASCAP member who is exploiting and performing portions of the ASCAP catalogue of songs which he himself has contributed to the ASCAP catalogue, is nevertheless, forced to pay for this privilege.

Much of the Marais catalogue has been available to the public through book publications. Ballantine Pocket Books just completed a new printing, ringing the edition up to one hundred thousand (indicating in some small measure the impact that his work has on the public), and another book is in preparation. He has also arranged for GUITAR and DULCIMER. These publications are also available.

Very special mention should be made of the importance of his works to the youth of the nation. His songs appear with regularity in many publications for elementary school. In addition, Josef Marais and Miranda are frequently featured on recordings which accompany these books and are disseminated in school systems in the country. In this way their impact on the children of the nation in the formative stages of their cultural life is quite important, and must ultimately accrue to the benefit of all of us interested in the finer things in music and directly (in pecuniary terms) thus benefit ASCAP.

I therefore urge as an individual with considerable ownership in publishing companies licensing exclusively through ASCAP, and as a long-term writer member of ASCAP whose income directly contributes to the awards pool, that the utmost consideration be given to Josef Marais, not only in terms of a cash award but in terms of an official citation from the membership of ASCAP for his continuing noteworthy contributions to ASCAP over the years.

Sincerely,
Frank Loesser

6 December 1965: To Mr. and Mrs. Josef Marais

Dear Josef and Miranda:

Answering your last, first of all the new offspring is a girl and a very pretty one, no doubt maternal influence. Her name is Emily.

The Open Air Concert record is absolutely a charmer and I have played it several times. Incidentally, a question: it seems to me the piece called "Sponono" differs a great deal from one you used to sing which had an extra syllable in it, and the refrain went re mi fa sol, with the sol on the downbeat.[85] But what's the difference, I like them both. Hannah enjoys some pieces more than others, and generally can be regarded as a fan.

Thanks and love and Merry Christmas from all of us.

9 May 1963: To Allan Sherman[86]

Listen!

Thanks for your note. It appears now that Padula[87] and my company are talking together about a production combine on your subject. Assuming that they close the deal together shortly, you may regard me as the western representative of this tower of managerial strength, and starting early in July we will commune.

I think your titles are real darling. If you pick a mess of our stuff (Frank Music and its affiliated publishing houses), I'm sure that we can find a way to approve eight or so of them for one of your song packages. But of course there is no absolute guarantee on that, so if you get serious about parodying any of our stuff before I get out west, please shoot me the titles and I'll put you in touch with my boss Mr. Kramer, who is the last word on these things.

And now to more serious things. How are you? I, too, miss our long fireside chats. As soon as I get out west, I'll stock up on seltzer and filtered cigarettes.

Best,

Loesser had considerable contact with playwright and novelist Paddy Chayefsky about this time – not only in connection with the film *Marty*, but also with respect to Chayefsky's play *The Passion of Josef D.* – that is particularly revealing of Loesser's relationship to

---

85 Marais and Miranda's Open Air Concert at the Bowman Arts Theatre, Idyllwild, California, in October 1965, was recorded and self-released; see https://www.discogs.com/release/9572408-Marais-And-Miranda-Open-Air-Concert.

86 Allan Sherman (1924–1973), American songwriter and satirist.

87 Edward Padula (1916–2001), theatre producer and stage manager; he won the Tony Award for Charles Strouse and Lee Adams's *Bye Bye Birdie* (1960).

language and words. By the same token, a long letter to television writer Cynthia Lindsay is an exegesis on Loesser's thoughts about writing Broadway songs. And he sent good luck to Noël Coward on the opening night of his new Broadway show, *The Girl Who Came to Supper*.

8 July 1963: To Paddy Chayefsky

Dear Paddy:

I have a gnawing feeling about your play title. I saw it in print in the newspaper a couple of days after you and Arthur agreed on it and it gave me a finicky pang. You have become accustomed to the pinpointedness of mine about some areas of the English language. So I know you will bear with me while I point out something about the word "Passion".[88]

Please note that this is a capitalized word and that you intend to precede it with the word "the" and follow it with the word "of." I love and applaud the use of the religioso motif, but let me tell you something about the meaning of the word "passion" – especially since the words you have it placed between make any ulterior or secondary meaning impossible. Passion in the New Testament sense, and I believe in some translations within the Old Testament – means suffering. I think it was two of the four gospels (Matthew and Mark) which report pretty much identically on the Lord's "passion" taking great pains to quote Jesus as saying "Lord, Lord why have you forsaken me" (known better to us yahudim as, "Eli, Eli. etc.").

Generally speaking the whole point of the gospels is just what the word originally means, which is: "God's spell" – the word spell meaning actually what the German spiel or the old Norse spel meant. This roughly means "words," thus the "words of God" are being reported by a variety of witnesses and although all are to some extent historians concerning other points in the life of Jesus – all lead climatically to what is called the "Passion" – the expression of final suffering.

---

88 Paddy Chayefsky's *The Passion of Josef D.*, based on the life of Stalin, had a short run at the Ethel Barrymore Theatre in February 1964.

In modern times a great many European composers, among them J.S. Bach, have made musical settings to the "Passion" and I believe many, if not all, are intoned by choruses. Of course the famous Passion Plays dramatize as exactly as possible the scenes preceding the crucifixion and, if I am not mistaken, the entombment and resurrection are also included. These latter two examples are a broadened use of the word "passion" and have had a tendency to diffuse that real meaning of the word.

Since you are probably as meticulous as anybody about how you come off in the use of our language[89] – on the stage as well as in print – I beg of you to consider carefully how that word lines up with the concept of Stalin and his deification of Lenin for his own purposes.

Remember that the 'passion' is that of the Lord and it is only according to – let us say Matthew – that we hear of it. I don't think it can be called Saint Matthew's passion. Please think of this and weigh it carefully before that good Catholic Walter Kerr, and that probably Catholic Bob Coleman, and that maybe once Catholic John Chapman[90] start quarreling with the point you are trying to make.

Before you do anything please check with some real authority other than me. Being an atheist I am highly unreliable, biased, badly informed and already in hell. The hell here at the moment on the beach at Santa Monica consists of fireworks and jazz music and jazz barbecues just about evenly divided as to smoke and decibels between my left and right side neighbors. Anyway hell is getting my kids tan at about $8,000 a month. I better write something commercial.

Love,

Frank

Unshriven but neatly circumcised

---

89 Loesser's description of Chayefsky's use of language finds a parallel in the review of *The Passion of Josef D.* in the *New York Times*, 12 February 1964, 29, which notes Chayefsky's 'intoxication with the thunder of the English language'.
90 Walter Kerr (1913–1996), Broadway theatre critic; Robert Coleman (1900/1–1974), drama critic for the *Daily Mirror*; and John Chapman 1901/2–1972), theatre critic for the *New York Daily News*.

13 September 1963: To Cynthia Lindsay[91]

Dear Cynthia:

I hope by this time you are prodding your brilliant and shapely skull in the interest of doing the Broadway musical theatre a favor. This note is to try to give you an idea of how I think on this subject. Some of what follows may sound like rule of thumb, and dogma and other nasty things – and some of it in fact is just that. But bear with me.

Like I mentioned on the phone, a great great number of principal show songs are written in the first or second person singular and sometimes plural – and express a wish, or a want, a prayer, a hope, or a purpose. For example:

"Someone to Watch Over Me"

"Surrey With the Fringe on Top"

"I'm Gonna Wash that Man Right Out of My Hair"

"Why Can't You Behave"

"Wouldn't It Be Loverly"

"Where Is The Life That Late I Led"[92]

Also, there are phrases not contained in the titles themselves, but which clearly indicate the purpose of the singer. To wit:

"—let me go way from the Mississippi"

"—and the hell with Burgandy" [sic]

"—if we only had a lousy little grand we could be a millionaire"[93]

---

91 Cynthia Lindsay (1915–2007), American writer known in particular for the television series *My Three Sons* (CBS, 1964–1972; she contributed episodes 1964–1967).

92 'Someone to Watch Over Me' from George and Ira Gershwin, *Oh, Kay!* (1926); 'The Surrey With the Fringe on Top' from Rodgers and Hammerstein, *Oklahoma!* (1943); 'I'm Gonna Wash that Man Right Out of My Hair' from Rodgers and Hammerstein, *South Pacific* (1949); 'Why Can't You Behave' from Cole Porter, *Kiss Me, Kate* (1948); 'Wouldn't It Be Loverly' from Lerner and Loewe, *My Fair Lady* (1956); 'Where Is The Life That Late I Led' from Cole Porter, *Kiss Me, Kate* (1948).

93 '—let me go way from the Mississippi' from 'Ol' Man River' from Jerome Kern and Oscar Hammerstein II, *Show Boat* (1927); '—and the hell with Burgandy' [sic] from 'Song of the Vagabonds' from Rudolf Friml, Brian Hooker and William H. Post, *The Vagabond King* (1926); '—if we only had a lousy little grand we could be a millionaire' from 'The Oldest Established' from Loesser's *Guys and Dolls* (1950).

You yourself can think of hundreds more. Also on thinking further, you will recollect that many many of them occurred quite early in their plays – quite a few in the very first scene. Almost all are delivered by people who propose that they have principal parts – and appreciable emotional stakes and pursuits.

Now look ever sharper. These songs differ from the pure "self-descriptive" or "commentary" or "biographical" numbers. I will name a few:

"I Can't Say No" [sic]

"I'm a Time-Study Man"

"Jennie"

"I'm Alive, I'm A-tingle, I'm A-glow"

"You've Got to Brush Up on Your Shakespeare" [sic][94]

Note that these songs do a great deal to <u>identify</u> the singer to the audience – as to his character, occupation, or opinion. But the vast majority of them stop short of declaring any motive, or wish, or purpose. In short, they fail to catapult us into a true concern over the fortunes of the people singing them. Recollect for a moment how many many many of these are sung by minor characters and not true principals. I guess in the English language, Gilbert and Sullivan are responsible for making healthy and frequent use of these "self-descriptive, commentary and biographical" songs. To help your memory along I will quote:

The judge's song in "Trial by Jury"

"Polish Up the Handles So Carefully"

"I've Got a Little List"[95]

etc., etc., etc.

---

94 'I Cain't Say No' from Rodgers and Hammerstein, *Oklahoma!* (1943); 'I'm a Time-Study Man' from 'Think of the Time I Save' from Adler and Ross, *The Pajama Game* (1954); 'Jennie' ('The Saga of Jenny') from Weill and Gershwin, *Lady in the Dark* (1941); 'I'm Alive, I'm A-tingle, I'm A-glow' from Jule Styne and Leo Robin, *Gentlemen Prefer Blondes* (1949); 'Brush Up Your Shakespeare' from Cole Porter, *Kiss Me, Kate* (1948).
95 'The Judge's Song' from Gilbert and Sullivan, *Trial by Jury* (1875); 'Polish Up the Handles So Carefully' from 'When I was a Lad' from Gilbert and Sullivan, *HMS Pinafore* (1878); 'I've Got a Little List' from Gilbert and Sullivan, *The Mikado* (1885).

True, in Gilbert and Sullivan the principal characters did indeed sing a great deal of this kind of stuff. But there was no intention that the characters should be anything but puppet or cartoon creatures. It was a kind of journalism. One applauded, but the heart did not bleed. It wasn't supposed to.

I will now be frank with you. I expect you to write stuff of the heart bleeding variety. Not necessarily with all the slobber of "Showboat," or of "Music Man," or of "Sound of Music" (those are three distinct kinds of deep slobber) – but with enough urgent care about the people involved so that the customers will <u>believe</u> the ballads. A show can have a grownupness about it and still be enough of a slob – as witness "West Side Story." A show can be funny enough and yet have its moments of pathos, as observe "Guys and Dolls." A show can be bitter and ironical and yet deliver to its audience the pitiful and terribly real female victim of the play's own irony – like look at "Pal Joey."

So don't think that my purpose is to dump you into a sticky puddle of "Desert Song" or "Student Prince."[96]

Now I know you know all this as a prose writer. I could read it in every chapter of "Mother Climbed Trees"[97] which you balanced just beautifully. But I'm telling you all of the above, just in case you might have some mistaken notion that a Broadway musical comedy comes under the heading of "divertissement," or "something clever," or "something amusing." The last thing that you should think is that you are dealing with "fantasy." THE SINGING AND DANCING AND COSTUMES, THE LIGHTING, THE ORCHESTRAL EFFECTS – ARE EXACTLY WHAT MAKE IT A FANTASY. But in my book it has got to start for real. Oh, I know fantasies have worked. Like "Peter Pan." But I don't believe the musical[98] was as good as the original and was simply a stunt designed in favor of Queen Mary who seemed to cherish being slung by the crotch all evening. I don't wish this kind of writing chore for you.

---

96 Sigmund Romberg, *The Desert Song* (1926) and *The Student Prince* (1924).
97 Cynthia Lindsay, *Mother Climbed Trees* (New York, 1958).
98 By Moose Charlap and Carolyn Leigh (1954). Starred Mary Martin ('Queen Mary').

Now once more back to songs which tell us of a principal character's emotional purpose and desires. Even if the tunes are only fair
and even if the lyrics are not quite brilliant – these songs indeed give
us <u>memorable</u> landmarks about emotional motive. And in my book
these motives should become evident shortly after their expressors
have first taken stage. I will give you one example and then retire for
the day. Hillbilly girl expresses wish for love but also confesses special
ineptitude, and therefore a certain amount of impatience.[99] This
sums up neatly in "You Can't Get a Man With a Gun." Shortly thereafter a handsome man appears and she gives one gockle that tells us
she would like him in the lifelong kip. Very quickly there is revealed a
coincidence that both of these people have a kinship in that they are
both expert sharpshooters. Emotionally she would follow him to the
ends of the earth. Practically she accepts the job of following him to
the end of the circuit. The result is a buoyant and enthusiastic expression called "There's No Business Like Show Business." The girl has
gained proximity to the maybe attainable man. We have accomplished a first scene and the game is on. We care. In the relative leisure
that follows she admits her ignorance about romance or its techniques and makes us care a little more tenderly by singing "They Say
That Falling In Love Is Wonderful." She is hopeful. She doesn't know
how she'll land the man, and <u>we</u> don't, but we hope with her. It
becomes all the more poignant when the man gives her a stiff arm
entitled "The Girl That I Marry."

All right little Cynthia, don't brush away that tear, it will come in
handy. You need it. You have been fed memorable little emotional
kumquats. You can repeat them to yourself in the intermission and
care some more – a lot easier than you could repeat a page full of
Jean Kerr's jokes in the "Mary, Mary" interval.[100]

Of course, remember the language of this show is an operation. It
could be that Rosalind Russell with the glasses is the only secretary at

---

99 What follows refers to Irving Berlin's *Annie Get Your Gun* (1946).
100 Jean Kerr's (1922–2003) play *Mary, Mary* premiered at the Helen Hayes
Theatre, New York, on 8 March 1961 and played for 1,572 performances (closed 12
December 1964).

the U.N. who can translate Nigerian dialect – she frets over the days and night at Berlitz that gave her this proficiency, but no boy friend. All of a sudden Nigeria is admitted to the U.N. and she is sat next to this beautiful black giant. She has had lots of dreams about him (alternating with horses and a few water scenes) and here he is in the flesh presently requesting that she accompany him on an important mission to beautiful Lake Victoria. Wow! The only trouble is he is on his special tribal dignity. Okay, you know the rest. Only observe that this is no longer the same cast. It is now a blacked up Yul Brynner and a willowy city girl.[101] Irving Berlin and Dorothy Fields can't do it. Maybe it goes to Cole Porter. Don't ask me who should write the book. At any rate, you have observed that fundamentally we are dealing with exactly the same array of problems.

I'm all done for now. In my next I will discuss with you why you can't talk too much or too long on the musical stage, and consequently why action and the use of quickly recognizable physical objects (the revolver in the drawer, the telltale empty whiskey bottle beside Uncle Harry's dead body, pink gloves that indicate without a doubt that Eloise spent the night here) – are terribly important. But as George Kaufman once said to me: "Of course do all the corny things. Just don't let them catch you at it."

Give up?

Love,

6 December 1963: To Noël Coward and Harry Kurnitz

GIGANTIC SMASH PLEASE.[102]

FRANK LOESSER

---

101 This (distasteful) scenario is made up.
102 Noël Coward and playwright Harry Kurnitz (1908–1968), *The Girl Who Came to Supper*, which played at the Broadway Theatre, New York, 8 December 1963 to 14 March 1964. The title is a word play on George S. Kaufman and Moss Hart's *The Man Who Came to Dinner* (1939).

CHAPTER ELEVEN

1964–65
PLEASURES AND PALACES, ANYA AND
SEÑOR DISCRETION HIMSELF

By 1964 *How to Succeed* had made a huge profit: *Variety* reported in February of that year that the return to the original backers of the show had been almost 195%, thanks to the ticket sales both on Broadway and on the two road companies.[1] By the beginning of May, the net income of the three productions was over $2 million.[2] And in October 1964 Mirisch-United Artists concluded a deal for over $1 million for the rights to make the show into a film.[3] The implication of these reports was not only a reminder of his artistic contribution but also the confirmation of Loesser's continued commercial value as a writer.

Teddy Holmes, who was director of Chappell & Co. in the UK and represented Loesser's catalogue there, was a regular correspondent; the pair were in touch both professionally and, as was typical of Loesser's dealings with his colleagues, socially. Holmes sent Loesser – a habitual smoker – an ashtray that he had purloined from a theatre (which one is unclear), and Loesser wrote to send him good wishes on an operation. Loesser also revealed his anxieties over his new, and as it happened last produced, musical: *Pleasures and Palaces*.

---

1 ‘ "Succeed" Profit Payoff Now 195%’, *Variety* 234/1 (26 February 1964), 77.
2 ‘ ‘Succeed’ Still Does, in Triplicate’, *Variety* 235/1 (27 May 1964), 1.
3 ‘Mirisches-UA Buy "How to Succeed" ’, *Variety* 236/10 (28 October 1964), 5.

The new show was referred to as *Ex-Lover* in the press in the autumn of 1964, when Loesser's office started putting out casting calls for the production. A column in *Variety* from December confirmed that the show had been budgeted at $450,000.[4]

16 March 1964: To Teddy Holmes

Dear Teddy:

Many many thanks to you and Rita for the handsome addition to my ash tray collection. I hope, for your sake, you waited until the house lights were out before you snitched it. I am very fond of the 50 New Bond Street address, and would hate to get your next letter from Wormwood Scrubs.

Love to you and Rita,

11 May 1964: To Teddy Holmes

Dear Teddy:

Of course the whole thing has been a terrible shock – especially about your injury. You must know how sorry Jo and I are, and how the best of our wishes go with this note. There is some cheer in the fact that you are not at this moment in full hustle and bustle. Maybe the enforced rest will ultimately have been a blessing for you.

You might try this riddle on your nurse.

Question: which has more <u>finger-prints</u> – the F.B.I. or E.T.A.?

The nurse will blink a few moments and then inquire "what is E.T.A.?" Upon which – you answer "Elizabeth Taylor's arse."[5]

Love as always,

---

4 'Legitimate: Seek 450G Bankroll for "Ex-Lover" Tuner', *Variety* 237/5 (23 December 1964), 52.
5 A reference to Hollywood star Elizabeth Taylor's (1932–2011) recent wedding to Richard Burton (1925–1984) on 15 March 1964, her fifth marriage.

23 November 1964: To Teddy Holmes

Dear Teddy:

Frank Rogers and I have brushed briefly – both of us being terribly busy – and that's all I have seen of him. Nevertheless there was time in our brief meeting to learn that you are doing nicely, and I'm delighted to hear it.

I don't even know whether Frank has left these shores as yet. If so, when you see him please give him my profoundest apologies for what seems to be a great impoliteness on my part for not even phoning him. My only excuse is that I'm having the usual enormous preoccupation with the preparing of a show. As usual, I'm full of self-doubt, anxiety and downright dread.

Anyway, my love to you,

Sincerely,

Loesser's long-standing friendship with John Steinbeck flourished during the 1960s. Famously a dog lover, Steinbeck's French poodle Charley was largely the inspiration for his *Travels with Charley* (1962). Charley died in 1961 and shortly afterwards Steinbeck acquired a bull terrier, Angel. A letter from Loesser to Angel may date from 1964, given its reference to Jerry Herman's *Hello, Dolly!* (which opened on Broadway on 16 January 1964), or possibly somewhat later.

Undated (1964 or later): To John Steinbeck's
dog Angel[6]

Dear Angel

Meeting you again last night was a fine experience as always. But, as always, it left me with the feeling of something un-said and un-solved . . . (at first, anyway)

(Members of my breed characteristically want things said and solved, and I am no exception. Like other people I get little satisfaction out of the simple spirit and smell of something – but at once

---

6 This letter was originally typed in full caps.

proceed to bombard it with notions about cause and effect. This human process has many names – drama, mathematics, recipe, research, logic, and worry. You dogs are smart enough to know that worry is something you do to a bone, and let it go at that. Even Pavlov couldn't do any more than prove that your brain is in your gut – something that you knew all the time. My breed insists that the brain is in the head, and that is what we worry.)

Now, since meeting you several times in mixed company, I've felt a constantly sharpening uneasyness [sic] about the inevitable resort to cheap memory-simile-symbolism that bounces around the room every time:

"He looks like a pig"

Now, Angel, you must excuse people for that. They have manufactured the phrase "looks like" to complicate their senses with. This is a process which escapes your understanding, so I won't labor it further – except to say it is a sickness, and a pitiable one. I have it, and your father has it, and please be sorry for us.

Your father has another sickness. Remember last night how he rolled you over and showed me your underside? You know what he said? He said: (showing me some negligable [sic] gray spots) "some dalmatian origin".

He is a dramatist-historian (incurable) and felt compelled to report on who made buckety with who around what town pump to produce your Great-Uncle Rover. You probably didn't catch this exercise in conjecture and conclusion because it had nothing at all to do with how good his hand felt on your belly. I have revealed and explained what he was muttering – in the knowledge that you will forgive him for changing the fundamental subject of a belly rub.

I feel, too, that you will forgive me for a similar infirmity. I am not a dramatist-historian, but a popular poet – popular only because dogs are not allowed in theatres, but only people; and this circumstance gives me a poll that is rigged as hell.

Nevertheless please accept me as a poet. I deal in sounds. You know, like "Let's go Mets".[7] (That isn't one of mine.) I string sounds

---

7 The New York Mets baseball team.

together. But to string them I have to remember a bunch of old ones I heard somewhere and then juggle them into a new rhythm and shape.

Where you will be satisfied with the concept: "I see the cat".

I juggle it into:

"Hello Dolly" (not one of mine either [shit!])

I supply the cat's name, imply that it's at least a second meeting, and a pleasant one. I do this to please people, not dogs – so don't give it another thought. But do please let me explain about the juggling process that produces a new and qualified version of "I see the cat".

We have learned to call it word-association. One word reminds us of another word or name. Then this leads us to another reminder. With me it's like this: I see a tree; I notice it's a maple; maple sounds like Mabel. Mabel hasn't been used in a song since – let me remember – oh yes – nineteen twenty-nine. That was the year of the crash. Christmas Eve I waited freezing, on line in the street to draw what I could out of my deposits in a busted bank. No gloves! Blue hands – and I'd have to write my signature in a minute ––– hence:

"Baby It's Cold Outside" (mine! mine! mine!)

Note how narrowly I escaped writing a Mabel song or (God forbid) one called "Blue Hands".

You, my dear Angel, wouldn't torture yourself this way. You'd see a tree, and without remarking on its being a maple or reminding you of anybody – would know exactly what to do about it.

Me, I'm complicated. But it's a living, I tell myself. Also, every once in a long while this disease manages to produce a fine and beautiful truth – as (they say) some oyster illness makes the wondrously perfect pearl.

Well, last night and this morning, my unrelenting tendency to invent itches to scratch instead of fighting real fleas – has led me to one of those rare fine and beautiful truths!

Remember when we wagged tails goodbye last night? (I was trying to squeeze into the seat of my small but exquisite car) At that moment – whilst having a last look at your lovable face – I said to myself:

Mrs. Weissberg

And my wife and I drove off.

I hasten to tell you that you don't look at all like Mrs. Weissberg. But I would like to tell you who she is, or was – and what it leads to.

Mrs. Weissberg owned the candy store on our block when I was a little kid. I suppose my feeling of fondness for you reflected a feeling of fondness for her which I now recollected. It was a different kind of fondness, of course. I wouldn't have wanted to rub her belly, for instance. Or wouldn't I have? I found myself not sure – and tried to remember how I responded to her great kindness. Then the idea of belly struck me, and I quickly gave up my research on whether I had ever even smiled and said thank-you[.] I was on the trail of belly.

I was about five; just old enough to be allowed to go alone with my nickel to Mrs. Weissburg's for a cone (Angel, a giant cone was once a nickel)

Last night, in the car, I found myself remembering those walks around the corner, and how I savored the new independence. The first solo flights – without big sister or Mama! (Remember no-leash!)

The pride of it tasted almost better than the ice cream. Almost.

But there were still some curbs and some heeling. My mother – like other mothers – used to have a notion that kids' treats were full of harmful poisons – notably artificial coloring, or paraffin they use to harden chocolate against the New York summer – or saccharine which was dirty-trick sugar and not really edible. My mother may have been right in principle – but out of her suspicions came the conclusion that the whiter something was, the purer it had to be. Any mother with a kid who has a diet deficiency – and who catches him gobbling spackle because his gut knows he needs calcium – will soon shake herself out of the whiteness-purity theory and thereafter let him have pool chalk if he fancies blue.

But my mother and the others on the block equated the two ideas – and although the walks were my own – the choice of flavors was not. I was limited, alas, to vanilla.

Vanilla was, and I guess still is – a fighting word to a kid. Even French vanilla which is the same thing with dirt spots. If mothers could have dopey credo about purity, kids certainly were entitled to believe that no color implies no flavor.

So with me, the joy of those walks was imperfect. I wanted chocolate, strawberry, pistachio!

Then one day something wonderful happened! Mrs. Weissberg knew Mama's rules – but she had two very fine Jewish qualities. She knew about compromise and she had a soul full of compassion. (These are not exclusively Jewish characteristics but the Jews have an exclusive way of putting them together.)

Mrs. Weissberg's heart went out to me one afternoon. After having held back tears of pity for almost a whole year, she just couldn't stand it any more – hearing me ask for vanilla —— gazing wistfully the while into one after another can of rich and flamboyant ice creams. I guess I must have been good at wistful gazing then. I'm not any more. We all get over it. (Remember how you got trained out of table begging?)

Anyway, she said, knowing her duty: "Vanilla I got to give you"

Then she added, singsong Talmudic: – out of nowhere – hope! Hope of heaven! Bu-ut what? What?

There was this pot of warm water into which the lady used to plunge the ice-cream scoops to clean them off after every use. The handles were sticking out. One for each: chocolate, pistachio, peach. The vanilla was out; in her hand. Now it was mashing the big ball of vanilla into my cone. Now it went back into the pot, bearing its little clustering remnants to be washed off.

That made four handles back in the pot. There was one missing! I knew that for a fact. I had had long experience watching, counting, noting every detail of soda-fountain backstage.

At that same moment:

"Bu-ut....."

Mrs. Weissberg's hand swept over to the big can of strawberry. There was its scoop – not put away for a bath, but still nestling in the pink, and clustered generously with what I had not learned to call residuals. Even one real quarter of a strawberry was stuck in the edge of the scoop.

Up it came. The giant number two scoop, and on to my vanilla – and then Mrs. Weissberg – artist that she was – performed a historical collage – mashing first concave – then sliding convex – until there it was – without losing a crumb – my first almost strawberry cone. Now it was in my hand and I was staring at it.

There are people who recollect with joyful wonder their first view of a Rangoon sunset, and in fact treasure a color print of it. But they show it to other people who give it a quick look, and thereafter refer to it as plain mottled pink and white and nothing to wonder at.

Fortunately for my friends, ice cream gets devoured or melted – and nobody takes pictures of it. Especially not a five year old kid.

So I can only tell you about this. And you don't have to be impressed or excited. Just take my word for what a beautiful sight it was. To me.

"Walk slow" said Mrs Weissberg, "and leck off all the pink before you get home" (only at a distance would anyone mistake it for plain vanilla)

That was the first of many many strawberry tainted vanilla cones. The ritual lasted until I was old enough to order crumbled butter pecan or cherry-fudge-walnut and all those.

Mrs. Weissberg was a neat and orderly woman, as I think of it now – maybe her first instinct to give me what I craved was pushed a little by her sense of guilt over leaving the strawberry scoop unwashed. Maybe it was an act not of compassion, but atonement. The Jews are good at that too.

Well, that's why I said to myself "Mrs. Weissberg" last night. And this morning I have found out why.

Angel, you do not look like a pig. That is cheap and over convenient imagery – and lousy songwriting

You look like vanilla ice cream dressed up with the strawberry scoop

And I'm the one who knows it.

There are people who get up to $50 an hour listening to memory chains like this, but no dogs that I know of are so favored or so burdened. But let me say thanks for listening.

As I told you, I am a poet – and my job is to write and say and sing things that people will like because they recognize a beautiful truth.

I have told one.

I hope your father recognizes it, and in the future abruptly corrects those who volunteer that you resemble a pig.

Love, Uncle Frank

Pleasures and Palaces, based on Sam Spewack's unsuccessful 1961 play *Once There Was a Russian* (which ran for only one performance), was widely anticipated. United Artists Records invested $300,000 in the production and bought the rights to release the cast album, while the cast and crew included Bob Fosse as director-choreographer (Fosse had choreographed *How to Succeed in Business Without Really Trying*) as well as British theatre stars Hy Hazell and Alfred Marks in addition to American stars Phyllis Newman and John McMartin. But the show – which concerned the relationship of Catherine the Great, Grigori Alexandrovich Potemkin, John Paul Jones and Russia's war with the Turks – was poorly received during tryouts in Detroit. The critic for *Variety* wrote 'The spirit and the resolution which produced one of the great rallying cries in history ["I have not yet begun to fight"] are urgently needed by Frank Loesser, Sam Spewack and Bob Fosse, who are principally responsible for the disappointing launching at Detroit's Fisher Theatre of a new musical comedy, "Pleasures and Palaces."' Both the music and lyrics came in for criticism, the lyrics for being repetitious and the song "What Is Life?", which is repeated twice in the show, for sounding "like a second-rate nursery rhyme".[8] *Pleasures and Palaces* closed out of town and, in his correspondence over the summer with playwright Alfred Uhry (who had first suggested the show to Loesser) and producer Cy Feuer, which included comments on the latter's new musical *Skyscraper* (also opening in Detroit), Loesser refers to the pain of closing the production (which lost $495,000).

---

8 *Variety*, 17 March 1965, 90.

14 April 1965: To Alfred Uhry

Dear Al:

It is now established that you are connected closely with one of Broadway's biggest failures. I am not astonished as I have never quite trusted your big mouth and its overwilling crop of pompous convictions.

If next time we meet I pretend not to know you – don't be surprised. I can't afford to acknowledge the acquaintanceship of such a squanderer of nice investors' money. Nor can I admit being on speaking terms with a man of such poor judgment.

In the future, therefore, please have Waldman contact me on all matters. He is a literate man. A man of probity as well as imagination. A natural winner. Why he remains by the side of a loser like you God alone knows.

Enclosed please find my check for $1.00. This is for the re-purchase of my introduction to you several years ago. I am sending this note special delivery so that it will reach you in time before your abashed exit from town. Let me suggest here that if you are thinking of a more dramatic and permanent exit – that you do not jump out of a window. You have done quite enough littering of the streets of Detroit and I do not wish to see this same mess inflicted upon my fair city.

Farewell,

8 June 1965: To Alfred Uhry

Dear Al:

Thanks for yours of June 2nd. Apparently in naming your west side kid you did not consult the Bronte-Hahn society – who had the west side covered long, long ago and have firm squatters' rights. If your spurious Emily is four years old I'm willing to bet she is squatting daily in the muck of Central Park (West) or possibly Riverside Drive Park, and has no damn right to. I, on the other hand, was smart enough to apply before hand for a royalty arrangement with the Post-

Dickinson society on the east side, and now have a perfectly valid kid who is even entitled to steal tulips from the middle of Park Avenue.

Also, for your information Jo Loesser, the Great White Mother, is in reality <u>Elizabeth</u> Josephine and has seniority rights on both sides of town. So your Elizabeth had better watch out. Although I imagine your Elizabeth has the reach on my Elizabeth.

Sincerely,

Frank Loesser

18 June 1965: To Cy Feuer

Dear Cy:

Not content with bugging me week after week to read your new musical, it seems you have now been forward enough to send a mimeographed copy of the whole thing to my house. So I suppose for the sake of friendship I am now obligated to glance through it. I hope this acknowledgement of the fact that it is, indeed, somewhere on my premises will satisfy you that there is now a chance that I will get around to it. I say this in the hope that you will no longer interject this subject into our otherwise comfortable and friendly conversations, as you have continually in the past few weeks.

But bear in mind that I am not really obligated to read the thing at all. I do, however, have every hope that I will get to it in the next few months. I hope that despite your seemingly obsessive sanguinity about getting me interested – that you will let the matter rest as it is.

Sincerely,

13 September 1965: To Cy Feuer c/o Skyscraper Company (FLE) (Telegram)

GOOD LUCK TONIGHT ON THE STAGE OF THE FISHER. DON'T SKID ON MY BLOOD. LOVE
FRANK LOESSER

Another musical with which Loesser was involved in the 1964–65 season was *Anya*, the latest effort of Wright and Forrest. Just as they had enjoyed success using the music of Borodin to create the score for *Kismet* (1953), they now planned to use compositions by Rachmaninov to create a musical about the Anastasia affair. Anna Anderson (1896–1984) claimed fraudulently to be the Grand Duchess Anastasia of Russia and the musical, with a book by Guy Bolton and George Abbott, further adds to the mythology by obscuring facts related to the real-life Grand Duchess. The show opened on Broadway on 29 November 1965 and ran for only sixteen performances, being branded old-fashioned. As always, Loesser was deeply involved in offering feedback to Wright and Forrest, who were published by Frank Music; there was some friction, too, with Abbott, who directed Loesser's *Where's Charley?* many years earlier. It is curious that both *Pleasures and Palaces* and *Anya* dealt with Russian themes at this point in the Cold War. United Artists also bought the cast album rights for *Anya* – another bad investment, although this album was actually made, unlike that for *Pleasures and Palaces*.

7 October 1964: To George Abbott, Bob Wright and Chet Forrest

Dear Gents:

In the interest of speed in getting my opinions to you, I am rushing the enclosed comments, etc., on the first act of the 9-1-64 script. My notes on the second act will be coming to you within a couple of days, provided we are still on speaking terms.

What I have done is what I think you all have learned to count on my doing. I have made notes in the course of reading, not as a result of reading and then going back. I prefer to do this because like a member of the audience, I can only reflect on what has happened so far in a play – and cannot honestly predict what will happen, nor can I arrive at any valuable generalities in passing. Nevertheless, upon finishing the first act I have made certain general reflections. Some of these are indeed the result of checking back to confirm my recollections. But all in all you can regard the enclosed notes as the result of a first reading. As a result, it is quite likely that I have not made a really thorough study of what is there. But neither will a member of the audience, who also will be relying on a first impression, and so I like to put myself in his position.

But I don't think for a moment I have limited myself to the expression of opinion, approval or disapproval. I have butted in with many a gratuity which you have every right to consider or accept or reject. I'm sure that many things I have had to suggest will not suit you. But give me credit for having explained in each case the reason for the suggestion. I must ask you to bear with me in reading a critique which is the only kind I'm capable of delivering. I cannot tell a man that his trouble is baldness without also suggesting that he get a toupee. This last sentence just concluded is my mystic parable for today. Aren't you all lucky? Second installment shortly. Meantime–

Love to you all,

12 October 1964: To George Abbott, Bob Wright and Chet Forrest

Dear Gents:

Enclosed you will find my comments after a reading of the second act of "Anya." As I have pointed out in the notes, there are too many questions in my mind relating to the meaning of a number of things. If I wrote them all out they would doubtless evoke further counter-questions, and the process might take a long time.

Is there any possible way you (George Abbott) and I can meet? If so, I feel that although I might seem inquisitorial – that I might be of some help at the same time. I prefer not to include you two composers in a first meeting for this reason: If, as a result of meeting with the playwright, there are amendments, additions, newly placed song cues, etc. – I feel it would then be more valuable if these results were presented to you composers all in one piece in order to get more of a "one piece" reaction.

If this is alright with everybody, please, George, phone me and we'll have a date. If not, phone me for your next available Dutch Treat luncheon. It has been a long time since I saw you drink a Daiquiri.

Love to you all,

1 June 1965: To George Abbott

Dear George:

This note is to clarify things as to communication between you and me, and also to establish a new method as per your own suggestion.

Firstly, in the event I didn't make it clear – I think your version of "ANYA" is the best and strongest yet written or produced, especially for musical purposes. Secondly, I believe anything <u>you</u> don't want in the script should not be forced on you, whether by me, or Wright and Forrest, or the producer or choreographer – or any committee formed among these. We all wanted you to write and direct it in the belief that you would do it well, and I for one continue to think that – possibly even more strongly than the rest.

What apparently has been less than valuable to you – if not painful – is my tendency when being specifically critical of an element in a play, to propose an alternate or substitute element as an example of what <u>might</u> be done as an improvement. As per your request I will now abandon this method. Nevertheless please keep in mind that I don't for a moment apologize for it in itself, but for its seeming effect on your comfort. As I try to recall your words, you said something like: "just tell me what you don't like about it, and if I agree I'll try to fix it." Okay, I will confine the notes that follow to that kind of criticism (the only exception might be as to songs and song cues which you must understand as necessarily requiring concrete and "constructive" suggestion).

As the proprietor of a loony bin I wouldn't hand over an insane patient in custody to a poor, foreign taxi driver, and then forget all about it.

I learned from Wright and Forrest that they expect Katrina to sing "Homeward," and more or less exclude Josef, whose voice is not as musical as hers. This now to some degree invalidates my former criticism about the Katrina-Josef "accord" in the expressed sentiment. Nevertheless I consider the present song cue lame in stemming from a path and mood of dialogue which does not remotely express homesickness.

1-4-26: Genia does not acknowledge Anya's presence, even though she is looking right at this object of enormous curiosity.

1-4-28: Anya's speech "she is the hardest one." She is volunteering something out of the blue to which Bounine shows no astonishment.

In scene 1-5 there is no indication of any reaction by Bounine and the plotters to the progress of Anya's astonishingly good performance.

1-7-52: In discussing the Grandmother's suspicion of fraud and refusal to communicate – is it presumed that this is <u>despite</u> some presumable reassurance to her from Paul after the garden interview? The script doesn't say so.

1-7-53: How can Anya's offstage singing of "Hand In Hand" be understood as "sarcastic" in manner? If so, fine. But if not the impression might be that she is romantically affected by simply having repeated the tune.

1-7-53: Exactly why is Bounine's trip kept a secret from Anya?

2-1: Anya has confessed to actual fraudulent impersonation and yet seems to have exit privileges by the police.

2-1-7: Anya: "why didn't I die in the canal?". I don't believe this event has been discussed previously in the present script.

2-1-8: Petrovin: "– betrayed us all, I know, but still –". Petrovin, the cruel one, has turned soft.

2-2-12: The Empress; song cue "sing it again" seems to be the third of almost identical cues in the play thus far. The insane woman asking Anya to finish the song, and then the request for Tinka's vocalization.

2-2: I have just carefully read over this entire scene. Except for one tiny example in the beginning of the scene (about the man from the Italian Embassy), nowhere is the Empress anything but vigorous of mind and definite of expression. The weakness she expresses is only one of sentimentality, but her memory never fails her for a second.

In scene 2-5 she suddenly appears in a totally new guise. That of a senile amnesiac with a generous dash of wandering dementia. How did she get that way suddenly in 2-5? If it is your intention to enrich 2-2 with further examples of the Empress' mental malfunction – it could easily disqualify the whole recognition scene.

Again on the subject of 2-2: although we get the drama of recognition by the Grandmother, somehow the "truth" is not dramatized in Anya. Also, there is no evidence of any doubt on her part from the minute she enters the scene that she is indeed Anastasia. At what point had she become convinced that she was actually Anastasia? The only positive expression of this was way back on 1-7-54, and judging from the dialogue following her disclosure on this and the following page – the whole thing is treated as a joke by herself, Bounine and Katrina – and then promptly dismissed upon Genia's entrance. SO WHEN DOES SHE HAVE HER FINAL REALIZATION, AND HOW DO WE KNOW THAT SHE HAS HAD IT?

In general, as I have told you, I feel that Bounine does not seem to be a strong and active motivator. He has originated a scheme and then seems to let lieutenants accomplish it. Also, as I have told you, I cannot distinguish between Chernov and Petrovin and their functions. No doubt I would be able to do so once I saw them on the stage, and possibly appreciate their difference in personality. But at the present moment the existence of two such men seems to augment the already necessarily large group of "plotters." By the word "plotters" I mean as distinguished from the innocent investors in the syndicate.

Well, that's about it for now, on the script. Please note that I have simply reported on what I don't understand, or what I don't like. I have taken great pains to leave out any suggestion of alternate or substitute ideas. Until I hear from you the question "all right then, what would you do?" I will keep things this way. Of course many or maybe all of the above criticisms may not be valid or even sensible – but that's for you to decide.

I will shortly prepare a separate digest relating to songs. This is the result of several exhaustive meetings with Wright and Forrest. It will take another day or so before I can prepare this set of notes. As I said before, these will necessarily involve some concrete suggestions – as opposed to just plain criticism. It would be idle of me simply to say that I don't care for a certain song, or think it wrongly placed. So brace yourself for my next. Meantime, I remain full of vast respect and profound affection.

Sincerely,

29 November 1965: To Wright
and Forrest (Telegram)

SERGE RACHMANINOFF
c/o ROBERT WRIGHT & GEORGE FORREST
DEAR SERGE YOU NEVER HAD IT SO GOOD
  FRANK LOESSER

Among the projects Loesser tried to promote but got nowhere with was the play *Madame Ponce* by actor Jean-Pierre Aumont (1911–2001). An internal memo shows it was sent to writers and directors including Burt Shevelove (1915–1982) and Jonathan Miller (1934–2019), and Loesser's correspondence with Abe Burrows, Ruth Gordon (1896–1985) and Peter Ustinov (1921–2004) reveals his commitment to the project, which was never produced.

3 April 1964: To Abe Burrows

Dear Abe:
  Here is the script of MADAME PONCE you said you would read. I realize that it is by no means perfectly executed but I do think it is realizable or whatever the word is.
  I really would like to know what you think in all departments, as I consider you a wise, cultured, perspicacious, literate and fairly well-enough-to-do so that you can spare the time to do this reading immediately and then rush me your opinions.
  Love,

15 May 1964: To Peter Ustinov

My Dear Ustinov,
  My producing company had found what I think is a charmer of a play for Broadway. All of us agree on the idea of asking you to read it. The object would be that you should agree to direct the play.
  In an unguarded moment, I told them that I happened to know you and would not at all mind bringing the subject up personally.

535

Actually, you and I know each other as the result of various luncheons upstairs at Wheelers's in London,[9] various small talk sessions with Leonard Lyons, and an assortment of how-do-you-dos on busy street corners. In the event you do not recollect any of these occasions let me submit that I am the composer-lyricist of "Guys and Dolls," "The Most Happy Fella," "How To Succeed In Business Without Really Trying," etc. Please be overwhelmed enough at this evidence of status, probity and talent to favor me with a note requesting a look at the script, upon which I will air mail it to you.

I believe the worst that can happen is that you will have amused yourself for an hour, even if you prefer not to take the play to your professional bosom.

Thanks and regards,

P.S. It is NOT a musical

10 June 1964: To Peter Ustinov

Dear Peter:

Thanks for your response. Of course it is disappointing that you have such a busy schedule before you, nevertheless I have a feeling that you ought to read the play. I believe that at the very worst you will have enjoyed yourself. Also I entertain the hope that you will at least give my people your opinions and feelings about it even though you don't accept an association with its production.

And so I will have the wizards of this Frank Music Corp. (named after me because I own it) forward you the script. It is by a friend of yours, Jean Pierre Aumont and it is called "Mme. Ponce."

About the credentials, please forgive me. You are a man with a great assortment of interests, all of which can't be Frank Loesser all the time. I did not want to subject you to the embarrassment of having to cable Leonard Lyons to find out whether or not you know me. But now many thanks for your flattering note of recognition and

9 A fashionable fish restaurant formerly on St James's Street, Piccadilly, founded in 1856.

even admiration. I hope shortly that you will admire me for having found a darling little play.

With good wishes,

30 July 1964: To Ruth Gordon

Dear Ruth:

Thank you so much for reading MADAME PONCE anyway, and please forgive me. None of us here at the office could possibly have known of your previous brushes with it. Next time around I will get you on the phone and say "Lissen. Did anybody ever send you 'The Frogs' by a new writer named Aristophanes? If not, please let me send it to you. It is a musical with a tragic ending. The heroine croaks in the end." And then you can say "Oh, that one. The author has been reading it out loud at parties for a month." And then I will say "See? I have saved us a lot of time, haven't I?" etc.

I dearly wish to hear you sing sometime this autumn when we are all back in the city. The idea sounds very exciting.

Love and thanks, and kiss Garson[10]

Correspondence with H. Reid Sterrett of Aldco, Inc. shows Loesser's fascination with their pitcher cooler, which he was using for unconventional means.

6 May 1965: To H. Reid Sterrett Jr

Dear Mr. Sterrett:

Thank you for your letter of May 5th acknowledging my order on which I anxiously await delivery.

Apparently by some error there was no literature enclosed on the travel cooler or additional products. Please send this information on as soon as possible.

---

10 Garson Kanin, writer and director and husband of Ruth Gordon.

As for your inquiry on serving Aquavit: it seems that Mr. Stoner misunderstood what I said. At present I am using the pitcher cooler for <u>vodka</u> <u>martini</u>. This I keep in the deep freeze along with the capsule, as well as martini glasses, and serve myself and others from it, keeping a pitcher pretty well filled in reserve all the time. The pitcher has never shown any inclination to crack or explode even though the constant temperature is about 5 degrees above zero.

My reason for wanting the bottle form was in order to serve Aquavit as well as pure vodka with a sprig of dill in the bottle. Observe that Aquavit and vodka would normally be poured into much smaller and narrower vessels than a martini, and that is my reason for wanting the bottle form. I imagine while in the freezer I would keep the screw cap on very lightly, if at all. Here the capsule as well as the steel bucket would be of essential importance since these drinks are more likely to be served in the dining room, which is a good distance away from the kitchen – and kept in the dining room for refills during the service of appetizers, etc. Under informal circumstances I don't mind at all keeping the whole combination as one does a fancy carafe – in the middle of the table, to be reached for by whoever wishes to get the drunkest earliest. In the past I have been putting Aquavit in an ordinary beer bottle set inside a body of water within an old pewter liter measure, and then freezing the whole thing so that a solid cake of ice forms around the bottle. The trouble with this has been that I cannot avoid leakage from the melting ice, upon pouring the Aquavit. Also the pewter vessel does quite a little sweating after a while.

So I am grateful that there is such a thing as a bottle form and anxiously await receiving it. Let me suggest here that my freezer unit is quite a generous one – the kind actually used in restaurants – and there is enough head room for your product. But I don't believe that everyone has such a convenience, and that probably there isn't enough standing room in the freezer section of the average refriger-ator even though one puts the ice trays to one side. So I might suggest a shorter and broader model for people interested in pre-freezing a supply the way I do. Certainly Aquavit, which is not a mixture and doesn't even need a shake, might be more convenient to the purchaser in this form. Also the capacity need not be so big. At least not over here. I can't speak for the Danes who seem not only to drink it endlessly, but chase it with beer almost every time.

I note that the Aalborg Company[11] is advertising quite broadly lately. They include in some of their copy the suggestion of a "Danish Mary" by which they propose to substitute Aquavit for vodka in a Bloody Mary. This would imply a certain ambitiousness on their part, and possibly there might be an advertising or selling tie-up with these people if you did indeed want to make an Aquavit model. Toward that, why don't you examine their standard bottle (it doesn't seem to have changed over the years) and test it by putting the whole thing full of Aquavit and sealed tight in zero degrees temperature (first standing up and then lying down). From my experience with a cheap beer bottle nothing awful will happen, although I can't be sure in this case. At any rate if a sample capsule were made <u>and protected by you</u> it might be something to discuss with the Aquavit makers or their American distributors.

Scientific question: if a completely frozen capsule were taken from the freezer and placed in a room at 70 degrees temperature – how efficiently would it affect the body of air in the unoccupied interior. In other words, do we need actual contact with the plastic inner surface to give the cooling effect? It would seem to me that the cooled air inside the vessel would be heavier than the room air and inclined to sit there and maintain its own coldness. I ask this question because it then might be recommended that the Aalborg special capsule might very well be used to sit your (narrower) bottle of Tuborg in. That makes it the Aalborg-Tuborg model, with special emblem and millions in royalties for you and yours.

Have you ever thought about Dubonnet? In this instance refrigeration would be enough, without freezer.

And I'm sure this letter is enough. But in a way you asked for it.

Cordially,

---

11 A major exporter of liquor based in Denmark.

20 May 1965: To H. Reid Sterrett Jr

Dear Reid:

Enjoyed our session of yesterday very much and also your contributions to my drinking future, for which I thank you again. Remember we talked about possibly getting me a hand-altered version of the glacier jug? Maybe two or three if at all possible. I now push my secretary off my lap and provide you with a picture of what I'd like to have:

[blank space on page]

Okay, she's back. As a matter of fact, she sends her kindest regards and so do I.

Along with this note I am sending you an LP version of the entire "Most Happy Fella." It wasn't recorded too well but was the first example of a show done in its entirety, talk and all. Notably [sic] (at least to me) is the fact that my wife, Jo Sullivan, is the leading woman. These years, she is doing some piteous shrieking about the house, but no more long runs in the theatre. On the other hand, no more long runs in her stockings.

Well there you have my funny saying for the day. I hope we'll be seeing each other in August. Meantime, please let me know what you can do about the conversion of a few glacier jugs.

My very best,

Frank Loesser

25 May 1965: To H. Reid Sterrett Jr

Dear Reid:

The thought occurred to me that your outfit might sometime want to make a rolling pin. Ask your wife. A great deal of pastry dough rolling is done ice cold. At the moment they are manufactured to be filled with ice or ice cubes. The cold isn't really lasting and the filling and emptying operations are drippy. Sometime ago I saw some made of glass, but now I understand they are made in aluminum as well as plastic. The thought struck me that possibly an easy conversion of your present machinery could make this simple cylinder:

[blank space on page]

The chances are that the type of plastic would have to be harder than the ones you are using for capsules. Would this destroy the long time cold value? Or could it indeed be done at all with a hard plastic? If it couldn't, there could still be a capsule within a hard plastic jacket such as you have in the beer mugs. The center rod would of course be hard, solid plastic.

The main thing that occurs to me is that the same store <u>buyer</u> who buys the jugs and the mugs would also buy this item. Why not take it along if your present machinery can be converted easily enough?

Over and out,

P.S. For your information, the half bottle of <u>pernod</u> is exactly the right diameter for the beer capsules. I already have my Aquavit nicely housed, thanks to you, and there is no sign of cracking glass.

A rich trove of Loesser's personal correspondence from this time includes letters to familiar names such as Broadway regular Edward Chodorov, journalist Shannon Fife, Richard Rodgers, choreographer Jerome Robbins, Johnny Green, producer Dave Karr, Pilade Levi of Paramount, Rome, Groucho Marx, popular singer Dinah Shore and Peter Starr, the son of a friend, on the occasion of his Bar Mitzvah.

19 February 1964: To Edward Chodorov[12]

Dear Eddie:

My pleasure in lunching with you so soon after your return is <u>one</u> thing. You picked up the check, and I didn't get heartburn. Hands down, I enjoyed. But my lingering nachis about your treatment of "Gondolier" is a relentlessly fervent one, and I hasten to add not untinged by GREED, and I can't get it out of my mind. To repeat briefly what I told you on the phone, I think it would make a marvelously

---

12 Edward Chodorov (1904–1988), Broadway and film writer and producer. *Broadway Gondolier* was a 1935 Warner Bros. film about a taxi driver aspiring to become a singer.

rewarding project for the musical theatre – and I can't tell you how much I regret your present tendency to make a movie out of it.

Let me point out to you now, if there is any hope for a talk between you and my outfit before you conclude a picture deal, that we have a very firm association by which I believe that we could organize a Broadway musical production with a pre-purchase arrangement. This is based on a very intimate association my firms have with a responsible and well-heeled motion picture company. I think it is possible to anticipate that certain reasonably large guarantees could be paid to you at the very outset.

But, of course, I certainly would not want to impede your present talks and plans unless you yourself wanted to give my company the green light. I don't know who you're doing business with, but they can't be as handsome or Jewish as me. Being handsome and Jewish at the same time is a lost art. Everybody I run into at the club locker room has one of those luminous plastic foreskins.

Wonderfully,

11 March 1964: To Shannon Fife[13]

Dear Shannon:

How nice to hear from you. Also, the news that your brother has beat the rap with his chest. It happens that I am a bronchiestasis plus an incipient emphysema man myself. I get winded simply looking at a tennis match on the television screen, so I know what that business is. As for your arthritis – I don't know what brand you have, but whatever it is get rid of it. Has any doctor told you that between the easy chair and the bed there should be a modified fandango of some kind (administered, if necessary, by a therapist) so that there is some semblance of muscle exercise? Or maybe that wouldn't work in your case. At any rate, take care of yourself.

Oh, oh, oh! Didn't we acknowledge receiving the Christmas wreath? If we didn't, it's a terrible boo boo and we hope you will forgive us on the basis of the information that we had a mess of

---

13 Shannon Fife (1888–1972), American journalist and humorist.

company keeping us frantic during the entire holiday season and beyond.

News. Jo is pregnant again and so Hannah is going to have a companion. Sometime in the autumn.[14]

You say in closing you are not certain what production I am working on now. I hasten to tell you that I am not certain either. I'm trying on a lot of things for size and hoping to find one I fall in love with.

Best as always,

29 June 1964: To Richard Rodgers (Telegram)

THANKS FOR YOUR WIRE. I TOO AM GLAD THAT BOTH OF US WERE BORN.[15]
FRANK LOESSER, MUSIC LOVER

22 September 1964: To Jerome Robbins (Telegram)

GOOD LUCK TONIGHT.[16] CALL YOU VERY SOON.
LOVE,
    FRANK LOESSER

23 November 1964: To Johnny Green

Dear Johnny:

Last night Jo and her mother and I went to see a movie, and an extra added attraction was a short of you conducting the MGM symphony in something of Rossini's.[17] We all thought you were handsome as well as enormously able. Also, it was fun recognizing klezmers of long acquaintance. Also, it was fun watching the second

---

14 John Loesser.
15 Loesser and Richard Rodgers had birthdays on consecutive days (Rodgers, 28 June; Loesser, 29 June).
16 For the premiere of Jerry Bock (1928–2010) and Sheldon Harnick's (1924–2023) *Fiddler on the Roof* at the Imperial Theatre, New York, on 22 September.
17 In 1954 MGM released a short film of Johnny Green conducting Rossini's overture to *La gazza ladra* (*The Thieving Magpie*).

percussion man, near the finale, walk thirty feet from bells to cymbals without the sound of a footfall.

But mostly we loved you and your eternal Green-ness, and we wanted you should know.

Love as always,

P.S. The bawds is still cvooked.

20 April 1965: To Gerald Heller

Dear Jerry:

Enclosed please find my ticket for the Mandyorama just in the event there is someone who wants to go, and who ought to go and who can't afford to go – here's his or her way to get little green peas in the lap and platitudes in the ear. If by any miracle I can avoid my trip that day, I'll be there, and as I said I'm willing to sit on Mandy's shoulder. Or if you want, I'll burst out of a cake resplendent in a Camp Wigwam[18] t-shirt. But as I explained to you it is very unlikely that I'll make it on May 6th.

Since talking to you I contacted your very nice Mr. Blum who directed me to a model maker friend of his in the shirt business, and I'm on my way to great and glorious doings. Thank you so much for making the introductions. Mr. Blum has been especially nice.

Sincerely,

9 June 1965: To Dave Karr[19]

Dear Dave:

I have your self-serving flier of June 8th regarding XMAS IN LAS VEGAS.[20] I say flier on the best advice of my experts here who assure me that it is the product of varitype or some other impersonal form of multiple approach. You should know better than to suggest invest-

---

18 See Chapter 1.
19 David Karr (1918–1979), theatrical and film producer.
20 Karr had produced writer Jack Richardson's (1934–2012) *Xmas in Las Vegas* at the Ethel Barrymore Theatre, New York; the play ran for four performances, 4–6 November 1965.

14. Emily and Frank Loesser, undated.

ment without letting me see what has been written. I approve of you. I approve of Mr. Coe and his record. I approve of Tom Ewell.[21] But so far I think your play stinks. Send it on or I will tell the SEC[22] that you are withholding information.

They tell me you sold that house of yours on the bay for something like $65,000 or $75,000. I believe the land alone is worth that

---

21 Fred Coe (1914–1979), producer and director of *Xmas in Las Vegas*; Tom Ewell (1909–1994), actor.
22 The Securities and Exchange Commission.

much, so I think you got robbed. I hated the house from top to bottom or I would have bought it. We'll be renting a place in Westhampton this summer. Where will you be? And send me the play.

Best,

14 July 1965: To Pilade Levi

Dear Pilade:

Thanks for your letter. Giulio looks absolutely marvelous and we all thank you for the picture.

It occurs to me that you may not have learned that we have a second baby, a girl, born June 2nd. I would swear I sent you a cable but then again in the excitement I might not have. Anyway, her name is Emily and she is doing beautifully. Jo is in Westhampton, Long Island with the two girls. In Westhampton one of our neighbors is Ernest Martin. I have talked to him casually about what goes on at Paramount, and frankly I don't really understand it except that he and his group seem to be making a survey of the entire company situation. In our conversation he had not ever sounded concerned or alarmed about anything, but of course can be counted on to want to get rich from whatever he does. That's about the best I can tell you. Except for one thing: I mentioned you to him, and he agreed that if I liked you that you must be a remarkable man. If he ever comes over I will warn you in advance so that you can do your best greeting. I think you would like each other.

Love from all of us to you and Carol and the baby.

As always,

15 July 1965: To Mel Fogel

Dear Mel:

Here's the package called Twist-o-lemon. Also, an example of the expensive advertising these people did in the New Yorker in an effort to do mail order business.

As an addendum to our scattered reflections on this subject please consider the valuable use of this item at bars. I know it is not your racket to go pick off some stale barkeep in the interior of Queens for the sale of one spritzer and two refills, but I think it would save him a lot of preparatory work in cutting lemons and subsequently twisting them into people's drinks, and same barkeep might sell a dozen a week to curious patrons once they had seen him operate the display spritzer. When I was a little boy a bartender introduced me to the subject of the hard boiled egg. I thought he had invented them. So in a state of wonder I went home to my mother and asked her to hard boil some eggs. She did so like any other mother would do without forgetting it would encourage me to drink more beer (which I didn't). But to this very day I'm aware that the bartender recommended the idea.

Please let me know what you think of this item.

Sincerely,

Frank Loesser

16 August 1965: To Groucho Marx

Dear Groucho:

I have your letter on Alexander Tucker stationery. Some business manager: Letting you get away with free paper and probably use of typewriter (both she and it). In keeping with your inexpensive, yea, niggardly style of correspondence I am going to switch back from Upmann to Bering in honor of your next visit to New York.

Anyway about your daughter Melinda, whom I love. I have before me now a copy of the Neighborhood Playhouse school's prospectus, and in it is a list of people who run it. I am not acquainted with a damn one of them, I'm sorry to say, and so there is not much of a word I can put in. But do you mind my doing it through someone else who also knows you? Like Paddy Chayefsky? Or Sidney Kingsley[23] or some such? Let me know, and forgive me for being so badly connected.

---

23 Sidney Kingsley (1906–1995), American dramatist. He won the Pulitzer Prize for his 1934 drama *Men in White*.

Yes, Fred Coe[24] had a meeting with Paddy Chayefsky and me, and we didn't agree on anything except that the idea had a promising ring. We weren't sure, though, what the substance of the play would be.[25]

Our brood is fine and send love and wish you and yours the same. See you on your next New York trip. Meantime, let me know about passing on knowledgeable and prideful information about Melinda.

Love again,

18 April 1966: To Groucho Marx

Dear Groucho:

You certainly have a slippery daughter. She called up once when I wasn't in and said she would call back and hasn't yet. I would call her but she left no word as to where she was staying. Maybe she is scared or rich or something. Anyway I wanted you to know the news to date.

You may include in this news the fact that I have heard from Harry Ruby's dog,[26] and I have had my dog answer him. This dog Mr. Chips has his own letterhead which includes a picture of himself, and he is quite a hairy and matted individual. But I suspect that his woof is worse than his warp. Or has that been used somewhere before?

Love to you and Eden,[27]

1 November 1965: To Dinah Shore

Dear Dinah:

It is still today and I am writing this note to tell you how happy a sight you were today at lunch. If I think of something that I think is very specially wonderful for you to sing I will send it on. The pickings are slim these days – notably in my repertoire – and I think the trick is

---

24 Frederick H. Coe (?–1979), major producer and director during the golden age of television in the 1950s and 1960s.

25 It is not clear which play Loesser, Fred Coe and Paddy Chayefsky were considering at this time.

26 Apparently this is a joke, since according to all available sources, Ruby did not have a dog.

27 Groucho Marx's wife Eden Hartford; they married in 1954 and divorced in 1969.

15. Susan and Frank Loesser in Hollywood, undated.

to find an obscure little nugget from the past heretofore overlooked. These things sometimes become "My Funny Valentine," etc.

Mainly I want to say what a joy it was to see you looking specially pretty and beamish and all the things you are.

Love,

19 April 1965: To Peter Steven Starr

My dear young man:

I am sending this to you at the address of your parents, on the assumption that you have not yet run away from home. That is quite proper, as you should not make your exit empty-handed. Sound and mature judgment has no doubt already prevailed in favor of your leaving full loaded with Bar Mitzvah loot and money.

I write you this note on receipt of a handsomely engraved and typographically impeccable invitation from your folks to attend your Bar Mitzvah on this coming May 22nd. It happens, alas, that neither Mrs. Loesser nor I will be able to attend. To assuage our sense of regret about this, there is the consoling thought that your folks can make the chopped herring supply stretch farther.

There is an almost fundamental reason why we can't attend. It is as follows: my daughter Susan – an only slightly Jewish girl – is getting married to a total Gentile on that very same day. You can understand why we must prefer this occasion, even though the speech will not be as stirring and determined, and the food won't be anywhere near as good.

But the whole picture represents a happy sort of balance. While you're up there proclaiming to your parents and your congregation and the world that you are indeed a Jewish man, my little daughter will be in effect establishing her alliance with a member of a goy family. That means that my future grandchildren will have to <u>learn</u> chopped chicken liver, the way to pronounce "meshuggeh," an appreciation for George Jessel[28], and various other chochmis[29] which [are] yours from the very beginning. On the other hand, my grandchildren may very likely be fine and upright people, like Lindbergh, or Thomas Edison. They probably will drill for oil or raise cattle. They probably will see something in the Republican Party. It's a cinch they will have less cholesterol.

The whole idea of populating the world with various kinds of people is part of what your father will tell you is my master plan. If there is any cockamamie motto that goes with this, maybe it is BE PROUD OF WHAT YOU ARE AND LET OTHERS BE PROUD OF WHAT THEY ARE. If everyone felt that way, world peace wouldn't be hard to arrive at. Of course, today there are too many mixed-up

---

28 George Jessel (1898–1981), American vaudevillian.
29 Yiddish, in this context, for 'wise men'.

people with strange and sometimes compulsive loyalties. Take for instance your father. I say this in absolute confidence that you will not spill the beans to the Rabbi. Your father worships ME. So much for calm, judicial Jewish solidarity and world peace.

But wait. That there should be this monstrous flaw in your father's otherwise fine character – is, in a way, very valuable to you. A Jewish boy must sooner or later find something fallible about his father – some weakness – some capacity for error. And there you have it. Now when you get up on May 22nd and tell everybody that you have become a man, you can do so with a tone of superiority – and even maybe with a baleful glance in mid-speech – at the old man.

I congratulate you in advance, and wish you a most joyous Bar Mitzvah.

Respectfully already,

With *Pleasures and Palaces* having closed prematurely, Loesser tried to get a television version of *Greenwillow* off the ground, rumoured to star Anthony Perkins from the original Broadway production (it never happened).[30] And in May 1965 *Guys and Dolls* enjoyed a well-received revival starring Jerry Orbach as Sky Masterson at City Center in New York, with *Variety* noting that it 'is bullseye entertainment from the first number' and adding that the show 'comes to life' particularly during 'Frank Loesser's durable numbers'.[31] His other major project of the time was as a producer through Frank Productions of the South African revue *Wait a Minim*, which had been a hit in London. *Variety* welcomed the production when it opened on Broadway on 7 March 1966, calling it 'one of the most unusual and entertaining revues seen on Broadway in years. Anyone who fails to see it will be missing a fine show'.[32] The review also noted that 'the show throughout is scornful of racist mentality'. Yet there was some unrest from the show from the S.N.C.C. (the Student Nonviolent Coordinating Committee), and Loesser called on his

---

30 Ted Green, 'Mister Main Stem', *Back Stage*, 16 April 1965, 3.
31 Hobe, 'Legitimate: Guys and Dolls', *Variety* 238/11 (5 May 1965), 64.
32 Hobe, 'Shows on Broadway: Wait a Minim', *Variety* 242/3 (9 March 1966), 62.

friend, the celebrated actor and singer Harry Belafonte (1927–2023), to intervene. He also wrote to journalist Leonard Lyons about the meaning of the title of the show. In the end, the show was a success at 456 performances.

19 November 1965: To Harry Belafonte

Dear Harry:

The thing I enjoyed most about the other night was my conversation with you. I hope we have another one soon because I would like not only to hear more about the Peace Corps, but also to exchange whatever variety of jokes you like and maybe knock a few people who are not there.

I don't know how free you are, or how much time you spend in New York, but if you and I and our ladies can have an evening some time it would please me.

I write you this note with some self-consciousness because as an old timer I recollect a primitive form of automation by which a fellow vending music would press his Be Pleasant button and out of his lip would come some friendly words directed to Abe Lyman,[33] as a result of which Abe was supposed to feel he ought to perform some of this man's music. I survived that time with an enormous contempt for the chummy pusher process – but also with a fear that sometimes I might sound like one of those boys. As a result I very rarely have invited the friendship or even association with people who make sounds in public.

I hope this reassures you that I like you and don't wish to sell you anything, and would like to spend some more time with you.

Best,

17 February 1966: To Leonard Lyons

Dear Leonard:

Welcome home. About "WAIT A MINIM," the title of the marvelous entertainment coming to the Golden Theatre – the word MINIM

---

33 Abe Lyman (1897–1957), bandleader.

confuses a lot of people. Most have never heard it. To a very old-fashioned physician, especially in England, it means a very small quantity of liquid equal to what we now call a <u>drop</u>, fifteen to the cubic centimeter – or one sixtieth of a fluid drachm. But in the field of <u>penmanship</u> a MINIM is any single downstroke. On the other hand, MINIM is the name for a member of a very austere order of mendicant monks founded by St. Francis of Paola; also, in connection with this sense MINIM is a tannish color named after the habit of these monks. In zoology MINIM is the name given to smaller size worker ants. The word MINIM in very general use – mostly in the past – means any sort of tiny particle. I think this term went out of use when science got hip to molecules. I learned very recently that one of our very important retail ladies' stores actually maintains what they call a MINIM department, which carries dresses and coats to fit very tiny ladies. Finally, the word MINIM is a musical term, in Medieval times originally applied to the note of the shortest duration. In those days it was square or diamond shaped, and today appears as two successive half notes. In addition, MINIM is used as a term for what we more frequently call a half rest.

I haven't asked any of the MINIM people or their director which MINIM they mean, because I'm quite sure that none of them knows exactly. But it seems to me that the <u>half rest</u> is the only damn MINIM you can <u>wait</u>.

The show, which I saw in London, is really a charmer, and I have every hope that Broadway will fall in love with it. If so – or even before hand [sic] – the above information may have some snob value.

I saw Warren[34] at lunch today and it is very pleasant to see that he is not only one of the handsomest young men around, but is also eating.

Love,

7 March 1966: To Allen Whitehead

Dear Allen:

This note relates to the recent surprise we got about new fire regulations, and the resultant trouble and expense there will be in

---

34 Warren Lyons, Leonard's son.

correcting the violations on "MINIM." Question: is there an executive among the members of the League of New York Theatres whose duty it is to learn <u>immediately</u> any new rulings – whether from the fire department, musicians' union,[35] Equity, building department, or anything else? If there is no person charged with this, I believe it quite important for you to suggest at the next League meeting that someone be appointed and accept the responsibility, not only to gather this kind of information about changed rulings as soon as they happen – but to distribute this information to the membership promptly and thoroughly.

23 March 1966: To Allen Whitehead

Subject: "MINIM" Pickets (S.N.C.C.)
Copies to: Milt Kramer
(I don't care [?] I'm picketing anyway)

At 2:00 today I spoke to Harry Belafonte on the phone and reported to him what you had told me about the news broadcasts implying that S.N.C.C. was picketing the Golden Theatre. He was shocked to hear it – having specifically told the S.N.C.C. people that although all African subjects in general were targets – that this show was a definite exception because it was very much on the Negro side. He agreed with me that the whole thing was a result of innocent enthusiasm by one person in the group. Harry then promised me that before he leaves for Paris (today or tomorrow) he will definitely have them send out a release to the effect that "MINIM" is certainly not to be picketed or protested in any way.

Harry further went on to say that of all things our show was one that S.N.C.C. would probably be buying benefit nights for. Also, he told me Miriam Makeba[36] and some others would be wanting to see the show and he would tell me (or Whitehead) when that occasion came up – and that no doubt there is some publicity benefit in that kind of thing.

---

35 Presumably the American Federation of Musicians, founded in 1893.
36 Miriam Makeba (1932–2008), South African singer-songwriter and actress.

[Note runs off page]

For dessert, Harry reminded me that I was lukewarm about his recording of "Summertime Love" some years ago, and calmly announced to me that he recently recorded it for his new album and hoped that I would like it better. Also, why don't my people send him some little Loesser [gems] ^("Piece Core") for further use by him. That last one, of course, is a common piece of flattery. Nevertheless we can talk about taking him up on that subject. This last paragraph is specifically for Kramer.

Loesser started work on a further musical after the failure of *Pleasures and Palaces*. Titled *Señor Discretion Himself*, the show was developed on and off for the remainder of Loesser's life, although it was ultimately abandoned. On 10 February 1967 it was even mentioned in the trade magazine *Back Stage*: 'A new and still untitled script based on a story by Budd Schulberg, "Señor Discretion Himself," will be produced on Broadway by Frank Productions, Frank Loesser's production company. The setting will be in present-day Mexico and will tell the story of a resident baker and what happens when a big city operator moves into the area. Mr. Loesser will supply the book, lyrics and music. Production is scheduled for the fall of this year. No casting yet but watch BACK STAGE for word on it.'[37] Correspondence and memos from 1965 to 1968 (some of them reproduced from Susan Loesser's biography of her father) reveal Loesser's struggles with the story.

20 September 1965: To Harold Norling Swanson[38]

Your letter of September 14 appalls me. If I had any idea that you intended to select my producer for me, I would not have communicated as I did. It is not at all likely that I would have read Budd Schulberg's story even once, much less several times.

---

37 Anon., 'Casting Bits', *Back Stage*, 10 February 1967, 15.
38 Harold Norling Swanson (1899–1991), literary agent; his clients included F. Scott Fitzgerald and William Faulkner.

I wish you would quickly tell Bob Banner[39] that I don't wish him to communicate with me on this. I hasten to add here that this is not based on any lack of regard for Mr. Banner's work in the past or his qualifications for Broadway producership. Let's just say that things have to be written before they get produced, and as far as I'm concerned, all my bedfellows are my choice ...

The only thing I can suggest is that I (or this company) acquire the basic rights for a long enough time to let me try a hand at the musicalization and some songs. Possibly alone. Possibly with someone else. The only way I can commit this to actual production is by liking the result well enough.

If the above sits well with Budd, let me know. If, however, Budd feels that he'd rather do it himself out West, I will of course understand. If after he accomplishes any adaptation without songs, he wants to shoot it to me, I would be very much pleased, but only if there are no commitments with producers, directors, and others beforehand.

6 December 1965: Office memo to Allen Whitehead, Milton Kramer and others

Frank Productions Inc. has entered into a more or less typical agreement with Budd Schulberg in acquiring basic rights to a story for the purpose of making a Broadway musical out of it.

Frank Productions is at present tacitly countenancing an effort by Frank Loesser to write the adaptation as well as the songs. There is at the moment no contract covering this activity.

We are in relatively virgin territory. That is to say there are not too many entanglements. There is no last will and testament of the original Brandon-Thomas,[40] nor is there a dissolute son of [Damon]

---

39 Robert James Banner (1921–2011), American producer and director known in particular for his television shows.
40 Brandon Thomas (1848–1914), author known for *Charley's Aunt* (1892), the play on which Loesser's *Where's Charley?* was based. Loesser is talking about a new project on which there were no anticipated rights issues associated with the adaptation (unlike *Where's Charley?* or *Guys and Dolls*).

Runyon. Nor is there a Sidney Howard estate with a suspicious agent and a complexity of variously mature and immature inheritors of copyright.

In addition there is a good span of time in which to make plans. I mean in this instance plans by which FPI can possibly embark on a novel managerial and fiscal scheme – one which has never been tried before or even thought of before; one which will make money.

For a change I (as an officer of FPI) have no scheme to propose. You may all consider this an invitation to propose one of your own invention or adaptation. I will give you a clue. Suppose we give our first performance on the moon so that extra-terrestrial rights are established – and then sold at a capital gain to the planet Venus? Suppose all the actors become stockholders in the corporation which produces the show? Suppose the physical inventory (scenery and costumes) becomes the ostensible capital of a business venture such as this and the play appears to be secondary? Suppose Cyd Cheiman[41] gets the leading part? Suppose it is produced for puppets heavily insured against fire and then we burn it on the road? Suppose Frank Loesser and his creative partners all become shareholders or partners instead of royalty getters? Etc., etc., etc. I invite all of you to have meetings or discussions about this beginning as of now (when I said there was a lot of time there is, only if you start thinking now). I would expect that the Orenstein office and the Wolman office would act as legal and tax-hip policemen and censors in discussing suggestions – at the same time this should not prohibit them from some imaginative thinking. Now is the time. This will not change the content of the play except to slow down its progress if our present (unofficial) writer Frank Loesser is consulted. In short, I urgently request all of you to kick this project around in search of a new and valuable method for producing a show – and not to discuss it with me until you have a reasonable affection and regard for what you propose.

Happy holidays.

F

---

41 Cyd Cheiman (dates unknown), a business manager and treasurer for Frank Music.

28 November 1966: To Don Walker

Without knowing the precise dates I can't, of course, ask my office to negotiate a contract with you at the moment, but consider yourself invited by me to join this project. When I see you next Monday (I hope) I will be asking you about religious processional music in small Mexican towns; the size of low-range marimbas; the use of a small diatonic harp (I have heard vaguely of such); instrumentation of mariachi music in the section two hundred miles south of Mexico City; etc., etc. Bring a pencil and give me a good hour.

12 December 1966: To Don Walker

In addition to all the other things, please find out for me what sort of music is played by marching bands in Mexico. I do not mean military or patriotic, but more the stuff that a carnival parade would use. If there are any recordings of such things please get them for me, along with other material.

Late February 1967: Memo to readers on draft of *Señor Discretion*

This will be tedious going. There are some 242 pages to read carefully. In the event that you believe you are up against the new Parsifal, I hasten to assure you that I have done some rough timing with generous allowance for songs and choreographic and pantomime passages – and that this show is at the moment no more than twenty-five minutes longer than what is considered normal. The extra jazz that stretches this manuscript to its present length consists of detailed visualization of the specific ACTION, MANNER, and PHYSIQUE of the show, as I imagine it at this moment.

If it seems to you that I itch to usurp the functions of director, choreographer, scenic designer, costume designer, makeup man and coffee girl, please take comfort in my assurance that I simply want these people to improve what I have written. Let's call this form of script a challenge – an invitation to my cohorts to amend, correct, excise or clarify – and generally make what is there more effective.

But at least there is something there – and you are stuck with the job of absorbing it . . .

Brace yourself for many of the locutions. My intention is that this entire show be played with a distinct Mexican accent. Please try to get used to "I go tomorrow to the house of my uncle" as opposed to "I'm goin' to my uncle's house tomorrow." If you doubt that all the performers can master the accent, consider that anybody who can say CHUTZPAH can also say CHAVE JOU MET MY SEESTER? .

And now, the big big demand on you: I want negative criticism only. Here are some examples:

"I hate the whole thing."

"On pages x, y, and z the intention seems to be to get laughs. It's not funny to me."

"The quotation on page 606 sounds like an infringement."

"This and this line is uncharacteristic of the character speaking. He is reversing himself."

"On page ABC you are informing the audience for the fourth time that the cat has fleas."

"I don't have a clear notion of Nebenzahl's attitude."[42]

"How did Orville know Wilbur could be at Kitty Hawk at such an ungodly hour? Hmm?"

WHAT I DON'T WANT is for you to run with the ball, for the time being. I will give you some examples of what to avoid telling me:

"If the boy's part were changed to the part of the girl and she came on stage two scenes later with a parasol it would make much better sense."

"I have a much more literate ending for your song JADA."

"It would be much more logical to have a table fifty-three inches long instead of fifty-four."

---

42 The following comments are largely jokes not to be taken seriously and sometimes referring to fictitious names. Nebenzahl may be a reference to Avigdor Nebenzahl (born 1935), a well-known Orthodox rabbi, or Heinrich Nebenzahl (1870–1938), an Austrian-born film producer, or simply a humorous made-up name or play on a German name; Wilber and Orville are, of course, the Wright Brothers.

"If Pferdfus is a backward child, why doesn't he come in backward?"

"This play should be narrated by a sort of master of ceremonies. This would shorten your exposition. Incidentally, my cousin Selig, who looks Mexican, has put in a great and long apprenticeship at the Concord."

"When the leading lady cries, she should wave an American flag so we know how she feels."

"I have a much dirtier way of telling that joke: The lady walks into the saloon with one of her –"

Finally, I beg you to return the script promptly without having made notes on it or marking it in any way. Your copy may very well be the one intended for the eyes of a prospective director or choreographer or even investor, and should remain pristine. In passing, let me state that I have used pristine for years and find that while it indeed closes my mind, it does open my sinuses.

22 May 1967: To Budd Schulberg

The reason I haven't sent along the script is that it is simply not good enough. I don't mean this only as a matter of degree. It is un-right, so please forgive me for not showing it.

... The play in its present condition is terribly diffuse. It lacks concentration on a prevalent rooting line, and I must supply that. My difficulty for the last month or so has been in deciding what line to follow. You read about three quarters of it some time back, so I think you will understand specifically what I mean.

For instance, there is a strong opening scene that presents a small problem of the clergy about no cojones in the confessions. The problem then disappears as a larger and more exciting one is assigned to Hilario. We then introduce Pancito and his problems as the town's drunken reprobate. But he shortly finds this problem ended by virtue of his quasi canonization through Hilario, who in turn abandons his own purpose of seeking nookie with a fifteen-year-old. The happy coalition of the two bakers provides Lupita with a release from her status anxieties. This leaves us with Martin, who has a clear-cut purpose which continues although I propose no interesting or entertaining penalty for failure in his professorship examinations. We are also left with Carolina as the standard old maid who continues to pray for a husband. Along with this I suppose we must consider the trio of priests as exerting a continuous drive toward putting their town on the religious map.

Well, I have never considered constructing the play as the story of Martin, or the story of Carolina, or the story of the three priests. But that is what the present script leaves me with, and in all honesty I don't believe any audience would stand for such stakes after careful presentation of at least three others as being our big principals . . .

To put it very briefly, I have asked for a rooting section at a ball game which gets rained out in the second inning; then begged them to travel to another field where darkness shortly stops the game; invited them on a bus ride which takes them around in a circle; and then coaxed them off the bus for a supper of chicken noodle soup, only to serve it in bowls with holes at the bottom.

There is some question as to whether Loesser continued to work on *Señor Discretion Himself* until the time of his death in July 1969 or whether he had abandoned the project earlier. Loesser's widow, Jo, claimed in the *New York Times* (26 November 1985, 69) that, shortly before he died, Loesser was refining the songs and writing a second draft of the book. Susan Loesser, however, reproduces a letter to Schulberg dated 19 March 1968 that suggests he had fully abandoned it.

19 March 1968: To Bud Schulberg

A sad time has come. I find myself obliged to report to you that I don't know how to budge my version of Señor Discretion in any further direction or into any other shape. I have begun to remechanize the poor thing in several different ways only to find the results deadly dull – and with not all the feeling I had wished for it.

I think I have already told you that I went to the three theatrical writers I consider most valuable in the musical comedy field – and offered each the job of doing a new book. In each case I got some friendly words, but neither Abe Burrows nor Doc Simon[43] came anywhere near considering my offer.

And now finally I must confess that I have grown cold on the subject. Not cold to it. I feel sure there is someone in our business who will know how to write a good adaptation but that someone is not me or any of the people I trust, and so I have told the company not to take advantage of its option which comes up in May, but to return it with regret to you.

I feel confident that you understand me and that my decision to quit is one I simply had to make after all this time. Also I feel sure that this will not change what I think is a happy regard you and I have for each other.

Although the show was never finished by Loesser, a workshop production of *Señor Discretion Himself* was mounted in 1985 and a version of the work had a short run in Washington, DC, in April–May 2004.

---

43 Neil ('Doc') Simon (1927–2018), American playwright of films, television shows and theatrical works. He won the Tony Award for Best Playwright for *The Odd Couple* (1965) and in 1975 was awarded a Special Tony for his lifetime contributions to American theatre.

CHAPTER TWELVE

1966–69
THE LAST YEARS

Meredith Willson continued to loom large in Loesser's plans for Frank Music and as a close friend. Letters from this time – to Willson and to Loesser's colleagues at Frank Music – touch on both the personal and on Willson's upcoming plans for a musical. These included a version of the Danish verse drama *King Rene's Daughter* and *1491*, an original musical centred on Christopher Columbus the year before he sailed for the New World. The letters concerning *1491* deal not only with the structure of the play and its suitability as a musical but also, and in particular, the financial and contractual arrangements surrounding its production by the Los Angeles Civic Light Opera, which eventually produced the piece in the autumn of 1969.

27 January 1965: Memo to Milton Kramer

Subject: "KING RENE'S DAUGHTER" – MEREDITH WILLSON
Dear Milt:
  Herewith I am returning the copy of "KING RENE'S DAUGHTER."
I have not given much thought to it in itself – as I have many conjectures about what Meredith sees in it for himself.[1]

---

1 *King Rene's Daughter*, first published in 1845, was a Danish drama by author Henrik Hertz (1797–1870). A fictional account of Yolande of Lorraine, a blind

Almost any treatment of it that I can imagine ––– would seem to be a departure in style for MW. In principle, I welcome the idea of a departure. I believe Willson has more scope than he has shown in the theatre, and I believe he has more than even he believes he has. Nevertheless, this story seems to remain a romantic <u>myth</u> no matter how it's handled. By this I mean that there are a whole lot of implausible things that would hurt this yarn if the whole aura of fantasy were lifted from it. Compare with "Sleeping Beauty."

I would like to know what ideas Meredith has for treatment. I could suggest one or two (modern form) but I would rather wait till we hear from him whether he has any set idea for treatment; change in period; ending <u>without</u> the lady's recovery of sight; change in character of our hero, etc., etc.

Are you in touch with him on this subject?

19 May 1965: To Meredith Willson

Dear Meredith:

Our friend Kramer[2] keeps me in touch with the process of Rini's recovery and return home, so that I am sure by this time all is well.

All is well here too, except fraught. My daughter gets married next week and our new baby should arrive within the next three weeks. Me, I have a schedule of dentist visits looming, plus the detail of <u>renting a boat by telephone</u>. All this busy-ness is what is sometimes described by Sam Goldwyn as an absence of calmth.

Meanwhile, Kramer has given me your new musical[3] to read. I have hopes about it. The central character hasn't been done as far as I know, and neither has that period geography been used. Certainly also I think you could invest your Willsonian idiom with the proper tinge of Period Espanol – and that would be news.

---

princess who lives in a garden paradise, it was widely translated and produced as a play, titled *Iolanthe*, in London in 1880 (a version unrelated to Gilbert and Sullivan's *Iolanthe*); in musical versions, by Henry Smart (1813–1879, produced 1871) and Pyotr Ilyich Tchaikovsky (1840–1893, produced 1892); and as a silent film, released in 1913.

2 Milton Kramer.

3 *1491.*

Nevertheless, taking a broad look at what I read – I seem not to be able to imagine the emergence of the guitar as a monumental point in history. Even Spanish history. Observe that Nathan's Coney Island[4] succeeded in putting a totally edible skin on the kosher frankfurter, but the classic American one you get at the baseball game is still as tough as ever, and three strikes is still out. Being a frankfurter connoisseur I am acutely and deliciously aware of the Nathan's revolution, and celebrate it privately every so often without a knowing nosch.[5] But until they inscribe some future Magna Carta on one of those filmy little hotdog skins Nathan's will have remained a relatively tiny breakthrough. On the other hand if anyone can prove anything about the guitar's importance in history – you can.

The title is marvelous and I believe it would suggest to anyone that it presents the circumstances which precede the discovery of America, notably the personality of Columbus. I am very fond of the smart way he finds out where the map is. But I seem to want to see more such episodes so that by the time we're half way through with the first act we know for sure what a nutty adventurer first came to these shores. In other words I feel that the play should be more personality-centralized, as is "MUSIC MAN" and "HOW TO SUCCEED." They sure buy the progress of a purposeful rogue in this century, notably in musical comedy. Only in westerns do we seem to find a real do-good hero like Gene Autry.[6] So as long as you start with a fellow who gets on by his wits you are probably right, only he should do it more constantly, vigorously, etc.

All this above is the result of one quick reading through. I will not read it again until I have the next edition which I'm sure is already in work, and then I hope Milt will pass it on to me.

Love and all the best wishes to Rini. Tell her I spent a week in St. John's once and they fried me a nun for breakfast every morning. I

---

4 Nathan's Famous was founded as a hot dog stand in Coney Island in 1916; the name derives from its co-founder, Nathan Handwerker (1892–1974).
5 Yiddish for snack.
6 Gene Autry (1907–1998), singer, actor and rodeo performer known as 'The Singing Cowboy'; he appeared in more than ninety films and hosted *The Gene Autry Show* on CBS television 1950–56.

was on the bland diet. Anyway seriously, I hope she stays fine now. So kiss her a lot. That sometimes does it. Make one of them from me.

Love,

26 January 1966: To Meredith Willson

Dear Meredith:

Firstly, thanks for your note and the text of the Roger Eldridge sermon. It <u>is</u> nice to get yourself into the language, even by way of a moralist's mouthings.

Our spy Milt[7] tells me you and Rini are heading this way. Please save time for a lunch or something with me. I still can't touch my toes with my fingertips but I may want to touch yours. Shine Mister? What I am meaning to say is that we owe each other an hour or so of merry banter, or whatever doesn't have a deadline or a state of emergency.

Meanwhile, the best of everything for your premiere of "Prelude to America." Will there be a tape, including introductory words and audience applause?

Love to you and Rini and those other Willsons who I know must be laying you the finest table along with the reddest carpet.

Soon,

18 April 1966: To Meredith Willson

Dear Meredith:

I am in more of a mad blind rush than ever what with the City Center business,[8] plus a household exploded by help problems, the children's health, etc. which explains why this has to be short and very much to the point.

For the past months Rinimer-Frank seems to have been attempting to renew its English and other foreign contracts.

Rinimer-Frank has no legal representation.

---

7 Milton Kramer.
8 A revival of *The Most Happy Fella*, 11–22 May 1966.

At one time you and I agreed on Harold Orenstein's office but they presented a bill which somebody in your camp refused to pay.

At the time I paid the entire bill myself, but I told Harold that he is no longer representing Rinimer-Frank since he would run the risk of having to work for nothing. In what seems to be interminable and really pointless correspondence with Martin Gang, our house counsel, Alan Bergman, has been pinch-hitting.

Rinimer-Frank must decide now on who its legal counsel is and for how much.

Have you any suggestions? I think we should establish this representation quickly if any legal question comes up affecting our joint enterprise. And believe me, every week or so there is a license requiring approval or an attempted parody to quash or a threatened unlicensed use to police, etc., etc. It is unfair for us to plague Alan Bergman who is a full time Frank Music employee.

Who would you like and for how much?

Please!

Love,

2 May 1966: To Meredith Willson

Dear Meredith:

Thank you, thank you, thank you for yours of April 27th. I can't tell you how relieved I am that all this mess is on its way to being settled. I am delighted that you agree on Harold [Orenstein] as official attorney for our joint business, and somebody from my outfit (probably our Cyd Cheiman) will be writing to Lefkowitz about the share of the fees paid by us.

Again, my congratulations for your prompt handling of this. For a long time, it has been a constant itch – sort of in the tenor clef – accompanying my happier thoughts, and this sort of ostinato I can well do without. Hooray!

Love to you and Rini.

Sincerely,

21 June 1966: To Meredith Willson

Dear Meredith:

I thought by this time you would have sent me that script.[9] Really, it will give me a much better concept of the whole thing – and a chance to form a possibly valuable opinion. I simply don't have one yet because I don't really know what I heard. Yes, I heard some exciting scenes – as well as some I didn't quite understand. As far as the songs go, I will have to hear them all again after knowing where they belong <u>emotionally</u> in the tale.

Of course if you don't feel like it at the moment, then don't send it along. But I am trying to support your sense of urgency as well as offer my own two cents worth.

After you left I got in two conversations. One with Feuer and a later one with Martin.[10] Both confirmed their opinions about the enormous expense indicated. I can understand that very well, but at the same time I don't believe that the show – from my one brush with it – absolutely has to have such gigantic production elements. In the last analysis the writing is what counts – as well as the playing of it.

But please (if you want) send it along again. Now that the City Center thing is over I am not being nagged and can put some hours into it.

Love to you and Rini as always,

20 July 1966: To Meredith Willson

Dear Meredith:

I had begun a lengthy array of notes in the study of the script. It was entirely too lengthy and picky, and so I quit in favor of asking questions out loud when we meet on August 2, 3 and 4.

I think this is a better idea than writing down little bits, especially in view of the fact that you are doing a lot of self-editing and filling right now and will come in loaded. Also, in view of the fact that a

---

9 For *1491*.
10 Cy Feuer and Ernest Martin.

great many of the items I picked on will be the same ones you pick on yourself.

Like it says in the song, we will "pick a little, talk a little."[11] Or maybe a whole lot. I look forward.

Love to you and Rini.

Sincerely,

5 August 1966: To Meredith Willson

Dear Meredith:

As I have told you, I approve of a writer-producer relationship between you and Ed Lester.[12] But this is a broad expression of my high regard for his abilities and the potential advantage to be gained through his power and influence in the far west.

But I must emphasize here that we are speaking of a pre-Broadway engagement. Your intention is to arrive on Broadway with "1491," and nothing by way of your contracts with Lester or anyone else should be allowed to impede the show's progress toward a successful Broadway opening and a long run there.

Therefore a great deal depends on every word, syllable and letter in your agreement with Lester. I will want to give everything careful scrutiny before approving. Notably the degree of control you have regarding his employment of performing artists; your privileges regarding later use of the physical show, scenery, props and costumes; your final approvals as to director, choreographer, scenic and costume designers, etc., etc.

As I mentioned this morning, the printed standard Dramatists Guild contract forms simply reflect <u>minimal</u> requirements of an author-composer. The present tendency has been to include these printed forms, however amended. I believe a lot of the stuff contained in them to be onerous, considering your veteran position in the theatre – and I am going to recommend to my cohorts here, as well as

---

11 A song from Willson's *The Music Man*.
12 Edwin Lester had founded the Los Angeles Civic Light Opera in 1938, where *1491* premiered on 2 September 1969.

to your agents, not to regard all of such contract content as absolutely sacred.

In short, I do indeed approve your relationship with Lester, but only if he recognizes and acts upon your unnumbered, unimpeded, unfeblungered <u>Broadway</u> plans. My people will be conferring with your Morris office people shortly on the entire project.

Love,

14 September 1966: To Meredith Willson

Dear Meredith:

Herewith are comments and suggestions based upon a proposal to Ed Lester prepared by the William Morris office. A copy of this proposal I assume is in your hands. Bear in mind it has never been delivered to Ed Lester but was simply drafted as a suggested document awaiting comment, improvement, refinement, correction, etc.

You will find enclosed six pages from me to my cohorts, Whitehead and Kramer. You will also find their independently arrived at notes.

Of course a complete copy of all this has been forwarded to Jerry Talbert at the William Morris office, but that must not be too much of a comfort to you. I feel that you yourself should carefully and earnestly read, study and understand everything we have put down and then confer with the Morris office to find out where we all agree on what to propose to Ed Lester.

The gist of what I have had to say, you will note, is that Meredith Willson ought to get at least as good a deal as Frank Loesser would get.

As your loyal mayvin[13] I have put in a lot of sweat and time in saying my say, and so have Milt and Allen. So I beg you to give all this your keen attention.

Love as always,

---

13 Yiddish for someone who is particularly skilled in some field, in this case also in the sense of mentor.

21 September 1966: To Meredith Willson

Dear Meredith:

Pretty soon it will be time for me to make some sort of formal announcement about the show I am trying to write.[14] Actually it is much too early for me, but there are other people whose pressures I must consider.

Now how about your announcement? If you feel you ought to go ahead quite soon, then I will delay my little spitball.

Of course your production plans are, as of this moment, not crystallized, and it can't be said for sure that Lacloa[15] will produce, or when or with what great stars, etc, etc. On the other hand, you might want an immediate announcement of the nature and maybe title of your work and the intention of doing business with Ed Lester, or for that matter Menasha Skulnick.[16] Please let me know about this. My point is that I would like to leave some daylight between our announcements in the hope that each will have a significant impact and not gleeble or brungle into each other. Generally in the fall theatrical production announcements in the New York press make sort of a typographical mash, and no one remembers exactly what he read, and if he does, cannot seem to consider it important because it was among so many other shrdlus, Doreschars and Kermbloos.[17] See? Please answer. Also, tell me your thoughts and feelings about my analysis of your prospective deal with Lester.

Love to you and Rini,

---

14 *Señor Discretion Himself;* see Chapter 11.
15 The Los Angeles Civic Light Opera Association, where *1491* was to be produced.
16 Menasha Skulnik (1890–1970), American actor known in particular for his performances in Yiddish theatre.
17 Shrdlus, meaning 'nonsense', derived from the arrangement of the keyboard of a Linotype machine. Doreschars refers to Dore Schary and Kermbloos refers to Kermit Bloomgarden.

13 December 1966: To Allen Whitehead
and Milton Kramer

Subject: RINIMER-LACLOA "1491" Contract

I have some broad questions, and some narrow. Some no doubt uninformed. Some based on some error of mine in interpreting what I have read. So please in reading this over prepare whatever rebuttals or corrections you may have to my opinions.

I. With the greatest possible clarity Lacloa should express its intent to produce the show for Broadway. I seem to see where Lacloa – after a glorious no-risk provincial run – can wash its hands of the project and continue no further.

What Rinimer must be sure of is continuity without lapse, so that the actors and other valuable contractees do not have to be paid for marking time while Lacloa in the final weeks suddenly puts the show up for grabs under its privilege of assignment.

I therefore feel that Lacloa should state its case concretely to Rinimer by exhibiting contacts to occupy theatres on the way to New York and in New York itself <u>at a specific advance date</u>. If this requirement (and possibly others) is not fulfilled by this date, all rights of any kind to produce the show should revert to Rinimer – which in turn will have plenty of time to choose the next producer. Along with this right to produce, Rinimer should receive all the physical properties, scenery and costumes of the show, and inherit all of the producer rights and privileges expressed in the various performers' and directorial contracts. Without in the least criticizing Lacloa's very fine western accomplishments, I reflect here that historically it is not typical of Lacloa to plow through bravely to Broadway. In the above suggestion I am expressing only one safeguard. Maybe there should be many others.

I-A. For instance, here's one: I believe very strongly that Rinimer should have approval of all contracts with performing artists, so that Rinimer does not have to face losing actors it wants because of too early a terminus to their employment. Rinimer should also insist that Lacloa get the proper collateral contracts with performing artists for recording services if and when there is a Broadway cast album. Also contracts restricting principal performers from performing material independently in tv, radio and clubs without express permission from Rinimer. If you wish to you may show Rinimer's agents my restriction agreements secured for me by Feuer & Martin in "HOW TO SUCCEED...."

II. In light of the hazards expressed above, I feel that Lacloa's right to assign its rights to another producer should be subject to the final approval of Rinimer. Meredith should not be tossed into the hands of a producer he doesn't like and doesn't trust, and can't work with. Suppose for instance Lacloa's run and control ends in the month of June, of whom Meredith can stomach even though they have indeed presented two successful shows on Broadway in the last ten years. He is going to have to endure the rest of a long, hot summer on the road and some of a dreary and discouraging autumn in order to arrive triumphantly in the right theatre in New York in November. This should not simply be a nominal change in management. It represents a long and arduous labor on the road. As we well know, certain gloriously effective elements of a Los Angeles extravaganza earn themselves a lot of glum audience reaction in Chicago. Meredith should have the producer of his own heart's choice all the way. It is tough enough fixing and changing a show on the road. It should not also be stupid and full of unsympathetic obstructions. And I will bet you a nickel that valuable and experienced Ed Lester is not likely to travel east of Pasadena for very long. And I will bet you a dime that there is nothing in Section 49 of the printed Schedule that can force him out of his nest.

(After making all the above notes I have read ABW's[18] memo of September 12th to Kramer and me which covers certain oversights of mine and also certain ignorance of Equity rulings. I think the idea in the postscript for Rinimer's <u>prevailing</u> position as General Partner – is a very good one).

III. I have in hand a proposed letter agreement between Lacloa and Rinimer. The intent seems to be that Rinimer Corporation will receive 10% of the profits of the play for rendering a number of services described in the first page. None of these services seem to

---

18 Allen Whitehead.

have any relation to writing or authorship of any kind or to the designation of any specific employee – and yet there is a constant reference to the word author and author's agent. On the second page there is a fleeting reference to the existence of a Dramatists Guild agreement entered into between the parties. I find that in the last six lines of this paragraph there is a reference to "rights which the Author may have under this contract."

In the final paragraph of the letter (7) I don't understand the phrase "personal to you, etc."

I may be wrong but considering the above could this letter agreement be better and less transparently organized?

IV. The exact meaning of APPROVAL should be defined. In many instances I think Willson should get DESIGNATION. It seems to me that the following hypothetical dialogue can possibly obtain:

WILLSON

I want Elia Kazan.[19]

LACLOA

I'm sorry but I don't like him. He is too expensive, too Greek, etc. The man I want is Morton Da Costa.[20]

WILLSON

But I have approval and I'm telling you that I want Elia Kazan.

LACLOA

Sorry but you are not in a position to approve a name that I have not proposed. After all, I am the producer and I pay the fees and until I propose a name, there is no sense or meaning to any so-called approval of yours. But in deference to your wishes – if they are not extraordinarily repugnant to me – I will propose a new name. How about Joseph Anthony?[21]

---

19 Elia Kazan (1909–2003), film and theatre director; his film credits include *A Streetcar Named Desire* (Warner Bros., 1951) and *On the Waterfront* (Columbia Pictures, 1954). Kazan won the Academy Award for best director for both films.
20 Morton Da Costa (1914–1989), director of Willson's *The Music Man*.
21 Joseph Anthony (1912–1993), theatrical director. Anthony had staged Loesser's *The Most Happy Fella*.

WILLSON

But I don't want Joseph Anthony. I told you I want Kazan.

LACLOA

And I told you I have not proposed that name, and don't intend to.

(— and so far into the night)

<u>V.</u> On the subject of an English production of the play: I am confused by some of the apparent opportunities available to the producer. A "lump sum" might not suit the purposes of the author at that moment. On the other hand, he might yearn for a lump sum and not have a voice in the matter. Is it not possible to give the author plain and simple approval of any deal for production in England? Please recall that this type of clause is part of a minimal Guild consideration, and Meredith Willson is a <u>big</u> man. I have just looked at an old document. It is the one by which Bloomgarden et al, the Broadway producers of THE MOST HAPPY FELLA, assigned all English stage rights to another producer. I note that the entire document was approved by Frank Loesser in writing.

<u>VI.</u> On Page 11(d) there is a paragraph numbered (ii). I think here it would be more valuable and more dignified to say that the producer, at the author's <u>request</u>, will engage a revisions writer and that Rinimer will approve the terms of this engagement. Period. After all, at this point we cannot predict whether Rinimer will wish to engage someone for hire at its own expense, or the producer will wish to do something similar in Rinimer's behalf at its expense and what conflict might arise because of this. We do not know what billing a revisions writer may demand. We do not know what collateral arrangement will have to be made between the author and the revisions writer for the sharing of subsidiary rights, etc., etc.

In passing, let me suggest that provision should indeed be made in the event that the author's employee, Meredith Willson, should by virtue of illness or death not be able to complete the intended writing and re-writing. I think that the producer should accept the Rinimer Corporation's choice of any revision writer-editor-additional composer-lyricist to substitute for Willson. Rinimer, as a corporation, could still control financial agreements with such contributors without affecting or changing in any way the existing contract. I am assuming here that in the event of Willson's demise the Rinimer Corporation would be left as part of his estate and in the control of knowledgeable people.

VII. On Page 11(d) there is something I loathe and despise and it is Paragraph V. It is a trap. Please acquaint Willson's agents with the special terms of my motion picture sale of "HOW TO SUCCEED IN BUSINESS WITHOUT REALLY TRYING," as well as the terms with co-writers and producers of the stage version which cleared the way for my "music demands." They may easily consult Beresford's (Burrows) agreements with me and acknowledgement of my music terms in the sale contract. In this day and age there is no possible way to tell what ten thousand dollars will be worth five years hence. Nor is there a way to tell that Meredith will be in Greece for a holiday, or up to his neck in a new piece of writing when called on by some studio to supply some little extra nugget. I will not labor this subject further, except to say that Meredith should do at least as well as I do on the terms of a motion picture sale.

VIII. Above you have my major objections and suggestions, although I am sure there must be some things I have overlooked thus far. I have proposed some seemingly strong demands on Lacloa. It must be remembered that they will have the right to bargain for a prevailing proprietary share in the interests of any succeeding producer. This especially if they should turn over scenery, costumes, etc. It is also predictable that Lacloa may rise in indignation in view of the fact that Rinimer has asked for unrecoupable advance royalties of $25,000.00, plus an additional 10% of the producer's profits. Am I to assume that Meredith really and truly wants that $25,000.00? Or is this just expressed as part of a whimsical plan? If he definitely needs it and wants it, there is no arguing the point, but then I am sure he will have to pay for it by agreeing to certain terms which I consider onerous.

By the same token: an afterthought about the award of 10% of the profits to Rinimer, a corporation which I wish the best of financial health. This bite of 10% may put a serious dent in any effort Lacloa may make in asking another producing organization to join it – and such a circumstance might critically affect the possibility of this show's arrival on Broadway. "Get the money and run for the train" is not always the wisest policy.

So much for now.

19 April 1967: To Meredith Willson

Dear Meredith:

Milt Kramer gets me up to date with the news that you are back from Seattle. Also that you have come to a finish with your labors on the book, and at least for now are satisfied with it. Oh how I wish I could say the same for myself. I am in the well-known throes, and I hate every word and note I have written at this point. This is quite an ordinary thing with me in everything I try, but it always somehow surprises and shocks me. Of course I will get over the doldrums by the simple process of waking up one morning with the following stroke of genius: change the boy to a girl; change the locale from Pittsburgh to Ghana; then place Scene 3 where Scene 7 was and omit the reference to the uncle giving all his money to a home for cats; instead, Katz leaves all his money to the uncle who then returns to Pittsburgh in the following scene where we do the "stogie" number, but in B♭ instead of G. See? Everything works out fine, only at this moment it hasn't.

Anyway, I was thinking of you and how you were, and when I would see you again. I have no plans for there, but I will wait to hear from Milt when to figure on your arrival here.

Love as always,

5 July 1967: Memo to Milt Kramer

HERE'S LOVE[22] – NBC
Wearing my red hat as personal advisor and kindly policeman to Meredith Willson, my immediate reaction is to ask whether Meredith has any artistic restrictions in mind, or whether he wishes to

---

22 For Willson's *Here's Love*, see Chapter 9.

collaborate artistically in a television treatment etc. I wish you would call him in my behalf and get his general intent. I will know better which of my guardhairs are to become erectile with caution. Please tell him in passing that I certainly have no objection to the association with either NBC or Bing Crosby. Also, send him my fondest love and tell him I am still in trouble.

5 December 1967: To Meredith Willson

Dear Meredith:

I have been reading and rereading your show[23] after quite a long time away from it. Also, after certain revisions. The object here has been to develop opinions both discrete and collective – for what they are worth to you. Milt Kramer endorses this process, so I hope you don't mind.

For openers, let me tell you that I believe the ending of your story is one of the most powerful and exciting finishes I have ever come across, and I applaud and congratulate you for an achievement that will not be equaled for a long time in the theatre.

Notice that I said <u>story</u>. I think that the way the play plays the story could improve some – and here it's a question of <u>clarity</u> more than anything else.

Now my big squawk: I feel very strongly that the play, as written up until the last couple of scenes, does not deserve such a fabulous ending. For the past ten days I have been trying to make notes pointing out where I lose bigness and richness; where I feel a waste of emphasis, or a drop in taste etc. But notes arrived at by the critic alone at his desk – very often turn out to be a collection of nit-pickings, a great proportion of which could be obviated upon a simple consultation with the nit. I will give you an example.

THE NOTE

Why does the author use the word "perpendicular" in describing the body of Sydney Carton which at the moment is quite supine and

---

23 *1491.*

permanently horizontal on the floor of the tumbril. It would seem to me not only a misnomer, but something of a joke since Sydney Carton hasn't taken a sober breath in two whole hours of Dickens. Of course, Mme. Defarge might be a joker, but then that goes against her character as a knitting voyeuse. A mean old woman should not make funnies. Of course, if it is intended to rewrite the Defarge character, I will have to refer the author to his second scene in which she says "Up your ass," and suggest that he correct it to "Down the hatch." On second consideration I should not encourage the author to change character already there. I must write him a long letter about this.

THE CONSULTATION

FRANK: Meredith, why do you use "perpendicular"?
MEREDITH: Because it rhymes with vehicular?
FRANK: Oh.
MEREDITH: Next question?

But this letter is not going to contain any notes except maybe one which is a parable of my own spurious, however earnest, manufacture. Here is the parable.

I am standing in the forest near a clearing. I hear the sounds of a woodsman's axe. Presently, a giant tree begins falling from the edge – straight north into the center of the clearing. It makes a surging, singing sound as it falls, brushing the foliage of every standing tree but hardly destroying so much as a twig on its enormous descent. And, in another moment, it crashes magnificently to the ground, its pinnacle landing at the dead center of the clearing, a halo of dancing, sunlit dust forming about and above the fallen giant – while an entire forest of leaves rustles an ever-echoing applause. I go over to the stump remaining where the giant has been felled, and I see something which puzzles me. The axe marks. They are odd. They are strange. They are – well, I will call the woodsman and ask him. I call, but he is gone. Fled somewhere. Fled to a saloon somewhere, in shame. I go back to the axe marks. Although the woodsman properly worked from the south so that the tree could fall north into the clearing – there being a southerly breeze – he did not, by any means, hew to the line. There were gashes far from the proper mark. Some of the east, grazing nothing but bark, some to the west, cropping neighborly ground vines, and some fully a foot above or below the mark. How did a woodsman so haphazard, possibly so preoccupied or undetermined – or maybe just boozed up – ever manage such an expert and majestic finale?

I would like very much for you to come and see me for, let's say, three days, early in January. I think possibly we could arrange for two two-hour sessions each day. Or maybe more, if we could stand the strain. Can you do it? Do you want to? Please write me.

Love,

P.S. In a way I am reminded of my intercession in your behalf with Walter Kerr.[24] We had put the knock on you because of what he considered a sort of rewrite of your earlier material of years. When I yelled at him that you were entitled to use your own <u>style</u> just as surely as [Cole] Porter was entitled to write many, many pieces in the "Beguine" rhythm, Walter said "Oh, I see what you mean," and then begged off with a lame: "But he didn't do it as well" – which was not at all the point he had made in his printed review. I am pointing out here the value of consultation, instead of an exchange of documents IN ADVANCE OF PHILADELPHIA.

18 December 1967: To Meredith Willson

Dear Meredith:

Okay okay. I had no idea that you weren't finished with the show. When you have it so you like it fine is when I think I ought to see it again, if that is all right with you. But I don't think there is any point in our sitting down together until you have what you want produced.

Let me make the observation here that it is those we love and cherish the most that we are the most critical of. That is because we want them to be perfect.

Have a good Christmas and a fine, successful new year. Those are un-frowning thoughts because they represent something merely

---

24 Walter Kerr (1913–1996), Broadway theatre critic.

wishful. If a happy and hopeful whimsey were all I had to give you about your work, I would not be:

Your loving friend,

9 December 1968: To Meredith Willson

Dear Meredith:

Thanks for the recent clips. The "territory" one is a real beauty and conforms to my specifications, as I always think of you in large size bold type.

Milt has me somewhat acquainted with your plans for the show.[25] At least I learn that you are definitely going in as the last piece of the Ed Lester season. I hope you are toweringly sanguine. As you may recall – after hearing you play the flute – I advised the world that your spit ought to be bottled. I now wish to advocate further that the stubs from your pencils should be collected and auctioned off at Sotheby's along with contributions from Stradivarius, Rembrandt, etc.

Also I insist that you and Rosemary should have a magnificent and joyous Christmas.

Love as always,

Bob Fosse and Gwen Verdon's *Sweet Charity*, one of the hits of the 1965–66 Broadway season, opened at the Palace Theatre on 29 January 1966. Loesser did not attend the opening although he saw at least two performances over the next few months. Verdon had taken the role of Lola in Adler and Ross's *Damn Yankees*; Fosse had recently staged Loesser's *Pleasures and Palaces*. Earlier, Fosse had choreographed *How to Succeed in Business Without Really Trying*, the film of which – again with Fosse as choreographer – was first mooted in 1964. Loesser's initial arrangements for the film were made by lawyer and talent agent Irving Lazar (1907–1993). Loesser engaged in a lengthy – and at times seemingly acrimonious – correspondence

---

25 *1491*, which was originally intended to open in California in 1967 but was not produced at the Los Angeles Civic Light Opera until 2 September 1969; the show did not make it to Broadway.

with screenwriter David Swift (1919–2001), and in the end appears to have been not entirely satisfied with the final version. The film opened on 9 March 1967 and was a critical success but a commercial disappointment.

25 January 1966: To Gwen Verdon and Bob Fosse

Dear Gwen and Bob:

This note is to tell you how wildly I am rooting for a smash hit for both of you on Saturday night. I know from talking to you long ago, Bob, that this is a very important step – in the personal and emotional sense as well as the professional. So my wishes are not only those of a show business colleague, but are truly heartfelt.

Let me add something about opening nights. I love to be asked but I really and truly hate to go. That is why when your office called about whether I wanted seats, we answered no thanks. Instead we already have seats for the following Friday. It happens that I get the nervous pip at openings. Somehow I feel responsible. I turn green just thinking about a missed cue or fumbled scenery. This is especially the case where so many good friends of mine are involved. Believe it or not, I have never sat through an entire New York opening of my own, except on one occasion where I was physically held down in my seat by a powerful and sincere friend I made the mistake of inviting along. So if you have heard about my turning down opening night seats, I hope you will understand.

Jo and I will be at home, pacing, momentarily half-listening to a shrieking infant or having an unconcerned glance at Marshall Dillon on the tv.[26] All the while, I assure you both of us will be concentrating on wishing you not only well but the very best. I don't know how the Protestant Sullivans[27] rate with God, but speaking for myself I can tell you that earnest Jewish prayers can't be beat. You will notice that in the last fourteen years or so that our tribe has gotten our own real

---

26 The popular television series *Gunsmoke*, the protagonist of which was Marshall Matt Dillon; the show ran from 1955 to 1975.
27 I.e. Jo Sullivan's family.

estate somewhere near Egypt. (Next year the New York Athletic Club). So I am confident that you will have a resounding hit.

Best love,

14 July 1966: To Bob Fosse

Dear Bobby:

Yesterday afternoon, I went to see "Sweet Charity" again and, once more, confirmed to myself that you are a genius. For me to call a gentile a genius is a big step. To say it out loud for everybody to hear is to invite the raising of eyebrows. After all, such excellent workshop of talent in our business is usually the sign of some barely concealed homosexual yearnings. You know what I mean – like the dress designer and the roommate he is trying to promote. Well, maybe in this case it is indeed true, so I might as well confess here that I love you dearly and have really nothing against fixed marriages.

So – please work with me again. Please. Why should I have to tell everybody that the most brilliant man in American Theatre today knocked me up and abandoned me?

Thanks and love,

Sincerely,

27 May 1964: To Irving Lazar

Dear Irving:

Looking forward to your representation of my interest in a motion picture sale of "HOW TO SUCCEED," let me give you a refresher on the various items we have discussed bearing on the terms I will want with respect to the disposition of the musical and lyrical contents of the play:

1. The motion picture must contain no music or lyrics other than those included in the original Broadway production. The music, of course, may be arranged orchestrally, and if further underscoring, main and end title music, etc., is required – and this material is permissible providing it is adapted recognizably from the music of the original play. In other words,

583

even bridges, cues or extensions of choreographic music must be arrangements or re-orchestrations of the original score content.

All rights in such "added musical components" as I have just described must be acquired by the motion picture producer by the employment-for-hire of orchestrators and adaptors, and subsequently re-assigned to me. This is simply in the interest of legal neatness, since the basic music copyrights belong to me – and therefore any treatment of them would be of no value to the producer beyond their use in the picture.

There can be no changes of lyrics, except for censorship reasons. In such instances, I would want the picture makers to consult me well in advance, and I will supply the changes free of charge. If I should fail to supply them, the picture company could then supply the lyric changes themselves. Nevertheless, they would have to have acquired all rights of all kinds in the substitute words (through an employee-for-hire) and assign such rights to me, retaining for themselves only such privileges and rights as they would be entitled to if the substitute lyrics had originally existed in the play's score.

2. The orchestral track of the final picture as first exhibited in the U.S.A. will have to be the permanent track and neither the producer nor its distributors may change or substitute any part of this in any territory.

The vocal track (as far as songs are concerned) may be changed by translation into foreign languages. If this is anticipated, I would insist that the picture producers or their designees employ for hire (in my behalf) a translator in each country. The resultant translation would have to have the approval of the music publisher owning publishing and allied rights in that territory, or else my personal approval. (I know all this sounds fussy, but the intention here is to make it possible to exploit the motion picture successfully through songs identical with those used in the picture.)

3. The picture producer may not have any rights of any kind or any restriction of my rights in songs omitted from the picture. By "omission" I refer not only to total omission but to songs which are not performed vocally, and to songs performed for too short a duration.

4. Of course I would agree that for a reasonable period of time after first release of the motion picture – not to allow uses of any of the songs in other theatrical motion pictures. Similarly, I would restrict for a limited period of time my privilege of using or assigning any of my song titles as the title of another theatrical motion picture. Naturally, I would not apply the two self-restrictions above to omitted numbers or their titles.

5. I would want copies of "music cue sheets" which accompany the film in each country in which it is shown.

6. I would want a usable copy of the entire musical track (vocal and orchestral) of the finished picture delivered to me for my disposition in negotiating and contracting for a "sound track album" of the picture.[28] In connection with this, I would be perfectly willing to make some reasonable arrangement with the motion picture producers by which they would share in the benefits of the ultimate track album. In return, it would be absolutely necessary for them, in casting the picture, to secure the services of performers who had no agreements in force which would prohibit my free disposition of the track album rights to any record company.

7. I would want to approve the musical director,[29] and/or orchestrator(s) of the motion picture. (I would be perfectly willing to do this from a pre-set list of names.) Also, I would want to approve the billing of these people. I say this for the following reason. I do not like the use of the word "arranger" or "arrangement." Further, I disapprove of such billing as "music by –" which I sometimes see as a credit for a musical director or musical conductor, or even orchestrator. You can

---

28 The soundtrack was released by United Artists records in 1967.
29 In the event, veteran bandleader and orchestrator Nelson Riddle (1921–1985).

understand why I would not want a conflict of <u>impressions</u> on the public.

Well there you have an array of what I consider harmless special terms. I have gotten all of them before, and so I see no special difficulties. Possibly I have left out a few details. Also it may be that the producer may present new food for thought along these lines in suggesting terms I have never been asked to think about before. But for the moment there you have it. Incidentally, my partners (F&M[30] and Abe Burrows) have been apprised in great detail long ago about these "music terms," and express no concern or objection.

Love to you,

Frank Loesser

15 March 1966: To David Swift, c/o Mirisch Corporation

Dear David:

Over this weekend I have read your screenplay of "HOW TO SUCCEED IN BUSINESS WITHOUT REALLY TRYING," marked FINAL DRAFT. This reading was not for the purpose of ferret-like examination for possible contractual excursions in the use of music and lyrics. My purpose was to form a general and broad opinion about the whole thing – and to report that opinion to you, as you requested.

Before I tell you my thoughts, I must remind you that I know less than nothing about what makes a "good" picture, or a "profitable" picture, or a "box office" picture, or an "Academy Award" picture. The fact is that I am totally ignorant about these values. In addition to that, in this instance I am enormously biased in favor of what I helped create for the stage. That includes what it says, the form in which it says it, the mood, the tempo, the style.

It is with apologies for this combination of ignorance and bias that I submit that I do not like the present screenplay. I estimate that it would take between twenty and forty working hours to discuss with you what I mean. I can't possibly put all that in a letter, except to say

---

30 Cy Feuer and Ernest Martin.

this: I think you are entitled to change the play for "motion picture purposes." I also think that very few of your changes have improved or even sustained the idea. I think that quite a few jokes are worded so that they miss, where they used to hit. I think that some photographic expansions are expensive without adding virtue – and some of them even blur the point.

But regard, please, that if I myself were to begin the story "Once there was a man named Gary Cooper[31] and in the same time and space there was a herd of buffalo" – that I would not accomplish it in the same magnificent way that Cecil DeMille[32] would. That is because I don't know anything about movies. In my last meeting with you here I thought in some respects I was being an effective influence. I wasn't. But then I am loaded with the capacity for making errors in judgment. For example, I no longer subscribe to the "pre-use" of "I Believe in You." As I read it now, it will make the mirror scene seem like something remembered instead of spontaneously thought of. Also, I notice that "Happy To Keep His Dinner Warm" follows so closely on the heels of this boy-girl use of the song that you will be tempted to cut one or the other of these adventures because you are too thick with song material at just the point where the narrative should advance. Also, in this whole complex collection of scenes I note with alarm that you show the end of the date between boy and girl, thus succeeding in blowing the whole "you didn't do anything" joke later on.

Toward the end of the picture your script accounts for the subject of Rosemary's resignation, but there is no evidence of the whole point [of] "I'll give him one more chance," which is what makes her return to the office and refer to the resignation letter. I don't mind at all if the "Cinderella" song is cut, but I do mind the absence of clear motivation, and the use of stray pieces of song lyrics as dialogue.

Oh my God, I am getting into a meeting. I didn't intend any such thing. There would be too much to ask about and talk about. Also,

---

31 Gary Cooper (1901–1961), American actor; among other honours, he won the Academy Award for best actor for *High Noon* (1953).
32 Cecil B. DeMille (1881–1959), legendary filmmaker whose credits include *The Greatest Show on Earth* (1952) and *The Ten Commandments* (1956).

I can't say that I am sure that my way is the only way. Once more I repeat that I do not know what makes successful pictures. And once more I plead a penchant for what was there and what got paid for.

Cordially,

15 March 1966: To Abe Burrows

Dear Abe:

Herewith is the softest way I could put it to [David] Swift after reading what he calls the final draft. Between you and me I consider it a lot more of a horror than I have let on. If you want to torture yourself I have an extra copy. But why should you? If they ever drop the bomb I hope it is on those vaults out West where they keep the negatives.

Love,

4 April 1966: To David Swift

Dear David:

I am probably just about as swamped these days as you are, so I can't go to any great length to reply to yours of March 22nd squawking back at my squawks. Except to say that your opinion is the one that counts, and that my collaboration ends with grabbing the contractual payments. I have your most recent revised pages about the date and will read them tomorrow.

Since my last communication to you I have looked over the "final draft" for any expressed tendency toward violation of my special music terms. I find a few things, a great many of them simply typographical boo-boos:

> On page 114 there is a reference to "Pomp and Ceremony" – by which I assume you intended "Pomp and Circumstance." In any instance this should not be outside stuff but certainly can be orchestrated out of existing score to express the desired mood.
>
> On page 98 I sincerely feel that the inclusion of lyrics from "Cinderella Darling" – but used as dialogue – is a violation. Please remember that in obviating the song (a circumstance

to which I do not object) you are still using elements of it, so that any later use by me of the song "Cinderella Darling" could not be regarded as a totally new use elsewhere in motion pictures, and therefore its market value would be reduced.

There is a reference to the Grieg piano concerto (page 87C). I remind you here that according to my agreement, the Mirisch company uses this at its own risk. I think its worldwide availability should be checked by your company.

On page 40A (eleven lyrics lines from the bottom), the word TROUBLES should be TROUBLE.

On page 45B (eleven lines from the bottom) "It's a fate" should be "It's fate."

Page 28A (seven lyric lines down from the top), the word CONFIRMITY should be CONFORMITY.

On page 12 there is a reference to "The Working Girls Cha-Cha-Cha." Do I assume correctly that this is in some way a musical version of "Coffee Break" as we discussed?

On page 54A I find the boy-girl version of "I Believe in You" which you and I discussed. As I have written to you, I now feel that it should not be used. You seem to have agreed that at least my comment was valid. I don't know whether this would be a technical violation of contract but I dearly hope and pray that you don't use that first version, especially since it crowds into the next song by the distance of less than a page.

Well, that's all I have found to date. Please ask Nelson Riddle to phone me if he has any scoring difficulties. Meantime, my fond good wishes.

Sincerely,

6 April 1967: To David Swift

Dear David:

I have been so deep in my writing that I haven't had the chance to send my congratulations for what appears to be a winner, as you predicted. I haven't seen it yet. First I have to see my wife and children and what I am having for dinner, if any, and get a few glimpses of on-rushing traffic. None of these have I had a chance to manage – and probably won't for a few more weeks. After that I will be going to see "How to Succeed . . .", and have no doubt but that I will enjoy it. Anyway, my congratulations, however, belated.

With fond wishes,

Sincerely,

17 April 1967: To David Swift

Dear David:

I have in hand your letter of April 11th. The first thing I note is that the letterhead, which says COLUMBIA PICTURES CORPORATION, etc. – thus pointing out who actually owns the stationery – is bountifully embossed, while a little lower down to the left the legend DAVID SWIFT PRODUCTIONS has been overprinted in ordinary, no-class, straight Roman, and probably in cautiously small quantity. An inveterate watermark reader, I can report to you that the paper itself is 50% cotton English bond by Fox River. On these two counts alone I can only surmise that you are not getting the best of it at Columbia.

But why should you? Any man who volunteers to do his own underlining in fast fading brush pen – as a cavalier afterthought – shouldn't get house room in those stately halls. The flamboyant mile-high signature DAVID does not in any way make you a Selznick,[33] nor does your attempt at self-identification – "David Swift", typed underneath that signature – show much class.

Nevertheless, being well disciplined, I felt obliged to read what you had to say. It is no more or less than I do for United Jewish Appeal and their sallies, the stagehand's union and their plaintive pitches to sell advertising space in the year book, and certain paranoid complaints from my ancient Aunt Minna in the laughing academy.

Your opening suggestion, "For God's sake," is superfluous. I have been pretending to watch sparrows fall, and to listen to prayers, and

---

33 David O. Selznick (1902–1965), American film producer known in particular for *Gone with the Wind* (1939).

punch belly buttons in infants for so long that I am aware of my own self-interest. Briefly let me remark here that you will never be as snotty as me, no matter how many letters you write. But being a god of mercy – as advertised – I forgive you for your attempted criticism.

You threaten to show up in New York fairly soon. By all means, do so. Arrange for an audience with me, and be prepared to genuflect and all the rest, bearing in mind that I will not tolerate piteous slobber all over my ring. On this count alone I once excommunicated Pavlov's elsewhere esteemed dogs.

Watch it,

26 April 1967: To David Swift

Dear David:

I see where you have taken a hint, and bought yourself your own cardboard stationery – on the face of it an independent move, but transparently indicative of your extreme insecurity.

There is no need for a violent self-serving declaration that the piece of cardboard purports to be a MEMO in 36 point Roman caps, green yet. I <u>know</u> it is a memo. What else would it be? Except possibly that the shape of the thing recalls to mind those tasteless "tall" greeting cards from the basement of Buzza Cardozo.[34] On second glance, I throw out the above possibility because there is no cartoon. Or am I mistaken? There is indeed a sort of awkward vignette at the end of your message – executed in green brush pen. I could easily credit it with being an attempt to represent a fat man trying to pick up a dime. But hold! I note that below it in relatively modest (however overspaced) type there appears the imprint of your name, so I deduce that the clumsy little design is simply a capital D followed by a period. Well sir, if that is your D, you have a lot of climbing to do before you even begin showing any class. I refer you here to the Ds of Albrecht <u>D</u>urer (buy one), <u>D</u>ostoievski (read one), and <u>D</u>octor

---

34 A greeting card company founded by George Earl Buzza (1882–1957) in 1909.

<u>Denton</u>[35] (wear one). Study these signatures along with others by your cultural superiors, and try to develop something of the authority you so desperately need.

As for your message itself, it contains the same gratuitous suggestion that keeps coming in from hosts of other well-meaning people, including my wife and certain other creditors. So you cannot claim even a spark of originality.

Nevertheless it is evident that you are some sort of well-wisher, therefore I feel obligated to return a gesture of equally good will. I enclose herewith a design for a decent correspondence card, so that in the future any message from you may be regarded as accurate and realistic – as well as reflect your true personality.

Let me hear from you.

F *
  **

  * for you know whom
** for you know what

15 June 1967: To David Swift

Dear David:

Surprise. I finally went and saw "How To ..." in Westhampton, Long Island, where I am staying for the summer. I liked most of it, but I'll bet you can't guess the parts I didn't like. Being handsome and enormously wealthy, I can afford to be objective, and so really and truly have very few of the typical squawks you get from preservers of relics of the true play. When I see you maybe you would like to talk about the details of my opinion. Maybe not. Your choice.

Also, a couple of weeks ago I saw "Sabrina"[36] on television. Yes, I think it could make a good musical – on stage or maybe directly as a

---

35 A manufacturer of blanket sleepers, also known as footie pajamas, and designed in particular for small children.
36 The 1954 film directed by Billy Wilder and starring Humphrey Bogart and Audrey Hepburn.

picture. But first it would have to overcome one element always very difficult to lick.

Your dice.

Best,

Loesser's long-time friend composer William Schuman, who had been serving as head of the Juilliard School since 1945, was appointed president of Lincoln Center, a post he held until 1969. Loesser did not entirely approve of the venture, had apparently – at least by mid-1965 – never visited the venue, and, according to Susan Loesser, made some disparaging comments about it. Schuman apparently wrote to Loesser: 'Since you accuse me of being a stuffed-shirt salesman, I will play the role and call you an artist. As an artist, which you certainly are, your cavalier dismissal of our enterprise shocked me.'[37]

18 August 1965: To William Schuman

Dear Billy:

Answering yours of August 13th, lissen:

I did not accuse you, but merely remarked on your guise as salesman You supplied the word stuffed-shirt. Further, I didn't give a cavalier dismissal to your enterprise, I was simply describing possible circumstances in the past that might have led people to think I had some personal grudge against you, and I had no intention of exposing you to my impressions of Lincoln Center except for that reason. Also I don't particularly take pride at not having been at Lincoln Center, and didn't say I did. I simply was reporting on the fact that I knew very little about [it], but that thus far I was impressed the wrong way chemically.

Anyway, I have read the literature you so kindly included. It is very neat, and as such things usually are, completely self-serving. When we meet in the fall, I will have made it a point first to have visited Lincoln Center. I'm sure I will have seen nothing evil in it, any more

---

37 Loesser, *A Most Remarkable Fella*, 260.

than I do in the type face used in your giant brochure. But I will want some definitions from you. For instance, the words:

ARTISTIC

DEVELOPMENT

ENCOURAGING

EDUCATION

etc., etc.

And another definition I will want will be yours for THE PERFORMING ARTS. It seems to me that your prospectus does not include a few of the performing arts, for instance:

PROFESSIONAL WRESTLING

BULL FIGHTING

AUTO RACES

BURLESQUE COMEDY

RADIO & TV ANNOUNCING, NEWS & WEATHER REPORTING

POLITICAL DEBATE

RELIGIOUS ORATORY

FIGURE SKATING

STRIP TEASE

DIVING

AUCTIONEERING

STILT WALKING JUGGLING

RESTAURANT GREETING AND SEATING

MARCHING AND DRILLING EXHIBITION

etc., etc., etc

Please, Billy, don't suppose that I am pushing for a more vulgarian tendency in your program. I am pushing for nothing, but simply pointing out that THE PERFORMING ARTS ARE NOT NECESSARILY THE NIFTY PERFORMING ARTS. Let me submit here that Hemingway – a high-class fellow, found something underline in bull fighting, and that Fred Allen, the much esteemed wit, started as a juggler, or that Victor Moore, who gave such a sensitive performance as Gramps in "Borrowed Time," learned his craft in burlesque; that Billy Graham is more effective as an actor than Sir Laurence Olivier; that the Indianapolis Speedway has a bigger and more avid audience in one day than do the combined performances of LA TOSCA in this country over a 10 year period – even though both audiences are there enjoying the smell of imminent death; that there is an abiding thrill for millions in the performance of those boys marching across the field at West Point; and that sky writing, parachute jumping, and fireworks (– all performing arts) make one look up in awe and wonder. But what I have just reported I don't mean as corrective criticism. It happens that I, myself, prefer ballet, drama, opera, and musical comedy – and not too many other kinds of performance. I am not proposing that you include Billy Graham or Manoleto [sic][38] (this dates me) in your programs. A sneaky thought reminds me that I would indeed like fireworks emanating from your real estate. But skip it, until you run short of plays.

What I really have a sense of dismay about is that there is a <u>center</u> of anything. I think maybe Cleveland can use one. Also possibly Los Angeles needs informed cultural guidance and a place to go get it. But not New York. New York <u>is</u> a center, a world's fair, and a den of thieves, and a house of miracles. Sometimes I like my hot dogs at Nathan's, and sometimes the gentile kind at ball games. Sometimes I go to one stadium, and sometimes the other. Sometimes with my wife and children, and sometimes with a man I'm trying to sell something. Sometimes I like my opera at Asti's,[39] and sometimes the Met, and sometimes on records at home, and sometimes a funny place in Brooklyn. I walk in Central Park and also on Madison Avenue, and sometimes around in circles in my study – and when I read, sometimes it's the Herald Tribune, and sometimes the Talmud and sometimes your Lincoln Center brochure. In short, I have lots of places to go. It isn't that one is <u>better</u> than the other, but simply that it is <u>different</u> from the other.

Now all this reflects on a chemical preference, and a very private one. Remember, about 36 years ago you and I met a girl named——? She was symmetrical and well spoken. Not only that, but her father owned a chain of liquor stores, and she was reported as conveniently nymphomaniacal. Yet, as I recall, neither you nor I especially wanted

---

38 Bullfighter Manuel Laureano Rodríguez Sánchez (1917–1947), known as Manolete.
39 An Italian restaurant in Greenwich Village, first open in 1924.

her phone number. Maybe she was too wondrously neat, or maybe she was too predictably available, or maybe she gave the impression of being so vastly prized that we couldn't prize her at all. Anyway, we agreed on that one. On the present lady we don't agree. But you're married to her and I have to go by whatever my antenna tells me, and admittedly by my built-in prejudices.

I am going to quit this now in the hope that you do not send me a letter in answer, but rather anticipating the meeting with you this fall. I think it will be fun, but I want you to think it will be fun. In the interest of giving you some encouragement in this direction I will close, not with

> Yours,
> but with –
> Very fondly yours,

11 April 1966: To William Schuman

Dear Bill:

This is to get you up to date on my acquaintanceship with Lincoln Center. A few Sundays ago I went on one of the girl-guided tours with my son. We both liked a great deal of what we saw and heard, including the girl guide who seemed not only well-informed but articulate without too much mechanized patter. Our visit was before the official opening of the new opera house, so we didn't get a look inside that. But we did get a pretty good notion of the entire geography and were allowed, along with the crowd, to drop in on two performances then in progress. I must say the tour policy is very generous and should cost more. My feeling is that some of the sculpture on view is also very generous and should cost less.

I will be going to one or more shows at your store in the near future, and then I will have a new set of opinions about what I saw and heard and how well.

See, you suggested I should case your domain before being so sure of what I think about the whole idea – and so you will have to suffer through another note from me.

Tell Frankie I saw her mother a couple of weeks ago and it was a sheer joy to see her snapping and crackling as ever.

More soon.

Love to you both,

8 December 1966: To William Schuman

Dear Bill:

Since responding to your last I have experienced an evening at your opera house. The occasion was "La Gioconda."[40] I hasten to report to you that I found the acoustics magnificent. I seemed to have heard noises to the contrary about this earlier.

For the past few years Jo and I have shared a very good box with the Howard Wilsons (box #15). Upon the removal to your premises we were awarded one equally good. My only objection to it is that I cannot see the orchestra well enough as I did at the old Met. There is something fascinating to me about watching a well disciplined orchestra – the impeccably uniform bowing, the responsiveness to the conductor, even the flashes of light from the preparatory movements of the brass on occasion, etc. I am sure that some of my enthusiasm for this is based on my lack of fascination with the acting and its trappings on stage. But that's an old story. On the other hand, there may indeed be many on the good box level and below who share my preference for at least the option of looking into the pit.

I will want to send you another note about all the paved real estate, waterways, etc. lying between the buildings, but I'll save that until after another visit.

One more thing: I take up the cudgel now for a friend of mine. (He has not asked me to do this and doesn't know I am doing it). His name is Marc Schwarz. He has been a box holder for twenty-one years at the old Met. Box #33. In the awarding of boxes in your place he was again given #33, but where it once was quite good this number turns out to be way over on the side. The men have to stand up in the

---

40 By Amilcare Ponchielli (1834–1886). The production starred Italian tenor Franco Corelli (1921–2003) and Italian lyric soprano Renata Tebaldi (1922–2004).

back in order to see the stage. Also, there is no place for coats. Marc Schwarz is a life-long friend which doesn't alter the fact that he is a gentleman, a quiet businessman, and too decent to raise any kind of hell with anyone. From what I understand he has written a modest letter to your Mr. Hubay.[41] And there was no answer of any kind. Can anything be done to improve his situation? Of course I don't believe that he is the only one who might have gotten scrambled out, but please observe that he has been a paying opera buff at the Met for twenty-one years.

That's about it for now. I think I mostly felt like keeping in touch and saying Merry Christmas to you and Frankie. So – MERRY CHRISTMAS TO YOU AND FRANKIE.

And love,

Other correspondence from this time chiefly concerns Loesser's business dealings, the search for properties, and even whimsical memos to his colleague Milton Kramer about calcium chloride. Loesser was keen on writer Archibald MacLeish's play *Scratch* (not published until 1971), based on Stephen Vincent Benét's short story *The Devil and Daniel Webster* (1936), and he promoted his friend Paddy Chayefsky's story 'The Case of the Latent Heterosexual' to the *New Yorker* magazine: 'The Case of the Latent Heterosexual' was published as a play in 1967 and staged at the Dallas Theatre Center in March 1968. Loesser also considered a film version of *The Most Happy Fella* although nothing ultimately came of the idea.

Early Mon A.M. (date unspecified but possibly from about this time): To Milton Kramer

Milt –

I have just finished reading "Scratch" once over – and with much pleasure. As you know, second only to the excitement of liking something I myself have written – is the nachis that bubbles up when I

---

41 Alfred Hubay (1925–2018), house manager and box office chief at the Metropolitan Opera.

come across somebody else's stuff that hits me. This nachis is not without its measure of professional cupidity, so:

How did you come by it?

Have we been in any way invited to produce or help finance it?

Do you know the author?

Anyway – this is too busy a day for much talk, and you wanted my opinion(s) – so I will try to tell you some of the things I think, – as the result of this one reading.

Firstly – a very rare goody – the play has an affection for itself – which <u>must</u> be preserved; largely thru direction and casting, but in relatively small posts by way of change in wording. In this connection, I think the word "mordant" in the sub-title is a misnomer. Some of the people in the play say biting and sarcastic things – but only out of their own vulnerability. I think the sense of this has to be kept. Compare with Saroyan ("Time of Your Life")[42] – but he had to put his play in a circus-like concourse to make it work, and delivered too many un-called-for generalities. This play doesn't seem to want or need all that.

Nor do I think it wants or needs Mike Nichols (this may be unfair to him; I mean the Mike Nichols who did "Luv")[43] – here let me submit that the opening scene is – or can be – deceptive as to <u>level</u>. It may be only the Song-of-Solomon quotation that needs thinking about. Anyway I think the first scene as it stands gives us a false start – and this plus some other parts of other scenes should not deliver <u>milking rights</u> to the wrong director.

Please regard what I believe is a big error in expression: the label <u>whore</u> and attendant references, doesn't seem to me to be what is actually meant in terms of the girl's characterization. Prostitution involves a <u>sale</u>, and a conscious one. This girl seems to be looking for some emotional exchange – and is not trying to <u>make</u> a <u>living</u> out of a perfectly valid "below-the-waist" <u>fix</u> – which in her experience has never worked for more than fourteen seconds. She is entitled to be

---

42 William Saroyan's play won the Pulitzer Prize for Drama in 1939.

43 Mike Nichols (1931–2014), German-American film and theatre director, actor and comedian. He directed Murray Schisgal's (1926–2020) *Luv* which ran at various New York theatres from 11 November 1964 to 7 January 1967.

cynical – and, while still alive, settle frequently for the fourteen seconds. This is not a whore. Nor does she have a simple animal pruriency, like a curious seventeen-year-old. (Am I behind the times?) Anyway, she can't be called nymphomaniacal either. On one reading, I think I understand the author's wish to create a sort of parallelism between the girl's (desperate) way of life and the chess-player's – whose technique wings for him something to pay the rent with. The parallel doesn't have to be that neat.

In reading, I stopped at a few places for a second because I was not sure I understood what was being said. Okay, I have had the same trouble with Shakespeare and other hit writers. It gave me great enjoyment not to notice any big luminous author's representative taking stage (as with T. Williams and G. B. Shaw and Hammerstein).[44] The play seems to stay in its own microcosm – and within the experience of its own people – their own intellects and feelings. And if any big fat universal truths showed up, they must have leaked out to me, and weren't shouted to the world. Hooray!

So I am back to what I do like about the play, which is plenty.

What happens next? It is now near 5:00 A.M. Shortly I will sleep for another hour, then to the office early, when I will shoot all this up to you. Then a busy day – some of it outside. But I should be in the clear by five. Call me then to talk about the play. Maybe you will tell me to read it again so I know what I'm talking about.

F.

Lissen. I would like to meet the author. F.[45]

11 July 1966: Memo to Milton Kramer

Dear Milt:

Please research something for me among your learned friends or by tapping your esteemed capacity for scientific recall.

---

44 Tennessee Williams, George Bernard Shaw and Oscar Hammerstein II.
45 *Scratch* was eventually performed at the St James Theatre, produced by Stuart Ostrow, but closed after only four performances, 6–8 May 1971.

Calcium Chloride

I am told this stuff is very good for reducing moisture in limited indoor areas by just leaving it around in an open container. I am told that the moisture in the air combines with it, in some way, as to leave nothing but moisture, dispersing the solids elsewhere. If the elsewhere is my adorable, selective and expensive wardrobe, do my pants shrink? Or do I invite moths? Or do my socks begin to smell like my son's socks? Do the walls of the closet turn puce? If I inhale anything, do I go directly to the hospital without passing Go or collecting $200? Or do I just cough more? How about inflammable? As the man with the haemorrhoids said, "This arson has got to stop." In short, what's not to like about calcium chloride?

So – you are doing me a favor? Maybe it is good for your Volkswagen, or the fish you catch or the termites in the Catskills. So, maybe you can learn something that is good for you as well as for me. If you already know all about the substance, please let me know; if not, hurry and find out.

    FL

(Like for instance, you have nothing else to do)

9 November 1966: Memo to Milton Kramer

Dear Milt:

I have in hand your note of October 28th to Allen Whitehead about MOST HAPPY FELLA orchestrations, etc., as well as Noel Silverman's[46] November 7th reply. My question was not merely one about the album. It was about the motion picture itself.

My intention in making any motion picture sale of this work is to retain the orchestrations (at least those accompanying vocal performance and existing dance performance). That is, I would like to make prevail Don Walker's instrumentation. This of course might be affected by augmentation, or as the result of necessary vocal key

---

46 Noel Silverman (born 1931), a lawyer specializing in copyright, intellectual property and entertainment law.

changes. Basically I would want what has always been there to remain there. Bear in mind that I do not refer to arrangements. There are no arrangements. There never have been. That is to say: all of the inner voices, rhythmic patterns, counter melodies, harmonies, passing harmonies are permanent and integral parts of the <u>writing</u>.

Of course there must be some additional adaptation of the original music to supply titles, action underscoring, bridges, etc. I would like to insist that Don Walker was to be hired for this job but I know I cannot demand this arbitrarily. Therefore for the moment let us assume that someone else (orchestrator B) will supply what is needed.

My question is: because of the limitations I put on orchestrator B, can Don Walker assume that there is a re-use of his orchestrations and charge for it? If so, I think provision has to be made in front. After that any track album would simply be regarded as being permitted as a faithful reproduction of the film content.

Any questions?

20 July 1966: To William Shawn[47]

Dear Bill:

Here is Paddy Chayefsky's "The Case of the Latent Heterosexual." Let me remind you again that the idea of forwarding it to the New Yorker is mine and not Chayefsky's, although he seemed pleased that I wanted you to see it.

Chayefsky had intended this piece of prose as a working outline for a dramatization for theatre or movies. Shortly after beginning to write the outline, he tells me he decided to put it in language readable among others than himself. I find it very.

My thanks for your willingness to read it. And if it is all wrong for the New Yorker, just recall that it was my idea.

My sincere best wishes.

Yours very truly,

---

47 William Shawn (1907–1992), editor of the *New Yorker* magazine 1951–1987.

Loesser's interest in calcium chloride (see 11 July 1966) was only one manifestation of his attachment to objects and gadgets, to building furniture (Loesser was an avid woodworker), to his physical possessions and more generally the 'science' of everyday life, both serious or to humorous or entertaining ends, as in the medical terminology of 'Adelaide's Lament' from *Guys and Dolls* or his letter to Charlotte Kent. He also continued to cultivate his friends, among them playwright S. N. Behrman (1893–1973) who, not coincidentally, perhaps, was also a long-term writer for the *New Yorker*.

18 August 1966: To Morty Sills

Dear Morty:

Here is the belt which is extremely precious to me, and even in your careful and thoughtful hands it could possibly get sour cream on it, or lose a part, or catch cold. The buckle presently on it is the wrong type. What it needs is the kind with a tongue (that's what I think it's called). Anyway, it is the sharp gedinkus that goes through a hole in the middle of the belt at any variety of points, depending on how much gut you have at the moment. Do I make myself clear? Now we go further: I would like to have a buckle of not too formal a type, but rather something simple and perhaps on the sporty side, – but not necessarily with any nautical or marine connotation.

Knowing you have nothing to do I depend on you to go right to work on this and trudge among the buckle people until you find what I want. It is all right for you to go unarmed, but if anybody tries to take this belt away from you I authorize you to hit them with it.

Or to put it briefly, if anything goes wrong with this process the three suits waiting for me automatically become yours. I hope they fit.
　　　　　Love and kisses

27 October 1966: To Charlotte Kent

Dear Charlotte:

How lovely of you to send me those medicaments. I will forever treasure them in my collection of thoughtful gifts from thoughtful friends. This will not at all be difficult to do as I have not swallowed one single drop of any of the gluck, and I don't intend to. That is because by the time it reached me I was again in fine fettle.

Here is a poem of pause:

> Hoover was a Herb
> Coolidge was a Simple
> Put them both together
> And they couldn't squeeze a pimple

About the medical book that came along, I find it fascinating. Some time between shows I am going to make it a point to contract the ague or quinsy. I just know that some little goodie in this book will fix me up in no time.

About the Kiehl Pharmacy,[48] I am going to visit there some day, maybe when I'm planning a new musical of Macbeth. If I run into you there let us have a mutual laying on of the hands. All over, because I love you.

22 September 1966: To S. N. Behrman

My dear Sam Behrman:

What a joy finding myself with you. Together again for the first time! My recollection about Leonard Lyons was indeed a sloppy one. I think I meant the building. One West 81st Street. Does that ring a bell? Anyway, I enjoyed myself so much the other afternoon that I thought I would tell you so. Brother Arthur will be arriving in New York this evening, and of course I will tell him of our meeting and give your regards.

I hope we see each other soon. And if I may I will phone you in an effort to accomplish same, whether about Daniels or anything else, or just nothing. I think one of the things I will want to talk about is how to feel at home with the musical comedy medium, just in the event that you and I fancy doing something together in the future.

Meantime, my warmest regards.

---

48 Founded in New York's East Village in 1851, Kiehl's is still in business at 109 3rd Avenue.

12 December 1966: To S. N. Behrman

My dear Sam:

In answer to your plaintive and beady-eyed entreaty, I deliver to you herewith the address of my brother, the saint, the genius, and altogether the darling fellow: [provides address in Ohio]

I must here announce my resignation from further function as your self-betterment agent. After Arthur I have nowhere to go but down. If you should choose to renew acquaintanceship with Leonardo da Vinci, Steinmetz,[49] or such fry, I suggest that you call the Morris office.

Of course if you are looking for Jehovah himself, by all means call. For that is Me.

With affection,

31 January 1967: To S. N. Behrman

Dear Sam:

I owe you this note even though it is merely to say that I can't arrange for a klatch[50] between us, as much as I would treasure such a thing. I am deep, deep, deep in my drunkard musical.[51] So much so that I consume about half a bottle a day, the better to visualize and feel the part. Also to keep the flavor musical I have a tendency to whack my kids' toy xylophone from time to time. As I think of this latter compulsion it occurs to me that it represents a release from frustration, rather than a joyous attempt at making music. In short, I am – like any normal Jewish writer – at work.

At this moment I am near the end of the daily half bottle – a time which I dedicate ritualistically to telling myself that the ordeal will soon be over. I pash thish information over to you, in the hope that you will forgive me for not having phoned in a while.

But shoon, my friend, shoon.

With affection,

---

49 Charles Proteus Steinmetz (1865–1923), German-American mathematician and electrical engineer known in particular for his work on the development of alternating electrical currents.
50 A 'get-together'.
51 *Señor Discretion Himself.*

Loesser was in touch again with his brother Arthur, who had just given a recital in Cleveland and later that year gave another recital at the Town Hall, New York. And he explored possible properties with writer and director Garson Kanin; with Paramount Pictures and film mogul Samuel Goldwyn; with legendary theatrical producer David Merrick (whose credits included the musical *Hello, Dolly!* and the play *Rosencrantz and Guildenstern Are Dead*); with writers Howard Lindsay and Russel Crouse; with film producer Robert Evans (1930–2019); and with Philip Rose (1921–2011) and Ossie Davis (1917–2005), whose play *Purlie Victorious* Loesser considered turning into a musical.

14 March 1967: To Arthur Loesser[52]

Dear Jean and Arthur:

Yesterday I got myself a good tape player, locked myself up in the office and had a delicious time listening to the piano recital.[53] As always, Arthur, I thought you were marvelous, except that I miss seeing you do it. That has always been part of it for me. That way I can <u>see</u> the love affair going on between you and the music. You were a little stingy with the talk before your encore. But I guess there was nothing to teach anybody – which is really what makes you talk.

However, you could teach me – what is the name of the little piece? The final applause was gratifying, and I am sure I could hear you, Jean, in the middle of it.

Anyway, the tape is a lovely present, and thank you both again. See you soon.

Love,

---

52 International Piano Archives, University of Maryland, Arthur Loesser Collection.
53 Possibly the recital Arthur Loesser gave on 11 January 1967 at the Cleveland Institute, the recording of which was supervised by Jean Loesser. The programme included works by Haydn, Mozart, Beethoven, Prokofiev, Schubert and Chopin.

? November 1967: To Arthur Loesser[54]

Dear Arthur:

This is a fan letter. Not simply from Jo and me, but a transmittal of <u>everybody's</u> happy (some almost delirious) exclamation points about you ever since the concert.[55] As you know, I made a distribution of tickets to people who can read and write and who have mastered the crossing of streets and the bringing of pablum spoons successfully to the mouth – not necessarily people equipped to be music critics, but let's say having relatively low boring points.

Well, dozens, literally, of them have been phoning to tell us their state of wonder and pleasure. Abe Burrows regaled me for <u>an hour</u> as if to convince me that I have a genius for a brother. Cy Feuer called with joyous words and I could almost hear him (as he does rarely about anything other than money) jumping up and down.

Paddy Chayevsky (the playwright, you don't know him) says you changed his entire life (he is a <u>dramatic</u> playwright) – Lucy Brown repeated her: "Of course, he plays with his ass." Abba Bogin (you may remember – my conductor) came into my office the day after the recital and just stood there shaking his head from side to side – for all the world a man recently come from some deeply religious experience. Jo's operatic coach – a woman not easily taken in by merely <u>instrumental</u> music phoned a very special and detailed thank you. The night before last we kept a long established and cherished dinner date with Dello Joio[56] and wife. Ordinarily the conversation dedicates itself to the subject of our children and/or the problem about domestic help. This time Norman couldn't stop about what a great time he had had and what a very special man you are.

Well, you <u>are</u>. And Jo and I are very proud to claim the family relationship. Me, I get a very special Nachis (Yiddish, look it up) about

---

54 International Piano Archives, University of Maryland, Arthur Loesser Collection.
55 Arthur Loesser's concert at the Town Hall, New York, on 29 October 1967. The programme was billed as a pre-Halloween celebration, with works by little-known composers including Jan Ladislav Dussek (1760–1812), Johann Nepomuk Hummel (1776–1837), Joachim Raff (1822–1882), Leopold Godowsky (1870–1938) and Moritz Moszkowski (1854–1925).
56 Norman Dello Joio (1913–2008), composer.

the (too infrequently) <u>public</u> Arthur Loesser. I feel like an old HOG watching new little piglets discover the truffle for themselves – and squealing for more more.

It seems to me, my dear Truffle – that there ought to be more of just such concerts – amusing, illuminating, etc. without making any special <u>point</u> of re-confirming the long established fact that you know how to tickle the ivories.

As the old lady said to the sailor – PLEASE PLEASE PLEASE
        DO IT AGAIN !!!
            Thanks and love

20 September 1967: To Garson Kanin

Dear Gar:

Lissen. I think you are mad at me for being captious and fussy about the approach to "BORN YESTERDAY." I think also that some of your disaffection has rubbed off on Ruth[57] who swore to God she would send me the script as well as your California address, and then didn't. I will now have to fish out your address from the Morris office, as a result of which Nat Lefkowitz will put a little memo down about my being obligated for a favor.

Anyway, lissen. Last time I tried to do a musical it was with two other people, quite experienced and highly professional, and we laid a big medicine ball.[58] This was because we had not agreed on any sort of level. One thought it was a comic opera, the other thought it was a farce with music, and the third fellow considered it a fruit stand from which to sell terpsichore. A fourth fellow, the producer, thought the whole idea splendid as he had never visited Detroit and would now do so at the investors' expense. He sure did!

That is why I am leery about loose plans to collaborate. Even with tight plans you and I once wrote one that turned out to be not good enough.

---

57 Garson Kanin's wife, actress Ruth Gordon.
58 Here Loesser refers to *Pleasures and Palaces*.

Lissen more. I am thinking over my old notions about the play and rereading my old notes, and find I don't exactly agree with them anymore. So I'm fiddling with a somewhat different approach which, if we are still speaking, I will submit to you. Or, if you have already dropped me in favor of Peter Tinturin,[59] please let me know.

Also, tell Ruth I am waiting to read her play.

Love,

P.S. My son Johnny the Schoolboy will be seventeen very shortly and, I think, has stopped growing. If you have a chance to see my son Frankie the Plant, see if he still needs his sleeves lengthened every year. I wouldn't be surprised.

Love again.

16 October 1967: To Garson Kanin

Dear Gar:

Lissen!

Love,

25 September 1967: To Martin Davis, Paramount Pictures Corp.

Dear Marty:

As promised, here is the delightful prizewinning novelette[60] I loused up on the musical stage (although Brooks Atkinson raved). Also enclosed is the original cast album. Since the show's short life on Broadway a couple of numbers have become standards by way of recordings etc. This piece is a pet of mine and I think I know a way to make this a commercial picture without loss of charm.

I await your Paramount property roster and will dig myself into it as soon as I get it. Delighted to talk to you and very happy for you.

Sincerely yours,

---

59 Peter Tinturin (1910–2007), Russian-born song and film composer active in Hollywood from the 1930s to 1990s.
60 *Greenwillow*.

4 December 1967: To Robert Evans

Dear Bob:

Answering your note of November 20, I am not quite sure what my opinion might be about SUNSET BOULEVARD.[61] Would you mind sending me the shooting script shortly?

About THE GREAT GATSBY, I reread it a year or so ago at the request of Samuel Goldwyn Jr. and reported that I did not feel it to be right for me. I guess it is possibly a good study of an interesting period and the behavior of people in the Prohibition era, but the personal, emotional plot among principals is what counts for me and not the costumes or manners of any given time.

Let me suggest here that a great many pictures on the face of it show no hope as musicals notably, ANNA AND THE KING OF SIAM, THEY KNEW WHAT THEY WANTED and, for that matter, PYGMALION.[62] Something tells me that you have more riches than you have thus far imagined in your list of properties. Nevertheless, I very much respect your reticence to attempt a creative approach – leaving such things to writers and directors.

Don't forget to shoot me the script of SUNSET BOULEVARD.

Thanks and best wishes.

Sincerely,

9 January 1968: To Robert Evans

Dear Bob:

I am returning herewith the script of SUNSET BOULEVARD. It is not my idea of a potential musical. I will continue to look through the big bundle of synopses of unproduced stuff.

Meantime, thanks and Happy New Year.

Sincerely,

Frank Loesser

---

61 Paramount Pictures' 1950 film, directed by Billy Wilder and starring William Holden and Gloria Swanson.
62 *Anna and the King of Siam* (1946), Rodgers and Hammerstein's *The King and I*; *They Knew What They Wanted* (1940), Frank Loesser's *The Most Happy Fella*; and *Pygmalion* (1938), Lerner and Loewe's *My Fair Lady*.

20 January 1968: To Samuel Goldwyn

Dear Sam:

This morning I received a copy of the story "UNCLE EDGAR AND THE RELUCTANT SAINT"[63] – forwarded in your behalf by your Mr. Foreman.

I read the story immediately. I now feel obliged to report to you that the general <u>nature</u> <u>and</u> <u>spirit</u> of the story coincides with one I am now preparing for Broadway theatre.[64] But I hasten to add that this is only a similarity in type. My present project takes place in a foreign country, does not involve any children or the occasion of Christmas. But it does indeed tell the story of a person with some socially negative and ungenerous characteristics, and how his personality changed for the better, the more amiable, and the more lovable.

My personal feeling is that there is no real conflict between the two projects, but as I have said I feel the obligation to report the existence and nature of my Broadway musical – so that you may judge for yourself whether my joining forces with you might be too exhausting an attack by me on the whole subject of sweetness and good will.

I will assume for the moment that you see no conflict, and that you are indeed serious about your invitation to me to supply a musical score for "UNCLE EDGAR AND THE RELUCTANT SAINT" as a musical motion picture for theatres and television. Firstly, I feel that I would have to collaborate on the treatment and script. In past experience I find that unless I have some control of the entire form of a piece, I cannot do my best work in laying out and supplying the song elements.

(As you know I am now very wealthy, having saved literally hundreds of dollars and with a full city lot in Bayside[65] all paid for – and therefore am quite fussy and independent about my choice of jobs.) To put it seriously, Sam, I can't simply supply a musical Band-Aid

---

63 A 1952 Columbia Pictures release based on the story of the seventeenth-century Italian saint Joseph of Cupertino.
64 Presumably *Señor Discretion Himself*.
65 A neighbourhood in Queens, New York.

to a script arrived at by someone else. If you have no objection to this approach it will mean that you and I would have to satisfy each other with a choice of adaptation partner.

So much for that. Now about time: you told me on the phone that you "wanted to do it when it was right." Nevertheless the work has to begin sometime – and sooner or later there are actual deadlines. So let me describe my working schedule for the future as well as I know it. As I told you I am doing the book and songs for a Broadway musical. I expect that it will open at the very latest thirteen months from now, but possibly as early as next October. Then there is always the possibility that I may tear up the whole thing because I don't like it well enough. Or, that I may abandon it temporarily. I have this privilege since I have no partners or collaborators to disappoint or to disagree with. But in any of the events mentioned above there is no reason why there can't be an overlap of efforts, so that preparation of your piece and mine could be to some degree coincidental.

Well, there you have my response thus far. It occurs to me at this moment that I have failed to tell you how much I enjoyed reading the story, and how many very, very good possibilities I see in it. Please forgive my impoliteness in not beginning the letter with this observation.

Thanks for thinking of me, Sam, and please let me know your reactions to this response. Meanwhile, my fondest wishes to you and Frances.

Sincerely,

Frank Loesser

17 January 1967: To David Merrick

Dear David:

Returned with great sadness herewith is the copy of Jerome Weidman's play version of "National Velvet."[66] I have struggled for

---

66 Jerome Weidman (1913–1998), writer. Enid Bagnold's (1889–1981) novel *National Velvet* was published in London in 1935; the film version, starring Elizabeth Taylor and Mickey Rooney, was released in 1944 (Metro-Goldwyn-Mayer).

quite a long time with the possibilities for musicalization and come up with no way to turn it into a musical show without ruining or losing the beauty of the prose script.

I am speaking of course in terms of my impression of it and my approach to it <u>as a writer</u>. In short, I myself can't tackle it. But that doesn't mean no one else can. I am luminously on record for having seen absolutely no way to musicalize "Pygmalion" when it was offered to me, so don't consider my reluctant abandonment of the idea as having any sort of valuable generality.

As you probably know, Jerry [Weidman] and I had a number of meetings at which we did a lot of searching into the subject. Between our sessions I tried any number of musical structures and even spotted them with dummy songs. It was disappointing finally that nothing came of it to satisfy me. Nevertheless, it was an exciting challenge and I don't regret my efforts.

The last time I spoke to Jerry I told him that I thought that the play as it stands without music is a beautiful and sensitive piece of writing – and yet structurally falls into the soap opera category. By this last comment I meant to indicate that it was probably too corny for Broadway as a straight play. But maybe I was wrong about that. Maybe there is such a thing as a soap opera written, cast, and directed with such sensitivity that it winds up being regarded as in a class by itself. Think about that, in the event you don't satisfy yourself with musical man power.

Finally, thanks very much for letting me see it, and please send on more whenever you think I might fit in.

Kindest regards,

22 May 1967: To Muriel Hollander[67]

DIGGEREL, DOGGEREL,
MURIAL HOLLANDER,
INTRAMEHUTINAL
GREETINGS ANON –

---

67 Muriel Hollander was the mother of John Hollander (1929–2013), husband of Arthur Loesser's daughter Anne (i.e. Frank Loesser's niece).

PLUS, IMMERWIEDER, MY
PLENIAVUNCULAR:
"WHAT ARE WE GOING TO
DO ABOUT JOHN?"

POETRY SCHMOETRY,
MURIEL HOLLANDER,
ISN'T THE BUBBELEH
PUTTING US ON?
HARK TO THE CLAMOROUS
GANZEMESCHPOCHEDICH
"WHAT ARE WE GOING TO
DO ABOUT JOHN?"

Characteristic'lly,

2 June 1967: To Howard Lindsay

Dear Howard:

With this note comes a separate and sanitary water pitcher for your cat. I took a long time picking one out to suit the capacity of the feline gut, as well as to allow some deep-dish lapping through a broad enough aperture so as not to provoke something I now coin as glasstrophobia. In other words, I believe it to be as nearly as possible cut-to-fit-the-kisser, an expression I learned in Atlantic City many years ago.

I was going to descend on you again to talk about "The Great Sebastians,"[68] but summer seems to have crept up on us, and I am now a ward and virtual captive of Remsenburg, Long Island – from which place I am dictating this on the phone to my secretary, who claims she can spell. She will presently forge my signature if I know her.

---

68 A melodramatic comedy by Howard Lindsay and Russel Crouse that played on Broadway 4 January to 2 June 1956.

So let me include here a few remarks about "The Great Sebastians" as a musical. You constructed it with beautiful mounting tension. I think it is very difficult to interrupt such things with songs, dances, etc. Even though you provided enough leisure for the development of a sort of personality battle between our hero and heroine – you kept it operative in passing and it enriched the play without slowing it up. I don't think the same thing can be done with such outrageous things as songs. Somehow most of the songs in a show seem to lead toward their own ultimate climax, demanding appreciation in themselves. I am speaking of songish songs. Not "Just You Wait Henry Higgins" or "Sue Me." I mean "Oh What A Beautiful Morning" or "They Say That Falling in Love Is Wonderful."[69] I would not know how to make room for songs in the manner of the latter two.

Nevertheless, I am going to read the play again this summer and make believe I am a heavy-handed money maker like Lionel Bart or Walter Donaldson,[70] and try again for a key to musicalizing this. I will holler on you within the next couple of months.

Meantime please present this pitcher to the cat. If she turns up her nose at it, empty the water, fill it with Clos Vougeot 1961 and watch how soon she changes her tune. My love to you and Dorothy.

15 June 1967: To Alfred Newman

Dear Al:

What are your recollections about our song "Your Kiss"[71] – the circumstances under which it was written and delivered for publication? I am being nagged by my attorneys because renewal time is coming up – or is already here. The first period publisher was 20th Century Music Corp. Do you have any sort of contract? Were you at

---

69 'Just You Wait' from *My Fair Lady*; 'Sue Me' from *Guys and Dolls*; 'Oh, What a Beautiful Mornin'' from *Oklahoma!*; 'They Say It's Wonderful' from *Annie Get Your Gun*.

70 Lionel Bart (1930–1999), English composer best known for *Oliver!* (1960); Walter Donaldson (1893–1947), American songwriter known for 'Yes Sir, That's My Baby' (1925) and 'My Blue Heaven' (1927) among others.

71 Loesser and Alfred Newman's 'Your Kiss' was written for the 1940 film *Johnny Apollo* (20th Century Fox).

the time bound hand and foot as an employee of 20th Century Fox, so that automatically your rights were those of an employee? Maybe George Cohen can help you, or maybe the attorney or other guardian of your career at the time (circa 1939–40).

I am navel-deep in re-writing something I have written badly[72] – and that is a job many times as tedious as the one of having written it in the first place. But I still listen to my legal eagles. Hence this note, which if it doesn't seem affectionate, cordial, and all the things I mean about you and me, it is because of my present state of FEAR OF FUCK-UP. So I close –

Cordially and with much affection,

19 January 1968: To Tom Mortimer

Dear Partner:

Let me be the first, by way of this message, to show you your ferschtoonkene[73] stationery. Firstly, who asked you to order it in red? Secondly, how dare you use words from a copyrighted song of mine? Thirdly, in the watermark on the paper it clearly says "Should I tell my partner?" I knew I couldn't trust you. I will now end this note because I do not want to use up a second sheet. You must realize our firm hasn't made a quarter in all our existence and I don't want you to complain to me about wasting paper.

Sincerely,

P.S. Enclosed please find dividend check. I can't.

28 February 1968: To Orenstein, Arrow and Silverman[74]

Gentlemen:

In view of what you have so often told me about my business behavior as an adaptor or writing collaborator, I address this memo-

---

72 *Señor Discretion Himself.*
73 Yiddish for 'contemptible' or 'nasty'.
74 A New York entertainment law firm including Loesser's close associate Harold Orenstein.

randum to you in order to get you up to date on my recent association with Phil Rose and Ossie Davis on the subject of the play "Purlie
Victorious."[75]

A few weeks ago Phil Rose phoned me to ask whether I had had
any interest in writing a score for a musical version of the above play.
I answered that I could not fairly give him my thoughts about this
without first rereading the play, and he volunteered to send me a
copy. This I read and subsequently (February 14) took Mr. Rose to
lunch to discuss my feelings about his suggestion. At the end of our
conversation I told him that I would like to write a sort of sketch –
including indications of song, and song ideas and titles – for the book
of a musical based on the play to see whether I myself liked the result.
I added, however, that I did not want to attack this at all without the
complete approval of its original author Ossie Davis. A few days later
Mr. Rose brought Mr. Davis to visit me in my office (February 16) and
both assured me that I might try an adaptation, leaving any terms,
royalty agreements, producing agreements for some later date, if
any. At that meeting I also indicated that I would want some collaboration from Ossie Davis – as well as approval from him of certain
excursions etc. from the original which I might wish to design. All
three of us agreed on this, and a few days later (February 20) I had a
meeting alone with Ossie Davis at which I presented him with a copy
of the enclosed five page sketch for an opening scene (dated
February 19, 1968).

I will continue to send you from time to time copies of my writing
contributions in this trial adaptation, indicating if and when they have
been forwarded to either Mr. Rose or Mr. Davis. So please keep this
memorandum in a special file to which you may add further notes
from me.

Thanks.

Sincerely,

---

75 Ossie Davis's play *Purlie Victorious* played on Broadway from 28 September
1961 to 13 May 1962; a musical version, *Purlie*, with music by Gary Geld (born
1935) and lyrics by Peter Udell (born c1929), played on Broadway from 15 March
1970 to 6 November 1971.

P.S. Note: As you know, I never agree to deliver the songs for a show without officially or unofficially taking an important part in the construction of the libretto itself. In this case I have some doubts about my abilities as a song writer and have expressed this to the two gentlemen, although the original invitation was for me to consider writing the songs. We have all tabled this abiding the development of a satisfactory book.

15 March 1968: To Phil Rose and Ossie Davis

Dear Gents:

Herewith are notes more or less describing a structure for the First Act. This is a first try and there probably is a lot wrong with it. Here are some more notes for your guidance. Please observe that I have entitled this "Project 7." This is to baffle curious noses around my office. I will continue to refer to the project as such for the time being.

You will notice that I did not accept the too-easy knockabout reasons for Gitlow's acquiescence in the first scene, and therefore put in some of what I consider more realistic blackmail.

Also, please note that I don't have Lutiebelle returning bedraggled from her experience with Ol' Cap'n, but simply rely on Gitlow's pimp report to set Purlie on fire.

Please remember that the dialogue I have written is not to be read for enjoyment. It is merely diagrammatic to indicate what elements of the plot have to be learned. If here and there I have thrown in a joke, it is probably a bad one.

You already know what I have in my mind about the Second Act. I would like it to begin exactly where we left off in the First Act, continuing the struggle between Purlie and his better judgment, to the accompaniment of the song, and then fading in favor of a transition to the front of Ol' Cap'n's mansion where we go right into the pantomimic/balletic attempted seduction dance.

Early Thursday morning, March 21, I am leaving town for about ten days. When you both have read the enclosed stuff I would like it if you phoned me. That is if we are still speaking.

Best,

30 April 1968: To Phil Rose and Ossie Davis

Dear Gents,

About my outline thus far:

I still have some of my original misgivings about this subject at this time in history – but I suppose I am thinking less commercially than morally. This is one of the reasons that I have not run for the senate in Connecticut.

In musicalizing a play it must be assumed that an aggregate good solid hour of singing and dancing will be needed. That reduces the length of the talk by one-half. In the instance of a comedy with an enormous number of proven laughs – as in this case – it seems quite a dangerous thing to forego almost half of them. That is, unless there is a compensating factor – song values, choreography, etc. It is much simpler and less destructive to musicalize a romance or a melodrama ("Oklahoma!," "The King and I," "Traviata," "She Loves Me"). I have no way of guessing at this point how we are improving what is already there. Nevertheless this is something we can try to project and visualize when next we meet.

Assuming that my outline form is good enough to begin on, I believe certain faults have to be cured. Firstly, I did not allow for the specific establishment of Purlie's character as an uncontrollable braggart. I think the audience must understand this from the very beginning – not only by virtue of Gitlow's criticism of Purlie but in some sort of pointed incidence within the structure of the first scene. Second: the play owes Purlie and Lutiebelle one more scene together. At least that's how it feels to me now.

Etc., etc., etc.

When shall we three meet again? (Now there's a reliable line)

Best,

By mid-1968 Loesser was suffering from ill health but he was active, as always, with Frank Music, considering properties or auditioning songs sent by aspiring composers or composers who wished to be associated with Frank Music, and with his friendships and personal material interests. Many of the letters from his last year are known only from their publication in Susan Loesser's *A Most*

16. Frank Loesser, c1968/69.

Remarkable Fella (the originals are apparently lost). As such, they are more personal – and more telling of Loesser's non-theatrical or musical interests as well as his private life – than the majority of otherwise surviving letters.

16 April 1968: To Sammy Timberg[76]

Dear Sammy,

How nice to hear from you.

Answering your question about your compositions, of course my firm and I are always interested. Nevertheless, if you have simply a

---

76 Sammy Timberg (1903–1992), stage, film and television composer.

collection of tunes with no lyrics it would be very difficult for us (or anyone) to market them, so don't figure on any meteoric results when you show us your stuff. Of course I realize that in your letter you ask for my <u>personal opinion</u>. This I will be glad to give you although I don't know how smart I am as in recent years I have become less and less attentive to tunes and their values.

But please do indeed come to New York some time in May. I will be able to see you almost any Tuesday or Wednesday as long as you tell me in advance when you are arriving. Until then my fondest regards.

Sincerely,

22 May 1968: To Sammy Timberg

Dear Sammy:

The powers-that-be in my publishing outfit have given me a blanket <u>no</u> on the stuff you sent in. This does not mean that they don't like some of it, but in their best judgment they would not be able to market it at this time. They felt that among all of the pieces "Carissima" had the most chance but in terms of modern record production and exploitation would be too much of an uphill fight. The comment on "Fortunate" was "old-fashioned." I didn't say anything.

Well there you have the emmis[77] truth of the matter. I'm returning your material herewith, along with my regrets.

But let's keep in touch.

Fondly,

3 June 1968: To Allen Whitehead

Subject: African straw hats

Dear Allen:

As you know, Andrew Tracey was kind enough to refer us to Mrs. Ford in Durban. I hope you will carry this matter to her attention as quickly as possible.

---

77 Yiddish for 'truth'.

Just for the sake of clarity, I will try to describe the kind of African hat I would like to have made. Toward this end, I am enclosing a picture of Dana Valery[78] wearing what seems to be a typical one. In addition, I am enclosing a postcard and folder from La Ronde, a beach club in West Hampton. Mrs. Ford will see that their main dining room is illustrated and the shape of its roof curiously resembles those African hats. Nevertheless, she will be able to see that the proportions are somewhat different.

In expectation of a sizeable order, I would like a sample hat made out of customary South African material but shaped as precisely as possible like La Ronde's roof. Also, I would not like the detail of banding design but a simple over-all surface. The one color should be brown or brownish – to resemble the weathered shingles that the roof is made of.

Please ask Mrs. Ford whether she could make the sample and ship it to you and also give you some idea of the price per hundred or per gross.

With many thanks.

Sincerely,

7 June 1968: To Leon Gross

Dear Mr. Gross:

Pursuant to the request of Sammy Cahn,[79] I hereby give permission to the Henry Street Settlement[80] to use the tape recording of my performance at the Sammy Cahn Testimonial Dinner held at the Hilton Hotel, April 28, 1968 provided that, 1) it shall not be used for public performance at any time or by any media; 2) the tape recording will be converted into a phonograph record and sold only by the Henry Street Settlement for the benefit of the Henry Street Settlement Scholarship Fund and 3) no commercial distribution of any kind whatsoever will be made through normal channels of business.

---

78 Dana Valery (born 1944), Italian-born South African singer and actress.
79 Sammy Cahn (1913–1993), songwriter.
80 A social service agency on the Lower East Side, founded as the Nurses' Settlement in 1893.

Please execute the license below and return one copy to me for my records.

Cordially yours,

ACCEPTED AND AGREED TO

[Signature]

———

LEON GROSS for the
Henry Street Settlement

27 June 1968: To Collier Young,[81] Four Star International

Dear Collie,

I have read with some pleasure the "AIMEE" script. I think it is a good story to tell but I don't think it is right for a Broadway musical at least not for <u>me</u> to dip into. Mostly my reasons are that the background itself is full of music per se – that is, songs and hymns and such actually and factually sung. This always opposes itself to those songs supplied to substitute for dialogue. I know this is not considered a conflict by many people but it is to me. I hated having to supply "A Bushel and a Peck" into a show full of sung expressions which played the play. Also I don't like "Honey Bun" where it occurs, and such intrusions on a sung play but a lot of other writers don't mind and do quite well not minding. So please skip me on this one but do not fail to keep in touch as the Union side up here is getting stronger and may insist on permanent secession. Which it should have, and then you and your damned uniform would have been Mexican. Or Seminale.[82] Speaking of Seminale, how are your vesicles.

Thanks, and love.

---

81 Collier Young (1908–1980), film writer and producer. A text *Aimee* by him is apparently unknown.
82 The seminal vesicle is the glandular structure found in the male reproductive system.

1968 [late July]: To Susan Loesser[83]

And now about the LEDERHOSEN. They were a hilarious surprise on my birthday. I didn't want to audition them in mixed company (we had guests) so I waited until next morning to try them on. It was about 4:00 A.M. and I think I almost laughed the neighborhood awake. <u>Yes, they are a trifle big</u>. So I stuck out my gut to keep them on – over my otherwise naked body – and paraded up and down past the mirror – reflecting that if Germany had engaged a Yiddishe Gauleiter[84] or two in every hamlet they could have gotten rid of the entire male Jewish population via CHAFE and saved GAS and their own world image as well. There is a limit to how long one can distend the middle section artificially – especially with raw bleeding thighs. So I figured I would support the narcissistic experience with BEER. This swells the belly real good – and is of course in the right tradition.

So I marched (YES) to the fridge where I had a moment of pause in realizing it was <u>Danish</u> beer, but presently got some moral comfort out of the realization that we Germans are liberal and international – also out of the fact that I was now negotiating a tour of the downstairs floor without any effort in keeping the pants up. I remembered I had a hat, shaped (vaguely) in the Tyrolean manner. I found it and put it on. True, it is made of <u>straw</u>, and the hatband says LET'S GO METS[85] – but I squinted that away and went happily on with my goose-step. It was now full daylight and I swear all the grackles, cardinals and bluejays I have been watching were out there on the other side of the window WATCHING ME! It is an odd experience, I can tell you, and very disconcerting. So I lowered the blinds and tried some mountain climbing over Jo's pink living room furniture – humming snatches of the Horst Wessel song[86] to myself as I went.

---

83 Loesser, *A Most Remarkable Fella*, 279–80. Given the reference to Loesser's birthday, this letter must date from late July 1968.
84 Gauleiters were regional administrators of the Nazi Party in Germany, ranking, politically, in importance only behind the Reichsleiter – national leaders – and Adolf Hitler.
85 The New York Mets baseball team.
86 Horst Wessel (1907–1930), a German gangster and *Sturmführer* in the SA who was murdered in 1930, was promoted by Joseph Goebbels as a Nazi martyr; a

Presently I realized I had to take a leak. (This is a fairly common sensation among beer drinkers.) I got down off the arm of the sofa and made for the bathroom – proceeding to undo the fly. What fly? There are two of them. Like on sailor pants, only zippered. <u>European</u> zippered yet, which is always a problem. But on heavy leather!! Anyway, the fly wouldn't open. So I rushed to undo the belt. The belt wouldn't budge. I should have known. I was once locked in a pair of French swimming trunks for three days in Antibes. Well, there I was with this now exaggerated urgency to piss. So I decided to go out on the lawn, dress right and piss down one leg, then smartly dress left and dribble down the other. It occurred to me that there might be some soothing balmlike effect on my SPARTANISCHEN BEINEN[87] – and if it worked, I might bottle the stuff – sell millions of gallons of it to alpine guides and retire (with the profits) to Bad Homburg. I prepared for squirt number one adopting the position known fondly here as the EMILY AKIMBO. The grackles seemed to find it quite natural and didn't remark much as they watched. But I myself was overtaken by the sudden thought that this whole thing was quite childish. I told myself (aloud) to be aware that I was now FIFTY-EIGHT YEARS OLD!! – and a voice answered mine:

"You don't look it."

It was Conzetta (our sometimes maid) who often comes out on the lawn early mornings to kick mushrooms.

Then she added "Happy Birthday," helped undo the belt (she worked for a locksmith once), and rushed me solicitously to the bathroom, where I made it just in time.

Look, I hope you kids won't mind if I don't put the lederhosen on again. Even when my legs get their skin back. Also I hope you won't think me ungrateful if I don't run them up the flagpole – because ours isn't strong enough. What I'd like to do is take the pants to Abercrombie and Fitch and see if I can trade them in on a beartrap.

---

march he had written was renamed the Horst Wessel Song and became the official anthem of the Nazi Party.
87 Literally, 'spartan legs'.

3 October 1968: To Betty Rosebrock[88]

Dear Mother Rosebrock:

How nice to hear from you and in such a sweet way! And how did you know that I am a fudge fancier? Many, many thanks for being so thoughtful.

And where is Betty? Working? I suppose I ought to know but I have been hiding away writing and have lost track of a great many people.

My fond wishes to you and again thank you for a very lovely gift.

Sincerely

11 November 1968: To Hillard Elkins[89]

Dear Hilly:

I have just read "Two for the Seesaw"[90] and enjoyed myself even more than I did seeing it on Broadway – if that is possible.

Now about making a musical out of it. I am about to give you some reasons why I should not think it would make a musical. These, you will see, are what I call "producer" reasons. They are based on empirical and probably stuffy thinking, but they are nevertheless reservations strongly in my mind at this moment.

There is no community of people with a common purpose. That is, no group to swing into us with "We know we belong to the land ..." or "Tradition" or even the meretriciously placed "Hello, Dolly."[91] Of course there are musicals which have done without this kind of mass emotion. Take "I Do! I Do!" for example. I guess it worked well enough but all it was for openers was one little corner of a soap

---

88 Betty Rosebrock (dates unknown) appeared in *Pleasures and Palaces*.
89 Hillard Elkins (1929–2010), American theatre and film producer.
90 A play by William Gibson; it opened on Broadway in 1958 and was adapted into a film in 1962. Later, it was adapted into the Broadway musical *Seesaw* (1973) by Michael Bennett, Cy Coleman and Dorothy Fields.
91 'We Know We Belong to the Land' from Rodgers and Hammerstein's *Oklahoma!*; 'Tradition' from Bock and Harnick's *Fiddler on the Roof*; Jerry Herman's *Hello, Dolly!*; Tom Jones and Harvey Schmidt's *I Do! I Do!* (1966). Further down, Loesser refers to 'A Puzzlement' from *The King and I*.

opera. In the present instance we have a play a hundred times as good and a play which should not lose its essential goodness as such by way of artificially imposed song and specialty.

This play is about two people who take turns in being hesitant, full of self-doubt, always damming up an imminent emotional flood. That is why the title of the play was chosen so aptly. I submit here that this is very bad for song singing at least for singing impressive and memorable pieces. While there are examples to the contrary ("A Puzzlement," "South Pacific's" "Double Soliloquy," etc.) these are not real big fat aces as score material goes. And a show ought to have a bank account of potential aces.

About the physique of the show: the essential drabness on both sides of the stage is part of the very fabric of the show. It is hard to imagine throwing a volley of spangles on it or treating it to high white lighting or making this about rich people instead of poor people so that the clothes can be elegant, the bed lines slick, and the milk warmed in the Portland Vase over a flame attended by semi-nude Vestals. Yes there can be some scenic relief if you want this couple to walk in Central Park or ride at Palisades. But mere scenic expansion for its own sake has never done much for a production except put it in hock.

There is a total lack of broad physical movement called for in the play. As a matter of fact if I remember correctly the only thing that moved was the skyline. The people spent much of their time phoning each other, and the rest of the time visiting each other. These visits featured nothing nearly so dynamic as a ping-pong game or even a good protracted rassle in bed. Certainly no-one rescued the lady from an oncoming locomotive nor could sixteen well-wishers come in with gifts and a mass mazurka nor did either apartment house catch fire.

All right. I have told you what I should be thinking if I were <u>you</u> but it would be stupid of me to rest on the categorical objections above, without finding out what Mr. Gibson[92] has in mind for a structure that will preserve the beautiful original – or at least the feel and

92 William Gibson (1914–2008), author of *Two for the Seesaw*.

meaning of it – without getting caught sticking pretty gumdrops all over it.

If he feels like telling me about it I would be more than happy to meet with him after this week. Meanwhile thanks for thinking of me, and maybe we will go onward and upward. With apologies – as the tired old man remarked while setting down the heavy bulky carton of Cutty Sark – "I rest my case."

Best

2 December 1968: To Groucho Marx

Dear Grou:

Jo and I are of course delighted about Melinda's[93] marriage, but can't possibly come to the event. There are a whole lot of complex reasons why it has taken us so long to acknowledge the invitation, so please forgive. The main thing is that you should please give Melinda a big hug for me. She probably doesn't remember me at all so do an imitation. And for you, as always

Much love,

9 December 1968: To Alice Crump

Dear Alice:

Once again the merry season is upon us. It seems to begin officially every year upon the arrival of your very lovely fruitcake. This time the children are old enough to enjoy this sort of delicacy and they are clamoring to open the container, awaiting Christmas Day itself. The children are fast beginning to recognize Alice Crump as the name of our Western Santa Claus!

And so we all thank you very much for an ever welcome gift.

With this letter we are sending you a less glamorous present, but one which we hope you will translate into your own choice of Christmas cheer. With fond good wishes.

Sincerely,

---

93 Groucho Marx's daughter Melinda (born 1946).

Loesser had been ill, on and off, for several years – a legacy of his heavy smoking, up to three packs a day according to his daughter Susan. He was finally diagnosed with lung cancer in 1968 and his letters to his children, and to his friend William Schuman, testify to an awareness of his physical and mental decline.

September 1968: To Susan Loesser[94]

In some ways I am starting to dodder. My memory is sloppy and so is my cabinetwork. And I resist sailing into a new writing project for fear nobody else will like it (I've never been that way before). Also, I find myself glued to the TV more and more. And more and more tolerant of Ed Sullivan.

20 May 1969: To William Schuman[95]

Dear Children:

So lo you now hear from me – with many thanks for the poetry samples. Yes, I have been ill and continue to be so. When ready for circulation either Jo or I will call and we'd love to put an evening in with you. Meantime thanks for thinking of me.

Much, much love,

Frank

Frank Loesser died of lung cancer on 28 July 1969 at the age of fifty-nine; the obituary in the *New York Times* for 29 July quoted his long-time friend William Schuman: 'You can't be condescending about Frank's musical genius. He was one of the greatest songwriters the United States ever produced. His songs were authentic Americana.' Apparently Loesser had thought about his mortality many years earlier. In 1962 he left instructions with Harold Orenstein describing his final wishes.

---

94 Loesser, *A Most Remarkable Fella*, 280–1.
95 William Schuman papers, New York Public Library.

23 April 1962: To Harold Orenstein[96]

Beyond the time necessary for medical and legal confirmation of the fact that I have indeed departed this life, I wish my remains viewed by no one - and that includes family members. Immediately upon becoming officially dead, I would like my remains turned over to an organization licensed to cremate. The ashes are to be disposed of by the cremators in any way that they may see fit, providing that under no circumstances they place them separately in any urn or vessel or in any spot of ground or other identifiable place. I would prefer that what is left of me be commingled with other refuse so that it is in every respect untraceable.

I wish there to be no ceremony of any kind marking the event of my death, nor any gathering of people pertinent to the occasion of my disappearance. There will, of course, have to be the official brief death notice in the daily newspapers. However, under no circumstances is anyone or any company or organization left behind to place any form of commemorative or mourning notice or advertisement as sometimes seen in <u>Variety</u> and other such trade papers. This last applies at the time of my death, as well as to subsequent anniversaries of same and to any other later time.

I am deeply grateful that you have agreed to do whatever you can toward carrying out the above requests. I realize, however, the possibility that you might, at the time, not be close at hand or indeed available to carry out everything. In that event, I trust that you will assign someone else the job of doing away with a body without benefit of ceremony, religion, speech-making, coffin-selecting, flower-sending etc. This person should be someone who isn't an old buddy or relative but is simply efficient and cold to sales talk about real silver casket handles.

The *Times* obituary, inadvertently perhaps, draws an implicit parallel between Loesser and one of his most popular characters, Sky Masterson in *Guys and Dolls*, both public figures but, in the end,

---

96 Loesser, *A Most Remarkable Fella*, 286–7.

intensely private: 'The dark-haired … Mr. Loesser was a fidgety worker who was usually up by 5 A.M. "You are alone then with the birds – no telephones, no interruptions and the world is yours," he said,' a sentiment that reflects Sky Masterson's introspection in 'My Time of Day':

> My time of day is the dark time
> A couple of deals before dawn
> When the street belongs to the cop
> And the janitor with the mop
> And the grocery clerks are all gone.
>
> When the smell of the rainwashed pavement
> Comes up clean, and fresh, and cold
> And the streetlamp light
> Fills the gutter with gold
>
> That's my time of day
> My time of day.

INDEX

Song titles are given in quotation marks ('Adelaide's Lament'); the names of shows, books and films are in italics (*Guys and Dolls*).